SOCIAL STUDIES FOR SECONDARY SCHOOLS

SOCIAL STUDIES FOR SECONDARY SCHOOLS

Teaching to Learn, Learning to Teach

THIRD EDITION

Alan J. Singer
and the
Hofstra New Teachers Network

Routledge
Taylor & Francis Group

NEW YORK AND LONDON

First edition published 1997
by Lawrence Erlbaum Associates, Inc.

This edition first published 2009
by Routledge
270 Madison Ave, New York, NY 10016

Simultaneously published in the UK
by Routledge
2 Park Square, Milton Park, Abingdon, Oxon OX14 4RN

Routledge is an imprint of the Taylor & Francis Group, an informa business

First edition © 1997 Lawrence Erlbaum Associates, Inc.
Second edition © 2003 Lawrence Erlbaum Associates, Inc.
Third edition © 2009 Taylor & Francis

Typeset in Times New Roman by Swales & Willis Ltd, Exeter, Devon
Printed and bound in the United States of America on acid-free paper by
Sheridan Books, Inc.

Library of Congress Cataloging in Publication Data
Singer, Alan J.
   Social studies for secondary schools : teaching to learn, learning to teach / Alan J. Singer and the Hofstra New Teachers Network. 3rd ed.
      p. cm.
   1. Social sciences – Study and teaching (Secondary) – United States.   I. Hofstra New Teachers Network.   II. Title.
   H62.5.U5S56 2008
   300.71′2 – dc22
   2008008900

ISBN10: 0–805–86446–6 (pbk)
ISBN10: 0–203–89187–2 (ebk)

ISBN13: 978–0–805–86446–5 (pbk)
ISBN13: 978–0–203–89187–2 (ebk)

This book is dedicated to the middle school and high school students who spent so much time teaching us how to become social studies teachers.

Contents

Preface   xi

Chapter 1: Who Am I?   1
  WHO AM I?   2
  Essay: Why Multiculturalism Still Matters   11

Part I: Thinking about Social Studies   21

  Chapter 2: Why Study History?   23
    WHY TEACH SOCIAL STUDIES?   23
    WHY STUDY HISTORY?   25
    WHAT IS HISTORY?   28
    WHAT IS A SOCIAL STUDIES APPROACH TO HISTORY?   31
    WHAT ARE HISTORICAL FACTS?   34
    WHAT IS THE DIFFERENCE BETWEEN FACT AND THEORY?   36
    HOW DOES AN HISTORIAN STUDY HISTORY?   36
    HOW DO HISTORIANS RESOLVE DISAGREEMENTS?   38
    SHOULD A TEACHER ALSO BE AN HISTORIAN?   39
    IS THE STUDY OF HISTORY SCIENTIFIC?   41
    ARE THERE LAWS IN HISTORY?   43
    WHAT ARE THE GOALS OF HISTORIANS?   44

    Essay 1: What Social Studies is all About   46
    Essay 2: Are We Teaching "Greek Myths" in the Global History
        Curriculum?   51

  Chapter 3: What Is Social Studies?   59
    WHAT ARE THE SOCIAL SCIENCES?   59
    HOW DID THE SOCIAL SCIENCES BECOME SOCIAL STUDIES?   60
    WHAT DO WE LEARN FROM THE SOCIAL SCIENCE DISCIPLINES?   61

    Essay 1: How can Teachers Promote the Economic and Civic
        Literacy of Students?   73
    Essay 2: How can Teachers Use Drama to Promote Literacy while
        Teaching Social Studies Content and Concepts?   77

  Chapter 4: What Are Our Goals?   81
    WHY HAVE GOALS?   81
    ARE WE TEACHING SUBJECT MATTER OR STUDENTS?   82
    WHAT IS IMPORTANT TO KNOW AND WHY?   83
    WHO ARE OUR STUDENTS AND HOW DO WE CONNECT TO THEM?   86
    WHAT USE IS EDUCATIONAL THEORY?   88

Contents

HOW CAN WE TEACH DEMOCRACY? 89
HOW ARE GOALS REFLECTED IN DIFFERENT APPROACHES TO TEACHING
    SOCIAL STUDIES? 90
WHAT ARE THE TRADITIONAL ACADEMIC GOALS IN SOCIAL STUDIES? 91
HOW DO TEACHERS INTEGRATE GOALS INTO CLASSROOM PRACTICE? 95
WHAT ARE THE STATE STANDARDS? 96

Essay 1: What We Should Teach 99
Essay 2: What are the Essential Questions? 102

Chapter 5: Is Social Studies Teaching "Political"? 107
IS EVERYTHING POLITICAL? 107
WHY WAS THE DEBATE ON NATIONAL HISTORY STANDARDS SO
    HEATED? 108
SHOULD TEACHERS DISCUSS THEIR OPINIONS IN CLASS? 111
WHY IS DEFENSE OF ACADEMIC FREEDOM IMPORTANT? 113
SHOULD TEACHERS ENCOURAGE STUDENTS TO WORK FOR SOCIAL
    JUSTICE? 117
HOW CAN CLASSROOM TEACHERS EMPOWER STUDENTS? 118
HOW DO TEACHERS TRANSLATE EDUCATIONAL THEORY INTO SOCIAL
    STUDIES PRACTICE? 119
WHAT DOES A CLASSROOM BASED ON TRANSFORMATIVE PRINCIPLES
    LOOK LIKE? 124

Essay 1: Social Studies Under Attack 125
Essay 2: TAH Means "Traditional" American History 129
Essay 3: Are Activist Teachers "Social Predators"? 132

Chapter 6: How Do You Plan a Social Studies Curriculum? 137
WHAT IS A CURRICULUM? 137
HOW DOES A CURRICULUM HELP TEACHERS MAKE DECISIONS? 139
HOW IS A SOCIAL STUDIES CURRICULUM ORGANIZED? 140
WHICH VERSION OF HISTORY? 142
HOW DO YOU PLAN AND USE A CURRICULUM CALENDAR? 143

Essay 1: Teaching Global History 149
Essay 2: Multicultural Social Studies 152
Essay 3: Are We Teaching Religious Myth Instead of the History of
    Religion? 161

Part II: Preparing to Teach Social Studies 169

Chapter 7: How Do You Plan a Social Studies Unit? 171
WHY PLAN UNITS? 171
WHAT SHOULD BE INCLUDED IN A UNIT PLAN? 173
WHERE SHOULD TEACHERS START PLANNING? 173
HOW DO SOCIAL STUDIES TEACHERS PLAN UNITS? 175
HOW DO TEACHERS USE PLANS EFFECTIVELY IN THE CLASSROOM? 176
HOW CAN SOCIAL STUDIES CURRICULA ADDRESS DIFFERENCES AMONG
    STUDENTS? 176
HIGH SCHOOL UNIT PLANS 180
WHAT DOES A UNIT THAT FOCUSES ON CONTENT LOOK LIKE? 180
HOW IS A DOCUMENT-BASED THEMATIC UNIT ORGANIZED? 183
WHAT IS A COMPARATIVE THEMATIC UNIT? 192

Essay 1: Original Intent and the United States Constitution 196
Essay 2: Teaching About Work and Workers 204

Essay 3: Using Student Dialogues to Teach Social Studies and
    Promote Democracy   211

Chapter 8: How Do You Plan a Social Studies Lesson?   218
    WHY HAVE WRITTEN LESSON PLANS?   218
    WHAT DOES IT MEAN TO PLAN A LESSON?   219
    WHY ARE THERE DISPUTES OVER LESSON PLANNING?   220
    WHAT DO STUDENTS UNDERSTAND FROM A LESSON?   221
    HOW DO LESSON PLANS REFLECT IDEAS ABOUT LEARNING?   223
    WHAT DO BEGINNING TEACHERS WORRY ABOUT?   224
    WHAT SHOULD BEGINNING TEACHERS CONSIDER WHEN PLANNING
        LESSONS?   225
    WHAT ARE THE INGREDIENTS OF AN ACTIVITY-BASED LESSON PLAN?   226
    HOW IS AN ACTIVITY-BASED LESSON ORGANIZED?   228
    HOW IS A DEVELOPMENTAL LESSON ORGANIZED?   236
    WHAT DOES AN "OUTCOMES-BASED" LESSON PLAN LOOK LIKE?   238
    DOES THE "WORKSHOP MODEL" MAKE SENSE IN SECONDARY SCHOOLS?   242
    HOW DO YOU TRANSLATE YOUR PLAN INTO PRACTICE?   242

    Essay 1: Using "Text" and "Context" to Promote Student Literacies   243
    Essay 2: Teaching About Presidential Elections   246
    Essay 3: What are the Lessons of 9/11?   248

Chapter 9: What Are the Building Blocks of an Activity-based
    Lesson?   254
    HOW CAN LESSONS ACTIVELY INVOLVE STUDENTS IN LEARNING?   254
    WHAT IS DOCUMENT-BASED INSTRUCTION?   256
    HOW DO TEACHERS ORGANIZE SOCIAL STUDIES ACTIVITIES?   258
    HOW DO TEACHERS OPEN AN ACTIVITY-BASED LESSON?   260
    ARE THERE PERFECT QUESTIONS?   266
    HOW CAN TEACHERS REINFORCE STUDENT UNDERSTANDING?   270
    ARE ACTIVITIES ALWAYS APPROPRIATE?   272

    Essay 1: Which Document Do You Choose?   274
    Essay 2: Cooperative Learning in Social Studies Classrooms   281
    Essay 3: Sample Cooperative Learning Activity: Founders Discuss
        the Reasons for a New Constitution   286

Part III: Implementing Your Ideas   291

Chapter 10: How Can Social Studies Teachers Plan Controversy-
    Centered, Thematic, and Interdisciplinary Units?   293
    HOW SHOULD CONTROVERSIAL ISSUES BE ADDRESSED IN SOCIAL STUDIES
        CURRICULA?   293
    WHY TEACH THEMATIC UNITS?   295
    HOW DO YOU ORGANIZE A CONTROVERSY-CENTERED, THEMATIC
        CURRICULUM?   296
    HOW SHOULD WE DEAL WITH SENSITIVE TOPICS?   300
    SHOULD THEMATIC UNITS FOCUS ON PARTICULAR SOCIAL GROUPS?   301
    HOW CAN DIFFERENT SUBJECTS BE CONNECTED IN THE SOCIAL STUDIES
        CLASSROOM?   305

    Essay 1: Expanding Our Concept of Inclusion   308
    Essay 2: Women's History Month Curriculum   309
    Essay 3: Responding to Crisis: What Can Social Studies Teachers
        Do?   313

Contents

Chapter 11: What Is a Project Approach to Social Studies?   317
HOW DO YOU INCLUDE PROJECTS IN SOCIAL STUDIES CURRICULA?   317
WHAT ARE THE ADVANTAGES OF A PROJECT APPROACH TO SOCIAL STUDIES?   320

Essay 1: Oral Histories: A Project Approach to Social Studies   335
Essay 2: Technology-based Project Ideas   338
Essay 3: Middle School Immigration Museum   344

Chapter 12: How Should Teachers Assess Student Learning and Our Own Practice?   351
DOES ASSESSMENT EQUAL TESTING?   352
WHAT DO THE TESTS ACTUALLY MEASURE?   353
WHY SHOULD EDUCATORS ASSESS STUDENT LEARNING?   354
HOW CAN TESTING BECOME PART OF LEARNING?   355
WHAT DO TEACHERS WANT TO MEASURE?   358
WHAT DOES A SOCIAL STUDIES PORTFOLIO LOOK LIKE?   360
HOW DO TEACHERS DESIGN FAIR EXAMS?   367
HOW CAN TEACHERS GRADE FAIRLY?   373
SHOULD STUDENTS BE INVOLVED IN ASSESSING THEIR OWN LEARNING?   374

Essay 1: How Do We Move from Instruction to Assessment?   375
Essay 2: What Does a Research Paper Look Like?   380
Essay 3: Assessing Our Teaching Practice?   381

Chapter 13: What Resources Exist for Social Studies Classrooms and Teachers?   386
HOW CAN YOU DEVELOP YOUR SKILLS AS A SOCIAL STUDIES TEACHER?   386
HOW USEFUL ARE COMPUTERS IN SOCIAL STUDIES CLASSROOMS?   390
HOW DO YOU PLAN FIELD TRIPS?   396
SHOULD I SHOW MY CLASS A MOVIE?   396
WHAT CAN I COPY FOR MY CLASS?   404
WHO PROVIDES RESOURCES FOR SOCIAL STUDIES TEACHERS?   404

Author Index   409
Subject Index   414

Preface to the Third Edition (2008)

> **"This book gives me ammunition to defend my view of teaching."**
>
> **Dean Bacigalupo, Lincoln Orens Middle School, Island Park, New York,
> Member of the Hofstra New Teachers Network**

WHY WRITE A THIRD EDITION?

Little is known about the ancient Greek philosopher Heraclitus of Ephesus except what survives as fragments within the work of others. In Plato's *Cratylus*, Socrates quotes Heraclitus as saying that "all things are in motion and nothing at rest." According to Socrates, Heraclitus believed that the path of a person's life was like a river and that "you cannot go into the same water twice" (see Jewett, http://classics.mit.edu/Plato/cratylus.html). The water in the river would no longer be the same water that was there before, and the person, shaped by experience and age, would not be the same person either.

I started writing the first edition of this book in 1993 while teaching high school social studies in New York City. By that time I had been a classroom teacher for 14 years. Much has changed since then, including me (since 2004 I have been a grandfather). Even if educational issues had remained the same since the early 1990s, which they haven't, I am not the person who I was 15 years ago. That was the last year I was a full-time high school teacher. Since then I have worked as a social studies teacher educator at Hofstra University in support of pre-service and beginning teachers and as a staff developer and curriculum consultant in New York City metropolitan area schools. If I were a student in a pre-service teacher education program, I would be very skeptical about practical advice offered by a grandfather who had not worked as a classroom teacher for such a long time. You are the ones who must decide if after 35 years as a social studies teacher, my insights and arguments are still valid and useful.

The last decade has been a tumultuous period in our society and secondary school social studies teachers have been asked to play a major role in helping students (our society's future leaders) understand events reshaping the country and the world. I agree very much with President John F. Kennedy, who in 1962 warned, "Those who make peaceful revolutions impossible, make violent revolutions inevitable" (see http://www.quotationspage.com/quotes/John_F. Kennedy, accessed September 17, 2007).

I have continued to work with the Hofstra New Teachers Network (NTN) and their contributions greatly strengthen my approach to teaching and enrich this book. In their classrooms they have had to grapple with the attacks on the World Trade Center and Pentagon, the United States response in Afghanistan, Iraq, and at home, as well as local issues in the New York metropolitan area such as charges of police brutality and racial profiling in minority communities, unequal school funding, and pressure to prepare students for standardized assessments.

Because I am no longer tied to a classroom for five periods a day, five days a week, I have been able to broaden my experience by meeting with classroom teachers around the country. Through the National Council for the Social Studies, I spoke with teachers in Phoenix, Kansas City, Anaheim, San Antonio, Washington, DC, Cincinnati, and Baltimore. I have had the opportunity to make extended visits with social studies teachers in Flint, Michigan, St Louis, Missouri, and Sonoma, California. I have learned a lot about their approaches to teaching social studies and I hope it is reflected in this new edition.

Dean Bacigalupo, quoted at the beginning of this preface, is a former student who has long been a big supporter of my approach to teaching. However, my ideas about teaching are not for everyone. An anonymous review posted on Amazon.com issued a warning to potential readers of this book of which that I am actually quite proud.

> "Save your money!! If this book is required for a college class do not waste the money on it. There is not a single useful piece of advice. The author apparently has never been in a real classroom or spoken to a real high school student. His advice is condescending and just plain wrong. The sample lesson plans are not practical for real life! The author gives instructions that are simply contradictory to the real world. This is one of the worst books that I have ever read. If I could give it zero stars I would."

If you end up agreeing with this reviewer, you can always resell the book. But maybe, just maybe, you will decide to keep it. I wonder if the anonymous reviewer reconsidered this initial reaction when, or if, they ever became a teacher.

In 1982, I started a new assignment at Franklin K. Lane High School. My first day there I was approached by an assistant principal who said that he had heard a lot about me. When I asked what my reputation was, he said word was I was a very good teacher, but also a "pain in the ass." I confessed that both assessments were true and that they were part of the same package. I continue to pride myself on being a "pain in the ass" and only hope that I remain a good teacher.

However, everyone does not think I am. On Sunday, December 19, 2004, I had a startling exchange with New York Senator Charles Schumer at the Hofstra University graduation (see http://www.counterpunch.org/singer12222004.html, accessed September 17, 2007). Senator Schumer makes a habit of appearing, uninvited, at graduations at the last minute, speaking to the audience about his experience when he himself was a recent college graduate, and then fleeing the scene before anyone can speak with him. I tried to approach him on a number of occasions but never had the opportunity until one time he arrived early while the faculty was lining up to enter the arena. I walked up to him and asked whether he was reconsidering his position on the war in Iraq now that the justifications presented by the Bush administration had all proved to be false. He immediately began shouting, blamed me for the destruction of the Democrat party, and said that "with your ideas you should not be allowed to be a teacher."

While Senator Schumer is a Democrat, I have also annoyed some Republicans. After a presentation on the lessons of September 11, 2001 at a Long Island, New York High School, I received an e-mail from a self-described "Republican" parent informing me that "a number of parents have and will be voicing our disgust with your presentation and do our best to insure (*sic*) that you are not allowed to poison the minds of our children any further!"

What kind of teacher am I? What kind of teacher do I argue you should become? Take a look at this course evaluation, submitted by an undergraduate student at the end of a social studies methods class. It was unsigned, handwritten, and I am reproducing it without editing.

> "The course did teach how to teach, but it was only coming from one philosophical angle – only Singer's (both of what to teach and how to teach and the materials to be taught). Singer knows a lot of info and I know he is probably a great teacher, but this course and the University in general could be discouraging for people with dissenting views/opinions/beliefs. Luckily, I'm not discouraged, but this university probably wishes I was because my beliefs are so opposed to those of the University. Did this come into play in this class with this teacher? No, I don't think so, but I did mention it here."

This evaluation is an accurate portrayal of my class and I want to highlight a few things from it. The student learned to teach in this class, albeit not the way he or she had anticipated. And while the course "could be discouraging for people with dissenting views/opinions/beliefs," it wasn't. Disagreements about views on teaching, history, and society did not "come into play" or affect how the student was treated or evaluated. I regard this as a very positive evaluation of my teaching practice by someone who had reason to be skeptical and as a good rebuttal to the Amazon.com reviewer, Senator Schumer, and the "Republican" parent.

As I have gotten older, I have begun to reflect more on the experiences that shaped my life and thinking and to be more selective about how I use my available time. Teachers have to know something. They have to have experiences they can build on as they try to help students draw connections. "The Motorcycle Diaries" (2004) is a movie version of a coming-of-age journey by Ernesto "Che" Guevara in 1952. It recounts a trip from Argentina through Chile and Bolivia into the Amazon where he first began to understand the vast social inequality in our world. The claim made in the movie and book versions is that it was this trip that laid the basis for his transformation into a revolutionary.

When I watched the movie, I revisited the experiences of my own youth. I had visited some of the same places Che had in 1969 when I was 19-years-old. While I cannot claim the trip transformed me into a revolutionary, it did play an important part in my eventually becoming a social studies teacher by simulating my desire to learn. I suddenly encountered a world of people, places, cultures, and historical events that I had never imagined or experienced in such a visceral way while reading books, going to school, and living in a working-class community in New York City. My traveling companions and I visited Cartagena, the city in Colombia where the Spanish Armada, loaded with silver and gold, gathered before crossing the Atlantic Ocean, the waterfront slums of Guayaquil and indigenous villages in the Andes, the Galapagos Islands where Charles Darwin pieced together his explanation for the evolution of life, and Machu Picchu and Cuzco, where we camped out in the middle of the ruins of the Inca civilization. I fell into quicksand on the Galapagos and chewed coca leaves for altitude sickness in the Andes. We spent almost two weeks on a barge floating down the Amazon where I contracted cholera and almost died from dysentery. On this trip it was as if my eyes were opened to the world in all of its magnificence and sorrow for the first time.

Since then I have traveled in the United States and other countries as often as possible. It has been a major part of my life-long learning as a teacher. A recent major trip, taken in the summer of 2006, was to La Sabranenque in southeastern France. My wife and I spent two weeks as part of an historical restoration team rebuilding castles using medieval construction techniques and materials and learning a little bit about what it meant to live and work in a preindustrial society. I strongly recommend travel as part of the preparation and ongoing education of social studies teachers, although I can understand avoiding some of the things that I did in Latin America.

NEW IN THE THIRD EDITION

If you compare this edition with the first two, you will see that I have changed a number of the references, anecdotes, and lesson suggestions. Sometimes it is because my ideas have changed, but frequently it is because I have been working with many new and exciting young teachers who have shared their approaches with me.

I have also been fortunate to work in schools preparing and field-testing the *New York State Great Irish Famine* and *New York and Slavery: Complicity and Resistance* curriculum guides. I have developed a new persona as a "rapper" known by local students as "Reeces Pieces" because "I am better than Eminem." A sketch of me as "Reeces Pieces," prepared by one of my students, appears at the beginning of Chapter 1.

The structure of the book and most of the topics examined in this third edition remain largely the same as before, but every chapter has a number of new lesson ideas. These are especially designed to help new teachers address learning standards, work in inclusive settings, and to promote literacy and the use of technology in social studies classrooms. Despite my best efforts, computers are ubiquitous in public school classrooms; so while I remain a "Luddite" and suspicious of technology at heart, I have been forced to adjust the way I teach. I started on this preface while sitting in a library in St Louis typing away on a laptop. I stopped for a few minutes to e-mail help to a student teacher planning a demonstration lesson that she was presenting in a classroom 1,000 miles away. Earlier that day, I used PowerPoint to illustrate a presentation on teachers as transformative agents to teachers and administrators participating in a conference on social justice. Ten years ago I would not have guessed it was possible to teach this way. Five years ago I would have been resistant. For those of you looking for a seer with a crystal ball, I confess I have no idea what the influence of technology will be on classroom practice in the future. The only things I am sure about is that things will continue to change and that I will be learning about them from my students.

I am pleased to see the new focus on document-based instruction and assessment in social studies, and I have worked with members of the NTN to develop sample activities that can also serve as tools for assessing student learning. Project or activity-based social studies instruction and multicultural education have been under ever increasing attack by proponents of traditional educational practices, so I have sharpened my defense of both of these approaches to teaching throughout the book.

The main change in my thinking about preparing to become a social studies teacher is a deeper awareness of the importance of teacher conceptual knowledge of history and the social sciences. In earlier editions, I was comfortable with the reality that most teachers would eventually learn what they needed to know over the course of their careers. While this still remains true, I am concerned that unless new teachers are committed to the continuous growth of their own knowledge and understanding, they will fall into the habit of using easily available print and on-line material that is attractive, even seductive, but is superficial and largely misleading. In 2003, President George W. Bush and Secretary of State Colin Powell sold a war to the American people by presenting evidence of "weapons of mass destruction" in Iraq that never existed. If social studies teachers do not know enough about the past and society so we can tell the difference between analysis and propaganda, how will students ever be able to develop the knowledge and skills needed to become active and critical citizens of a democratic society.

OVERVIEW

This book integrates discussions of educational goals and the nature of history and social studies with ideas for organizing social studies curricula, units, lessons, projects, and activities. Sections include lesson ideas developed by new and experienced middle school and high school social studies teachers. A major theme woven throughout the book is that what we choose to teach and the way we teach reflects our broader understanding of society, history, and the purpose of social studies education.

The book is intended as either a primary or supportive text in methods courses for undergraduate and graduate pre-service social studies teachers. However, it should also be useful for in-service training programs, as a reference for new social studies teachers, and as a resource for experienced social studies educators who are engaged in rethinking their teaching practice.

Following the introduction (Chapter 1), the first part of this volume, "Thinking about Social Studies," includes chapters that focus on philosophical issues like the reasons for teaching and studying history (Chapter 2) and social studies (Chapter 3), social studies goals and standards (Chapter 4), the political nature of social studies (Chapter 5), and the design of social studies curricula (Chapter 6). The second part, "Preparing to Teach Social Studies," is intended to be more practical. It examines strategies for planning social studies units (Chapter 7) and lessons (Chapters 8 and 9) and includes many sample lesson ideas. These sections have new, extended discussions of inclusion and literacy. The third part, "Implementing Your Ideas," explores topics like thematic and interdisciplinary teaching (Chapter 10), a project approach to social studies (Chapter 11), and assessing student learning and our own performance as teachers (Chapter 12). The book concludes with a discussion of social studies resource materials (Chapter 13) and ideas for promoting literacy and the use of technology in social studies classrooms.

Every chapter addresses a broad question about social studies education. Sub-chapters begin with narrower questions that direct attention to specific educational issues. Chapters conclude with essays about related social studies topics. They also include sources for further reading, lesson "examples," and teaching, learning, and classroom activities designed to provoke discussion and illustrate different approaches to teaching social studies. Inserts labeled as *TEACHING ACTIVITIES* are assignments and topics for discussion by students in university methods courses and social studies teachers. *CLASSROOM ACTIVITIES* are sample lesson ideas designed for middle-level and high school students. Teachers and pre-service teachers should experiment with some of these activities to see how they work and consider how they would use them in secondary school classes. *LEARNING ACTIVITIES* are intended to be useful activities and important topics for discussion in both secondary school social studies classrooms and in university social studies methods courses. Activities are followed by four categories:

"*Think it over*," "*Add your voice to the discussion*," "*Try it yourself*," and "**It's your classroom.**"

GOALS AS AUTHOR AND TEACHER

I am an historian with specializations in the history of slavery, particularly in the Northern states, and the social history of the industrial United States, as well as a former high school social studies teacher. When I write about social studies, I generally use historical examples. I do not think this focus invalidates the points I raise about the social sciences, but I am prepared for criticism. I know this may sound heretical, but I do not think the specific content focus of a social studies curriculum should be the main concern; it is certainly not as important as taking a critical approach to any subject matter that is being explored. Social studies curricula need structure. Although my organizing preference is chronology, this is not a rule.

Many parts of this book are designed to hone in on points of contention. My intent is to promote dialogue between myself as author and you as reader. Literacy specialists call this active approach to examining a text and making meaning of it "reader response." I hope that new teachers think about the ideas I am raising and agree or disagree with me and with each other. If you disagree with my biases, criticize them. That is one of the overall goals of social studies education and a purpose of this book. It is how we get to be social studies teachers.

If you want to reach me, my address is Alan Singer, Department of Curriculum and Teaching, 119 Hofstra University, Hempstead, NY 11549. My e-mail address is catajs@hofstra.edu and my website is http://people.hofstra.edu/facultu/alan_j_singer.

We have a lot to do if we are going to become social studies teachers who have some say in shaping the debates in our profession and active citizens who influence decisions in our society. So let us roll up our sleeves and get to work.

ACKNOWLEDGMENTS

I am the Graduate Director of the secondary school social studies program in the Department of Curriculum and Teaching of the Hofstra University School of Education and Allied Human Services (SOEAHS). The Hofstra New Teachers Network (NTN) is a network of students and student teachers currently in the program, alumni, secondary school social studies teachers and administrators, cooperating teachers, field supervisors, and Hofstra faculty. NTN maintains an e-mail newsletter, sponsors two annual conferences, organizes support teams for new teachers, and promotes participation in teacher development activities.

Although I no longer teach in secondary school classrooms on a full-time basis, I have been fortunate that members of the NTN have "lent" me their classrooms to experiment with new lessons, activities, and approaches to teaching. These "guest appearances" have helped me remain in practice as a teacher, to develop and field test the *New York and Slavery: Complicity and Resistance* curriculum guide, which received the Program of Excellence Award from the National Council for the Social Studies, and to edit material for *Social Science Docket*, a joint publication of the New York and New Jersey Councils for the Social Studies. I hope that readers familiar with earlier volumes of this text feel that I have continued to grow as a social studies teacher despite being marooned in a university teacher education program.

Many of the hundreds of members of the NTN are contributors to the third edition of *Social Studies for Secondary Schools* and are mentioned in the text. Contributors also include cooperating teachers, colleagues from the New York and New Jersey Councils for the Social Studies, and teachers I have worked with in the past.

This edition could not have been completed without support from the Hofstra University Offices of Editing and Computer Services; the staff of the Curriculum Materials Center in Hofstra University's Axinn Library, the secretarial and administrative staff of the Hofstra University SOEAHS and the Department of Curriculum and Teaching; critical readings and suggestions by Dennis Banks (SUNY Oneonta), Kenneth Carlson (Rutgers University), Kathy Bickmore (University of Toronto), Stephen Thorton (University of South Florida), and Pearl Oliner (Humbolt State University); and the invaluable assistance of Naomi Silverman and her staff.

I want to thank Naomi Silverman and the editors for giving me the opportunity to produce a third edition of *Social Studies for Secondary Schools: Teaching to Learn/Learning to Teach.*

My most important collaborators continue to be Maureen Murphy, the Graduate Director of English Education who also completed a shift as Dean of the SOEAHS at Hofstra and Judith Y. Singer, former director of the MLE Learning Center in Brooklyn and Associate Professor of Elementary Education at Long Island University-Brooklyn Campus. Judi was a full partner in the development of the educational philosophy and teaching approaches presented in all three editions of this book. Our grown children, Heidi, Rachel, and Solomon, deserve special credit for years of ingenuity and patience as I experimented with them on approaches to teaching, as do my grandchildren, Gideon and Sadia, who are my latest victims. Their willingness to continually argue with me has helped keep many a flight-of-fancy grounded in the reality of schools "as they are," while recognizing the potential of education "as it can be."

1. Who Am I?

Overview

- Trace the evolution of a social studies teacher
- Consider the cultural, social, and historical nature of individual identity
- Examine the roots of personal identity and its intersection with history
- Explore reflective practice
- Introduce the political nature of curriculum

Key Concepts

Identity, Culture, Change, Experience, Competence, Experimentation, Curriculum

Essay

Why Multiculturalism Still Matters

Figure 1.1 Alan Singer a/k/a "Reeces Pieces" teaching hip-hop history.

I began the first and second editions of this book with the statement that anybody who writes a book about teaching has to expect certain questions. Who are you? What have you studied? What is your experience? Will your ideas about teaching social studies be useful to me?

I am not the same person I was when I began writing the first edition of *Social Studies for Secondary Schools* in 1993. In 2007, I celebrated my sixteenth year as a university-based teacher. Most of the middle school and high school teachers I started with in 1971 have retired. I have thin, graying hair and I am a grandfather. Most of you who are reading this book were not born yet when I started teaching. You have a right to be skeptical about what I have to offer. I certainly would have been in your position.

I think my teaching, research, writing, and activism over the last decades have made me a better teacher. They have certainly caused me to rethink my ideas and practices. But only you can decide how useful they are. I certainly have had more of an opportunity to talk with

teachers from all over the country because of my involvement in the National Council for the Social Studies and the Teaching American History grant program. I have learned that suburban teachers from the St Louis region have the same difficulties getting their students to understand the African-American Civil Rights struggles of the 1950s and 1960s as do my former students who teach in Long Island schools. I know how hard it is to make the achievements of the Labor movement meaningful to inner-city students who live in a world where work is scarce and trade unions are virtually non-existent, whether they are from Brooklyn, New York or Flint, Michigan.

I argue with new teachers that they need to be curriculum creators rather than curriculum consumers. That means you need to decide what is important to teach to the particular group of students you are working with, rather than depending on other people's answers or commercial teaching packages, and that includes my work as well. I think my methodology holds together as an overall approach to social studies education, but as you develop your own pedagogy and curriculum, you may decide to just use pieces, or not to use it at all. It will be your decision.

I was marching with a group of teachers at the 2004 Republican National Convention in New York City in protest against the war in Iraq. After we had been standing in one place for a while, a young social studies teacher named Monica Mejias asked me how long we had been marching. I thought for a few seconds and responded "40 years." She laughed and said, "I mean really." "40 years," I said, "I've been marching for 40 years."

WHO AM I?

My name is Alan Singer. I am a white, male, husband, father, grandfather, son, brother, college-educated, politically active, ethnic Jew, atheist, citizen of the United States, New Yorker, city dweller, sports fan, hiking and biking enthusiast, high school social studies teacher, college education professor with a Ph.D. in US history and a specialization in the organization of the coal miners' union.

Learning Activity: Ballad for Americans

Toward the end of the Great Depression and just before US entry into World War II, the African-American singer and political activist, Paul Robeson, performed the song *Ballad for Americans* (available at: http://lyricsplaybround.com, accessed September 17, 2007) in a series of concerts across the country. It became so popular, that in 1940 it was selected as the theme song for the Republican Party's national convention (Robeson 1990). During the song, the chorus asks Paul Robeson to identify himself, and he responds that he is a member of every ethnic, religious, and occupational group in the United States, and represents an amalgam of all the people who built America (LaTouche and Robinson 1940). The song takes on particular importance in the contemporary United States as the country grows increasingly more diverse.

Try it yourself:
1. Who are you? Which groups of people are you a member of?
2. Explain how you became a member of each group.
3. How did different members of your family become "Americans"?

Add your voice to the discussion:
1. In the song *Ballad for Americans*, Paul Robeson suggests that a large number of groups of people should be included in the history of the United States and our definition of what is an American. Do you agree or disagree with Paul Robeson? Explain the reason for your answer.
2. The song was written in the 1930s. How would you change it if you rewrote it for today? Why?

I grew up in a working-class community in the Bronx, New York, within walking distance of Yankee Stadium. Neither of my parents went to college, but I was always considered "college material." I attended one of New York City's academically selective public high schools, where I was a mediocre student. On the relatively rare occasions when I liked a teacher or a subject, I usually did well. More often, I just got by.

I have few memories of secondary school teachers or classes. I remember my 9th-grade algebra teacher. She was also my homeroom teacher and coach of the math team. I was on the math team, and she always made sure that I had money for lunch. If I did not, she lent it to me. I remember my 10th-grade social studies

teacher because he gave students extra credit for bringing magazines to class and including pictures in their reports. I never got the extra credit because we did not have magazines in our house, and this was the era before copying machines made it possible to get pictures from the library. I was very bitter because, without the extra credit, I was kept out of the advanced placement history class. I remember my 11th-grade US history teacher because he challenged the class to find something incorrect or vague in the Declaration of Independence, which he considered to be the "greatest document ever written." I argued that the passage that states that "the People" have the right "to alter or to abolish" governments, never spells out what percentage of the people are required for this kind of change. The teacher gave me a copy of Carl Becker's book on the Declaration, where Becker makes a similar point, and he discussed it with me (Becker 1942).

I started college at the City College of New York (CCNY) in September 1967, partly because it was the thing to do after high school, partly because my parents said it would provide me with a "profession" and a middle-class standard of living, and partly because college meant a deferment from the war in Vietnam. When I thought about the future, I considered becoming a research scientist or maybe a lawyer. I never imagined myself becoming a secondary school teacher. How could I? I did not like high school the first time.

The years 1967–1971 were exciting times at CCNY and in the United States. Demonstrators protested against US involvement in the war in Vietnam. The African-American community debated integration vs. separation. Women and gays and lesbians were challenging second-class citizenship. Students were demanding the right to participate in the college decision-making process. In December 1967, I was arrested in a protest at Whitehall Street, the New York City draft induction center immortalized by Arlo Guthrie in the ballad *Alice's Restaurant* (available at: http://www.arlo.net/resources/lyrics/alices.shtml, accessed September 17, 2007). I was charged with "obstructing pedestrian traffic" by standing on the sidewalk. The charges were later dropped. As a result of my arrest, which was unplanned, I emerged as a radical student leader and was elected to the student government.

My freshman, sophomore, and junior years were spent planning and protesting, working (in a cafeteria and as a taxi cabdriver), traveling, and only occasionally attending classes. At the start of my junior year, I began to think about what I would do after I finished college. My long-term plan was to become a revolutionary. My short-term plan was to be employable. My father persuaded me to get my teaching credentials as a back-up plan.

At some point, and I am not sure when, I started to become a serious student. If I was going to change the world, I had to understand it. I began to read history, study, do research, and think about the world. I became a member of the United Community Centers, a community organizing group based in the working-class, largely minority community of East New York, Brooklyn. At the center, we worked with community youth, knocked on doors in the public housing projects raising money and discussing our ideas, distributed a community newspaper, organized people to participate in broader social movements, and operated a summer "sleep-away" camp. I spent my next five summers working in camp as a counselor, bus driver, and maintenance worker and remained active in the center for over 30 years.

The education program at CCNY will surprise no-one. After a series of disagreements between us in class, my first education professor said I should never become a teacher and recommended that I drop out of the program. The history of education professor lectured about things those who remained awake considered irrelevant. The educational psychology professor was enamored with B. F. Skinner and Konrad Lorenz, so he spent all of his time discussing experiments with pigeons and geese rather than discussing how children learn. The social studies methods teacher was especially disappointing. His specialty was operating outdated audiovisual equipment, so we had workshops on each machine. At the end of his class, I swore I would never use an overhead projector in class, even if it meant permanent unemployment. But I did not really have to worry. The first time I worked in a school where I had access to an overhead projector was 1992. Thanks to him, I still have an aversion to technology, although I have broken down and started to use PowerPoint in the classroom (but never to lecture!).

Because of my reputation at City College as a troublemaker, I was exiled to student teach in an "undesirable" junior high school in the south Bronx. My cooperating teacher was starting her second year as a teacher. She was nice to the students, but had not yet learned how to teach or organize a class. An adjunct in the School of Education was assigned to observe me three times.

My most memorable lesson as a student teacher was a mock demonstration in the classroom. We were studying Martin Luther's 95 theses. I met the students at the door and handed them flyers inviting them to come to a rally protesting against the injustices of the Roman Catholic Church. We yelled, sang protest songs, evaluated Martin Luther's demands, and then discussed similarities between protests against the authority of the Catholic

3

Church in 1517 and against US policy in Vietnam in 1971.

The draft remained a problem until the Fall of 1971, when the law authorizing military conscription expired and the United States started its experiment with an all-volunteer army. My friends and I had decided that if we were drafted we would organize against the war in Vietnam from inside the military. I was terrified of this prospect and was tremendously relieved not to have to go into the army. One of the lessons that I always enjoy doing with students is examining where their lives, or the lives of people in their families, intersect with and are directly affected by historical events.

Classroom Activity: My Life and History

Try this exercise at the beginning of the semester. As a homework assignment, ask students to write about ways that their lives, or the lives of friends or family members, have been influenced (or changed) by historical events. This is a good homework activity because it gives students a chance to discuss their ideas with family members. In recent years, I have had many discussions with students about the events of September 11, 2001. Students who were ten or older at the time usually select it as the historic event that most influenced their lives. However, I find that students who were less than ten years old in 2001 have only vague personal memories.

As a follow-up in class, students can share their stories in groups, and the stories that groups find especially interesting can be read aloud to the class. After hearing the stories, students can discuss why they think these events took place. This discussion allows the class to formulate their own questions about history that can become the basis for organizing the term's work. Following are excerpts from essays by students who wrote about their experiences living in other countries. I initially had some concerns about the veracity of the first story and confirmed it with the boy's father. Jacqueline Murekatete, the student who wrote about surviving the Rwandan genocide, did not begin to speak about her experiences until after an elderly Jewish survivor of World War II era of European Holocaust spoke with her class. She later became an active campaigner and public speaker against genocide (Murekatete 2004: 66–68).

My summer vacation in an Israeli prison

It was a hot and humid night on the West Bank in Palestine, where I was spending my summer visiting my grandparents. I was a 14-year-old boy looking for a good time, but what I got that night no-one could have expected. I was on my way home from my cousin's house when I heard a truck pull up. Out of the truck came 12 Israeli soldiers. I was stunned and had no idea what to do. I began to walk quickly, hoping not to be bothered by the soldiers, but to my disappointment the soldiers stopped me. I had no identification with me, and a soldier asked me a question in Arabic. Before I could even answer him, they all began to beat me with clubs. I was in extreme pain and the blows to my head were so brutal that finally I fell unconscious. When I awoke, I found myself in the back of a military truck surrounded by soldiers. After three hours of driving, I was put in a prison. I was very scared, but one guy named Ali, another Palestinian-American, kept me straight. Ali was 17 years old, and for the month that I was imprisoned, he was like my brother.

It was the 29th day of our 30-day sentence and Ali and I were hoping to get out the next day. We thought we could stay out of trouble for one more day, but avoiding these soldiers was nearly impossible. One of the soldiers kicked my food on to the floor. I tried to keep cool, but I just couldn't anymore. I punched him in the face and he quickly fell to the ground. I jumped on him and continued to hit him. All of a sudden I heard a shot. I thought I was hit, but when I turned around, it was Ali who was bleeding. I ran right to Ali and held him in my arms. I stood silent in shock as I felt Ali's heartbeat get weaker and weaker on my chest until the beat just completely stopped and Ali was gone. A tear found its way down my cheek as I put Ali down on the ground.

I had trouble getting to sleep that night. I kept asking myself, "Why Ali?" I blamed myself for his death. Finally, I fell asleep. When I woke up in the morning, Ali's body was gone.

El Salvador—country in crisis

El Salvador is the smallest and most densely populated mainland country in the Western Hemisphere. Salvadorian politics are not easy to explain. During the 1970s, guerrilla bands formed among the peasants because of their frustration at unfairness and the hopeless situation under which they lived. The guerrillas are both men and women, and they can be children or senior citizens. Sometimes they wear bandannas over their faces to hide their identities from the military. If guerrillas are captured, they will be tortured to release the names of their friends. The military is willing to kill innocent people, so they can get their hands on the person that they want to catch.

In 1979, when I was five years old, the Catholic Church decided to take an active role in the politics in El Salvador. Archbishop Romero and Father Grande decided that the Catholic Church had to help people get a better life while they were still in this world.

My family was extremely religious. Every Sunday, without fail, we put on our best clothes and went to a mass in San Salvador that lasted about two hours. During one mass, I feel asleep. I woke up about 45 minutes later to the sound of gunshots. I was still sleepy, but I remember that my aunt scooped me up and we left the church. Later, I woke up on the living room floor at home. Only then did I learn what had happened at church. Archbishop Romero had preached that people had to oppose the government of El Salvador. In the middle of the sermon, he was assassinated by military officers. They killed the archbishop in cold blood in a holy place in front of all the worshippers, and the government claimed that the murderers were justified!

100 days of genocide in Rwanda

I spent most of the 100 days of genocide at the orphanage. Each day we had more kids arrive whose parents had been killed and it grew very crowded. Some of the children had hands or arms cut off by the killers. Sometimes parents dropped off their children for safety and then they would try to find a place to hide from the Hutus. There were many instances where I witnessed Tutsi men and women being dragged to their deaths by the killers as they tried to climb the fences of the orphanage. In the orphanage, little children cried every night for their parents. We did not have enough food in the orphanage and many children died from malnutrition or diseases that spread because of the overcrowding. It got to the point that the priests built a cemetery inside the orphanage. Every day or so we all went to the cemetery, the priests would say a prayer, and they would bury a child. It became almost like a daily routine. I was fortunate to never get really sick. Every night, I prayed that the whole thing would soon be over and then I would go back home and see my family.

Hutu soldiers, who were trying to escape, came to the orphanage and told the Italian priests that they were going to finish the job and exterminate all the Tutsis, including the children and babies. They herded us into the cafeteria and made us sing their victory songs. Soldiers walked up the aisle in the middle of the cafeteria pointing guns at us and pushed around the priests. The children cried and we thought, "they are going to kill us." But the priests convinced them we could do them no harm and offered them money to leave us. I was almost ten years old when all of this happened. I do not know how I managed to escape the killers in the several instances when I came face to face with them. I believe that God was responsible for my safety.

Think it over:

What questions do you have about the events described in the stories told by these students?

Try it yourself:

Write an essay about the way that your life or the life of someone in your family has been influenced (or changed) by historical events.

It's your classroom:

What would you do if students did not believe these stories or were upset by them?

Although I liked student teaching, I still did not plan to become a teacher. An unanticipated result of my changed attitude toward studying was that I was accepted into the US History Doctoral program at Rutgers University and offered a teaching assistantship. Suddenly, I was in graduate school and was going to be both a scholar and a revolutionary. During the next few years, I learned that coffee house intellectualizing, academic revolutionary theorizing, and long lonely hours of library research were not all that appealing. What I liked most was teaching history classes. When I completed my coursework and passed my written and oral exams, I resigned my assistantship and became a substitute teacher in a middle school in

Brooklyn. Within a few months, I had my own Language Arts and Reading program, but then in 1975 New York City went bankrupt and thousands of teachers were laid off. My name was placed on a list that remained frozen until 1978.

During the next few years, I got married, started a family, began my doctoral dissertation about coal miners, worked as a substitute teacher, truck driver, a bus driver for the New York City Transit Authority on the midnight shift, at the community center, and in the summer camp. It was in camp that I finally learned how to become a teacher. I figured out that the keys to working with young people were treating them as human beings, listening to their concerns, and finding ways to connect what I was interested in, with who they were and their interests. Teaching requires interaction, students and teachers working together, and developing shared classroom goals. Otherwise, I might be talking, but I would not be teaching and they would not be learning.

In the Fall of 1978, I made my semi-annual call to the New York City Board of Education to see if my list had been "unfrozen." They said "no," but three days into the school year, a high school contacted me and said I had been appointed to work there. Finally, I was a social studies teacher and now I wanted to be one. The school that I was assigned to had serious academic, discipline, and attendance problems, and my first few years as a teacher were very hard. Many teenagers from low-income public housing projects with high crime and unemployment rates were zoned into the school. Attendance was erratic, fighting was frequent, and teachers were often just as glad when the kids did not show up.

But I wanted to be a good teacher and I worked hard at it. I had students in my 10th-grade economics class analyze the Board of Education budget report. We prepared our own recommendations, and then we testified at government budget hearings. The students were so excited that they organized a school club so they could remain involved with public issues when they were no longer in my class. Two years later, the club helped organize a rally against educational budget cuts at New York City Hall that involved approximately 5,000 people.

During the first three years, my lessons were largely hit or miss. Sometimes it seemed like I had the entire class in the palm of my hand and I could do no wrong. On other days, the students acted like I was not even present. The worst part was that I could not predict which lessons would work or why. I read a book called *The Last Unicorn* by Peter S. Beagle (1968) that captured the way I felt about my teaching. It is the story of a hapless young magician who is trying to save unicorns from extinction. Sometimes he finds that he has great magical powers, but then, inexplicably, the magic is gone. The magician eventually realizes that humans cannot control magic. It only comes when there is a great need. During those years, I frequently felt that I was that hapless magician. I was always hoping for the magical lesson, but I never knew when it would appear.

Part of the problem during those early years was of my own making. I believed that I knew better than everybody else about how to manage a classroom, organize a curriculum, and connect with teenagers, so I would not take any advice. I had to think everything through for myself and continually reinvent the wheel. Another part of the problem is that, even when you work at becoming a teacher, it takes between three and five years of hard work, planning, and practicing for the things you want to happen in a lesson to happen on a consistent basis.

Finally, after experimenting and failing and experimenting again, I learned how to organize lessons centered on the interests and concerns of my students, rather than simply on what I would like to have discussed. More and more of the lessons worked. The need for magic disappeared.

Teaching Activity: Should the Curriculum Depend on Your Students?

In response to campaigns for a more multicultural social studies curriculum, there was a contentious debate over whether the content of the curriculum should vary depending on the race and ethnicity of students. Proponents of a uniform curriculum, such as Arthur Schlesinger Jr. (1992), argued that alternative paths would increase social divisions and undermine national unity. I think Schlesinger and his supporters were crediting social studies teachers with much more power to shape the consciousness of our students and national identity than we actually have. They also misunderstood classroom dynamics and how a curriculum is organized.

It is impossible to teach everything. Every curriculum involves choices about what is important to include. Every curriculum essentially uses "content" case studies to illustrate broader historical concepts. The same concept, such as why ancient civilizations developed in river valleys, can be taught by focusing on Egypt, the Tigris-Euphrates, the Indian sub-continent, or China.

When I taught United States history, I promised students that at some point in the curriculum, their families would be part of what we studied. This generally meant simply focusing on one immigrant group or another during different historical eras. Opponents of alternative curriculum paths usually have fewer problems with the idea when it means using historical examples from the local region. The history standards for every state encourage teachers to do just this.

In my experience, when students see themselves, their ethnic group, or their town, in the curriculum, they are much more interested in the historical narrative. A narrower case study focus also means they are not inundated by vast amounts of unrelated factual information. These are among the reasons I am a strong proponent of multicultural education and tailoring curriculum to address who our students are.

Add your voice to the discussion:
Do you think curriculum should vary depending on the race and ethnicity of students? Explain.

It's your classroom:
What alterations, if any, in the curriculum would you make in the United States history curriculum?

As I became more competent in lesson planning and more confident in my performance as a teacher, I found I was able to appreciate the competence of other people more and learn from them. I was also able to experiment much more. I developed integrated thematic units, long-term group projects, and cooperative learning activities. I worked on motivations, transitions, promoting student discussions, and improving written expression. I tried to develop new means of assessing what my students had learned and what I had taught. Eventually, I was able to move myself out from the "center" of every lesson. I eased up my control over the class and created more space for my students to express their voices.

At the same time that I matured as a classroom teacher, I completed my doctoral dissertation on the transformation of consciousness among bituminous coal miners in the 1920s. At first glance, the topic might seem narrow and distant from my teaching, but in my dissertation I was actually examining one of the questions I was exploring in the classroom: How do people (coal miners, community residents, or high school students) develop fundamentally new perceptions of their world and their place in it?

Over the years I learned along with my students, and much of this book is an effort to share what they have taught me. However, I remain committed to many of the goals I struggled for as a young revolutionary in college in the 1960s and as a community organizer in the 1970s. My primary goal as an educator continues to be empowering young people so that they can become active citizens and agents for democratic social change. I recognize that the most effective way to empower students is to encourage them to think about issues and to help them learn how to collect, organize, analyze, and present information and their own ideas. If I can encourage them to think and act, the habit of thinking and acting will stay with them long after I am just a dim memory. If they only agree with an idea because I present it in class and they want to identify with me, they will just agree with someone else's idea the next year.

Two of my proudest moments as a teacher were when I read an article in the newspaper about a former student who had become a lawyer and an activist defending the rights of immigrants in the South Asian community in Queens, New York, and when a former student, an immigrant from the Dominican Republic who could barely speak English when I knew him, was interviewed on television as the leader of the New York City livery cabdrivers' union.

Because of my beliefs, I am a strong supporter of state and national learning standards that encourage document-based instruction, the ability of students to locate, organize and present information, critical thinking, and the promotion of literacy in the content area subjects.

I consider myself both a "transformative" and a "democratic" educator, and I believe that the teaching package I offer here is consistent with radical notions of education developed by contemporary thinkers like Paulo Freire, Maxine Greene, and Henry Giroux, and progressive ideas championed by John Dewey and his students. Paulo Freire argues that the role of the transformative educator is to help students pose and explore the problems that impact on their lives so they can develop "critical consciousness" about the nature of their society and their position in it (Freire 1970). Henry Giroux calls on transformative educators to allow students to explore their lived experiences, locate themselves culturally, dissect their personal beliefs and the dominant ideology of their society, and confront established power relationships (Giroux 1992).

Learning Activity: Another Brick in the Wall

Michael Pezone is a high school teacher and a mentor teacher in the Hofstra New Teachers Network (NTN). He uses lyrics from the song *Another Brick in the Wall (Part 2)* (available at: http://www.pink-floyd-lyrics.com/html/the-wall-lyrics.html, accessed September 17, 2007) by the British rock band 'Pink Floyd' to provoke his students into thinking about who they are, how school affects them, what education is and should be, and why the world is the way that it is. The song focuses on the alienation of students in schools and accuses teachers of contributing to their oppression (Waters 1979).

It's your classroom:
1. What popular song, if any, would you use to begin this discussion? Why would you select this song?
2. How would you respond to a colleague who thinks that using a song like this in class turns the kids against school and teachers?

I am a democratic educator in the traditions of Maxine Greene (1988) and John Dewey (1916; 1927/1954; 1938/1963). I share Greene's beliefs that democratic education must be based on acceptance of the plurality of human understanding, experience, and ideas, and that freedom represents a process of continuous individual and collective struggle to create more humane societies; it is neither a commodity that can be hoarded by a limited number of individuals nor a right institutionalized by governments and enjoyed by passive citizens. I share Dewey's understanding that the primary classroom responsibility of the teacher is to create democratic learning experiences for students and his commitment to educating an "articulate public" capable of fighting to extend human freedom. I have learned a lot about implementing Deweyan ideas in the classroom from the work of Alfie Kohn (1986), George Wood (1992), and the Rethinking Schools collective (http://www.rethinkingschools.org, accessed September 17, 2007) who discuss the importance of building democratic communities where students are able to express and explore ideas and feelings.

I hope you see the impact of their work on my ideas about teaching and social studies, but, as I wrote earlier, it is not necessary to buy the entire package for this book to be useful. I think most readers, regardless of whether they agree with my broader goals, will find valuable and challenging ideas that will enable them to enrich social studies curricula in their classrooms.

Time is an incredibly valuable commodity for teachers; we never have enough of it. There are always papers to mark, lessons to plan, tests to design, departmental responsibilities, students and parents to meet with, school-imposed deadlines, and assorted emergencies. A job that is supposed to be over at three o'clock and to include regular days off and extended vacation time has a way of stretching until it fills every waking moment.

I have been lucky to have time to reflect on my teaching and write this book. After 13 years in a New York City high school classroom, I was offered a position at Hofstra University as a social studies educator. Working with people who wanted to become teachers gave me the chance to become a more conscious teacher and to root my practice in educational theory. I began to think about many of the ideas about teaching, social studies, and adolescents that I had come to accept, and the things that I just did year after year. Hofstra also gave me the opportunity to go back to teach high school for a year so I could test out what I had been talking about. Since that time I have been a strong proponent of both "reflective practice," the systematic and ongoing evaluation of our work as classroom teachers, and "action research" on our classroom practice to better assess what our students are actually learning.

Over the years, I have experimented with different ways to begin the semester by involving students in exploring social studies and its implications for their lives. Sometimes I change my introductory lessons because they are not working the way I want them to work. Sometimes I give them a particular twist for a special course. Sometimes I change them because I like to experiment with new ways of doing things or with an idea someone has shared with me.

Let me confess at the outset that I believe nothing is ever completely new in teaching, especially teaching social studies. We are always recycling ideas and materials "borrowed" from other teachers (ideas and materials that they also "borrowed" from someone else). As you play around with some of the ideas and lessons introduced in this book, and as you invest in yourself and your students, I think you will discover that rethinking your own lessons and recycling other people's lessons are two of the things that help to make teaching social studies so exciting.

In the 1955 movie *Blackboard Jungle* (Brooks 1955), Glenn Ford portrays an English teacher working in a tough urban high school who explains his desire to be a teacher as an attempt to do something "creative." He tells his university mentor, "I can't be a painter or a writer or an engineer. But I thought if I could help to shape young minds, sort of sculpt lives—and by teaching I'd be creating." The character's pedagogy is a bit dated. Students certainly play a much more active role in their own learning, or refusing to learn, than this statement suggests. But I love watching the movie, and I think these sentiments capture the spirit I want to convey here.

On the first day(s) of class (whether I am teaching social studies in a secondary school or a university), I usually have four goals:

- I want to introduce the class to what I mean by social studies.
- I want to help students discover why the social studies are important in understanding who we are as individuals and members of groups.
- I want to help students begin to define social studies questions they would like to explore during the course.
- I want to begin the process of creating a supportive democratic classroom community where young people (of any age) will work together in an effort to understand the nature of our world.

One successful opening lesson is asking students to answer this question: Who am I? I use this lesson on a number of different academic levels, ranging from middle school through graduate school, although, of course, I structure it differently for different age groups. Sometimes I ask students to make a list of at least ten things about themselves. Sometimes I ask students to write a paragraph about who they are. Sometimes I introduce the activity by saying, "We all belong to different kinds of groups. Some of these groups we are born into. Some of these groups we are placed in. Some of these groups we join voluntarily. Make a list of all of the groups that you belong to." When I start this way, students usually ask for an example of a group. I try to throw the question back to the students and have them come up with suggestions.

Whichever way I begin, I always have students write something. I find that writing helps people focus their thoughts. It allows time for thinking about, organizing, and editing ideas. It also ensures that every student has something they can contribute to the discussion. When everybody has written something, I usually have students come together in small groups to examine the similarities and differences in their responses. I also ask groups to look for categories that can be used to organize the different ways that people in the class define themselves.

Classroom Activity: Who Am I?

I have students complete one of these exercises. In class, we discuss why they describe themselves in these different ways, and I ask them why they think these categories and groups are important. I try to get them to think about how their identities are defined, whether people have to be defined in these ways, and whether their identities are set for life. We use the conversation about our identities to formulate questions about the nature of our society and what we should learn about in class.

1. Each of us thinks about ourselves in a number of different ways. Suppose you had to describe yourself in a letter to someone who does not know you. Think about who you are and then write a letter to introduce yourself. In your letter, include a minimum of ten (or 20) things about yourself.
2. All of us belong to many different groups or categories of people. Some groups we choose to join. Some groups we are born into. Some groups other people place us in. Examples of groups or categories that you may belong to include: a school club or the group that consists of all people who are female. Make a list of all the different groups or categories to which you think you belong. Try to think of 10–20 groups or categories.
3. Interview the student sitting next to you. Find out as much as you can about the person and how they describe themselves. In what way is this person like you? In what way are they different?

Try it yourself:
Select one of the identity exercises and complete it yourself.

It's your classroom:
Would you share your autobiography with students? Why or why not?

While people are working in their groups, I am very busy. I travel from group to group, asking questions that help students uncover patterns and understand the reasons for the characteristics and categories they have selected. I usually carry a notepad and jot down some of their ideas so I can refer to them during full class discussion. Eventually, I have to make judgments based on how the small-group discussions are progressing. At some point, I want the class to become a committee of the whole. I also have to decide how to start discussion in the larger group. Sometimes, I simply ask a group to report on their discussions and this broadens into a full class exploration of the individual, social, and historical nature of the way we identify ourselves. At other times, I have the class "brainstorm" a list of the different characteristics or categories people have used to describe themselves. We list their ideas on the board and then try to find ways of grouping them.

Most students primarily focus on personality, interests, or physical appearance when they list the characteristics that define them. However, their lists also include references to social categories like voluntary group memberships (clubs), family relationships (they are sons or daughters, mothers or fathers, sisters or brothers), occupational roles (student, worker), and broad categories based on their gender, race, religion, and ethnicity. A lot of students like to include their species: human being.

In the discussion that follows, we use the lists to explore how people see themselves, the ways that societies see people, and the ways that people are both similar and different. We discover a lot of things about who we are and the nature of identity. Some of the characteristics and categories are very individual and particular, whereas others are much broader and include many people. Some group memberships are voluntary, but people are born into other groups or placed in them by their society. We choose some definitions of who we are, but the community where we live imposes other definitions on us. Some categories appear to be unchanging, whereas others seem to change on a regular basis.

From this discussion of who we are, the class begins to explore where we come from—that we have histories as individuals and as members of social groups. Sometimes students also begin to talk about how they would like things to be and how they can achieve their goals. By the end of the lesson, students begin to realize that studying social studies helps them understand themselves, their social relationships, and the nature of their world. The lesson creates a reason for them to explore the things the class will examine during the course of the semester.

I did not invent this activity; it is "borrowed" and then reworked to fit my classes and the way that I like to teach. At the center's summer camp in 1971, the campers and staff held a "Convention of Minorities," where we explored the histories and cultures of different racial and ethnic groups in the United States. During the "convention," campers ranging in age from seven to seventeen began to formulate and discuss three interrelated questions: Who am I? Where do I come from? Where do I want to go? I have never forgotten these discussions and the way that they involved such a racially, culturally, religiously, and chronologically diverse group in exploring social studies issues.

Essay: Why Multiculturalism Still Matters

When an idea becomes so all-encompassing that everyone can claim to be a supporter, it loses its meaning. In the United States today, an overwhelming majority of the population defines itself as middle class. That is a very big "middle" that hides very broad differences.

When it comes to multiculturalism, it seems that everybody claims to support it, at least in principle. But as with the term "middle class," this umbrella covers very different concepts. There are probably as many definitions of multiculturalism as there are advocates, which has been part of the problem defining the purpose of multicultural education.

Over the years, Christine Sleeter has done a very good job of cataloguing broad schools of thought on the subject. According to Sleeter (1996), in many school systems, multicultural education has simply meant adding a lesson or activity here and there about people and regions that were previously overlooked. Other than celebrating Martin Luther King's birthday, curricula largely remain the same.

In other schools and districts, human relations workshops or classes are used to increase student and staff sensitivity towards others and respect for cultural differences. In this "can't-we-all-just-get-along" model, a series of workshops, or even only a single mandated lesson, often follows a period of increasing racial and ethnic tension among students or in a community.

Another approach has been called "Teaching the Culturally Different." In this case, teachers tweak the standard curriculum content to focus on the racial and ethnic groups represented by children who are in their classrooms. This approach often means little more than introducing in-group role models. Every group has its heroes, sports stars, cabinet members, or Supreme Court justices, and in "our" classroom we learn about our own. As a Jewish boy who loved sports, I was a big Sandy Koufax fan. My friends and I were convinced he was the greatest pitcher in the history of baseball.

Learning Activity: Lens to the Past

People have a tendency to view the past through the lens of the present. It is one of the major reasons that we need to study history. Secondary school students frequently assume that people from their ethnic background or social group lived like them and always held the same relative position in American society. Over the years, I have looked for newspaper articles and other primary source documents from the past that illustrate the experiences of people with the same ethnic identity as students in my classes. Discussion of these articles brings people like them into the historical process, and helps students reconsider who they are, where they come from, how their ethnic group has been affected by events in the United States, and how its position has changed. The first excerpt is a first-hand account of Irish immigrants in New Orleans in the 1830s. The second describes a police attack on Guyanese immigrants in New York City. The third is a call for a strike at a meeting of Jewish garment workers. The excerpts are edited.

1. "The Irish in New Orleans," Tyrone Powers, *Impressions of America* (1836)
   "At such works all over this continent the Irish are the laborers chiefly employed, and the mortality amongst them is enormous. At present they are, where I have seen them working here, worse lodged than the cattle of the field; in fact, the only thought bestowed upon them appears

to be, by what expedient the greatest quantity of labor may be extracted from them at the cheapest rate to the contractor. Slave labor cannot be substituted to any extent, being much too expensive; a good slave costs at this time two hundred pounds sterling, and to have a thousand such swept off a line of canal in one season, would call for prompt consideration."

2. *The New York Times*, "Negro Aliens Complain," August 18, 1900
Dr. M. S. N. Pierre of 318 West Forty-first Street, a Negro from British Guiana, and 200 of his fellow-British subjects have prepared a petition to Percy Sanderson, British Consul, asking him to take the necessary steps for their protection. The petition alleges that the signers were brutally attacked by the mob in the recent riots, and that the police, instead of giving them protection, actually urged and incited the mob to greater fury.

3. *New York Call*, "The Cooper Union Meeting," November 23, 1909
Clara Lemlich, who was badly beaten up by thugs during the strike in the shop of Louis Leiserson, started to speak, saying: "I wanted to say a few words." Cries came from all parts of the hall, "Get up on the platform!" Willing hands lifted the frail little girl with flashing black eyes to the stage, and she said simply: "I have listened to all the speakers. I would not have further patience for talk, as I am one of those who feels and suffers from the things pictured. I move that we go on a general strike!" As the tremulous voice of the girl died away, the audience rose en masse and cheered her to the echo. A grim sea of faces, with high purpose and resolve, they shouted and cheered the declaration of war for living conditions hoarsely.

Try it yourself:
What ethnic groups are you a member of? How were these groups treated in the past? Find a newspaper article or primary source document that illustrates the position of one of these groups in American society during another historical period.

It's your classroom:
How would you respond to students who do not understand why they have to learn about "them"?

Each of these approaches to multicultural education has something to offer students and I use aspects of each in my own classrooms. But they all fall short of the goals of impacting the lives of students and of promoting a commitment to democratic involvement. They do little to transform who we are as individuals and as a society, and are more easily labeled as expendable frills and add-ons when there is pressure on teachers and administrators to improve student test scores.

Paulo Freire, the Brazilian educator, political activist, and educational philosopher argued, "without practice there is no knowledge" (Bell 1991: 98). He meant that unless people utilize what they learn about themselves, others, and the world, they do not truly understand ideas or believe in them.

Building on this notion, Sleeter and I advocate what she calls "Multicultural Education as Social Reconstruction." We believe that a conscious and prominent ingredient in the study of global cultural diversity should be the examination of injustice and oppression that feed on prejudice, undermine political and social equality, and victimize people all over the world. Multicultural education in this sense, means learning to question and critique dominant ideologies and social institutions and developing the skills required for social activism. Activism does not only go one way. I am not talking about training revolutionary cadre committed to the overthrow of government. But I am arguing that it is our responsibility as teachers to prepare an active citizenry that resists efforts by those with political and economic power to dictate what they should believe and how they should behave.

This version of multicultural education is consistent with Thomas Jefferson's belief that the goals of education should be "to enable every man to judge for himself what will secure or endanger his freedom" (1810) and to empower the people as the "ultimate guardians of their own liberty" (1784).

In 1999, I wrote an article for the National Council for the Social Studies in which I argued, "with public and professional attention now riveted on national standards, curricula that emphasize history instead of social studies, and proposals for national testing programs, the demand for multicultural inclusion in social studies curricula may have run its course" (Singer 1999: 28–31).

I admit that since then I have wavered in my commitment to a multicultural approach to social studies; not to the principle, but in my public advocacy, writing, and teaching. When I discussed a third edition of *Social Studies for Secondary Schools* with the publisher, I proposed that given the current debates in education, the extended discussions of multi-culturalism in the first two editions needed to be consolidated.

After considerably more thought, new developments in the first six months of 2007 prompted me to change my mind again. I know some politicians do not like to say this, especially presidential candidates, but I was wrong.

Each of these events led me to think deeper and harder about why multiculturalism still matters:

- The Cherokee people of Oklahoma put to a vote the question of who is legitimately a member of the Cherokee nation.
- The New York City Council debated a symbolic ban on use of the "N-Word."
- The Anglican Church faced a schism over the ordination of gay priests and the elevation of gay bishops.
- The United States was sharply divided over immigration reform.
- Senator Barack Obama announced his candidacy for the Democratic Party's nomination for President of the United States.
- President Bush proposed an increase in United States armed forces in Iraq.

The Cherokee nation is the second largest tribe in the United States with over 250,000 members. Membership, as the saying goes, has its advantages. It entitles people to federal benefits and tribal services, including medical and housing aid and college scholarships. When the Cherokee, one of the so-called "civilized tribes," was forced to move to Oklahoma on the "Long March" in 1838, many of them brought along enslaved Africans to work their new lands. Slavery ended on the reservation in 1866 and Black freedmen and women were granted full citizenship in the independent Cherokee nation. Over the next hundred years they intermarried with other members of the tribe. In 1983, a tribal decree stripped away membership rights from descendants of the freedmen and women, claiming they were not "Cherokee by blood." When this was overturned by a federal court decision, a vote was taken to amend the Cherokee constitution and limit citizenship to those who could trace their heritage to the "Dawes Rolls," a federal tribal census conducted in 1906 (Nieves 2007).

The problem is that the Dawes Rolls reflected the virulent racism of the time. Although tribal members of mixed European and Native American ancestry were listed as Cherokee, Black freedmen and people of mixed African and Native American ancestry were placed on a separate list.

More than 75 percent of those currently enrolled in the Cherokee Nation are genetically less than one-quarter Cherokee. The vast majority of these people are of partial European ancestry. If the new "definition," which was approved by three-quarters of the voters, is implemented, White Americans, with a "single drop" of Cherokee blood, will be able to claim tribal membership and benefits, while Blacks who live on the reservation, who have been part of the tribe and its cultural traditions for decades, and who may actually have a large number of ancestors who are biologically Cherokee, will be excluded. In what is essentially a battle over distribution of limited resources, racism raises its ugly head in America once again.

As teachers, we are often confronted by young Black people casually calling each other "nigger" or "nigga." They hear it in the street and in popular music, and they repeat it in school corridors and classrooms. Use of the "N-word" within the community has been defended by some African-Americans as a term denoting group membership and mutual respect. It has been described as an attack on racism because the meaning of the word has supposedly been transformed into something new and empowering.

Everyone is not happy with this formulation, particularly in the Black community. The New York City Council recently approved a symbolic ban on use of the "N-Word" in the city as a statement that racism and racist terms are unacceptable (Schuster 2007).

I find the claim of empowerment shallow and a poor substitute for political action against racism and injustice. The pain associated with the "N-Word" continues to haunt American society. Most Whites teachers I know, who have heard the word used as a racist epithet and who reject this use, cannot say it out loud, even to discuss the issue of its meaning with their students. Most young Blacks I know who tolerate the use of the term within their group remain deeply offended when Whites use the "N-Word" as a term of comradery. When a word evokes this level of emotion, it is because the underlying feelings and biases behind the word remain in effect.

Secondary school students need to see the way the word has been used throughout United States history as a weapon against Black people. This quote from a 1981 interview with Lee Atwater, a Republican Party consultant and confidant of President Reagan and the first President Bush, shows how the sentiments behind the word continue to influence contemporary United States politics. According to Atwater, the way you traditionally swayed White voters, especially in the US South, was by shouting "Nigger, nigger, nigger." However, "[B]y 1968 you can't say 'nigger'—that hurts you. Backfires. So you say stuff like forced busing, states' rights and all that stuff." By the 1980s, politicians were "getting so abstract" that they were "talking about cutting taxes, and all these things you're talking about are totally economic things and a byproduct of them is [that] blacks get hurt worse than whites" (Herbert 2005: 37). Atwater's point is that both the politicians and their targeted voters know they are using code words for no longer acceptable racial epithets, and even though the phrases had become more "abstract," politicians were essentially still shouting "Nigger" to get White votes.

Learning Activity: Decision-making in a Democratic Classroom

Sojourner Truth was an African-American woman and a former slave who was active in the women's rights movement of the 1850s. Her participation was frequently challenged by White activists who did not want woman's suffrage associated in the public's mind with abolition. At the 1851 Akron, Ohio women's rights convention, Sojourner Truth delivered one of the most famous speeches in US history. Truth could neither read nor write; however, Frances Gage, the president of the convention, included a report on the address and the audience's response in her reminiscences. In her report, Gage presented readers, as best as she could, with Sojourner Truth's accent, syntax, and grammar. Her version of the speech has been edited and re-edited numerous times over the years.

The first version that follows is by Frances Gage (Stanton et al. 1889:116), and was published in *History of Woman Suffrage, Vol. 1*. The second version is adapted from an attempt to modify and modernize the language for use in a high school classroom (Millstein and Bodin 1977:116–117). The third version is from Diane Ravitch's *The American Reader: Words that Moved a Nation* (1990:86–87). In the original Gage version, Sojourner Truth refers to herself and other African-Americans as "niggers." Ravitch changed the word to Negroes. Other editors have substituted Blacks or Africans.

Which version should we use in our classes? If we use Gage's original text, how do we handle the painful impact of certain words on many people? Should we remain committed to historical accuracy? Should we involve students in making these decisions?

1. Frances Gage's version of Sojourner Truth's speech:
   "Wall, chilern, whar dar is so much racket dar must be somethin out o' kilter. I tink dat 'twixt de niggers of de Souf and de womin at de North, all talkin' 'bout rights, de white men will be in a fix pretty soon. But what's all dis here talkin' 'bout? . . . Den dey talks 'bout dis ting in de head; what dis dey call it? ['Intellect,' whispered someone near.] Dat's it, honey. What's dat got to do wid womin's rights or nigger's rights? If my cup won't hold but a pint and yourn holds a quart, wouldn't ye be mean not to let me have my little half-measure full?"

2. An edited version of Sojourner Truth's speech:
   "Well, children, where there is so much racket there must be something out of kilter. I think that between the niggers of the South and the women of the North, all talking about rights, the white men will be in a fix pretty soon. But what's all this here talking about? . . Then they talk about this thing in the head; what do they call it? ['Intellect,' whispered someone near.] That's it, honey. What's that got to do with women's rights or nigger's rights? If my cup won't hold but a pint and yours holds a quart, wouldn't you be mean not to let me have my little half-measure full?"

3. Diane Ravitch removes the word "nigger":
   "Well, children, where there is so much racket there must be something out of kilter. I think that 'twixt the Negroes of the South and the women of the North, all talking about rights, the white men will be in a fix pretty soon. But what's all this here talking about? . . Then they talk about this thing in the head; what do they call it? ['Intellect,' someone whispers.] That's it, honey. What's that got to do with women's rights or Negro's rights? If my cup won't hold but a pint and yours holds a quart, wouldn't you be mean not to let me have my little half-measure full?"

Think it over:
Which version of Sojourner Truth's speech would you prefer to use? Why?

It's your classroom:
1. Would you involve your students in deciding which version to use? Why? How would you involve them?
2. What would you say and do if their opinions were divided along racial lines?

The schism in the international Anglican Church over the ordination of gay priests and the elevation of gay bishops is just a small piece of a broad cultural and political debate over homosexual rights and the norms of human sexuality. It includes the legitimacy of gay marriages, adoptions, partnership rights, and service in the military, as well as the right of adults to have consensual sexual relations without government or religious interference. In the past, gay rights was a divisive issue among multiculturalists, some of whom prized ethnic and cultural diversity, but because of traditional religious upbringings were uncomfortable extending the same recognition to gays and lesbians (Banerjee 2007: A11).

While all human differences are not cultural, one of the great strengths of the multicultural movement in the United States has been its ability to expand the notion of who should be included in our communities and its championing of a wide range of diversity. It is because of multiculturalism that many Americans, including myself, have come to accept the legitimacy of what makes us uncomfortable.

The debate over changes in immigration laws have been at least as sharp as the debate over homosexuality and it has been much more extensive. In May 2006, President George Bush proposed an immigration reform package that eventually became so complicated and, according to its critics, contradictory, that it had virtually no support. It was finally defeated in the US Senate in June 2007 (http://abcnews.go.com/Politics/story?id=3326113&page=1, accessed September 17, 2007). Debate over the bill exposed deep-seated prejudice in the United States against recent immigrants, whether legal or undocumented. This problem will only intensify as the population of the United States becomes increasingly more diverse. According to the 2000 census, the population of the United States was approximately 69 percent non-Hispanic White, 12 percent African-American, 12 percent Hispanic, and 4 percent Asian (http://www.census.gov/prod/2001pubs/cenbr01–1.pdf, accessed September 17, 2007). However, Texas and California already had non-White majorities (http://www.censusscope.org/us/map_nhwhite.html, accessed September 17, 2007). Furthermore, according to the census bureau's estimates for 2005, 45 percent of American children under the age of five were minorities (http://www.prb.org/Articles/2006/IntheNewsUSPopulationIsNowOneThirdMinority.aspx?p=1, accessed September 17, 2007).

Another reason I decided multiculturalism still mattered was the Obama phenomenon, but not for the reason you would initially suspect. Senator Barrack Obama was the first non-White candidate in United States history to have a realistic chance of being nominated for president by a major political party. He was a "walking-talking" advertisement for a multicultural America. His Black father was an African from Kenya. His White mother was a Middle American from Kansas whose ancestors owned enslaved Africans. He was raised in Indonesia and Hawaii where he attended ethnically diverse schools. He was married to an African-American woman and the Senator, his wife, and children identified themselves as African-American.

While Senator Obama personified multiculturalism, his campaign for president rested on an ideological platform that minimized its importance. At the 2004 Democratic Party National Convention, Senator Obama charged that "pundits like to slice-and-dice our country into Red and Blue States: Red States for Republicans, Blue States for Democrats. But I've got some good news for them, too . . . We are one people, all of us pledging allegiance to the stars and stripes, all of us defending the United States of America." Later, in his best-selling book, *The Audacity of Hope* (2006: 22), the Senator wrote: "Perhaps more than any other time in our recent history, we [meaning American citizens] need a new kind of politics, one that can excavate and build upon those shared understandings that pull us together as Americans."

His message, as I read it, is that our differences are minimal. Underneath the skin we are all the same. Taking this position points to the best in our nation and may be the only way Senator Obama thought he could get elected president. But that does not make this an accurate portrayal of the way race, class, gender, and ethnicity are experienced in the United States. Our differences are real, and the way they are manipulated for political gain are more than just superficial.

If multiculturalism is meaningful, it must stand for social justice as well as respect for difference. But conditions in the United States are far from just. According to studies by the Harvard Civil Rights project, school segregation that has contributed to "savage inequalities" in every major metropolitan area in the United States has increased since the 1970s. Despite the promises of "No Child Left Behind," many children, especially children from racial and ethnic minority groups, remain in substandard schools where they are tracked for failure. Even those fortunate enough to attend functioning schools are more than likely assigned to "test prep" classes where the curriculum focuses on remediation rather than education.

A report by Northeastern University's Center for Labor Market Studies concluded that in the past 50 years African-American men have suffered a serious decline in labor force participation (Herbert 2007: 27). In 1954, 52 percent of Black male teenagers held jobs. By 2003, only one out of five Black male teenagers were employed. In 1954, the employment rate for White teenagers was less than the employment rate for Black teenagers. In 2007 it was double. Employment rates among Black males aged 20–24 and among older Black men have seen parallel precipitous declines. Can you imagine the outrage if half the White male population of the United States was regularly out of work?

Americans were embarrassed by government ineptitude and failure in New Orleans following Hurricane Katrina and the racial implication of its mega-failures. A curriculum package on Hurricane Katrina and its racial implications, with lessons paired to the Spike Lee movie *When the Levees Broke*, was distributed by the National Council for Social Studies (Crocco 2007). It includes a lesson on "Third World Conditions in a First World Country." I believe that based on school and job statistics, every inner-city minority community in the United States is potentially another New Orleans.

Classroom Activity: Family Artifacts

Most people, but especially people who are members of the dominant groups in a society, assume their own culture is the norm. They absorb it from their families and the media while they grow up. Unless they are exposed to other cultures, they live their lives without really thinking about who they are and the ways that they do things. One way to help students begin to think about cultural identity and the values, ideas, and practices of their own cultures is to have them bring a family artifact to class. Students can present their artifacts and explain their origins and why they are important to their families. The class can compare artifacts from different cultures and use them to begin an exploration of cultural similarities and differences.

In a variation of this activity, Cynthia Vitere has high school students bring in family artifacts that are circulated around the room anonymously. Student teams examine the artifacts and speculate about cultures of origin. After teams report hypotheses to the class, the students who brought in the artifacts discuss their actual significance to their families. Rachael Thompson and Laurence Klein have students in their middle school classes use the family artifacts to organize a Museum of Immigration. Sometimes parents and grandparents come to class to explain customs and holidays, model clothing, and prepare food. All of the teachers have their students write about the cultural and historical background of the artifacts as part of their commitment to promote student literacy through work in the content areas.

Try it yourself:
Bring an artifact to class that shows something about the cultural background of your family.

This vast social inequality has been maintained by a majority White electorate, fearful of change, that votes for candidates committed to maintaining its privileged position and ignoring the impact of racism and bigotry on American society. It is buttressed by laws that disenfranchise citizens convicted of felonies, deny the right to vote to recent documented immigrants and all undocumented residents, grant disproportionate legislative representation to rural communities that are largely White, and declare millions of Black and Hispanic voters living in Washington, DC and Puerto Rico ineligible to participate in federal elections.

Almost one and a half million Black men cannot vote because of felony convictions. In Florida, which gave the election to George Bush in 2000 and 2004, 30 percent of all Black men are permanently disenfranchised. If Puerto Rico had electoral votes in 2000, Al Gore would have been elected President of the United States. When it comes to electoral politics, it is as if the entire nation has become like the pre-Civil Rights Era South.

Learning Activity: The Changing Complexion of the United States

Since immigration laws changed in 1965, the population of the United States has become increasingly more diverse. Few people realize the extent of the change. According to the Census Bureau (Roberts 2007: A21), in 2006 the nation's minority population was over 100 million people, or about one-third of the nation. However, there was a significant demographic divide. Eighty percent of the population over 60 years of age was White, but only 58 percent of the population under 19 were. If this trend continues, and the Census Bureau projects that it will, it may become meaningless to talk about a "majority" population in the United States. By 2006, "minorities" were already a majority in four states: Hawaii, New Mexico, California, and Texas.

Add your voice to the discussion:
What actions, if any, should the United States take to address these demographic changes? Explain.

Try it yourself:
Imagine it is the year 2050. How will the demographics of your community have changed? What cultural and political changes do you anticipate will accompany demographic changes?

Meanwhile, hostility toward ethnic difference has soared. Media and political commentators anxious to boost ratings or win elections have played up the idea of a "clash of civilizations." Sometimes they claim it exists between the West and the Islamic world. Sometimes the "clash" is supposedly between Anglo and Latin America. But it is always posed as a threat to the "American Way of Life."

Since September 11, 2001, Islamic, Middle Eastern, and South Asian men and women have routinely been held suspect and sometimes assaulted because of their appearance. Hispanic has become synonymous with illegal alien, even though more than 60 percent of the Hispanic population of the United States was born in this country.

The danger of minimizing the impact of difference on society, of claiming we are all really the same, and of abandoning an active commitment to promoting multiculturalism, can be seen in events that occurred in France during the last few years. The population of France is roughly 10 percent Moslem, most of whom are members of families originally from former French colonies in North and West Africa, the Caribbean, and the Middle East. French Moslems are crowded into substandard housing, in ghettoized communities, with poorly performing schools and high rates of unemployment (Smith 2005: 3). Sound familiar?

France has prided itself that all French citizens are socially and politically equal. The French claim that the law does not see "race" or ethnicity, and affirmative action and a commitment to multiculturalism are unnecessary. Perversely, because of its commitment to equality and claim that there are no differences among its citizens, the French government has been unable to address the multiple problems faced by immigrants and their children, who while nominally French, are never truly accepted. The result of this failed policy has been rioting by frustrated young people in the Moslem ghettos and increasing electoral success for anti-immigrant political parties. Violent unrest has happened in the United States before and it may well happen again. As H. Rap Brown of the Black Panther Party commented in the 1960s, "Violence is as American as apple pie" (http://encarta.msn.com/encyclopedia_761580646/Black_Power.html, accessed October 25, 2007).

By spring 2007, the Democratic Party, and some Republicans, seemed to have finally woken up to the debacles taking place in Afghanistan and Iraq and their impact on American standing around the world. Heroin production had reached record levels in Afghanistan, the western region of Pakistan was no longer under government control, and Iraq had plunged into a bloody civil war. Meanwhile, the international coalition that President Bush assembled to fight a war on terrorism had dissolved at the same time that Americans were being asked to escalate troop strength and financial commitments in the region.

The absence of a real debate in the United States about the implications of the events of September 11, 2001 and the long-term impact of an invasion of Afghanistan and Iraq emphasizes the importance of two other essential aspects of multiculturalism that must be part of the education of our children because they are essential for the promotion of active, educated, citizens and for the survival of democracy—respect for diverse opinions and uncertainty about universal truths.

In the rush for vengeance following September 11, 2001, discussion about what made sense was suspended and freedom of speech was tempered because no one with political or career aspirations wanted to be branded as soft on terrorism. George Bush silenced dissent by declaring God had endorsed American military policies because, although "We're a peaceful nation . . . there can be no peace in a world of sudden terror." He warned that "Every nation," and by implication every American, "has a choice to make. In this conflict there is no neutral ground."

Teachers were put on notice by conservative spokesperson and former Under-Secretary of Education Diane Ravitch, who accused advocates of multicultural education specifically, and anyone else who questioned the push for war or tried to understand the reasons for the attacks, of being cultural relativists incapable of making moral judgments (Ravitch 2001).

Only one Congressional representative, Barbara Lee of California, had the courage to oppose the "blank check" authorizing President Bush to use military force against Afghanistan in retaliation for the attacks (Singer 2002: 3). Lee warned Americans, "Far too many innocent people have already died. Our country is in mourning. If we rush to launch a counter-attack, we run too great a risk that women, children, and other non-combatants will be caught in the crossfire. Nor can we let our justified anger over these outrageous acts by vicious murderers inflame prejudice against all Arab Americans, Muslims, South-east Asians, or any other people because of their race, religion, or ethnicity." But in the climate of the time, she was ignored.

A few months later, the United States Senate voted 77:23 and the House of Representatives 296:133 to authorize a pre-emptive attack against Iraq. President Bush praised the Congressional action, declaring "America speaks with one voice," as if the silencing of other voices somehow was a sign of democratic decision-making (Bush 2002).

Senator Robert Byrd of West Virginia attempted to argue against the authorization resolution but discussion was cut off in the Senate by a 75:25 vote. A year later, as the American military prepared to launch its attack, an exasperated Byrd wrote: "To contemplate war is to think about the most horrible of human experiences. On this February day, as this nation stands at the brink of battle, every American on some level must be contemplating the horrors of war. Yet, this Chamber is, for the most part, silent—ominously, dreadfully silent. There is no debate, no discussion, no attempt to lay out for the nation the pros and cons of this particular war. There is nothing. We stand passively mute in the United States Senate, paralyzed by our own uncertainty, seemingly stunned by the sheer turmoil of events." He concluded, "We are truly 'sleepwalking' through history" (Byrd 2003). But in the climate of the time, he was ignored.

In a time when people seem determined to erase the uncomfortable past from historical memory; when symbolic language has become a substitute for social action; when bigotry is used to mobilize voters to support a conservative political agenda; when increased diversity has become an excuse for minimizing multicultural education; when world peace and stability are endangered by defenders of universal truth and "deciders" who claim to act in the name of God, we cannot allow ourselves to be ignored. This is why I believe in multiculturalism. This is why multicultural still matters.

Classroom Activity: Cartoon Metaphors

These cartoons are from a lesson on European immigration to the United States from 1880–1920. They can be used in either middle school or high school.

See Figures 1.2 and 1.3 opposite.

Try it yourself:
1. Which metaphor best illustrates your vision of American society? Why?
2. Design a cartoon presenting your pictorial metaphor for the United States today.

Figure 1.2 Salad bowl.

Figure 1.3 Melting pot.

References and Recommendations for Further Reading

Banerjee, N. 2007. "Visit by Anglican bishop draws Episcopal anger," *The New York Times*, April 28.

Beagle, P. 1968. *The last unicorn*. New York: Viking.

Becker, C. 1942. *The Declaration of Independence*. New York: Knopf.

Bell, N. 1991. *We make the road by walking*. Philadelphia, PA: Temple University Press.

Brooks, R. (dir. 1955). *Blackboard jungle*, MGM, 100 min.

Bush, G. 2002. "President Bush outlines Iraqi threat," October. http://www.whitehouse.gov/news/releases/2002/10/20021007–8.html, accessed April 12, 2007.

Byrd, R. 2003. "Reckless administration may reap disastrous consequences," February 12. http://www.commondreams.org/views03/0212–07.htm, accessed April 12, 2007.

Crocco, M. ed. 2007. *Teaching the levees*. New York: Teachers College Press.

Dewey, J. 1916. *Democracy and education*. New York: Macmillan.

Dewey, J. 1927/1954. *The public and its problems*. Athens, OH: Swallow Press.

Dewey, J. 1938/1963. *Experience and education*. New York: Collier/Macmillan.

Freire, P. 1970. *Pedagogy of the oppressed*. New York: Seabury.

Freire, P. 1995. *Pedagogy of hope*. New York: Continuum.

Giroux, H. 1992. *Border crossings: Cultural workers and the politics of education*. New York: Routledge.

Greene, M. 1988. *The dialect of freedom*. New York: Teachers College Press.

Herbert, B. 2005. "Impossible, ridiculous, repugnant," *The New York Times*, October 6.

Herbert, B. 2007. "The danger zone," *The New York Times*, March 15.

Jefferson, T. 1784. "Notes on the State of Virginia." http://press-pubs.uchicago.edu/founders/documents/v1ch18s16.html, accessed April 12, 2007.

Jefferson, T. 1810. http://www.cr.nps.gov/nR/twhp/wwwlps/lessons/92uva/92facts1.htm, accessed April 12, 2007.

Kohn, A. 1986. *No contest: The case against competition*. Boston, MA: Houghton Mifflin.

LaTouche, J. and Robinson, E. 1940. *Ballad for Americans*. New York: Robbins Music Corporation.

Millstein, B. and Bodin, J., eds. 1977. *We the American women. A documentary history*. Chicago, IL: Science Research Associates.

Murekatete, J. 2004. "100 Days of Genocide in Rwanda," *Social Science Docket* 4(1).

Nieves, E. 2007. "Putting to a vote the question 'Who Is Cherokee'?" *The New York Times*, March 3.

Obama, B. 2006. *The audacity of hope*. New York: Crown.

Powers, T. *Impressions of America during the years 1833, 1834, and 1835* (London: R. Bently, 1836), in F. Binder and D. Reimers. 1988. *The way we lived, essays and documents in American social history*, I. Lexington, MA: DC Heath, pp. 238–40.

Ravitch, D. 1990. *The American reader: Words that moved a nation*. New York: HarperCollins.

Ravitch, D. 2001. "Now is the time to teach democracy," *Education Week* October 17: 21(7).

Robeson, S. 1990. *The whole world in his hands*. New York: Citadel Press, pp. 117–18.

Roberts, S. 2007. "New demographic racial gap emerges," *The New York Times*, May 17.

Schlesinger, A. 1992. *The disuniting of America*. New York: Norton.

Schuster, K. 2007. "City council bans use of 'N' word," *Newsday*, February 27. http://www.newsday.com/news/local/newyork/ny-nyword0227,0,2286981.story, accessed April 12, 2007.

Singer, A. 1999. "Teaching multicultural social studies in an era of political eclipse," *Social Education* 63(1).

Singer, A. 2002. Now is the time to teach democracy. *Organization of American Historians Newsletter* 30(1).

Sleeter, C. 1996. *Multicultural education as social activism*. Albany, NY: SUNY Press.

Smith, C. 2005. "Has an underclass, but its roots are still shallow," *The New York Times*, November 6.

Stanton, E., Anthony S. and Gage, M., eds. 1889. *History of woman suffrage*, v. 1. Rochester, New York: Charles Mann.

Waters, R. 1979. "Another Brick in the Wall (Part II)," Pink Floyd Music Publishing/Unichappel Music, in *No.1 Songs from the 70's & 80's*. Winona, MN: Hal Leonard Publishing.

Wood, G. 1992. *Schools that work*. New York: Dutton.

I. Thinking about Social Studies

2. Why Study History?

Overview

- Define history and the social sciences
- Examine theories about the role of history and the social sciences for creating knowledge and understanding our world
- Explore the similarities, differences, and relationships between the disciplines included in social studies
- Discuss the significance of social studies in secondary education

Key Concepts

Multiple Perspectives, History, Social Science, Social Studies, Curriculum

Questions

- Why Teach Social Studies?
- Why Study History?
- What Does It Mean To Be An Historian?
- What is History?
- What is a Social Studies Approach to History?
- What are Historical Facts?

What is the Difference Between Fact and Theory?

- How Does an Historian Study History?
- How Do Historians Resolve Disagreements?
- Should a Teacher also be an Historian?
- Is the Study of History Scientific?
- Are there Laws in History?
- What are the Goals of Historians?

Essays

1. What Social Studies is All About
2. Are We Teaching "Greek Myths" in the Global History Curriculum?

WHY TEACH SOCIAL STUDIES?

The song *This Land Is Your Land* (1956, available at: www.arlo.net/lyrics, accessed September 17, 2007) has become a popular standard at public school assembly programs in the United States. It is hard to imagine that it was written by Woodrow Wilson "Woody" Guthrie, a formerly unemployed and homeless "Okie" who was involved in left-wing political causes during a career that spanned from the 1920s to the 1950s. Guthrie spent his youth in Oklahoma, absorbing the culture and music of farm workers and rural mountain people before joining the great dust-bowl migration to the US west coast. In California, he was an active supporter of the labor movement and the Communist Party (Blum 1990: 284–285). Many of Guthrie's songs celebrate the United States, but in a way that questions the fundamental inequalities he witnessed in our society. A simple statement like "this land is your land, this land is my land," which says that the nation belongs to everyone, challenges a world where some people have great wealth and limitless opportunity while others are impoverished, discriminated against, and disempowered. In stanzas that rarely appear in school productions, Woody's political message is much more explicit. For example, one stanza openly challenges the idea of private property (Seeger 1985: 160–162).

Removing Woody Guthrie and his music from their historical and political contexts changes the meaning of his songs and ignores what he tried to achieve during his life. However, when teachers provide a context for Guthrie's songs, it opens up the possibility for broad discussions of the social, economic, and political nature of US society, including philosophical explorations of morality, individual action, and social justice. Providing a context that broadens people's understanding of our world and gets us to question our assumptions about it is a primary reason to study and teach history and the social sciences or, in the lexicon of education, the social studies.

According to the National Council for the Social Studies (NCSS 1994):

> Social studies is the integrated study of the social sciences and humanities to promote civic competence. Within the school program, social studies provides coordinated, systematic study drawing upon such disciplines as anthropology, archeology, economics, geography, history, law, philosophy, political science, psychology, religion, and sociology, as well as appropriate content from the humanities, mathematics, and natural sciences. The primary purpose of social studies is to help young people develop the ability to make informed and reasoned decisions for the public good as citizens of a culturally diverse, democratic society in an interdependent world.

Because of the complexity of our world, and because of a democratic society's dependence on thoughtful, informed, active citizens, the social studies are multidisciplinary and interdisciplinary. Social studies teachers are the intellectual imperialists of secondary education. Everything is included in our subject's domain. But to teach social studies in schools, it has to be organized into curricula with calendars, units, and lessons that include goals, content, and concepts that (a) promote academic and social skills, (b) raise questions, (c) provoke disagreements, (d) address controversial issues, (e) suggest connections, and (f) stimulate action.

Adding to the difficulty of defining and teaching social studies are the political implications of many curriculum choices. For example, in January 1995, the US Senate voted 99 to 1 to reject National History Standards that were prepared by the National Center for History in the Schools with participation from the NCSS, the Organization of American Historians (OAH), and the American Historical Association (AHA). The Senate resolution claimed that the standards, which were written under a grant from the federally funded National Endowment for the Humanities, failed to provide students with a decent respect for the contributions of western civilization to the development of the United States (Rethinking Schools 1995: 7).

In the last few years the federal government has tried to influence the teaching of history in secondary schools by financing staff development through the Teaching American History grant program. I have participated in a number of the projects and on the local level they tend to be flexible in their approach to history and teaching. However, guidelines for grant applications are restrictive and insist that funds should only be made available to programs that promote "Traditional American history" (see Chapter 5, Essay 2 for a more in-depth discussion).

According to former Secretary of Education Rod Paige, "Traditional American history . . . teaches how the principles of freedom and democracy, articulated in our founding documents, have shaped—and continue to shape—America's struggles and achievements, as well as its social, political, and legal institutions and relations. Traditional history puts its highest priority on making sure students have an understanding of these principles and of the historical events and people that best illustrate them" (Rees 2003; Paige 2003: 24054). My problem is that this definition would exclude teaching about slavery, segregation, racism, the extermination of Native Americans, the internment of the Japanese, xenophobia, nativism, religious bias, imperialism, the Klan, the exploitation of workers, continuing social inequality, and any efforts to challenge them. With these non-traditional topics eliminated from the curriculum, it would be difficult to explain why this country had a Civil Rights movement, suffragists, and labor unions.

The disputes over National History Standards (discussed again in Chapter 5) and "traditional" American history are just the tip of a very large iceberg. Within the social studies, there are ongoing curriculum debates pitting supporters of multicultural vs. traditional European-centered curriculum; advocates of a focus on historical content versus champions of history as a process of discovery (inquiry-based learning); organizations that want history at the center of any curriculum and groups that prefer a broader social science perspective; celebrators of America's glories vs. critics of its inconsistencies; political historians vs. social historians vs. economic historians vs. feminist historians; and people who want teachers to play a strictly neutral role in classroom discussions against those who argue that claims for neutrality mask support for the status quo. Rightwing websites including http://edwatch.org branded me a "social predator" because of an article I wrote for *Rethinking Schools* advocating the promotion of student activism as part of citizenship education.

Many of these debates, especially those on multiculturalism, were re-ignited following the attacks on the World Trade Center in New York and the Pentagon in Washington DC on September 11, 2001. Chester E. Finn Jr. accused proponents of multiculturalism of shortchanging patriotism (Hartocollis 2001a: A32). Lynne Cheney denounced educators who wanted American schools to expand efforts to teach habits of tolerance, knowledge, and awareness of other cultures (Hartocollis 2001b: 9). Diane Ravitch, a former official in the federal Department of Education, charged, "multiculturalism, as it is taught in the United States, . . . teaches cultural relativism because it implies that 'no group may make a judgment on any other.' "

Even when politicians keep their distance from the schools, social studies teachers, by themselves, are a contentious lot. I think that this is the way it should be. How can we teach students to value ideas and knowledge, and to become participants in democratic decision making, if we hide what we believe? Sometimes the best way to include students in discussions is for teachers to express their opinions and involve classes in examining and critiquing them.

WHY STUDY HISTORY?

When our children were younger, my wife and I sang a song with them by Robert Clairmont called *The Answers* (Engvick 1965: 38–39). In this song, a child questions a lamb, a goat, a cow, a hog, a duck, a goose, and a hen about the origin of the world and records their

responses: quack, honk, oink, and moo. The idea of copying down responses from barnyard animals seemed so ridiculous that we all used to laugh. Unfortunately, writing down meaningless answers to what are potentially such wonderful questions goes on in social studies classrooms across the United States. For far too many students, social studies means copying from the board.

As a witness during his libel suit against the *Chicago Tribune* in July 1919, Henry Ford is quoted as saying, "History is more or less bunk" (Seldes 1966: 253). Ford's statement was probably just part of an effort to collect from the newspaper. But, possibly, he also understood the power of history if it got into the wrong hands; the hands of the automobile workers in his factories, ordinary citizens, or people who disagreed with his economic and political views. History gives us both the information and the means for understanding our world. History is the past, and it is the human effort to study, understand, and utilize the past to help us make choices about, and to shape, the future. History is neither bunk nor moo, despite what Henry Ford or the cow may have said.

If we are going to teach students about history and the social sciences, we have to have some idea what each discipline includes. I am not only referring to information about the past and present—that part is laid out effectively in textbooks—but also ideas about how practitioners of these disciplines work, insights into the motivation of people and societies, opinions about the way the world operates and changes, and theories about the connections among past, present, and future.

A number of historians have shaped my thinking about the meaning of history (the past) and the use of history (the field of study). Much of the discussion in this section is based on my reflections on the work of two historians, E. H. Carr, an historian of modern Russia and the Soviet Union in the twentieth century, and Stephen Jay Gould, a paleontologist who also was an historian of science. Their ideas on the meaning of history are much more developed than mine, and I strongly recommend that social studies teachers examine their work. I first read E. H. Carr's book, *What is History?* (1961), as a graduate student in the early 1970s. When I re-read it while preparing this chapter, I was surprised to discover how much of an impact it had had on my thinking about history. Carr introduced me to the idea of thinking about the past and present as part of a continuum that stretches into the future. He believes that concern with the future is what really motivates the study of the past.

I enjoy reading Stephen Jay Gould's books and articles for a number of reasons. Gould asked interesting historical and scientific questions, had the ability to connect what appear to be narrow issues with sweeping global concerns, and used philosophical and literary metaphors to create mental images that illustrate complex ideas. In his writing, especially *Wonderful Life* (1989), he demonstrated how a point of view directs our questions and allows us to see things that we might otherwise miss.

Wonderful Life is the story of 525-million-year-old fossils discovered at a rock quarry in the Rocky Mountains near the British Columbia-Alberta border. Known as the Burgess Shale, they are possibly the oldest soft body animal fossils in existence. When they were first collected in the early part of the twentieth century, evolution was considered a gradual, incremental process, so scientists assumed they were similar to animal families (phyla) that survive today. Since that time, scientists have become aware of numerous catastrophic extinctions in the distant past and have developed a new understanding of the evolution of life. This theory, called punctuated equilibrium, posits long periods of stability followed by relatively rapid change. When the *Burgess Shale* fossils were reexamined from this

new perspective in the 1970s, scientists realized that these were entirely different life forms with no contemporary descendants. I was actually inspired by the book and the theory of punctuated equilibrium to make the trek to the fossil site, a trip that included a ten-hour guided mountain hike through Yoho National Park.

A good example of Gould's approach to historical study was his effort to explain William Jennings Bryan's apparent shift from progressive to conservative during the course of his career (1991: 416–431). Bryan was a Midwestern Populist who ran unsuccessfully for US President as a Democrat in 1896, 1900, and 1908. He also served as Secretary of State under Woodrow Wilson. In the 1920s, Bryan was a leader in the campaign to prevent the teaching of evolutionary biology in the schools, and he served as the prosecuting attorney in the 1925 Tennessee v. Scopes "Monkey" trial.

In the *Age of Reform and Anti-Intellectualism in American Life*, Richard Hofstadter (1955, 1962) used Bryan's opposition to evolution to support his position that American agrarian populism was an anti-intellectual revolt against modernity and as a reason to reject radical reform movements in general. Gould re-examined Bryan's ideas and developed a different explanation for his political positions. According to Gould, Bryan, along with many of his contemporaries, incorrectly identified Darwinian evolution with the biological determinism and racism of

Figure 2.1 Alan Singer at the Burgess shale quarry.

Figure 2.2 Close up of a 500-million-year-old trilobite.

nineteenth- and twentieth-century Social Darwinism. Bryan campaigned against the teaching of evolution because, as a progressive, he considered it a dangerous ideology that undermined democracy and justified imperialism, war, and the exploitation of farmers and workers.

Teaching Activity: What Does It Mean to Be An Historian?

Historians are faced with an infinite number of potential facts and have to decide which ones are historically significant. Examine the following headlines from *The New York Times* and notes based on the articles. You need to decide whether these are important historical facts and whether there are historical explanations that connect any of the articles. These articles also raise an important philosophical issue, "Do ends justify means?" This question can lead to powerful classroom discussions.

Headline: "Where Arab Militants Train and Wait" (August 11, 1993)
According to Hamid Gul, a retired Pakistani general who was responsible for providing $3 billion in American money and weapons to Afghan anti-communist guerrillas, the guerrilla army included large numbers of Islamic militants from other parts of the Arab world. According to Western intelligence officials, among the militants trained and armed in Pakistani refugee camps were a number of the radicals later convicted of bombing the World Trade Center in New York City and of other bomb plots in the United States.

Headline: "One Man and a Global Web of Violence" (January 14, 2001)
Nine months before the attacks on the World Trade Center in New York and the Pentagon in Washington DC, an article described Osama bin Laden, his goals and supporters. In the early 1980s, while Islamic groups were fighting a Soviet invasion of Afghanistan with support from the Central Intelligence Agency, bin Laden was considered a man the West could use. However, around 1987, he began to take aim against what he considered "the corrupt secular governments" of the Muslim Middle East and the Western powers. By January, 2001, American officials considered him responsible for masterminding the 1998 bombings of two United States embassies in Africa that killed more than 200 people, and suspected him of involvement in the October (2000) bombing of the destroyer Cole in Yemen, which killed 17 sailors.

Headline: "US Spied on Its World War II Allies" (August 11, 1993)
According to newly declassified documents, the United States operated an enormous and previously unknown spy network aimed at our allies during World War II. It included reports on General

Charles DeGaulle, leader of the free French forces, Belgium, Greece, Mexico, China, and Switzerland, as well as information from Germany and Japan. Documents from the Soviet Union were not made public; however, information on our Soviet allies is contained in some of the other reports. Communications with Latin American governments show that, toward the end of the war, the United States was working to develop a united front to oppose the Soviet Union in the postwar world. The files also contain a memorandum from a German diplomat indicating that leaders of the Japanese army were willing to surrender more than three months before the United States dropped nuclear bombs on Hiroshima and Nagasaki, even if the terms were hard.

Headline: "Arthur Randolph, 89, Developer of Rocket in First Apollo Flight" (January 3, 1996)

An obituary for Arthur Randolph appeared in *The New York Times* on January 3, 1996. When he died, Randolph was living in Hamburg, Germany. He had left the United States and returned to Germany in 1984 after the US Justice Department accused him of working thousands of slave laborers to death while director of a German factory that produced V rockets during World War II.

Randolph, who was the project manager for the Saturn rocket system used on Apollo flights, was one of 118 German rocket scientists who were secretly brought to the United States after the war. At the time he entered the United States, Randolph was considered an ardent Nazi by the US military and a war criminal by both West German and US officials.

Try it yourself:

1. In your opinion, what motivated US actions in each case?
2. Develop an historical explanation that connects the information from the articles. Explain your hypothesis.

Think it over:

1. Do you consider the information contained in these headlines and summaries important historical facts? Why?
2. In your opinion, can historians make sense out of historical facts without also developing theories of historical explanation? Explain your views.
3. Do you believe, given the nature of "real world" crises, ends justify means? Explain.

It's your classroom:

1. Would you use these articles in a middle school or high school class? Why? How?
2. Would you express your views during the course of discussion? Why?

WHAT IS HISTORY?

Teaching Activity: Defining History

- Lord Acton (Sir J. E. E. Dalberg), 1896: "It [*The Cambridge Modern History*] is a unique opportunity of recording . . . the fullness of the knowledge which the nineteenth century is about to bequeath . . . Ultimate history we cannot have in this generation; but . . . all information is within reach, and every problem has become capable of solution" (Carr 1961: 3).
- Sir George Clark, 1957 (Introduction to *The New Cambridge Modern History*): "Historians . . . expect their work to be superseded again and again. They consider that knowledge of the past has come down through one or more human minds, has been processed by them . . . The exploration seems to be endless, and some impatient scholars take refuge in skepticism, or at least in the doctrine that, since all historical judgments involve persons and points of view, one is as good as another and there is no objective historical truth" (Carr 1961: 4).
- E. H. Carr (1961: 111): "Scientists, social scientists, and historians are all engaged in different branches of the same study: the study of man [*sic*] and his environment, of the effects of man on his environment and of his environment on man. The object of the study is the same: to increase man s understanding of, and mastery over, his environment."

- Rod Paige (2003). "Traditional American history teaches the significant issues, episodes, and turning points in the history of the United States, and how the words and deeds of individual Americans have determined the course of our Nation. This history teaches how the principles of freedom and democracy, articulated in our founding documents, have shaped—and continue to shape—America's struggles and achievements, as well as its social, political, and legal institutions and relations. Traditional history puts its highest priority on making sure students have an understanding of these principles and of the historical events and people that best illustrate them" (Paige 2003: 24054).
- Lawrence "Yogi" Berra (1989: 6–7) (Hall of Fame catcher and former manager of the New York Yankees and Mets), during the 1973 National League pennant race: "It ain't over til it's over."

Add your voice to the discussion:
Which of these quotes (or other statements of your choice) comes closest to your view of history? Explain your answer.

Frequently it is confusing when a term is used in more than one way, especially when it is used to describe related concepts. In essays discussing political battles over the teaching of evolution and creationism in public schools, Stephen Jay Gould (1983: 253–262) explains that scientists since Charles Darwin have used the term *evolution* to mean both the fact that life on earth changes over time as new species develop, and to describe theories like natural selection that explain how and why these changes take place. Gould believes that the dual meaning of evolution as both fact and theory has either been misunderstood or misused by advocates of creationism, who dismiss the fact of evolution as just one among a number of possible theories.

The definition of *history* is even more complicated because it refers to a number of different but related concepts. If we accept E. H. Carr's view that historians, along with scientists and social scientists, are engaged in an active process of asking questions, seeking out information, and forming explanations that enable society to understand and master our environment, then what we commonly refer to as *history* actually includes a series of distinct but related ideas: (1) events from the past—"facts," (2) the process of gathering and organizing information from the past—historical research, (3) explanations about the relationships between specific historical events, and (4) broader explanations or "theories" about how and why change takes place. History is the past, the study of the past, and explanations about the past.

Other factors adding to the complexity of studying history are the differing experiences and ideas of historians from different societies, and the fact that historians are trying to understand an incomplete process that continues to take place around them. In 1896, living in a world where European, especially British, cultural, economic, and political dominance in world affairs seemed unshakable, Lord Acton argued that ultimate history, the ability to know and explain everything of importance, was within our grasp. But following two horrific world wars and numerous revolutions that shook the confidence of European society, the situation had changed. While Acton and his colleagues possessed certainty, Sir George Clark, a successor of Acton's as an editor of *The Cambridge Modern History*, was overwhelmed by the difficulty of establishing an objective account of history, and accepted that historians would continually reinterpret the past. Clark recognized that every generation and community answers certain questions (What happened in the past? How does it shape the present and future?) based on new research and experiences and different ideological explanations about human actions and social change.

Rod Paige is not an historian. His idea of history, which was promoted while he served as Secretary of Education during the George W. Bush presidency, is a restrictive one. I would argue its intent was to promote uncritical patriotism rather than historical thinking. It was proposed at a time when many historians and other scholars were questioning the legitimacy of American foreign policy in Iraq and of choices made by American leaders in earlier eras.

Yogi Berra is a former baseball player, not an historian, who is well known for apparent malapropisms (misstatements) that manage to capture meaning in imaginative ways. Berra is supposed to have made the statement, "It ain't over til it's over," when besieged by sports writers who wanted him to explain the failure of the N.Y. Mets to capture a pennant before the season was over or the race was even decided. Berra could not explain the team's defeat because he was not convinced that they were going to lose. Historians have a similar problem. Identifying history as the past arbitrarily breaks up an ongoing process that includes the present and that extends into the future, a process that is incomplete and difficult to evaluate.

During the last two centuries, there have been numerous theories about the importance of history and numerous explanations of historical change. I think social studies teachers and students need to think about and discuss these theories and the question: What is history? Andrea Libresco, a former high school teacher who is now a colleague at Hofstra University, argues that one of our major goals as social studies teachers should be to undermine student certainty about past events and to help them understand that, if anything, history is messy.

Classroom Activity: History is Messy

Highly regarded historical figures have often been engaged in questionable activities. How should this affect their reputations and the way we teach about them in our classrooms?

1. On October 12, 1492, Christopher Columbus and his crew arrived at an island in the Bahamas inhabited by the Arawak Indians. In his log, Columbus wrote about the people he encountered: "They do not bear arms, and do not know them, for I showed them a sword, they took it by the edge and cut themselves out of ignorance . . . They would make fine servants . . . With fifty men we could subjugate them all and make them do whatever we want" (available at: http://www.hartford-hwp.com/archives/40/182.html, accessed October 7, 2007).

2. United States Presidents George Washington, Thomas Jefferson, James Madison, James Monroe, and Andrew Jackson were slave owners who profited from and defended slavery as an institution. In 1761, George Washington placed an advertisement in a Virginia newspaper calling for the return of four runaway "Negroes," Peros, Jack, Neptune, and Cupid. According to the notice, "they went off without the least Suspicion, Provocation, or Difference with any Body, or the least angry Word or Abuse from their Overseers, 'tis supposed they will hardly lurk about in the Neighbourhood, but steer some direct Course (which cannot even be guessed at) in Hopes of an Escape" (available at: http://gwpapers.virginia.edu/documents/slavery/aug1761.html, accessed October 7, 2007).

3. Before and during his presidency, Andrew Jackson was a strong advocate for "Indian removal" from the eastern United States. From 1814 to 1818 he commanded military forces that defeated the Creek and Seminole nations and forced them to abandon their homelands in Alabama, Georgia, and Florida. In 1832, when the Supreme Court of the United States found in favor of Cherokee who were being displaced by the state of Georgia, Jackson, as President of the United States, refused to enforce the court ruling. As President, Jackson was responsible for the forced removal of 50,000 native people from their east coast homes on what came to be known as the "Trail of Tears" (available at: http://www.allthingscherokee.com/articles_culture_events_020201.html, accessed October 7, 2007).

4. In 1942, President Franklin D. Roosevelt signed Executive Order 9066 authorizing the forced removal of United States residents and citizens of Japanese ancestry living on the west coast. They were imprisoned in internment camps located in remote areas of the interior of the country for the duration of World War II. In 1944, the United States Supreme Court upheld the constitutionality of this action because of "pressing public necessity." In 1988, President Reagan signed legislation apologizing for the internment and providing reparations for survivors (available at: http://www.history.com/tdih.do?action=tdihArticleCategory&id=191, accessed October 7, 2007).

5. The "Nuremberg Defense" in judicial proceedings refers to the claim by defendants that they were not responsible for their actions because they were only following orders from superiors. Its origin was the post-World War II trial of former Nazis at Nuremberg for crimes against humanity.

Similar claims were made by US military personnel accused of killing civilians or torturing prisoners at My Lai during the Vietnam War and at Abu Ghraib prison during the United States occupation of Iraq.

Think it over:
1. What is happening in each of these passages?
2. Are any of these actions acceptable in today's world? Explain.
3. In your opinion, should historical figures be judged according to the standard of their times or by a universal moral code? Explain.

It's your classroom:
1. Should the people involved in these actions, such as Christopher Columbus, George Washington, Andrew Jackson and Franklin Roosevelt, be presented to students as heroes or villains? Explain.
2. In your classroom, how will you deal with the "messiness' of history?

WHAT IS A SOCIAL STUDIES APPROACH TO HISTORY?

As editor of *Social Science Docket* (published by the New York and New Jersey Councils for the Social Studies), I have been involved in trying to define exactly what is meant by a social studies approach to history, particularly global history. For me, a social studies approach to history starts with questions, particularly student-generated questions, and it starts with the present.

There are a number of problems with the traditional global history curriculum. The worst problem is probably that, with the wealth of possible detail to include in a crowded curriculum, it is difficult for teachers to decide what is important for students to know. What bears mentioning? What requires a lesson? What topics demand an entire unit? The abundance of information influences the way we teach history. There is tremendous pressure to race through epochs and regions, dictating names and dates, with little time available for an in-depth exploration of concepts and historical themes, the evaluation of primary and secondary sources, and for students to draw their own historical conclusions.

A second problem is that most social studies teachers have a significantly more extensive background in European and United States history than in the history of the non-Western world. The tendency to highlight the Western heritage in the global history curriculum is supported by the idea that what is really important to know about the history of the world happened in Europe. According to this Western triumphalist position, civilization started in ancient Greece, traveled through Rome to medieval and modern Europe, landed in the Americas along with Columbus, and reshaped the world through Enlightenment ideas (including democracy) and the power of industrial capitalism and imperialism. It finally culminated in US global expansion after World War II. At best, the examination of the history of rest of the world is tangential to this process.

An alternative to straight chronology is to organize the curriculum around broad social studies concepts and themes and student questions about humanity, history, and the contemporary world. This approach is directly concerned with ideas and issues being discussed today. Teachers often ask me for interesting lesson ideas on relatively obscure topics such as absolute monarchy in seventeenth- and eighteenth-century Europe or nationalist movements in Korea. The first question I ask them is what they believe it is important for students to know about the topic. Most cannot think of reasons other than that it is in the textbook or might appear on a standardized test.

But if you think about the current world scene, significant reasons to examine absolute monarchy in Europe or nationalism in Korea do emerge. In both cases we are looking at case studies in nation-state building. As the United States, allegedly, tries to develop democratic governments in Iraq and Afghanistan, it is important to explore the process by which other countries developed, or tried to develop, democratic institutions in the past. Are there necessary stages that nations have passed through during this process? The United States experienced a bloody civil war. Have alternative strategies been attempted or successful? Can some stages be "skipped" and nation-building be collapsed in time? Have national unity and cohesion and the development of a viable political and economic infrastructure sometimes been enhanced by authoritarian regimes?

The history of the world prior to 1750 is really the history of relatively isolated regions that increasingly come into contact with each other. A possible overall theme is cultural and historical similarity and difference, although the impact of geography on history is also important. In a lesson comparing the pyramids and written languages of Egypt and Mexico, students can decide whether their similar designs are examples of cultural diffusion or parallel development. Lessons on the impact of the Columbian Exchange should explore the devastation that was caused by global interaction and challenge students to reconsider the idea of historical progress. Questions for discussion could include "Why does change often appear to emerge from the periphery?"; "Are historical events pre-determined or contingent on accident?"; and "What happens when world's collide?" While these are questions about the past, they are also questions about the present. Globalization has accelerated the processes of global interaction and students, as well as the rest of us, wonder what the future holds.

A social studies approach to history, because it is not trapped in chronology, makes it easier for teachers to balance the breadth of historical coverage with in-depth case studies. Everything cannot be covered extensively, but for students to appreciate the historical process and the work of the historian, some things must be. Because it is a case study approach, examples can be drawn from outside what the teacher normally perceives of as the main historical narrative, creating space for more extensive examination of the non-Western world throughout the curriculum. Instead of studying how trade networks promoted global exchange by focusing on Marco Polo, students can learn about non-Western global travelers such as Rabban Sauma, an ethnic Turk and Eastern Orthodox monk who was born in Northern China in the first half of the thirteenth century, Abu Abdullah Ibn Battuta, a North African merchant whose memoirs include reports on his visits to eastern and western Africa and the Indian sub-continent, or Zheng He, the fifteenth-century Chinese admiral whose ships plied the Indian Ocean.

A theme that students can explore as they examine the impact of history on the lives of ordinary people is the idea of *transculturation*.

In *Cuban Counterpoint* (Ortiz 1940), the sociologist Fernando Ortiz examined the impact of tobacco and sugar production on the development of Cuban history, culture, and society. Ortiz described the dialectical nature of colonialism and imperialism as both destructive and constructive forces in human history. An example of how transculturation operates is symbolized by the annual celebration of Puerto Rican Discovery Day in June. Puerto Ricans, as a culture and people, and other Latin Americans, are a direct result of the Colombian exchange, an exchange that also led to the extermination of indigenous people in many areas and the trans-Atlantic slave trade.

While terms such as cultural diffusion, acculturation, and assimilation suggest benign processes, transculturation focuses on the dislocation of people's lives. Latin American societies, for example, combine elements of indigenous American, European, and African cultures in a seething caldron that frequently "bubbles over" in social conflict, not a slow simmering melting pot or a bowl of mixed fruit. The concepts of acculturation and assimilation also imply that the acquisition of another culture is a uni-dimensional process experienced by new arrivals to a country. Transculturation, on the other hand, suggests that entirely new cultures are created as old patterns of behavior are destroyed and new ones are formulated. Good examples of this aspect of transculturation are the numerous "Creole" or blended languages that are invented in slave communities in the Americas.

The world since 1750 has been an increasingly integrated one that has been transformed by two major historical forces, the struggle for human rights since the Enlightenment and the French Revolution and the seemingly inexorable tide of capitalist industrialization. These forces have directly changed the way people live in Western Europe and North America, and because of imperialism and globalization, in the rest of the world as well. The study of recent global history should focus on the way North American and Western European products, culture, and political influence have spread to every portion of the globe, sometimes as forces for liberation and sometimes for destruction. Socialist revolutions and religious fundamentalist movements have all been framed as responses to capitalist industrialization. Essential questions for this period of study should include "Is capitalist industrialization a force for positive or negative change?," "Should dominant powers force their values and ways of life on conquered people?," and "Are democracy and human rights compatible with capitalist economic competition between people and nations?"

Learning Activity: Reading History and the Social Sciences

Over the years, I have tried to read at least one "serious" book during the winter break and another each summer. Usually they are works of fact, either a monograph directed at experts in a field, a book written for a popular audience, essays, or collections of lectures; sometimes they are historical fiction.

Eric Hobsbawm is probably my favorite historian. *The Age of Extremes, A History of the World, 1914–1991* (1994) is a comprehensive survey of the twentieth century where Hobsbawm attempts to explain the development of the modern world. I also recommend *On the Edge of the New Century* (with Antonio Polito) (1999) and *On History* (1997), collections of essay that examine historical interpretation and controversial issues.

Eric Foner has written numerous books on United States history. In *The Story of American Freedom* (1998), Foner offers a thematic overview of the history of the United States as he discusses the evolution of the meaning of freedom. Other interesting books by Foner are *Who Owns History? Rethinking the Past in a Changing World* (2002) and *Forever Free, The Story of Emancipation and Reconstruction* (2005).

In the social sciences, Jared Diamond's *Guns, Germs, and Steel, The Fates of Human Societies* (1997) won a Pulitzer Prize and is eminently readable. He makes a powerful case for the role of geography in shaping history and provides plenty of material that is easily translatable into classroom activities. Amartya Sen is a Nobel Prize winning economist concerned with social justice. His book, *Development as Freedom* (1999), argues that advancing private profit should not be the primary engine of an economic system in a democratic society. Ira Katznelson is a political scientist who has grappled with the reasons for continuing racial inequality in the United States. In his book, *When Affirmative Action was White: An Untold History of Racial Inequality in Twentieth-Century America* (2005), he argues that progressive programs such as the New Deal and post-World War II support for returning veterans actually reinforced the racial divide.

In recent years, I have been especially moved by the historical fiction of a number of authors.

Denise Giardina's *Storming Heaven* (1988) and *The Unquiet Earth* (1994) explore the struggle of Appalachian coal miners to survive under difficult conditions, organize unions, and establish their humanity. Her novel, *Saints and Villains* (1999) is the story of Dietrich Bonhoeffer, an anti-Nazi Lutheran theologian who was executed because of participation in a plot to assassinate Adolph Hitler. Russell Banks confronts difficult moral and political issues in *Cloudsplitter* (1998), a fictional account of John Brown's war against slavery and the United States government and *The Darling* (2004), which explores the motives of the radical left in the United States during the 1960s and the dehumanization that accompanied recent African civil wars. Madison Smartt Bell, *All Soul's Rising* (1996), *Master of the Crossroads* (2000), and *The Stone that the Builder Refused* (2004), has produced a majestic three-volume fictionalized account of Toussaint Loverture and the Haitian war for independence. In a quartet of novels, *Shadows of the Pomegranate Tree* (1992), *The Book of Saladin (1998), The Stone Woman* (2000) and *A Sultan in Palermo* (2005), Tariq Ali paints a portrait of Islamic culture while exploring its conflicts with the West between the Crusades and the fall of the Ottoman Turkish empire. Ngugi wa Thiong'o is a Kenyan who has used literature to challenge post-colonial corruption. The lead character in his novel *Matigari* (1994) was seen as such a threat by the government that the author and the fictional character were both threatened with arrest. A more complete recommended reading list is included in Chapter 13.

Add your voice to the discussion:
1. List three books from history and/or the social sciences that influence the way you think about the world and social studies.
2. Why do you choose these books?
3. How do they influence your thinking?

WHAT ARE HISTORICAL FACTS?

Many social studies teachers, feeling pressure to prepare students for standardized exams, present their classes with long lists of key facts to memorize. I call this the Dragnet School of Social Studies Education. Dragnet was a 1950s television series where police inspector Joe Friday would greet a prospective witness with the request, "Just the facts." The idea that the goal of history is the collection of an enormous volume of information can probably be traced back to Aristotle in ancient Greece and certainly was behind the encyclopedia movement of the eighteenth-century French Enlightenment. In recent years, E. D. Hirsch, Chester Finn, Diane Ravitch, and Allan Bloom have championed this approach to social studies.

One problem with this view of history is that not everyone agrees on which facts are important to include when analyzing the past. While researching US history, I became engrossed in the sports pages of old newspapers. During the summer preceding the New Orleans General Strike of 1892, Dan Brouthers of Brooklyn and Clarence Childs of Cleveland battled for the National League batting title, but it was Boston, the first team to win over 100 games in a season, that won the pennant. Babe Ruth hit 60 home runs the same summer that worldwide protests were being held against the scheduled execution of Sacco and Vanzetti. These are interesting facts, but do they have historical significance? Are they historical facts? If we dismiss the Bambino as historically insignificant, what about barely remembered US presidents like William Henry Harrison, James Garfield, Chester Arthur, or Warren G. Harding? It is certainly possible that future generations will be uninterested in the administrations of Gerald Ford, Jimmy Carter, Ronald Reagan, George H. Bush, Bill Clinton and George W. Bush. What establishes them as historically important? What about events or individuals that fail to make the newspapers or textbooks—does that automatically mean they were unimportant in their time and for all time?

I do not believe there are any independent objective criteria for establishing a particular event or person as historically important. The status of a fact rests on its importance in explaining the causes of events that interest historians and societies. The Italian historian Benedetto Croce (Carr 1961: 23) argued that essentially all history is contemporary history because people read the past and decide on what is important in the light of current problems and issues. The attitude of US historians towards the nineteenth-century presidency of Andrew Jackson is an example of this at work. During the New Deal, Jackson's presidency was cited as an historical precedent for democratic participation and a reformist spirit. However, since the Civil Rights movement of the 1960s, Jackson's ownership of enslaved Africans and attacks on the rights of native peoples have led to a reevaluation of his role in US history.

Figure 2.3 The Parthenon on the Acropolis in Athens. Should it be viewed as a crowning achievement of a society experimenting with democracy or as a symbol of imperialist ventures and slave labor? How did the people who did the labor view its creation?

Weighing the historical importance of facts is also a problem because they are continually screened through the decades and centuries. Historians are forced to draw major conclusions based on limited information that was pre-selected by contemporaries, considered important by earlier generations of historians, or survived because of fortuitous accident. For example, our picture of life in ancient Greece and the belief that it was the inspiration for modern democracy is unduly influenced by what we know about a very small group of free male citizens living in the city-state of Athens.

In a workshop for social studies teachers at an annual meeting of the NCSS, I asked an audience of almost 200 global history teachers from around the country to raise their hands if they taught about Mansa Musa, the fourteenth century leader of the Kingdom of Mali in western Africa. About two-thirds of the audience claimed that they did. But when I asked if anyone really considered him important and could explain why, there were no volunteers. I suspect most teachers include Mansa Musa in the curriculum because they feel political pressure to provide students with an example of an African civilization, but do not really believe he was historically significant. I did not at the beginning either. However, I changed my mind as I studied more about the growth of Islam following September 11, 2001.

Most empires in the past were land-based with centralized political authority. The Islamic empire that stretched from Spain to Indonesia and included India and regions of sub-Saharan Africa during the early centuries of the last millennium was very different. It was based on trade and facilitated by the spread of a shared religion and literacy. Regions had different governments, but were unified by religious beliefs and practices and they exchanged goods, ideas and people through the trade network. Islam penetrated sub-Saharan Africa by offering princes who adopted the religion entry into the trade network and the support of Islamic scribes for governmental administration. Mansa Musa and the Kingdom of Mali are important historical actors because they illustrate the workings of the Islamic world during a period when it was politically ascendant, and their study provides students with an alternative to the European-dominated version of history offered in most textbooks.

Recognizing that facts take on meaning within the context of explanations, and that the historical record is, at best, incomplete, does not mean that all facts carry the same weight and that all interpretations are equally valid. Within the historical craft, accuracy is an obligation, interpretations must be supported by evidence, and evidence is subject to review. US historian Carl Becker argued that the facts of history do not exist for any historian until he or she creates them (Carr 1961: 23). If we want our students to become historians, we need to involve them in deciding which facts are important for understanding history and what criteria to use when making decisions, instead of focusing our efforts on providing them with lists of someone else's important facts.

Classroom Activity: A Worker Reads History

In his poem, *A Worker Reads History* (available at: http://poems.wiki.zoho.com/A-Worker-Reads-History.html, accessed October 28, 2007), Bertolt Brecht asks a series of questions about the past that might be asked by a workingman or woman. Each of Brecht's questions introduces the same point. Too often historians present great achievements and catastrophes as if they were the result of the efforts of only one person. Brecht and his hypothetical worker want to know about the lives of the masons who helped build Thebes, ancient Lima, and the Great Wall of China, the soldiers and sailors who triumphed or perished alongside Alexander of Macedonia, Julius Caesar, and Frederick the Great of Prussia.

Think it over:
What point is Brecht making in this poem? Do you agree or disagree with him? Why?

It's your classroom:
How could this poem be used to promote a discussion of the nature of history?

WHAT IS THE DIFFERENCE BETWEEN FACT AND THEORY?

One problem when discussing "facts" is that the scientific and colloquial meanings are different. In ordinary conversation, a fact is something that is incontrovertible and unchanging. It is supposedly eternal truth. But scientists, as well as historians and social scientists, recognize that what is incontrovertible and unchanging today, may no longer be the case when new evidence is discovered. When I was a high school student "back in the days," scientists knew there were three sub-atomic particles, neutrons, protons, and electrons, and that electrons were the smallest particles. That was indisputable scientific fact. Today we know that there are even smaller particles, including fermians, quarks, leptons, neutrinos, and anti-neutrinos, just to name a few. In an earlier era, it was common knowledge that the sun traveled around the earth. Few of us would accept that as fact today.

In some ways, the scientific notion of fact is closer to the colloquial idea of theory, a strongly held idea supported by extensive evidence. As an historian, I like the scientific idea that "facts" are what we understand to be true at a particular time and that we have to be open to change our minds as new information is uncovered.

Over the years, many students in my social studies classes, both in secondary schools and in the teacher education program, have been uncomfortable with the claim that human evolution is a scientific fact. Partly, this is because they do not understand the difference between the scientific and colloquial usage of "fact." But I also think another factor is at play. They are thinking in absolute terms, they want absolute proof, but scientists and historians do not. They cannot. Neither scientists nor historians know what new discoveries the future holds.

While the future is unknown, there are still rules for establishing scientific knowledge. Scientists cannot make claims that violate the rules or fall outside the boundaries without changing the way the game is played. A group of people could eliminate foul territory in baseball and still play some kind of game, but it would no longer be baseball as we know it. A scientist might not believe in the existence of God, but knows that according to the rules of science, it is impossible to prove that a supreme being, or for that matter unicorns, do not exist.

Sometimes someone gets the information wrong. But in history and the social sciences, major disputes about facts are not generally about inaccuracies. They usually center on conflicting definitions, people really talking about different things, or on disagreements about causality. Disagreements about causality, the impact of one event on others, are addressed through research, but research is often more suggestive than conclusive. Both types of disagreements are usually resolved through debate or when one idea comes to dominate what people think, similar to the way the Windows operating system took over in the computer world. But defeated ideas and discarded facts sometimes come back for reconsideration. In the world of science and of history, majority rule does not make an idea right.

Teaching Activity: Facts and Theories

Add your voice to the discussion:
1. Should biological evolution be presented to students as scientific fact or theory?
2. Should a conclusion about historical causality (e.g., nationalism and imperialism were the underlying causes of World War I) be presented as a fact or a theory?

HOW DOES AN HISTORIAN STUDY HISTORY?

The role of theory or point of view in the study of history is sharply debated, yet crucial for understanding how historians know what they claim to know. Most social studies teachers would argue that students should get their facts straight before they worry about interpretation. I am not sure most practicing historians agree.

According to E. H. Carr (1961: 32–33), a frequent assumption is that an "historian divides his (*sic*) work into two sharply distinguishable phases or periods. First, he spends a long preliminary period reading his sources and filling his notebooks with facts: then, when this is over, he puts away his sources, takes out his notebooks, and writes his book from beginning to end." The idea that research should be completed before analysis begins is rooted in the dominant empiricist ideas of late nineteenth-century Europe. I think these ideas are epitomized in the research methods of Sherlock Holmes, Sir Arthur Conan Doyle's fictional Victorian-age detective.

Doyle explains Holmes' approach to problem-solving in the story *A Study in Scarlet* (1890). According to Sherlock Holmes, the only way to remove bias from research is to make scientific deductions based on accurate observations. Holmes advises his friend Dr James Watson that, "It is a capital mistake to theorize before one has data. Insensibly, one begins to twist facts to suit theories, instead of theories to suit facts" (Hardwick 1986: 32).

I love to read the Holmes adventures, but I challenge anyone to employ this method to understand the world, solve mysteries, or study the past. Despite the assertion that his conclusions are induced from empirical evidence untainted by point of view, Holmes simply does not recognize his own assumptions. When Watson is struck by his ignorance of literature, philosophy, astronomy, and politics, Holmes defends himself by arguing that the human brain is an attic with limited space, and he does not want to crowd it with information that "would not make a pennyworth of difference to me or to my work" (Hardwick 1986: 24–25). To discard information as irrelevant, Holmes must have a point of view about causality that lets him know which facts to ignore and what needs to be stored for later reference. In *Silver*

Blaze (1892), Inspector Gregory asks Holmes, "Is there any point to which you would wish to draw my attention?" When Holmes answers, "To the curious incident of the dog in the night-time," a puzzled Gregory says, "The dog did nothing in the night-time." Holmes replies, "That was the curious incident" (Hardwick 1986: 79). Without assumptions (theories) about the behavior of dogs, Holmes would have missed this "curious incident" altogether.

Nowhere are Holmes assumptions more apparent than in his views about women. In *A Scandal in Bohemia* (1891), Holmes claims to have discovered a series of truths about women. They "are naturally secretive, and they like to do their own secreting." During emergencies, a woman's instinct is "to rush to the thing which she values most. It is a perfectly overpowering impulse." A "married woman grabs at her baby" while "an unmarried one reaches for her jewel-box" (Hardwick 1986: 54). Poor Sherlock is so committed to the idea of objectivity that he cannot even see his own biases.

When E. H. Carr describes his own research, he explains that data gathering and analysis "go on simultaneously. The writing is added to, subtracted from, re-shaped, canceled as I go on reading. The reading is guided and directed and made more fruitful by the writing: the more I write, the more I know what I am looking for, the better I understand the significance and relevance of what I find . . . I am convinced that . . . the two processes . . . are, in practice, parts of a single process." Historians are engaged in a "continuous process of molding facts to interpretation and of interpretation to the facts . . . The historian without facts is rootless and futile; the facts without their historian are dead and meaningless" (Carr 1961: 32–35).

Teaching Activity: Sherlock Holmes

Add your voice to the discussion:
1. How do you evaluate Sherlock Holmes' approach to understanding our world?
2. Do you agree or disagree with E. H. Carr's concept of writing history? Why?

Think it over:
Was the job of the historian presented to you in high school or college? How was it explained?

It's your classroom:
1. How can Carr's view be used to shape a social studies curriculum?
2. Is it possible to present Carr's view of history to secondary school students in a useful way? Explain how you would do it.

HOW DO HISTORIANS RESOLVE DISAGREEMENTS?

In the post-World War II decades, left-wing historians, primarily from Great Britain, debated the causes of the transition from feudalism to capitalism in Western Europe. The debate originated with a book by Maurice Dobb (1946), *Studies in the Development of Capitalism*, and included a series of critiques and responses in leading historical journals. This debate is an excellent example of the historical process, as leading academics analyzed competing theoretical explanations based on their research in different time periods and regions. Many of the contributions were published in a collection of essays, *The Transition from Feudalism to Capitalism* (Hilton 1978). Most of the arguments revolved around whether the transformation from feudalism to capitalism had its roots in internal "contradictions," such as the impact of the growth of trade and urban areas on feudal society, or was principally the result of external forces such as the Bubonic Plague and conflict with the Islamic world for control over the Mediterranean region.

During the debate, Eric Hobsbawm (1962: 159–164) proposed that part of the problem was that the transition was neither universal nor sudden. Feudalism developed, evolved, and receded at different rates in different places over the course of over one thousand years. Hobsbawm proposed a rough timeline with six components to provide some order to historical understanding of the process, at least as it occurred in Western Europe. I have expanded somewhat on his explanations, and included both internal and external causes.

1. Relapse (600–1000). The early Middle Ages was a period of economic, social, and political decline following the breakup of the Roman Empire in the Western Mediterranean. During this period Western Europe was isolated from the rest of the known world by Islamic expansion in North Africa and conquest of Spain and Sicily.
2. Rapid Development (1000–1350). These years marked the peak of medieval civilization in Western Europe. Population, agricultural production, manufacturing, and trade were all expanding. Governments were more integrated. Islam was being challenged by the Crusades in Palestine and was being turned back in Spain.
3. Crisis (1350–1450). During this period the Bubonic Plague killed approximately one-third the population of Western Europe, disrupting the political and economic infrastructure of society. It was also a period of intense religious and dynastic warfare in France and England that included the Battle of Agincourt made famous by William Shakespeare in Henry V and the execution of Joan of Arc.
4. Renewal (1450–1650). This is the period of both the European Renaissance and Reformation. Expanding trade with Asia, silver and gold stolen from the Americas, and profits from the trans-Atlantic slave trade and slave-produced commodities, produced new concentrations of wealth and supported the consolidation of central state power and empires. Hobsbawn argues that development during this period marks a major break with the past, especially in smaller trading nations like the Netherlands.
5. Adjustment (1650–1750). The wealth and expansion generated during the previous period contributed to civil, religious, and colonial wars and the emergence of new centers of power. Spain, Portugal, and the Netherlands were eclipsed as major powers, while France was on the verge of bankruptcy. Land-based feudal nobility is increasingly dependent on powerful monarchs for patronage. New classes begin to recognize their distinct interests and compete for influence.
6. Triumph (post-1750). With the Industrial Revolution in England, feudalism is overturned. Capitalism emerges as the dominant force in global economic affairs and begins to re-make the world. The French, American, Haitian, and Latin American Revolutions sweep aside old ruling classes and end traditional restraints on people, production, and trade.

An interesting feature about Hobsbawn's essay, and all of the articles in the Hilton collection, is the way some of the research is now outdated. The authors virtually ignored both the Columbian Exchange and the trans-Atlantic slave trades, topics which more recent research places in the forefront of the causes leading to the transition from feudalism to capitalism. With these changes included within his framework, Hobsbawn offers teachers a useful way to conceptualize this time period and organize instruction, while the debate helps us understand how historians resolve disagreements.

SHOULD A TEACHER ALSO BE AN HISTORIAN?

I first encountered the British working-class historian Edward (E. P.) Thompson when I was a graduate student studying history at Rutgers University. His book, *The Making of the English Working Class* (1963), was a seminal study of the ideas and actions of ordinary people and an inspiration to a generation of historians, including myself. Despite his influence on my education, I cited, but did not discuss, Thompson in the first two editions of this book. In retrospect, I think it is because I separated my work as a teacher from my interest in historical study and these were intended as books about teaching social studies.

My experience working with beginning teachers researching, designing, and implementing a *Great Irish Famine* curriculum and the *New York and Slavery: Complicity and Resistance* curriculum, has prompted me to reevaluate the importance of teachers taking ownership over their own historical understanding and of the role Thompson played in shaping my views. If we are to be curriculum creators rather than just curriculum consumers, social studies teachers must be lifetime students. We also must become historians and social scientists ourselves. Rather than seeing this as a chore, I think it is part of the great fun of our profession.

As I prepared for this edition, I decided to revisit E. P. Thompson's *The Making of the English Working Class* to rediscover what had captured my imagination so many decades ago. The book described the development of the English working class from artisan and agrarian roots at the end of the eighteenth and beginning of the nineteenth centuries. Thompson illustrated how the uneven geographic, industrial, and business adaptation of new modes of production gave workers the ability to organize effectively to continue traditions and values in the face of turbulent social transformation brought on by capitalist industrialization. The things that always stayed with me

were his assertions that just because their struggles had been defeated, did not mean that people were wrong to fight for their ideals and ways of life, and that their losing struggles had actually shaped the future. These people and their struggles should never have been erased from the historical record.

In 1976, I met E. P. Thompson and was inspired by him all over again. He was in the United States for a year as a visiting scholar, and a group of friends and I who worked together as community organizers in Brooklyn went to hear him speak at Rutgers University. After his presentation, we cornered Thompson and invited him to speak in Brooklyn with the people we were organizing. He probably was receiving a lot of invitations from universities in the area and he hesitated. At that point, being young and arrogant, I hit him "below the belt." I said, "we understand, you teach about the working class, but not to the working-class." The remark "hit home" and he decided to come.

The subject of Thompson's presentation was "Thomas Paine and the Rights of Man." He spoke in the community room of a local daycare center to an audience of about one hundred people, most of whom were community residents without any higher education. He began with a song by British Jacobins (supporters of the French Revolution) and spent the next two hours singing history with occasional side comments to explain contexts and lyrics. It was the most brilliant presentation I had ever seen and connected what on the surface was an obscure topic to what could have been a very difficult audience. I later learned that Thompson prided himself on his work with working-class and community groups in England, and rather than being an isolated academic, he was a political activist constantly engaged with "ordinary people."

Besides writing about working-class movements, Thompson was also fascinated with British Romantic poets who wrote at the end of the eighteenth and beginning of the nineteenth centuries, especially William Blake. Before Thompson, most historians considered them unpractical romantics rather than revolutionaries, and dismissed the political content of their work. Thompson, who fancied himself a romantic revolutionary, identified with their contributions to both poetry and politics, and demonstrated their contributions to British political evolution. Blake, who often employed religious metaphors in his poetry, argued "He who desires but acts not, breeds pestilence" (1790–1793). In a poem he wrote in the early 1950s, Thompson echoed Blake's sentiments. He opening with the declaration that "[I]t is time to speak one's mind."

E. P. Thompson never separated his historical work from his teaching and his political activism. As an historian he challenged all orthodoxies and as a teacher and activist he drew on his historical understanding to speak his mind about issues affecting his world. He believed that history, as the memory of a culture, could "never be free from passions and commitments" and refused to be "inhibited by the fact that my own passions and commitments are clear" (Palmer 1994: 92).

Teaching Activity: Teaching about the Arab-Israeli Conflict

Some topics are by their nature controversial—abortion rights, the role religion has played in history, contemporary US military actions. They can be very difficult to teach about, especially when a teacher is relatively new and is concerned about job security. Because of this, I was surprised when Maram Mabrouk (NTN), a student whose family is Islamic, was assigned a demonstration lesson about the Arab-Israeli conflict when she applied for a position in a community with a large Jewish population.

Maram is an activist who marched in protests against the US occupation of Iraq and participated in campus dialogues about the nature of Islam, restrictive US government domestic policies, and conflict in the contemporary world after the events of September 11, 2001. It was very important to her that she develop a lesson that broadened student perspectives on the Middle East while respecting their views, that allowed her to maintain her own intellectual integrity, and gave her a real possibility of getting the position. This was clearly not an easy assignment.

Maram and I met together to design the lesson. She wanted students to understand that the conflict between Palestinians and Israelis had deep historical roots, that the local conflict involved many regional and national powers, and that there are legitimate grievances amongst all parties. She also hoped students would be able to connect discussion of the situation in the Middle East with similar territorial conflicts they had examined in global history, including those in Northern Ireland, South Africa, Northern Iraq, and North America. We decided on five ideas that would promote thoughtful student discussion and allow Maram to introduce perspectives on the issues that students would not ordinarily be exposed to. Maram, by the way, did not get this position, although she was hired in a neighboring town.

1. To establish the subject of the lesson, students would be asked when they entered the room to read an excerpt from a relatively neutral newspaper article on the topic. Maram selected "Rice Pursues Shuttle Diplomacy in Mideast" (Cooper 2007), an article from *The New York Times*. The article was about efforts by United States Secretary of State Condoleezza Rice to revive Middle East peace talks.
2. To encourage sensitivity and respect for difference, Maram would open by asking students if any of them had family connections or friendship ties with people living in Israel or Palestine. She would stress that this lesson would involve students in a discussion and not a debate.
3. To motivate discussion, Maram would ask students to consider why people develop attachments to their neighborhoods, cities, and "land'" and to discuss whether they have these kind of attachments.
4. Maram would provide a document package for a group work activity. The package would introduce students to multiple perspectives on the Arab-Israeli conflict and would include, but certainly would not be limited to, excerpts of articles critical of the Israeli occupation of Palestine. These articles would be from both European and Arab sources.
5. Instead of having a one-period lesson reach a superficial conclusion about the Arab-Israeli conflict, this lesson would end with a discussion of why some issues generate such intense controversy.

Think it over:
Do you agree or disagree with this approach to addressing the Arab-Israeli conflict? What might you have done differently? Explain your answer.

Add your voice to the discussion:
Edward Thompson, Maram Mabrouk, and I believe that teachers should not, really cannot, separate their historical work and teaching from their political beliefs. The challenge is to be responsible as a teacher and engage students in understanding the past and present, not to proselytize or hide what you think. Where do you stand on this issue? Why?

IS THE STUDY OF HISTORY SCIENTIFIC?

Early in his career as a philosopher and mathematician, Bertrand Russell hoped for the development of a mathematics of human behavior as precise as the mathematics of machines (Carr 1961: 71). However, the prevalence of contingent factors (accidents and uncontrolled or unanticipated incidents) and the recognition that individual points of view and cultural assumptions strongly influence what historians see have made Russell's dream highly unlikely. Meanwhile, the possibility of objective and predictive history has been popularized by science fiction writers. In high school, I devoured the Foundation series, where Isaac Asimov developed the science of psychohistory. However, even Asimov's psycho-historians had to contend with "The Mule," an unexpected mutant who threw off all of their calculations.

When most of us think of real science, we think of people in white coats, usually men, operating sophisticated machinery and running carefully controlled experiments in sterile laboratories. According to the scientific method taught in high school, scientific experiments require a formal hypothesis to be tested, a predicted and quantifiable outcome, control over the immediate environment, the ability to regulate variables, and assurance that the same result will be obtained each time the experiment is replicated.

Historians can never conduct this kind of experiment. They do not control events that happened in the past, are known incompletely, are much too complex, and are never repeated in exactly the same way. They cannot remove a Lenin or Hitler from the historical equation and play back the twentieth century, and they are not very successful at predicting specific historical events (the collapse of the Soviet Union or the election of particular candidates).

Significantly, many sciences do not have this kind of control either. Evolutionary biology, geology, and astronomy all have a historical dimension and a breadth of field that cannot be contained within a laboratory. Extinct species cannot be resurrected to see if they would survive under different circumstances, earthquakes cannot be replayed for closer observation, the big bang will not be repeated, at least not for many billions of years, and no one seems very good at predicting the weather.

The level of control and precision in the "laboratory sciences" is also exaggerated. You might remember that in high school chemistry, certain processes occurred only when an experiment took place at standard temperature and pressure (STP). Although the notion that a particular range of temperature (between the freezing and boiling points of water) and a specific pressure (sea level on Earth) defines what is normal may be useful, it is also arbitrary. High-altitude cooking in Denver, Colorado, differs from sea level cooking in New York City because the boiling point of water is lower; as a result, recipes have to be changed. In fact, it is only in a limited number of locations that water even occurs in its liquid form. What we see as the standard on Earth is not standard for the rest of the universe.

In addition, as scientists work with increasingly smaller and faster subatomic particles and charges, the certainty of Newtonian laws has been replaced by the uncertainties of quantum mechanics, relativity, and chaos theory. According to Werner Heisenberg, a German scientist writing in the 1920s, when scientists examine a physical or chemical process, their observations and measurements interfere with and change what is taking place; they can never know exactly what was happening before they intervened. The classical scientific method still has value, but we need to remember that it can only be applied in its traditional rigor under special and limited circumstances (Hawking 1988: 53–61).

The question for us is, how can any historical science where contingency is always a factor, including human history, be scientific?

Stephen Jay Gould (1989: 277–291; 1991: 385–401) argued that the historical sciences have their own appropriate scientific methods based on constructing narratives of events that allow us to locate patterns, identify probable causes, and create broader explanations and encompassing theories. Historical explanation uses specific events to describe general categories and general categories to explain specific events. For example, labeling a group of events as *social revolutions* means they have similar qualities that historians and social scientists can identify in other locales and eras, and that these qualities explain human actions and point to new, potentially revolutionary situations.

However, if the label proves to be too inclusive or of little use in predicting revolutionary situations, new general categories and explanations must be sought. Historians and other historical scientists also search for evidence that defies our explanations and forces us to redefine them. Gabriel Kolko's *The Triumph of Conservatism* (1963) uncovered significant corporate support for federal regulation of business and stimulated a reconceptualization of the Progressive Era in US history.

Because history and the historical sciences do not rely on experiments that can be replicated in other laboratories, they also require a different form of verification. The ultimate check on the historian is the marketplace of ideas where explanations are debated and analyzed, and colleagues are convinced that interpretations explain the data, are logical, are consistent with other things that we know, and provide possibilities for new explanations and further research.

Classroom Activity: Steps to Revolution

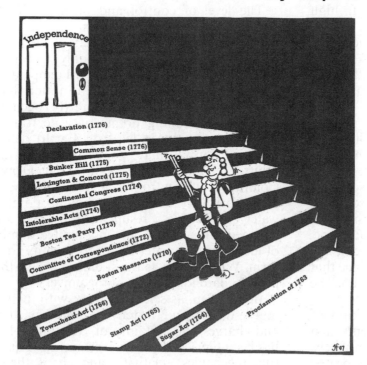

Figure 2.4 Steps to Revolution.

Try it yourself:
1. Which step was most important in causing the American revolution? Why?
2. When was a backward step no longer possible? Why?

ARE THERE LAWS IN HISTORY?

Historians, historical scientists, philosophers, politicians, and theologians look for causes, patterns, and laws in nature and history. However, that may be where their agreement stops.

In the sixteenth century, Protestant theologian John Calvin presented a doctrine of predestination. Calvin argued that the fate of every individual human being, born and yet to be born, was predetermined by God at creation. All events past, present, and future were already fixed. Current Christian millennialists continue to embrace these beliefs as they prepare for Armageddon, a battle between the forces of good and evil, final divine victory, judgment day, and ultimate rapture. To some extent, a notion of predestination, although not as dramatic and couched in scientific terminology, is also implied in the ideas of contemporary genetic determinists and sociobiologists.

In the eighteenth century, philosophers and scientists increasingly viewed the universe, the natural world, and the social world as Newtonian machines operating according to scientific laws. The astronomer Pierre-Simon La Place, who coined the term *celestial mechanics*, claimed that if anyone could identify the position and motion of every particle of matter in the universe, knowledge of natural law would permit them to predict all future history (Gould 1995: 26). Montesquieu argued that "there are general causes, moral or physical, which operate in every monarchy, raise it, maintain it, or overthrow it, and that all that occurs is subject to these causes" (Carr 1961: 114).

Predetermination or determinism entered the nineteenth century in the philosophy of Georg W. F. Hegel, who viewed humans as actors in events they did not understand or control in a world moving forward under its own spiritual dynamic toward the achievement of a "Universal History." Hegel discounted human free will, and argued, "The great man of the age is the one who can put into words the will of his age, tell his age what its will is, and accomplish it" (Carr 1961: 68). In recent years, Francis Fukuyama (1992: 59–69) has championed Hegelian philosophy. He argues that, with the collapse of the Soviet Union and the triumph of the West, humanity has achieved "the end of history," and human beings are now freed from the forces that had propelled development in the past.

In my opinion, the dominant intellectual forces of the nineteenth and early twentieth centuries include Karl Marx, Charles Darwin, and Sigmund Freud. Each of these thinkers presented a different image of history and historical change. Marx claimed to stand Hegel on his head, locating the dynamic element of historical change in the economic law of motion of modern society. In Marx's view, new social systems emerged as the result of inherent economic, social, and political conflicts among social classes existing in earlier societies. As a result of Darwin's work explaining the evolution of life on earth, his name became associated with the idea of history as continuous, gradual, and progressive change in society. Both Marxist and Darwinian progressive ideas have been associated with a sense of historical inevitability. In contrast, Freudian psychology added an element of the irrational to history, which won adherents especially after European and American experiences during the two world wars of the twentieth century.

For social studies teachers, there are many questions to think about as we involve our students in the study of history:

1. Do individual events have identifiable and understandable causes?
2. Are they single or multiple causes? If there are multiple causes, are some causes more significant than others?
3. Are there patterns in history? What are they? What causes them?
4. Do natural laws determine what happens in history? What are they? What are their origins?
5. Are individuals and groups able to make choices based on free will, or are they subject to historical and social forces beyond their control?
6. Is the future predetermined, or is it contingent on accident and unpredictable incident? Can individual or group action influence the course of the future? Would the world be different if Hitler had died at childbirth?
7. With sufficient information about the past and present, will historians be able to predict the future?
8. Is there a goal or purpose to history?

Learning Activity: The Nature of History

"For the want of a nail the shoe was lost. For want of a shoe the horse was lost. For the want of a horse the rider was lost. For the want of a rider the battle was lost. For the want of a battle the kingdom was lost. And all for want of a horseshoe-nail." Benjamin Franklin (Stevenson 1952: 2041), *Maxims . . . Prefixed to Poor Richard's Almanac* (1758).

Try it yourself:
1. In your opinion, what lesson is expressed in this proverb? In your opinion, what does the author believe about the nature of history?
2. Draw a picture illustrating your view of the nature of history.

WHAT ARE THE GOALS OF HISTORIANS?

All historians try to make sense out of the past, but many also have other goals. The issue here is whether these other goals are valid. For example, must historians remain impartial, objective, and apolitical, or can history legitimately be used to achieve political or social goals and support moral judgments? In *The Education of Henry Adams*, nineteenth-century United States historian, Henry Brooks Adams (Seldes 1966: 40, 41) argued, "No honest historian can take part with—or against—the forces he has to study. To him even the extinction of the human race should be merely a fact to be grouped with other vital statistics." However, during the American Civil War the same historian dismissed the idea of impartiality and wrote, "The devil is strong in me . . . Rebellion is in the blood, somehow or other. I can't go on without a fight."

Point of View
In *The Disuniting of America, Reflections on a Multicultural Society*, Arthur Schlesinger Jr. (1992: 80) decried the political uses and distortions of history in authoritarian countries and people in the United States he described as *ethnic chauvinists*. Schlesinger was particularly concerned with what he described as efforts to define "the purpose of history in the schools" as "therapeutic." However, in the same book, Schlesinger supported the use of history to promote patriotism. He argued that "a nation denied a conception of its past will be disabled in dealing with its present and future. As a means of defining national identity, history becomes a means of shaping history" (Schlesinger 1992: 45–46). Why is it wrong to use history to develop a sense of self-worth among African-American children, but right to use it to build national unity? Schlesinger denounced his opponents in the name of objective and impartial history, while ignoring the possibility that he also has biases and a political agenda.

Is it unacceptable for historians to try to establish the legitimacy of their points of view? Or is it a more serious problem when historians deny that their conclusions are influenced by their ideologies and, as a result, the conclusions go unexamined?

During the Enlightenment, Denis Diderot praised Voltaire, writing, "Other historians relate facts to inform us of facts. You relate them to excite in our hearts an intense hatred of lying, ignorance, hypocrisy, superstition, tyranny; and the anger remains even after the memory of the facts has disappeared" (Zinn, 1970: ix). During the nineteenth century, Karl Marx argued that, although "Philosophers have . . . interpreted the world differently . . . the point is to change it" (Carr, 1961: 182–183). Even Arthur Schlesinger Jr. (1992: 52) believes that "Honest history is the weapon of freedom."

All of these statements seem consistent with the social studies goals of promoting critical thinking and active citizenship. Perhaps a political agenda is a virtue for an historian, a social studies teacher, and students in a social studies class.

Teaching Activity: New Teacher's Debate "Point of View"

Since I have discovered how to make T-shirts with political messages on my computer using iron-ons, I have started to wear my views on my chest. One of my best (most outrageous?) creations quoted Venezuelan President Hugo Chavez at the United Nations where he said "Was Bush here, I still smell the sulfur?" However, teachers in the New Teachers Network tend to be sharply divided about whether to present their views during classroom discussions. In a seminar for new teachers where we discussed the 2008 Presidential election, most participants argued that teachers should to be strictly neutral. Suzy Mellen responded, "If teachers are afraid to offer their opinions for examination because they will be accused of partisanship or unpatriotic behavior, students will never be willing to formulate and openly express controversial ideas." My guideline is: If expressing your views opens up discussion, they should be introduced. If they shut it down, they should be withheld.

Add your voice to the discussion:
Where do you stand in this debate? Why?

Moral and Political Judgments

Does the study of history provide information and explanations that can be used to make moral and political judgments about the past and present and hopes for the future? Of course, I think that is one of the main reasons that people are interested in history. Does that give historians special authority to make moral and political judgments? In this case, not only do I think the answer is no, but I think historians have an obligation to slow the rush to judgment. First, because historians are accustomed to studying societies within specific social and chronological contexts, they tend to reject absolute universal moral standards of right and wrong. Second, because they are aware that "it ain't over til it's over," historians are sensitive to the need to reevaluate the past based on new findings, ideas, and historical developments.

There have been innumerable efforts to define moral standards throughout human history. I suspect that every country that ever went to war considered itself the aggrieved party and argued that right was on its side. The US expansion into the Great Plains and to the west coast of North America was considered "manifest destiny" or God's will. However, its growth was achieved at the expense of numerous small Native American nations that were nearly exterminated.

Some eighteenth- and nineteenth-century British philosophers, in an effort to counter the arbitrary nature of many political and economic judgments, argued that decisions should be evaluated based on whether they provided the greatest good for the greatest number (Mill 1963). At first glance, this seems like a reasonable equation, but it is difficult to apply. The enslavement of millions of Africans made possible the development of North America and financed the European commercial and industrial revolutions. Was it justified? Frederick Engels called history "the most cruel of all goddesses" because those called on to pay the price of progress are rarely the people who receive its benefits (Seldes 1966: 240).

Further, judgments changed as events unfolded. In 1910, an historian studying the impact of Bismarck on Germany and Europe might have praised the Iron Chancellor's political agenda and organizational skill. But the same historian, re-evaluating events after 1945, would be inclined to notice destructive tendencies that were missed in the earlier study. Future developments in China and Eastern Europe, economic depression in Western economies, or communist success in other parts of the world may lead to a re-evaluation of a system that was largely discredited with the collapse of the Soviet Union. Historians have the same right as anyone else to make judgments, but they also have a professional responsibility to question them. Eric Hobsbawm, author of *The Age of Extremes* (1994), is an excellent example of a contemporary historian who consciously applies a point of view to understand the past, and who uses understandings about the past to draw tentative conclusions about the present and to raise questions about the future. If Yogi Berra is right, maybe only the future holds the key to understanding the past.

Teaching Activity: Goals of Historians

Combatants in war often claim that God is on their side. Following the attacks on the World Trade Center and the Pentagon, President George W. Bush concluded a public statement explaining air strikes against targets in Afghanistan by saying, "We will not waver, we will not tire, we will not falter and we will not fail. Peace and freedom will prevail. Thank you. May God continue to bless America" (*The New York Times*, October 7, 2001, B6). Meanwhile, Osama bin Laden, the Saudi-born dissident accused of masterminding the attacks, announced, "I swear to God that America will not live in peace before peace reigns in Palestine, and before all the army of infidels depart the land of Mohammed, peace be upon him. God is the Greatest and glory be to Islam" (*The New York Times*, October 7, 2001, B7).

Try it yourself:
In their statements, both George W. Bush and Osama bin Laden called on God for strength and support. How do you respond to their invocation of God for their causes? Explain.

It's your classroom:
How would you respond to a student who claims "God is on the side of the United States?"

Add your voice to the discussion:
1. In your opinion, should historians strive for impartiality or seek to establish particular theories or points of view? Why?
2. In your opinion, should historians be involved in making moral and political judgments about the past and about contemporary societies? Why?

Essay 1: What Social Studies is all About

This essay is based on a teaching journal I kept during the Fall 1996 semester. I find keeping a teaching journal a useful way to discipline myself to reflect on my teaching and student learning on a regular basis. When teaching high school, I tried to write for a few minutes at the end of the school day while events were still fresh in my mind. At a minimum, I wrote about things that were successful in a lesson and things that needed to be changed before I taught it again. This journal entry is longer than usual because I realized as I was writing it that I wanted to include it in the first edition of this book.

In recent years, I have modified the lesson described here. Before we discuss Aurora D'Angela, I ask students to complete an activity sheet, "Foreign Criminals In New York," designed for use in an eleventh grade United States history class. It is based on an article from a magazine called *The North American Review*. I have also used the activity sheet in workshops with high school students where we followed with a discussion of stereotypes about different ethnic groups. The activity sheet is at the end of the essay.

The undergraduate section of the secondary education social studies methods class at Hofstra University is a small group. There are 11 students, 7 females and 4 males. I asked students to introduce themselves, including their name, major, place in the program, and how they identify themselves ethnically and culturally. It is an interesting group of students more diverse than many of my previous classes at this suburban university. One woman is Caribbean American and her parents are from Jamaica in the West Indies. One woman was born in Medellin, Columbia. One of the men and one of the women are from Greek-American families. Their parents are immigrants and they speak Greek at home. Two women identified themselves as Italian American. One of the male students is a Russian immigrant who arrived in the United States when he was a pre-teenager. Three White students, two women and a man, described themselves as Americans from "many different backgrounds". Two of these students are in their late twenties, the man and one of the women. All of the students in the class are history majors. Eight are seniors. Three are juniors.

I began the second part of the lesson by distributing a 1927 newspaper article about a teenage girl named Aurora D'Angela, and I asked the students to answer questions based on the article (*Johnstown Tribune* 1927). Aurora D'Angela was a teenage Italian immigrant who was arrested during a demonstration in Chicago protesting against the impending execution of Sacco and Vanzetti. I use this article in my teaching because many of the high school students on Long Island come from Italian-American families, but they have not really thought about what that means. They live in a culturally isolated time warp, with little sense of who they are, where they come from, or how their culture and history is similar or different from anyone else's. They have little sense of how the world today differs from the past. I find that this story promotes discussion and gets them to ask questions.

While the students were answering the questions, I circulated around the room looking at what they were writing. This gave me some idea about what they were thinking, and it helped me organize my thoughts and formulate questions. Sometimes I wrote down notes on a memo pad.

We began a discussion by brainstorming about events in the United States during the 1920s. Our list included prohibition, international isolation, "between the wars," the Scopes ("monkey") trial, an economic boom followed by depression, anti-immigrant feelings and quotas, prejudice against Catholics, Jews, and African-Americans, and of course, the Sacco and Vanzetti trial. Three students confessed that they did not know who Sacco and Vanzetti were, so two students gave a pretty complete account. They included charges that the court was biased against Sacco and Vanzetti because they were immigrants, Catholics, and political radicals.

One of the students who explained the Sacco and Vanzetti case to the class identified herself as Italian American. She remembered learning about this case in high school. I asked her why this story had stuck with her. She said that her grandparents were Italian immigrants, and that the treatment of Sacco and Vanzetti always struck her as unjust and as anti-Italian: "It hit me in the gut."

Another student, who also identified herself as Italian American, now remembered reading a statement by Vanzetti to the court. She spoke about the problem these two immigrant men had had expressing themselves during the trial because of their limited English.

One of the Greek students spoke up. She explained that the problem of discrimination against people who have trouble with English still continues. She told a story of how her father had been to court, how difficult it was for him because of language, and how her older sister had to go and help him to make sure he was treated fairly.

Learning Activity: Political Protest

This newspaper article was published in the Johnstown, PA. *Tribune*, on August 10, 1927, p. 1. It is about a female teenage Italian immigrant who led a political protest in Chicago against the threatened execution of Sacco and Vanzetti.

CHICAGO GIRL URGES GENERAL PROTEST STRIKE
By United Press

CHICAGO, Aug. 10. A bright-eyed 18-year-old high school girl paced her cell at police headquarters today shouting she was an anarchist after having been arrested while leading thousands of shouting Sacco-Vanzetti sympathizers through the streets last night. It was the girl who brought chaos to an orderly Sacco-Vanzetti protest meeting.

As the meeting ended she dashed to the street, shouting: General strike! General strike! This added a splash of color to the otherwise drab proceedings of the meeting and inflamed the gathering. With the girl, Aurora D'Angela, at the lead, the crowd surged into the street and marched along shouting the "Third Internationale" and appealing for a general strike. For a few blocks the protest parade was orderly. Then a motor car was ripped and torn by the crowd. A street car was boarded and the girl slapped the motorman.

One small police motor car attempted to stop the parade, but its passage was blocked. Additional police motor cars swept into the tide of shouting enthusiasts and tear gas bombs were unloosed into the crowd. The tear gas bombs caused the crowd to disperse and 15 of the leaders including the

18-year-old girl were arrested. She maintained she had long attended Liberal meetings in Chicago and said: I am an anarchist. My father was an anarchist.

Throughout the entire din there was a cry that Sacco and Vanzetti were being persecuted by capitalism. No signs were in evidence and the only means of identifying the crowd was in the constant shouting. The parade capped a day in which demonstrations became more acute.

Try it yourself:
1. What important information is included in this article? In your opinion, why is this information important?
2. What broader issues/ideas/questions are raised by this article?
3. As an 11th-grade US history teacher, how might you use this article in your class?
4. Are the events and issues described in this article important enough to include in the US history curriculum? Why or why not?

One woman, who had been quiet for much of the period, explained the importance of making it possible for teenagers to identify with what went on in the past. She said it was important to her that the newspaper story was about a teenager who was a female and an immigrant. She identified with this girl. She knew girls like her.

I asked another woman who identified herself as "part-Italian" whether she thought it was significant that Aurora was Italian. She answered, "Italian kids on Long Island don't think of themselves in this way so much anymore. They really didn't know about what their families had gone through. They need to learn about this." Two students added that they do not remember ever learning about people like themselves, "ordinary people," in school.

At this point our discussion shifted. I asked group members if they thought that the demonstration in Chicago in 1927 could be compared to any demonstrations today. The Caribbean-American student said that people associate this kind of demonstration today with African-Americans. She gave protests in Crown Heights, Brooklyn, and Los Angeles as examples of current protests. The Russian immigrant strongly objected to this comparison. He argued, "looting is different from protesting." Other students thought he was exaggerating the differences. There was a lot of disagreement in class.

Learning Activity: Attitudes Towards Immigrants

1. Bartolomeo Vanzetti was tried in Massachusetts twice, first for bank robbery and then for murder. In the first trial, Webster Thayer, who was the judge in both cases, told the jury:
"This man, although he may not have actually committed the crime . . . is nevertheless morally culpable, because he is the enemy of our existing institutions" (Boyer and Morais 1955: 226).
2. These statements were by Congressional Representatives during the debate over immigration quotas in December 1920 (Congressional Record 1921).
Congressman James McClintic, Democrat, Oklahoma: "I say the class of immigrants coming to the shores of the United States at this time are not the kind of people we want as citizens in this country" (177).
Congressman Lucian Parrish, Democrat, Texas: "We should stop immigration entirely until such a time as we can amend our immigration laws and so write them that hereafter no one shall be admitted except he be in full sympathy with our constitution and laws" (180–181).

It's your classroom:
1. How could you use these quotes to promote student discussion of conditions facing immigrants to the United States during the 1920s?
2. What questions would you ask your class? Why?
3. Would you connect discussion of these quotes with current debate about immigration? Explain the reasons for your answer.

Teaching Activity: Student Voice

It's your classroom:

You are the teacher and you have to make a decision. Are these personal statements by students taking us off on tangents, or are they making it possible for us to better understand the issues in the Sacco and Vanzetti case and the situation facing immigrants to the United States? What do you think? What do you decide?

Teaching Activity: Ordinary People

It's your classroom:

1. Would you include the history of ordinary people in social studies curricula? Why or why not?
2. If you would, how would you do it?

I asked if people thought Aurora should have been arrested for protesting. The Greek-American man identified himself as a "traditionalist" from a "strict family." He argued that if Aurora had broken the law she should be punished, no matter how much she felt Italians were discriminated against. "Breaking the law is wrong in all cases." Another student felt that protesters should not be arrested. "They have a constitutional right to protest." She felt that contemporary protests and the Sacco and Vanzetti protests of the 1920s were similar. "It is important for students to recognize this. It will help them deal with their prejudices today."

One student questioned whether the report that Aurora and the other protesters were rioting was true. I asked her what made her suspicious of the accuracy of the article. She responded that the article credited the "United Press" as its source. "If a reporter witnessed the events and wrote the story, he would have had a by-line. This story was probably from a police account." I asked the group, "If the account comes from a police report, does that make it inaccurate"? There was scattered uncertainty. I asked if anyone ever had a reason to doubt the police version of a story. One of the Italian-American women became very upset and told the story of a visit she made to another college. "The police broke up a beer blast on campus and started arresting participants and then beating them. When other students gathered, the police started attacking, beating, and arresting people in the crowd. They marched in full riot gear and I was terrified. A young man near me was grabbed, beaten, and arrested. I narrowly escaped. We tried contacting the media, but they didn't come. It was a police riot, but the whole incident was covered up by the press." When she finished,

other students began to recount experiences that made them feel skeptical about a police account. They wanted to read what other witnesses had to say before they made any judgments.

At this point, I asked the group to step back so we could examine what we had done. I asked if any of them could remember a free-flowing discussion like this on a social studies issue in either high school or college. No one could. All they remember about social studies classes is lectures and notes.

When I asked, "What made our discussion possible?" The following points were made:

> "We had the article as a starting point."
>
> "You gave us time to answer questions and write down our ideas so we could have something to contribute."
>
> "It was the first meeting of the class, but you knew our names. It seemed like you cared about what we were saying."
>
> "You asked us to speak louder so everyone could hear."
>
> "You asked us 'What do you mean?' and then you gave us a chance to think and explain more. You didn't guess what we were thinking and repeat it for the class."
>
> "When _____ interrupted, you asked him to wait so _____ could finish her idea."
>
> "The discussion connected to things we knew about, things from our experience. We talked about our religions and families. We used what we knew to help us understand the past."
>
> "These are important things that concern us."
>
> "We went back and forth between the past and the present. We used our knowledge from today to understand the past and the past to increase our knowledge about today."

As a summary question, I asked the group if it thought this was an important discussion for a high school social studies class. One student argued it was because we "had talked about a lot of important things and we reached agreement about the importance of this historical event."

I asked, "What if we hadn't reached agreement, would it still be an important discussion?"

There was a broad consensus that it would be.

People in the class said they had gotten a chance to think about different sides of an issue and to express their views. But they had not just expressed their views. They felt my questions had pushed them to use evidence from history and their lives to support their ideas.

Teaching Activity: Breaking the Law

Add your voice to the discussion:
1. Is breaking the law wrong in all cases? What do you think? Why?
2. Should we always accept statements from people in authority? What do you think? Why?

It's your classroom:
1. How would you handle student skepticism about authority?
2. How would you respond to these questions if they were raised by students in your classroom?

Teaching Activity: Student Discussions

Add your voice to the discussion:
Think about your secondary school experiences as a student, observer, and teacher. In your opinion, can this kind of discussion take place in a middle school or high school social studies classroom? Should it? What do you think? Why?

Teaching Activity: Foreign Criminals in New York
by Police Commissioner Theodore A. Bingham (1908)

Instruction: This reading passage is edited from an article in a magazine called *The North American Review*. Some words have been removed. After you read the passage, fill in the blanks and try to figure out what year the article was written. Then write a paragraph explaining why you selected this year and these groups of people.

1. When the circumstance is taken into consideration that 85 percent of the population of New York City is either foreign-born or of foreign parentage, and that nearly half of the residents of the five boroughs do not speak the English language, it is only a logical condition that something like 85 out of 100 of our criminals should be found to be of exotic origin. It is not astonishing that with a million (a) _____ in the city (one-quarter of the population), perhaps half of the criminals should be of that race.
2. The crimes committed by the (b) _____ are generally those against property. They are burglars, firebugs, pickpockets and highway robbers—when they have the courage; but, though all crime is their province, pocket-picking is the one to which they seem to take most naturally.
3. Among the most expert of all the street thieves are (c) _____ boys under 16, who are being brought up to lives of crime. Many of them are old offenders at the age of ten. The juvenile (d) _____ emulates the adult in the matter of crime percentages, forty percent of the boys at the House of Refuge and 27 percent of those arraigned in the Children's Court being of that race. The percentage of (e) _____ children in the truant schools is also higher than that of any others.
4. Although, while the (f) _____ are outnumbered in New York by the (g) _____ by two to one, the (h) _____ malefactor is by far the greater menace to law and order. For more than ten years, wherever a few (i) _____ laborers have gathered together, whether it be at work on

a railroad, or in a mine, or on a farm or an irrigation ditch, or in the vineyards of the Pacific slope, the desperadoes of the race have fastened themselves upon the honest and industrious. In New York, presumably the very center of Western civilization, crimes of blackmailing, blowing up shops and house and kidnapping of their fellow countrymen, have become prevalent among (j) _____ residents of the city to an extent that cannot much longer be tolerated.

5. The audacity of these desperadoes is almost beyond belief. Arrested for crimes that, proved against them, might given them capital punishment or life terms of imprisonment, they will obtain bail and return to the scene of their depredations to jeer at and threaten their victims.

6. (k) _____ children come next after the youthful (l) _____ in the percentage of arraignments in the Children's Court and commitments to the truant schools and the House of Refuge—the lower rounds of the ladder of crime. They are 20 percent of the total brought into the court, and 10 percent of those at the House of Refuge. There are no figures available as to percentages of commitments to the truant schools.

Add your voice to the discussion:

1. The year this article was written was 1908. The group mentioned in (a)–(e), (g), and (l) is Hebrews (Jews). The group mentioned in (f) and (h)–(k) is Italians. Why were most criminals in that period from these groups? What individuals and groups become criminal in any historic era?
2. In your opinion, is the situation similar or different today? Explain.

It's your classroom:

How would you address answers by students that were based on racial and ethnic stereotypes?

Essay 2: Are We Teaching "Greek Myths" in the Global History Curriculum?

In March 2001, *The New York Times* (Broad 2001: F1) reported that a submerged robot, searching the bottom of the Mediterranean Sea off of the island of Cyprus, found the remains of an ancient Greek vessel. The research team identified it as a Hellenistic trader carrying a shipment of wine between Rhodes and Alexandria. They estimate that it sank 2,300 years ago in the era of Alexander the Great.

The discovery supports the idea that in the ancient world the Mediterranean Sea was a giant highway for transporting products, peoples, and cultures from one site to another. This supported the process of cultural diffusion and contributed to the growth of early empires. In *The Odyssey*, Homer claimed that the Greek hero Odysseus sailed a similar route from Crete to North Africa. That voyage would have taken place about 1300BC The Greeks were not the only prolific sailors of this era. During the 1,000-year period before the consolidation of the Mediterranean world under Roman rule, the Phoenicians regularly sailed between the Middle East and Carthage in present day Tunisia, and as far as Spain.

This find is of major historical significance because the isle of Rhodes is about 200 miles north of the wreck, near the coast of present day Turkey. Alexandria, Egypt is an additional 200 miles south of the wreck in North Africa. The trip necessitated navigating across open water away from the sight of land.

The research team is continuing to search the region, hoping to uncover a Minoan shipwreck. The Minoans were seafarers who ruled an empire in the eastern Mediterranean and Aegean Seas from the island of Crete between 2500 and 1200BC This period is known as the Bronze Age because it predates the manufacture of iron tools and weapons in the Mediterranean region. No Minoan ship from this period has ever been recovered.

The subheading of *The Times* article was "Accidental Find Lends New Credence to Greek Tales of Sailing Feats." This statement is the crux of the issue that I address in this essay. Do social studies teachers present history "backwards" when our starting point is Greek accomplishments? If the Mediterranean was truly a highway in this period, then the likelihood is that it was dominated by the era's military, economic, and cultural superpowers, Egypt on the Nile River and Sumeria or Babylon in Mesopotamia (the Fertile Crescent). Greece, at best, would have been a peripheral trading partner. If Greece was at the margins and Egypt and Mesopotamia were at the center of cultural and technological advancement in this period, are social studies teachers presenting "Greek myth" as history when we attribute the origin of "Western Civilization" to ancient Greece?

The significance of the Nile and Fertile Crescent civilizations in early human cultural development and the power of cultural diffusion are well established. To cite a recent example, Jared Diamond (1997) shows that agricultural and animal husbandry emerge in the Fertile Crescent, and spread to the Nile River Valley, over 10,000 years ago (8500BC). Eventually this "food package," and a sedentary way of life based on it, spread throughout the Mediterranean world. Diamond traces a similar route for the spread of writing systems. Starting about 5,000 years ago (3200BC), they develop in Mesopotamia and Egypt (later, but independently, in China, 1300BC and Meso-America, 600BC) and diffuse across the globe. Other cultural developments in the ancient Mediterranean world followed a similar pattern of dispersion. Pottery first appears in the Nile Valley and Mesopotamia about 7000BC; metallurgy about 4000BC; formal governments about 3700BC; and iron tools about 900BC. Since the historical record makes it virtually impossible to decide whether a development first emerged in Egypt or Mesopotamia, they are considered as a single point of origin.

Given the early achievements of Mesopotamia and Egypt, why the unbalanced focus on ancient Greece in history textbooks and social studies classrooms? There are three general answers to this question. Historians and teachers often focus on ancient Greece because they perceive Greek civilization as fundamentally different (as somehow more "Western") than the civilizations that preceded it or existed at the same time, and they believe these differences produced the modern world as we know it. Historian Peter Burke (1998:2) calls this view the "'Grand Narrative' of the rise of Western civilization: a triumphalist account of Western achievement from the Greeks onwards in which the Renaissance is a link in the chain which includes the Reformation, the Scientific Revolution, the Enlightenment, the Industrial Revolution, and so on."

Within this framework, Houghton Mifflin's high school text, *History of the World* (Perry, 1990: 71), reports, "The earliest civilizations that grew up on the Greek islands developed a unique culture. Although these people were conquered by foreign invaders, many of their traditions endured. Greek ideas would come to have a powerful influence on the politics, thought, and art of Europe and the Western Hemisphere. For this reason, Greece is known as the 'cradle of Western civilization'."

Learning Activity: Athens during the Age of Pericles (450BC)

There is considerable disagreement among historians about the actual population of Athens during this time period, so these figures are only estimates.

Table 2.1 Population of Athens in 450BC

Total population	450,000	
Adult male citizens with ability to vote	40,000	9%
Disenfranchised citizens (women, children and some men)	80,000	18%
Free foreign-born residents of Athens	80,000	18%
Slaves	250,000	55%

Questions/Activities:

1. What is the largest demographic group in Table 2.1?
2. What conclusions about ancient Athens can you draw from the information in Table 2.1?
3. Create a pie chart illustrating the population of Athens during the time of Pericles.

It's your classroom:

How would you use the information in Table 2.1 to promote student discussion? What questions would you ask?

Is there sufficient evidence to document historical continuity from ancient Greece to the modern era? Diane Ravitch and Abigal Thernstrom (1992) edited a collection called *The Democracy Reader* that includes classic and modern speeches, essays, poems, declarations, and documents on freedom and human rights. In this book, Ravitch and Thernstrom try to support a thesis championed by Harvard sociologist Orlando Patterson (1991), who argued that we can trace the history of democratic ideals as an essential component of Western philosophy from ancient Greece to the modern world. But an examination of the table of contents raises an interesting problem. The book contains no documents for the 1500-year period between Aristotle's *The Politics* (written c. 320BC) and Thomas Aquinas' *Summa Theologia* (written about 1250AD). Even if the ancient Greek city-states possessed a system with recognizably democratic elements, it is exceedingly difficult to establish a direct political or intellectual connection between societies separated by over 1,500 years of history. In fact, Greek texts were largely unknown in Europe prior to the Crusades, and only survived because they were preserved by Arab scholars.

A second explanation for the unbalanced focus on ancient Greece is that people in modern societies can see themselves in its art, literature, philosophy, and ideologies. Classical Greek sculpture appears realistic rather than symbolic or exotic. Socrates and Plato sound as if they could be giving interviews on C-SPAN. Athens seems the model for democratic society, while martial Sparta reminds some of twentieth-century totalitarian societies or *Star Trek*'s Klingon Empire. Even their Gods, with soap opera-like battles and love affairs, remind us of our own passions and conflicts.

Are we reading more into their culture and history than actually can be supported by the historical record? Are we seeing what is there, or what we want to see? Let me offer two examples that illustrate what I mean. The first is an example of seeing what is not there—an ancient philosopher championing modern democratic values. The second is an example of ignoring what is clearly there—a different attitude toward sexual mores.

The popular conception is that Socrates was a Greek philosopher and teacher persecuted, and then executed, by an authoritarian government for questioning leaders and pursuing the search for truth. Unfortunately, the historical record is not so clear-cut. In *The Trial of Socrates* (1988), I. F. Stone concluded that Socrates was actually involved in an attempt by the oligarchy to undermine efforts to broaden representation in Athenian government.

A second issue, rarely addressed because of our culture's homophobia, is the Greek attitude toward same-sex sexual relationships. According to M. I. Finley (1963: 123–125), Aristotle believed that true friendship was only possible between equals, hence impossible between men and women. Bisexuality was common, especially among the upper class, where men and women were expected to seek both physical and spiritual companionship from people of the same gender. Sexual relationships between adult men and younger boys were a feature of military elites in Sparta and Thebes and among the nobility in Athens. This aspect of ancient Greek culture is missing from most high school textbooks.

Teaching Activities: Addressing Homosexuality in History

There are numerous examples that homosexual relationships were accepted as normal human behavior in ancient Greece, especially relationships between established men and male youths. Among the Thebians, a special "Sacred Band' of elite troops consisted entirely of male homosexual couples. According to legend, Alexander the Great and his childhood friend Hephaistion had a physical and emotional bond, as did Achilles and Patroclus in Homer's account of the Trojan War.

Add your voice to the discussion:
Discussion of attitudes toward homosexuality in other societies may make students, teachers, and parents uncomfortable. But it also helps students reconsider their concepts of normal human behavior, which is an important part of the study of anthropology. As a teacher, will you introduce this issue in your classroom? Explain. If not, how will you address it if introduced by a student?

Probably the most comprehensive effort to read the present into the past is the celebration of Greek "democracy." According to Houghton Mifflin's *History of the World* (Perry 1990: 86–87), "Democracy, which had been developing in Athens over many years, reached its peak under the leadership of Pericles. He opened all political offices to any citizen. He paid jurors so that poor citizens as well as the wealthy could serve. Athens had a direct democracy—that is, all citizens had the right to attend the Assembly and cast a vote."

In the next paragraph, however, we learn that "Athenian democracy was far from complete. Citizens had time for public service largely because they owned slaves . . . Most residents of Athens were not citizens and had no say in government . . . Women, too, had no political rights." In fact, during the era of Pericles, the population of Athens was about 450,000 people, and less than 10 percent were adult male citizens with the power to vote. About 18 percent of the population was foreign-born with no legal rights and 55 percent of the residents of Athens were enslaved. Athenian "democracy" was so restricted in scope and in time (the age of Pericles lasted about 30 years), that students should consider whether it should legitimately be labeled democratic at all.

A third explanation for the focus on ancient Greece as the source of Western civilization is *Eurocentrism*: the effort to center history on European societies and to minimize the contributions of non-European "others." For example, the debate over the relationship between Egypt, Mesopotamia, and Greece in the ancient world is highly charged. Claims by Afrocentric authors that Egypt was the source of Greek civilization, that ancient Egyptians were "Black Africans," and that this history has been hidden by mainstream "White" institutions in order to strip people of African ancestry of their proper place in history, have been challenged by essays in most of the major historical and archeological journals (Levine 1992: 440–460; Pounder 1992: 461–464; Lefkowitz and Rogers 1996).

I want to sidestep the debate over whether ancient Egyptians were "Black Africans" because I believe it takes us away from the more important issue of Egyptian influence on Greek culture and development. We will probably never know for certain the skin color or genetic heritage of ancient Egyptians. Their art is largely symbolic and I suspect the colors used to portray people were selected from pigments available to artists, not because of the skin color of subjects. Most likely, since ancient Egypt was a crossroads civilization, it was a genetically and culturally blended society with diverse people who probably did not place the same significance on race as we do in the United States today.

Much of the debate over the relationship between Egypt, Mesopotamia, and Greece is in response to the work of Martin Bernal (1987, 1991; Bernal and Moore 2001), who has published two volumes of a proposed three-volume collection called *Black Athena: The Afroasiatic Roots of Classical Civilization*. Bernal marshals extensive evidence to present a detailed case for Egyptian and Semitic (Middle Eastern) contributions to Greek culture during the Bronze Age (prior to 1100BC) based on an examination of religion, art, mythology, language, and artifacts. Among other things, he provides powerful arguments for the origins of the Hercules legend and the Sphinx in ancient Egypt.

The ancient world is not my area of expertise as either a teacher or historian, so I cannot evaluate Bernal's documentation. What I find most interesting are the concessions made by his opponents. Among his more vocal critics, Molly Myerwitz Levine (1992) and Mary Lefkowitz and Guy Rogers (1996) accept some of Bernal's claims about Bronze Age influence, but argue that they are not at the core of what we identify as classical Greece—its art, politics, and philosophy.

In an essay entitled, "Did Egypt Shape the Glory that was Greece?" John Coleman, a classicists from Cornell University, presents an alternative historical scenario to Bernal's and concludes that "recognizing that Greek civilization was influenced from abroad and made use of previous advances in mathematics and science, . . . is a far cry from asserting that it had Afroasiatic roots'" (Coleman, 1996: 281). Coleman claims that all scholars recognize the contributions of Egypt and the Middle East to the ancient Greek world, especially to Minoan or Crete civilization, and argues that the dispute with Bernal is primarily a matter of degree.

According to Coleman's narrative, cultural contact between the Aegean and Egypt started in the early Bronze Age, around 2100BC, as a result of migration and trade. Crete needed to import tin, a major ingredient in the manufacture of bronze, which was lacking in the Aegean world. The widespread diffusion of pottery from 2100 to 1725BC shows increasing contacts between Greece and Egypt. During this period, Minoan culture, which was shaped by its contacts with Egypt, exerted a powerful influence on the developing mainland Greek societies. Later, with the decline of Crete, Mycenaean (or mainland Greek societies) took over the trade connections with Egypt. We know less about Greece between 1100 and 750BC, but after 750BC Greek soldiers were used as mercenaries in

Egypt and, according to Coleman (1996: 296), there is a "flood of influence on all Greek arts and crafts from Egypt." These conclusions are supported by an exhibit I visited, "Crete-Egypt: Three Millennia of Cultural Interactions" at the Herakleion Archaeological Museum in Crete. It contains 527 artifacts that demonstrate interaction between the two Mediterranean peoples. Some of the exhibit can be viewed at the museum's website (available at: http://www.ancient-greece.org/images/museums/heraklion-mus/index.htm, accessed September 17, 2007).

I find Coleman's statement balanced and reasonable, and believe it establishes a significant relationship that was ignored before the Bernal work. It is in sharp contrast to what is currently taught in secondary schools. Houghton Mifflin's *History of the World* (Perry 1990: 71) section on Minoan civilization reports that they were "seafaring traders, exporting wine, honey, and olive oil to Egypt, Asia Minor, Syria and Greece," but ignores any Egyptian influence on Crete or Greece. After the collapse of Crete, Egypt plays no further role in Greek history until it is conquered by Alexander the Great. The chapter on ancient Egypt (p. 34–42) reports that Egypt traded with other civilizations in the Mediterranean region including Crete, but does not identify the Greek world or discuss any cultural exchange between the two civilizations. The spread of Greek culture through Alexander's conquest of the Mediterranean world, known as *Hellenization*, is presented as a major accomplishment of ancient Greece that stimulated trade, science, philosophy, and cultural diffusion. But should conquest and forced assimilation into the Greek world be presented uncritically?

Would similar conquests and assimilations be viewed that way if they took place today? The much celebrated Hebrew revolt under the Maccabees (the story of Hanukah) about 170BC was a response to efforts by Greek rulers to enforce Greek culture, law and religion in ancient Israel (Johnson 1987: 102–107).

The celebration of ancient Greece's role within the "Grand Narrative" of the Western world is reinforced in standard interpretations of the European Renaissance, which define the era as a rebirth of classical Greek and Roman civilization (Thompson 1996). According to Burke (1998: 2), "the major innovators of the Renaissance presented—and often perceived—their inventions and discoveries as a return to ancient traditions after the long parenthesis of what they were the first to call the Middle Ages." Houghton Mifflin's text credits Italian humanists, especially Petrach of Florence, with reading ancient texts and "rediscovering knowledge that had been lost or forgotten" (p. 327).

Even if Renaissance innovators believed that social change was a result of the rediscovery of ancient traditions, that does not mean that it actually happened that way. In *Worldly Goods, A New History of the Renaissance* (1996: 12), Lisa Jardine presents a materialist interpretation of the period, arguing that the celebrated culture of the European Renaissance was the result of a "competitive urge to acquire" stimulated by the growth of trade, cities and a new affluent, secular, elite. She believes that "Early Renaissance works of art which today we admire for their sheer representational virtuosity were part of a vigorously developing world market in luxury commodities" (Jardine 1996: 19).

Classroom Activity: Inventing the European Renaissance

Webquest:
Filippo Brunelleschi (1377–1446), Lorenzo de Medici (1449–1492), Leonardo da Vinci (1452–1519), and Niccolo dei Machiavelli (1469–1727) are four figures closely identified with the development of the European Renaissance in Italy. Your historical challenge is to discover the "connections" between these four individuals; explain why the European Renaissance began in Florence, Italy; and use your answers to these challenges to define the European Renaissance and identify its accomplishments and historical impact. (Be sure to document your internet sources and to check your data and interpretations using multiple sites. Remember, *Wikipedia* is the starting, not the end point, in your research.)

It's your classroom:
What web links would you provide to students to direct their research?

But why would this increasingly affluent, secular world claim spiritual and intellectual descent from classical Mediterranean civilizations? The answer is

related to the power of religious authority in that era. The Roman Catholic Church was threatened by competing religions and new world-views, and brutally resisted change. Framing new ideas and discoveries as a rebirth of knowledge from classical Greco-Roman and Biblical eras was necessary for survival. In Florence, where the European Renaissance first emerged, major religious authorities attacked the study of "pagan authors" as an impediment to salvation, and humanists were forced to defend the texts as compatible with church teachings (Burke 1998: 31–32). In the end, Church and secular authorities preferred to credit Aristotle and Ptolemy with the origin of civilization, rather than acknowledging the role of contemporary Moslems and Jews.

Debates over ideas during the European Renaissance were not just intellectual exercises. In the early thirteenth century, Pope Innocent III launched a Crusade to crush heresy in southern France that resulted in the slaughter of tens of thousands of people (O'Shea 2000). After warring against its Islamic population, Spain's Roman Catholic monarchs expelled Jews and in 1477 established the Inquisition. Under Torquemada, the third Grand Inquisitor, over 2,000 people were burned at the stake for suspicion of rejecting Catholic religious orthodoxy (Thompson 1996: 509). Noted Renaissance artists and scholars were not immune from suspicion or attack. In 1516, Leonardo da Vinci, whose actions and work were frequently impious, and who made no pretense of connection with classical antiquity, fled the Italian peninsula and sought sanctuary from King Francis I of France (Thompson 1996: 147–158). In 1633, Galileo was tried for heresy by the Holy Office of the Inquisition in Rome for challenging the Ptolemaic system and asserting that the Earth traveled around the Sun (Sobel 1999: 273–278).

Where does this leave social studies teachers? We need to re-conceptualize both the "grand narrative" of Western civilization presented in global history and the way we teach social studies. Instead of presenting the past as a series of facts and truths to be memorized and celebrated, teachers should engage students in a critical examination of different explanations of the past and present. The Global History curriculum can be organized so students explore essential historical questions (Wiggins and McTighe 1998: 28–32; Singer 1999: 28–31), including: What were the origins of Western civilization? Was there only one origin? Was Athens or any ancient society democratic? Does conquest make a leader (Alexander) great? What are the costs of cultural diffusion and assimilation? How does democracy emerge? How do societies change? Why do societies accept and promote myths about their past?

An earlier version of this essay appeared in the Winter-Spring 2002 issue of *Social Science Docket*, published by the New York and New Jersey Councils for the Social Studies.

References and Recommendations for Further Reading

Ali, T. 1992. *Shadows of the pomegranate tree.* New York: Verso.

Ali, T. 1998. *The book of Saladin.* New York: Verso.

Ali, T. 2000. *The stone woman.* New York: Verso.

Ali, T. 2005. *A Sultan in Palermo.* New York: Verso.

Banks, R. 1998. *Cloudsplitter.* New York: HarperCollins.

Banks, R. 2004. *The darling.* New York: HarperCollins.

Bell, M. 1996. *All soul's rising.* New York: Penguin.

Bell, M. 2000. *Master of the crossroads.* New York: Pantheon.

Bell, M. 2004. *The stone that the builder refused.* New York: Pantheon.

Bernal, M. 1987. *Black Athena: The Afroasiatic roots of classical civilization, Volume 1: The fabrication of ancient Greece, 1785–1985.* New Brunswick, NJ: Rutgers University Press.

Bernal, M. 1991. *Black Athena: The Afroasiatic roots of classical civilization, Volume 2: The archeological and documentary evidence.* New Brunswick, NJ: Rutgers University Press.

Bernal, M. and Moore, D. 2001. *Black Athena writes back: Martin Bernal responds to his critics.* Durham, NC: Duke University Press.

Berra, Y., with T. Horton. 1989. *Yogi: It ain't over . . .* New York: Harper & Row.

Bingham, T. 1908. "Foreign criminals In New York," *North American Review*, September.

Blake, W. 1790–1793. *The Marriage of heaven and hell.* http://books.google.com/books?id=-zTaF39CC9EC&dq=&pg=PP1&ots=F7u9dvxoUF&sig=J99HkbsmGbYaeGBaP3VB3yaVmzs&prev=http://www.google.com/search%3Fhl%3Den%26q%3Dblake%2BThe%2BMarriage%2Bof%2BHeaven%2Band%2BHell%26btnG%3DGoogle%2BSearch&sa=X&oi=print&ct=title#PPA10,M1, accessed September 18, 2007.

Blum, J. 1990. "Guthrie, Woody (1912–1967)," in M. Buhle, P. Buhle and D. Georgakas, eds. *Encyclopaedia of the left.* New York: Garland.

Boyer, R. and Morais, H. 1955. *Labor's untold story.* New York: Cameron.

Broad, W. 2001. "In an ancient wreck, clues to seafaring lives," *The New York Times*, March 27.

Burke, P. 1998. *The European Renaissance, centres and peripheries*. Oxford, UK: Blackwell.

Carr, E. H. 1961. *What is history?* New York: Vintage.

Coleman, J. E. 1996. "Did Egypt shape the glory that was Greece?" in M. Lefkowtiz and G. MacLean Rogers, eds., *Black Athena revisited*. Chapel Hill, NC: University of North Carolina Press.

Congressional Record. 1921. *3rd session, 66th Congress, vol. LX – Part 1, December 6, 1920 – January 6, 1921*. Washington DC: Government Printing Office.

Cooper, H. 2007. "Rice pursues shuttle diplomacy in Mideast," *The New York Times*, March 25.

Diamond, J. 1997. *Guns, germs, and steel: The fates of human societies*. New York: Norton.

Dobb, M. 1946. *Studies in the development of capitalism*. London: Routledge.

Engvick, W. ed. 1965. *Lullabies and Night Songs*. New York: Fawcett.

Finley, M. 1963. *The ancient Greeks*. London: Chatto & Windus.

Foner, E. 1998. *The story of American freedom*. New York: Norton.

Foner, E. 2002. *Who owns history?* New York: Hill and Wang.

Foner, E. 2005. *Forever free, the story of emancipation and reconstruction*. New York: Knopf.

Fukuyama, F. 1992. *The end of history and the last man*. New York: The Free Press.

Gardiner, P., ed. 1959. *Theories of history*. New York: The Free Press.

Giardina, D. 1988. *Storming heaven*. New York: Ballantine Books.

Giardina, D. 1994. *The unquiet earth*. New York: Random House.

Giardina, D. 1999. *Saints and villains*. New York: Random House.

Gould, S. J. 1983. *Hen's teeth and horse's toes*. New York: Norton.

Gould, S. J. 1989. *Wonderful life*. New York: Norton.

Gould, S. J. 1991. *Bully for brontosaurus*. New York: Norton.

Gould, S. J. 1995. *Dinosaur in a haystack*. New York: Harmony Books.

Hardwick, M. 1986. *The complete guide to Sherlock Holmes*. New York: St. Martin's Press.

Hartocollis, A. 2001a. "Campus culture wars flare anew over tenor of debate after the attacks," *The New York Times*, September 30.

Hartocollis, A. 2001b. "Lynne Cheney disputes official's call for more teaching of multiculturalism," *The New York Times*, October 10.

Hawking, S. 1988. *A brief history of time: From the big band to black holes*. New York: Bantam Books.

Hilton, R. 1978. *The transition from feudalism to capitalism*. London: Verso.

Hobsbawm, E. 1962. "From feudalism to capitalism," *Marxism Today*, August.

Hobsbawm, E. 1994. *The age of extremes: A history of the world, 1914–1991*. New York: Pantheon.

Hobsbawm, E. 1997. *On history*. New York: New Press.

Hobsbawm, E. and A. Polito. 1999. *On the edge of a new century*. New York: New Press.

Hofstadter, R. 1955. *The age of reform*. New York: Random House.

Hofstadter, R. 1962. *Anti-intellectualism in American life*. New York: Random House.

Jardine, L. 1996. *Worldly goods, a new history of the Renaissance*. New York: Doubleday.

Johnson, P. 1987. *A history of the Jews*. New York: Harper and Row.

Katznelson, I. 2005. *When affirmative action was white: an untold history of racial inequality in twentieth-century America*. New York: Norton.

Kolko, G. 1963. *The triumph of conservatism: A reinterpretation of American history, 1900–1916*. New York: The Free Press.

Lefkowitz, M. and Rogers, G. 1996. *Black Athena revisited*. Chapel Hill, NC: UNC Press.

Levine, M. M. 1992. "The use and abuse of Black Athena," *American Historical Review* 97(2).

Mill, J. S. 1963. *The six great humanist essays of John Stuart Mill*. New York: Washington Square Press.

National Council for the Social Studies. 1994. *Curriculum standards for social studies: Expectations of excellence, NCSS bulletin 89*. Washington, DC: NCSS.

Ortiz, F. 1940. *Cuban counterpoint*. Durham, NC: Duke University Press.

O'Shea, S. 2000. *The Perfect Heresy*. New York: Walker.

Paige, R. 2003. *Federal Register* 66(7): May 6.

Palmer, B. 1994. *E.P. Thompson, objections and oppositions*. New York: Verso.

Patterson, O. 1991. *Freedom*. New York: Basic Books.

Perry, M. 1990. *History of the world*. Boston, MA: Houghton Mifflin.

Pounder, R. 1992. "Black Athena 2: History without rules," *American Historical Review* 97(2).

Ravitch, D. and Thernstrom, A., eds. 1992. *The democracy reader*. New York: HarperCollins.

Rees, J. 2003. "What did Bush mean by 'Revisionist Historians'?" *History News Network*, June 30. http://hnn.us/articles/1532.html, accessed September 19, 2007.

Rethinking Schools. 1995. "History standards," *Rethinking Schools* 9(3).

Schlesinger, A. Jr. 1992. *The disuniting of America: Reflections on a multicultural society*. New York: Norton.

Seeger, P. and Reiser, B., eds. 1985. *Carry it on!* New York: Simon and Schuster.

Seldes, G., ed. 1966. *The great quotations*. New York: Lyle, Stuart.

Sen, A. 1999. *Development as freedom*. New York: Knopf.

Singer, A. 1999. Teaching multicultural social studies in an era of political eclipse. *Social Education* 63(1).

Sobel, D. 1999. *Galileo's daughter*. New York: Walker.

Stevenson, B., ed. 1952. *The home book of quotations*. 6th ed. New York: Dodd, Mead.

Stone, I. F. 1988. *The trial of Socrates*. New York: Doubleday.

Thiong'o, N. 1994. *Matigari*. Lawrenceville, NJ: Africa World Press.

Thompson, B. 1996. *Humanists and reformers, a history of the Renaissance and Reformation*. Grand Rapids, MI: Eerdmans.

Thompson, E. P. 1963. *The making of the English working class*. New York: Vintage.

US Bureau of Education. 1916. *Report of the committee on social studies*. Washington, DC: Government Printing Office.

Wiggins, G. and McTighe, J. 1998. *Understanding by design*. Alexandria, VA: ASCD.

Zinn, H. 1970. *The politics of history*. Boston, MA: Beacon Press.

3. What Is Social Studies?

Overview

- Define history and the social sciences
- Explore the similarities, differences, and relationships between the disciplines included in social studies
- Discuss the significance of social studies in secondary education

Key Concepts

Social Science, Social Studies, Geography, Anthropology, Political Science, Sociology, Philosophy, Economics, Psychology, Curriculum

Questions

- What Are the Social Sciences?
- How Did the Social Sciences Become Social Studies?
- What Do We Learn from the Social Science Disciplines?

Essays

1. How can Teachers Promote the Economic and Civic Literacy of Students?
2. How can Teachers Use Drama to Promote Literacy while Teaching Social Studies Content and Concepts?

WHAT ARE THE SOCIAL SCIENCES?

The social sciences started to develop as areas of study during the seventeenth- and eighteenth- century European Enlightenment when new scientific approaches were applied to understanding the ways that societies were organized and people made decisions. For an essay in an undergraduate European intellectual history class at City College in the 1960s, my instructor asked us to discuss, "To what extent were later Enlightenment thinkers Newtonian?" Sir Isaac Newton believed that the physical universe obeyed natural laws that could be described with mathematical precision. The teacher wanted us to examine efforts by thinkers like John Locke, Thomas Hobbes, and Adam Smith in Great Britain; Voltaire, Montesquieu, Diderot, and Rousseau in France; and Benjamin Franklin, Thomas Jefferson, and James Madison in the United States to adapt Newton's view of the physical world so they could develop a calculus describing the world of human interrelationships.

The social sciences—Political Science, Sociology, Economics, Geography, Anthropology, and Psychology—emerged as individual disciplines during the nineteenth century, coinciding with efforts to explain mass social upheavals, the development of industrial society, and the need of growing European nation-states to gather and organize statistical information and manage complex economic, political, and social systems. During this period, social scientists formulated research questions about areas of society that had previously been ignored, and developed new methodologies for study. Important theorists like Auguste Comte, Emile Durkheim, David Ricardo, John Stuart Mills, Karl Marx, Herbert Spencer, and, later, Sigmund Freud changed the way we understand the world and ourselves. By the late nineteenth and early twentieth centuries, the different disciplines were institutionalized in the United States and Europe with their own university departments and professional organizations. The American Historical Association (AHA) was founded in 1884, the American Political Science Association in 1903, the American Sociological Association in 1905, and the National Council of Geography Teachers in 1914.

Twentieth-century movements for expanded government intervention in economies and regulation of society, whether called progressivism, bureaucratization, technocracy, fascism, or socialism, increased the importance of the social sciences. In the United States, the Great Depression, the New Deal, government-industry partnership during World War II, and the influence of British economist John Maynard Keynes all contributed to an expanding role for the social sciences in managing the capitalist economic system and in measuring the impact of economic development and government-sponsored social programs on the general population.

Generally, the social sciences have distanced themselves from the study of history by focusing on analysis of contemporary events, rigorous application of social theory and research methods, and the "scientific objectivity" of their findings. At the dedication of a new Social Science Research building at the University of Chicago in 1929, economist Wesley Mitchell argued that the social sciences represented the victory of the "man of facts" over the "man of hunches." John Merriam, president of the Carnegie Foundation, believed that many of the highly contested issues of the era would "melt away" as soon as social scientists had collected sufficient data to objectively resolve social policy debates. Many economists and political scientists concentrated on designing mathematical descriptions and models of society. Some sociologists and psychologists distinguished their fields from history and philosophy by identifying them as behavioral sciences. However, although boundaries remained between the disciplines, areas of study continued to overlap. In recent years, historians have increasingly incorporated the theories, methodologies, and insights of the social sciences, while many social scientists have added an historical dimension to their work. In addition, there have always been social scientists like sociologists Robert Lynd, Gunnar Myrdal, and C. Wright Mills, who reject the possibility of total objectivity and believe that their research should support progressive political goals (Smith 1994).

HOW DID THE SOCIAL SCIENCES BECOME SOCIAL STUDIES?

In the United States, the importance of history and the social sciences in education has roots in the early national period. Benjamin Rush, a physician in colonial America who represented New York at the Continental Congress and signed the Declaration of Independence, argued that education was vital to the development of citizenship. Thomas Jefferson was an early champion of including history and geography in a basic education. During the nineteenth century, history, geography, and civics tended to be independent subjects, with history gradually supplanting geography as the dominant influence on curriculum.

The idea of social studies as a comprehensive secondary school subject, including history and the social sciences, was a product of the move toward rationalizing and standardizing education during the Progressive era at the start of the twentieth century. In 1912, the National Education Association created a Committee on the Social Studies to reorganize the secondary school curriculum. The committee, with representatives from different social science disciplines and educational constituencies, issued a report in 1916 that defined the social studies as "those whose subject matter relates directly to the organization and development of human society, and to man [sic] as a member of social groups" (US Bureau of Education 1916: 9). It also established that the preparation of citizens was the primary goal of the social studies. In a preliminary statement, Thomas Jesse Jones, chair of the committee, claimed "high school teachers of social studies have the best opportunity ever offered to any social group to improve the citizenship of the land." The committee's focus on citizenship education is not surprising, given the Progressive era's concern with the assimilation of millions of new Eastern and Southern European immigrants to the United States, especially as the country prepared for possible involvement in the Great War being fought in Europe.

The National Council for the Social Studies (NCSS) was founded in 1921, with the support of the national historians organization as a response to the NEA-sponsored report and as an effort by historians to assert the central role of their field in social studies. From 1925 to 1975, it served as the NEA's Department of Social Studies. The relationship between the AHA and the NCSS continued until 1935, when the NCSS became an advocate for a broader definition of the social studies. One of the organization's most important activities was publication of the journal *Social Education*, which expanded its influence in shaping social studies curricula (NCSS 1994).

Although the debate over citizenship education versus discipline-based instruction and over the relative importance of different subject areas continues, since the end of World War II secondary schools generally integrate history and the social sciences into a multi-year, history-based social studies curriculum. Although economics and political science are often assigned specific courses in the social studies sequence, geography, sociology, anthropology, psychology, and philosophy are usually taught within the confines of other subject areas or in elective courses. In the last decade, however, social science requirements for teacher certification, especially knowledge of geography, government, and economics, have been increased as part of the general push to raise educational standards.

WHAT DO WE LEARN FROM THE SOCIAL SCIENCE DISCIPLINES?

Geography

The focus of geography in secondary education is generally on the location of cities, states, countries, continents, natural resources, major land formations, bodies of water, international boundaries, and interconnecting routes. One of its more important functions in social studies curricula is academic skill development, through map reading and design, and the creation and analysis of information on charts and graphs. Geography is also used to help students develop their ability to observe, organize, and analyze information presented in pictures, slides, and videos.

As an academic discipline, the importance placed on geography in secondary education has had peaks and valleys, and it now seems to be rising. In the early national era, geography, not history, tended to be the main focus of what is now called the "Social Studies." In a physically expanding, largely agrarian nation that was also dependent on international trade, a subject that focused on map skills, international and domestic trade routes, and land formations had more concrete value than stories of great deeds by heroic figures from the past. However, as the study of history became associated with explanation and nation-building during the nineteenth and twentieth

centuries, geography was eclipsed. In social studies classes, geography continued to provide students with information that teachers believed they needed to memorize, but curricula were organized around history.

In recent decades, four factors have contributed to a resurgence of geography within the social studies: (1) focus on global interdependence, including increased attention to the non-Western world, its contributions to world history and culture, and its role in contemporary world affairs; (2) concern for the impact of environmental issues, like pollution, resource depletion, and global warming, on the quality of human life; (3) the importance of understanding global demographics and population diversity, and (4) as a result of the work of Jared Diamond, author of *Guns, Germs, and Steel* (1997) and *Collapse* (2004), increased attention to the idea of geographical causality (e.g., accidents of geography have a major impact on cultural and historical development). Geography, although still generally taught within the context of history or current events, has become crucial for defining and comparing regions of the world; understanding the relationship between people and place; examining the migration of people, plants, and animals; explaining ways that the physical world influences human development; and exploring the ways that human development has changed the physical world.

An example of an area where geography enriches our understanding of history is the study of the impact of the post-Colombian exchange that, among other things, brought crops like sugar cane to the Americas and potatoes to Eurasia and Africa. Results of the introduction of potatoes into Ireland included concentration on one-crop agriculture, a rapid increase in population from approximately 1.5 million people in 1760 to 8 million people in 1840, a devastating potato famine between 1845 and 1852, and the death or emigration of millions of people (Hawke and Davis 1992).

Geography also contributes to the inter-disciplinary nature of the social studies by introducing understandings drawn from the natural and physical sciences about climate, agriculture, and the use of resources like air, water, and land. In the last few years, the threat of global warming has turned attention towards the impact of climate change on earlier civilizations. Recent books of interest on the topic include *Late Victorian Holocausts:*

El Niño Famines and the Making of the Third World by Mike Davis (2002), *Collapse: How Societies Choose to Fail or Succeed* by Jared Diamond (2004), and *The Winds of Change: Climate, Weather, and the Destruction of Civilizations* by Eugene Linden (2006). The issues raised in these books about the impact of climate change and human and governmental responses are particularly important when preparing students to participate in decision-making as active citizens.

Sample Geography Lesson Ideas

1. Map or Globe: Which is More Accurate?
Compare the island of Greenland and the continent of Africa on a globe and on a standard Mercator projection map. On the map, they are roughly the same size. On the globe, Africa is considerably larger. Which is a more accurate representation of the relative sizes of Greenland and Africa? Why? If students cannot resolve the issue through discussion, try the following demonstration.

a. With a magic marker, draw a line representing the Equator on a grapefruit and mark the poles.
b. Slicing through the poles with a knife, cut the grapefruit into six sections.
c. Have student volunteers eat the grapefruit and return the peel (be sure to provide napkins).
d. Flatten the peels and lay them out so the lines of the equator are touching. What happened when we tried to reproduce a three-dimensional sphere, the earth (the grapefruit), as a two-dimensional map? Why is Greenland larger on the map? Which is a more accurate representation of the Earth, the map or the globe? Why?

2. Ecological Disasters: Acts of Nature or Acts of People?
The world is a changing place. The Sahara Desert is expanding into the Sahel region of Africa. The Ariel Sea is disappearing. Flooding threatens human life and property along the Mississippi River in the United States and the Ganges River in Bangladesh. Forests have disappeared in Northern India and Haiti. Are these changes caused by acts of nature or acts of people? The simple activity that follows illustrates the importance of preserving marshlands to minimize the devastation caused by flooding.

a. Place a dry sponge in an open plastic container. This represents the marshlands along the banks of a river. Slowly pour in a measured amount of water. This represents spring floods caused by snow melting in the Mississippi River's watershed area. The sponge expands and absorbs the water.
b. Ring out the sponge and pour the water back into a measuring container.
c. Replace the sponge with something the same size and shape that is non-porous (e.g., a plastic container filled with sand, a block of wood sealed with paint and weighted down so it doesn't float). This represents economic development (e.g., the construction of shopping centers that pave over the marshlands).
d. Slowly pour the same measured amount of water into the plastic container. A devastating flood sweeps across the landscape.

3. Where Would You Build the City?
Draw a map showing mountains, two branches of a river meeting, a coastline, and other natural features. Have students discuss where they would build a city and why. Compare their decisions to selected cities around the world.

4. How Do We Define a Region?
Many geographic subdivisions (e.g., some national boundaries, or lines of longitude and latitude) are arbitrary. Others have a historical or cultural logic that is not apparent at first glance. For example, what is the Middle East? Allow students to look at a map, and have the class brainstorm the names of countries they believe should be included in the region. List all the countries on the board. When the list is complete, examine the suggestions, discuss their similarities and differences, decide on criteria for including countries in the region, and define the Middle East.

5. How Did Agriculture Spread in The Ancient World?

Table 3.1 Spread of fertile crescent crops

Era	Location
Before 7000BC	Fertile Crescent
7000–6000BC	Asia Minor, Egypt, Crete, Greece, Caspian Sea, Persia
6000–5000BC	Central Europe, Iberian and Italian Peninsulas
5000–2500BC	Northern and Western Europe

Source: Adapted from Jared Diamond (1997). *Guns, Germs, and Steel*. New York: Norton, p. 181.

a. Locate the different areas on a map.

b. How long does it take for agriculture to travel from the Fertile Crescent to Northern and Western Europe?

c. In your opinion, how did agriculture spread from region to region?

6. Webquest: Why do civilizations disappear?
Working as an individual or as a team, students use Internet sources to write brief histories of two civilizations (choose from among Akkadian in Mesopotamia, Mayan in the Yucatan, Anasazi in the US Southwest, Norse in Greenland, and Easter Island in the South Pacific) that "disappeared" as local environments changed. They should include a chronology of events and descriptions of locations, environments, resources, cultures, and governments. In a summary report, students should identify features the two societies shared in common, points of difference (especially geographic differences), and possible actions that could have prevented the end of their ways of life.

Teaching Activity: Geography in the Curriculum

Add your voice to the discussion:
Do you think geography should be integrated into a history-based social studies curriculum or taught as an independent subject? Why?

It's your classroom:
Would you use these geography activities as is? Would you modify them? Would you discard them? Why?

Anthropology

Franz Boas, one of the founders of modern anthropology, described it as the study of the growth and development of human cultures, human inventions, materials, spiritual and artistic creations, institutions, relationships, beliefs, values, and practices. As anthropologists delved deeply and systematically into the way of life of different peoples and compared different cultures, they contributed to ongoing debates about human nature. There are (a) anthropologists who argue that human cultures develop primarily as responses to similar basic needs and diverse environments, (b) supporters of the idea that human genetic makeup determines cultural development, and (c) researchers who stress the individual and contingent nature of societies.

Generally, anthropologists draw conclusions about the development of culture from studies of small, traditional societies where they can make in-depth observations of entire communities and account for outside influences. They also examine the artifacts, or material culture, of societies that no longer exist. In earlier decades, anthropologists looked for relatively isolated communities. However, in today's world, these communities are extremely rare. The best-known anthropological study is probably Margaret Mead's (1973) work about adolescence on the Samoan Islands in the southern Pacific. Mead spent nine months living with the people of Pago Pago, and observed the experiences of adolescent girls as they prepared to enter adulthood. Her study demonstrated that the rite of passage in this society was less stressful than in Western industrial societies. She concluded that the Western concept of adolescence, rather than being rooted in the nature of human development, was a product of cultural experience.

In the secondary school social studies curriculum, anthropology is generally integrated into and expands the study of history. In regional studies, anthropology helps students focus on the range of human diversity and the similarities and differences in the ways that societies around the world organize to survive and prosper. A global history class can compare naming ceremonies in European Christian societies with similar practices among the Yoruba people of West Africa, or they can examine why, in both traditional Japanese society and among the Kikiyu people of East Africa, newborn babies were not considered fully human. A United States history class can study Native American spirit masks and students can design and create masks that express their own struggles or beliefs (see Chapter 11).

Anthropology draws attention to the transformation of cultural practices as people migrate and adapt to new worlds. Students can explore cultural diffusion by examining the influence of traditional West African religious beliefs, such as Vodun from Benin, on the practice of Christianity in many communities in the Americas.

The analysis of artifacts extends human history further back into the past so that prehistoric societies and even the cultures of our pre-human ancestors can be examined. It makes it possible for students to examine and compare the development of different civilizations, and to explore topics like the contributions of women to husbandry, agriculture, and metallurgy, and the origins of family patterns and religious beliefs.

Anthropological approaches like the examination of material culture (artifacts) and community rituals enrich social history. Pictures of clothing can be used to illustrate social stratification in colonial America and pre-Revolutionary France. Hand tools and crafts can be used to demonstrate technological development in societies. In the book, *The Souls of Black Folk* (1961), W. E. B. DuBois examined the religious music of nineteenth-century southern African-Americans to explore their ideas and the impact of racism on their lives. In *The Making of the English Working Class* (1963) E. P. Thompson traced the changing political consciousness of pre-industrial British workers by analyzing popular and protest music.

An anthropological approach also introduces major debates into the social studies curriculum. Boaz and Mead believed that anthropologists had to get as close as possible to a society in order to understand it from the inside from the perspective of its members. However, Marvin Harris, who has written a series of books that explain anthropological puzzles such as food taboos and belief in witchcraft, argues that an anthropologist can never understand a society from within. His theory of cultural materialism ignores why people believe they are doing something. Instead, his focus is on the ways that different practices either support or interfere with the survival of a community. The idea of studying people by entering into cultures has been challenged for other reasons as well. Patrick Tierney (2001) argues that efforts to study the Yanomami people of the Venezuelan and Brazil rainforest were really a form of unwarranted interference that introduced new diseases and social turmoil into their culture and transformed the way they lived.

Another sharp debate in anthropology, which must also be addressed by multiculturalists, is the issue of cultural relativism. For example, how should Western societies respond to cultures and religions that deny women what they consider to be basic human rights? On the other hand, do societies that reject capital punishment as a violation of human rights have the right, or even the responsibility, to interfere with countries that execute people?

Taboos

In the "Old Testament" of the *Judeo-Christian Bible* many foods and cultural behaviors, including certain sexual practices, are considered "taboo" or a violation of religious codes. These include bans on eating pork and some sea foods, viewing close relatives naked, and sexual relations between a man and woman while the woman is menstruating. Violation of some taboos, either consciously or unconsciously, are punishable by death or banishment. Anthropologist Marvin Harris argues that cultures declare practices taboo, not because they are unnatural, but to enhance group cohesion and survival. Starting with practices banned in *Leviticus*, students try to discover why certain behaviors were banned in some societies and allowed, and even promoted, in others.

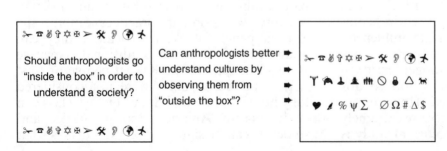

Figure 3.1 Sample anthropology lesson ideas.

Participant/observers "Inside the Box"

Andrea Libresco (NTN) has students observe the cultural practices and mores of their classmates and keep observational logs. Students can also observe family customs and rituals, and develop hypotheses that explain different practices. A possible topic is eating rituals and practices. Items that are considered good to eat, cooking practices, and even utensils vary from culture to culture and environment to environment. Through systematic observation of family members and note-taking, students can discover and record:

- What we eat and what we don't eat.
- How we produce (or obtain) what we eat.
- How we prepare what we eat.
- How we eat.
- When we eat.
- Who we eat it with.
- What we think about what we eat.

Isomo Loruko—Yoruba Naming Ceremony

Patricia Kafi (NTN) is a native of Nigeria. According to Patricia, among the Yoruba people of Nigeria, an entire community participates in naming a new baby (Kafi and Singer 1998). In their culture, a name is not just a name. It tells the circumstances under which a child was born. There are names for just about every situation. Sometimes a new named is even created. A name can also tell group or family history. It is always selected by family elders. Yoruba people always celebrate the naming ceremony when a child is seven days old.

At the traditional ceremony, people bring the child symbolic gifts like spices, sweets, and water, which represent hope for the future. The pen and a book, especially the *Bible* or the *Koran*, are fairly recent additions to the ceremony. As with many other aspects of Nigerian life, the items used as well as the ceremony itself vary depending on the ethnic group and family preferences. The theme they share in common is that the birth of a child is a time of great joy and celebration for the entire family and community.

Isomo Loruko, the Yoruba Naming Ceremony, can be reenacted in a global history class and used to stimulate discussion comparing Yoruba culture with the traditions observed by students in the class and the importance of tradition for families and communities. Many of the ingredients used in this version of the Yoruba Naming Ceremony are difficult to find

in the United States so other items can be substituted. For example, vegetable oil can be used instead of palm oil. When acting out the ceremony in a classroom, use fruit juice instead of wine.

Ingredients: Fruit juice, water, palm oil or vegetable oil, honey, bitter kola and kola nut (unsweetened baker's chocolate), whole peppercorns (or a clove of garlic), dried fish (preferably catfish), pen, book.

Participants: Elder (Agba), Mother (Iya), Father (Baba), Grandmother (Iya-iya: mother's mother), Grandfather (Baba-baba: father's father), Aunt (Aburo-iya: mother's younger sister), Uncle (Egbon-baba: father's older sibling), Honored Guests (5) (Alejo Pataki), Community members.

Elder (Agba): We are gathered here today because Fola and Ayinde have brought us a new life. We have brought certain gifts today to use in this naming ceremony, and we ask our ancestors to bless these things. We thank our ancestors for this addition to the family. We ask our ancestors to join us and bless this child. May the names given today enhance this child's life.

Community: Ase (so it shall be).

(*Traditionally, each of the items used in the ceremony is rubbed on the child's lips. Today, for health reasons, the mother of the child tastes the food items instead of the infant.*)

Mother (Iya): We offer wine to our ancestors as libation so that they might join us today in blessing this child.

Community: Ase (so it shall be).

Father (Baba): Water (omi) has no enemies because everything in life needs water to survive. It is everlasting. This child will never be thirsty in life and like water, no enemies will slow your growth.

Community: Ase (so it shall be).

Grandmother (Iya-iya): Palm oil (epo) is used to prevent rust, to lubricate and to massage and soothe the body. May this child have a smooth and easy life.

Community: Ase (so it shall be).

Grandfather (Baba-baba): The bitter kola (orogbo), unlike most other kolas, lasts a very long time. This child will have a very long life.

Community: Ase (so it shall be).

Aunt (Aburo-iya): Kola nut (obi) is chewed and then spit out. You will repel the evil in life.

Community: Ase (so it shall be).

Uncle (Egbon-baba): Honey (oyin) is used as a sweetener in our food. Your life will be sweet and happy.

Community: Ase (so it shall be).

Honored Guest (Alejo Pataki) 1: Peppers (ata) have many seeds within its fruit. May you have a fruitful life with lots of children.

Community: Ase (so it shall be).

Honored Guest (Alejo Pataki) 2: We use salt (iyo) to add flavor to our food. Your life will not be ordinary, but it will be filled with flavor, happiness, and substance.

Community: Ase (so it shall be).

Honored Guest (Alejo Pataki) 3: The fish (eja) uses its head to find its way in water, no matter how rough the water is. You will find your way in life and never drown, even through tough times.

Community: Ase (so it shall be).

Honored Guest (Alejo Pataki) 4: The pen (biro) is very important today because it can be used for both good and evil. You will not use the pen for evil and no one will use it for evil against you.

Community: Ase (so it shall be).

Honored Guest (Alejo Pataki) 5: This book (iwe) contains (the word of God or human knowledge). May you be God smart and book smart. May God be with you as you follow in God's path.
(The last two items (pen and bible) are new additions to the ceremony).

Community: Ase (so it shall be).

Elder (Agba): We will now name this child together. I want you all to repeat the names after me so that this child can hear them. The names are [Abejide (male), Ifeoluwa (female)] Balogun.
(The last name is the surname. The class should select a given name for the child.)

Community: [Abejide (male), Ifeoluwa (female)] Balogun!
(This is followed by prayers and celebration for the rest of the day.)

Teaching Activity: Anthropology in the Curriculum

Add your voice to the discussion:
1. Should anthropologists enter a community and study its members even if it means potentially interfering with their way of life?
2. Should societies challenge the cultural practices and religious beliefs of other groups whom they consider in violation of basic human rights? Explain.
3. Do you think anthropology should be integrated into a history-based social studies curriculum, or taught as an independent subject? Why?

Think it over:
What customs in the United States parallel the Yoruba naming ceremony?

Try it yourself:
Study eating practices, or other rituals, in your family.

It's your classroom:
1. Based on your experience with the eating practices activity, how do you think it would work with middle school or high school students? Why?
2. Our society still has "taboos." Many are related to sexual practices. How would you address these in your classroom?

Political Science
Political science examines who has the power to make decisions in societies (power and citizenship), how they are made (government), rules and procedures for enforcing decisions (laws), and the impact of decisions on societies

(justice and equity). The study of political science often includes philosophical queries, and examines the values, dilemmas, choices, and broader belief systems (ideologies) that shape political decisions. It is also closely related to the social science disciplines of sociology and economics.

In secondary school social studies curricula, separate political science courses generally focus on the principles (e.g., representative democracy), institutions (e.g., the presidency), and processes (e.g., electoral politics) of the US government and current US social issues. Because a major goal is the development of the knowledge, skills, and habits of mind required for active citizenship, a recent trend has been to encourage student involvement in participatory citizenship projects like voter registration and lobbying. Many schools offer electives or include thematic social studies units on aspects of the American legal system. Political science is also integrated into the global studies curriculum, where major themes include comparison of decision-making and government in contemporary societies and in different historical eras.

Sample Political Science Lesson Ideas

1. Political Cartoon Dialogues
Michael Pezone (NTN) provides students with political cartoons with empty dialogue boxes.

Figure 3.2 Cartoon dialogue.

1. Complete the empty cartoon dialogue box.
2. What is a good title for your cartoon?
3. What is the main idea you want to present? Why?

Students add their own dialogue ideas, which are acted out in class. Michael uses political cartoons clipped from newspapers or from cartoon collections. Many contemporary political cartoons are available at: http://www.nytimes.com/pages/cartoons/index.html. The Library of Congress has a Herblock exhibit with cartoons from the 1930s through 1990s, available at: http://www.loc.gov/loc/lcib/0010/herblock.html. Daryl Cagle's Professional Cartoonists Index is available at: http://cagle.msnbc.com and is an excellent source for contemporary political cartoons (sites accessed September 17, 2007).

2. Hidden Government
One of the topics in a government class is the "hidden government" (parts of the government that are not mentioned in the US Constitution). This unit can include an examination of the evolution of the Cabinet, the growing responsibilities of presidential and congressional advisory committees, and the behavior of lobbyists and political action committees. This activity involves students in using mathematical information supplied by a chart to draw social studies conclusions. It is designed to be completed by either individuals or small groups. The questions direct students to locate information, to help them use the information to describe what is taking place, to encourage them to draw conclusions about the impact of this information on the country, and to stimulate them to form opinions that they can support with data from the chart and with other information they have learned.

WHO INFLUENCES GOVERNMENT DECISIONS?
Table 3.2 shows donations to political action committees by defense contractors in 2003 and 2004 during a presidential election campaign. Experts estimated that the winning candidate in the 2008 president election would spend $500 million, most of it raised from corporations and the wealthy. Amongst the aerospace companies, the largest contributors were Lockheed Martin and General Dynamics with donations to political action committees of approximately $1 million each.

1. What was the total amount of money contributed by defense contractors to political action committees in 2003–2004?
2. Which political party benefited the most from these contributions?
3. The United States was at war while these

Table 3.2 Defense contractor contributions to political action committees

Industry	Total contributions	Percentage to Democrats	Percentage to Republicans
All Defense Contractors	$8,091,537	36%	64%
Aerospace	$3,683,871	38%	62%
Electronics	$2,314,679	35%	65%
Miscellaneous	$2,092,987	32%	68%

Source: Federal Election Commission (http://www.opensecrets.org, accessed September 17, 2007).

contributions were made. In your opinion, did these contributions by companies receiving war contracts from the government unfairly influence the election? Explain.

3. Philosophical Issues: The Responsibility of Government and People
"When it shall be said in any country in the world, my poor are happy; neither ignorance nor distress is to be found among them; my jails are empty of prisoners, my streets of beggars; the aged are not in want, the taxes are not oppressive . . .; when these things can be said, then may that country boast of its constitution and its government." [Thomas Paine] (Foner 1945: 446).

1. What is the main idea introduced by Thomas Paine in this quote?
2. According to Paine, are the poor responsible for their own condition? Do you agree or disagree with him? Why?
3. In your opinion, do individuals who are successful in a society have an obligation to change rules that leave some people at a disadvantage? Why or why not?
4. Draw a political cartoon that presents your views on these issues.

Teaching Activity: Political Science in the Curriculum

Add your voice to the discussion:
Do you think political science should be integrated into a history-based social studies curriculum or taught as an independent subject? Why?

Try it yourself:
How would you answer the questions in these political science activities?

It's your classroom:
Would you use these political science activities as is? Would you modify them? Would you discard them? Why? Would you interject your point of view into the discussion? Why?

Behavioral Sciences
Sociology and psychology are often called *behavioral sciences*. Sociology examines human relationships and institutions in complex contemporary societies. Its goal is to establish theories that explain events, activities, and ideas about human interaction and group behavior. It often overlaps psychology, which examines the motivation and behavior of individuals. In secondary school social studies, insights and topics from sociology and psychology are usually included in courses that focus on government, citizenship, and current issues. They can also be incorporated into units on recent history. Some schools offer upper level social studies electives in these fields.

Social inequality, and its impact on individuals and social groups, is an area where political science, philosophy, sociology, and psychology overlap. For a research report, and in class discussions focusing on current issues, students can examine how different social scientists view the problem of social inequality in the United States and the relationship among inequality, racism, and crime.

For example, Herbert Gans (1995) argues that poor and minority people are unfairly labeled as *dangerous* and *different*, and this allows the majority in our society to blame them for social problems that are beyond their control. As a result, programs that are supposed to assist poor people receive little public support and are frequently designed to punish them. Manning Marable (1983) believes that racism and inequality persist because they benefit segments of US society. Cornel West (1993) is concerned that racism and inequality debilitate people so that it becomes difficult to rebuild communities, families, and the lives of individuals.

Sample Sociology and Psychology Lesson Ideas

1. Student Surveys
Students can conduct surveys that examine the attitudes, beliefs, and practices of other students or of community residents. Studies can focus on a specific target population or they can be comparative. Individuals, teams, or classes identify the goals of the study and research questions, define subject populations, construct questionnaires, interview subjects, analyze data, draw conclusions, and report findings. Topics can include:

- "Opinions on the impact of music lyrics on the ideas and values of teenagers"
- "Evaluations of community institutions (e.g., schools)"
- "Ideas about community or national issues (e.g., abortion rights)."

2. "Parental Bonding"
Bobbie Robinson (NTN) distributes lemons to pairs of students and they become its parents.

They name it, study its unique features, and make up its life story. They write down their dreams for their lemon based on its particular qualities and share their lemon's story with the class. The next day, all of the lemons are thrown together in a basket and "parents" must quickly identify and reclaim their lemon. In the unit that follows this activity, student imagine how they would feel as parents if their lemon was shunned for being in the wrong ethnic group, had no resources to meet its needs, could not live in a particular neighborhood, or had to spend its days alone and isolated. The lemons provide a concrete focus for discussion that helps students express their feelings.

3. Is the Enforcement of "Drug Laws" racially biased?
The United States imprisons a higher percentage of its citizens than any other country in the world. Many inmates are imprisoned for possession and use of illegal drugs. A report by Human Rights Watch in May 2000 charges that non-White minorities (Blacks, Latinos, and Native Americans) are arrested and imprisoned for drug use at rates significantly higher than Whites. Examine Figure 3.3 and answer the questions that follow.

1. Describe the pattern illustrated by the information in this graph.
2. What questions do you have based on your examination of this data?
3. In your opinion, do these figures document racism in the United States? Explain.

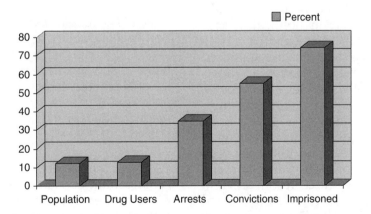

Figure 3.3 Drug Use and Punishment in the United States, 2000.
Blacks as a percentage of each category.
Source: http://www.drugpolicy.org, accessed September 26, 2007.

Teaching Activity: Sociology and Psychology in the Curriculum

Add your voice to the discussion:
Do you think sociology and psychology should be integrated into a history-based social studies curriculum or taught as independent subjects? Why?

Try it yourself:
How would you answer the questions in these sociology and psychology activities?

It's your classroom:
Would you use these sociology and psychology activities as is? Would you modify them? Would you discard them? Why?

Economics

Economics examines how societies produce and distribute the goods and services that people, communities, and nations need to survive. Because economic recommendations impact sharply on government policies, they involve some of the most controversial issues in the social sciences. Economists are engaged in disputes over the merits of different economic systems, including communist and socialist centrally managed economies, capitalist economies where decisions are made by private corporations in the pursuit of profits, and various mixed economies that attempt to balance private and public interests. Within all of these societies, economists address problems related to depression, inflation, unemployment, governmental subsidy of business, tax policy, and social service budgets. Economics-related controversies extend into the school curriculum, where teachers often disagree over the relative importance of mathematical models for describing economic systems, and whether natural economic laws are actually human creations.

In many high schools, economics is taught as a separate subject. As in political science (government) classes, the curriculum tends to describe the way US institutions are supposed to function. Other major economic topics include the impact of technology on society; global trade, and economic interdependence; the environmental impact of economic decisions; the role of government in managing modern economies; relationships between privately owned corporations and workers; acquisition and use of scarce resources; and individual investment strategies. Some social studies programs offer electives or thematic units where students learn business and occupational skills.

Economics, Sociology, and Political Science topics or classes offer teachers opportunities to systematically address social justice issues with students. For example, the federal government generally defines a four percent unemployment rate as "full employment." It considers lower unemployment rates inflationary and uses fiscal and monetary policies, especially manipulation of interest rates, to maintain what it considers "fluidity" in the work force.

While many Americans may benefit from these economic policies, the benefits are not spread equally throughout the population. Black unemployment in the United States tends to be double White unemployment, and in inner-city urban areas, unemployment rates for young Black men range between twenty-five and fifty percent. This occurs at the same time that the federal government raises interest rates to combat inflation, causing higher unemployment rates (Bernstein and Baker 2002).

Sample Economics Lesson Ideas

1. What Do People Need to Survive?
For an introductory lesson on economics, individual students list what they believe people need to survive. The entire class brainstorms a list on the board and evaluates ideas. In a follow-up lesson, students discuss how these items are made (produced) and acquired (distributed) in our society.

2. Look at the Labels
An important economic concept is global interdependence. Students examine labels in their clothes to discover where items were manufactured. For homework, they can examine major appliances in their homes. This lesson can be

70

used as an introduction to the study of globalization.

3. Describing the Soccer Ball

Students toss a soccer ball around the class. When a student catches the ball s/he tells the class one piece of information about the ball. Terms are listed on the board. Eventually one of the students mentions where the ball was manufactured. Often it was made in a third-world nation where factories use child labor. Students discuss whether this is important to know when they purchase a product. Organizations maintaining websites that focus on child labor include Human Rights Watch (available at: http://hrw.org/children/labor.htm, accessed September 17, 2007), Child Labor Coalition (available at: http://www. stopchildlabor.org, accessed September 17, 2007), and UNICEF (available at: http://www. unicef.org/protection/ index_childlabour.html, accessed September 17, 2007). A photographic essay on child labor around the world is located at www.childlaborphotoproject.org/childlabor. html. Important sources on the history of child labor in the industrialized world include http:// www.historyplace.com/unitedstates/childlabor and http://www.spartacus.schoolnet.co.uk/IRch-ild.htm (all sites accessed September 17, 2007).

4. Why Workers Join Unions

As unionized labor declines as a percentage of the workforce, fewer students have personal experience with family members who are union members. A union member or official can be invited as a guest speaker to class to discuss the role of labor unions today. Either to prepare for the speaker or as a follow-up, students can do on-line research on the labor movement. Important websites include http://www. wakeupwal-mart.com, which focuses on the campaign to unionize workers at Wal-Mart stores, http:// www.seiu.org, which is the website of the Service Employers International Union, a union commit-ted to organizing less skilled immigrant workers, and http://www. aflcio.org, the official site for the American Federation of Labor-Congress of Industrial Organizations (all sites accessed September 17, 2007).

5. "Natural Economic Laws"

In 1776, Scottish philosopher Adam Smith intro-duced the idea that a market economy is a self-regulating machine whose rules are unchange-able scientific laws rooted in the nature of human behavior. In the United States, the idea that the role of government is to support these natural laws was succinctly expressed in a 1925 speech by President Calvin Coolidge. Coolidge believed, "The business of America is business." These ideas reenter public discussion whenever politi-cians and economists argue against government efforts to rectify economic imbalances and in favor of letting the economic mechanism work out its own irregularities.

Students should consider whether economic development in the United States and the world economy is the result of natural law or of a series of business, government, and individual decisions that can be altered to produce different results, including a cleaner environment and a more equitable distribution of wealth.

6. Mortgage Interest Deductions: Is the System Fair?

The US government allows individuals and cor-porations to deduct certain expenses from their income when calculating federal income tax payments. One of the most common tax deduc-tions for individuals is interest payments on home mortgages. This tax break has broad popu-lar support, even among advocates of a flat tax that would eliminate most other deductions. Examine Table 3.3 and answer the questions that follow.

QUESTIONS

1. What percentage of income tax returns are for incomes less than $10,000?
2. Which income bracket receives the largest percentage of total savings on mortgage tax deductions?
3. Which income bracket receives the largest per person savings?
4. What percentage of income tax returns are for incomes over $100,000?
5. What is the total percentage savings for incomes over $100,000?
6. Based on Table 3.3, are mortgage tax deduc-tions equitable to all tax payers? Why?
7. In your opinion, why do mortgage interest tax deductions have broad support, even though the benefits are distributed this way?
8. Changes in economic policies can have broad repercussions. In what ways could an end to mortgage income deductions change the US economy?
9. In your opinion, are deductions like the mortgage interest tax deduction a product of natural economic laws, or of political and

Table 3.3 Mortgage interest deductions on federal income taxes.

Annual income ($)	Percentage of all tax returns	Percentage of total savings on mortgage deductions	Average savings per person ($)
Under 10,000	18.5	Less than 1	258
10,000–20,000	19.1	Less than 1	411
20,000–30,000	15.9	1.5	514
30,000–40,000	12.8	3.8	721
40,000–50,000	9.1	6.3	944
50,000–75,000	13.8	22.0	1,265
75,000–100,000	5.7	21.9	2,183
100,000–200,000	4.1	27.6	3,511
200,000 and over	1.1	16.5	8,348

Source: *The New York Times*, January 12, 1996, D1.

economic decisions to benefit particular groups and industries? Explain the reasons for your answer.

7. "Mr. Block" Learns About Workfare

During the early years of the twentieth century, the Industrial Workers of the World had a cartoon series in their labor union newspaper featuring the character "Mr. Block." Mr. Block's head is made of wood so he never understands what is going on until it is too late. Figure 3.4 reintroduces Mr. Block into a contemporary setting.

QUESTIONS

1. Describe what is happening in the cartoon.
2. What is the main idea presented by the cartoonist?
3. Do you agree with the point of view of the cartoonist? Why?
4. Explain a possible solution to Mr. Block's problem.
5. Create a cartoon that illustrates your ideas about a problem facing the US economy?

Figure 3.4 Mr. Block learns about workfare.

Teaching Activity: Economics in the Curriculum

In my experience, two of the biggest trends in the teaching of "economics" have little to do with what the study of economics should be all about. Too often teachers present economics as a series of formulas to be mastered without focusing on the main ideas that they are supposed to represent. In many schools, students participate in one or another version of the Stock Market game (available at: http://www.smg2000.org/ accessed September 17, 2007), an activity that does little more than promote gambling and propagandize for a speculative brand of finance capitalism. Neither of these approaches promotes any kind of critical thinking about issues confronting American society or the world.

Add your voice to the discussion:
1. Do you think economics should be integrated into a history-based social studies curriculum or taught as an independent subject? Why?
2. In your opinion, in subjects such as economics, should teachers focus on technical concerns or on social justice issues?
3. Would you have students "invest" (gamble) in stocks as part of an economics program? Explain.

Try it yourself:
How would you answer the questions in these economics activities?

It's your classroom:
Would you use these economics activities as is? Would you modify them? Would you discard them? Why?

Essay 1: How can Teachers Promote the Economic and Civic Literacy of Students?

The Bush Administration's "No Child Left Behind" (NCLB) policy has led to the extensive testing of students from elementary school through high school. Many have questioned how meaningful this testing program really is. For example, how can teachers measure the economic and civic literacy of high school students as called for in many national and state standards?

I recommend using current events articles from newspapers and the internet to both help gauge and improve student academic literacy (reading, writing, and mathematics) and promote conceptual understanding of economics, political science, and social justice.

Newspapers target different audiences and use different vocabulary. When radio and television broadcaster Don Imus was fired for using racially and sexually charged language that demeaned members of the Rutgers University women's basketball team, it was widely covered in the print media. The story was covered by both *The New York Times* and *USA Today* in their on-line editions. The *New York Times* reported "NBC News dropped Don Imus yesterday, canceling his talk show on its MSNBC cable news channel a week after he made a *racially disparaging* remark about the Rutgers University

women's basketball team" (italics added, Carter and Story 2007). According to *USA Today*, "MSNBC said Wednesday it will drop its simulcast of the 'Imus in the Morning' radio program, responding to growing outrage about the radio host's *racial slur* against the Rutgers women's basketball team" (italics added, Crary 2007). The major difference in their coverage was that one newspaper described Imus' on-air statement as a "racially disparaging remark," while the other called it a "racial slur." While the meaning of the two phrases is the same, the level of vocabulary is certainly more sophisticated in *The New York Times* coverage.

The first two newspaper articles in "Classroom Activity: Economic Literacy" are excerpted and adapted from the business section of *The New York Times*. The third article, from the *Washington Post*, is accompanied by a chart. They all have broad social, economic, and political policy implications. High school seniors in economics and government classes should be able to read and discuss these articles and the chart with understanding. If they cannot, it will be difficult for them to function as active and aware citizens in a democratic society, which is certainly a goal of NCLB.

Classroom Activity: Economic Literacy

1. *"Reinventing the Mill"*
by Eduardo Porter (*The New York Times*, October 22, 2005, C1)

Instructions: Read the excerpts from the article "Reinventing the Mill" and answer the questions below.

1. *The Social Contract*

   What was once Bethlehem Steel is more competitive now than it has been in a long while. Flailing under the onslaught of cheap foreign steel just four years ago, today it has consolidated into a larger company with a leaner work force and more pricing power. To arrive at this stage, however, the work force at Bethlehem's plants was trimmed to some 8,200, down from 11,500 three years ago. More important, Bethlehem had to cast off many of its roughly 70,000 retirees. In doing so, it abandoned the part of industrial America's social contract that implied that if workers gave the company decades of hot and dirty factory work, the company would, in return, provide generously for them in old age . . .

2. *Productivity*

   In 1980 steel companies employed about 400,000 American workers and it took about nine hours of labor to produce a ton of steel; by last year, the work force had withered to some 120,000 workers but it took each of them only about two hours to make a ton of steel. The surge in productivity also had a cost, however. Early retirement was always the favored tool to ease workers off the payroll. As layoffs continued from one decade to the next, the number of retirees grew rapidly . . .

3. *Bankruptcy*

   Bethlehem was among more than 40 steel companies that went bankrupt from 1997 to last year . . . Two dozen failing steel companies moved the pension plans for a quarter of a million workers and retirees to the Pension Benefit Guaranty Corporation from 2001 to 2003, dropping into the government's lap a long-term payment gap of about $10 billion . . . Many retirees lost portions of their pensions when the Pension Benefit Guaranty Corporation took them over, especially the youngest batch . . . Of the 100,000 Bethlehem retirees and dependents who lost their healthcare plan, about one-quarter are under 65, too young to qualify for Medicare.

4. *The Future*

   And it is still uncertain whether the industry can survive over the long term, even in its current leaner, no-retiree form . . . As China and other developing countries continue building steel plants, workers and executives worry about what would happen if China's economic growth were to waver and its demand for steel to wane.

Questions

1. According to this article, why is Bethlehem Steel more productive now than it was in the past?
2. What has been the impact of the reorganization of the steel industry on retired workers?
3. What has been the impact of the reorganization of the steel industry on American tax payers?
4. Why are workers and executives concerned about the future?
5. In your opinion, what solutions exist for the problems raised by this newspaper article?
6. Do you believe the United States government should take responsibility to protect pensions and provide health care insurance for retirees? Explain.
7. In your opinion, should the United States government provide health insurance for the American people? Explain.

2. *"Wal-Mart Memo Suggests Ways to Cut Employee Benefit Costs"*
by Steven Greenhouse and Michael Barbaro (*The New York Times*, October 26, 2005)

Instructions: Read the excerpts from the article "Wal-Mart Memo Suggests Ways to Cut Employee Benefit Costs" and answer the questions below.

1. *Wal-Mart has a Problem*

   An internal memo sent to Wal-Mart's board of directors proposes numerous ways to hold down spending on healthcare and other benefits while seeking to minimize damage to the retailer's reputation. Among the recommendations are hiring more part-time workers and discouraging unhealthy people from working at Wal-Mart. In the memorandum, Ms Susan Chambers, Wal-Mart's executive vice president for benefits, also recommends reducing 401(k) contributions and wooing younger, and presumably healthier, workers by offering education benefits. The memo voices concern that workers with seven years' seniority earn more than workers with one year's seniority, but are no more productive.

2. *The World's Largest Retailer*

The memo acknowledged that Wal-Mart, the world's largest retailer, had to walk a fine line in restraining benefit costs because critics had attacked it for being stingy on wages and health coverage. Ms Chambers acknowledged that 46 percent of the children of Wal-Mart's 1.33 million United States employees were uninsured or on Medicaid. Wal-Mart executives said the memo was part of an effort to rein in benefit costs, which to Wall Street's dismay have soared by 15 percent a year on average since 2002. Like much of corporate America, Wal-Mart has been squeezed by soaring health costs. The proposed plan, if approved, would save the company more than $1 billion a year, by 2011.

3. *Costs and Profits*

Wal-Mart's benefit costs jumped to $4.2 billion last year, from $2.8 billion three years earlier, causing concern within the company because benefits represented an increasing share of sales. Last year, Wal-Mart earned $10.5 billion on sales of $285 billion.

4. *A New Proposal*

Under fire because less than 45 percent of its workers receive company health insurance, Wal-Mart announced a new plan on Monday that seeks to increase participation by allowing some employees to pay just $11 a month in premiums. Some health experts praised the plan for making coverage more affordable, but others criticized it, noting that full-time Wal-Mart employees, who earn on average around $17,500 a year, could face out-of-pocket expenses of $2,500 a year or more.

5. *Corporate Image*

Acknowledging that Wal-Mart has image problems, Ms Chambers wrote: "Wal-Mart's critics can easily exploit some aspects of our benefits offering to make their case; in other words, our critics are correct in some of their observations. Specifically, our coverage is expensive for low-income families, and Wal-Mart has a significant percentage of associates and their children on public assistance."

Questions
1. According to the memorandum, what economic problems are facing Wal-Mart?
2. Why are critics unhappy with Wal-Mart's policies?
3. Why are Wal-Mart's policies such a major concern in the United States?
4. In your opinion, should Wal-Mart be required to change the way it treats its employees? Explain.
5. In your opinion, would Wal-Mart employees be better off with labor union representation? Explain.

3. "Federal Subsidies Turn Farms into Big Business"

by Gilbert M. Gaul, Sarah Cohen and Dan Morgan (*Washington Post*, December 21, 2006, A01)
Instructions: Read the excerpts from the article "Federal Subsidies Turn Farms into Big Business" and answer the questions below.

1. *The Myth of the Family Farm*

The cornerstone of the multibillion-dollar system of federal farm subsidies is an iconic image of the struggling family farmer: small, powerless against Mother Nature, tied to the land by blood. Without generous government help, farm-state politicians say, thousands of these hardworking families would fail, threatening the nation's abundant food supply. "In today's fast-paced, interconnected world, there are few industries where sons and daughters can work side-by-side with moms and dads, grandmas and grandpas," Rep. Jerry Moran (R-Kan.) said last year. "But we still find that today in agriculture . . . It is a celebration of what too many in our country have forgotten, an endangered way of life that we must work each and every day to preserve."

2. *Misleading Images*

This imagery secures billions annually in what one grower called "empathy payments" for farmers. But it is misleading. Today, most of the nation's food is produced by modern family farms that are large operations using state-of-the-art computers, marketing consultants and technologies that cut labor, time and costs. The owners are frequently college graduates who are as comfortable with a spreadsheet as with a tractor. They cover more acres and produce more crops with fewer workers than ever before.

3. *The Reality*

The very policies touted by Congress as a way to save small family farms are instead helping to accelerate their demise, economists, analysts and farmers say. That's because owners of large farms receive the largest share of government subsidies. They often use the money to acquire more land, pushing aside small and medium-size farms as well as young farmers starting out.

Large family farms, defined as those with revenue of more than $250,000, account for nearly 60 percent of all agricultural production but just 7 percent of all farms. They receive more than 54 percent of government subsidies. And their share of federal payments is growing—more than doubling over the past decade for the biggest farms.

Questions

1. What is the traditional belief about farm production in the United States?
2. What is the reality?
3. How have government policies affected trends in agricultural production?
4. In your opinion, should federal subsidies for agriculture be continued? Explain.

4. Riceland Foods

Riceland Foods is an agricultural cooperative based in Arkansas with 9,000 members. It was started in the 1930s to help impoverished farmers during the Great Depression. Today, it is the largest recipient of federal agricultural subsidies in the nation. While the average size of a farm belonging to a member of the cooperative is 750 to 1,000 acres, some of the farms are owned by giant agribusinesses with land holdings of between 40,000 and 80,000 acres.

Table 3.4 Federal subsidies for Riceland Foods, Inc, 1995–2005

Year	USDA subsidies ($)
1995	9,511,270
1996	32,942
1997	0
1998	5,599,524
1999	63,933,311
2000	100,556,047
2001	128,115,702
2002	133,988,962
2003	68,942,419
2004	14,566,018
2005	15,815,471
Total	541,061,667

Source: http://www.ewg.org, accessed April 21, 2007.

Questions

1. In what year did Riceland Foods receive its largest federal subsidy?
2. What was the total federal subsidy during this period?
3. In your opinion, should an agricultural subsidy program that helps some small farmers but overwhelmingly transfers federal money to large and profitable businesses be continued? Explain.

Essay 2: How can Teachers Use Drama to Promote Literacy while Teaching Social Studies Content and Concepts?

Dramatic presentations encourage students to read and speak while teaching social studies content and concepts. In this play, characters (except for Alabama Governor George Wallace, state trooper John Cloud, Sheyann Webb #4 and Mr and Mrs Webb) stand in a double line in order of speaking parts. Narrator #1 and #2 are at the front of the line. Wallace and Cloud are off to the left. Sheyann Webb #4 and Mr and Mrs Webb are off to the right. The script is based on interviews with Sheyann Webb, Charles Bonner, John Lewis, and Hosea Williams. The actual television footage of "Bloody Sunday" in Selma, Alabama was included in the PBS *Eyes on the Prize* series and can be viewed on-line at: http://www.pbs.org/wgbh/amex/eyesontheprize/story/10_march.html#video, accessed October 14, 2007. The title of this play, "Ain't Gonna Let No Body Turn Me Around," refers to an African-American Civil Rights song (words and music are available on-line at: http://www.pbs.org/wgbh/amex/eyesontheprize/story/05_riders.html, accessed January 7, 2008). Allow students with reading parts to take the script home the night before to practice. After performing, students discuss the questions included in the *Learning Activity* at the end of the script. Martin Luther King, Jr issued his statement on the events in Selma the night they occurred (Miller 1968: 210). The quote by Lyndon Johnson is from a speech to a joint session of Congress on March 15, 1965 (available at: http://www.answers.com/topic/lyndon-b-johnson-voting-rights-act-address?cat=biz-fin, accessed January 6, 2008).

"Ain't Gonna Let No Body Turn Me Around"

A. Narrator #1: Marching for freedom was an important part of the struggle for African-American Civil Rights in the 1950s and 1960s. Sometimes the marches were small. Sometimes they involved tens of thousands of people. Sometimes only local people or only Black people were involved. Sometimes people came from all over the country and many different kinds of people joined together to protest against injustice. This is the story of two protest marches against police brutality and for voting rights that started in Selma, Alabama in March 1965.

Alabama Governor George Wallace: (Shouting) "I say segregation now, segregation tomorrow, segregation forever ... I am not going to have a bunch of Blacks walking along a highway in this state as long as I'm governor."

A. Narrator #2: On Sunday, March 7, 1965, 600 people gathered together at Brown Chapel AME Church. There were men, women, and children. Everybody was African-American. The group was led by John Lewis of the Student Non-Violent Coordinating Committee and Hosea Williams, a civil rights activist who worked with the Reverend Martin Luther King, Jr. They planned to march from Selma to the state capital at Montgomery. To leave Selma, they had to cross the Edmund Pettus Bridge.

B. Charles Bonner #1: "I arrived at Brown Chapel church on that Sunday morning along with all of my other high school classmates and comrades. There was nervousness in the air because we had been told that we would probably be tear-gassed. We had been instructed to carry a moist hand-kerchief with us in the event we were tear-gassed. And we were told that there were posses on horses. We were scared, because we didn't know what was going to happen."

B. John Lewis: "We left church and walked silently downtown. Hosea Williams and I were in the lead. Our group turned south and headed for Pettus Bridge to cross over the Alabama River. At the bridge state troopers ordered us to disperse."

John Cloud (Shouting): "I am Major John Cloud of the Alabama state troopers. This is an unlawful march, and it will not be allowed to continue. You are ordered to disperse. You have two minutes."

C. Hosea Williams #1: "When we refused to turn back, we were attacked by the police. They came towards us, beating us with nightsticks and bullwhips. Sheriff Clark and his posse started trampling us with horses and they used tear gas. John Lewis was beaten unconscious by a state trooper. He suffered a skull fracture but lived to march again and eventually became a congressman from Georgia."

C. Charles Booner #2: "The kid who was next to me was totally overcome. I was trying to help him to get down to the water, I thought we could get some water and try to get his eyes clean, because he was just crying and rubbing his eyes. But when we got down by the water's edge, the troopers were coming after us, the posse members on the horses. They were herding us back on to Highway 80 and back over the bridge. They beat us back across the bridge, beat us back down Water Avenue, and then back to the church. The posse members rode their horses right up on the church premises. It was like a war zone, the most frightening experience I've had in my life."

D. Sheyann Webb #1: "That morning my mother brushed my hair, hugged me, and let me go join the march from Selma to the state capital in Montgomery. I went with my friend Rachel West. I was eight-years old."

D. Rachel West #1: "I was frightened by everything that was taking place. I couldn't stay. I just went home."

E. Sheyann Webb #2: "I heard all this screaming and the people were turning and I saw this first part of the line running and stumbling back toward us. I was just off the bridge and on the side of the highway. They came running and some of them were crying out and somebody yelled, 'Oh, God, they're killing us!' I think I just froze then. There were people everywhere, jamming against me, pushing against me. Then, all of a sudden, it stopped and everyone got down on their knees, and I did too, and somebody was saying for us to pray."

E. Sheyann Webb #3: "It seemed like just a few seconds went by and I heard a shout. 'Gas! Gas!!' and everybody started screaming again. And I looked and I saw the troopers charging us again and some of them were swinging their arms and throwing canisters of tear gas. And beyond them I saw the horsemen starting their charge toward us. I was terrified."

F. Hosea Williams #2: "Horsemen were coming towards us and they were wearing teargas masks. Some of them had clubs, others had ropes or whips, which they swung about them like they were driving cattle. I saw a little girl running, Sheyann Webb. She was crying and her eyes were blinded by tears. I grabbed her and lifted her up and ran back over the bridge. She kept kicking her legs and shouting 'Put me down! You can't run fast enough with me!' But I held on to her until we were off the bridge and down on Broad Street. Then I let her go."

F. Bettie Mae Fikes: "People were running and fall-ing and ducking and you could hear the horses' hooves on the pavement and you'd hear people scream and hear the whips swishing and you'd hear them striking people. They'd cry out; some moaned. Women as well as men were getting hit. They kept rolling canisters of tear gas on the ground, so it would rise up quickly. I heard more horses and I turned back and saw two of them and the riders were leaning over to one side. It was like a nightmare seeing it through the tears."

G. Sheyann Webb #4: "I didn't stop running until I got home. All along the way there were people running in small groups. I saw people jumping over cars and being chased by the horsemen who kept hitting them. When I got to the apartments there were horsemen in the yards, galloping up and down, and one of them reared his horse up in the air as I went by. He had his mask off and was shouting something at me."

G. Mrs Webb: "When Sheyanne came in the house she was hysterical and was repeating over and over, 'I can't stop shaking, Momma, I can't stop shaking.' I grabbed her and sat down with her on my lap."

G. Mr Webb: "I grabbed my shotgun and yelled, 'By God, if they want it this way, I'll give it to them!' I was ready to die. I was ready to die."

G. Mrs Webb: "My husband was heading out the door when I leaped in front of him. He finally put the gun aside and sat down. Sheyann was lying on the couch. She was crying."

G. Sheyann Webb: "I felt so disgusted. They had beaten us like we were slaves. I wondered if there would ever be another march."

H. Narrator #3: In the evening the people gathered in church. Everyone was quiet, stunned. Nobody was praying. Nobody was singing. But then about nine-thirty or ten, somebody started humming. At first it sounded like they were moaning, but it turned into humming and became a freedom song.

H. Narrator #4: It was real low, but some of the children began humming along, slow and soft. It was like a funeral song. They were humming the traditional song "Ain't Gonna Let Nobody Turn Me 'Round." It just started to catch on and the people began singing the words.

[The entire group moves to the front of the stage and sings.]

Ain't gonna let Governor Wallace turn me 'round,
   turn me 'round, turn me 'round.
Ain't gonna let Governor Wallace turn me 'round,
   gonna keep on walking, keep on talking,
Marching to the freedom land.

Ain't gonna let no state trooper turn me 'round,
   turn me 'round, turn me 'round, turn me 'round.
Ain't gonna let no state trooper turn me 'round,
   gonna keep on walking, keep on talking,
Marching to the freedom land.

Ain't gonna let nobody turn me 'round, turn me
   'round, turn me 'round.
Ain't gonna let nobody turn me 'round, gonna
   keep on walking, keep on talking,
Marching to the freedom land.

[The group remains at the front of the stage.]

I. Rachel West #2: "Everybody was singing now. Some of us were clapping our hands. We were still crying, but it was a different kind of crying. It was the kind of crying that's got spirit, not the weeping we had been doing."

I. Sheyann Webb #5: "I knew the state troopers outside the church heard us. Everybody heard us. More people were coming in, leaving their apartments and coming to the church. Something was happening. We was singing and telling the world that we hadn't been whipped, that we had won. We had really won, after all. (Shouts) We had won!"

J. Narrator #5: Television cameras captured the terrible beating peaceful marchers had taken on the Edmund Pettus Bridge. The whole country saw what happened that day in Selma. Dr. Martin Luther King, Jr. called on religious leaders from around the country to come to Selma for a peaceful, non-violent march for freedom. President Lyndon B. Johnson denounced the attack and promised to submit a federal voting rights bill to Congress.

J. Martin Luther King, Jr: "I am shocked by the terrible reign of terror that took place in Alabama today. Negro citizens engaged in a peaceful and orderly march to protest racial injustice were beaten, brutalized and harassed by state troopers and Alabama revealed its law enforcement agents have no respect for democracy nor the rights of its Negro citizens. I had no idea that the kind of brutality and tragic expression of man's humanity as existed today would take place. Alabama's state troopers, under the sanction and authorization of Governor George Wallace allowed themselves to degenerate to the lowest state of barbarity."

K. Lyndon Johnson: "Many of the issues of civil rights are very complex and most difficult. But about this there can and should be no argument. Every American citizen must have an equal right to vote. There is no reason which can excuse the denial of that right. There is no duty which weighs more heavily on us than the duty we have to ensure that right. But even if we pass this bill, the battle will not be over. What happened in Selma is part of a far larger movement which reaches into every section and state of America. It is the effort of American Negroes to secure for themselves the full blessings of American life. Their cause must be our cause too. Because it is not just Negroes, but really it is all of us, who must overcome the crippling legacy of bigotry and injustice. And we shall overcome."

K. Narrator #6: On March 21, Dr King led an interracial march of over three thousand people from Selma. It was protected by the National Guard. It arrived in Montgomery on March 25. On August 6, President Johnson signed the Voting Rights Act into law. It outlawed discriminatory voting rules that had prevented African-Americans from participating in elections since the era after the Civil War.

Learning Activity: Understanding the Civil Rights Movement

Try it yourself:
1. Why did the people of Selma want to march from Selma to Montgomery?
2. What happened on Edmund Pettus Bridge?
3. How was Sheyann Webb able to get off of the bridge safely?
4. How did the events in Selma change the United States?
5. If you were an adult living in New York in 1965, would you have gone to Selma to march? Explain.
6. If you went to Selma, would you have been willing to follow the principles of nonviolent civil disobedience? Explain.

References and Recommendations for Further Reading

Bernstein, J. and Baker, D. 2002. "Full employment. Don't give it up without a fight," *Working Paper No. 122,* January. http://www.epi.org/content.cfm/workingpapers_full-employment, accessed on April 12, 2007.

Carter, B. and L. Story. 2007. "NBC news drops Imus show over racial remark," *The New York Times*, April 12.

Crary, D. 2007. "MSNBC drops Imus 'simulcast'." *USA Today,* April 12. http://www.usatoday.com, accessed April 12, 2007.

Davis, M. 2002. *Late Victorian holocausts: El Niño famines and the making of the third world.* London: Verso.

Diamond, J. 1997. *Guns, germs, and steel: The fates of human societies.* New York: Norton.

Diamond, J. 2004. *Collapse: How societies choose to fail or succeed.* New York: Penguin.

DuBois, W. E. B. 1961. *The souls of Black folk.* New York: Fawcett.

Foner, P., ed. 1945. *The complete writings of Thomas Paine.* New York: Citadel Press.

Gans, H. 1995. *The war against the poor: The underclass and antipoverty policy.* New York: Basic Books.

Hawke, S. and Davis, J. 1992. *Seeds of change: The story of cultural exchange after 1492.* Menlo Park, CA: Addison-Wesley.

Kafi, P. and Singer, A. 1998. Isomo Loruko: The Yoruba naming ceremony. *Social Education Middle Level Learning Supplement* 62(1).

Linden, E. 2006. *The winds of change: Climate, weather, and the destruction of civilizations.* New York: Simon & Schuster.

Marable, M. 1983. *How capitalism underdeveloped Black America.* Boston: South End Press.

Mead, M. 1973. *Coming of age in Samoa.* New York: American Museum of Natural History.

Miller, W. 1968. *Martin Luther King, Jr.: His life, martyrdom, and meaning for the world.* New York: Weybright and Talley.

National Council for the Social Studies. 1994. *Curriculum standards for social studies: Expectations of excellence, NCSS bulletin 89.* Washington, DC: NCSS.

Smith, M. 1994. *Social science in the crucible: The American debate over objectivity and purpose, 1918–1941.* Durham, NC: Duke University Press.

Thompson, E. P. 1963. *The making of the English working class.* New York: Vintage.

Tierney, P. 2001. *Darkness in El Dorado.* New York: Norton.

US Bureau of Education. 1916. *Report of the committee on social studies.* Washington, DC: Government Printing Office.

West, C. 1993. *Race matters.* Boston, MA: Beacon.

4. What Are Our Goals?

Overview

- Describe classroom goals
- Examine the goals of different educational theorists
- Explore ideas about democratic and transformative classrooms
- Connect educational theory and social studies practice
- Discuss models for social studies teaching
- Define social studies concepts, skills and understandings
- Examine state learning standards

Key Concepts

Goals, Standards, Transmission, Inquiry, Scaffolding, Intelligence, Relevance, Democratic Community, Transformative Education, Concepts, Understandings, Skills

Questions

- Why Have Goals?
- Are we Teaching Subject Matter or Students?
- What is Important to Know and Why?
- Who are our Students and How do we Connect to Them?
- What Use is Educational Theory?
- How can we Teach Democracy?
- How are Goals Reflected in Different Approaches to Teaching Social Studies?
- What are the Traditional Academic Goals in Social Studies?
- How do Teachers Integrate Goals into Classroom Practice?
- What are the State Standards?

Essays

1. What We Should Teach
2. What are the Essential Questions?

WHY HAVE GOALS?

The first written homework assignment for pre-service teachers in my social studies methods class is to prepare notes in outline form for a chapter from an 11th-grade US history textbook. At the next class meeting, we compare chapter outlines. Generally, they range in length from one typed page to eight typed pages. To open up discussion, I ask "Which outline is a more appropriate model to use with students in a high school social studies class?"

There is always a wide range of opinions. One position is that the more notes a student takes, the better. "This way they know something." "Facts are important." "They won't have to go back and study from the book for the test."

A number of the pre-service teachers "confess" that they do assignments like these because they are required to, but they do not really think about the material. They skim the book, copy a phrase, and skim some more. Information goes directly from book to paper without being processed by the brain. When they were in secondary school, they handed in the work and they got good grades, but they did not learn much social studies. According to one participant, "People who were considered 'good students' in high school, this is how they got by."

Some of the people in the class admit that in high school they were "bad students." They tried to do the work, but if they saw no point in it, they got bored, stopped handing in assignments, and learned to live with the consequences. You may have already guessed, but in high school I was generally part of this group.

Sometimes the pre-service teachers challenge the idea of note-taking at all. They charge that it is always a mechanical assignment. "It's not designed to teach students anything, just to prepare them for tests." "Teachers use assignments like these to sort students out, label them, and justify grades. They have nothing to do with social studies." "If the assignments are too long, I just don't do them."

Other discussants defend the idea of assigning high school students to take notes on chapters if the note-taking has clear goals and the assignments are both flexible and manageable. "Students need to decide which information is more important and how to organize it so it is useful to them." "When I take notes I write down the things that make sense to me and help me remember. I keep my notes short. When I study, if I don't remember something, I can always look in the book again."

The concluding point of nearly every discussion like this one is that teachers have to be clear about their long-term goals and short-term objectives when they give students assignments, and that students need to understand, or even participate in defining, what the goals and objectives are. Are we just trying to memorize facts, or are we learning how to gather, organize, and use information? Depending on the goals and objectives, chapter notes look very different.

As social studies teachers, we each have a variety of educational goals; some are widely shared, some are individual, and some are hotly contested. In addition, we have short- and long-term subject-specific goals. Our assignments and lessons need to take all of these goals and objectives into account. Maxine Greene, whom you will meet in Chapter 5, describes this process of consciously and continually rethinking our teaching practice as being "wide awake." John Dewey, whom we will also meet later in this chapter, calls this "reflective practice."

This chapter introduces different types of goals and objectives: broad pedagogical goals that reflect our teaching philosophies; con-ceptual and content goals for understanding history and the social sciences (examined again in Chapter 6); skills goals—social studies, general academic, and social skills that students need so they can process information and work with other people (examined again in Chapters 8 and 9); and personal goals for our own professional growth. In this chapter, I also discuss my goals and the educational and social studies theorists I found useful in shaping them.

ARE WE TEACHING SUBJECT MATTER OR STUDENTS?

In secondary school social studies classrooms across the United States, teachers who consider themselves subject area experts believe they impart vital information to their classes in a clear and logical fashion. In these classrooms, it is the responsibility of individual students to decide whether they learn it. This view of social studies education is supported by popular writers like E. D. Hirsch (1987), Chester Finn and Diane Ravitch (1987) and Allan Bloom (1987), who bemoan declining academic standards while compiling lists of "facts" that students should know at each grade-level. It is also the premise behind the "No Child Left Behind" Act (NCLB), the Teaching American History grant programs (TAHG), and the push for more standardized assessments. What I call the "Dragnet School of Social Studies Education" (lecturing the facts) is frequently referred to as the "transmission model." It is a teacher-centered approach to classroom practice; teaching is defined as organizing and presenting information to essentially passive learners. Brazilian educator Paulo Freire (1970) describes it as the "banking method."

Advocates of the transmission model in secondary schools usually consider university lectures the most efficient format for presenting students with information. Many practitioners are quite entertaining and skilled at holding student attention. To modify the approach for use in high schools and junior high schools, they adjust for lower levels of student interest, skills, and maturity. They also allow class time for academic skill development, especially in lower track classes. But in their upper level honors and advanced placement classes, where teachers are free to exercise their expertise, they pitch their "chalk and talk" toward a "college-level" audience.

By this point, you know I have many problems with this approach to teaching. Memorizing long lists of facts is not the way that historians understand our world and passive listening is not the way that most students learn. Concentration on streams of facts is not even a good lecture technique. The best lecturers pull their audiences into their arguments, and they think about ideas together. Philosophically, the transmission model supports the beliefs that (1) knowledge is a scarce resource; (2) learning ability is unevenly distributed throughout the population; and (3) the goal of teachers should be to invest in people with the greatest potential and sort out those who cannot do the work. This approach to education serves a stratified society that is based on competition for resources, but not committed to either learning or democratic values.

I support a model for teaching based on an alternative view of how people learn and a different set of educational and social goals. Inquiry-based social studies education centers on student questions and research, and on student-student and student-teacher interaction. In an inquiry-based classroom, teachers work with students to organize learning experiences and then join with students in exploring the world and making meaning out of what they discover. Academic and social skills develop as students become historians and social scientists; students understand the meaning of citizenship and community because they experience democratic relationships; and success in teaching is measured by what students learn.

Supporters of the transmission model sometimes accept "hands-on" social studies as appropriate for middle school students who are experiencing the transition from the seemingly unstructured experiential learning of elementary school to the disciplined academic learning of high school. However, I argue that structured experiential learning is the most effective way to teach social studies on every level. My middle and high school lesson and unit recommendations differ in skill difficulty and conceptual sophistication, but not in basic structure or philosophy. Both are based on student activities; lessons are organized around primary source document analysis, and units include long-term individual and group projects.

Teaching Activity: Models of Social Studies Learning

Add your voice to the discussion:
1. Which of your secondary school social studies teachers influenced your views of social studies education the most? Why?
2. What happened to you in classrooms you didn't like? Why?
3. What most strongly motivated you to learn? Why?

WHAT IS IMPORTANT TO KNOW AND WHY?

In the preface to this edition of *Social Studies for Secondary Schools*, I noted that the main change during the last few years in my ideas about preparing to become a social studies teacher is a deeper awareness of the importance of teacher conceptual knowledge of history and the social sciences. To highlight these changes, I will repeat some of the points I raised there.

In earlier editions of this book, I was comfortable with the reality that most teachers would eventually learn what they needed to know over the course of their careers. While I still hold this position, I am increasingly concerned that unless new teachers are committed to the continuous growth of their own knowledge and understanding, they will fall into the habit of using easily available print and on-line material that is attractive, even seductive, but is superficial and largely misleading. The web is a wonderful resource—I am on-line and constantly referring to it as I write—but by providing easy access to selected material, and easy answers to what are really complicated questions, it can become a substitute for independent thought and analysis by both teachers and students.

I think the crucial moment for me was when President George W. Bush and Secretary of

State Colin Powell sold a war to the American people by presenting phony evidence of "weapons of mass destruction" in Iraq that never existed. I remember Powell speaking at the United Nations and showing the world satellite images of supposed "nuclear weapons" being loaded on truck beds so they could be hidden. Now I have *Google Earth* on my computer, as do most of you, and I have to believe the United States military has more sophisticated satellite footage than we do. The question I kept on asking, but which most of the world seemed to ignore, was if they have pictures of the weapons being loaded on the trucks, where were the pictures of them being unloaded in the secret sites.

If social studies teachers do not know enough about the past and contemporary society to tell the difference between analysis and propaganda, how will students ever be able to develop the knowledge and skills needed to become active and critical citizens of a democratic society?

Teaching Idea: How Important is Race in American Society?

In 2007, the United States Supreme Court narrowly overturned public school choice plans in Louisville, Kentucky, and Seattle, Washington because race was one of the factors used in the assignment of students. In the majority opinion, Chief Justice John Roberts wrote, "The way to stop discrimination on the basis of race is to stop discriminating on the basis of race . . . Before Brown, schoolchildren were told where they could and could not go to school based on color of their skin. The school districts in these cases have not carried the heavy burden of demonstrating that we should allow this once again—even for very different reasons" (available at: http://seattletimes.nwsource.com/html/localnews/2003767426_opinions29.html, accessed October 8, 2007).

Race and racism have long had an impact on American society. In 1835, Alexis De Tocqueville (available at: http://etext.lib.virginia.edu/toc/modeng/public/TocDem1.html, accessed October 8, 2007) wrote, "I do not believe that the white and black races will ever live in any country upon an equal footing. But I believe the difficulty to be still greater in the United States than elsewhere . . . A despot who should subject the Americans and their former slaves to the same yoke might perhaps succeed in commingling their races; but as long as the American democracy remains at the head of affairs, no one will undertake so difficult a task; and it may be foreseen that the freer the white population of the United States becomes, the more isolated will it remain." In 1903, W. E. B. DuBois (1961: v) argued, "the problem of the Twentieth Century" in the United States, "is the problem of the color-line." In the opinion that accompanied the unanimous Brown v. Topeka, Kansas Board of Education (1954) decision, Chief Justice Earl Warren wrote, "Does segregation of children in public schools solely on the basis of race, even though the physical facilities and other tangible factors may be equal, deprive the children of the minority group of equal educational activities? We believe that it does . . . To separate them from others of similar age and qualifications solely because of their race generates a feeling of inferiority as to their status in the community that may affect their hearts and minds in a way unlikely to be undone" (available at: http://www.nationalcenter.org/brown.html, accessed October 8, 2007).

Add your voice to the discussion:
1. In your opinion, does race continue to be such an importance influence on life in the United States? Explain.
2. Do you agree with Chief Justice Roberts that programs that assign students to schools based on race in order to promote school integration perpetuate racism in American society? Explain.

I now ask students in my classes and teachers I meet at staff development activities to start unit and lesson planning by answering two simple questions. (1) What is important to know about the topic and why? (2) How will I make the important content and concepts available to students in a way that is meaningful to them? The first question we will start to address here. The second question will be examined over and over again in the "how to teach" sections of the book.

Big problems when teaching the global

history curriculum are that there are far too many events to include; many, if not most, appear to be unrelated, and most of us, including myself, have large areas of the world and great swaths of time about which we know little. This is why we end up following the textbook or using pre-packaged lessons we find in the department office, are handed at conferences or staff development, or download from the internet. What happens is we become the victims of other people decisions, usually without knowing the underlying ideas and biases that motivated their choices.

The best example is probably the history of industrial capitalism during the last 200 years. Winston Churchill is quoted as having said, "Democracy is the worst form of government except all the others that have been tried" and "History is written by the victors" (available at: http://www.brainyquote.com/quotes/authors/w/winston_churchill.html, accessed April 13, 2007). Of course his conclusion about democracy, by which he really meant free-market capitalism, was not based on any kind of objective analysis, but on his position as leader of the British Empire in the twentieth century, an empire that used capitalism to subvert both democracy and traditional economies in its colonies, including much of India, East Africa, the Middle East, and the Caribbean. The triumph of capitalism and its essential role in support of democracy is the standard narrative in most Western civilization courses, but that does not mean it is true. Certainly nineteenth- and twentieth-century Marxists disputed it, as do contemporary critics of unregulated globalization. Criticisms will probably increase if China remains committed to both capitalism and dictatorship, if much of the Third World continues to be impoverished, and if development motivated by the singular desire for private profit decimates the environment and endangers the survival of human civilization.

Most packaged curricula trumpet unrestrained capitalist growth without questioning its impact or exploring alternatives. One example is the Foundation for Teaching Economics (available at: http://www.fte.org, accessed October 8, 2007) that runs free workshops for teachers and provides them with on-line lesson plans and supporting material. Their mission statement claims their goal is to "introduce young individuals, selected for their

leadership potential, to an economic way of thinking about national and international issues, and to promote excellence in economic education by helping teachers of economics become more effective educators." However, their approach to the teaching of history and economics is decidedly ideological. It is based on the idea that "the mid-eighteenth century was an historical turning point of economic advance. Organizational and technological changes in that period allowed growing numbers of people to move from mere subsistence activities to thoughts and actions that furthered economic, political and social progress." Based on the premise that industrial capitalism is overwhelmingly a positive force, they have developed unit plans that present a case against environmental restrictions that interfere with a "rational economic approach" and encourage teachers to claim that unrestrained capitalism has been, and will continue to be, good for the world's impoverished people. The Foundation for Teaching Economics approached Hofstra University offering to do workshops at our campus, but withdrew the offer when the social studies program insisted that Hofstra faculty had to be part of any presentations in order to provide teachers with alternative views.

I see both industrial capitalism and movements to extend human rights as the principle forces transforming the modern world, starting with the mid-eighteenth century. The expansion of both should be the underlying theme in the study of this era in history. But they do not always work together. Imperialism, class conflict, and gross disparities of wealth within and between societies are all products of capitalist development and have been challenged by human rights advocates. Contrarian and revolutionary movements are often framed in support of one and in opposition to the other. Instead of promoting capitalism, the goal of the social studies curriculum should be to analyze and understand it.

Too often, I have observed student teachers and beginning teachers start lessons with aim (or overarching) questions that they, themselves, have not really thought through and cannot answer. We should not be teaching students to believe in our answers. But if we have not considered what is important to know and why, we will just be teaching them someone else's answer.

Teaching Activity: Where Do You Stand?

As someone preparing to become a social studies teacher, you probably were either a history major or minor as an undergraduate college student.

Add your voice to the discussion:
1. Identify three major controversial issues from your study of history.
2. What were the controversies?
3. Where do you stand?
4. How will you address these controversies in your teaching?

WHO ARE OUR STUDENTS AND HOW DO WE CONNECT TO THEM?

In an interview with the editor of *Rethinking Schools* (1994), US historian Howard Zinn explained that he "started studying history with one view in mind: to look for answers to the issues and problems I saw in the world around me. By the time I went to college I had worked in a shipyard, had been in the Air Force, had been in a war. I came to history asking questions about war and peace, about wealth and poverty, about racial division" (Rethinking Schools 2007).

I think that Paulo Freire, who has worked in adult literacy programs in Third World communities since the 1950s, would argue that Howard Zinn was motivated to read the word (to study books) because he wanted to read (understand) the world. Freire (1995) believes that there is a dynamic interactive relationship between increasing academic literacy and the desire to understand and change the world around us.

Freire's insight into the way people learn is supported by similar findings in history, psychology, and education. Chapter 2 described a reciprocal relationship between research and the development of historical understanding and theories. Early childhood educators and educational psychologists like Lucy Calkins (1983), Lev Vygotzky (1987, cited in Reiber and Carton 1997), and Loris Malaguzzi, the founder of an internationally acclaimed early childhood program in Reggio Emilia, Italy (Gandini 1993: 4–9) find the same dynamic at work as young children explore the world around them and learn to read. In their teaching autobiographies, Septima Clark (1986) and Myles Horton et al. (1990) argued that freedom schools in the US south during the civil rights movement of the 1960s successfully promoted literacy because they built on the struggle of African-Americans to win the right to vote.

The careers of Freire, Clark, and Horton demonstrate that intense and complex learning is possible when motivated adults are helped to draw connections among their life experiences, social concerns, political points of view, and academic knowledge and skills. However, the question remains whether connecting the study of the word with study of the world will also motivate (1) 13-year-old 7th-grade boys from affluent suburban communities who are yeasting with hormones; (2) self-effacing young women in 11th-grade classes who behave in school and do all their work, but whose interests are elsewhere; or (3) angry students whose lives are overwhelmed by feelings of oppression, and with the difficulty of dealing with prejudice, poverty and urban (or rural) violence. How do teachers convince these students to invest in school and learn social studies?

Many educators have grappled with ways to reach students in the classroom, suggesting strategies for changing the ways that teachers teach, the content of the curriculum, and classroom relationships. Lev Vygotsky, working in the 1920s and 1930s in the Soviet Union, was concerned that educators were often trapped by narrowly conceived and universally applied ideas about human social and psychological development, and, as a result, had rigid views about appropriate learning strategies. Vygotsky recognized that students are strongly influenced by the social and historical circumstances of their lives; he believed that to stimulate academic learning, educators had to "scaffold," or build on the individual and social experiences of students and what they already knew about the world (Newman and Holtzman 1992; Berk 1994; Reiber and Carton 1997).

The idea that teachers should respond to individual differences in the ways that students learn is also a crucial component of Howard Gardner's theory of multiple intelligences. Gardner (1987: 187–193) disputed the ideas that human intelligence can be accurately summarized with one reference point and that all people learn in essentially the same fashion. He suggests seven at least types of intelligence possessed by students in a variety of combinations, including linguistic, logical-mathematical, spatial, body-kinesthetic, musical, interpersonal (social), and intrapersonal (reflective). Gardner argues that curricula and teachers must "recognize and nurture all of the varied human intelligences, and all of the combinations of intelligences," so that schools and societies are able to appropriately address "the many problems that we face in the world."

Advocates of curriculum reform, especially since the 1960s, frequently argue that relevance—drawing connections between school learning and life experience—is crucial for motivating students to learn, particularly in social studies. For example, Howard Zinn recommends that teachers organize curricula so that students "go back and forth and find similarities and analogies" between the past and present. Henry Giroux (1983; 1992) believes that curriculum should be organized so that students are continually involved in examining their lived experiences. According to Giroux, this makes it possible for students to understand the relationship between their ideas and cultures and the ideology and culture of the broader society. Peggy McIntosh (1983) wants teachers to involve students in creating curricula that include everyone, and also in critiquing earlier forms of instruction and the social theories that lay behind them.

Nel Noddings (1992a; 1992b) and Alfie Kohn (1986) take a different approach to motivating students, focusing on the nature of classroom community, rather than particular subject content. Noddings proposes a "feminist approach to education" based on an ethic of caring and concern for others, the acceptance of a wide range of human differences, and the nurturing of individual student strengths.

Kohn believes that academic and social competition among students is inherently destructive. He emphasizes cooperative instruction as the basis for creating supportive, democratic learning environments.

Gloria Ladson-Billings (1994) integrates these approaches in what she calls "culturally relevant pedagogy." Ladson-Billings, who is concerned with both curriculum content and classroom organization, believes that teachers must familiarize themselves with the "home" cultures of students, and adjust both the subject matter and their classroom practice so that students feel their lives and sensitivities are included in what is taking place. Ladson-Billings' specific research area is on successful approaches to teaching African-American students; she argues that a culturally relevant pedagogy is especially important when students come from communities outside the cultural mainstream.

Drawing on my understanding of educators like Vygotsky, Gardner, Giroux, McIntosh, Noddings, Kohn, and Ladson-Billings, it seems that if we start with the assumption that our primary responsibility is to teach students, instead of specific subject matter, social studies teachers have to be knowledgeable about who our students are emotionally, socially, and academically, and need to address issues related to race, class, gender, cultural differences, prior preparation, and student interest in our classrooms and curricula. It means we have to adjust our teaching to meet the individual and collective needs of our students.

The issue in classrooms is not really relevance; essentially any topic can be made relevant if teachers establish a context for student understanding. For example, I began lessons on famine-era Irish immigration in the 1840s by asking students to discuss contemporary attitudes towards immigrants in the communities where they live.

One of my pedagogical goals is to reach every student in every classroom every day. I do not have all of the answers about how to do this, and I am not even sure that it is possible. But I do know that the starting point is accepting responsibility for what students learn, and always asking the questions—"Who are my students?" and "How do I connect to them?"

Teaching Activity: Heterogeneous or Homogenous Grouping?

Many schools assign students to social studies classes based on their performance on exams, their perceived intelligence or talent, parental pressure, or teacher recommendation. Supporters of homogenous grouping (tracking) argue that it allows teachers to focus on the specific academic needs of the students in their classes. In theory, homogenous grouping benefits students on every academic track while preparing them to succeed in a competitive society where rewards are distributed based on achievement.

Supporters of heterogeneous grouping respond that tracked classrooms are inherently inequitable, reinforce social divisions, and injure students. The experience of being tracked teaches students to believe that intelligence is innate, people are fundamentally different, and that some are incapable and undeserving of rewards. Tracking encourages competition and increases resentment of others. Denied experiences with diverse groups of young people, students never learn to work with people different from themselves. Students in lower tracks believe that they are born inferior and destined to fail. They develop low self-esteem, give up trying to learn, and many drop out of school. Students in upper tracks are hurt as well. Many become lonely and alienated. Others students grow anxious. They feel as if they are always being tested, and that eventually their inadequacies will be exposed. Instead of enjoying learning, they fear that they will be thrown out of the upper track, and thus let down their parents. Even the students who respond to the competition and do well are vulnerable. When, like any ordinary human beings, they stumble, their entire self-image is subject to question. One result of tracking is that even the best students experience school as an oppressive, stressful place.

Over the years I proposed another way of organizing instruction that challenges students academically while avoiding the negative affects of tracking. So far no school district has taken me up on my plan.

My proposal is to organize social studies classes in the same way we organize laboratory science classes. Three days a week, all students taking a particular social studies subject would be grouped heterogeneously and study the major issues in history, political science, and economics together. Two days a week, students would meet in social studies "labs" organized to address their specific academic needs. Students taking classes for advanced placement college credit would be in sections that examined appropriate college-level documents. Students who need assistance in reading and writing would meet in smaller groups where the focus would be on skill acquisition and improvement. Other students would meet in sections designed to meet state-level academic standards.

Think it over:
1. What track were you assigned to in secondary school?
2. What was your relationship with students in other tracks?
3. What was the impact of tracking on your learning and on your life?
4. Thinking back, could your school have been organized differently? How?

Add your voice to the discussion:
Where do you stand on the issue of heterogeneous versus homogenous grouping in social studies classes? Why?

WHAT USE IS EDUCATIONAL THEORY?

In *Sometimes a Shining Moment: The Foxfire Experience*, Eliot Wigginton (1985), who helped promote the project approach to teaching (discussed in Chapter 11), discussed his reaction as he began to reread John Dewey after a number of years of teaching secondary school. Wigginton was amazed that "All of those discoveries I thought I had made about education, Dewey had elucidated into complete clarity fifty years and more before." He asked himself, "Why didn't I hear what Dewey et al. were saying when I was first introduced to them?" (Wigginton 1985: 281).

Wigginton's comments underscore the importance, but inaccessibility, of educational theory for many teachers. While in pre-service teacher education programs, we lack the practical experiences that make ideas meaningful. Later, there is little time structured into the school year to read, systematically explore issues with other teachers, or conduct action research on classroom practice. We feel pressured to develop our practical competence, rather than develop theoretical understanding—to teach while wearing educational blinders. Just as our students do, we end up learning so we can pass the test.

I was lucky during the 1992–1993 school year, when I was able to return to the high school classroom after a two-year leave of absence as a pre-service teacher-educator at Hofstra University. In my social studies classes, I had the opportunity to systematically experiment with the ideas, theories, and teaching methods discussed in my teacher education classes, especially the work of John Dewey, Paulo Freire, and Maxine Greene. Their work, and the work of some of the other people discussed in the next two sections, gave me a new appreciation for the value of educational theory in directing teaching practice. I include a brief introduction to their ideas in this book so that each new generation of social studies teachers does not have to reinvent every wheel.

Teaching Activity: Educational Theory

In *Experience and Education*, John Dewey (1938: 51) wrote that unless teachers base "educational plans and projects" on theories of how people learn, they are "at the mercy of every intellectual breeze that happens to blow." In high school, we call these intellectual breezes "the gimmick of the month"—miracle cures that somehow fail to make much of a difference.

Add your voice to the discussion:
In your opinion and based on your experience, should social studies teachers study educational theory? When? Why?

HOW CAN WE TEACH DEMOCRACY?

In his November 19, 1863, address at the dedication of the Gettysburg National Cemetery, Abraham Lincoln defined democracy as "government of the people, by the people, for the people" (Stern 1940: 786–787). John Dewey's progressive educational philosophy was concerned with the need to educate people for life in such a society. Key concepts for Dewey (1938: 25) were experience, freedom, community, and "habits of mind." Dewey believed there was an "organic connection between education and experience"; that effective teachers are able to connect the subject matter to the existing experience of students and then expand and enrich their lives with new experiences.

According to Dewey, students learn from the full spectrum of their experiences in school, not just the specific thing they are studying in class. They learn from what they are studying, how they are studying, whom they are studying with, and how they are treated. In racially segregated or academically tracked classes, students learn that some people are better than others. In teacher-centered classrooms, they learn that some people possess knowledge and others passively receive it. When teachers have total control over classrooms, even when they are benevolent or entertaining, students learn to accept authoritarianism. During his career, Dewey continually examined the experiences educators need to create for students so they become active participants in preserving and expanding government of, by, and for the people.

For Dewey, the exercise of freedom in democratic societies always involves education. He identifies freedom with "power to frame purposes" or achieve individual and social goals. This kind of freedom requires a probing, critical, disciplined "habit of mind." It includes intelligence, judgment, and self-control, qualities that students never acquire in classrooms where they are subject to external controls and are forced to remain silent. In progressive schools that use a Deweyan approach, students engage in long-term thematic group projects, where they learn to collectively solve problems, and classrooms become democratic communities where "things gain meaning by being used in a shared experience or joint action."

Kim Cahill of the New Teachers Network conducted an interesting experiment in her classes that demonstrated the power of Dewey's ideas. She had student teams in her senior government classes write a constitution for a hypothetical newly emerging third world country. Instead of designing democracies, nearly every team chose to have a dictatorial regime that would keep people in line and get things done. In retrospect, it should not have been so surprising. In their families, at work, and in schools students are constantly exposed to authoritarian leaders (parents, employers, and teachers) who boss them around.

Teaching Activity: Problem Solving and Critical Judgment

In the social studies, Harold Rugg became a leading advocate for Dewey's educational theories. Rugg (1923) argued that, "Not the learning of texts, but the solving of problems is what we need . . . For the pupil to think, he [*sic*] first must be mentally blocked and thwarted until he is obsessed with a desire to clear up the matter; he must also have at hand data, the facts on all sides of the issue, before he can think constructively on it; and third, he must be practiced in deliberations on situations that are somewhat similar . . . Only those who are trained through five, ten, twelve years of practice in deliberation will tend to use critical judgment about contemporary problems."

Add your voice to the discussion:
1. Why does Rugg want students "mentally blocked and thwarted"?
2. In your opinion, does Rugg's approach offer real options for the classroom? Explain.

Traditionally, Dewey's ideas have been implemented in small, private elementary schools, where student populations tend to be academically and socially well prepared for school. However, under the leadership of Ted Sizer, the Coalition of Essential Schools (CES) has championed Deweyan principles in public secondary education. CES promotes smaller schools where students feel connected to a learning community, and argues that, in terms of curriculum content, "less is more." Coalition schools encourage students to be active learners, and encourage researchers and teachers to be their co-learners and coaches. The most noted participants in the CES are the Central Park East Secondary Schools in New York City, where Deborah Meier (1995) and her colleagues were recognized for creating democratic classroom communities that allowed working-class and poor, urban, and minority youth to achieve a high level of academic success. Can social studies teachers teach democracy? If Dewey is right, this can only happen in classrooms where students experience democracy.

HOW ARE GOALS REFLECTED IN DIFFERENT APPROACHES TO TEACHING SOCIAL STUDIES?

Although models for social studies teaching vary depending on goals, teaching approaches do not fit into neat compartments. The transmission model is often associated with demands for increased classroom control, social assimilation, and political conservatism, but it also has supporters who want to ensure that academic knowledge is available to working-class and minority students who have traditionally been denied access to a rigorous education. Similarly, educators with points of view across the political spectrum can adapt the inquiry method and student-centered approaches. Who gets included in a social studies curriculum, which documents and ideas are introduced for examination, and whether activities focus on individual achievement or group struggles can differ sharply from classroom to classroom.

Although advocates for a transformative approach to teaching social studies tend to support similar classroom goals and practices, there are no rules that guarantee consistency. Some transformative social studies teachers do minimal advanced planning because they want students to take the initiative in class. I prefer to over-plan lessons. I bring extra documents and activities to class, and decide what to include, shift to another day, or drop based on class discussion and student questions. Because this approach involves many options, I can teach a lesson five times and it may never include the same materials.

WHAT ARE THE TRADITIONAL ACADEMIC GOALS IN SOCIAL STUDIES?

Careful advanced planning helps me integrate short- and long-term content, conceptual, and academic and social skills goals into my teaching. In secondary school social studies classes, students are expected to (1) develop their ability to examine and explain historical and social science concepts and understandings, (2) utilize information from history and the different social science disciplines, (3) develop the academic and analytical skills necessary to discover information on their own, make reasoned decisions, and present their ideas, and (4) enhance the social skills needed to share ideas and work with others.

Social Studies Concepts and Understandings

Social studies concepts are overall organizing categories. I compare them to the "folders" used to store computer files. They suggest relationships among people, ideas, and events that allow students to make meaning of, sort, and remember information. Understandings are main ideas about a topic that describe the relationships and patterns. For example, actions have consequences in both everyday life and in the historical arena. When a teenage woman consciously violates the family curfew, she anticipates conflict with her parents and

decides that the risk is worth the reward. Similarly, a large country that invades a smaller neighbor understands that it risks provoking a response from that country's allies.

There are several systems for identifying key social studies concepts and understandings. In general, these systems share a belief that students should reexamine basic ideas from different vantage points throughout a curriculum. In the approach developed by the National Council for the Social Studies (NCSS 1994), concepts are called thematic strands. Aspects of at least one strand, and preferably multiple strands, should be explored in each social studies lesson.

A problem with NCSS thematic strands is that they present social studies concepts as neutral principles that are independent of broader historical explanations or theories. In a social studies curriculum that encourages students to view the world through a critical lens, other basic concepts need to be included. For example, individuals and societies are not just interdependent; relationships are often exploitative. Secondary school students need to examine concepts like injustice, racism, and imperialism, and to decide when they are operating. Although continuity and change are significant concepts, students also need to examine different theories about change and compare concepts like progress, reform, reaction, and revolution.

NCSS THEMATIC STRANDS

The 10 NCSS thematic strands are as follows: (available at: http://www.socialstudies.org/standards/strands/, accessed September 19, 2007):

1. *Culture*: Ways that human groups learn, create, and adapt, in order to meet their fundamental needs and beliefs they develop to explain the world.
2. *Time, Continuity, and Change*: Ways that human groups locate themselves historically.
3. *People, Places, and Environments*: The influence of geography on human cultures and history.
4. *Individual Development and Identity*: Relationships between the ways that people perceive themselves and their membership in social groups.
5. *Individuals, Groups, and Institutions*: Roles played by social institutions like schools and families in a society and their impact on individuals and groups.
6. *Power, Authority, and Governance*: Ways that individuals and societies make decisions about rights, rules, relationships, and priorities.
7. *Production, Distribution, and Consumption*: Ways that individuals and societies make decisions about the things people need to survive and how they will be provided.
8. *Science, Technology, and Society*: Methods and tools used by people to produce and distribute what they need and want within an economic system.
9. *Global Connections*: The increasingly important and diverse relationships between societies.
10. *Civic Ideals and Practices*: The relationship between the expressed beliefs of a society and the implementation of these beliefs in actual practice.

NCSS Thematic Strand on Culture
- Human cultures are similar. They all include systems of beliefs, knowledge, values, and traditions that influence individual and group behavior.
- Each human culture is unique because people view the world from different vantage points.
- Cultures are dynamic. They change to accommodate new beliefs, ideas, and conditions.
- Religious beliefs and political ideals influence other aspects of a culture.
- Language is an important ingredient for expressing cultural values and practices.
- Cultures change through adaptation to new environmental and social conditions, assimilation of group members into other cultures, diffusion of cultural practices through cross-cultural interaction, and cultural dissonance between different groups of people.

Teaching Activity: Concepts, Understandings, and Controversies

Translating broad concepts into specific content understandings and lesson plans introduces controversy into social studies curricula. Examine the example that follows.

- *Concept*: Economic System. The decision-making process related to, and the production and distribution of, the goods and services that people in a society need to survive and/or prosper.
- *Understanding*. In a managed capitalist economy like the United States, a drop in the official unemployment rate below approximately 6 percent has led to increased inflation, a decline in the value of money, and decreased confidence in political leaders.
- *Controversies*. Is unemployment a result of uncontrollable market forces or conscious economic policies that benefit business and people with secure jobs, at the expense of a significant minority of the population? Is it fair to pursue economic policies like cutting government budgets for social service programs and tightening credit, which disproportionately injure the poor and members of racial and ethnic minorities?

Lesson design:
Examine a graph showing the relationship between inflation and unemployment, a statement by the head of the Federal Reserve system explaining a decision to raise interest rates, and a political cartoon showing the president calling on poor African-American children to become "inflation fighters."

Try it yourself:
1. List five understandings that you think high school students should learn about the US economic system.
2. Why do you consider these understandings important?
3. How would you introduce these understandings into lessons?
4. What controversies are related to at least one of these understandings?

Academic and Social Skills

The term *social studies skills* covers a broad range of classroom activities and goals. For example, proposed National History Standards (discussed in Chapter 5) focus on five historical thinking skills that "students should be able to do to demonstrate their understandings and to apply their knowledge in productive ways . . . These thinking skills are the process of active learning" (NCHS 1994). They include chronological thinking, historical comprehension, historical analysis and interpretation, historical research, and historical issue analysis and decision making. The National Standards for Civics and Government describes similar academic capacities, but identifies them as intellectual and participatory skills. According to these standards, students should be able to acquire, describe, explain, and evaluate information, arrive at and defend conclusions that are based on evidence, and take action based on their conclusions (Center for Civic Education 1994).

In its Curriculum Standards for Social Studies, the NCSS (1994: 148–149) offers a comprehensive list of "essential skills for social studies." Skills for acquiring information are divided into reading, study, research, and technical skills, and each of these sections has numerous subdivisions. For example, reading skills include comprehension, vocabulary, and rate of reading, and comprehension is redivided into twelve distinct activities that students should be able to perform (e.g., "use picture clues and picture captions to aid comprehension"). Other broad skill categories include organizing and using information (thinking, decision making, and metacognitive skills), interpersonal relationships (personal and group interaction skills), and social and political participation. As a demonstration of their social and political participation skills, secondary school students are expected to be able to: (1) keep informed on issues that affect society; (2) identify situations in which social action is required; (3) work individually or with others to decide on an appropriate course of action; (4) work to influence those in positions of social power to strive for extensions of freedom, social justice, and human rights; and (5) accept and fulfill social responsibilities associated with citizenship in a free society.

All these approaches argue that content and conceptual learning in social studies does not take place in isolation. Students learn about history, government, and society; to really learn about them, they must develop literacy, numeracy, oral and written communication skills, analytical abilities, and the capacity to work independently and with others. Social studies students need skills for (1) getting information: observing, listening, reading, researching, and measuring; (2) using information: thinking, evaluating, organizing, questioning, creating, and evaluating hypotheses; (3) expressing information and ideas: writing, explaining, and discussing; and (4) interpersonal and group relations: cooperating, sharing, empathizing, democratic community building, and decision making.

Michael Pezone and Vance Gillenwater (NTN) work with students who generally do not speak the Standard English dialect at home, in their communities, or in school. This interferes with their ability to write clear, edited, statements and more extended essays. To enhance writing skills, Michael and Vance have their students read famous speeches aloud and prepare their own "speeches," written in "standard," that they deliver in class. Not only does this seem to improve their general academic literacy, but it also helps students to appreciate the seriousness of learning and the need to listen to and help each other.

It is important to remember that developing academic and social skills requires planned instruction by teacher and considerable practice by students. Skills have to be integrated into specific lessons, and carefully and systematically woven throughout a social studies curriculum.

Teaching Activities: Including Academic Skills in Social Studies Lessons

Literacy and numeracy are basic skills in all academic subjects. In social studies, students need to use language and numbers to acquire and present information. Individual and team activities can be integrated into most lessons.

Mathematical Skills (Graph analysis):

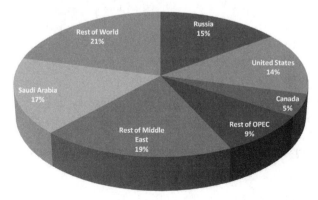

Figure 4.1 World oil production, 2004.
Source: Energy Information Administration (http://www.infoplease.com, accessed April 12, 2007).

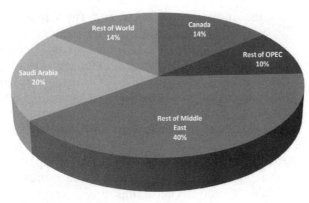

Figure 4.2 Known world oil reserves, 2005.
Source: Oil and Gas Journal (http://www.infoplease.com, accessed April 14, 2007).

Questions

1. What is the title of pie chart A?
2. What is the title of pie chart B?
3. What information is provided by each of the pie charts?
4. What percentage does the entire circle represent for each pie chart?
5. Which country has the largest current production?
6. What percentage of oil production comes from the United States?
7. What percentage of known oil reserves are controlled by nations in the Middle East?
8. Which current large producers are not among the countries with large reserves?
9. Which country has the most undeveloped reserves?
10. The Organization of Petroleum Exporting Countries (OPEC) includes Saudi Arabia, other Middle East oil producing nations, as well as other countries. What percentage of world oil reserves is controlled by OPEC?
11. In your opinion, how can decisions made by OPEC affect other countries?

Map Skills:

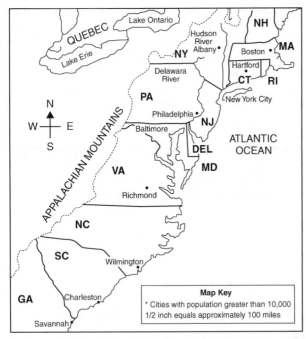

Figure 4.3 Map Skills.

1. Based on the information in the map in Figure 4.3 and what you know about US history, approximately what year does the map represent?
2. What section of the current United States is shown in Figure 4.3?
3. Use the compass to figure out the direction a person travels going from Boston, Massachusetts to Albany, New York.
4. In what direction does the Hudson River flow?

5. Use the map key to estimate the distance from New York, New York to Richmond, Virginia?
6. In your opinion, why are most of the cities in the British colonies in North America near the Atlantic Ocean?

Writing Skills:
Use pictures of artwork from different eras to encourage students to write. Students write brief essays describing the pictures, explaining what they thought an artist was trying to portray, and discussing what the pictures illustrate about a historical period. Images of many famous paintings are available on the internet at *WebMuseum, Paris,* http://www.ibiblio.org/wm/paint, accessed September 19, 2007.

Teaching Activity: Content, Concepts, or Skills?

Add your voice to the discussion:
Do you think social studies teachers should incorporate basic mathematical and literacy skills in social studies lessons? Why?

Think it over:
Are you comfortable teaching basic mathematical and literacy skills? How would you prepare yourself to teach them?

It's your classroom:
Select one of the activities. How would you integrate this activity into a lesson?

HOW DO TEACHERS INTEGRATE GOALS INTO CLASSROOM PRACTICE?

One of the most successful examples of integrating social studies concepts, understandings, and academic and social skills into classroom practice that I have been involved with was a group project with elementary school children in the after-school program at the MLE Learning Center in Brooklyn. The group and their teacher used a traditional African-American folktale, "The People Could Fly" (from a collection of folktales, *The People Could Fly,* "retold" by Virginia Hamilton, 1985), to learn about the desire of people for freedom. In the story, enslaved Africans are working in a cotton field in the American South. When the master and overseer whip a young mother who is too tired to continue working, an old man tells her magic words so that she can fly away to Africa.

After reading the folktale, the group decided to rewrite it as a play and perform it for the rest of the school. It was an interracial group of young people, and an important part of the project was their discussion of how to cast the roles in the play. They discussed how they were related to each other, and decided not to use race as a criteria for casting because "that's not the way we are at the Learning Center."

Since seeing their performance and discussing it with them, I have had teams of students at different grade-levels rewrite and perform this story and others from the same collection. I always have them discuss how they want to cast the play. Teams have made different decisions; once they even made giant puppets to play the master and overseer while students played "the people who could fly." The discussion of casting has always made possible discussion of student views on slavery, oppression, and freedom, and their feelings about race relations in their schools and our contemporary society.

Example: 7th-Grade Lesson Outline—The People Could Fly

Lesson Aim: How did African-Americans express their desire for freedom?
Concepts: Freedom, slavery, culture, racism, justice.

Content: Learn about the song, *Go Down Moses*, and the story, *The People Could Fly*; conditions for enslaved Africans on cotton plantations in the American South; the religion of enslaved Africans; efforts to build community.

Academic Skills (class): Analyze a reading passage. Discuss the meaning of a play. Discuss casting and racism. Write a story about freedom.

Social Skills (group): Work together to create production. Arrive at consensus decision about casting. Present production and decision.

Social Skills (class): Participate as an audience and in discussion. Share writing.

Understandings/Main Ideas: Throughout human history, people have found ways to express their desire for freedom. Enslaved African-Americans (slavery) used stories, songs, and religious practices (culture) to express their desire for freedom. Although racial tension continues in our society today, overt discrimination (racism) is both illegal and considered unacceptable (justice).

Activities:

1. Read and discuss the song, *Go Down Moses*.
2. Student cooperative learning team performs *The People Could Fly*.
3. Class discussion(s) of the play, casting decisions, racism, and freedom.
4. Write a story that explains why freedom is important to you.

Teaching Activity: Including Goals and Understandings

Think it over:

In your opinion, is it necessary to include goals and understandings in a lesson outline? Explain the reasons for your answer.

Try it yourself:

- Take a story from a folktale collection and rewrite it as a play.
- What concepts and understandings could you teach using this folktale?

It's your class:

Would you use the prior lesson outline as is, modify it, or discard it? Explain the reasons for your answer.

WHAT ARE THE STATE STANDARDS?

As you have moved through your teacher certification program, you quickly discovered that everybody in the United States (the media, politicians, parents, and teachers) is worried about higher standards and the assessment of student learning. It seems like every educational organization has its own published list of what children should know and every political unit (city, county or state) has its own standardized tests that students are expected to pass. But there is very little public discussion of exactly what we mean by standards. Most experienced social studies teachers I know respond to the call for higher standards by saying that this is the same thing we always do.

I think the general public finds the call for higher standards confusing because the term means different things in different contexts. In track and field, the *standard* is the record performance that other athletes try to surpass. In baseball, it is the Yankees with a century of accomplishment. In basketball and golf it is identified with one player, Michael Jordan or Tiger Woods. But everybody cannot be like Mike, Tiger, or the Yankees, and that is the problem with using the top performer as a measure or standard.

In education, *standards* can best be described as goals, the things we hope all students will achieve, the things we plan for them to achieve. Achieving standards is not a competition. In theory, in a well-run classroom with effective teaching strategies, every student should be able to obtain the goals.

Most State Departments of Education now publish general and subject-related learning standards on the Internet. New York State, where I work, offers elementary, intermediate, and commencement (high school graduation) standards in each subject area, but not unit or lesson plans. Teachers, departments, schools, and districts are expected to develop their own strategies for achieving the standards. Student achievement, and the success of social studies programs, are measured by comprehensive tests administered in 5th, 8th, 10th, and 11th grades.

Links to social studies curriculum, standards, and assessments for many of the states and for major national organizations are available on-line at http://edstandards.org/StSu/Social.html (accessed October 30, 2007). Most open with a statement of purpose defining the goals for social studies education. The introduction to Georgia's Performance Standards for Social Studies identifies the primary purpose of social studies as the development of "informed Georgia citizens who understand the history of the United States and our place in an ever increasing interconnected world" (available at: http://public.doe.k12.ga.us, accessed on April 14, 2007). To achieve this goal, social studies teachers are called on to "bridge essential understanding about the past to contemporary events, . . . assist students in understanding the nature of historical inquiry and the role of primary and secondary sources," and "encourage the consideration of multiple perspectives on events." The social studies standards then offer teachers a matrix that correlates the content, concepts, skills, and values to be taught at different grade-levels.

State Department of Education social studies standards around the country tend to be organized around two models. Thematic strands, similar to those produced by the NCSS (available at: http://www.socialstudies.org/standards, accessed October 30, 2007), focus on broad concepts. Content is primarily offered to provide examples of what should be taught in different classes. Content-based approaches to standards, similar to those developed by the National Council for History in the Schools (available at: http://www.sscnet.ucla.edu/nchs/, accessed October 30, 2007), generally provide lists of information and definitions of terms, grouped either chronologically or thematically, that students should master at different grade-levels. These models have a broad area of overlap and both approaches expect students to develop appropriate academic skills. Published standards, whether offered by state Departments of Education or national social studies organizations, vary widely in the amount of sample lessons, activities, and assessments they provide to teachers. I think it is useful to look more closely at an example of each of these approaches to standards at greater depth. While I prefer the thematic approach, standards that I have examined offer a teacher enough leeway that I feel I could be comfortable adapting my style of teaching to the requirements of either set of standards.

The state of Michigan's social studies curriculum framework (available at: http://www.michigan.gov/documents/Social_Studies_Standards_122915_7.pdf, accessed September 25, 2007) is an example of a primarily thematic or conceptual approach. Michigan's social studies curriculum builds four capacities in young people: disciplinary knowledge, thinking skills, commitment to democratic values, and citizen participation." All of the standards are pursued at every grade-level of the curriculum from kindergarten to graduation. Although the standards refer to areas of knowledge and skill that no one ever masters completely in a total sense, benchmarks are established for each to designate clearly what students are expected to know and be able to do at different grade-levels.

A *Historical Perspective* includes the ability to sequence chronologically the eras of American history and key events within these eras in order to examine relationships and to explain cause and effect; constructing and interpreting timelines of people and events in the history of Michigan and the United States; characterizing eras in United States history; comparing interpretations written by others from a variety of perspectives and creating narratives from evidence; using primary and secondary records; challenge arguments of historical inevitability by formulating examples of how different choices could have led to different consequences; and selecting contemporary problems in the world and composing historical narratives that explain their antecedents.

Michigan's Social Studies Strand II, the *Geographic Perspective*, has five standards that explore the following themes: Diversity of People, Places, and Cultures; Human/Environment Interaction; Location, Movement, and Connections; Regions, Patterns, and Processes; and Global Issues and Events. Strand III, the *Civic Perspective*, is designed to make it possible for students to "use knowledge of American government and politics to make informed decisions about governing their communities." Five standards explore the purposes of government, the ideals of American democracy, democracy in action, including decision making, consensus building and conflict resolution, the functioning of American Government and politics, and the role of the American Government in world affairs. In Strand IV, the *Economic Perspective*, students acquire knowledge of the production, distribution, and consumption of goods and services to make personal and societal decisions about the use of scarce resources. Standards focus attention on individual, household and business choices, the government's role in the economy, economic systems, trade and development.

Strands V and VI focus on the acquisition of social studies-related academic skills. Under the *Inquiry* strand, students learn to "use methods of social science investigation to answer questions about society." This component includes development of information processing skills, including learning to "acquire information from books, maps, newspapers, data sets, and other sources, organize and present the information in maps, graphs, charts, and time lines, interpret the meaning and significance of information, and use a variety of electronic technologies to assist in accessing and managing information." Students also learn to "conduct investigations by formulating a clear statement of a question, gathering and organizing information from a variety of sources, analyzing and interpreting information, formulating and testing hypotheses, reporting results both orally and in writing, and making use of appropriate technology." Under the *Public Discourse and Decision Making* strand, students learn to "analyze public issues and construct and express thoughtful positions on these issues." This component includes the ability to identify and analyze an issue, to participate in group discussion, and competence in written persuasion. The final social studies strand is *Citizen Involvement*, which requires that students "act constructively to further the public good" and includes "responsible personal conduct."

The State of New Mexico's Social Studies Content Standards and Benchmarks (available at: http://www.nmlites.org/downloads/standards/stand_ss.pdf, accessed September 25, 2007), which takes a more content-based approach, is actually adapted from the Massachusetts State Department of Education's History and Social Science Curriculum Framework. It provides Social Studies Content Standards, Benchmarks, and Performance Standards that "describe the disciplinary content and skills students should learn at specific grade-levels" and "serve as the basis for statewide assessment of student learning."

New Mexico's Social Studies Content Standards, Benchmarks, and Performance Standards are organized within a spiraling framework so that skills and course content at each grade-level increases in complexity and important topics, texts, and documents are continually reexamined. Content Standard 1 is History. Under this standard, students are expected "to identify important people and events in order to analyze significant patterns, relationships, themes, ideas, beliefs, and turning points in New Mexico, United States, and world history in order to understand the complexity of the human experience."

In 7th grade, students compare and contrast the contributions of the civilizations of the Western Hemisphere (e.g., Aztecs, Mayas, Toltecs, Mound Builders) with the early civilizations of the Eastern Hemisphere (e.g., Sumerians, Babylonians, Hebrews, Egyptians) and their impact upon societies; describe the characteristics of other indigenous peoples that had an affect upon New Mexico's development; explain the significance of trails and trade routes within the region ; describe how important individuals, groups, and events impacted the development of New Mexico from sixteenth century to the present (e.g., Don Juan de Oñate, Don Diego de Vargas, Pueblo Revolt, Popé, 1837 Revolt, 1848 Rebellion, Treaty of Guadalupe Hildago, William Becknell and the Santa Fe Trail, Buffalo Soldiers, Lincoln County War, Navajo Long Walk, Theodore Roosevelt and the Rough Riders, Robert Goddard, J. Robert Oppenhiemer, Smokey Bear, Dennis Chavez, Manuel Lujan, Manhattan Project, Harrison Schmitt, Albuquerque International Balloon Fiesta); explain how New Mexicans have adapted to their physical environments to meet their needs over time; and explain the impact of New Mexico on the development of the American West up to the present.

In 8th grade, students compare and contrast the settlement patterns of the American Southwest with other regions of the United

States; analyze New Mexico's role and impact on the outcome of the Civil War; explain the role New Mexico played in the United States participation in the Spanish American War; and analyze how people and events of New Mexico have influenced United States and world history since statehood.

In 9th through 12th grades, students compare and contrast the relationships over time of Native American tribes in New Mexico with other cultures; analyze the geographic, economic, social, and political factors of New Mexico that impacted United States and world history; analyze the role and impact of New Mexico and New Mexicans in World War II; analyze the impact of the arts, sciences, and technology of New Mexico since World War II; and explain how New Mexico history represents a framework of knowledge and skills within which to understand the complexity of the human experience. Similar lists of topics, events and people are provided for each grade-level for United States and World history.

As a teacher, my preference is for broader thematic strands rather than detailed content-based frameworks. They emphasize that we are supposed to be revisiting the same basic ideas and questions across the curriculum and provide more space for flexibility in planning, which increases the possibility of responding to student-generated ideas and questions. The reality, however, is that the standards are being defined by politicians who are distant from the classroom and with little, if any, knowledge of how students learn. Rather than using them as blueprints for instruction, social studies teachers have to adapt these standards for practical classroom use.

Essay 1: What We Should Teach*

The graduate section of the social studies methods class at Hofstra University has 31 students who plan to become middle school or high school social studies teachers. The size of the class can make discussion difficult; this is a group of people who like to talk, but I still have them sit in something that approximates a circle. As students enter the room, I hand them a three-question "surprise quiz." The first question is multiple-choice. The second and third questions require brief written responses.

After students complete the "quiz," I break the class up into groups of four designed so there are students with different choices in each group. I give the groups very general instructions: Examine your points of agreement and disagreement. Try to resolve your differences.

While the students deliberate, I join each group. One issue that keeps reappearing is whether the land "should be considered America before it was named America." This generally leads students to discuss, "What is America?" I find myself asking roughly the same questions in each group. "Did the voyage of Columbus bring about such a major change that there is basic discontinuity between what existed before and after the voyage?" "Can we agree on a set of criteria that we can use to evaluate the Native American's contribution to American history?"

Classroom Activity: When Does American History Begin?

1. What year(s) does American history begin?
   - 40,000–20,000BC: People first migrate from Asia across the Bering land bridge.
   - 985–1000AD: Vikings from Scandinavia explore the western North Atlantic.
   - 1492AD: The first voyage of Christopher Columbus.
   - 1565AD: Spanish settlement is established at St Augustine in Florida.
   - 1607AD: The first permanent British settlement at Jamestown, Virginia.
   - 1619AD: The first enslaved Africans are brought to Jamestown.
   - 1620AD: Pilgrims arrive in what will become Massachusetts.
   - 1776–1783AD: Declaration of Independence followed by a successful war for separation.

---

* Names of participants are fictitious in this essay.

- 1787–1789AD: The Constitution is written and a new government is formed.
- 1861–1865AD: The US Civil War.
- Another date/event _____

2. Why do you select this event?
3. Would your answer be different if the question asked, "What year(s) does United States history begin?" Why?

Try it yourself:
Which date would you select? Why?

Add your voice to the discussion:
Do you believe that a question like this has a "right answer?" Why?

It's your classroom:
How could you use this activity to promote discussion in a high school classroom? Why?
How would you resolve disagreements among students? Why?

After reassembling as a full class, groups report on their discussions. The first group agreed on the migration of nomadic peoples from Asia as the start of American history. One group member explains that, "We shouldn't just define things in European terms. People were here before the arrival of the Europeans. It is important for students to know about their cultures." A student from another group thinks that including the native peoples is carrying the idea of American history to an illogical extreme. He counters, "Why not just start with the continent's geological formation. It had existence independent of people."

This comment opens up a wide-ranging discussion. Donald argues that the voyage of Columbus is the single most important event setting off conquest, migration, and change. It defines what comes after it. Another student adds that the idea of America does not even exist until it is named by a German mapmaker based on the accounts of Vespucci and Columbus.

A woman in the class interrupts. She says she was uncertain about her answer, but "in a real sense, what we know of as America doesn't start until the Declaration of Independence." Someone says we have to consider whether "America would be America if there had been no Native Americans." Cathy responds "there were crucial native contributions that made it possible for the Europeans to survive and prosper. This meant they had to be included."

Darlene says the question for her is, "What do we choose as important in US history for students to understand? We cannot include everything." She believes that "American identity and experience as we know it really starts with British settlement." But she recognizes that this is her opinion, not something that can be presented as historical fact. One of the

men adds, "How can we call it American history before the European arrival? The earlier nomadic people who settled here were important, but not crucial." He concludes that, "America begins with the Declaration of Independence." Jean agrees there are many things Europeans had learned from the Indians, but she believes the crucial developments took place somewhere between the British settlement and independence. Harvey adds "the British remained British in India; in the US they became American. This is what has to be explored."

Anthony believes that "American history starts at different times in different localities. It isn't one uniform nation until after the Civil War. Maybe that is the starting point." Tom says he feels that the key is identity: "When did Americans identify as a separate and distinct people?" Alice feels that this idea also contains problems: "America is pluralistic; there are still some people that don't share this common identity. We define everything by the experiences of white Anglo-Saxon males. But that's not the way it is."

Bart insists that, as teachers, we have a responsibility "to teach students the facts," but Sharon counters, "What are the facts? What if we don't agree on the facts?" Carol adds, "Students need to discover the facts for themselves, to form their own opinions and to listen to each other." Marie suggests letting students debate a question such as: "When does American history begin?" Bart still is not satisfied. "Students don't know anything yet. They have to learn the facts first. How can they decide when American history begins and who contributed?"

Lisa says that there are no right answers to some questions: "The key goal is to get students to think and explore the different answers about what makes America 'America.' They need to form opinions based on the information they have available to them.

Then as they get new information they can rethink their opinions. It isn't useful to talk about right or wrong answers."

At this point, I enter the discussion. I ask the class, "Are all answers equally good?" Jim responds, "We have different interpretations of when American history begins because we have different concepts of America, as a place, a people, an idea, a continent. We need to help students develop criteria to evaluate answers. This is part of what they are learning; it's what historians do."

We spend the rest of the time trying to establish criteria to decide if the pre-Columbian experiences of the native peoples should be considered part of American history. Most of us conceptualize history as a single timeline of events. I suggest that it might be more useful to think of history as a river with a number of different tributaries. The native contributions are one of the tributaries; so are the European and African contributions. Students can examine the past and try to decide how large or important a stream it is.

One student asks, "Are you saying that African history is also part of the river? It must be a very small part," he says. At this point the class erupts into discussion again. Anthony outlines the triangular trade and the importance of African labor in creating the wealth of the Americas. Jim argues that the profits from the slave trade financed the Industrial Revolution in Europe. Cathy says, "You're stretching the point. They were brought as slaves. How much can they be credited for these developments." Marie asks, "Should we include everybody? How do we include the newest immigrants?" Darlene answers, "Why not at least include the kids in our classes. Show where their families entered the stream." Someone else asks what the state wants us to teach, but it is already ten minutes past the end of the class time. These issues will have to be part of other discussions.

Teaching Activity: History is a River

Add your voice to the discussion:
What do you think of this metaphor: "History is a river with a number of different tributaries?" Why?

It's your classroom:
Teachers are always making choices. Which experiences would you include in the "American River?" Which would you emphasize? Why?

Teaching Activity: The Tree of Liberty

After studying the United States Constitution, I have students create posters that illustrate their views about the fundamental nature of American society. They identify its roots, trunk, branches, leaves and fruit. Posters are hung on the wall and each student makes a presentation to class. Often the images are profoundly different. For example, should racism and/or freedom be considered "roots"? How much "bitter fruit" should be included on the tree?

Add your voice to the discussion:
Create you own symbolic "Tree of Liberty." What do you include? Why?

It's your classroom:
Would you use an assignment similar to this one in your class? At what grade-level? Explain.

Essay 2: What are the Essential Questions?

As a high school social studies teacher, I distributed newspapers and news magazines to teams of students in my 11th grade United States history classes at the start of the semester. The student teams were assigned to select five articles that they believed reported on important issues facing the United States in the contemporary world. Teams had to write down the headlines of the articles and their reasons for selecting them. At the end of the period, students listed the topics of the articles on the board and I asked at least one group to report on their deliberations.

On the second day, the rest of the groups reported. After the presentations, students categorized the issues facing the United States, identified underlying problems raised by the news articles, and discussed questions they wanted to answer during the year. Articles on racial discrimination, sexual harassment, and police brutality led to questions such as, "Can the United States become a more just society?" Topics like welfare reform, healthcare, unemployment, tax breaks, and crime prompted students to ask, "What is the responsibility (or job) of government?" Other questions developed by students have included, "Should the United States be the world's police force?" and "Is technology making the world a better place?" Essential questions can be placed on poster boards and hung prominently around the room. Students took pride in the questions they came up with, and the project increased their willingness to participate in class and furthered our exploration of social studies and history.

During the course of the school year, student-generated questions, especially about social justice and the responsibility of government, led to other "big" questions, and provided a focus for studying about the past, understanding the present, and deciding how to engage the future. The key to the "essential question approach" is to respect student questions and to encourage student voices. Teachers in the New Teacher Network have used this same approach successfully in Global History, Economics and United States government classes.

Kenneth Dwyer recommends the following questions developed by Kevin Sheehan and the social studies department in Oceanside, New York for use in Global history classes. Teachers at Oceanside also assemble a packet of documents for each unit that students examine and use to discuss one of these questions.

OCEANSIDE HIGH SCHOOL'S ESSENTIAL QUESTIONS FOR GLOBAL HISTORY

- What is civilization?
- To what extent are civilized societies uncivilized?
- Is contemporary civilization superior to civilizations of the ancient world?
- Is geography destiny?
- How do societies change?
- Is cultural diffusion a positive or negative force in world history?
- Do advances in technology really improve society?
- Is the diffusion of ideas more powerful than the diffusion of goods?
- Was imperialism an inevitable consequence of industrialization and nationalism?
- Is nationalism a positive or negative force?
- Can wars be prevented?
- Can political revolutions achieve their goals?
- Do people control governments or do governments control people?
- Does the world's diversity make for a stronger planet or lead to inevitable conflict?
- Is the world today a better world than the world we studied in previous ages?
- Can the world learn to live without global conflict in our life times?
- Will the world be able to more successfully deal with its problems in the coming century?

Join the discussion:
1. What questions would you add to the list?
2. Which questions would you drop or modify? How?

Similarly, Maureen Murphy, the English education coordinator at Hofstra and I (Murphy and Singer 2001) organized the New York State Great Irish Famine curriculum guide to address a series of essential questions in global history. For example, in 1861, Irish nationalist John Mitchel charged that "(N)o sack of Magdeburg, or ravage of the Palatinate ever approached the horror and dislocation to the slaughters done in Ireland by mere official red tape and stationery, and the principles of political economy. . . The Almighty sent the potato blight, but the English created the famine."

Whether or not one agrees with Mitchel's accusation about British policy in Ireland during the Great Irish Famine, his statement contains a number of key ideas about Irish, British, and world history. The sack of Magdeburg, a German Protestant city, by the forces of the Catholic League—which included Italy, France and Spain—in 1631, was part of the Thirty Years War in Reformation Europe. The ravaging of the Palatinate, also in Germany, by the forces of Louis XIV of France from 1688–1697, was more directly related to imperial ambition during an era of European colonial expansion. Both of these conquests, as well as the British conquest and rule over Ireland, force students and historians to consider human motivation and behavior during times of war; the legitimacy of religions and religious leaders who urge war to promote or enforce beliefs; and the relationship between large powers and their smaller, vulnerable neighbors. Significantly, these are all major questions confronting the world today: the Balkans and central Africa (war), South-west Asia and Afghanistan (religion), and the United States' role in the Americas (use of power). In addition,

Mitchel is asking us to explore causality in history, the workings of a laissez-faire political economy, the nature of bureaucracy, and collective responsibility for government action (or inaction). One small quote unleashes a slew of major issues and powerful questions.

An essential questions approach to Irish and world history uses current events to help high school students and teachers frame and examine complex and controversial questions about the contemporary world, and uses these questions to direct their examination of the past. It draws on Grant Wiggins's work on social studies teaching methods; Paulo Freire's belief that education must involve students in posing and examining questions about the problems facing their own communities; and the National Council for the Social Studies *Handbook On Teaching Social Issues*.

Wiggins argues that teachers should present students with broad questions without simple answers that are reintroduced over and over throughout the curriculum. For social studies, he suggest questions such as these: Is there enough to go around (e.g., food, clothes, water)? Is history a story of progress? When is law unjust? Who owns what and why? We have students develop their own questions about the past, present, and future. We recommend starting the school year with teams of students searching through newspapers and selecting articles they believe report on important issues facing the contemporary world. Teams categorize the issues, identify underlying problems, and formulate the questions they want to answer. Their big questions are placed on poster boards, hung prominently around the room, and referred to continuously.

ESSENTIAL QUESTIONS FROM THE NEW YORK STATE GREAT IRISH FAMINE CURRICULUM

The Great Irish Famine Curriculum (available at: http://www.emsc.nysed.gov/nysssa/gif/index.html, accessed April 14, 2007) started with a few thematic questions. However, it was designed so that new questions would continually be introduced as students explored global history. These twelve essential questions emerged when teachers field-tested the Great Irish Famine curriculum in secondary school social studies classes.

- Can a small thing or event transform the world?
- What role does religion play in human history?
- How does technology change the way people live and work?
- Are famines more often acts of nature or the result of decisions by people with power?
- What are the consequences of ethnic prejudice?
- What is the responsibility of government in times of disaster?
- What is the responsibility of the media when it reports the news?
- What are the responsibilities of individuals when faced with injustice or calamity?
- What causes imperialism?

- What are human rights?
- What is genocide?
- Can individuals and groups shape the future?

Try it yourself:
Select three of the essential questions from this list and write a brief essay expressing your views.

At workshops with high school teachers, participants generally express three major concerns with an essential questions approach to social studies curriculum. They worry about the need to prepare students for standardized tests; the problem of establishing historical truth when multiple voices and controversial positions are introduced into discussion; and their ability as teachers to conduct an open and civil classroom discourse if sharp conflicts emerge.

I find the problem of preparing students for standardized exams is the easiest to address. On most standardized tests, students do not pass or fail because of the specific social studies content presented in class or in textbooks. Students do well on these examinations when they are engaged by discussion in class, understand the general social studies concepts integrated into the curriculum, and have adequate reading and writing skills. No specific piece of information is ever absolutely crucial.

In 14 years as a high school social studies teacher, I never taught a specific lesson on the collapse of the Ottoman Turkish Empire (though I did discuss the Armenian genocide with students). Students need to understand both the positive and negative effects of nationalism and modernization, and they should examine the global impact of World War I, but they can examine these historical concepts and events while looking at Germany, Italy, Russia, Eastern Europe, Africa, China, India, or Turkey. They can touch on them again when they discuss post-World War I Kenya, Vietnam, Iran, China, or Algeria. It is both impossible and undesirable for students to memorize extensive details about each place on Earth and its history. An engaged student is much more likely to be successful in school and in life than is someone who passively copies volumes of notes from the board.

The debate over what makes something true is a lot harder to resolve, and I do not have a simple solution. The dispute over what constitutes truth is not new; the meaning of truth and the possibility of acquiring it have been debated throughout world history, especially in Western intellectual traditions. For example, according to the multi-volume *Great Books of the Western World* (Adler 1952: 915, 920), a collaboration between the University of Chicago

and the Encyclopedia Britannica, "the great issues concern whether we can know the truth and how we can ever tell whether something is true or false. Though the philosophers and scientists, from Plato to Freud, seem to stand together against the extreme sophistry or skepticism which denies the distinction between true and false or puts truth utterly beyond the reach of man, they do not all agree on the extent to which truth is attainable by men, on its immutability or variability, on the signs by which men tell whether they have the truth or not, or on the causes of error and the means for avoiding falsity." While Aristotle argued that we should accept theories as true "only if what they affirm agrees with the observed facts," many of our students, and many of our colleagues, probably would agree with Augustine and Spinoza, "God is the warranty of the inner voice which plainly signifies the truth." If these noted philosophers could not decide whether something is true or not, why should students take our word that what we say is true, and what they believe is false. Perhaps one of our essential questions should simply be, "What is truth?"

I am not suggesting an everything-goes attitude or that every statement about the past is equally valid. But what social studies teachers need to acknowledge is that we are a lot less certain than we like to pretend and that we are also susceptible to being trapped by comforting myths. Instead of insisting that students accept one version of immutable facts, we need to help them become practicing historians and social scientists who weigh evidence, evaluate theories, and work collectively to establish and continually reevaluate criteria for understanding our world.

Discussion of essential questions requires introducing historical topics (e.g., government policy during famines, the African slave trade, or the European Holocaust) and points of view that have the potential to produce sharp conflict in social studies classes. Teachers are often concerned that they will not be able to control classroom discussions. But conflict is not necessarily bad; it can be a creative force that pushes people to delve deeper into issues and to find evidence to support their opinions. Control, on the other hand, is not necessarily good—especially when it stifles intellectual freedom and student voice.

Heated discussion, if it is going to be productive, requires that people listen to each other and respond to each other's ideas. In my experience, this happens more effectively in a democratic community than it does in an authoritarian, teacher-controlled environment. In order for a social studies curriculum based on an examination of essential questions and controversial issues to be effective, students need to feel related to each other and to their teachers, and must have respect for other people and their intelligence, even when there is disagreement about the validity of particular ideas. Students need to engage in dialogues, rather than debating to win, and need to see themselves as part of a shared quest to study and understand the world (Pezone and Singer 1997: 75–79).

References and Recommendations for Further Reading

Adler, M., ed. 1952. *Great books of the western world*, vol. 3. Chicago, IL: Encyclopedia Britannica.

Berk, L. 1994. Vygotsky's theory: The importance of make-believe play. *Young Children*, November: 30–39.

Bloom, A. 1987. *The closing of the American mind*. New York: Simon and Schuster.

Calkins, L. 1983. *Lessons from a child: On the teaching and learning of writing*. Exeter, NH: Heinemann Educational Books.

Center for Civic Education. 1994. *National standards for civics and government*. Calabasas, CA: CCE.

Clark, S. 1986. *Ready from within: Septima Clark and the Civil Rights movement*. Navarro, CA: Wild Trees Press.

Dewey, J. 1916. *Democracy and education*. New York: Macmillan.

Dewey, J. 1938/1963. *Experience and education*. New York: Collier/Macmillan.

Dewey, J. 1939. *Freedom and culture*. New York: G. P. Putnam.

DuBois, W. E. B. 1961. *The souls of Black folk*. New York: Fawcett.

Finn, C., Jr. and Ravitch, D. 1987. *What do our 17-year-olds know? A report on the first national assessment of history and literature*. New York: Harper and Row.

Freire, P. 1970. *Pedagogy of the oppressed*. New York: Seabury.

Freire, P. 1995. *Pedagogy of hope*. New York: Continuum.

Gandini, L. 1993. "November. Fundamentals of the Reggio Emila approach to early childhood education," *Young Children* 4–9.

Gardner, H. 1987. "Beyond IQ: Education and human development," *Harvard Educational Review* 57(2).

Giroux, H. 1983. *Theory and resistance in education, A pedagogy for the opposition*. South Hadley, MA: Bergin and Garvey.

Giroux, H. 1992. *Border crossings, Cultural workers and the politics of education*. New York: Routledge.

Hamilton, V. 1985. *The people could fly*. New York: Alfred A. Knopf.

Hirsch, E., Jr. 1987. *Cultural literacy: What every American needs to know*. Boston, MA: Houghton Mifflin.

Horton, M., with J. Kohl and H. Kohl. 1990. *The long haul: An autobiography*. New York: Doubleday.

Kohn, A. 1986. *No contest: The case against competition*. Boston, MA: Houghton Mifflin.

Ladson-Billings, G. 1994. *The dreamkeepers: Successful teachers of African-American children*. San Francisco: Jossey-Bass.

McIntosh, P. 1983. "Interactive Phases of Curricular Re-Vision: A Feminist Perspective," *Working Paper No. 124*. Wellesley, MA: Wellesley College Center for Research on Women.

Meier, D. 1995. *The Power of their ideas: Lessons for America from a small school in Harlem*. Boston, MA: Beacon.

Murphy, M. and A. Singer, A. 2001. "Asking the big questions: Teaching about the Great Irish Famine and world history," *Social Education* 65(5): 286–91.

National Center for History in the Schools. 1994. *National standards for United States History: Exploring the American experience*. Los Angeles, CA: NCHS.

National Council for the Social Studies. 1994. *Expectations of excellence: Curriculum standards for social studies. NCSS bulletin 89*. Washington DC: NCSS.

New York State Department of Education. 1987. *9 & 10 grade global studies syllabus*. Albany, NY: State Department of Education.

Newman, F. and Holtzman, L. 1992. *Lev Vygotzky: Revolutionary scientist*. New York: Routledge.

Noddings, N. 1992a. *The challenge to care in schools*. New York: Teachers College Press.

Noddings, N. 1992b. "Social studies and feminism," *Theory and research in social education* 20(3): 230–41.

Pezone M. and Singer, A. 1997. "Empowering immigrant students through democratic dialogues," *Social Education* 61(2).

Reiber, R. and Carton, A. eds. 1997. *The collected works of L. S. Vygotsky, vol. 1. Problems of general psychology*. New York: Plenum.

Rethinking Schools. 1994. *Rethinking our classrooms: Teaching for equity and justice*. Milwaukee, WI: Rethinking Schools.

Rethinking Schools. 2007. "Why students should study history: An interview with Howard Zinn," in W. Au, B. Bigelow and S. Karp, eds. *Rethinking our classrooms, vol. 1.* 2nd edn. Madison, WI: Rethinking Schools, pp. 179–185.

Rugg, H. 1923. *National society for the study of education twenty-second yearbook*. Bloomington, IL: Public School Publishing Co.

Stern, P., ed. 1940. *The life and writings of Abraham Lincoln*. New York: Modern Library.

Wigginton, E. 1985. *Sometimes a shining moment: The Foxfire experience*. New York: Anchor/ Doubleday.

5. Is Social Studies Teaching "Political"?

Overview

- Examine the goals of different educational theorists
- Explore ideas about democratic and transformative classrooms
- Connect educational theory and social studies practice
- Examine the political nature of curriculum debates

Key Concepts

Goals, Politics, Academic Freedom, Transformative Education, Democratic Community

Questions

- Is Everything Political?
- Should Teachers Discuss their Opinions in Class?
- Why is Defense of Academic Freedom Important?
- Should Teachers Encourage Students to Work for Social Justice?
- How can Classroom Teachers Empower Students?
- How do Teachers Translate Educational Theory Into Social Studies Practice?
- What Does a Classroom Based on Transformative Principles Look Like?

Essays

1. Social Studies Under Attack
2. TAH means "Traditional" American History
3. Are Activist Teachers "Social Predators"?

IS EVERYTHING POLITICAL?

In August 2003, *New York Times* columnist Paul Krugman (2003), who is an award winning author and professor of economics at Princeton University, wrote an essay critical of the Bush administration where he expressed concern that all its decisions, including those that should have been based on the technical competence of experts in different fields, had been politicized. He cited examples from the Treasury Department, the Central Intelligence Agency, the Environmental Protection Administration, and the National Institutes of Health. Critics have also charged that the Clinton administration, where advisors constantly evaluated public opinion polls before the president defined his positions on issues, functioned in a similar way.

Professor Krugman should not have been so surprised by either the influence of politics in the Bush administration or the absence of principle. The political nature of human decision-making is not a new discovery. In the fourth century BC, Aristotle wrote about ethics and politics in the Greek city-states and argued that people must be understood as political animals that were perfectible, but also capable of injustice and savagery. Machiavelli, whose advice to the rulers of Florence during the European Renaissance focused entirely on the art of politics, warned politicians that if they were going to be successful, they could not be moral. In the nineteenth century, British Prime Minister Benjamin Disraeli recognized that politics and politicians had no honor, claimed that principles had no meaning, and argued that party loyalty should be valued above all else (Seldes 1966: 66, 208, 454).

My answer to Paul Krugman is "Yes. Everything is political." This is especially true when it comes to teaching social studies. As you read this chapter, I think you will agree. Our choice as social studies teachers is whether we allow political forces to dictate to us, or we become activists who shape what takes place in our classrooms and who influence broader policy debates.

Teaching Activity: Who Decides What Gets Taught?

Control over the curriculum, what gets taught, is often contested by teachers, school-based administrators, district officials, and state education departments. Should students also have a say? In the tumultuous 1960s, many African-American secondary school students petitioned and even struck demanding Black history classes. Many teachers allow students to select report topics or books to read. But should they also participate in decisions about what units will be taught and documents used?

As a high school teacher, at the beginning of the school year, I used newspaper articles to help students define the major issues confronting the nation and the world. They developed questions about the past and present based on their thoughts about the issues (e.g., Should the United States act as a police for the world? What should be the responsibility of government? Can the United States become a more just society? Should environmental concerns outweigh development?). As their teacher, I responded by organizing units to address their questions.

On one occasion, I proposed possible case studies the class could focus on (the impact of imperialism on China, India, or sub-Saharan Africa; revolutionary movements in Algeria or Iran, Congo or Kenya, Cuba, Mexico or Nicaragua, and Vietnam or Malaysia). Students did preliminary reports on the regions and the class decided which ones we would study.

Add your voice to the discussion:
1. Should creating a democratic classroom be a goal for social studies teachers? Explain.
2. How much of a role should students have in deciding what gets taught? Explain.

WHY WAS THE DEBATE ON NATIONAL HISTORY STANDARDS SO HEATED?

Recognizing the political nature of debate over the social studies curriculum is only the beginning. An example of how difficult it is to modify a social studies curriculum is the explosion that followed the release of voluntary "national history standards" in October 1994.

According to the US Department of Education (1994), the purpose of "content standards" in different subject areas is to "define what all students should know and be able to do. They describe the knowledge, skills, and understandings that students should have in order to attain high levels of competency in challenging subject matter." In addition, performance standards identify expected "levels of achievement in the subject matter," and the ways that students "demonstrate their competency in a subject." The Department of Education and most advocates for national standards stressed that they were not proposing mandatory curriculum guidelines with lesson plans. Even if general standards were adopted, it would remain the job of state committees, school districts, and individual teachers to decide what was taught in the classroom and how it would be done.

The idea of developing national educational standards in social studies and other subject areas was fueled during the 1980s by concern that American secondary school students trailed their foreign contemporaries in academic performance. National standards were endorsed by the Republican administration of George W. H. Bush at a national governors' conference in 1989, and in 1994 they were included in "GOALS 2000" legislation signed by Democratic President Bill Clinton.

At first glance, the creation of broad voluntary national standards sounds like an activity appropriate for classroom teachers familiar with what is taught in different secondary school subjects on a daily basis. However, the development of national standards for social studies quickly became a contested battleground involving academics, public and private funding agencies, politicians, and competing professional organizations. As a result of pressure from historians, the social studies were divided into different fields: the National Center for History in Schools wrote history standards, the National Council for Geographic Education wrote geography standards, the Center for Civic Education wrote civics and government standards, and the National Council for Economic Education wrote economics standards. Meanwhile, the National

Council for the Social Studies independently created a separate set of standards which integrated history and the social sciences.

When the US and world history standards were released by the National Center for History in Schools, they included suggested approaches to the study of history, statements outlining broad historical themes, lists of topics to analyze, and suggestions for how some of the themes and topics could be examined in social studies classes. Although the broader themes and topics were generally ignored by critics, the classroom suggestions quickly became a lightening rod for conservative discontent with public education, multiculturalism, immigration, ethnic identity movements, a declining US economy, and "eroding family values." The standards were widely denounced in the popular media; a columnist for *US News and World Report* (Natale 1995) charged that they placed "Western civilization . . . on a par with the Kush and the Carthagians," and they were overwhelmingly rejected by the US Senate.

Teaching Activity: What did the United States Purchase in 1803?

Controversy about historical issues frequently intensifies as curricula become more specific. For example, according to an 11th-grade United States history textbook (Danzer et al. 2005: 201):

> "In 1800, Napoleon Bonaparte of France persuaded Spain to return the Louisiana Territory, which it had received from France in 1762. When the news of the secret transfer leaked out, Americans reacted with alarm . . . Jefferson wanted to resolve the problem by buying New Orleans and western Florida from the French. He sent James Monroe to join American ambassador Robert Livingston in Paris. Before Monroe arrived, however, Napoleon had abandoned his hopes for an America empire . . . [I]n 1803, Napoleon had decided to sell the entire Louisiana Territory to the United States."

National Standards for United States History, Grades 5–12 (1996a, available at: http://www.sscnet.ucla.edu/nchs/standards/era4–5-12.html, accessed April 19, 2007) supports this perspective on the Louisiana purchase. It says that students should be able to: "Demonstrate understanding of the international background and consequences of the Louisiana Purchase," which includes "analyzing Napoleon's reasons for selling Louisiana to the United States, comparing the arguments advanced by Democratic Republicans and Federalists regarding the acquisition of Louisiana," and "analyzing the consequences of the Louisiana Purchase for United States politics, economic development, and race relations, and describing its impact on Spanish and French inhabitants."

Neither the text nor the standard has students examine this question: What did the United States purchase in 1803? Yet, despite European imperial pretensions, neither France nor Spain occupied or controlled the area they identified as Louisiana. In reality, it was occupied and controlled by Native American nations who never recognized foreign sovereignty over their traditional lands. What the United States purchased was France's "claim" to this territory, but it had to wage decades of war against native peoples before it established control.

Add your voice to the discussion:
Was US expansion west an act of imperialism? If so, did the ends justify the means? Explain your answers.

Think it over:
Should a discussion of these issues be introduced in middle school and high school social studies classrooms? Why or why not?

It's your classroom:
1. What do you think we should teach about the Louisiana Purchase? Why?
2. How would you teach it? Why?

Initially, the historians and educational groups who developed the history standards vigorously defended them at professional conferences and in social studies publications. The Organization of American Historians dedicated an entire theme issue of its magazine for secondary school teachers to a discussion of the standards (Nash 1995). Spokespeople for the National Center for History in Schools (Thomas 1996) stressed that the standards were voluntary, and accused critics of a "disinformation campaign." In response to charges that references to "McCarthyism and the rise of the Ku Klux Klan put too much emphasis on failings in our nation's history," they responded that "these episodes demonstrate for students the strength of the democratic system to protect itself, as long as concerned and vigilant citizens use the power of its institutions to turn back such assaults." They also argued that, "situating European history within its global context does not 'diminish' Western history. On the contrary, students are likely to gain a far better understanding of the relationship of European to world developments if the framework for their studies is the human community as a whole."

As the attacks continued, politically important proponents of national educational standards distanced themselves from the history proposals. Diane Ravitch, an Undersecretary of Education during the Bush administration, and Albert Shanker, former President of the American Federation of Teachers, both favored revising the history standards so that their "flaws" could be eliminated.

In April 1996, the National Center for History in Schools issued a new single volume of revised national history standards. *The New York Times* (Thomas 1996) noted that, based on recommendations by two review panels, the revised standards eliminated "their most criticized feature: the examples of classroom activities." The review panels wanted the teaching examples dropped because of concern that they invited students "to make facile moral judgments."

The new standards, minus the teaching suggestions, were almost as widely acclaimed as the original draft was condemned. Christopher T. Cross, President of the Council for Basic Education, declared, "The revised history standards are excellent. The UCLA National Center for History in the Schools has listened well to the criticisms of the earlier documents, has made substantial improvements throughout, and created a new document that will serve schools well as a guide to improving the teaching of US and world history."

Diane Ravitch and Arthur Schlesinger, Jr. celebrated the changes in an article for *The Wall Street Journal* (Ravitch and Schlesinger 1996). They praised the removal of references to Mansa Musa's African Empire, the Ku Klux Klan, Senator Joseph McCarthy, and numerous obscure people who, they believe, had been included because they were non-white, non-males. Ravitch and Schlesinger felt that the revised edition correctly focused on "America's developing democratic tradition, the movement from exclusion to inclusion . . . While attention is rightly directed to our nation's troubled history of racial, ethnic and religious tension, these issues are now placed within the context of the nation's continuing quest to make our practices conform to our ideals" (Ravitch and Schlesinger 1996: 14).

If I read the initial criticisms and the later praise correctly, the first versions of the national history standards were rejected because they moved beyond broad generalities and discussed the ideas and information that teachers would present in social studies classes. The teaching suggestions were unacceptable because they involved students in examining fundamental assumptions about history, American society, and world civilizations, exactly what I believe social studies is supposed to be about in a democratic society.

Has the United States been engaged in a "continuing quest to make our practice conform to our ideals" or have the country's ideals frequently been subjects of sharp disagreement (e.g., slavery, women's rights, reproductive freedom, immigration quotas)? Changes in practice are frequently the result of long-term struggles. Should the view that there is an evolving national consensus be assumed, or should multiple views be presented to students so they can sift through evidence and explanations to formulate their own interpretations?

Teaching Activity: Can a Social Studies Curriculum be Non-political?

"A nation denied a conception of its past will be disabled in dealing with its present and its future. As the means of defining national identity, history becomes a means of shaping history. The writing of history then turns from a mediation into a weapon. 'Who controls the past controls the future,' runs the Party slogan in George Orwell's *1984*; 'who controls the present controls the past'" Arthur Schlesinger, Jr. (1992: 46).

Add your voice to the discussion:
In your opinion, can social studies curricula be nonpolitical? Explain your answer.

Think it over:
As a beginning teacher, how do you explain your curriculum choices?

It's your classroom:
How do you make it possible for your students to become critical thinkers prepared for active citizenship in a democratic society?

SHOULD TEACHERS EXPRESS THEIR OPINIONS IN CLASS?

New teachers are often uncertain whether they should express their opinions during class discussions, especially when their views are politically controversial. As educators and employees, beginning teachers are concerned with the professional ethics of stating their views, the pedagogical implications of both expression and silence, and the impact their statements will have on the ideas of their students. In addition, they worry how their views and their willingness to express them publicly will be perceived by students, colleagues, supervisors, and parents.

Teachers, especially new teachers, can be frightened by school and public officials who try to silence them or who cave into pressure from parents and political pressure groups. There are always stories like this one in the media. In 2003, the contract of an elementary school teacher in Bloomington, Indiana was not renewed after she told students in her class that she sometimes "honks for peace." A state court later upheld her dismissal because the judges felt "teachers . . . do not have a right under the First Amendment to express their opinions with their students during the instructional period" (Rothschild 2006). Many new teachers opt to take the "safe" way out of this conundrum, and keep their views to themselves.

At this point, we need to put aside our political fears (at least temporarily) and examine the educational issues involved. Politically safe choices may not be the soundest educational policies. I do not have a set rule about when teachers should offer their opinion in class, but I have no question that a teacher's views can be vital contributions to discussion in a democratic and critical classroom.

Myles Horton and Paulo Freire (1990), whose ideas are discussed again later in this chapter, believe that knowledge is never neutral. Horton and Freire argue that every curriculum decision made by a teacher (e.g., which documents to introduce, facts to emphasize, questions to ask, students to call on) reflects a point of view. If that is the case, and I think it is, the question is not whether we express our opinions in class, but whether we express them openly so that students can evaluate them and feel free to agree or disagree with them.

When teachers state their views and open them up for evaluation by the class, it is a judgment based on their short- and long-term goals for their students and on the dynamic of a particular lesson. The long-term goals always are to promote student critical thinking and to model the making of informed choices based on an evaluation of evidence. Consider the following series of ideas as you think about whether you want to add your opinions to classroom discussion.

1. As teachers, we have to consider our goals and how we will achieve them when we decide whether we want to add our views to the intellectual hopper. Will a statement of our views open up discussion, close it down,

111

or send it off on a tangent? Will it make it possible for students to consider new ideas? Will it empower students, particularly those who feel silenced by the classroom majority, to express unpopular views?

2. When teachers express personal views, it demonstrates their willingness to share in classroom dialogue and open their opinions up for evaluation. It says to students that it is okay to take intellectual risks.

3. John Dewey argues that people learn from what they experience in class, rather than from what is said. If teachers are afraid to speak out because of intolerance or political pressure, how will students learn to function within and to defend a democratic society?

4. Sometimes I withhold my opinion because I am concerned whether the class discussion is doing justice to a position with which I disagree. Rather than play devil's advocate, I search for material that presents that view. On occasion, I have invited another teacher, a parent, or someone from a local advocacy group to meet with the class. When these people express their views clearly, it gives me more freedom to respond.

5. There is a tendency to present disagreement as bi-polar, representing two opposing positions. Teachers want students to understand that there is really a broad range of ideas and a spectrum of positions.

6. A healthy democracy requires tolerance of diverse ideas. When a teacher takes an unusual or unpopular position on an issue, it helps students develop respect for people whose ideas are different from their own.

7. Some issues are emotionally charged, so sensitivity is required whenever teachers express their views. But that does not mean it is automatically wrong to upset students. Sometimes people need to get a little upset before they can reconsider their beliefs.

Whatever decision I make about expressing my views, I try to keep in mind that my goal is for students to think about ideas and consider their options, not to parrot my views. I want students to be critical thinkers, not disciples. I am not trying to create a cadre of fourteen-year-olds committed to my ideas. If students accept something as true because I say it, that only means they will also accept what they hear from their next teacher.

Teaching Activity: Should Teachers Express their Views?

Controversial issues continually emerge in social studies classrooms. Topics such as affirmative action, racial and ethnic tension, reproductive rights, freedom of speech and religion, and gender bias or harassment are almost always in the news, and they are frequently at issue in schools. Verdicts in highly publicized trials, the actions of celebrities, and government policy decisions (sending US troops to other parts of the world, or modifying social welfare programs) also stir widespread debate.

When I was a high school teacher, I made political buttons to respond to some of these events. Now, thanks to recent developments in technology, as mentioned previously, I make iron-on decals for T-shirts to wear in class. I have also purchased some really good "message" shirts from a company called Northern Sun (1/800–258–8579; available at: http://www.northernsun.com, accessed September 25, 2007). I usually wear the T-shirts under my regular shirts and at the end of a lesson climb on a chair, take off my tie and shirt, and use the T-shirt to enter classroom debate. The students generally cannot decide if I am being "cool" or ridiculous.

Add your voice to the discussion:
1. Should topics like these be discussed if they arise in a social studies classroom? Why or why not?
2. Should topics like these be included in social studies curriculum? Why or why not? How?
3. In your opinion, can teachers remain neutral in classroom discussions? Explain.
4. In your opinion, should teachers try to remain neutral? Why?
5. Under what circumstances would you give your opinion during classroom discussion? Why?

Classroom Activity: Current Events and Talking Points

One way to encourage students to express their views and to support them with evidence is by having them create current events packages on specific topics, such as the issues in a presidential campaign. I usually require students to collect a minimum of ten news articles, opinion articles, editorials and cartoons, from diverse sources. They have to write a summary of each article and a brief essay (250–500 words) stating their views on the issues and how they would address them. From their essays, I assemble a series of "talking points" for class discussion. To get the widest participation, each student signs up to address one of the "talking points." During the discussions I ask questions to stimulate deeper explanations and to get students to address each other's comments. Depending on the nature of the discussion, I may join in and express my views.

It's your classroom:
1. Would you use an activity such as this one in your class? Explain.
2. How might you modify it? Why?

WHY IS DEFENSE OF ACADEMIC FREEDOM IMPORTANT?

The National Council for the Social Studies is a strong supporter of academic freedom for both teachers and students. In 2007, its Board of Directors approved a statement declaring:

> "Academic freedom for social studies teachers includes the right and responsibility to study, investigate, present, interpret, discuss, and debate relevant facts, issues, and ideas in fields of the teacher's professional competence. Academic freedom for students in social studies courses provides the right to study, question, interpret, and discuss relevant facts, ideas, and issues under consideration in those courses. These freedoms imply no limitations, within the guidelines of the subject area ... Academic freedom, like the freedoms of speech, press, and religion, is not absolute. However, it is recognized by the NCSS as a fundamental element in teaching excellence and in the maintenance of our culture and government" (NCSS 2007: 282).

Other national professional organizations that are strongly identified with the defense of academic freedom include the American Association of School Librarians, American Association of University Professors, American Bar Association, American Civil Liberties Union, American Federation of Teachers, American Historical Association, American Library Association, National Council of Teachers of English, and National Education Association.

One of the things that frightens teachers is that academic freedom, even when exercised responsibly and cautiously, may be disapproved of by politicians, parents, and right wing ideologues. A parent criticized a member of the New Teachers Network who assigned an adolescent novel in her sociology elective class made up of high school seniors who were studying about teenage behavior. The parent found the book offensive because a passage referred to masturbation. The district officials initially supported the parent and ordered that the book be dropped from the class's reading list; however, they reversed their position because of organized pressure from other students, their families, the teacher's union, and local and national library associations (Hildebrand 2003: A25; Finn 2007; Doyle 2004).

Academic freedom was challenged on a number of fronts after the attacks on the World Trade Center and the Pentagon on September 11, 2001. In Maine, Governor John Baldacci criticized teachers for not maintaining neutrality in discussions about the impending United States war on Iraq (Dillon 2003: A1), although he did not make the same demand of elected officials, who are also public employees. In Colorado, after a teacher was reported wearing a button that said "Not My President, Not My War," school district officials issued instructions that teachers "avoid politicizing the classroom or disrupting the learning environment" and told them they should not be seen as espousing particular views (available at: http://www.foxnews.com/story/0,2933,80226,00.html, accessed September 21, 2007). According to Chester E. Finn Jr., a former assistant secretary of education, "The purpose of schools is not to turn our 10-year-olds into policy wonks." He did not believe students should discuss impending war until after it began (Dillon 2003: A1).

After the invasion of Iraq, efforts to limit academic freedom did not stop. At Overland High School in Colorado, a teacher was put on a paid leave for over a month because of his comments about the 2005 State of the Union address by President Bush (available at: http://www.spokesmanreview.com/blogs/hbo/archive.asp?postID=7192, accessed September 21, 2007). In Parsippany, New Jersey, a teacher's judgment was questioned because he had his class conduct a "mock trial" of President Bush for "crimes against civilian populations" and "inhumane treatment of prisoners" (available at: http://www.msnbc.msn.com/id/11654656/, accessed September 21, 2007). Each of these cases was an effort to prevent teachers and students from examining crucial events affecting the nation and their lives. They were efforts to enforce silence that run counter to the entire purpose of social studies education and the principles of a democratic society.

Academic freedom for students is usually governed by the 1969 Supreme Court ruling in Tinker v. Des Moines. In this decision, the majority of the court argued that students do not "shed their constitutional rights to freedom of speech or freedom of expression at the schoolhouse gate." It established as a standard that actual and symbolic speech were permitted as long as they do not "materially and substantially disrupt the work and discipline of the school." However, this yardstick has not been easy to employ by students, school districts, or lower courts. In Bethel School District v. Fraser (1986), the Supreme Court refined its position and allowed schools to prohibit "vulgar and offensive" speech. In attempting to apply this decision, a federal appeals court supported a high school that would not permit a student to wear a Marilyn Manson t-shirt because it was deemed contrary to the "educational mission of the school." In Vermont, local courts ruled that a middle school student could not wear an anti-Bush T-shirt on a school trip, but this decision was overturned on appeal (Applebome 2007: 37).

I expect to be challenged when I take controversial positions either as a teacher or a citizen. I would be disappointed if I was ignored. An article I wrote for *Rethinking Schools* about supporting student activism by encouraging them to organize official school clubs was attacked on conservative and Christian Right websites where I was branded a "social predator," who along with other "activist teachers," were exploiting children (Donnach 2003). Their response helped get the article a much broader readership than it ordinarily would have had.

Academic freedom only survives because teachers defend it and use it in their classrooms. In September 2007, when General Petraeus reported to the United States on efforts to end the civil war in Iraq, I developed the lesson that follows for members of the New Teachers Network. In this lesson, which makes extensive use of primary source documents, I tried to be both political and responsible. It creates space for teachers to join in conversations with their students as they "study, question, interpret, and discuss relevant facts, ideas, and issues."

Lesson aim: Should the US occupation of Iraq continue?

Introduction:

On September 12, 2007, President Bush spoke to the American people about the US military occupation of Iraq and its efforts to create a modern, democratic, nation. In the speech President Bush promised a gradual, but slight, reduction, in the number of American troops stationed in Iraq during the next year. President Bush's speech followed testimony to the US Congress by General George Petraeus, who is in charge of US military operations in Iraq. General Petraeus argued that the escalation of US forces in Iraq during the past year had helped to stabilize the country and made eventual US success more likely.

There is tremendous disagreement in the United States about the success of US policy in Iraq. There is also sharp debate about the broader issues of whether US military power can ever resolve deep-seated local divisions and whether is possible to impose democracy on another nation.

Assignment:
Read the excerpts from the statement by President Bush and some of the supporters and critics of US policy. President Bush makes a number of assertions in this speech that have been questioned by critics. As you read the speech, underline points that might be disputed and discuss them with team members. Working individually, answer the questions that follow the sections of this document package and complete the activity that follows all of the quotes.

A. Statement by President George W. Bush on the US Occupation of Iraq
Source: *The New York Times*, September 14, 2007, p. A8

"In Iraq, an ally of the United States is fighting for its survival. Terrorists and extremists who are at war with us around the world are seeking to topple Iraq's government, dominate the region and attack us here at home. If Iraq's young democracy can turn back these enemies, it will mean a more hopeful Middle East and a more secure America.

This ally has placed its trust in the United States, and tonight our moral and strategic imperatives are one. We must help Iraq defeat those who threaten its future and also threaten ours. Eight months ago, we adopted a new strategy to meet that objective, including a surge in US forces that reached full strength in June. This week General David Petraeus and Ambassador Ryan Crocker testified before Congress about how that strategy is progressing. In their testimony, these men made clear that our challenge in Iraq is formidable. Yet they concluded that conditions in Iraq are improving, that we are seizing the initiative from the enemy, and that the troop surge is working.

The premise of our strategy is that securing the Iraqi population is the foundation for all other progress . . . The goal of the surge is to provide that security and to help prepare Iraqi forces to maintain it . . . Our troops in Iraq are performing brilliantly. Along with the Iraqi forces, they have captured or killed an average of more than 1,500 enemy fighters per month since January. Yet ultimately, the way forward depends on the ability of Iraqis to maintain security gains. According to General Petraeus and a panel chaired by retired General Jim Jones, the Iraqi army is becoming more capable, although there is still a great deal of work to be done to improve the national police. Iraqi forces are receiving increased cooperation from local populations, and this is improving their ability to hold areas that have been cleared. Because of this success, General Petraeus believes we have now reached the point where we can maintain our security gains with fewer American forces . . . General Petraeus also recommends that in December we begin transitioning to the next phase of our strategy in Iraq. As terrorists are defeated, civil society takes root and the Iraqis assume more control over their own security, our mission in Iraq will evolve. Over time, our troops will shift from leading operations, to partnering with Iraqi forces, and eventually to over-watching those forces. As this transition in our mission takes place, our troops will focus on a more limited set of tasks, including counterterrorism operations and training, equipping, and supporting Iraqi forces . . .

The success of a free Iraq is critical to the security of the United States. A free Iraq will deny al Qaeda a safe haven. A free Iraq will counter the destructive ambitions of Iran. A free Iraq will marginalize extremists, unleash the talent of its people and be an anchor of stability in the region. A free Iraq will set an example for people across the Middle East. A free Iraq will be our partner in the fight against terror, and that will make us safer here at home. Realizing this vision will be difficult, but it is achievable. Our military commanders believe we can succeed. Our diplomats believe we can succeed. And for the safety of future generations of Americans, we must succeed."

Questions
1. Why does President Bush believe it is vital that American troops continue to fight in Iraq?
2. What was the strategy that President Bush chose to increase the chance of success?
3. How does President Bush evaluate that strategy in this speech?

B. Comments by 2008 Presidential Candidates on the Report by General Petraeus to Congress
Source: *The New York Times*, September 14, 2007, p. A16

Rudolph Giuliani (Republican): "General Petraeus provided the first look at a strategy that is getting results and an Iraq that is making progress."

Senator Hillary Rodham Clinton (Democrat): "I think that the reports that you provide to us really require the willing suspension of disbelief."

Senator John McCain (Republican): "General Petraeus and his troops ask just two things of us: the time to continue this strategy, and the support they need to carry out their mission. They must have both."

John Edwards (Democrat): "General Petraeus may propose the withdrawal of a single brigade by the end of the year in exchange for keeping the failed surge going another six months. This is not the withdrawal the American people voted for."

Fred Thompson (Republican): "General Petraeus' report strengthens my conviction that we can achieve our objectives in Iraq and we must not withdraw precipitously.

Senator Barack Obama (Democrat): "This continues to be a disastrous foreign policy mistake. At what point do we say, 'Enough'?"

Questions

1. What pattern emerges when you read these statements?
2. Which candidate's views come closest to your own? Why?
3. In your opinion, why are political leaders so sharply divided?

C. An opinion essay published in The New York Times written by seven US soldiers who served in Iraq. None of the seven were officers
Source: "The War As We Saw It", by Buddhika Jayamaha, Wesley D. Smith, Jeremy Roebuck, Omar Mora, Edward Sandmeier, Yance T. Gray and Jeremy A. Murphy, *New York Times*, August 19, 2007.

"To believe that Americans, with an occupying force that long ago outlived its reluctant welcome, can win over a recalcitrant local population and win this counter-insurgency is far-fetched. As responsible infantrymen and noncommissioned officers with the 82nd Airborne Division soon heading back home, we are skeptical of recent press coverage portraying the conflict as increasingly manageable and feel it has neglected the mounting civil, political and social unrest we see every day. The claim that we are increasingly in control of the battlefields in Iraq is an assessment arrived at through a flawed, American-centered framework. Yes, we are militarily superior, but our successes are offset by failures elsewhere ... This situation is made more complex by the questionable loyalties and Janus-faced role of the Iraqi police and Iraqi Army, which have been trained and armed at United States taxpayers' expense ... We operate in a bewildering context of determined enemies and questionable allies, one where the balance of forces on the ground remains entirely unclear ... Political reconciliation in Iraq will occur, but not at our insistence or in ways that meet our benchmarks ... We need to recognize that our presence may have released Iraqis from the grip of a tyrant, but that it has also robbed them of their self-respect. They will soon realize that the best way to regain dignity is to call us what we are—an army of occupation—and force our withdrawal."

Questions

1. According to the authors, what problems face American troops stationed in Iraq?
2. What do they believe will be the eventual outcome of the US occupation of Iraq?
3. In your opinion, is it significant that the authors of this essay are regular soldiers and not officers? Explain.

Final activity:
Based on these quotes, your responses to the questions, and your knowledge about the United States invasion and occupation of Iraq, write a letter to either your congressional representative or one of your US Senators explaining your view on what is taking place there and what the United States should do now and in the future. Your letter should be a minimum of 250 words. It will be shared with your classmates and discussed in class. It will be your decision whether you want to send it to your representative.

What Should You Do If You Are Under Attack Because of Your Political Ideas?

Your first line of defense should be your colleagues, school and district administrators, and your chapter of the teachers' union (either the National Educational Association or the American Federation of Teachers). If you feel you need support from local and national advocacy groups, you should contact one or all of the following for help: American Civil Liberties Union (http://www.aclu.org); Teaching Tolerance (http://www.tolerance.org); National Organization for Women (http://www.now.org); Anti-Defamation League (http://www.adl.org); Rethinking Schools (http://www.rethinkingschools.org); Lambda (http://www.lambda.org) or Human Rights Campaign (http://www.hrc.org). You can also contact me, at catajs@hofstra.edu

SHOULD TEACHERS ENCOURAGE STUDENTS TO WORK FOR SOCIAL JUSTICE?

"The tree of liberty must be refreshed from time to time, with the blood of patriots and tyrants. It is their natural manure."—Letter from Thomas Jefferson to Col. William S. Smith, 1787 (Feder 1967: 45)

As a social studies teacher, I define the idea of social justice very broadly and place it firmly within the traditions of American society. The Declaration of Independence dedicates the nation to the self-evident truth that "all men are created equal" with the right to "life, liberty, and the pursuit of happiness." These principles were reaffirmed by Abraham Lincoln in the Gettysburg Address and Martin Luther King, Jr. in his 1963 "I Have A Dream" speech. They were continually extended to new groups of people through activist movements for social change such as the abolitionist, labor, suffragette, and Civil Rights movements, and by constitutional amendments and Supreme Court decisions.

Thomas Jefferson, the author of the Declaration of Independence, believed that, in a democratic society, teachers do not really have a choice about encouraging students to work for social justice. According to Jefferson, freedom and republican government rest on two basic principles: "the diffusion of knowledge among the people" (Seldes 1966: 368) and the idea that "a little rebellion now and then is a good thing" (Feder 1967: 45). Jefferson supported the right to rebel because he recognized that the world was constantly changing. The crucial question was not whether it would change, but the direction of change. Education was essential so that ordinary citizens could participate in this process, defending and enhancing their liberties.

In the United States, there has frequently been a close connection between advocacy for mass public education and demands for expanding democracy, social justice, and political reform. For example, in the mid-nineteenth century, Horace Mann championed public education because he believed that the success of the country depended on "intelligence and virtue in the masses of the people" (Prescott 1953: 29). He argued that, "If we do not prepare children to become good citizens, . . . then our republic must go down to destruction."

John Dewey (1939) saw himself within this intellectual tradition. He believed that democratic movements for human liberation were necessary to achieve a fair distribution of political power and an "equitable system of human liberties." However, criticisms have been raised about limitations in Deweyan approaches to education, especially the way they are practiced in many elite private schools. Frequently, these schools are racially, ethnically, and economically segregated, and therefore efforts to develop classroom community ignore the spectrum of human difference and the continuing impact of society's attitudes about race, class, ethnicity, gender, social conflict, and inequality on both teachers and students. In addition, because of pressure on students to achieve high academic scores, teachers maintain an undemocratic level of control over the classroom. Paulo Freire, who calls on educators to aggressively challenge both injustice and unequal power arrangements in the classroom and society, addresses both of these issues.

Paulo Freire was born in Recife in northeastern Brazil, where his ideas about education developed in response to military dictatorship, enormous social inequality, and widespread adult illiteracy. As a result, his primary pedagogical goal was to provide the world's poor and oppressed with educational experiences that make it possible for them to take control over their own lives. Freire (1970; 1995) shared Dewey's desire to stimulate students to become "agents of curiosity" in a "quest for . . . the 'why' of things" (1995: 105) and his belief that education provides possibility and hope for the future of society. But he believes that these can only be achieved when students are engaged in explicitly critiquing social injustice and actively organizing to challenge oppression.

For Freire, education is a process of continuous group discussion (dialogue) that enables people to acquire collective knowledge they can use to change society. The role of the teacher includes asking questions that help students identify problems facing their community (problem posing), working with students to discover ideas or create symbols (representations) that explain their life experiences (codification), and encouraging analysis of prior experiences and of society as the basis for new academic understanding and social action (conscientization) (Shor 1987).

In a Deweyan classroom, the teacher is an expert who is responsible for organizing experiences so that students learn content, social and academic skills, and an appreciation for democratic living. Freire is concerned that this arrangement reproduces the unequal power relationships that exist in society. In a Freirean classroom, everyone has a recognized area of expertise that includes, but is not limited to, understanding and explaining their own life, and sharing this expertise becomes an essential element in the classroom curriculum. In these classrooms, teachers have their areas of expertise, but they are only one part of the community. The responsibility for organizing experiences and struggles for social change belongs to the entire community; as groups exercise this responsibility, they are empowered to take control over their lives.

Teaching Activity: Defining a Freirean Curriculum

Add your voice to the discussion:
1. Should students participate in defining the curriculum? Why or why not? To what extent?
2. In your opinion, do all people have an area of expertise that can be integrated into the curriculum? Explain your answer.

Try it yourself:
A key idea in Freire's work is defining the curriculum through problem posing. Examine a newspaper for current events articles that raise broader questions about the nature of life in the United States, its history, and/or its relationship with the rest of the world. Make a list of your questions and the underlying issues and conflicts that are involved in each area.

Think it over:
Can the questions and underlying issues that you identified become the basis for creating a social studies curriculum? How?

HOW CAN CLASSROOM TEACHERS EMPOWER STUDENTS?

I agree with Freire's concern that teachers address social inequality and the powerlessness experienced by many of our students. I also recognize that it is difficult to imagine secondary school social studies classrooms where teachers are responsible for covering specified subject matter organized directly on Freirean principles. Maxine Greene (1993a, b, c), an educational philosopher who advocates a "curriculum for human beings" integrating aspects of Freire, Dewey, and feminist thinking, offers ways for teachers to introduce Freire's pedagogical ideas into the classroom.

Greene believes that, to create democratic classrooms, teachers must learn to listen to student voices. Listening allows teachers to discover what students are thinking, what concerns them, and what has meaning to them. When teachers learn to listen, it is possible for teachers and students to collectively search for historical, literary, and artistic metaphors that make knowledge of the world accessible to us. In addition, the act of listening creates possibilities for human empowerment; it counters the marginalization experienced by students in school and in their lives, it introduces multiple perspectives and cultural diversity into the classroom, and it encourages students to take risks and contribute their social critiques to the classroom dialogue.

Greene's ideas are especially useful to social studies teachers. Just as historians discuss history as an ongoing process that extends from the past into the future, Greene sees individual and social development as processes that are "always in the making." For Greene, ideas, societies, and people are dynamic and always changing. She rejects the idea that there are universal and absolute truths and predetermined conclusions. According to Greene, learning is a search for "situated understanding" that places ideas and events in their social, historical, and cultural contexts.

Greene believes that the human mind provides us with powerful tools for knowing ourselves and others. She encourages students to combine critical thinking with creative imagination in an effort to empathize with and understand the lives, minds, and consciousness of human beings from the past and of our contemporaries in the present. She sees the goal of learning as discovering new questions about ourselves and the world, and this leads her to examine events from different perspectives, to value the ideas of other people, and to champion democracy.

Learning Activity: Creative Imagination and Literature

Because of her continuous search for metaphors that illuminate meaning, Greene's interests are interdisciplinary. She examines the sciences, social sciences, art, and history, and argues that literature allows us to explore imagination with the least constraints, to ignore superficial detail, and to focus on the greater reality. In her work, she examines the ideas of fictional characters like James Joyce's Stephen Dedalus, Albert Camus' Tarrou and Dr Rieux, and the mother in Toni Morrison's *Beloved*.

As a high school teacher, I used Mark Twain's Huck Finn (1996), Okonkwo from Achebe's *Things Fall Apart* (1996) and the title character from Katherine Paterson's *Lyddie* (1991) in a similar way.

Try it yourself:
Select a character from a work of literature from the past. How do the ideas, experiences, and relationships of this character help you understand that society and era?

It's your classroom:
1. As a social studies teacher, do you believe these insights would be useful to students in your class? Why?
2. What characters from literature would you introduce to middle school students? High school students? Why?

HOW DO TEACHERS TRANSLATE EDUCATIONAL THEORY INTO SOCIAL STUDIES PRACTICE?

During the Great Depression, striking Harlan County, Kentucky coal miners sang a song called *Which Side Are You On?* (available at: http://www.ocap.ca/songs/whichsid.html, accessed April 13, 2007). In a book he co-authored with Paulo Freire, Myles Horton (1990: 102) of the Highlander School argued that educators, like the miners, cannot be neutral. He called neutrality "a code word for the existing system. It has nothing to do with anything but agreeing to what is and will always be. It was to me a refusal to oppose injustice or to take sides that are unpopular."

James Banks (1991; 1993), an educational theorist whose focus is on the development of social studies curriculum, shares the ideas that "knowledge is not neutral," and that "an important purpose of knowledge construction is to help people improve society." Although Banks is a strong advocate of a multicultural approach to social studies, he argues that a "transformative" curriculum depends less on the content of what is taught than on the willingness of teachers to examine their own personal and cultural values and identities, to change the ways they organize classrooms and relate to students, and to actively commit themselves to social change.

The main ideas about education and society at the heart of the philosophies of Dewey, Freire, Greene, Horton, and Banks are that society is always changing; knowledge is not neutral—it either supports the status quo or a potential new direction for society; people learn primarily from what they experience; active citizens in a democratic society need to be critical and imaginative thinkers; and students learn to be active citizens by being active citizens. Assuming that we agree with these ideas, we are still left with these questions: How do we translate educational theory into social studies practice? What do these ideas look like in the classroom?

I know many excellent secondary school social studies teachers who work hard to connect to the ideas and lives of their students, and who try to teach based on these understandings. Yet none of them, including myself, has created a model transformative classroom. It may simply be that, although the educational goals discussed so far provide a vision of a particular kind of classroom, transformative education, like history, is part of a process that is never finished. This section concludes with examples from social studies classrooms where teachers and their students are engaged in struggles to build transformative learning communities and as social activists.

Addressing Racism in Brooklyn, New York

I met Don Murphy when his commitments to educational equity and to social justice led him to teach English and produce a literary magazine at a high school for incarcerated youth. Earlier in his career, as a middle school social studies teacher in Crown Heights, Brooklyn, Don found that building a transformative classroom community meant he had to deal with the impact of racism on the lives of his African-American, Caribbean, and Latino/a students. In an article in the New York City teachers' union newspaper, Don Murphy (1991) reported that his "students wanted to talk about racism. They needed to talk about it—they face it every day. They have little close interactions with white people. They can't walk into Kings Plaza Mall without being watched like criminals, or onto a subway car without white people moving away."

As a result of their experiences, many of Don's students expressed anti-white and anti-Jewish sentiments. As a teacher and as an African-American male, his choices were to ignore their statements and continue with an academic examination of bias, moralize in class against prejudice, use his authority to silence students, or find ways that he and the class could examine their own biases as they analyzed the formation and continued existence of racism in our society. Don decided to make the active examination of racism the center of his class' social studies curriculum and the vehicle for creating a transformative classroom community.

In response to student bitterness during discussion of the enslavement of Africans, Don challenged them to "concoct a plan for enslaving whites"—an idea they gradually rejected because of the kind of people they would become in such a slave society. After this activity, students became interested in examining beliefs that justified other forms of exploitation, including their own ideas about gender, sexual orientation, ethnic and religious groups, and themselves.

Eventually, the class studied Nazi anti-Semitism and the Holocaust in Europe. Don selected the topic because he wanted students to understand the oppression of other groups, and because of tense relationships that existed between local African-American and Hasidic Jewish communities. Students viewed documentaries, read and discussed *The Diary of Anne Frank*, and made posters that compared the Holocaust and the Middle Passage, and the Nazis and the Ku Klux Klan. One young man wrote in his journal: "[I] started thinking of all the things I used to say, 'Heil Hitler' to the Jews and now I know what it feels like."

Don believes that combining "the opportunity to articulate and honor their personal experiences" with an open examination of racism in a variety of forms and settings helped his students develop empathy for the "suffering of others, and a universal, humanist perspective." This was a crucial step in the development of a transformative classroom community. Social studies made it possible to develop community, while community enhanced the ability of students to learn social studies.

Equality and Democracy in Portland, Oregon

William Bigelow (1988; 1990; *Rethinking Schools*, 1994) and Linda Christensen (2000) are social studies and English team teachers who teach together at Jefferson High School in Portland, Oregon. Linda and Bill attempt to systematically incorporate Freirean educational principles into their teaching practices and write about their classroom experiences on a regular basis for the educational newspaper *Rethinking Schools*.

Linda and Bill describe their classrooms "as a center of equality and democracy" where students are engaged in "an ongoing, if small, critique of the repressive social relations of the larger society." They use literature and history "as points of departure to explore themes in students' lives and then, in turn, use students' lives to explore history and our society today." Their goal is to have students become "social researchers, investigating their own lives." Among the history books they recommend are Howard Zinn's *A People's History of the United States* (1999) and Ronald Takaki's *A Different Mirror* (1993).

Linda believes that it is a mistake for teachers to ignore the toll the outside world exacts on students. She begins the semester by having students interview each other, to establish that their identities and questions are at the center of the curriculum. Readings are selected to explore the issues that students raise. One semester, when Jefferson High School students were caught up in a storm of violence plaguing Portland, she had her class read *Thousand Pieces of Gold* by Ruthann Lum McCunn (1981). The novel includes an uprising by Chinese peasants who rampage through the countryside. Some of the outlawed peasants organize into bandit gangs, where they recreate relationships that were lost when their families were destroyed. As her students read about these Chinese rebels, they discussed conditions in their own communities. As they better understood their own lives, they began to recognize what was happening in the Chinese society they were studying.

Bill frequently has his students become "textbook detectives" (*Rethinking Schools* 1994: 158–159). They learn about different interpretations of historical events, and then examine standard textbooks to see how these events are presented. A major topic is the coverage of Christopher Columbus and descriptions of Native American people. Bill's goal is to have students question their assumptions about the past and examine why certain interpretations have become standard beliefs. To encourage student activism, Bill has his

students present their findings in teach-ins for other classes in the school.

A valuable learning activity employed by both Bill and Linda (Christensen 2000: 134) "to promote student empathy with other human beings" is the interior monologue. For an interior monologue, students imagine the thoughts of a character in history, literature, or life during an event that they are studying. Linda and Bill believe that this activity develops social imagination, which allows students to connect with the lives of people "with whom, on the surface, they may appear to have little in common." Students read their dialogues out loud in class, which allows the entire group to discuss their observations and arrive at new understandings about history.

One of things I like about Linda and Bill is their willingness to discuss the difficulties they have as secondary school teachers with a commitment to transformative education. They describe how they struggle along with their students to build supportive and democratic learning communities, to become intellectually and emotionally aware of their own choices and prejudices as European Americans and middle-class professionals, and to be engaged social activists. They recognize how difficult it is to relinquish a teacher's control over the curriculum, their uncertainties when student decisions push classes into uncharted waters, and their concern that after all of their efforts, a cohesive classroom community might not emerge.

Learning Activity: The Intersection of Life and History

Try it yourself:
1. Interview someone about their life. Where does the person's life intersect with broader historical events? How has history shaped the person? How have they shaped history?
2. Select a character from a work of literature or from history. Describe a specific historical moment in which they lived or participated. Write an interior monologue about their thoughts at this time.

Think it over:
Do you think these activities have validity in a social studies classroom? Why?

Expanding Student Horizons in Cities and Suburbs
Adam Stevens (NTN) is a progressive political activist and community organizer. He teaches social studies in an inner city high school and lives nearby. As a teacher, Adam starts

from the perspective that schools "play an indispensable part in providing the economy with pre-sorted individuals who have been prepared to fit into a range of socioeconomic slots in the world at large, and generally, who accept the slot they wind up with. To encourage students to question this set-up, or even more sharply, to facilitate students in the process of allying themselves with grassroots movements that fight for social justice is to subvert the basic mission of public education." Adam advises new teachers that the "tactics they choose to employ in pursuing such a goal will vary according to conditions in the school building, district, and ultimately, in the nation." He also emphasizes that new teachers understand "the strategic importance and professional hazards of walking such a road are not to be made light of."

Adam's high school students are nearly all immigrants or the children of immigrants from the Caribbean who have little experience outside the neighborhoods where they live. Many work or have family responsibilities and school is not always a priority. While they often have a healthy skepticism about this society's claim to promote equality and justice, it is a challenge for teachers to channel this skepticism away from an anti-school/anti-intellectual mode of thinking and toward a more empowered and engaged attitude when studying history. To address the issues in their lives and to engage them in learning, Adam spends a lot of time having students study about social injustice in American society and efforts to rectify it.

Adam believes a crucial element of democracy and a way of making it meaningful to students is to focus on political action. They study about historical movements and Adam invites students to join with him in campaigns outside of school. Groups of students have participated in local activities and in mass rallies in Washington, DC, especially in opposition to the war in Iraq and to restrictions placed on immigrants under the Homeland Security Act. Students who participated in these actions with Adam brought their new experiences and sense of efficacy with them to class. One of Adam's goals is that they should see themselves as class, school, and community leaders.

Many teachers accept the possibility of working for social justice in inner-city urban schools, but argue that this approach can never work in suburban communities where watchful parents promote more traditional academic goals. Jessica Cartalucci and Jackie Hamill (NTN) teach in suburban communities where their students, while economically better off and more directed toward school achievement, are also isolated from the experiences of people in the broader world. They both search for projects to challenge students to see themselves as active participants in a democratic society. Jessica is the advisor to her high school's Human Awareness and Understanding Club. Club members studied about genocide in the modern world and became active in a campaign to pressure the United States government to help stop the genocide in Darfur in the Sahel region of sub-Saharan Africa. They created and distributed an information sheet, raised money for relief organizations, and read daily bulletins during morning school announcements. Jackie's high school students learned about United States troops in Iraq, not much older them themselves, who were serving in the war zone. Many soldiers spent long hours in between assignments with little to do. Classes decided to launch "Operation-DVD." They wrote letters to the soldiers, hung posters in the school, and collected new and used DVD's that they shipped to Iraq.

Laura Vosswinkel, Pat Turk, and Ken Dwyer (NTN) are members of the social studies in another suburban community. Every year, they help organize a school-wide Human Relations Day that includes speakers, student panels, and workshops to promote civic activism. At the conference, students debate human rights issues, responses to racism, and teen responsibility. Campaigns promoted on Human Relations Day have included support for animal rights, victims of natural disasters, and community improvement projects. Laura, Pat, and Ken have also been willing to put themselves "at-risk" of parental protest by inviting me to speak with students about more controversial topics such as the "lessons of 9/11" for the United States and the impact of the war in Iraq on the American people and conflict in the Middle East.

Defending Student Rights in Queens, New York

Michael Pezone (NTN) shares Linda Christensen and Bill Bigelow's emphasis on creating classrooms where students are able to expose their ideas, feelings, and academic proficiencies in public without risking embarrassment or attack and being pressed into silence. Students in his classes at Law, Government and Community Service Magnet High School frequently write position papers on controversial issues and deliver them in class where they are discussed as the basis for social action.

During the Fall 2001 semester, in response to the destruction of the World Trade Center, the New York City Board of Education required all public schools to lead students in the Pledge of Allegiance at the beginning of each school day and at all school-wide assemblies and school events. Michael's students were confused about the law governing behavior during the flag salute and concerned with defending the first amendment rights of fellow students. They contacted the New York Civil Liberties Union to clarify legal issues and learned that the law does not require participation. They decided to monitor both compliance with the directive's requirement that the Pledge of Allegiance be recited each day and protection for the freedom of student's to dissent. They also circulated a questionnaire in the school that asked students about their opinions on the issues, encouraged students to behave respectfully and responsibly during the pledge, informed them of their legal right not to participate, and asked them to report violations of the law. The results of the student survey and student comments were later distributed in the school's magazine.

Teaching Activity: What Role Would You Play?

This article appeared in the *New York Daily News* on September 20, 2005. An estimated 1,500 high school students participated in the protest.

"We're Kids—Not Convicts! Protest School Metal Detectors"
by Sondra Wolfer (2005)

Griping that new metal detectors and lunchtime lockdowns make them feel like jailbirds, angry DeWitt Clinton High School students took to the Bronx streets in a protest yesterday. "We felt institutionalized. It's like a prison," said Anthony Stafford, 17, a senior who helped organize the demonstration.

School officials and Mayor Bloomberg decided the metal detectors were necessary after a rash of weapons-related incidents during the 2003–04 school year. Records show 13 major crimes were tallied at the school that year, well above the average of 8.3 major crimes for a school of similar size.

But students said the detectors delayed them from getting into the school, and a new rule keeping students inside at lunch caused dangerous overcrowding in the cafeteria. "All these changes all at once had us feeling overwhelmed," Anthony said. Cecily Severe, 17, a senior, said the three metal detectors can't accommodate the crowds and students are missing part of their first morning classes because of the logjam. "We need to come a half hour early just to get to class on time," she said.

To voice their dismay, some 300 students protested outside the district superintendent's office on Fordham Road while a small delegation met education officials inside.

City Department of Education spokesman Keith Kalb said extra metal detectors will be installed and two more doors will be open to entering students starting this morning. But students will not be allowed out for lunch because there isn't enough time to rescan them for weapons when they return. "It's just not feasible for them to be going in and out," he said.

Bloomberg said that even though the security measures are a hassle, the DOE plans to stick with them. "I know it is annoying to some people, but the truth of the matter is the first thing—the most important thing—is to make sure that all students and the people that work in the schools are safe," he said.

Join the conversation:

Did the students have the right to walk out of school in protest? Explain.

It's your classroom:

1. What would you have done if the students asked you for advise on their planned walkout? Why?
2. Would you have supported the students on the day of the protest? How? Why?
3. What would you have done if the school tried to take disciplinary action against students? Explain.

Participating in Local Government

In my high school social studies classes, I promoted transformative goals through direct student involvement in social action projects as part of New York State's "Participation in Government" curriculum. In New York City, periodic budget crises, ongoing racial and ethnic tension, and the need for social programs in poor communities have provided numerous opportunities to encourage students to become active citizens. Class activities have included sponsoring student forums on controversial issues, preparing reports on school finances and presenting them as testimony at public hearings, writing position papers for publication in local newspapers, and organizing student and community support for a school-based public health clinic.

During each activity, social studies goals included making reasoned decisions based on an evaluation of existing evidence, researching issues and presenting information in writing and on graphs, exploring the underlying ideas that shape our points of view, giving leadership by example to other students, and taking collective and individual responsibility for the success of programs (see Essay 3 below).

Community Activists

Adeola Tella (NTN) is a middle school social studies teacher who has worked in an inner-city community with students who have serious academic problems. In order to promote student literacy and responsibility, she enlisted students as multicultural literacy volunteers to read with four-year-old children from a neighboring daycare center.

When the project was introduced to the classes, some of the students insisted, "we should be paid to volunteer." However, they each eventually decided that they were willing to volunteer "to do something important" and one hundred percent of the students returned signed permission slips allowing them to visit the preschool program. To prepare for their role, students studied international and American folk tales and practiced reading aloud to each other. They also rewrote some of the stories as plays and performed them wearing plastic masks and using giant puppets.

Adeola reports two student comments that underscore the importance of the project for their middle school students. Nearly every year when the project is introduced, one student will ask in surprise, "Why are you asking us? Do they know we aren't good students?" Later, after a visit to the day care center, an excited student will say, "This was special. They really looked up to us."

A number of members of the New Teachers Network have pursued similar goals through community improvement projects. Christina Agosti-Dircks has involved her classes in community clean-ups and fund-raising for homeless families. Darren Luskoff's students assisted in a food kitchen while studying about hunger and famine. Laurence Klein has middle school students read to the elderly. Each of these teachers reports these projects are particularly successful in integrating students with a broad spectrum of academic levels, including students with educational disabilities.

The Mifflin International School in Columbus, Ohio (Crook 1994) has made student involvement in community projects an integral part of its thematic social studies curriculum. Seventh graders walk to raise money to combat hunger around the world, while 8th graders work in a community kitchen.

WHAT DOES A CLASSROOM BASED ON TRANSFORMATIVE PRINCIPLES LOOK LIKE?

Democratic classroom communities based on transformative principles are not easy to build, but they are essential if we want to engage students in wanting to learn social studies and to prepare them for active citizenship in democratic societies. Consider the following:

1. One of my favorite African-American spirituals is "Freedom is a Constant Struggle" (available at: http://www.ed.uiuc.edu/mccomb/freedomconstantstruggle.html, accessed September 19, 2007). Freedom is not something you achieve and then have forever; it is something that people continually work for and must always recreate. I look at democratic classroom community in the same way. It is a long-term ongoing process of construction and reaffirmation. Democratic classroom communities are not finished products.

2. In democratic classroom communities, students learn to respect themselves and each other. Communities provide students with emotional support so they can trust the group and take intellectual and social risks.

For these communities to develop, teachers must play active roles. They must model what it means to develop a point of view, and must support a position with evidence and what it means to listen and learn from others.

3. Student voice (written and oral expression of their ideas) is crucial to social studies learning for at least two reasons. Sharing ideas is the way that people, especially historians and social scientists, check their theories about the world. In social studies classrooms where teachers define their role as the transmitter of information, students never learn to evaluate ideas, create metaphors that express connection and understanding, share differences of opinion, arrive at consensus or respectful disagreement, experience intellectual and social decision-making, and become critical and imaginative thinkers. In addition, social studies teachers cannot assume that students are making the intellectual connections that we make or that we would like them to make. If we do not learn to listen to our students, we cannot know what they are thinking and we cannot create experiences that help them examine their beliefs and discover new ideas.

4. Academic knowledge by itself, even knowledge of social struggles against racial and gender prejudice, does not enable students to reconsider their basic ideas and values and the way they act toward others. Most students primarily learn from reflection on what they experience, not from what

teachers say. Social studies curricula must provide experiences that enable students to discover the parallels between school learning and life.

5. Teachers need to encourage student leaders who can engage their peers to take responsibility for community learning and create new levels of understanding. Leadership and responsibility are crucial to community, citizenship, and social change.

6. The kind of activities discussed here can create conflict between students in the class, students and their teachers, and teachers in a school. Conflict and conflict resolution are inherent to the community process; they cannot be avoided and should not be ignored. They help us focus in on differences, make our ideas clear, and demonstrate that multiple perspectives are genuinely respected. Paulo Freire argues, "conflicts are the midwife of consciousness."

Of course, this chapter is based on my goals as an educator and activist, my experiences as a social studies teacher with a commitment to transformative education, and discussions with teachers, pre-service teachers, and high school students. As you think about the kind of social studies teacher you want to become, you may agree with all of these ideas, disagree with some of them, or reject the entire package. But whatever you decide, you should do it consciously, based on your educational goals, your ideas about history and the social sciences, and recognition that "everything is political."

Essay 1: Social Studies Under Attack

During the last 100 years, perceived national emergencies in the United States have contributed to periodic questioning of the efficacy of social studies education. In an article in *Social Education* (Singer 2004: 158–160), I documented a vitriolic 1943 debate over the ability of social studies curriculum to prepare Americans for world leadership as the

United States prepared to re-educate and democratize Nazi-dominated Europe. The latest challenge to the social studies was precipitated by the attacks on the World Trade Center and Pentagon on September 11, 2001 and was spurred on by the Bush Administration's war on terrorism.

Learning Activity: Historical Knowledge of College Freshmen

In April 1943, *The New York Times* (Fine 1943: 1) published the result of a test that was supposed to measure the historical knowledge of 7,000 college freshmen. The scores upset historians, educators, and politicians. Many worried whether a nation so ignorant of its own past could rebuild Europe on a firm democratic foundation. During a week-long debate over the causes of the problem, the social studies were excoriated. Below is a slightly modified version of the test with the percentage of students who answered each question correctly. Take the test and see how you do. Correct answers are at the end of this essay.

1. Name the 13 original states (6%).
2. Name the body of water where Memphis, Tennessee is located (16%).
3. Name two of the specific powers granted to the Congress by the Constitution of the United States (44%).
4. Name four of the freedoms mentioned in the Bill of Rights (45%).
5. Identify two contributions by Abraham Lincoln to the political, economic or social development of the United States (22%).
6. Identify two contributions by Thomas Jefferson to the political, economic or social development of the United States (16%).
7. Place the Dred Scott decision, the Nullification Act, Mexican-American War, and the Compromise of 1850 in chronological order (6%).
8. Name the home state of John C. Calhoun (20%).
9. Identify Henry Thoreau (16%).
10. Identify the two largest immigrant groups to the United States between 1845 and 1860 (14%).

Think it over:

Was this test a valid measure of (1) the "social studies" as taught in American schools, (2) the historical knowledge of the American people, or (3) the ability of the United States to promote democracy around the world after World War II?

Add your voice to the discussion:

1. Does content knowledge define historical understanding? Explain.
2. Why do conflicts over the social studies curriculum seem to arise on a regular basis?

The current challenge to the social studies is much more ideological and better financed than previous campaigns. While its leaders are a loosely structured, diverse coalition, with contradictory political goals, it is funded by foundations and "think tanks" with strong rightwing ideological leanings.

At the nexus of the strange bedfellows attacking the social studies is the Gilder Lehrman Institute of American History. Founded in 1994, it claims to promote the study and love of American history through initiatives targeting audiences ranging from public school students to scholars to the general public.

According to its website (http://www.gilder lehrman.org/institute/index.html, accessed April 16, 2007), the Gilder Lehrman Institute creates history-centered schools and academic research centers; organizes seminars and enrichment programs for educators; produces print and electronic publications and traveling exhibitions; and sponsors lectures by eminent historians. It also funds book prizes and offers fellowships for scholars to work in the Gilder Lehrman Collection and other archives. The Institute maintains this website to "offer high-quality educational material for teachers, students, historians, and the public; and to provide up-to-the-minute information about the Institute's programs and activities."

The Gilder Lehrman Institute's ability to influence the history profession rests on the financial resources of its founders, their control over the Gilder Lehrman Collection, the largest privately owned collection of American historical documents, and the organization's ability to shape policy at the Gilder Lehrman Center at Yale University for the Study of Abolition and Slavery, the New York Historical Society, and the Organization of American Historians.

The co-founders of the Gilder Lehrman Institute of American History are Richard Gilder and Lewis E. Lehrman. Richard Gilder heads a brokerage firm and is a founding member, and former chair, of the Board of Trustees of the Manhattan Institute, a conservative think-tank. According to the magazine *Mother Jones*, he is a major Republican Party operative and financier with ties to the Reagan and both Bush administrations (available at: http://www.motherjones.com/news/special_reports/mojo_400/145_gilder.html, accessed April 16, 2007).

Lewis Lehrman, formerly president of a drugstore chain, is a partner in a private investment firm. He has been a trustee of the American Enterprise Institute, the Manhattan Institute, and the Heritage Foundation, and in 1982 was a conservative Republican candidate for Governor of New York (see http://www.lewiselehrman.com/biography, accessed April 16, 2007).

The institute's advisory board, which gives it an air of legitimacy, includes many of the most prominent names in the history profession in the United States. While the historians tend to be from the liberal-left end of the political spectrum, the advisory board also includes conservatives such as Roger Kimball, managing editor of *The New Criterion*, Richard Brookhiser, senior editor at *National Review*, and Roger Hertog, former chairman of the Manhattan Institute. They are joined by Diane Ravitch, a former Under-Secretary of Education in the Bush I (1989–1993) Administration.

Are Gilder and Lehrman history fans who are content with buying a ticket and rooting from the sidelines? Are they patrons of the historical arts, who expect to hobnob with retainees and bask in their achievements, but who will otherwise leave them alone to pursue their professional interests? Or, are they entrepreneurs, intent on buying up, reorganizing, and marketing the historical profession in ways that they deem economically and politically profitable?

In an interview published in *The New York Times*, Richard Gilder acknowledged that he and Lehrman were using the Gilder Lehrman document collection as leverage to redirect the New York Historical Society, where they sit on the Board, to achieve their goal of influencing the national debate over history. While Lehrman claimed that the partners were "not interested in upholding any self-appointed establishment—on the left or on the right," an up-coming exhibition about slavery has been recast to reflect his views. Lehrman argues that slavery "was an institution supported throughout the world, but Americans took the initiative in destroying it." He deplores the view that "American history consists of one failure after another to deal with the issue of slavery . . . One of the triumphs of America was to have dealt directly with that issue in the agonies of a civil war, and to have passed the 13th, 14th and 15th Amendments" (Pogrebin and Collins 2004: E1).

Another graphic illustration of their wealth, reach, and influence is that after eighteen years of publication by the Organization of American Historians (OAH), the cover of *The Magazine of History* now reads that it is produced "with the generous support of the Gilder Lehrman Institute of American History." As a result of Gilder Lehrman Institute financing, the magazine, which targets pre-college history teachers, has expanded from 4 to 6 pages a year, now has a full-time editor, and includes a column called "Documents from the Gilder Lehrman Collection." It also has color images and uses higher quality paper (Byrne 2004: 3). Three members of the magazine's six member advisory board, including its chair, are from the Gilder Lehrman Institute.

I focus on the Gilder Lehrman Institute because of the prominent role it has played in the OAH and the NYHS. However, I could just as easily have featured the Bradley and Fordham Foundations and the Manhattan Institute, which have all been involved in the war against social studies.

According to its website (http://www.bradleyfdn.org/about.html, accessed April 16, 2007), the Lynde and Harry Bradley Foundation was established to preserve and defend the "tradition of free representative government and private enterprise that has enabled the American nation and, in a larger sense, the entire Western world to flourish intellectually and economically . . . The Lynde and Harry Bradley Foundation is likewise devoted to strengthening American democratic capitalism and the institutions, principles and values that sustain and nurture it. Its programs support limited, competent government; a dynamic marketplace for economic, intellectual, and cultural activity; and a vigorous defense at home and abroad of American ideas and institutions."

To strengthen capitalism and the "institutions, principles and values that sustain and nurture it," the Bradleys decided to redefine American history and the way it is taught in the schools. One of the Foundation's principle achievements was the establishment of the Bradley Commission on History in Schools that morphed into the National Council for History Education (NCHE) in 1990. NCHE maintains liaisons with the Gilder Lehrman Institute and the History Channel, two of its major funders. NCHE is a strong supporter of the federal Teaching American History Grant program as an effort to address what it perceives as the "Crisis in History," especially "the inadequate time given to history instruction, especially in the early grades; and the inadequate training in content demanded of teachers of history."

The Manhattan Institute (MI) (see http://www.manhattan-institute.org/html/about_mi.htm, accessed April 16, 2007) has provided a home base, publicity, credentials, and money for a host of right-wing intellectuals. It promotes its causes by "combining intellectual seriousness and practical wisdom with intelligent marketing and focused advocacy." Kay Hymowitz, one of MI's education policy fellows, used the 9/11/01 attack on the World Trade Center and the Pentagon as the basis of a bitter diatribe against the National Council for the Social Studies (NCSS) that was published in *The Weekly Standard* (2002). According to Hymowitz, "The leaders of this 26,000-member organization of teachers of history, sociology, geography, political science, psychology, and economics . . . were sure the attacks would provide the excuse Americans wanted to indulge their reflexive racism and 'revenge-oriented ideology.'"

The Thomas B. Fordham Foundation (available at: http://www.edexcellence.net/foundation/global/index.cfm, accessed April 16, 2007) is little more than the private political vehicle of Chester Finn, Jr. and Diane Ravitch, veterans of the 1980s war against multiculturalism. Following the attacks on the World Trade Center in New York and the Pentagon in Washington DC on September 11, 2001, Finn, Ravitch and their colleagues virtually equated multi-culturalists with the terrorists (Ravitch 2001, 2002). Finn accused proponents of multiculturalism of shortchanging patriotism and Ravitch charged "multiculturalism, as it is taught in the United States, . . . teaches cultural relativism because it implies that 'no group may make a judgment on any other'" (Hartocollis 2001: A32).

Finn wrote the introduction to *Where Did The Social Studies Go Wrong?* (Leming et al. 2003) (WDTSSGW), that is distributed by the Fordham Foundation. In it, he claimed that "(i)n the field of social studies itself, the lunatics had taken over the asylum. Its leaders were people who had plenty of grand degrees and impressive titles but who possessed no respect for Western civilization."

WDTSSGW also included a review by J. Martin Rochester (2003) of the first edition of this book. He described it as "an exemplar of progressive group-think" because of its "constructivist orientation" and dismissed it as offering "all the standard progressive clichés about direct instruction equaling 'chalk and talk' and fostering dreary, dictatorial classrooms."

One passage in the book drew Rochester's greatest ire. "Deriding attention to facts as belonging to the 'Dragnet' (or 'Jeopardy') school of pedagogy, Singer goes so far as to state, 'I do not believe there are any independent objective criteria for establishing a particular event or person as historically important' (p. 26)." Rochester declares that "factual competence is essential to civic competence" and quotes a Princeton historian who charges that if social studies educators have their way, "the widely lamented historical illiteracy of today's students will only worsen in the generations to come."

The review concludes, "Given the fact that the standards for what constitutes historical accuracy and mastery are so low, we should not be surprised that Singer believes students, by the time they reach high school if not sooner, are ready to "become historians and social scientists."

WDTSSGW's attack on my book, to which I plead guilty in every case, is exactly why I am proud to call myself a social studies teacher. I value historical knowledge, but I always remember that my job is to teach kids, not a specific list of facts. I teach students to do research, to evaluate and to form their own views, to become historians, social scientists, and citizens, not to memorize a long list of things that someone in authority has deemed important.

These groups are allied with private corporations who are trying to mass market and profit by packaging pseudo-history with patriotism and titillation. For example, in December 2004, *The History Channel* ran an advertising campaign for a special on "Ben Franklin. Inventor. Patriot. Playboy." It featured a 60-something Franklin partying with two scantily dressed, buxom, 20-something actresses.

While historians may think that their job is to decipher the past, according to a report from the Now Foundation (see http://www.nowfoundation.org/issues/communications/tv/ mediacontrol.html, accessed September 17, 2007), a few powerful and interlocking companies dominate the airways, decide what Americans can view, what really happened in earlier periods of time, and how the general public should understand it. General Electric owns NBC and between 25 and 50 percent of A&E and the History Channel (along with Disney and Hearst). Time Warner, the largest media corporation in the world, owns film and music production companies, theme parks, sports teams, magazines, websites and book publishers as well as 75 percent of HBO and between 25 and 50 percent of CNN. The Walt Disney Co., which merged with Capital Cities/ABC in 1995, is a fully-integrated media giant controlling theme parks, retail outlets, magazines, book publishers, websites, motion pictures, sports teams, TV, cable, radio, music and newspapers. These include 37.5 percent of A&E and the History Channel (along with GE and Hearst) and between 25 and 50 percent of the Biography Channel (again with GE and Hearst). Viacom owns the Paramount movie studio, the CBS television network, and Blockbuster Video as well as MTV. Rupert Murdoch's always "balanced" News Corporation, also known as FOX, controls "20th Century Fox" movies, the *New York Post*, the *London Times*, TV Guide and The National Geographic Channel. In 2004, the powerful role played by these companies in influencing what Americans are allowed to learn about was demonstrated when the Disney corporation refused to distribute "Fahrenheit 9/11," which was produced by one of its subsidiaries (Holson 2005). While this decision backfired and the documentary ended up becoming a box office success, curiously it received no Academy Award nominations.

Teaching Activity: Conspiracy, Conservative Campaign, or Coincidence?

I am not claiming that all of the groups making war on the social studies are working in collusion, or that they even think of themselves as allies. But there are connections. I believe the war on the social studies is part of the rightward swing in the United States since 1980 and that it is financed by powerful, wealthy, and conservative business interests.

Add your voice to the discussion:
1. Do you agree or disagree with my major theses? Explain.
2. Why do you think the social studies have been under attack?

Answers to Historical Knowledge of College Freshmen

1. New Hampshire, Massachusetts, Rhode Island, Connecticut, New York, New Jersey, Pennsylvania, Maryland, Delaware, Virginia, North Carolina, South Carolina, Georgia.
2. Mississippi River.
3. Borrow money, raise armies, regulate commerce, provide for a Navy, establish naturalization laws, coin money, establish post offices, regulate land and sea forces, provide for a militia.
4. Freedom of religion, freedom of speech, freedom of press, freedom of assembly, freedom of petition, right to bear arms, security in persons and houses, freedom from unreasonable seizure, right to speedy and public trials, not deprived of life, liberty or property without due process of law, trial by jury, no excessive bail.
5. President of the United States, Emancipation Proclamation Act, Civil War leader, preserved the Union, Reconstruction plans, Homestead Act.
6. Author of Declaration of Independence, Louisiana Purchase, President of the United States, founder of University of Virginia.
7. Nullification Act, Mexican-American War, Compromise of 1850, Dred Scott decision.
8. South Carolina.
9. Essayist, political dissident.
10. German and Irish.

Essay 2: TAH Means "Traditional" American History

A major player in the campaign to re-shape the teaching of American history and the promotion of patriotic platitudes as historical content is the US Department of Education. The Teaching American History Grant (TAHG) program is a discretionary grant program funded under the federal government's Elementary and Secondary Education Act (available at: http://www.ed.gov/programs/teaching history/index.html, accessed September 17, 2007). The key word here is "discretionary."

Initially, the goal of the program was "to support programs that raise student achievement by improving teachers' knowledge, understanding, and appreciation of American history." However, since 2003, the program, which provides money for the professional development of teachers, no longer funds proposals unless they "promote the teaching of *traditional* [italics added] American history in elementary and secondary schools as a separate academic subject." Based on the new criteria, proposal designs that were approved in the initial call for applications were rejected when resubmitted for new funding either because they taught history within a "social studies" framework or because they focused on themes or historical material the Department of Education did not want prominently displayed.

Part of my concern is that this change promotes self-censorship by workshop organizers and historians who want to be involved in the program. Members of at least one audience I addressed as part of a TAHG were outraged when I referred to Thomas Jefferson's sexual relationship with Sally Hemings, a 14-year-old enslaved African teenager. I believe it is vital information for understanding both the nature of slavery in the United States and ideas of the nation's founders. Evidently, they disagreed and felt I was introducing material that was outside the traditional focus of history.

In what I can only describe as an act of professional cowardice, the American Historical Association, instead of publicly challenging the Department of Education's demand for the teaching of "traditional history," printed an article in its newsletter explaining how to work around the new grant guidelines (Ebner 2003: 28–34).

An editor's note that accompanied the article explained, "The AHA has been actively supportive of the Teaching American History Grants program, one of the most important (and generously funded) history-related projects that the US Congress has initiated in recent times. The following essay is published as a useful guide for the many historians, educators, and educational administrators who may be thinking of (collaboratively) applying for a grant to enhance history teaching in their communities. The author has been involved in various capacities with the program since its inception and is currently the academic director of a project that was funded in the first, pioneering round of grants."

According to the article, "One of the first things to be keenly aware of is the stipulation from the Department of Education that projects must be devoted to what is labeled—for better and for worse—'traditional American history.' Do not anguish endlessly over the contentious word 'traditional' ... Endlessly debating about what 'traditional' does or does not mean will yield a most dissatisfying and pointless chase. Pursue an alternative path—carefully study the abstracts of funded TAH projects because collectively they reveal the diverse conceptions of the word 'traditional.'"

Learning Activity: Are these Quotations "Traditional" Enough?

Frederick Douglass and Dr Martin Luther King, Jr. have certainly become part of the "traditional" American history curriculum. We teach about Douglass' escape from enslavement and his role as a prominent abolitionist. The United States now has a holiday honoring the accomplishments of Dr King and many students can recite passages from his "I Have A Dream" speech delivered in Washington, DC in August 1963. But how accurately are their ideas presented in the "traditional" American history curriculum? The first quotation is from a speech by Frederick Douglass that he gave at a July 4th celebration in Rochester, New York in 1852 (Dunbar 1914: 42–47). The second quotation is from a speech by Dr King to the Southern Christian leadership Conference (King 1967).

Frederick Douglass Discusses the "Fourth of July" (1852)

"What to the American slave is your Fourth of July? I answer, a day that reveals to him more than all other days of the year, the gross injustice and cruelty to which he is the constant victim. To him your celebration is a sham; your boasted liberty an unholy license; your national greatness, swelling vanity; your sounds of rejoicing are empty and heartless; your denunciation of tyrants, brass-fronted impudence; your shouts of liberty and equality . . . There is not a nation of the earth guilty of practices more shocking and bloody than are the people of these United States at this very hour."

Dr Martin Luther King, Jr. Asks "Where Do We Go From Here?" (1967)

"[T]he movement must address itself to the question of restructuring the whole of American society. There are forty million poor people here, and one day we must ask the question, 'Why are there forty million poor people in America?' And when you begin to ask that question, you are raising a question about the economic system, about a broader distribution of wealth. When you ask that question, you begin to question the capitalistic economy. And I'm simply saying that more and more, we've got to begin to ask questions about the whole society. We are called upon to help the discouraged beggars in life's marketplace. But one day we must come to see that an edifice which produces beggars needs restructuring . . . [W]hen you deal with this you begin to ask the question, 'Who owns the oil?' You begin to ask the question, 'Who owns the iron ore?' You begin to ask the question, 'Why is it that people have to pay water bills in a world that's two-thirds water?'"

Try it yourself:

1. Why is Frederick Douglass questioning the celebration of the "Fourth of July"?
2. What aspects of American society is Dr King questioning in this speech?

3. What do these quotations suggest about the ideas of Frederick Douglass and Martin Luther King, Jr.?

Add your voice to the discussion:
1. Have you ever seen these quotations before? If not, why not?
2. In your opinion, should these quotations be included in the study of "traditional" American history? Explain.

The article also warned, "Wherever possible, avoid reliance upon the concepts, methodologies, and rhetoric associated with social studies. The disciplines encompassed by the National Council for the Social Studies include geography, economics, history, political science, sociology, psychology, anthropology, and law-related education."

The question is: why would historians, whose profession has reinvented itself since the 1960s by rejecting a traditional approach to the past and incorporating the social sciences into historical analysis, make these recommendations? A clue is how TAHG funds are used. According to the grant guidelines, "Typically, practicing professional historians will provide the teacher with content instruction, demonstrations in best practices, instruction in using primary source materials and objects in classrooms, and instruction in using and integrating educational technology." That few if any "practicing professional historians" have much of an idea of what is taking place in elementary and secondary schools or how to teach kids does not seem to be an issue addressed by either the grantors or the history profession.

I have been a participant in a number of the grants (as a partner, presenter and consultant) and swapped experiences with other participants, including some who attended national meetings for grant recipients. I am careful about identifying individuals or school districts because decent people who do good things in schools are dependent on the grants for their jobs. I would like to call your attention to a website created by a North Carolina project that is especially useful for social studies teachers (available at: http://www.dlt.ncssm.edu/lmtm/, accessed September 17, 2007). It is organized as a chronological examination of United States history with introductory thematic essays prepared by local university professors and museum educators that help teachers "learn more" so they can "teach more." It also includes lesson plans and activity sheets.

Some of the grant recipients, once the awards were made, employed what Herbert Kohl (1994) called "creative maladjustment" to support staff development in financially and academically troubled school districts. Among other things, they sent specialists into schools to provide enrichment for children and modeling for teachers. But creative maladjustment can also become creative bookkeeping. I am directly aware of one school district that exaggerated grant overhead costs to move money into their general fund in order to cover budget shortfalls, and I have heard reports of other districts doing the same thing.

Many of the staff development programs bear little relevance to what is appropriate for elementary or secondary education. They have "professional historians" lecture, in large auditoriums, to barely awake teachers, on obscure topics that do not translate into classroom practice. One historian was actually banned from addressing New York City teachers in any staff development program by the mayor and school chancellor because of his political views on the Israeli-Palestinian conflict, views he had not even expressed during his presentations to teachers.

The grant selection process itself appears to be rife with inconsistency and political patronage. Two districts with similar student demographics but located in different parts of the country submitted nearly identical proposals focusing on the intersection of their community's local history with national events. Inexplicably, one proposal was accepted while the other was rejected and the supposedly objective ratings showed diametrically opposite evaluations. It was suggested "off the record" by "insiders" that the awarding of grants largely depends on the "luck of the draw" of evaluators and that the disappointed district should just resubmit the next year. In one case I am personally aware of, the only regional grant that was awarded went to a school district whose grant administrator was coincidentally an officer in a national historical organization, but of course this was not a factor in the selection process.

Meanwhile, politically connected "community" partners have used grants to promote their ideological agendas or cover overhead and administrative expenses, often providing little in return. From 2001 through 2004, the New York Historical Society, and the Gilder Lehrman Institute of American History (discussed in the previous essay) that controls its Board of Directors, were listed as partners on nine

131

Teaching American History grants awarded to the New York City schools for a total of $10.6 million.

As discussed in the previous essay ("Social Studies Under Attack"), the founders of the Gilder Lehrman Institute of American History have close ties to the Republican Party and conservative foundations and think-tanks. Perhaps we need more "traditional" historians, in the tradition of Charles Beard, William Appleman Williams, and Howard Zinn, to fully uncover the political manipulation that is taking place in the rightwing effort to rewrite the United States history curriculum.

Teaching Activity: Taking Risks

Challenging the idea of teaching "traditional" history or introducing "non-traditional" ideas and approaches in your classroom can place a teacher at risk of close scrutiny by administrators and even of losing a position.

Add your voice to the discussion:
How far are you willing to go to stand up for principles?

Essay 3: Are Activist Teachers "Social Predators"?

An earlier version of this essay appeared in the magazine *Rethinking Schools* (Singer 2003). Soon after publication, I received an email from a member of the New Teachers Network telling me that an article titled "Social Predation 101: Now showing in classrooms near you" was circulating on right-wing websites and blogs (Donnach 2003). According to the article, "Singer outlines for teachers how to promote personal agendas using students" at "workshops and assemblies through which he helps teachers 'understand their right to disagree with and protest against government policies' and 'involve their students in political action' that promotes the teacher's interests. In other words, Singer seems to be teaching social predators how to use the classroom to recruit children to their personal perspective by supplanting the values taught at home with their own." I was so excited by the response to my initial article that I downloaded the logo for the Nashville Predator hockey team and created a "Social Predator" T-shirt to wear to social studies conferences.

As the United States government and military prepared for a war on Iraq in 2002 and 2003, I spoke with classes and assembles at a number of secondary schools and presented workshops on the war at staff development conferences in the New York City metropolitan area. Many of the same questions were raised repeatedly. Teachers worried about the issue of neutrality. They wanted to know, "Do we have the right to express our own point of view in class?" A few asked how they could involve their students in political action.

Students wondered whether, "Once war begins, do we still have a right to protest against government policy?" In response, I often discussed my own experience as a high school teacher organizing students in public schools to be political activists around different social issues. These included campaigns between 1978 and 1993 against cuts in school budgets, against US military interventions in Central America, in opposition to apartheid in South Africa and racial violence in our community, and in support of reproductive freedom, abortion rights, and condom availability.

One of my primary goals as a high school social studies teacher was to empower young people so that they could become active citizens and agents for democratic social change. I recognize that the most effective way to empower students is to encourage them to think about issues and to help them learn how to collect, organize, analyze, and present information and their own ideas. If, in my classroom, I can encourage them to think and act, the habit of thinking and acting will stay with them long after I am just a dim memory.

This approach requires that teachers be part of, but not dominate, classroom discourse, and it means being willing to express your views on controversial issues. Everyone has a point of view and I believe it is much more honest to present it than to try to keep it hidden below the surface. Rather than neutrality, our goal should be open, honest, and respectful dialogue. If we are afraid to express our views in open discussion, how will students learn how to participate as active citizens in a democratic society?

Many new teachers without tenure are afraid that if they involve students as political activists, they will jeopardize their positions. While I do not want to minimize this concern, I want to present a model that I was able to use effectively to engage students as activists. The Forum Club was an independent student group, chartered by the Student Government, that sponsored student-led forums on controversial issues, prepared reports on school finances and presented them as testimony at public hearings, wrote position papers for publication in local newspapers, and organized student and community support for a school-based public health clinic. Usually, the students who joined the club were from my classes, but they also involved their friends. In addition, as the club gained a reputation in the school, new students would come to meetings to raise their own issues. As a result, one year the Forum Club sponsored a bulletin board display on gays and lesbians in history and on another occasion helped Islamic students organize a meeting to address stereotypes about their religion.

In general, the Forum Club provided students who were excited by classroom discussions of social justice and democratic rights, or who were upset by events in our school, with a place where they could further explore their questions and act based on their beliefs. As the club's faculty advisor, I was able to both encourage students to see themselves as activists and to help them learn through experience how to organize for social change.

As a chartered student group, the Forum Club was entitled to some school funds, to do fund raising in school, distribute a newsletter and leaflets, hang up posters, make and sell political buttons, and to use rooms, copying machines, and computers. It gave us access to other students, the ability to meet with parent groups, and the right to send speakers to classes to report on club activities. An elected executive committee met regularly (sometimes daily during heated campaigns) and we tried to hold monthly meetings of the full club. Students actually received community service credit for their political involvement.

Being a student club meant that it had to have a clear educational purpose. Our educational goals included making reasoned decisions based on an evaluation of existing evidence, researching issues and presenting information in writing and on graphs, exploring the underlying ideas that shape our points of view, giving leadership by example to other students, and taking collective and individual responsibility for the success of programs. Significantly, all of these are part of the New York State Civics and citizenship standards. To promote academic achievement, as well as to help students present their ideas, club members continually put their opinions into writing and edited each other's work. One collective essay, that accused a local newspaper of bias in its negative coverage of pro-choice demonstrations, was published on its op-ed page.

Being an official student club also saddled us with responsibilities, but they were not onerous. Students had to abide by school rules. We had to be willing to discuss plans and handouts with school administrators and students had to get parental permission to participate in after school or weekend activities. We tried to get as much publicity for the club as possible on television and in mainstream and community newspapers. This generally gave the school good press and made it difficult to silence the students and me. Once the entire club appeared on a cable television program to discuss their opposition to laws requiring "parental consent" before teenagers could receive abortions. They also were quoted in local newspapers when they testified at public hearings in favor of making condom's available to students in public high schools.

Despite efforts to be responsible, the club and I were not completely protected from interference. When we invited a Sandanista mayor of a Nicaraguan town and a representative of the African National Congress to speak at the school, it was suggested by the social studies supervisor that students prepare "fact sheets" that presented alternative views (though we never did figure out what an acceptable "alternative view" of apartheid entailed). During a school-wide campaign in support of reproductive freedom and condom availability we were asked to invite an anti-abortion speaker to balance a presentation by the National Organization of Women. Preparation for this meeting was an opportunity for students to discuss issues and sharpen their ideas. A small group of "pro-life" students affiliated with the club acted as hosts, while other students raised questions and forcefully presented their views during the course of debate. Some anti-abortion teachers tried to take over the discussion, but the student moderator made it clear that she would call on people and that "students would speak first."

Once we were pressured by the school district to cancel a club trip to Washington to participate in a pro-choice demonstration. Their request was withdrawn when the club threatened to take the issue to the newspapers. However, the club's leadership agreed to take a supportive school administrator on the trip to ensure its educational legitimacy.

Many activist teachers are involved in outside political groups. These relationships sustain us during challenging political times. They also pose problems when organizing in schools. Since 1969, I have been a member of a community-based social action group. Initially, the community group tried to organize in high schools and local colleges by creating chapters. I know if you are an activist this model sounds familiar, but in my view it rarely works well. Students, parents and teachers are often suspicious of outside groups and school administrators are actively hostile. The students in the Forum Club never joined the community group, but they were informally related to it. We often attended local rallies and community meetings organized by the community group and joined its members at citywide and national marches.

My role as faculty advisor to the club meant I had to put the needs of the students and the club's decisions ahead of my own views. Sometimes, when students did not agree with my ideas, I had to back off. For example, in 1991, during the first Gulf War, the club decided not to participate in anti-war activities while troops were involved in military conflict. In addition, some demonstrations were potentially too dangerous. I did not bring students to one local rally against racial violence because I knew there would be hostile counter-demonstrators. As the club's faculty advisor, I knew that I always had to protect myself. I had typed lesson plans the day after a club activity because inevitably that was the day I

would receive an unannounced visit by the central administration.

It was distressing, but not surprising, that as the United States prepared to attack Iraq during the early months of 2003, many students did not understand their right to disagree with and protest against government policies. Following the events of 9/11, government leaders with the support of the media used fear and innuendo to promote an uncritical patriotism. But active citizenship in a democratic society requires critical thinking and the constant questioning of authority. In my view, far greater than any potential threat to the United States from Iraq, was the threat to democratic institutions when teachers are afraid to explain their views and students and adults are afraid to express disagreement with government policies.

I have not seen or heard from most of the students involved in the Forum Club's activities in at least a decade. But over the years I have learned about a few of them. One helped organize livery drivers into a union. Another became a lawyer and activist in the local South Asian community. A third, after graduating from college and medical school, took a position at UNESCO that allowed her to promote public health around the world. Finally, one became an English teacher who works with recent Latino immigrants from Central America. I am not sure if their parents are happy with the choices they made, and I certainly do not take credit for them, but I believe their experience as activists in high school played a role in their later choices and validate these activities and this approach to organizing students for social change.

If this makes me a "social predator," I am proud to be one.

Teaching Activity: Does Social Justice Require Activism?

Many teachers identify with the principles of social justice, but refrain from personal activism, or if they are activists, from involving students. When I speak with teachers around the country, the issue of whether a meaningful commitment to social justice requires a commitment to activism has been very contentious. I say it does. I am not demanding involvement in particular issues that I may find important. But I am saying that teachers, and students with the support of their teachers, must decide on the issues that are important to them, and become actively involved in shaping the world. For me, that is the essence of democracy and the preparation of students for active citizenship in a democratic society.

Add your voice to the discussion:
1. Have you ever participated in social action? What was the issue(s)? Why did you participate?
2. In your opinion, should teachers be open about their involvement? Explain.
3. Does a meaningful commitment to social justice require activism? Explain.
4. Should teachers involve students in activist projects? Explain.

References and Recommendations for Further Reading

Achebe, C. 1996. *Things all apart*. Portsmouth, NH: Heinemann Educational Books.

Applebome, P. 2007. "In court: When clothes speak to more than fashion," *The New York Times*, September 23.

Banks, J. 1991. "A curriculum for empowerment, action and change," in C. Sleeter, ed. *Empowerment through multicultural education*. Albany, NY: SUNY Press, pp. 125–42.

Banks, J. 1993. The Canon debate, knowledge construction, and multicultural education. *Educational Researcher* 22(5): 4–14.

Bigelow, W. 1988. "Critical pedagogy at Jefferson High School," *Equity and Choice* 4(2): 14–19.

Bigelow, W. 1990. "Inside the classroom: Social vision and critical pedagogy," *Teachers College Record*, 91(3): 437–46.

Byrne, K. 2004. From the Editor. *OAH Magazine of History* 18(5).

Christensen, L. 2000. *Reading, Writing, and Rising Up*. Milwaukee, WI: Rethinking Schools.

Crook, J. 1994. "The social studies teacher as curriculum creator: Reflections on teaching middle school social studies," in E. W. Ross, ed. *Reflective practice in social studies, NCSS Bulletin no. 88*. Washington, DC: National Council for the Social Studies, pp. 13–21.

Danzer, G., Klor de Alva, J. Krieger, L. et al. 2005. *The Americans*. Evanston, IL: McDougal-Littell.

Dewey, J. 1939. *Freedom and culture*. New York: G. P. Putnam.

Dillon, S. 2003. "Threats and responses in the classroom; Schools seek right balance as students join war debate," *The New York Times*, March 7.

Donnach, A. 2003. "Social Predation 101: Now showing in classrooms near you," *Sierra Times*, http://www.myshortpencil.com/schooltalk/messages/2/3361.html?1100218496, accessed April 13, 2007.

Doyle, R. 2004. *Books challenged or banned in 2003–2004*. http://www.ila.org/pdf/2004banned.pdf, accessed September 24, 2007.

Dunbar, A. ed., 1914. *Masterpieces of Negro Eloquence*. New York: The Bookery Pub.

Ebner, M. 2003. "Submitting a proposal for a Teaching American History grant," *Perspectives, Newsmagazine of the American Historical Association* 41(8).

Feder, B. 1967. *Viewpoints: USA*. New York: American Book Company.

Fine, B. 1943. "Ignorance of U.S. history shown by college freshmen," *The New York Times*, April 4.

Finn, R. 2007. "Summer reading title prompts resistance from parents, not students," *The New York Times*, July 8.

Freire, P. 1970. *Pedagogy of the oppressed*. New York: Seabury.

Freire, P. 1995. *Pedagogy of hope*. New York: Continuum.

Greene, M. 1993a. "Diversity and inclusion: Towards a curriculum for human beings," *Teachers College Record* 95(2): 211–21.

Greene, M. 1993b. "Reflections on post-modernism and education," *Educational Policy* 7(2): 106–11.

Greene, M. 1993c. "The passions of pluralism: Multiculturalism and expanding community," *Educational Researcher* 22(1): 13–18.

Hartocollis, A. 2001. "Campus culture wars flare anew over tenor of debate after the attacks," *The New York Times*, September 30.

Hildebrand, J. 2003. "Sorry, Charlie: Book becomes a target," *Newsday*, October 14.

Holson, L. 2005. "How the tumultuous marriage of Miramax and Disney failed," *The New York Times*, March 6: 34.

Horton, M., and Freire, P. 1990. *We make the road by walking*. Philadelphia, PA: Temple University Press.

Horton, M., with J. Kohl and H. Kohl. 1990. *The long haul: An autobiography*. New York: Doubleday.

Hymowitz K. 2002. "The nation's social studies teachers have lots of ideas for improving he curriculum—all of them bad," *The Weekly Standard*, May 6.

King, M. Jr. 1967. *A Call to Conscience: The Landmark Speeches of Martin Luther King, Jr.* http://www.stanford.edu/group/King/publications/speeches/Where_do_we_go_from_here.html, accessed September 16, 2007.

Kohl, H. 1994. *I won't learn from you and other thoughts on creative maladjustment*. New York: New Press.

Krugman, P. 2003. "Everything is Political," *The New York Times*, August 5. http://select.nytimes.com/search/restricted/article?res=F4091FFF355A0C-768CDDA10894DB404482, accessed September 16, 2007.

Leming, J., Ellington, L. and Porter-Magee, K. 2003. *Where did social studies go wrong?* Washington, DC: Thomas B. Fordham Institute.

McCunn, R. 1981. *Thousand pieces of gold*. San Francisco, CA: Design Enterprise.

Murphy, D. 1991. "Teaching the hard lessons of racism," *United Federation of Teachers Bulletin* September 30: 9a.

Nash, G. 1995. "Creating history standards in United States and world history," *Organization of American Historians Magazine of History* 9(3).

Natale, J. 1995. "Bone of contention," *The American School Board Journal* January: 18–23.

National Council for the Social Studies. 2007. "Academic freedom and the social studies teacher," *Social Education* 71(5).

Prescott, O. 1953. "Books of the Times," *The New York Times*, September 15.

Paterson, K. 1991. *Lyddie*. New York: Puffin Books.

Pogrebin, R. and Collins, G. 2004. "Shift at historical society raises concerns," *The New York Times*, July 19.

Ravitch, D. and Schlesinger, A. Jr. 1996. "The new,

improved history standards," *The Wall Street Journal*, April 3.

Ravitch, D. 2001. "Now is the time to teach democracy," *Education Week*, October 17, 21(7).

Ravitch, D. 2002. "The world in the classroom: September 11: Seven lessons for the schools," *Educational Leadership*, 60(2): 6–9.

Rethinking Schools. 1994. *Rethinking our classrooms: Teaching for equity and justice*. Milwaukee, WI: Rethinking Schools.

Rochester, M. 2003. "The training of idiots," in Leming, J., Ellington, L. and Porter, K. *Where did social studies go wrong?* Washington, DC: Thomas B. Fordham Institute.

Rothschild, M. 2006. "Judge Rules Teachers Have No Free Speech Rights in Class," *Progressive* March 27. http://www.commondreams.org/views06/0327–33.htm, accessed April 9, 2008.

Schlesinger, A., Jr. 1992. *The disuniting of America: Reflections on a multicultural society*. New York: Norton.

Seldes, G., ed. 1966. *The great quotations*. New York: Lyle Stuart.

Shor, I. 1987. "Educating the educators: A Freirean approach to the crisis in teacher education," in I. Shor, ed. *Freire for the classroom*. Portsmouth, NH: Heinemann Educational Books, pp. 7–32.

Singer, A. 2003. "Student clubs: A model for political organizing," *Rethinking Schools* 17(4).

Singer, A. 2004. "Past as Prologue, History vs. Social Studies," *Social Education* 68(2).

Takaki, R. 1993. *A Different Mirror*. Boston, MA: Little, Brown.

Thomas, J. 1996. "Revised history standards defuse explosive issues," *The New York Times*, April 3, B8.

Twain, M. 1996. *Adventures of Huckleberry Finn*. New York: Oxford University Press.

US Department of Education. 1994. *High standards for all students*, June. Washington, DC: Government Printing Office.

Wolfer, S. 2005. "We're kids—not convicts! Protest school metal detectors," *New York Daily News*, September 20.

Zinn, H. 1999. *A people's history of the United States: 1492-present*. New York: HarperCollins.

6. How Do You Plan a Social Studies Curriculum?

Overview

- Define curriculum
- Evaluate teacher decision-making
- Examine the components of a social studies curriculum
- Participate in current curriculum debates
- Explore curriculum options
- Develop social studies curriculum calendars

Key Concepts

Curriculum, Directed Experience, Reflection, Hidden Curriculum, Standards, Curriculum Calendar

Questions

- What is a Curriculum?
- How Does a Curriculum Help Teachers Make Decisions?
- How are Social Studies Curriculum Organized?
- Which Version of History?
- How Do You Plan and Use a Curriculum Calendar?

Essays

1. Teaching Global History
2. Multicultural Social Studies
3. Are We Teaching Religious Myth Instead of the History of Religion?

WHAT IS A CURRICULUM?

Major league baseball manager, Joe Torre, likes to remind reporters after a bad loss that every baseball team plays 162 games a year and no one game is crucial. The regular season is a "marathon, not a sprint" (http://www.cigaraficionado.com, accessed April 15, 2007). Torre planned for the post-season playoffs at the same time that he tried to win games on a daily basis. One major concern was getting players with nagging injuries enough rest so they could perform at the highest level when the playoffs began.

The school year, like the regular season in baseball, is a long haul. A curriculum requires a long-range plan for achieving content, concept, academic skill, and social goals. It helps social studies teachers decide how to organize units, lessons, and activities for their classes. The most effective curricula offer teachers a range of options, rather than fixed guidelines. They provide direction for classroom decisions while allowing for continuous reevaluation, and are open to change in response to student needs, new ideas, and classroom developments.

John Dewey (discussed in Chapter 4) believed that understanding the relationship between learning and human experience is fundamental for developing classroom curriculum. Dewey wanted teachers to direct learning by organizing experiences for students and by encouraging them to reflect on these experiences. In a real sense, in a Deweyan school, curriculum is everything that happens to students and helps them make meaning out of their lives. In these schools, all aspects of the program are continually evaluated because they all impact student learning. In most secondary schools, however, curriculum is much more narrowly defined. In these schools, *curriculum* refers to the content knowledge teachers are expected to convey to students in a particular subject area. Although broader subject-related concepts and specific academic skills may be included in prescribed guidelines, most of these curricula are text and test directed, and student recall of information is what is valued. Many of these curricula even attempt to eliminate the decision-making role of teachers by providing "teacher-proof" lessons.

Michael Apple, a contemporary educational theorist, is highly critical of this narrow view of curriculum. He claims that much of what takes place in traditional content-centered programs is based on an unstated and assumed "hidden curriculum." In *Ideology and Curriculum* (2004), Apple shows how a hidden curriculum shapes subject content, classroom relationships, and teacher practice in ways that limit a teacher's choices, suppress critical thinking by students, and train people to accept without question the social status quo.

In social studies classrooms, the hidden curriculum includes the encouragement of highly stratified competitive relationships among students, the authoritarian position held by many teachers, and the passive nature of most learning, which reinforce, and are reinforced by, unquestioned assumptions about the nature of society. For example, social and ideological conflicts are generally presented as negative factors that undermine societies and consensus is promoted as a paramount social virtue. Even when conflicting views are examined in social studies classes, students are usually offered only a narrow spectrum of officially condoned choices.

If Dewey and Apple are correct, an official curriculum may be narrowly defined, but the actual classroom curriculum continues to be everything that happens to students. The issue for social studies teachers is whether we act openly and consciously examine hidden curriculum assumptions, or we allow them to operate in the shadows.

Teaching Activity: What was Life Like in Colonial New York City?

Successful teaching is based on a dynamic three-way relationship between a teacher's classroom decisions, student involvement in learning, and a long-range social studies curriculum. I have taught this lesson on a number of academic levels ranging from middle school through graduate classes for teacher education students. A lesson like this one can take alternative directions in different classes. When I prepare, I organize optional document-based material, either printed on the same activity sheet or a separate sheet, or on PowerPoint slides, which I present in response to student questions.

At the start of the lesson, students are presented with a map of New York City (Berlin and Harris, 2005: 58), drawn in 1813, but showing the layout of the city in the 1740s. Students are divided into groups of three or four members and asked to identify "interesting or puzzling" aspects of the map. When the groups reported back to the class, three things generally stand out in their comments.

The northernmost boundary of the city in the 1740s was a wall near what we now called Chambers Street. New York City in the era prior to the American Revolution was a village at the tip of Manhattan Island, a small fragment of the city we know today.

Although many streets retain the same names over two centuries later, some familiar streets and landmarks have different names. The North River of colonial America is now known as the Hudson River.

During discussion, students recognize that New York City in the 1740s was very different from the way they envision it when they casually read about the past. They also identify perplexing labels and symbols just north of the city's wall; a "collect," a tiny gibbet or gallows with a hanging body, and a picture of a small fire. Once they realize that there were streams entering and leaving the collect, students quickly figure out that it was a reservoir. However, the gallows, which were labeled, "Plot Negro Gibbeted," and the fire, which was labeled "Plot Negro's burnt here," generally do not have easy explanations. Students are always surprised to learn that enslaved Africans lived in New York City during this period.

In response to student speculation about the symbols, I provide documents from the *New York and Slavery: Complicity and Resistance* curriculum guide (available at: http://www.nyscss.org, accessed April 15, 2007). They include selections from a 1741 "conspiracy trial" that ended with the execution of 35 enslaved Africans for plotting an uprising.

After students read the documents, I ask if they think the Africans should have been executed for plotting rebellion and murder. There is usually sharp disagreement ranging from arguments that they were fighting for their freedom to "laws are laws, and people who break them should be punished."

Rarely do students reach consensus, especially in classes where there are diverse student populations. I try to end discussion with a series of questions to be examined in future lessons. Can historians place themselves "in the shoes" of other people? Should historians judge people from the past based on standards from today? Is there a universal morality? How important was slavery in shaping New York and the other British northern colonies?

Add your voice to the discussion:
1. How should we define curriculum?
2. In your opinion, is there such a thing as a "hidden curriculum?" Why or why not?
3. In your opinion, is there a "hidden curriculum" in the classroom described here? Explain your answer.

Think it over:
Compared with the South and the Caribbean, there were relatively few enslaved Africans in the northern British colonies. The existence of slavery in the North could be acknowledged in a few sentences. In your opinion, does this topic merit major focus in the secondary school social studies curriculum? Why or why not?

Try it yourself:
1. What decisions were made by the teacher prior to and during the course of this lesson?
2. What goals are reflected in these decisions?
3. Would you have made similar choices? Why or why not?

It's your classroom:
In a high-school classroom, would you spend a class period on this lesson? Why or why not?

HOW DOES A CURRICULUM HELP TEACHERS MAKE DECISIONS?

Teaching involves choices that are based on our goals as teachers, our understanding of our students and their academic and social needs, and our efforts to achieve the goals spelled out in a course outline. Ideally, a curriculum helps teachers visualize a broader picture, allowing us to focus on what we are teaching today within a context of what we will examine with our students tomorrow, the next week, the next month, and at the end of the school year. A curriculum helps teachers understand the relationship between lessons, and to build on activities, understandings, and skills over the course of time. It also helps us examine the ramifications of our choices. If in November a teacher decides to spend an extra day on the Bank Controversy during the Jackson administration, it could mean that in June the class will not have time to discuss the impact of the Vietnam War on US society.

The lesson on colonial New York I described in the preceding teaching activity, involved a number of choices. The first was simply the decision to include a period-long discussion on slavery in New York City in a crowded United States history curriculum. Other choices include selecting documents, directing discussion, asking follow-up questions, whether to call on volunteers or non-volunteers, and even the sequence of speakers. When a student strongly argues that the Africans were freedom fighters at the beginning of the discussion, the class can take on a different dynamic than it does when initial speakers focus on law and order.

Does a teacher's efforts to direct class discussion, through questioning and the selection of participants to speak, mean that they have an undemocratic hidden curriculum? I do not think so. Having goals is not the same as having a hidden curriculum, if teachers are conscious of their choices and are willing to examine and reevaluate them along with their students and colleagues.

Curriculum choices and changes can also be on a much grander scale. In Fall 2001, in response to the destruction of the World Trade Center in New York and the Pentagon in Washington and the war in Central Asia that followed, many social studies teachers revamped their course outlines. Some simply infused more current events into class discussions and assignments. Others shifted or emphasized discussion of fundamental social studies concepts such as nationalism, imperialism, isolation, globalization, democracy, and justice, and focused more attention on geographic content and map-reading skills. This kind of shift is easier when a teacher has a sense of the year as a whole and focuses on themes and essential questions rather than on the accumulation of discrete content.

Teaching Activity: How Representative is a Primary Source Document?

A key question teachers must consider when organizing lessons around the analysis of primary source documents is whether a document is representative of an era or a group of people. Should social studies students be presented with a quote that offers biblical defense of slavery in the United States, a patriotic song, a political cartoon representing a minority point of view, a terrorist or a dictator's justification for his or her actions, or a selection from a personal memoir, such as *The Diary of a Young Girl* by Anne Frank (1995), which tells the story of one adolescent girl?

Stephanie Hunte wanted students in her 10th-grade global history class to explore the roots of Nazi ideology in nineteenth-century German nationalism. She provided them with an excerpt from a poem, written in 1878. Stephanie located the poem in *Source Records of the Great War, Vol. 1* (Horne 1931: 89) published by the American Legion. In the introduction to the collection, the editors wrote that "the German character" includes "vain and reckless arrogance in power," and that German society stood in opposition to "the sunlight of democratic civilization." The editors did not provide the title of the poem, the name of the poet, or a source for the fragment.

During class, a student asked: "How do we know if this poem is the view of one person or represents the German point of view? Didn't other ideas exist in Germany also?" As a result of the student's question and class discussion that followed, Stephanie decided to drop this poem from the lesson in the future.

Add your voice to the discussion:
1. Do you consider this poem an acceptable primary source for a high school social studies class? Explain your answer.
2. When teachers select "representative" documents for students to examine in class, are we editing the past and deciding in advance what students will discover? Explain your views.

Think it over:
How would you have addressed the student's questions?

It's your classroom:
How would you decide which documents to use in a document-based inquiry lesson?

HOW IS A SOCIAL STUDIES CURRICULUM ORGANIZED?

Responsible, student-centered teachers who are prepared to explain their curriculum decisions usually have a considerable amount of free space in which to maneuver. In any case, although the social studies include everything, everything cannot be included in a year-long social studies curriculum. A curriculum needs a focus and basic organizing principles. This section examines general strategies for organizing social studies curriculum.

The US Constitution does not mention education. It is a responsibility reserved for individual states, which can approach it in a variety of ways, including how to develop and promote social studies curricula. California provides local school districts with a formal social studies curriculum and financial incentives to adopt it. Texas tries to mandate its curriculum through centralized control over the approval of textbooks. New York State gives local school districts broader freedom to develop their own curriculum guidelines, but expects teachers to prepare students for standardized final examinations in grades 8 (social studies skills and US history), 10 (global history and geography), and 11 (US history and government). Within all of these approaches, secondary school social studies departments take the basic guidelines and translate them into curriculum calendars; individual teachers use the calendars to develop daily lesson plans and student projects.

The National Council for Social Studies (NCSS) advocates teaching an integrated social studies curriculum, including anthropology, economics, geography, history, philosophy, political science, psychology, and sociology. The NCSS (1994: vii) argues that an integrated interdisciplinary approach is the best way "to help young people develop the ability to make informed and reasoned decisions for the public good as citizens of a culturally diverse, democratic society in an interdependent world." The organization's publications and curriculum guidelines, including *Charting a Course: Social Studies for the 21st Century* (1989) and *Expectations of Excellence: Curriculum Standards for Social Studies* (1994), stress purposeful and experiential learning over course content. According to *Expectations of Excellence*, to promote civic competence, a social studies curriculum must "foster individual and cultural identity along with understanding of the forces that hold society together or pull it apart; include observation and participation in the school and community; address critical issues and the world as it is; prepare students to make decisions based on democratic principles; and lead to citizen participation in public affairs" (*Expectations of Excellence* 1994: 159).

These goals require a curriculum that promotes knowledge of diverse subjects, the ability to integrate ideas from different disciplines, democratic values and beliefs, thinking skills, and social and civic participation skills. In *Charting a Course* (1989: 3), the NCSS emphasizes:

"content knowledge from the social studies should not be treated merely as received knowledge to be accepted and memorized, but as the means through which open and vital questions may be explored and confronted. Students must be made aware that just as contemporary events have been shaped by actions taken by people in the past, they themselves have the capacity to shape the future."

Advocates of content-focused teaching tend to prefer a history-based curriculum (Evans 2004). When Diane Ravitch endorsed the revised national history standards, she contrasted them to "mushy," insubstantial social studies. Lynne V. Cheney, while chair of the National Endowment for the Humanities, argued that the idea of social studies is so broad that it includes "everything from driver education to values clarification" (Cheney 1987).

The National Council for History Education (Reinhold 1991; Cornbleth and Waugh 1995) successfully recruited prominent university historians—including Gary Nash of UCLA, Eric Foner and Kenneth Jackson of Columbia, and Mary Beth Norton of Cornell—to a campaign to have history "occupy a large and vital place in the education of the private person and the public citizen." The organization's greatest success was in California, where the state's Department of Education developed curriculum guidelines based on a statement from the California History-Social Science Framework (Berenson 1993) that "history is the discipline best able to integrate the social sciences, literature, and the humanities into a coherent whole for the purposes of K-12 education." This curriculum uses a heavily chronological content focus to teach US and world history in grades 7–12.

Alternative approaches for organizing social studies curricula include thematic (examined in Chapter 10) and project-based (examined in Chapter 11) approaches that can focus on either history or social studies. The project-based approach, which has been identified with the Coalition for Essential Schools and Brown University, actively involves students as historians and social scientists, and engages them in hands-on activities and research. Advocates of a thematic approach to social studies include the National Issues Forum (McKenzie and Hellerman 2002: 4), which publishes booklets that present multiple perspectives on controversial issues. The NCSS, in *Charting a Course*, endorsed the general idea of a thematic curriculum "selective enough to provide time for extended in-depth study."

WHICH VERSION OF HISTORY?

Even if history is placed at the center of a social studies curriculum, the problem still remains: Which version of history? From September, 2004 through February, 2005, an exhibit at the New York Historical Society (NYHS) on the career of Alexander Hamilton claimed that he was "The Man who Made Modern America." The program, which was created under the auspices of the Gilder Lehrman Institute of American History, drew a lot of criticism.

Jesse Lemisch, a historian, charged that it ignored the previous 35 years of historical scholarship and described it as "a paean to triumphalist capitalism." Richard Rabinowitz, president of a company that develops museum exhibitions on American history, accused the Gilder Lehrman Institute of creating "shrines" that promote "patriotic fervor" rather than exploring history and David Nasaw, a professor at the Graduate Center of the City University of New York, warned they were "overemphasizing the role of great white men" (Pogrebin and Collins 2004: E1).

On closer inspection, it is not surprising that the exhibit identified the American nation with the person its promoters believed epitomized capitalist industrial development. Major funders included Richard Gilder, an investment banker, Lewis Lehrman, heir to the Rite Aide drug store chain, Bear Stearns, Bloomberg, a billion dollar communications company, Commerce Bank, the History Channel, and the *New York Post*, which was owned by the mega-billionaire rightwing ideologue Rupert Murdoch (New York Historical Society 2004: 9). The curator who assembled the exhibit was the Senior Editor at *National Review*, a major conservative magazine, and a member of the advisory board of the Gilder Lehrman Institute.

There are other options to this way of presenting history. Nel Noddings (1992), a feminist educator, has called for a sweeping reorganization of the social studies curriculum because of its overwhelmingly male context. She recommends introducing women's culture into social studies by focusing on social interaction and human relationships, family and community building, the role of love and caring in different cultures, and movements for world peace. As an example of how the male cultural bias shapes social studies curriculum, she cites the career of Emily Greene Balch, winner of the Nobel Peace Prize in 1946, whose work is ignored because in our society, peace is not valued as much as war. The question of which version of history we teach is discussed in greater detail in essays at the conclusion of this chapter. In support of Noddings, Margaret Smith Crocco (2006) has proposed that units on recent global history focus on the treatment of women in the developed and underdeveloped world.

Teaching Activity: Facts or Thinking Skills?

Among advocates of a history-based curriculum, there is continuing disagreement whether its focus should be on historical facts or historical thinking skills.

1. Lynne V. Cheney (1987: 5–6) is concerned that current social studies curricula focus too much on "'process': the belief that we can teach our children *how* to think without troubling them to learn anything worth thinking about, the belief that we can teach them *how* to understand the world in which they live without conveying to them the events and ideas that have brought it into existence . . . Dates and names are not all that students should know, but such facts are a beginning, an initial connection to the sweep of human experience."

2. E. D. Hirsch (1993: 19) wants social studies teachers to teach a content-based core curriculum that replaces learning skills with content goals. Hirsch believes that problem-solving skills depend on a wealth of relevant knowledge; kids already "possess higher order thinking skills . . . what these students lack is not critical thinking but academic knowledge."

3. Gary Nash (National Center for History in the Schools 1996b) counters that "The study of history involves much more than the passive absorption of facts, dates, names and places. History is at its essence a process of reasoning based on evidence from the past."

HOW DO YOU PLAN AND USE A CURRICULUM CALENDAR?

Whatever the content of a curriculum, or its concept and skills goals, its value for social studies teachers and their willingness to follow it depend on whether it provides a useful lesson schedule, or curriculum calendar, and classroom materials. Curricula are usually organized by grade level, and annual calendars are subdivided into units (discussed in Chapter 7), lessons (discussed in Chapter 8), and activities (discussed in Chapter 9). Strategies to introduce, develop, and reinforce content, concepts, and academic and social skills are woven throughout the calendar.

New York State uses an "expanding horizons" social studies curriculum based on three principles: (1) young children learn about the world by examining ever larger "circles" or "communities," and by comparing what they find with what they already know about themselves and their social relationships (e.g., self | family | school | neighborhood | city | state | nation | world); (2) as students mature intellectually and socially, they will discover new meaning and develop enhanced skills by reexamining familiar topics; and (3) to prepare students for life in a multicultural society and world, social studies curricula must examine the history and cultures of a broad spectrum of people and civilizations.

From kindergarten through 3rd grade, the New York State social studies curriculum moves from self to family, school, community, and world community, as children compare the similarities and differences among people and cultures. US history is formally introduced in grade 4, and is studied in greater depth in grades 7 and 8 and again in grade 11. World history, divided into the history of the western hemisphere and the eastern hemisphere, is introduced in grades 5 and 6 and is studied in greater depth in grades 9 and 10. The US government and its political and economic systems are explored in grade 12. Students are expected to pass a standardized statewide final examination in global history and geography at the end of grade 10 and in US history and government after grade 5, 8 and 11. Using this guideline as a starting point, each school district establishes its own curriculum calendars.

The state of California's curriculum is considered a model sequential history-based social studies curriculum (available at: http://www.cde.ca.gov/re/pn/fd/documents/histsocsci-stnd.pdf, accessed April 15, 2007) with students alternating between the study of United States and global history. In 5th grade, students study the development of the United States up to 1850, with "an emphasis on the people who were already here, when and from where others arrived, and why they came." A major goal in the fifth grade is developing student "understanding of how the principles of the American republic form the basis of a pluralistic society in which individual rights are secured" (p. 16). In 6th grade, students study the history and geography of ancient civilizations, in seventh medieval and early modern times, and in 10th grade, the modern world. In grade 8, students study United States history from the Constitution through World War I and in grade 11, they look at the United States from World War I through the present.

Sample 11th-Grade Curriculum Calendar

In my experience, the most useful curriculum calendars give teachers a sense of how an entire year looks, while leaving plenty of room for collective departmental decisions and individual teacher choices based on developments in their classes. A curriculum calendar is an evolving document designed to meet specific program needs, rather than a precise model to be copied. When I started at Franklin K. Lane High School in 1982, the department began the year with the exploration and settlement of the New World by Europe and ended the first semester with 1865 and the conclusion of the Civil War. Later, we shifted the semester break to 1877 and the end of Reconstruction. A 1989–1990 calendar divided the academic year at the presidential election of 1896.

As the social studies department curriculum committee re-designed the Lane United States history calendar, we tried to take the following into account:

- New York City has semiannual reorganization in high school, so social studies teachers had to have their classes in roughly the same place at the end of the semester in January.
- Depending on holidays and the weather, each semester included approximately 88 lessons. The calendar had to include space for orientation, review lessons, tests, and projects.
- Although the US Constitution, the structure of government, and the economic system needed to be introduced, they would be studied primarily in separate government and economics classes.
- Within the department, teachers prefer to emphasize different aspects of US history. For example, some wanted to spend time examining the origins of American society during the colonial era, whereas others emphasized the issues facing the new government and nation.
- We wanted to guarantee that there would be sufficient time at the end of the year for students to examine the post-World War II United States.
- We decided to identify lesson topics by suggesting possible AIM questions.
- Students had to be prepared for a state-wide final examination. Some teachers wanted to reserve extra days for review, whereas others wanted time allocated for student presentations and discussions of current events.

Each unit and lesson in the Lane curriculum calendar involves numerous teacher choices. For example, in the first unit, a teacher has to decide how much time to spend on native peoples and the colonial era, and whether to introduce African civilizations in a US history curriculum. We recommended one lesson on Virginia and one on Massachusetts, but some teachers wanted to spend more time. Even the title of a unit, which reflects a point of view about the topic, involves choices. When we wrote it in 1989, we called it "Discovery and Settlement," but I now refer to it as "Encounter and Settlement." Another teacher might call it "Encounter and Conquest."

By the end of the 1990s, the New York State high school social studies curriculum had changed again. Study about Meso-American civilizations, the "Encounter" between the Eastern and Western Hemispheres following the Colombian exchange, the colonization of the New World and the Atlantic Slave Trade was shifted to the Global History curriculum. These changes were designed to allow social studies teachers' time to cover events through the conclusion of World War I in the first semester of United States history and ensure a comprehensive examination of events in the twentieth century. Many teachers use the extra time for intensive review for year-end standardized tests. I prefer to "open the curriculum up" and involve students in special research and classroom projects. Student dialogues are discussed in Chapter 7, Essay 2. Oral history reports and web-based research projects are discussed in Chapter 11, Essays 1 and 2. The sample 11th-grade United States History calendar presented here reflects changes and state mandates and my own teaching preferences.

11th-Grade US History Calendar First Semester Calendar of Lessons

1. Orientation: How can I do well in this class?
2. What are the "BIG" questions? (See Chapter 4, Essay 2.)

Unit 1: British America: From Settlement to Revolution (12 lessons)

3. When does American history begin? (See Chapter 4, Essay 1.)
4. Mercantilism and Empire: Why did Great Britain want new world colonies?
5. What was life like in the British colonies?
6. How did Enlightenment ideas change America?
7. Why did Great Britain redefine its relationship with its American colonies?
8. How did the colonists respond to changes in British colonial policy?
9. Why did Thomas Paine call independence "Common Sense"?
10. What is the "promise" of the Declaration of Independence?
11. Social Conflict in the Colonies: Were all people "created equal"?
12. Global War: How did the British colonies win independence?
13. Unit Review: Was the revolutionary war "inevitable?"
14. Unit Test: British America: From settlement to revolution

Unit 2: Creating a Government (10 lessons)
15. Why did national leaders write a new constitution?
16. Original Intent: Why is the US Constitution a bundle of compromises?
17. How are checks and balances structured into the American government?
18. How was the constitution ratified?
19. Why was a Bill of Rights added to the US Constitution?
20. What problems did a new government have to solve?
21. How did the Supreme Court emerge as a constitutional "umpire?"
22/23. (2 days). Trial of the Founding Fathers: Did the US Constitution violate principles established in the Declaration of Independence?
24. Unit Test: Creating a government

Unit 3: Building a New Nation (12 lessons)
25. How did the American people become a nation?
26. How did the US role in world affairs change?
27. Why did Congress try to retain sectional balance?
28. How did the expansion of the right to vote change American society?
29. Why did women demand equal rights?
30. How did sectional conflict threaten union?
31. Manifest Destiny: Why did the new nation expand westward?
32. How did US expansion affect native peoples?
33. Texas: How should we remember the Alamo?
34. What were the consequences of war with Mexico?
35. Unit Test: New nation
36. Review previous unit tests

Unit 4: Sectionalism, Slavery, and War (12 lessons)
37. How did the Industrial Revolution change the United States?
38. How did changes in transportation connect the North and West?
39. Why did cotton production lead to the expansion of slavery in the South?
40. How did the South justify slavery?
41. What was life like for enslaved Africans?
42. How did enslaved Africans resist slavery?
43. Was slavery a regional or national institution?

44. Why did balance and compromise fail to settle sectional differences?
45. How did abolitionists battle against slavery?
46. Why did the election of 1860 lead to the Civil War?
47. Unit Review: What were the principle causes of the Civil War?
48. Unit Test: Sectionalism, Slavery, and War

Unit 5: Civil War and Reconstruction (9 lessons)
49. Why did the South try to leave the union?
50. How did the North win the war?
51. What role did women, immigrants, and African-Americans play in the war effort?
52. What were the goals of conflicting Reconstruction plans?
53. Could the wounds of war be healed?
54. How did the Reconstruction Amendments rewrite the US Constitution?
55. Was Reconstruction a "dawn without noon"?
56. What was the cost of the "failure" of Reconstruction?
57. Document-based Essay Unit Test: Civil War and Reconstruction

Unit 6: Industrialization Reshapes the United States (17 lessons)
58. How did technology change the United States?
59. What was the impact of industrial growth on native peoples?
60. How did industry change the way Americans did business?
61. How was government corrupted by "monopoly" power?
62. How did workers respond to industrialization?
63. Why did farmers demand reforms?
64. What was the Populist vision for the United States?
65. Why did a new wave of immigrants come to the United States?
66. What was life like in urban America?
67. Why did conflicts between workers and corporations sometimes lead to violence?
68. Why did muckrakers and progressives demand reform?
69. Why did women emerge as champions of reform?
70. How did Progressive reforms change the United States?

71. Why did some Americans demand radical change?
72. How did women achieve political rights?
73/74. (2 days) Presentation of student projects on the impact of industrialization and reform
75. Unit Test: Industrialization and Progressive Reform

Unit 7: The United States Emerges as a World Power (13 lessons)
76. Why did the United States look overseas for expansion?
77. What was the ideology of imperialism?
78. Was US policy in Asia imperialistic?
79. Why did the United States go to war with Spain?
80. Should the United States have intervened in Latin America and the Caribbean?
81. Panama: Does the end justify the means?
82. What were the origins of the "Great War"?
83. Why did the United States enter the World War?
84. What were Woodrow Wilson's goals for the United States?
85. What was the US role in the World War?
86. How did participation in the World War change life in the United States?
87. Should the United States have joined the League of Nations?
88. Unit (or mid-term) test: The United States emerges as a world power

11th-Grade US History Calendar Second Semester Calendar of Lessons
1. What are the "BIG" questions? (See Chapter 4, Essay 2.)
2. Organizing the 20th-Century America Oral History Project (See Chapter 11, Essay 1).
3. Researching and writing oral histories.

Unit 1: Prosperity and Depression (15 lessons)
4. Could America return to "normalcy" at the end of World War I?
5. Why were immigrants targeted during the Palmer Raids?
6. Who were Sacco and Vanzetti?
7. Why did the Scopes trial create so much controversy?
8. Great Migration: How did African-Americans create culture and community in the northern cities?
9. What was happening to the US economy and workforce during the 1920s?

10. Why did the economy collapse?
11. What was the Republican concept of the role of government?
12. What was the impact of the Great Depression on life in the United States?
13. What was the promise of the New Deal?
14. How did the Great Depression and New Deal affect life in New York (or any locality)?
15. How did the New Deal change US government?
16. Unit review: Did the New Deal solve the Great Depression?
17. Unit Test: Prosperity and Depression
18. Review unit test

Unit 2: World War II (13 lessons)
19. Organize student dialogue teams on the atomic bombing of Hiroshima and Nagasaki (See Chapter 7, Essay 3).
20. What were the underlying causes of World War II?
21. Why did many Americans demand isolation during the 1930s?
22. What were the underlying causes of US entry into the war?
23. What were the immediate causes of the US entry into the war?
24. How did the allies win in Europe?
25. How did the allies win in the Pacific?
26. Was total war justified?
27. Rosie the Riveter and Civil Rights: How did the war change life in the United States?
28. The internment of the Japanese: How could it happen here?
29. Cold War or United Nations: What will the postwar world look like?
30. Unit review (Dialogue): Should the United States have dropped the atomic bomb on Japan?
31. Unit test: World War II

Unit 3: Post-War America—A Changing Society (14 lessons)
32. Student teams read and edit oral histories for presentation in class.
33. How did life in the United States change after World War II?
34. How did suburbs and highways transform life in the United States?
35. Was the United States becoming a consumer society?
36. How did science and technology change life in the United States?

37. Were internal communists a threat to the "American way of life"?
38. Should the New Deal grow or be reined in?
39. What was the promise of the Kennedy era?
40. Could the United States be a "Great Society"?
41. Was Watergate a threat to democracy in the United States?
42. How did conservative forces reshape government and society?
43/44. (2 days) Presentation of oral histories on life in the 1940s, 1950s and 1960s
45. Document-based essay: Post-War America—A Changing Society
46. Introduce web-based research reports (See Chapter 11, Essay 2).

Unit 4: The African-American Struggle for Civil Rights (13 lessons)
47. Organize student dialogue on the Civil Rights Movement.
48. What was life like for African-Americans at the end of World War II?
49. How did African-Americans respond to these conditions?
50. What were the responses of Southern whites and state and local governments?
51. How did the federal government respond to the Civil Rights movement?
52. What were the ideas of the Civil Rights movement?
53. What were the strategies of the Civil Rights movement?
54. What was Martin Luther King Jr.'s vision for US society?
55. Did the Civil Rights movement significantly change the laws of the US?
56. Why did African-American communities explode?
57. Why did a new generation of African-American activists challenge the ideas and strategies of the Civil Rights movement?
58. Who was Malcolm X and what did he teach?
59. Unit review (Dialogue): Did the Civil Rights movement succeed?
60. Unit test: The African-American struggle for Civil Rights

Unit 5: Vietnam, the Cold War, and the "New World Order" (15 lessons)
61. Why did wartime allies fight a "Cold War"?
62. Why did "hot spots" emerge in Berlin, Korea, and Cuba?

63. How did the nuclear and space races shape the world?
64. How did the United States respond to anti-colonial movements in the Third World?
65. Did events in the Middle East threaten US security?
66. Why did East Asia play a central role in US foreign policy?
67. Why was the United States in Vietnam?
68. What happened to American troops in Vietnam?
69. What was the impact of US involvement in Vietnam on the American people?
70. Did US policy in Vietnam "fail"?
71. How did Middle Eastern conflicts affect life in the United States?
72. What happened to the Russian "Evil Empire"?
73. Can the United States establish a "New World Order"?
74. Document-based essay: The Vietnam War
75. Unit test: Cold War and Vietnam

Unit 6: Life in the Contemporary United States (10 lessons)
76. Why did the United States take a turn to the "Right"?
77. How did the women's rights movement change the United States?
78. Why did Supreme Court decisions spark controversy?
79. What is life like for the United States' newest immigrants?
80. How has computer technology changed the way we live?
81. Race: Can the United States become a more equal society?
82. What are the responsibilities of government in an economically developed society?
83. Why was politics so contentious during the Clinton and Bush administrations?
84. What was the impact of 9/11 on the United States?
85. Unit test: Document-based essay on life in the contemporary United States

Standardized Test Preparation (3 lessons)
86. Day I: Examine essay format/practice essays
87. Day II: Discuss short answer strategies/ review prior exams
88. Day III: Student study teams complete prior exams

Teaching Activity: Examining a Curriculum Calendar

Think it over:

1. The unit on "British America: From Settlement to Revolution" includes ten regular lessons, a review lesson, and a unit test. Write a paragraph describing what you think each of the first ten lessons might include?

2. What primary source documents could you use as resources in the unit "Creating a Government?"

3. Slavery is the focus in 9 of the 12 lessons in the unit "Sectionalism, Slavery, and War." Do you agree or disagree with this emphasis? Why?

4. In the first semester, lesson 51 directs attention toward the role of women, immigrants, and African-Americans in the Civil War. Lesson 69 asks, "Why did women emerge as champions of reform?" In the second semester, lesson 8 explores how African-Americans created "culture and community" in the northern cities and lesson 27 examines changes in the lives of women and African-Americans as a result of World War II. What do you think about focusing lessons on particular groups of people? Why?

5. The units "Prosperity and Depression" and "World War II" include lessons on the Palmer Raids, Sacco and Vanzetti, the Scopes trial, and the bombing of Hiroshima, as well as discussions of wartime discrimination against Japanese and African-Americans. In your opinion, does this focus present the United States in an unnecessarily negative light? Explain.

6. This calendar includes a 13 lesson thematic unit on the African-American struggle for Civil Rights in the 1950s and 1960s (outlined in greater detail in Chapter 6). Do you agree or disagree with this emphasis? Why?

7. How would you answer the question: "What are the 'BIG' questions for the twenty-first century?"

8. What is your general opinion of this lesson calendar? Why?

It's your class:

1. What would you include that is missing in this calendar? Why?

2. Would you leave only three days for review for a standardized final exam? Why?

"Some Educators Say Recent Events Are Not Yet The Stuff Of History"

The *Boston Globe* (Greenberger 2001) reports the following debate in Massachusetts: "The Clinton administration is over, but is it history? It is, according to a draft of the state's new American history curriculum. High school students would have to study NAFTA and Clinton's welfare reform law, and 'explain the causes and consequences' of his impeachment. Studying recent events energizes teenagers, supporters of the new guidelines say. But Abigail Thernstrom, a member of the State Board of Education and a political scientist, argues that it is much too soon to put Monica Lewinsky, let alone Bush vs. Gore, in their proper historical context. Those characters and events are still 'too politically and emotionally charged' to be taught well, Thernstrom said. 'I wouldn't trust myself to teach the last 20 years.'"

Join the conversation:

1. This calendar, updated in 2007, includes discussion of 9/11, 2001 and the Iraq war. Are these events too "recent" to be analyzed as "history"?

2. Which recent events do you consider "history"? Why?

3. Where would you end the curriculum calendar? Why?

Classroom Activity: Mock Trial in a US Government Course

New York State offers options in its 12th-grade "Participation in Government" curriculum. They include a political science class that focuses on the US government and legal system; classes that explore local, state, and national public policy issues, the rights and responsibilities of citizens, or the political process; and a program that emphasizes community service activities. Working within the framework of the US government and legal system model, Michael Butler (NTN) organized a two-week criminal "mock trial" with students in his high school class.

At the start of the project, students selected a "case" after viewing videotaped coverage from the local evening news and reading articles in the newspaper. The case they selected involved the high-speed police chase of a truck transporting suspected illegal migrants from Mexico. Two police officers were accused of beating up passengers from the truck. In the "mock trial," the officers were charged with attempted murder, first-degree assault, and criminal negligence.

Lesson schedule

Day 1: Students examine different cases and select the case for their mock trial
Day 2: The class discusses the case and the participants in a trial, and divides up the roles.
Days 3 and 4: Students learn about the responsibilities of different participants in a trial.
Days 5 and 6: Student teams representing the prosecution, the defense, and witnesses write opening statements, prepare questions, and outline testimony.
Day 7: Trial participants practice their parts in a dress rehearsal.
Day 8: The trial. Michael Butler, the teacher, plays the judge.
Day 9: The jury deliberates, reaches a decision, and announces its verdict.
Day 10: The class views segments from a video of the trial and evaluates the entire project.

Add your voice to the discussion:

1. In your opinion, would students learn more by studying the transcripts of an actual court case or by creating and role-playing a case like this one? Why?
2. How do you respond to suggestions that this kind of activity reinforces student antipathies toward the police?

Think it over:

1. Would you have allowed students to select the case? Why or why not?
2. How much leeway do you think students should be permitted during the trial and the deliberations? Why?
3. What do you think of Michael Butler's decision to be the judge? Why?

It's your classroom:

Would you schedule so much class time for one project? Why or why not?

Essay 1: Teaching Global History

An earlier version of this essay appeared in Singer, A., Libresco, A., and Balantic, J. 1988. "SSR Forum: Teaching Social Studies with the New Global History Curriculum," *Social Science Record* 35(1): 6–8. Used with permission.

A curriculum is written on paper, not etched in stone. Often they are the product of sharply contested political battles. About the same time as the first edition of *Social Studies for Secondary Schools* (1997) was published, New York State changed its high school global studies curriculum. The original curriculum was an area studies approach integrating geography, culture and history. Students studied the non-Western world (Africa, Asia, the Islamic world and Latin America) in 9th grade and the history of Western civilization in 10th grade. The new curriculum was intended as a two-year chronological study of global history, but it generally followed the parameters of developments in European society. It concluded the ninth grade with the era of the European Enlightenment and began tenth grade social studies with the French Revolution and impact of industrialization.

TWO-YEAR CHRONOLOGICAL GLOBAL HISTORY CURRICULUM

9th-grade Topics:
- Ancient World: Civilizations and Religions (4000BCE–AD500)
- Expanding Zones of Exchange and Encounter (500–1200)
- Global Interactions (1200–1650)
- The First Global Age (1450–1770)

10th-grade Topics:
- An Age of Revolutions (1750–1914)
- A Half Century of Crisis and Achievement (1900–1945)
- Twentieth and Twenty-first Centuries, Since 1945

The old curriculum was a victim of battles over multicultural inclusion and whether students should be studying social studies or history. In *The Great Speckled Bird* (1995), Catherine Cornbleth and Dexter Waugh argued that campaigns to rewrite social studies curricula were part of a conservative nationwide drive for fact-based direct instruction and a celebration of the Western core of American civilization.

In an unlikely coalition, conservatives were joined by progressive historians who saw an opportunity to extend the influence of the history profession in pre-collegiate education and a chance to root out what they describe as "the old mishmash known as 'social studies'." The heart of their position was a belief that teachers must present the "pastness of the past" and not turn the study of history into a "mere prologue of the present." In an essay published in *The New York Times* (1997), Sean Wilentz of Princeton University argued that "the past is not a 'process'," and that social studies topics should not be selected based on their current "relevance to our own world."

The change in the curriculum presented social studies teachers with the difficult task of integrating essential questions and themes, conceptual understandings, social and academic skills, hands-on activities and student projects, *the things many of us consider most important*, into a chronologically organized curriculum, while stimulating and maintaining student interest.

It also raises a number of important questions teachers must consider as they develop units and lessons:

1. Will students be able to acquire a cultural understanding of, and appreciation for, the regions of the world as they continent-hop through history? Does it make sense to combine independent developments, occurring in different parts of the world, in the same chronologically organized unit?

2. In a chronological curriculum will there be room to integrate art projects, cultural investigations and comparisons, and world literature?

3. Will students be able to understand the role of geography in the development of a region if they do not study an area as a cohesive unit?

4. Will comparative study of different regions during the same epoch (e.g., twentieth-century nationalist movements) be organized so that students learn the historical narrative is complex and comprised of many voices? Will the focus on chronology lead to an abandonment of historical actors and movements that were defeated and reinforce a sense that the world today was somehow predetermined?

5. Will a predominance of information about the Western world, greater teacher knowledge about this region, the availability of European primary source documents, and Europe's role in the development of the United States, transform global history into a two-year European history class with occasional side trips to examine other parts of the world?

In theory, the new curriculum allows teachers to teach a concept and give multiple examples of its application within the same chronological period. The European motivations for imperialism will be followed directly by a study of the effects of imperialism in Africa and Asia. However, a danger is that non-Western societies will be completely defined by their interactions with European imperialist powers.

Another strong argument for a chronological approach is that students can learn the historical context of major principles and discover how they play out over time. Students will study the industrial revolution as a background to Marxism and the ideas of Marx before examining Lenin, Stalin, Mao, and Pol Pot. This change may help students better understand the interconnectedness of the regions of the world. A problem, however, is that its emphasis on linear progression may rob these movements and countries of their individual national dynamics and feed into a Cold War-like notion of a ideological communist monolith.

State curriculum guidelines also include basic concepts that are woven throughout the curriculum. This does provide a mandate to incorporate many of the social science understandings developed in the area studies approach. In alphabetical order, the concepts are Belief Systems, Change, Culture and Intellectual Life, Diversity, Economic Systems, Environment, Geography, Imperialism, Interdependence, Justice and Human Rights, Movement of People and Goods, Nationalism, Political Systems, Science and Technology, and Urbanization.

One way to ensure that these concepts are covered in the chronological curriculum is to make thematic stops along the journey through time. Mortimer Adler, author of *The Paieda Proposal* (1982), argues that in-depth examination of specific topics leads to more substantive learning than broad surveys that race across time and place.

Origami is the Japanese art of paper folding. In Japanese, *oru* means "to fold" and *kami* means "paper." Paper folding originally developed in China, probably soon after the invention of paper in the first century AD. In an example of cultural diffusion, Buddhist monks brought paper and paper folding to Japan in the sixth century AD. In Japan, paper and paper folding became important aspects of architecture and the Shinto religion. *Kami* (paper) is a homonym for spirit or god.

During the Edo period in Japanese history (approximately 1600–1868), with the increased availability of inexpensive paper, origami developed as a more elaborate art form. The creation of symbolic objects, such as cranes and boats, replaced simpler designs. The first written work about origami was published in 1797. Akira Yoshizawa developed modern origami in the 1930s. He is responsible for the creation of thousands of modern day techniques and patterns.

In an example of parallel cultural development, paper folding (papiroflexia) also developed independently in Spain after Islamic merchants imported paper in the eighth century AD Papiroflexia is still popular in Spain and Argentina.

To learn more about origami, start with *http:// library.thinkquest.org/27458/nf/origami/history.html* (accessed April 16, 2007). To get help with making origami, try Joseph Wu's Origami Page at *http:// www.origami.vancouver.bc.ca/* (accessed April 16, 2007).

Figure 6.1 "Cranes for Peace" Christmas tree at the American Museum of Natural History in New York City.

151

I use origami workshops in global history classes to reinforce the concepts of cultural diffusion and parallel development, to illustrate Buddhist philosophy, and to introduce the Japanese concept of *shibui*, beauty through simplicity. One aspect of Zen Buddhism is coming to terms with life's contradictions. Both Zen Buddhist meditation and origami teach relaxation through concentration and focusing on the process rather than the result.

I usually teach a few simple origami designs to student volunteers during a free period and they serve as an expert team that assists in teaching the designs in class. Once they get the hang of it, most of the students are better at paper folding than I am. Origami can also be part of a broader class project (discussed in Chapter 8), especially if you are teaching 6th grade.

While leading the class in paper folding, I stress three basic rules:

1. Symmetry (what you do to one side you must do to the others).
2. Concentration (the open side must always be down).
3. Precision (folds must done carefully and firmly).

Learning Activity: Origami Paper Crane

The crane is usually not for beginners but I think it is worth a try. Everyone is not going to be able to create one the first time. It is easier if you work in pairs with one person reading the directions aloud.

Start with a square of paper. Usually it is brightly colored or patterned on one side. While you can use any size, I prefer a six-inch square. A larger piece can be awkward to work with and a smaller is just plain difficult for inexperienced or clumsy fingers. Excellent directions with illustrations are available at: http://monkey.org/~aidan/origami/crane/index.html (Accessed April 16, 2007).

Try it yourself:
Experiment with creating a paper crane and other origami figures.

It's your classroom:
Would you use an activity such as origami? Explain.

Essay 2: Multicultural Social Studies

Based on A. Singer (1994). Used with permission.

One of the difficulties in discussing multicultural social studies is that there is not general agreement about what *multiculturalism* means, let alone what a multicultural social studies curriculum should look like. Despite a nearly three-decade-long debate, multiculturalism remains beset with conflicts about its value and implementation that will probably never be resolved.

In her book *Empowerment through Multicultural Education* (1991), Christine Sleeter identified five different approaches to multiculturalism: (1) a human relations approach intended to increase student sensitivity toward others; (2) curriculum designed to enhance the self-esteem of minority youth; (3) single group studies programs; (4) culturally inclusive classrooms with pluralistic curricula; and (5) a transformative approach that combines pluralism with critiques of social injustice. Sleeter did not mention more modest infusion approaches that try to incorporate the heroes and holidays of different groups into more traditional social studies curricula.

Most social studies teachers who identify themselves as multiculturalists are committed to the idea that the study of history must respect the integrity of the past. No matter how comforting or convenient, educators should not present myth as history. However, we also need to remember that historical interpretations continually change, and that the ideologies of historians and societies shape these interpretations.

When it is shaped by this perspective, multicultural social studies becomes a way of looking at the world that is rooted in scientific exploration, a challenge to cultural limitations distorting our vision, and a call for more inclusive and reflective teaching. Multiculturalism has the most relevance for subjects like social studies, art, music, and literature, but it is not limited to these areas. Multicultural social studies is an effort to present a fuller picture of the world's history, people, and cultures.

Since the 1960s, social history, the study of ordinary people, has played an expanding role in the history profession's understanding of the past. However, most public school social studies curricula continue to be based on political, economic, intellectual, and institutional history.

Social history is multicultural history. Its exploration of the United States is based on the notion that all people contribute to making a nation, not just presidents, generals, inventors, and business leaders. For social historians, the history of the United States is the history of people: Africans, Latinos, Native Americans, the Irish, Poles, Slavs, Italians, Germans, Asians, Jews, the English, and others, their relationships to one another, and to our society as a whole.

Multicultural social studies is based on the idea of "multiple perspectives": that there is more than one way to view and understand an event, idea, or era. As an example, consider this question: Did industrialization unleash waves of progress and prosperity? For some people, the answer is yes, but the answer is no if you were a shepherd or small farmer in Europe, the Sahel region of Africa, or South-east Asia, driven off your traditional lands by large-scale commercial agriculture; a hand-loom operator in England or India displaced by water-powered machinery; an African, kidnapped and sold into slavery to produce cash crops for capitalist factories and markets; or a member of any one of thousands of ethnic groups that were drawn into crowded, polluted, and disease-ridden cities out of fear of starvation and the desperate need for work.

Differences in perspective can also be subtle. For example, most US slave narratives were published by abolitionists who used them to illustrate the horror, irrationality, and inhumanity of human bondage. Because morality plays are designed to outrage readers, historians cannot simply rely on them to shed light on the experience of enslaved African-Americans or the motives and culture of southern white slave owners. Works of fiction can be particularly useful for understanding the way other people view the world. Three of my favorites authors are Rohinton Mistry (*A Fine Balance*, 1997), who writes about India, Chinua Achebe (*Things Fall Apart*, 1994), who writes about Nigeria, and Mongane Serote, who writes poems about apartheid in South Africa (available at: http://www.club.it/culture/culture97/itala.vivan97, accessed April 16, 2007).

Multicultural social studies is a call for "inclusion" in the curriculum. It says, "I should be visible in this classroom, but so should you, and so should all the people that inhabit this nation and world." It is important that students know where their ancestors fit into the historical picture. It generates a sense of pride. It engages them in the study of the past. But it is also important that students know how Irish canal builders, white Protestant New England women mill workers, Chinese railway construction crews, Jewish garment workers, and enslaved African agricultural workers made possible the industrial development of the United States. Multiculturalism allows students and teachers to explore the similarities and differences in human experience, and it shows the broad range of human contributions to historical development. I was touched by both the cartoon dialogues of *Maus* (Spiegelman 1986) and the biographical narratives of *The Joy Luck Club* (Tan 1989). One author was a male American Jew and the other a Chinese American woman. Both helped me reconsider my own experience trying to understand the choices and struggles of my parents' and grandparents' generations. Multiculturalism is not "feel-good" history or the watering down of literature; it is an expanded and more detailed picture of the social, cultural, and intellectual histories of our country and our world.

Learning Activity: Impact of Capitalist Development

A curriculum that explores multiple perspectives tries to help students understand how different groups of people experienced the same historical forces. Capitalist development and industrialization in Great Britain and Europe were financed by the African slave trade and the wealth expropriated from the Americas. It affected people all over the world.

General Ludd's triumph

This song was sung by British weavers (Thompson 1963: 534, 547) called "Luddites" as they destroyed new textile machinery at the end of the eighteenth and the beginning of the nineteenth centuries. They rose in scattered rebellion against industrial progress that had undermined their skills and standard of living.

The guilty may fear but no vengeance he aims
At the honest man's life or Estate,
His wrath is entirely confined to wide frames
And to those that old prices abate.
These Engines of mischief were sentenced to die
By unanimous vote of the Trade
And Ludd who can all opposition defy
Was the Grand Executioner made.

Then the Trade when this arduous contest is o'er
Shall raise in full splendor its head,
And colting and cutting and squaring no more
hall deprive honest workmen of bread.
Chants no more your old rhymes about bold Robin Hood,
His feats I but little admire.
I will sing the Achievements of General Ludd,
Now the Hero of Nottinghamshire.

Oloudah Equiano describes being kidnapped into slavery

Oloudah Equiano was born in Benin on the west coast of equatorial Africa in 1745, and was kidnapped and sold into slavery when he was eleven. While enslaved, he worked on a Virginia plantation as the servant for a British naval officer and for a Philadelphia merchant. After purchasing his freedom, he wrote his memoirs (Gates 1987: 32–36) and became active in the anti-slavery movement. A selection from his memoir follows. The full text of *The Interesting Narrative of the Life of Oloudah Equiano, or Gustavus Vasa, Written by Himself* (London 1789) is available at: *http://docsouth.unc.edu* (accessed April 16, 2007).

The first object which assaulted my eyes when I arrived on the coast was the sea, and a slaveship, which was riding at anchor, and waiting for its cargo. These filled me with astonishment, which was soon converted into terror, which I am yet at a loss to describe . . . When I was carried on board I was immediately handled, and tossed up, to see if I were sound, by some of the crew; and I was now persuaded that I had got into a world of bad spirits, and that they were going to kill me . . .

I was soon put down under the decks, and there I received such a salutation in my nostrils as I had never experienced in my life; so that with the loathsomeness of the stench, and the crying together, I became so sick and low that I was not able to eat, nor had I the least desire to taste anything . . . but soon, to my grief, two of the white men offered me eatables; and on my refusing to eat, one of them held me fast by the hands . . . and tied my feet, while the other flogged me severely . . .

Among the poor chained men, I found some of my own nation, which in a small degree gave ease to my mind. I inquired of them what was to be done with us? They gave me to understand we were to be carried to these white people's country to work for them . . .

The closeness of the place, and the heat of the climate, added to the number in the ship, which was so crowded that each had scarcely room to turn himself, almost suffocated us . . . The shrieks of the women, and the groans of the dying, rendered the whole scene of horror almost inconceivable . . . I was soon reduced so low here that it was thought necessary to keep me almost always on deck . . .

One day, when we had a smooth sea, . . . two of my wearied countrymen, who were chained together, preferring death to such a life of misery, somehow made it through the nettings, and jumped into the sea; immediately another quite dejected fellow . . . also followed their example; and I believe many more would very soon have done the same, if they had not been prevented by the ship's crew, who were instantly alarmed . . . Two of the wretches were drowned, but they got the other, and afterwards flogged him unmercifully, for thus attempting to prefer death to slavery. In this manner we continued to undergo more hardships than I can now relate; hardships which are inseparable from this accursed trade.

It's your classroom:
1. How could you use these documents in your classroom?
2. Would you edit these documents or use their original language? Why?
3. What questions would you ask to promote student understanding and discussion?
4. Can you connect these sources with other historical or contemporary issues? Explain.
5. What other sources (documents, historical and contemporary literature, movies) from different parts of the world might you include in a unit on the impact of capitalist development?

Although not all human differences are cultural, a multicultural approach supports respect for and inclusion of other kinds of differences as well. Feminist research has shown the importance of "positionality" in shaping human understanding (Code 1991; Alcoff 1988). Gender, racial, ethnic, class, sexual orientation, physical ability, and religious differences, the collectivity of group social experience, and the individuality of personal experience all contribute to the way that people see the world and the insights that students bring to our classrooms.

Multicultural social studies insists that we see the world in all of its global complexity. There are billions of actors on the world stage, and a viewpoint that ignores most of them leaves us unable to understand the forces that are shaping our planet. For example, environmental problems like the destruction of the rain forests and the threat of global warming cannot be solved in the United States alone or without taking into consideration the needs of people in other countries and other regions of the world.

Global complexity is not just pertinent, however, when we discuss the contemporary world. New histories emphasize that the Nile River Valley was a crossroads where diverse cultures met, interacted, and created new cultures. The Seeds of Change exhibit, organized by the National Museum of Natural History at the Smithsonian Institution, explored the cultural exchanges that followed the Colombian Encounter of 1492 and the ways they reshaped the lives of people in Africa, Europe, and the Americas. Before students can understand the US war in Vietnam, they need to examine the Cold War between the United States and the Soviet Union; the competition between the United States, Japan, and European nations for economic influence in South-east Asia; and the deep-seated nationalistic aspirations of the Vietnamese people.

Figure 6.2 A statue at the entrance of the American Museum of Natural History in New York City shows Theodore Roosevelt "leading" a Native American and an African to civilization. An interpretation of world events that was considered acceptable in the early twentieth century is viewed very differently today.

Classroom Activity: Eating Social Studies

As part of the 500th anniversary of 1492, the Smithsonian Institution, the National Council of Social Studies, and Addison-Wesley published *Seeds of Change, The Story of Cultural Exchange after 1492* (Hawke and Davis 1992). It focuses on the impact of five major exchanges on world history: disease, maize (corn), the potato, the horse, and sugar cane. "Old World" diseases decimated Native American populations, sugar cane production led to the introduction of slavery in the Americas, and potato cultivation contributed to skyrocketing population growth in Europe.

Pasta with red sauce is one example of what happened when an "Old World" crop (wheat) was combined with an American product (the tomato). Students can discuss their assumptions about the origins of different foods, ways that the post-Colombian encounter modified cultures and led to the creation of new dishes, and the broader concepts of cultural diffusion and blending.

- **Foods from the Americas:** avocados, beans, chile peppers, coca, maize (corn), peanuts, pineapples, potatoes, pumpkins, squashes, sweet potatoes, tomatoes, turkeys
- **Foods from Europe, Asia, and Africa:** bananas, barley, beets, cabbage, cattle, grapes, oats, olives, onions, pigs, rice, sheep, wheat

Try it yourself:
Name dishes made from these items that illustrate cultural diffusion and blending.

Viewed within this context, multicultural social studies requires dialogue between people with different points of view, acknowledgment of different experiences, and respect for diverse opinions. It creates space for alternative voices, not just on the periphery, but in the center. Multiculturalism values creating knowledge through research, analysis, and discussion. It rejects the idea that there is only one possible answer that everyone must accept, and recognizes that what people believe to be "true" is constantly changing.

Students need to understand that (1) there are many different African cultures and that their histories did not begin with the Atlantic slave trade, (2) Jews existed between the times of Christ and Hitler, (3) Native American civilizations flourished before Europeans arrived, and (4) Egypt did not disappear when Cleopatra died.

Educators need to know where the lives of different groups of people intersect on the world stage. But unless we also understand how different groups of people developed, how they perceived themselves, and how they lived before and after the points of intersection, we cannot understand their roles and contributions to human history and culture.

A key precept for a multicultural education should be respect for the richness of difference. This is a crucial value for the survival of a diverse and democratic society and a fundamental component of how we learn. Learning in general, and learning and developing a sense of self-identity in particular,

are part of a process of comparing similarities and differences. I become conscious of who I am and what I am as I compare me with you. Without difference, identity has no meaning.

Some educators are concerned that valuing cultural difference contributes to moral relativism and leads to the acceptance of oppressive practices simply because they are part of another group's culture. They have raised the issue of the continuing subjugation of women in many societies, including genital mutilation, female infanticide, the absence of reproductive freedom, and the denial of political and economic equality. The issue of how to address the treatment of women around the world in our classrooms is clearly a complicated one. There are a number of factors that students need to think about as they discuss gender equity and explore different cultures.

Respecting the right of other people to do things differently, and recognizing that a practice plays a role in a particular culture, does not mean we must surrender our right to voice disagreement, accept every aspect of a culture, or encourage its extension or survival. Cultures are not stagnant, and cultural traditions based on racism and patriarchy often generate internal tension, within national or ethnic cultures, that can stimulate social change. This has been the case in most of the Western industrial societies.

When looking at cultures that continue to subjugate women, especially in Third World countries, we have to ask what actions on our part create the greatest possibility for change. When "outsiders" challenge a group's cultural practices, it can have the undesired consequence of reinforcing the practice by transforming it into a symbol of national opposition to imperialism. This is one of the factors that has contributed to the growth of religious fundamentalist movements in a number of countries.

In the United States, an expressed goal of education is the creation of an active citizenry committed to democratic values. Promoting democratic values means that social studies educators need to be involved in developing antiracist, nonsexist curricula that allow students to explore social contradictions. A major theme in US history classes can be examining the conflict between the promise of America outlined in the Declaration of Independence and the reality of life in the United States. Through involvement in this kind of historical exploration, students learn how societies change and how they can become agents of change.

Multicultural social studies also promotes democratic values as students come to recognize the dynamic nature of culture. Students are exposed to a broad range of possibilities that enhance the likelihood of conscious cultural choices. A focus on similarity and difference and multiple perspectives can ultimately make possible a more integrated national culture in the United States.

The notion of multicultural social studies described here points to a different way of organizing our classrooms. In most classes, the teacher is the expert, the conveyor of all knowledge, and the job of the student is to absorb passively what the teacher presents. Too frequently, social studies teachers present history as a collection of isolated and seemingly random facts to be memorized. Students see little logic in this approach, and are unclear why some facts are included and not others. Teachers need to abandon reliance on lectures, allowing students to discover patterns and create connections through their own thinking and research. Our goal should be for students to become active learners who see history as a way of examining the past so they can better understand the present and participate in shaping the future. Educators should help students learn to frame and evaluate hypotheses about why things happen and why people and nations act the way that they do. We must be willing to take the risk that students will arrive at conclusions that might not make us happy.

I would like to share an example of how this kind of multicultural perspective has helped me learn in my social studies classroom. Over the years, a number of African-American students have expressed in class that they resent only learning about slavery and how their people were oppressed. They were not really interested in learning about the glories of ancient African civilizations either.

Learning Activity: The Missing Passage

The following charges against the King of England were removed from the original draft of the Declaration of Independence before it was signed on July 4, 1776 (Franklin 1974: 88):

"He has waged cruel war against human nature itself, violating its most sacred rights of life and liberty in the persons of a distant people who never offended him, captivating and carrying them into slavery in another hemisphere, or to incur miserable death in their transportation thither . . . Determined to keep open a market where men should be bought and sold, he has suppressed every legislative attempt to prohibit or to restrain this execrable commerce."

Think it over:
1. Why do you think this passage was dropped from the original draft of the Declaration of Independence?
2. What does its removal suggest about the principles of the founders of the new nation?

Their challenges forced me to reconsider a number of my ideas about teaching social studies, and to think about how I had felt as a teenager learning about the history of my own people. I remember growing up in the Bronx after World War II, and the upset that I felt because Eastern European Jews, including my relatives, had walked to their deaths into the gas chambers of Nazi Germany. Knowledge of oppression did not satisfy me then. I felt humiliated and I wanted to scream out, "Why didn't we fight back"?

What finally helped me come to terms with the Holocaust was reading about Jewish resistance in Leon Uris' book *Mila 18* (1961) about the Warsaw Ghetto, and, whatever my problems with it now, the creation and defense of the State of Israel (Uris 1958). I realize that the key for me was the recognition of struggle, or, as Alice Walker identified it so powerfully in her book *Possessing the Secret of Joy* (1992), resistance.

In response to my students and the connections they have helped me to make in my own life, I shifted the emphasis in our classroom from examining the burdens of oppression to exploring the history of people's struggles for justice.

Learning Activity: Songs of Resistance and Struggle

Singing has always been part of human resistance to tyranny and struggles for social change. Following are four songs sung by different peoples but expressing similar ideas.

Zog Nit Keyn Mol

This partisan hymn from the Vilna Ghetto of Lithuania was inspired by Jewish resistance to Nazi forces in the Warsaw, Poland, Ghetto uprising. *Zog Nit Keyn Mol* was sung in Yiddish, the language of Eastern European Jews. Rhoda L. Epstein translated it from Yiddish for this book. It is recorded in Yiddish on "Voices of the Ghetto, Warsawa 1943," CD 7 Productions, US Holocaust Memorial.

Never say that you are going your last way,
When leaden skies hide the blue of day;
Our designated time will also come,
Our steps shall thunder—we are here!
This song was written with blood and not with lead;
It's not a song of birds flying free,
But a people standing amid falling walls,
Sang this song with pistols in their hands.

Certainly, Lord

Songs were an important part of the African-American Civil Rights movement of the 1950s and 1960s in the United States. Many of these songs of resistance and struggle originated as spirituals in southern African-American Protestant churches. *Certainly, Lord*, a traditional song, was adapted by members of the Congress of Racial Equality. A version that includes music appears in *Sing for Freedom* (Carawan and Carawan 1990: 69).

Well, have you been to the jailhouse? Certainly Lord,
Well, have you been to the jailhouse? Certainly Lord,
Well, have you been to the jailhouse? Certainly Lord,
Certainly, certainly, certainly, Lord.

Well did they give you thirty days? . . .
Well did you serve your time? . . .
Well will you go back again? . . .
Well will you fight for freedom? . . .
Well will you tell it to the judge? . . .
Well will you tell it to the world? . . .

Kevin Barry

This song tells the story of an 18-year-old student who enlisted in the Irish Republican Army to fight for Irish independence from Great Britain. Kevin Barry was captured by British troops and executed in 1920. Ireland finally became an independent nation in 1921. A version that includes music appears in *Songs of Work and Protest* (Fowke and Glazer 1973: 194–195).

Early on a Monday morning,
High upon a gallows tree,
Kevin Barry gave his young life
For the cause of liberty.

Another martyr for old Ireland,
Another murder for the crown!
Brutal laws to crush the Irish
Could not keep their spirit down.
Lads like Barry are no cowards—
From their foes they do not fly,
For their bravery always has been
Ireland's cause to live or die.

The Story of a People

Modern Egypt became a completely independent nation in 1951 after centuries of being colonized by the Ottoman Turks and Great Britain. This song, which expresses Egyptian nationalism, has its origins in 1956 when Egypt was fighting Britain for control over the Suez Canal and was involved in constructing the Aswan Dam on the Nile River. Maram Mabrouk (NTN) translated it into English for this book.

We said we would build the Aswan High Dam and now we have.
O Imperialism we built it with our own hands.
We built it with our own money and our workers' hands.

Brothers, Brothers!
Would you allow me a word?
The story is not the story of the dam; it's the story of the struggle behind the dam
It's our story
A story of a people who rose up in a holy battle and revolted
A people who fought and blazed a trail behind them
A people who strived and were destined for victory
Will you hear the story?

It's the story of war and revenge between us and imperialism
Do you remember when we became foreigners in our own lands?
And the betrayal of the colonizers who enjoyed all of our wealth
And the gallows for all those who spoke out
The day we freed those who were killed in Dinshaway.

This was the beginning; the people began their story
It was our struggle, the pain of our wounds, written in the blood of those sacrificed
We succeeded when the army rose up and revolted, on the day we called this a revolution
The day we removed the corruptors
The day we freed the lands
The day we achieved victory.

Think it over:

Are injustices like racism and imperialism central features of Western civilization, or incidental and peripheral developments? Explain your answer and provide specific examples to support your views.

Add your voice to the discussions:

1. Everything cannot fit in the curriculum. In your opinion, do teachers distort history by including the contributions of women and minorities? Explain your answer and provide specific examples to support your views.
2. In your opinion, are we in danger of minimizing the history of oppression if we focus on resistance movements? Explain your answer and provide specific examples to support your views.
3. Teaching about Egyptian nationalism is complicated by its alliance in the 1950s with the Soviet Bloc, recent tension between the West and Islam, and the wars between Israel and Egypt in the twentieth century. How would you address these issues in your classroom?

It's your classroom:
1. Would you use songs like these in your social studies classes? How?
2. Can connections be drawn among these songs? What are they?

When I explain these ideas about multiculturalism to groups of teachers, they generally respond, "It seems so reasonable," and they do not understand why it has generated such intense controversy. I think the reason for the controversy is that most of the debate about multiculturalism has little to do with the nature of history, the relative merits of different types of art and literature, or the most effective ways to teach about them. They are political debates about who will hold power and shape educational policies in American society.

There is nothing wrong with educators being political activists. Given the nature of our democratic society, educators must always be political. Political ideology informs the topics we choose to teach, the ways we organize our classrooms and relate to young people, our relationships with colleagues, and the battles we wage with Boards of Education and various local and state funding agencies. But we need to be conscious of our political preferences because they shape and are shaped by our professional judgments. We have to insist that educators reflect on their assumptions and goals, and evaluate standards for knowing.

I do not pretend that the kind of multicultural education I have described in this chapter will solve all of America's educational and social problems. But by embracing a multicultural perspective, social studies educators can make a statement that we take the divisions in American society seriously and we are committed to bridging them.

Teaching Activity: Join the Multicultural Debate

Consider the issues raised in this chapter and read the following statements by different authors who discuss multicultural social studies:

- **Kwame Anthony Appiah** (2006): "The right approach, I think, starts by taking individuals—not nations, tribes or 'peoples'—as the proper object of moral concern . . . Cosmopolitans take cultural difference seriously, because they take the choices individual people make seriously . . . A tenable global ethics has to temper a respect for difference with a respect for the freedom of actual human beings to make their own choices."
- **James A. Banks** (1993: 22–28): "One misconception about multicultural education is that it is an entitlement program and curriculum movement for African-Americans, Hispanics, the poor, women and other victimized groups . . . Multicultural education . . . is not an ethnic- or gender-specific movement. It is a movement designed to empower all students to become knowledgeable, caring, and active citizens in a deeply troubled and ethnically polarized nation and world."
- **Maxine Greene** (1993: 17): "Learning to look through multiple perspectives, young people may be helped to build bridges among themselves; attending to a range of human stories, they may be provoked to heal and to transform. Of course there will be difficulties in affirming plurality and difference and, at once, working to create community. Since the days of De Tocqueville, Americans have wondered how to deal with the conflicts between individualism and the drive to conform."
- **Octavio Paz** (1993: 57–58): "You are already a hybrid culture, which to me is a positive thing. I believe all cultures are richer when they assimilate others, and change. I don't believe in a pure culture. Here we are sitting and talking in New York, a city populated by the minorities that are the world's majority. It is marvelous, no?"
- **Diane Ravitch** (1990: 3): "Almost any idea, carried to its extreme, can be made pernicious, and this is what is happening now to multiculturalism . . . Advocates of particularism propose an ethnocentric curriculum to raise the self-esteem and academic achievement of children from racial and ethnic minority backgrounds. Without any evidence, they claim that children from minority backgrounds will do well in school only if they are immersed in a positive, prideful version of their ancestral culture."

- **Arthur Schlesinger, Jr.** (1992: 29): "The use of history as therapy means the corruption of history as history . . . Let us by all means teach black history, African history, women's history, Hispanic history, Asian history. But let us teach them as history, not as filiopietistic commemoration."
- **Albert Shanker** (1995): "As practiced by some, 'multiculturalism' takes the shape of something approximating a new ideology of separatism. It challenges the idea of a common identity and rejects the possibility of a common set of values . . . Often, the claims of multiculturalists and other separatists reflects the attitude that no one group may make a judgement on any other, since all 'depends on your point of view'. This extremely relativistic viewpoint conflicts with the need that all societies have of establishing some basic values, guidelines and beliefs."
- **Christine Sleeter** (1991: 12): "Education that is multicultural and social reconstructionist forges a coalition among various oppressed groups as well as members of dominant groups, teaching directly about political and economic oppression and discrimination, and preparing young people directly in social action skills."

Add your voice to the discussion:

1. Which statement(s) come(s) closest to your understanding of the meaning of multiculturalism? Why?
2. Which statements do you agree with? Disagree with? Why?
3. What are the implications of this chapter and the quotations for planning social studies curricula?

Essay 3: Are We Teaching Religious Myth Instead of the History of Religion?

Based on A. Singer (2008). Used with permission.

My children describe me as an "evangelical atheist" because I actively recruit converts to my disbelief. Despite this, I am a strong advocate of greater attention to the role of religion in history. What I want to see included in the global history curriculum, however, is significantly different from what is currently there, and I suspect is very different from what religious advocates would like to have taught.

I am a strong believer in what Thomas Jefferson described as "wall of separation between Church and State," a wall that was later incorporated into law by Supreme Court rulings on the scope of the first and fourteenth amendments to the United States Constitution. Many social studies teachers have interpreted the "wall of separation" to mean they should not talk about religion in the classroom. But their decision minimizes, or even leaves out, one of the major forces shaping human history.

Other teachers—and this is a serious problem in the sciences as well as social studies—shy away from the topic of religion because they fear repercussions from supervisors, parents, and even students, who may be unhappy when the historical record does not buttress religious dogma. For example, there is NO independent historical verification of the existence of Jesus of Nazareth to support accounts later incorporated into the New Testament by Christian believers. There are documents and contemporary historical accounts, but no mention of Jesus. NONE. The officially accepted Christian gospels offer an edited version of the story codified by church leaders 300 years after Jesus' supposed virgin birth, crucifixion, and resurrection, when they discarded other, conflicting, accounts. Paul, the great proselytizer of church expansion, never met Jesus. There is also no archeological evidence, despite intensive searching by Israel's academics and military personnel, to support the Old Testament Exodus story of a forty-year sojourn in the Sinai Desert by the "children of Israel."

NCSS Thematic Strands

National Council for the Social Studies Thematic Strands (available at: http://www.socialstudies.org/standards/strands/, accessed September 25, 2007) include discussion of religion in an anthropological examination of culture and in efforts to promote respect for cultural diversity, but not in their historical strands. For the NCSS, the "study of culture prepares students to ask and answer questions such as: What are the common characteristics of different cultures? How do belief systems, such as religion or political ideals of the culture, influence the other parts of the culture? How does the culture change to accommodate different ideas and beliefs?" Unfortunately, it also anticipates an answer, "we all pray to the same god but in different ways," that is neither interrogated or substantiated.

Disagreements with the Curriculum

I have a number of disagreements with this way of presenting religion in a social studies classroom. It is ahistorical. It assumes that religion has meant the same thing and religions have functioned the same way throughout time. It is not analytical. Students are directed to look for cultural similarities, common characteristics, but not substantive differences in either time or place. It is uncritical. It assumes the universality of religion rather than examining why it develops. It is misleading. Because the focus is on culture, including theology (ideas) and ritual (practices), students never question the actual role organized religion as an institution has played within different societies during the past and present. And finally, it is proselytizing. The result of this approach is that the existence of God is assumed. In effect, we teach religion when we do not question it.

There are similar problems with the National History Standards for Global History (NHS) developed by National Center for History in the Schools (available at: http://nchs.ucla.edu/standards/worldera6.html, accessed September 25, 2007) and in most high school global history textbooks. In both the NHS and textbooks, religious beliefs and practices are a major focus in discussion of traditional societies and the ancient world (1000 BCE–300 CE). According to the NHS, "[t]he classical civilizations of this age established institutions and defined values and styles that endured for many centuries and that continue to influence our lives today. Six of the world's major faiths and ethical systems emerged in this period and set forth their fundamental teachings." Other faiths, such as Islam, are introduced to students in a similar way at the chronologically appropriate moment. Yet given the lack of later coverage of religion in the NHS, it is as if once the world's "major faiths" were founded, they ceased to be of importance.

Textbook Coverage

McDougal Littell's *World History, Patterns of Interaction* (Beck et al. 2005) is one of the major textbooks used in global history classes (grade 9 in New Jersey and 9 and 10 in New York). Its index clearly shows the ongoing importance of religion in global history. There are 50 citations listed under religion, religious beliefs, religious persecution and tolerance as well as separate categories for Christianity (34 citations), Islam (31), Muslims (20) and Muslim world (19), Buddhism (17), Confucianism (14), Hebrews, Jews and Judaism (a combined total of 42 citations), and Hinduism (14). In addition to these, the papacy and individual popes are discussed 26 times, the Crusades have 12 citations, burial rites 7, monotheism 5, the Roman Catholic Church in the Middle Ages 4, and the Taliban and masks have 3 each. Contemporary ethnic and religious conflict in Central Asia, Jainism, Krishna, Animism, and Zen Buddhism all merit individual listings.

Yet, despite the breath of coverage, depth is concentrated in few areas, and while religion is continually mentioned, its role in history, or in individual societies, is rarely analyzed. The major discussion of religion is in a 16-page supplement (pp. 282–297) called "World Religions and Ethical Systems" that focuses on similarities and differences in six major religious traditions (Buddhism, Christianity, Hinduism, Islam, Judaism, and Confucianism). It includes excellent maps and charts, more than two-dozen pictures of gods, rituals, and celebrations, but almost no text. A quote from historian Karen Armstrong's *History of God* that students are questioned about betrays the bias of the supplement and of the text as a whole. Armstrong asserts, "Human beings are spiritual animals. Indeed, there is a case for arguing that Homo Sapiens is also Homo religious. Men and women started to worship gods as soon as they became recognizably human . . ." (p. 297). Students are then asked, "With which of the following opinions would Armstrong probably agree?" The only possible choice, selection A, is that "People are naturally religious."

Similar quotes appear in other sections of the text. In a discussion of the "Neanderthals' Way of Life" (p. 9), Richard Leakey says that "A concern for the fate of the human soul is universal in human societies today, and it was evidently a theme of Neanderthal society too."

But the bigger problem is the lack of analysis. We are told that in Ur, "Rulers, as well as priests and priestesses, wielded great power" (p. 22), but not how or why. In Sumer, the earliest government was supposedly controlled by temple priests because of the superstitions of the farmers who believed the priests were go-betweens with the gods. How this might have come to be is never discussed. States in many parts of the world and at different times claimed the "mandate of heaven," yet comparisons are not made or used to discover explanations. Flood stories from Mesopotamia, and Hebraic and Hindu beliefs are juxtaposed, but the questions and activities ignore the role of river flooding in early agricultural societies. Mostly we read engaging stories about exotic rituals such as mummification in Egypt (p. 38) and colorful individuals like Siddhartha Gautama (p. 68).

The role of Confucian ideas in cementing state authority in China and of the Roman Catholic Church in the Roman Empire provide ideal opportunities for exploring the material basis for religious belief and the institutional role of religion in empire, but the textbook largely ignores them. Confucianism is cited as the "foundation for Chinese government and social order," but the assertion goes unexplained (p. 105). A chapter on "The Rise of Christianity" (pp. 168–172) argues that this religion grew in the Roman world because it emphasized a "more personal relationship between God and people" that Romans found attractive and because its followers were strengthened by their "conviction" that its founder had "triumphed over death." The existence of Jesus of Nazareth and his life story are cited as historical fact recognized by historians, but no references are provided. Curiously, chapters on "The Fall of the Roman Empire" and "Rome and the Roots of Western Civilization" have almost no mention of Christianity. Meanwhile, the savagery and brutishness of the Christian Crusades are described as part of an "Age of Faith" (p. 379).

The "Rise of Islam" merits its own chapter (pp. 263–268), as do "Islam Expands" (pp. 269–272), and "Muslim Culture" (pp. 273–281), with detailed discussions of the life of Muhammad, the "beliefs and practices" of the faithful, and cultural contributions. But the role of Islam, in promoting literacy and integrating an empire based on trade, shared language (Arabic), and a relatively simple, demystified, belief system, is missing.

The one instance where the integral relationship between state and religion is directly presented is in discussion of new world Aztec and Incan societies (p. 462). But these are brief discussions about societies that develop in isolation from the main sweep of human history. Chapters on the European Reformation (pp. 488–503) focus on corruption, beliefs, and reformers, and mention the printing press, but make no connection to the Columbian Exchange, the growth of commercial capitalism, and state formation in Europe. It is also unclear why during the French Revolution, the National Assembly would target church property, an action that supposedly "alarmed millions of French peasants, who were devout Catholics" (p. 656). In the era following the French Revolution, religion receives much less coverage in the text, although it played a major role as a now junior partner in European imperialist penetration of Africa and Asia, and the emergence of religion as a political force, particularly in the Islamic World during the second half of the twentieth century, is noted but goes unexplained. We learn that "ethnic and religious conflicts have often led to terrible violence" (p. 1,083), but not why.

My conclusion is that the history of religion is so problematic, so distressing, that those with the power to decide what gets included in the curriculum would rather distort the historical record than come to terms with the roles religion did play in the past and continues to play in the present.

An Unconventional Historian Examines the History of Religion

In preparation to writing this essay, I examined a number of historical works that purported to examine the role of religion in history. I found that most of these books shared problems similar to the social studies textbooks. They focused on theology, ritual, and institutional history, rather than an analysis of the role religion and religious institutions have played in history. I finally found the kind of book I was seeking when I came across an obituary for Norman Cohn, who died July 31, 2007 at the age of 92 (see www.nytimes.com/2007/08/27/world/europe/27cohn.html, accessed September 7, 2007).

Norman Cohn was an unconventional historian who had his academic training as a linguist. The Times Literary Supplement included his book, *The Pursuit of the Millennium: Revolutionary Millenarians and Mystical Anarchists of the Middle Ages* (1957) in a 1995 list of the 100 non-fiction works with the greatest influence on how postwar Europeans perceive themselves. The edition I found in the library was revised and republished by Oxford University Press in 1970.

The Pursuit of the Millennium examines Christian society in Europe from the Middle Ages through the Protestant Reformation including the Crusades. Cohn's primary thesis was that during periods of "mass disorientation and anxiety," the poor and displaced expressed dissatisfaction with their conditions and even formulated revolutionary goals through millenarian and messianic beliefs and religious-inspired mass movements that challenged temporal authority. Starting with the Crusades, the desire of the poor and displaced to improve their lives led them to embrace prophecies about a final struggle between Christ and Antichrist and the end of the world as they knew it. Cohn argued that these beliefs, which often included anti-Semitism (Jews, as non-Christians living in the midst of Christian Europe, were identified as supporters of the Antichrist), formed a strong undercurrent in Christian belief, but required specific historical factors in order to emerge as a historical force. The material conditions that contributed to the transformation of religious belief into political action included demographic pressures that caused increasing population density, rapid economic growth and social change that undermined traditional support systems, and crises such as prolonged famine and epidemic disease (Cohn 1970: 53–54). Significantly, once these forces were unleashed, they took on a life of their own and assumed power that traditional religious authorities could not control.

One of the things that made Cohn an unconventional historian is that he did not hesitate to draw connections between his historical scholarship and his analysis of the contemporary world. He believed that part of the appeal of twentieth-century autocratic leaders like Hitler and Stalin was their "messianic" ability to connect their vision with the aspirations of the disoriented and anxious poor of the modern epoch. According to Cohn, "The old religious idiom has been replaced by a secular one, and this tends to obscure what otherwise would be obvious . . . [S]tripped of their original supernatural sanction, revolutionary millenarianism and mystical anarchism are with us still" (p. 286).

In the 1970 edition of his book, Norman Cohn referred to a series of essays by Eric Hobsbawn, published in 1959, that examined millenarianism in southern Europe, particularly Italy, since the French Revolution. In *Primitive Rebels* (New York: W. W. Norton), Hobsbawn supported Cohn's position that historians need to look at the material, as opposed to the spiritual, causes of millenarian uprisings. Looking at the nineteenth and twentieth centuries, Hobsbawn describes millenarian movements emerging in traditional societies that are ripped apart by either internal or external economic and political forces beyond their control.

Hobsbawn argued that a weakness in Cohn's analysis was his failure to distinguish between reformist and revolutionary movements, and between movements with defuse aims as opposed to those with clear political goals. Hobsbawn believed that lumping together such a vast array of social movements makes it difficult for historians to explain the power of modern leftwing and socialist movements that challenged the hegemonic dominance of industrial capitalism in the twentieth century (p. 57).

As far as I know, neither Cohn nor Hobsbawn analyzed the impact of "mass disorientation and anxiety" on the poor and displaced in the Islamic world today, although in *The Age of Extremes* (New York: Pantheon, 1994), Hobsbawn claimed that "Islamic 'fundamentalism', the most flourishing brand of theocracy, advanced not by the will of Allah, but by the mass mobilization of the common people against unpopular governments" (p. 582). However, the theses advanced by Cohn and Hobsbawn effectively explain the power of Islamic fundamentalism as a political movement and the difficulty local governments and Western powers have had bringing it under control; especially after having previously encouraged it as a weapon against leftwing protest movements. The studies by Cohn and Hobsbawn suggest that instead of dealing with it as a religious phenomenon, the world needs to address the causes of the dissatisfaction, causes that are transforming ideas into violent action.

Social Studies Approach

The Winter-Spring (v.6 n.1), Summer-Fall (v.6 n. 2) and Winter-Spring (v.7 n.1) issues of *Social Science Docket* (a joint publication of the New York and New Jersey Councils for the Social Studies) presented a "social studies approach to global history" designed to engage students as historians, exploring events from the past in an effort to answer their questions about the world we live in today. Rather than giving students information, this approach stresses involving them in examining "essential questions." This essay extends this approach to an examination of the role of religion in history.

My own area of expertise as an historian is United States history with some "teaching focus" on the history of Europe. There are big gaps in my knowledge of the rest of global history, and that is reflected in the questions about the history of religion that I present here. They are organized into two groups. The first is a short list of "essential questions" about religion in general. They are questions people, including our students, think about as they go about their lives. The second list is more historical. These questions are intended as a starting point for writing religion into history, rather than as a comprehensive list.

Social studies teachers are faced with a difficult challenge. Everything about religion has not been bad. Sometimes religious leaders have expressed the noblest aspects of humanity. But far too often in history, religious institutions have participated in morally unacceptable actions. Should we ignore the past or continue teaching fairy tale versions of the past in response to religious pressure and our own fears? Or do we engage students in conversations and questioning and let the chips fall where they may?

Essential Questions about Religion

- Why do many people believe in God? Is widespread belief in a Supreme Being evidence that one exists? Can these questions be answered definitively?
- Why are so many people followers of organized religious movements, most of which are thousands of years old? Do these movements, their texts, and their leaders "speak" for God? What roles do they play in people's lives that make membership attractive?
- Do differences in theology (religious ideas) and ritual (religious practices) by themselves shape history? Are religious differences superficial like differences in style? Are all religions basically the same?
- Why are contemporary political conflicts, as well as conflicts in the past, often presented in religious terms? Why are "religious" conflicts in today's world frequently violent (tension between India and Pakistan and within both countries, Northern Ireland, Israel v. Palestine, the Iraqi Civil War, throughout the Sahel region of Africa, and in Indonesia)?

Questions about Religion in History

- Human cultures evolved in a world without scientific knowledge, a world where the inexplicable continually happens to individuals and groups. What are the origins of religious belief in this world? Why does human belief in religion appear to be nearly universal? What is the relationship between religion, belief in a spirit world and supreme beings, and magic and myth?
- How does organized religion as an institution develop as part of the River Valley Civilization package? As described by Jared Diamond (1997) in *Guns, Germs, and Steel*, the "package" includes agriculture and animal husbandry, urban concentrations, state or government formation with law, bureaucracy, and military, specialization of work, technological improvement, literacy and numeracy, and religious hierarchy as either part of the state bureaucracy or as an independent institution, and as an agency for enforcing common belief, promoting cohesion, and organizing mass cooperation in projects.
- How similar and how different are the histories of different religions in different parts of the world as opposed to similarities and differences in theology and ritual?
- How did the Catholic Church become the official state religion of the Roman Empire? Was it accidental, preordained, or the result of complex historical forces? What was the Church's role in the Empire before and after its selection as a partner in imperial rule?
- Would the history of Western Civilization have been significantly different if worship of Ra, Yahweh, Mithraism, or Allah had triumphed over Jesus and the Christian Trinity as the dominant belief? Would Europe have been different, or even better off, if Islamic had defeated Christian forces at Tours in 732?
- Why do theological disputes seem to constantly divide religious authorities, both within Churches and between Churches? Why are there constant charges of heresy in the history of the Christian and Islamic worlds? What are the relationships between theological disputes and contemporaneous political and economic conflicts?
- What role does the Roman Catholic Church play in feudal society? Does it "save" European civilization from barbarians, or is it better understood as a partner in oppression and exploitation? Was anything noble about the feudal nobility and a Church hierarchy that was related to secular authority through filial, political, and economic bonds?
- How do we explain the survival of the Jews and other minority religions in hostile climates dominated by powerful religious institutions that brand them as illegitimate? Is it because of the power of their beliefs or because they fulfill special economic and political roles within these societies?
- What is the role of the Papacy in the Roman Catholic world and why does it change? Does the emergence of dual papacies in the 14th century, one based in Avignon and the other in Rome, reflect theological issues or commercial and political competition? Why does the Papacy appear to become more authoritarian and "infallible" on religious matters as its secular power is eclipsed?
- Was the Roman Catholic Church corrupted by an absence of piety and concerns for the physical world in the years preceding the Protestant Reformation, or was it fundamentally, structurally, "corrupt" because of its interconnections with, and support of, temporal authority? Are the Crusades, the burning of dissenters like Joan of Arc, the inquisition, the rape of Langedoc, the attack on Cathars during the efforts to root out the Albigensian heresy, and the repeated victimization and later abandonment of European Jews accidents and missteps, or do they reflect the fundamental nature of the Roman

Catholic Church? Are "saints" the exception that has been used to justify an institution complicit with gross inequalities and barbaric behavior?

- Why did organized religions tolerate and support injustices such as enslavement (Protestantism, Catholicism and Islamic beliefs) and class and caste inequality (Hinduism, Buddhism, and Confucianism)?

- Has Reformed (Protestant) Christianity acted substantially different from the Roman Catholic Church in its relationship with the secular world? In seventeenth century, Puritan forces commanded by Oliver Cromwell exterminated Roman Catholic communities in Ireland. The Anglican and Dutch Reformed Churches were full partners with national leaders in promoting the Trans-Atlantic Slave Trade and European imperialism in Africa and Asia. Lutherans officials supported Nazi policies in Germany. In the modern world, Protestant and Roman Catholic clerics have been allied with fascist dictatorships in South America and apartheid regimes in Southern Africa.

- Why are some religious movements identified with struggles for social change and more equitable societies (African-American Baptism and the Civil Rights Movement, Liberation Theology among Roman Catholic clerics in South America, Anglican support for anti-apartheid campaigns in South Africa, periodic millenniumist peasant revolts)?

- Do theology and ritual play any significant role in history or are they simply contingent (accidental) developments in response to specific historical, geographic, and cultural circumstances?

References and Recommendations for Further Reading

Achebe, C. 1994. *Things fall apart*. Garden City, New York: Doubleday.

Adler, M. 1982. *The paidea proposal*. New York: Macmillan.

Alcoff, L. 1988. Cultural feminism versus post-structuralism: The identity crisis in feminist theory. *Signs: Journal of Women in Culture and Society* 13(3): 405–436.

Appiah, K. 2006. "The case for contamination," *The New York Times Magazine*, January 1. http://www.nytimes.com/2006/01/01/magazine/01cosmopolitan.html?_r=1&oref=slogin, accessed December 29, 2007.

Apple, M. 2004. *Ideology and curriculum*. 3rd ed. New York: RoutledgeFalmer.

Banks, J. 1993. Multicultural education, development, dimensions, and challenges. *Phi Delta Kappan*, 75(1): 22–8.

Banks, J. and McGee Banks C. A. 1989. *Multicultural education: Issues and perspectives*. Boston, MA: Allyn & Bacon.

Beck, R., Black, L., Krieger, L., et al. 2005. *World history, patterns of interaction*. Evanston, IL: McDougal Littell.

Berenson, R. 1993. The California history-social science project: Developing history education in the schools. *American Historical Association Perspective*, 31(9): 21–24.

Berlin, I. and Harris, L. 2005. *Slavery in New York*. New York: The New Press.

Carawan, G. and Carawan, C., eds. 1990. *Sing for freedom*. Bethlehem, PA: Sing Out.

Cheney, L. 1987. *American memory: A report on the humanities in the nation's public schools*. Washington, DC: Government Printing Office.

Code, L. 1991. *What can she know? Feminist theory and the construction of knowledge*. Ithaca: Cornell University Press.

Cohn, N. 1970. *The pursuit of the millennium: Revolutionary millenarians and mystical anarchists of the Middle Ages*. New York: Oxford University Press.

Cornbleth, C. and Waugh, D. 1995. *The great speckled bird*. New York: St Martin's Press.

Crocco, M. 2006. Gender and social education: What's the problem?, in E. W. Ross, ed. *The Social studies curriculum*. 3rd ed. Albany, NY: SUNY Press, pp. 171–93.

Derman-Sparks, L. and The A.B.C. Task Force. 1989. *Anti-bias curriculum: Tools for empowering young children*. Washington, DC: NAEYC.

Diamond, J. 1997. *Guns, germs, and steel: The fates of human societies*. New York: Norton.

Evans, R. 2004. *The social studies wars*. New York: Teachers College Press.

Fowke, E. and Glazer, J., eds. 1973. *Songs of work and protest*. New York: Dover Publications.

Frank, A. 1995. *The diary of a young girl*. New York: Bantam Books.

Franklin, J. 1974. *From slavery to freedom*. 4th ed. New York: Knopf.

Gates, H., ed. 1987. *The classic slave narratives*. New York: New American Library.

Greenberger, S. 2001. "Thinking in the present some educators say recent events are not yet the stuff of history class," *Boston Globe* December 28: B1.

Greene, M. 1993. The passions of pluralism: Multiculturalism and expanding community. *Educational Researcher* 22(1): 13–18.

Hawke, S. and Davis, J. 1992. *Seeds of change, the story of* cultural exchange after 1492. Menlo Park, CA: Addison-Wesley.

Hirsch, E. 1993. "Teach knowledge, not 'mental skills'," The New York Times, September 4.

Hobsbawn, E. 1959. Primitive rebels. New York: Norton.

Horne, C. ed. 1931. Source record of the Great War, vol. 1. Indianapolis, IN: American Legion.

McKenzie, R. with L. Hellerman, 2002. "Civic learning through deliberation," Social Science Docket 2(2).

Mistry, R. 1997. A fine balance. New York: Vintage.

National Center for History in the Schools. 1996a. National standards for United States History, grades 5–12. Los Angeles: NCHS.

National Center for History in the Schools. 1996b. "Newly revised voluntary history standards released today, endorsed by leadership of national review panels," Press release, April 3.

National Commission on Social Studies in the Schools. 1989. Charting a course: Social studies for the 21st century. Washington, DC: NCSSS, November.

National Council for the Social Studies. 1994. Expectations of excellence, NCSS Bulletin 89. Washington, DC: NCSS.

National History Standards Project. 1994. "Fact Sheet on National Standards for United States History," Press release, November 1.

National History Standards Project. 1994. Press release, November 16.

New York Historical Society. 2004. Alexander Hamilton, the man who made modern America. New York: New York Post.

New York Historical Society. n.d. Teaching local history: New York City as a national model, teacher resource manual. New York: NYHS.

Noddings, N. 1992. "Social studies and feminism," Theory and Research in Social Education 20.

Paz, O. 1993. "Talk of the town," New Yorker, December 27.

Pogrebin, R. and Collins, G. 2004. "Shift at historical society raises concerns," The New York Times, July 19.

Ravitch, D. 1990. "Multiculturalism: E pluribus plures," The Key Reporter 56(1).

Reinhold, R. 1991. "Class struggle," The New York Times Magazine, September 29. http://query.nytimes.com/gst/fullpage.html?res=9D0CE6D61431F93AA1575AC0A967958260, accessed December 27, 2007.

Shanker, A. 1995. Education and democratic citizenship: Where we stand. June 3. http://www.ashankerinst.org/Downloads/EfD%20final.pdf, accessed April 16, 2007.

Schlesinger, A. 1992. The disuniting of America: Reflections on a multicultural society. New York: Norton.

Singer, A. 1992. "Multiculturalism and democracy: The promise of multicultural education," Social Education 56(2): 83–5.

Singer, A. 1993. "Multiculturalism and Afrocentricity: How they influence teaching U.S. history," Social Education 57(6): 283–6.

Singer, A. 1994. "Reflections on multiculturalism," Phi Delta Kappan 76(4): 284–8.

Singer, A. 1997. Social studies for secondary schools. 1st ed. Mahwah, NJ: Lawrence Erlbaum Associates.

Singer, A. 2008. "Are we teaching religious myth instead of the history of religion?," Social Science Docket 8(2): 8–13.

Sleeter, C., ed. 1991. Empowerment through multicultural education. Albany, NY: SUNY Press.

Spiegelman, A. 1986. Maus: A survivor's tale. New York: Pantheon.

Takaki, R. 1993. A Different mirror: A history of multicultural America. Boston: Little, Brown.

Tan, A. 1989. The joy luck club. New York: Putnam.

Thompson, E. 1963. The making of the English working class. New York: Vintage.

Uris, L. 1958. Exodus. Garden City, New York: Doubleday.

Uris, L. 1961. Mila 18. Garden City, NY: Doubleday.

Walker, A. 1992. Possessing the secret of joy. New York: Harcourt Brace Jovanovich.

Wilentz, S. 1997. "The Past Is Not a 'Process'," The New York Times, April 20.

II. Preparing to Teach
Social Studies

7. How Do You Plan a Social Studies Unit?

Overview

- Explore issues related to unit planning
- Present a rationale for formal unit plans
- Compare strategies for unit organization
- Develop sample unit plans for different grade levels

Key Concepts

Planning, Structure, Flexibility, Choice, Middle Schools, Tracking, Inclusion

Questions

- Why Plan Units?
- What Should be Included in a Unit Plan?
- Where Should Teachers Start Planning?
- How do Social Studies Teachers Plan Units?
- How do Teachers Use Plans Effectively in the Classroom?
- How can Social Studies Curricula Address Differences Among Students?
- What Does a Unit that Focuses on Content Look Like?
- How is a Document-based Thematic Unit Organized?
- What is a Comparative Thematic Unit?

Essays

1. Original Intent and the United States Constitution
2. Teaching About Work and Workers
3. Using Student Dialogues to Teach Social Studies and Promote Democracy

WHY PLAN UNITS?

For a number of years, the New York City union local of the American Federation of Teachers (AFT) challenged formal lesson and unit plan requirements as inappropriate restrictions on a teacher's professional judgment. They finally secured a contract provision that supervisors could not insist on a specific format for lesson and unit plans, or require that they be reviewed unless a teacher's performance during classroom observations was considered unsatisfactory.

AFT President Albert Shanker (1985) explained the union's position on planning in a pamphlet entitled *The Making of a Profession*. In the pamphlet, Shanker recounted the story of James Worley, an experienced and highly regarded teacher who was fired for insubordination.

According to Shanker, supervisors, parents, peers, and students all considered James Worley an excellent teacher. However, when a new principal required teachers to prepare units in advance and submit them to their supervisors for review, Worley refused. Worley defended his position, arguing that the directive was based on a rigid notion of teaching that ignored the fundamental role of classroom interaction and student participation in lesson and unit development. He felt that compliance with a directive that was educationally unsound would injure his students and violate his professional integrity.

Paul Goodman, author of the book *Growing Up Absurd*, was one of many educators who rallied in support of Worley's decision. In a letter to the State Commissioner of Education, Goodman wrote: "It has been my universal experience that formal preparation of a lesson plan beyond the next hour or two is not only unrealistic but can be a positively harmful and rigidifying, for it interferes with the main thing, the contact between the teacher and his class ... A teacher who would seriously comply with the order would likely be a poor teacher" (Shanker 1985: 3).

During my teaching career, I have also experienced unit and lesson plan requirements that I considered to be interfering and less than useful. I worked in schools where teachers submitted unit plans to supervisors who held onto them for days and then returned them without comments. I knew teachers and supervisors who wrote elaborate plans, but were not considered adequate educators by either their colleagues or their students. Despite these experiences, I strongly disagree with Goodman, Shanker, and Worley's position on planning. I am convinced that most teachers need to plan even more than they do; that extensive advanced planning is an essential feature of effective teaching; and that planning is where we, as teachers, get the chance to think and act as historians and social scientists. It is our opportunity to consider broader ideas, frame questions, suggest hypotheses, and research potential resources before we go into the classroom to teach about them.

Unit plans do not have to be rigid templates that stifle the imaginations of teachers and students. When a teacher is teaching a lesson and decides to leave something out, changes the order that materials are presented in class, or takes time to respond to student questions and listen to student views, a building is not going to collapse. Unit plans are only ideas about useful ways to subdivide and integrate concepts, skills, and content information. They are neither eternal documents nor etched in stone.

Sometimes I think of unit plans as guides to a mountain hike. They suggest supplies you will need, warn you about potential dangers and difficulties, alert you to alternative paths, provide strategies for using your energy most effectively, offer a time frame, and direct attention toward interesting views. The guides help you know where you are going and to predict how long it will take you to get there. They leave room for turn-offs. But when time is a factor, hikers know they can only take a limited number of side trips.

Unit plans are the primary conceptual and organizing frameworks in teaching social studies. A 180-day curriculum calendar is too long and contains too many things to think about and teach to be useful in planning lessons, activities, and projects. Although people need to be aware of the "big picture," the reality is that we live and plan our lives in much smaller parcels of time.

Planning on a day-by-day, lesson-to-lesson basis means that a teacher is never really prepared. Without setting aside time to consider our own thoughts about a topic, it is difficult to give direction in class. Main ideas about history, society, and social studies, and general academic skills that could have been integrated into a series of lessons if they were organized in advance, are forgotten and end up never being included. Teachers feel squeezed for time, so they lecture instead of involving students in figuring things out. Concepts that take a number of days to develop while students examine a point from different perspectives are either rushed or dropped. At the last minute, that wonderful video segment, photograph, or quote that provides evidence for a historical interpretation or illustrates an economic concept cannot be located so it cannot be used. It is too late to reserve the DVD player, camcorder, LCD projector, or computer room.

Can you imagine a football team going into a big game without a game plan or only having decided on its first play from scrimmage? It is not the best strategy in football, and it is not the best strategy for teaching. The questions we need to consider here are not whether teachers should plan, but what to plan, how to plan, and how to effectively utilize our advanced plans in the classroom.

Teaching Activity: The Politics of Lesson Planning

During the 2004–2005 school year, New York City schools teachers were once again up-in-arms over restrictive lesson plan requirements. A regional superintendent ruled that all teachers in the district, including elementary, middle, and high school teachers, had to plan using a lesson format called the "workshop model" that was originally designed for elementary school classrooms. Experienced secondary school teachers were given disciplinary letters when they refused to use a format they considered inappropriate for their classrooms. After picketing at the regional superintendent's office by teachers' union members and officers and extensive media coverage, the city's Deputy Chancellor for Instruction finally issued a statement that the central office had never intended to impose a "rigid approach" to planning and instruction (Herszenhorn 2005: B4).

Add your voice to the discussion:
1. What do you think about decisions by teachers and the teachers' union to challenge efforts to impose specific guidelines for lesson and unit planning? Why?
2. Do you agree or disagree with the union position that formal lesson and unit plan requirements are inappropriate restrictions on a teacher's professional judgment? Why?
3. In your opinion, why does this issue continue to be so contentious?

WHAT SHOULD BE INCLUDED IN A UNIT PLAN?

At the preliminary stages, a unit plan is an outline of teaching ideas that are organized into a schedule for presenting them in class. The outline has integrated conceptual components (e.g., chronological, causal, or thematic relationships) which makes it more than just a list of possible lessons. Eventually the ideas get reworked into a series of detailed individual lesson plans that retain the unit's conceptual connections. A complete unit plan contains completed lesson plans.

What gets included in a preliminary unit plan varies depending on what a teacher finds most useful for planning actual lessons. This changes as a teacher gains experience. It can also differ from unit to unit. The following are some items to consider when starting a unit plan:

1. **Scope** and **Time** include the range of topics or questions that will be examined during the unit and the number of lessons available to explore them (e.g., 10 lessons covering the United States from 1920 to 1941).
2. **Concepts** are broad, overarching social studies terms or statements that are continually reexamined throughout a curriculum, like democracy, environment, nationalism, or scarcity, or like the thematic strands developed by the National Council for the Social Studies.
3. **Essential Questions** are also generally defined for an entire curriculum, so they help connect concepts and content for a particular unit with the larger course of study.
4. **Main Ideas/Understandings** include the relationships among people, places, ideas, and events, and the conclusions about history and society that inform the way a teacher, textbook, or curriculum presents a topic.
5. **Goals** are general projections about the main ideas, content, academic, and social skills that teachers want students to learn during the unit.
6. **Objectives** are specific results you expect students to achieve.
7. **Content** refers to the factual information about a topic that will be considered during the unit.
8. **Skills** include the general academic (e.g., thinking, writing, speaking, mastery of technology), social studies (e.g., gathering information, document analysis, decision-making), and social skills (e.g., group participation and leadership) that will be focused on during the unit.
9. **Materials** include the software (e.g., documents, visual images, songs, etc.) and hardware (e.g., DVD player, laptop and LCD projector, etc.) that will be needed on specific days.
10. **Lesson Design** refers to the different ways that lessons can be organized (e.g., cooperative learning projects, group work, full class activities, student presentations, etc.).

WHERE SHOULD TEACHERS START PLANNING?

This is a question, as I have mentioned earlier in this edition, to which I have been giving a lot of attention in the past few years. Most new teachers and many experienced teachers start their planning from a textbook, following its organization of the subject and emphasizing its concept, main idea, content, and skill choices.

In history classes, this generally leads to content-based chronological lessons. In economics, political science, and sociology classes, it generally means focusing on the major institutions in a society. Starting from the textbook is helpful when teachers do not feel comfortable with their own knowledge of the subject or the scope of the curriculum. It can also make it easier for students to follow the sequence of lessons. There are problems with this approach, however: Students become inundated with facts, main ideas are lost in a swirl of details, lessons are dry, and students grow bored. In addition, when teachers are dependent on packaged textbook-based units, they sacrifice much of their own creative energy. They become part of an information conveyor belt, instead of being historians and social scientists.

More and more, I advocate that student teachers and new teachers should start planning by asking themselves three questions: What is important to know about this topic? Why is it important to know? How will I make the concepts and content accessible to the students in my classes? Asking these questions first helps teachers avoid the compilation of long and essentially meaningless lists of "facts" and encourages us to think as historians and do our own research as we struggle to understand what we will teach.

Thinking about planning in this way makes it easier to leave things out. Secondary school students are not supposed to become experts on every topic. Professional historians study for years, even after completing doctoral degrees, and their areas of expertise are generally narrow. What we really should be exploring with middle and high school students are a series of case studies woven together by either a connecting narrative or underlying questions and themes.

One of the essential questions that I identify with students at the start of every school year is "What is the responsibility of government in a democratic society to meet the needs of its citizens?" As they answer this question during the course of the school year, students examine NCSS thematic strands for *Power, Authority, and Governance, Production, Distribution, and Consumption*, and *Civic Ideals and Practices,* each of which explores the ways that decisions are made in a society. Because essential questions and thematic strands continually re-emerge throughout the curriculum, starting unit planning with them is an effective way of focusing in on what it important to know about a topic and how different topics are connected.

In the United States history curriculum, whether in middle or high school, the debate about government responsibility plays a major role in George Washington's administrations and is usually identified with the decisions that had to be made as a new government was created and ongoing cabinet-level debates took place between Secretary of the Treasury Alexander Hamilton and Secretary of State Thomas Jefferson. Whatever issues are resolved, the resolution was usually only temporary because new circumstances led to the reconsideration of previous decisions. The nature of government responsibility returned as a major focus during Andrew Jackson's presidency when political leaders argued about the re-chartering of the national bank, tariffs, and internal structural development. After the Civil War, the role of the government in managing the economy and regulating big business was a central concern. Government regulation of the economy was the major point of contention between the Republican and Democratic Parties when Herbert Hoover was defeated for reelection in 1932 and Franklin D. Roosevelt launched the New Deal. The New Deal and its spin-offs, the Fair Deal and the Great Society, dominated American political and economic until the 1980s, when Ronald Reagan and conservatives gained power by arguing that business regulation and the taxes needed to provide a high level of social services had become an anchor on economic growth.

Teaching Activity: Defining a Unit in US History and Economics

Try it yourself:
1. You are teaching 7th-grade students about how the American colonists became independent of Great Britain.
   a. What is important to know and why?

    b. Where would you start the unit? Where would you finish it?

    c. How much time would you spend on the entire unit?

    d. What are your concept, content, and skill goals?

    e. What are the main ideas you want students to learn about this period? Why?

2. You are teaching a 12th-grade economics class about the role of a central government in a complex modern "mixed" economy.

    a. What is important to know and why?

    b. Where would you start the unit? Where would you finish it?

    c. How much time would you spend on the entire unit?

    d. What are your concept, content, and skill goals?

    e. What are the main ideas you want students to learn about this topic? Why?

HOW DO SOCIAL STUDIES TEACHERS PLAN UNITS?

The length of time a unit takes to teach varies depending on the topic, the importance assigned to it by a teacher, department, or district, decisions about how lessons will be organized, student interest, and time pressures (e.g., approaching the end of a semester or a scheduled departmental exam?). I generally find that 2–3 weeks, or between 8 and 15 lessons, is a manageable amount of time for a unit. It allows a class to explore a topic with some depth and to reach intellectual closure on an issue. With every unit, I try to provide students with a lesson schedule and a home-work assignment sheet, design some form of unit project, and include a unit test.

In most high-schools and middle schools, social studies teachers are assigned to teach two different subjects or grades. When I teach secondary school social studies, I try to flip-flop planning; every other week I plan a two-week long unit (with daily lesson plans) for each subject area.

Often the hardest point in planning for beginning teachers is simply starting. I suggest using a chart like the one in Figure 7.1 and brainstorming on your own or with colleagues. List the things you want to include in the unit, group them, and then start to break the groupings up into lessons. Once a unit plan is outlined this way, it becomes easier to create individual lessons.

It is also very difficult to decide in advance how much planning is enough. Certainly unit planning is more an art than a science, and decisions become easier as a teacher gains experience. As you plan, it is useful to ask yourself some of the following questions:

Questions to Consider while Unit Planning

- Does this unit build on previous work and understanding?
- Does this unit lay the basis for future explorations?
- Do I understand the period, the broader issues, or the topic? Will students understand them based on these lessons?
- Is there sufficient material for students to analyze in class? Do the lessons include enough active things for students to do?
- Does the unit cover the same scope and/or information as the textbook assignments? How closely do I want them to parallel each other?
- Are my lesson designs varied and interesting?

If planning seems daunting, remember that there is no reason that supervisors, experienced teachers, and beginners should not work together to develop a curriculum. Lesson and unit planning does not have to be a private, individual experience or a competitive sport. When teachers work together, old-timers benefit from new insights and perspectives and rookies do not have to discover every document for themselves and reinvent every teaching strategy. At a minimum, new teachers should not be afraid to borrow. That is why they invented the copying machine and internet.

Teaching Activity: Outlining Units on India and sub-Saharan Africa

Try it yourself:
1. Make a list of the major historical, social, cultural, and geographical points you would include in a unit on the river valley civilizations and empires of ancient India. Divide the list into potential lessons.
2. Make a list of the principal questions a class should consider in a unit on the history of sub-Saharan Africa prior to the European "Age of Imperialism." Divide the list of questions into potential lessons.

HOW DO TEACHERS USE PLANS EFFECTIVELY IN THE CLASSROOM?

In the controversy over lesson planning, there is a very important area where I agree with James Worley. The interaction within the classroom between students and between teachers and students is crucial to effective learning and teaching. I often advise student teachers: "Put your lesson plan away when the class begins."

Carefully constructed unit plans provide structure for our teaching, but they also make it possible for creative flexibility in the classroom. Advanced planning means that, when students raise unexpected questions or introduce valuable new ideas, lessons can change and important material that gets skipped over can be inserted into other lessons. It also means that, when necessary, we can say to a student, "That's a good idea, but I want to hold it for a couple of days until more of the class is with us."

Sometimes the most difficult thing to decide when unit and lesson planning is what *not* to include. At the planning stage, I recommend over-planning. It avoids potentially long and embarrassing silences when something takes less time or invokes less student interest than anticipated. While teaching, I try to remain aware that all of the material I have available and all of the goals I would like to achieve will not necessarily fit in a particular lesson or unit; that I need to make choices about what to introduce based on student involvement. I do most of my editing—shifting things around, sliding them into other lessons, or dropping them altogether—while teaching or after a class, when I can reflect on how students responded to what we are learning. Even when you have to drop something that took time to prepare, it is good to know you had it available if you needed to use it to answer student questions or to illustrate an important point.

HOW CAN SOCIAL STUDIES CURRICULA ADDRESS DIFFERENCES AMONG STUDENTS?

In Chapter 4, I argued that a curriculum based on structured experiential learning is the most effective way to teach social studies on every grade and academic level. In my experience, this approach provides social studies educators with the flexibility necessary to meet the individual and group needs of diverse student populations. Teachers have to find ways to engage students who have different intellectual interests, academic strengths, social and cultural experiences, and levels of emotional maturity. If social studies curricula are student-centered, they will differ in middle schools and high schools, in cities and suburbs, and in different neighborhoods and sections of the country. Units and lessons will even vary for classes taught at different times of the day, as teachers adjust to the ebb and flow of teenage emotions, anxieties, and predilections. The key to curriculum design is connecting to students. At the conclusion to Chapter 8 this is discussed in greater depth in an essay on "Text and Context."

Middle School Social Studies
In general, middle school social studies programs are more attuned to the developmental profile of adolescents than junior and senior high schools. In middle schools, learning is frequently interdisciplinary; students and teachers are encouraged to work in teams, and teachers try to consciously connect historical events and social studies concepts with their students' experiences.

According to a National Council for the Social Studies Task Force report on *Social Studies in the Middle School* (1991), middle school social studies curricula should

Subject _____ **Topic** _____ **Grade** _____

Lesson	Time/ Scope	Concepts	Essential Questions	Main Ideas	Goals	Objectives	Content	Skills	Materials	Lesson Design
1										
2										
3										
4										
5										
6										
7										
8										
9										
10										

Figure 7.1 Brainstorming a unit

emphasize concern with student personal growth and identity; the development of ethics and knowledge of right and wrong; the fostering of citizenship and community; and an understanding of global connections. Experiential and cooperative learning (see Chapter 9), performance-based assessment (see Chapter 12) and heterogeneous grouping are encouraged. In addition, the report suggests that teachers begin instruction with ideas that students are familiar with, help students develop their historical perspectives, emphasize clear communication in the classroom, provide opportunities for student participation in decision-making, and create a sense of classroom community. I wholeheartedly support this view of teaching, but I do not agree that it should be restricted to middle schools (see Chapter 11 for a discussion of a project approach to social studies in middle school and high school).

Academic Level and Inclusion

Recent decades have produced continuing debate on the academic organization of middle, junior, and senior high schools, especially the placement of students who are considered either "gifted" or "challenged." Most of my secondary school teaching experience was in academically "tracked" programs, where efforts were made to mainstream special education students into "appropriate" classes.

Philosophically, I oppose academic tracking because it stigmatizes students in the lower tracks, encourages competition for grades rather than learning, and teaches students to value hierarchy and individual benefit instead of democracy and community. However, I recognize that social studies teachers must be prepared to work in both tracked and non-tracked settings. In both types of programs, I encourage students to work in teams, drawing off each other's strengths. In non-tracked classrooms, students with more developed academic skills have an opportunity to polish their understanding as they work with other students to master complex skills and concepts. I also prefer heterogeneous grouping and the inclusion of special education students because they maximize student diversity, bring multiple perspectives into the classroom, and enrich everyone's experience.

A problem in planning social studies units and lessons for a heterogeneous class is that there may be a wide disparity in student reading and writing levels. I use a number of approaches to address this problem.

- In class, I vary the difficulty of assigned readings, recognizing that certain material will be too difficult for some of the students to understand.
- When documents are particularly hard to interpret, I make excerpts brief and provide vocabulary clues.
- Sometimes, I provide students with *differentiated text*, activity sheets with a series of documents that were originally written, or have been edited, so that they offer a range of academic difficulty.

- Before the class discusses documents, I either have students go over the material in small groups or I review it in some detail as a full class.
- For group projects, I assign students to teams so that each team has members with a range of academic skills.
- On individual projects, I provide a variety of choices and encourage students with greater academic skills to pursue more challenging assignments.

In many school districts, content specialists are increasingly being paired with support staff, either co-teachers or teaching assistants, who have greater expertise in working with students with special academic needs. Sometimes classrooms become too crowded and the teachers end up stepping all over each other. However, I have also seen partnerships where co-teachers work together seamlessly. I think the partnerships work best for the students when teachers share the planning and instruction, drawing on each other's strengths, but both being fully involved with all of the students in the class.

Teaching Activity: Editing a Primary Source Document

When Cheryl Smith works with heterogeneous cooperative learning teams in her middle school classes, she assigns individual students different reading passages or versions of an edited document, depending on their reading skills. This enables all the students on the team to participate in research and discussion. Examine the primary source documents that follow.

Magna Carta (Greaves et al. 1990: 277)
In 1215, nobles forced King John of England to accept a "Magna Carta" that placed limits on the power of the monarch. The Magna Carta, considered one of the seminal documents in the development of democratic institutions in Western society, is usually discussed in high school social studies classes.

1. In the first place, we have granted to God, and by this our present charter confirmed for us and our heirs forever, that the English church shall be free, and shall hold its rights entire and its liberties uninjured . . .
12. No scutage or aid shall be imposed in our kingdom save by the common council of our kingdom, except for the ransoming of our body, for the making of our oldest son a knight, and for once marrying our eldest daughter; and for these purposes it shall be only a reasonable aid . . .
39. No free man shall be taken, or imprisoned, or dispossessed, or outlawed, or banished, or in any way injured . . . except by the legal judgment of his peers, or by the law of the land.

Starving Time (Meyers et al. 1967: 16–17)
Captain John Smith's *General Historie of Virginia* (1624) recounted the "starving time" in Jamestown, Virginia, during the winter of 1609–1610. It is a graphic story that illustrates the precariousness of early settlements. Its gruesome qualities can capture the imagination of middle school students.

Now we all found the loss of Captain Smith, yea, his greatest maligners could now curse his lose: as for corn provision and contribution from savages, we had nothing but mortal wounds with clubs and arrows; as for our hogs, hens, goats, sheep, horse, or what lived, our commanders, officers, and savages daily consumed them, some small proportions sometimes we tasted till all was devoured; then swords, arms pieces, or anything, we traded with the savages, whose cruel fingers were so oft imbrewed in our bloods that what by their cruelty, our Governor's indiscretion, and the loss of our ships, of five hundred within six months after Captain Smith's departure, there remained not past sixty men, women, and children, most miserable and poor creatures; and those were preserved, for the most part, by roots, herbs, acorns, walnuts, berries, now and then a little fish.

Nay, so great was our famine that a savage we slew and buried, the poorer sort took him up again and eat him; and so did divers one another boiled and stewed with roots and herbs. And one amongst the rest did kill his wife, powdered her, and had eaten part of her before it was known, for which he was executed, as he well deserved. Now whether she was better roasted, boiled or carbonadoed, I know not, but of such a dish as powdered wife I never heard of.

Add your voice to the discussion:
Would you provide students with different versions of a reading based on their reading skills? Why or why not?

It's your classroom:
How would you edit these documents to make them accessible to students in your classes?

The inclusion of special education students can enhance learning for all students when districts provide necessary support services. At Edward R. Murrow High School, teaching assistants were assigned to work in mainstream classes to help students with disabilities. Some of these students felt that this added a stigma to what was already a difficult situation for them. After meeting with the students and teaching assistants, we developed a strategy that addressed this problem and benefited all of the students in class. Instead of teaching assistants working solely with an individual student partner, they worked with whichever group of students the student with disabilities was assigned to. Because students with disabilities changed groups during the year, all of the students in class eventually had an opportunity to work with one of the teaching assistants. As a result of experiences in inclusive classrooms, students with disabilities and the general student population can learn that all people have the ability to make contributions to society and should be included in our definition of *community*.

Cultural Diversity and Gender
The dynamic nature of culture and identity, as well as the challenge of developing social cohesiveness in a diverse and democratic society, are important reasons for encouraging diversity in schools. In racially, ethnically,

religiously, or gender-segregated classes, students experience separation as the norm and difference as strange and undesirable. In culturally diverse and gender-mixed classrooms, there is at least the possibility that student experiences will encourage respect for difference.

Classroom diversity places a heavy responsibility on teachers. There is often tension between students from different racial, ethnic, religious, or class backgrounds. Students feel pressure to conform, take sides, or be silent. Young women may withdraw from active involvement in class and play roles they think will make them more attractive to young men. Even when tension remains below the surface, students who feel marginalized can suffer academically and socially. The challenge for teachers is to build classroom communities where students feel welcomed and have confidence that conflicts will be openly and sensitively examined and resolved.

The social studies play a crucial role in this process. In social studies classrooms, social conflict is part of our field of study. Students can study the historical roles of different people; the meaning of concepts like equity, justice, and citizenship; and ways to creatively reduce tension so that people who are different are able to work together effectively. In social studies classrooms, conflict can provide learning opportunities that help students better understand each other, and the present and past.

During the recent national standards debate (discussed in Chapter 5), some proponents of a national curriculum expressed concern that allowing social studies curricula to diverge contributes to the polarization of our society. A student-centered social studies curriculum does not mean that students only study about themselves and their own racial, ethnic, or religious groups. Rather, in student-centered classrooms, social studies teachers use what students are familiar with, the *contexts* of their lives, as the starting point for examining the world in all of its complexity and diversity.

Teaching Activity: Dealing with Diversity

Laurence Klein (NTN) teaches in an ethnically diverse middle school in Queens, New York. The school is tracked, and the lowest track classes tend to have a mixture of students who are either recent immigrants or American-born students, largely African-Americans, with a history of failure in school. Often there is tension between these two groups.

In a lesson designed to help his 8th-grade class understand conditions in the United States at the end of the American Civil War, Lawrence asked students who had immigrated from countries with civil strife to discuss the impact of these conflicts on their families. Among the students who reported to the class were young women born in El Salvador, Yugoslavia, Israel, and Afghanistan. Although it was sometimes difficult to follow them because of their accents, the other students were mesmerized by their presentations. The discussion that followed allowed students to bridge many of their cultural gaps, and helped them perceive each other as fellow human beings for the first time.

As a follow-up homework assignment, students wrote statements explaining their views on contemporary conflicts in the United States, and whether they have the potential to lead to another civil war. This activity and follow-up discussion gave the American students an opportunity to explain their frustrations with the conditions of their lives. The tension between students in this class was not resolved by two discussions. However, Laurence Klein believes that possibilities were expanded for creating a cohesive classroom community.

Add your voice to the discussion:
Do you agree with the inclusion of students from diverse backgrounds with a range of abilities and interests in heterogeneous social studies classrooms? Why or why not?

It's your classroom:
1. How would you design lessons to accommodate differences among students?
2. Would you have your class discuss racial, religious, ethnic, or gender conflicts between students? Why or why not? How would you introduce it? How would you follow-up?

HIGH SCHOOL UNIT PLANS

The next three sections examine sample high school unit plan outlines that illustrate three approaches to unit planning. It includes a content-based unit from a Western civilization curriculum; a document-based thematic unit on the post-World War II struggle for civil rights for African-Americans; and a thematic unit for a global history class. In addition, a thematic middle school unit on the history of women in the United States is presented in Chapter 10.

WHAT DOES A UNIT THAT FOCUSES ON CONTENT LOOK LIKE?

High school history unit plans are generally organized chronologically. They focus on content while weaving in broader social studies themes and concepts. Traditionally, the content emphasizes political events and intellectual and economic trends. Units like these frequently follow the outline of the textbook.

John McNamara, who was my department chair when I taught at Edward R. Murrow High School, designed this unit. John begins planning units by dividing a broad time period into smaller periods of time or topics, and by listing the content he wants to include in each lesson. He recommends units and individual lessons that are sequentially structured and carefully organized. After John decides on the social studies content of each lesson, he works on how he will teach them. He formulates broad introductory aim questions that have more than one possible answer. He uses these questions to promote discussion and disagreement, and to encourage students to examine, organize, and understand the content materials. At some point in each lesson, John introduces a primary source document, cartoon, or reading passage for student evaluation. He prefers that his students work in groups. He also schedules writing activities whenever possible. Each unit is accompanied by a homework assignment sheet and concludes with an exam. I have added an introduction focusing on what we believe is important to know and why. It was written with the help of Michael Pezone, a high school teacher who has long been related to the Hofstra social studies education program.

REVOLUTIONARY FRANCE—A HIGH SCHOOL CONTENT-BASED UNIT

The wars of the eighteenth century, particularly the Seven Years War (1756–1763), depleted France's finances and almost completely destroyed its lucrative colonial empire. Support for the American revolt against Great Britain reduced the country to near-bankruptcy while provoking increased interest among the French people in Enlightenment principles of equality and freedom. On the eve of the French Revolution, the *ancien regime*, the centralized, absolutist state headed by King Louis XVI, was faced with an economic and political crisis. This crisis ended its control over the machinery of the state and unleashed social forces that ended the exclusive rule of landed privilege in France. A new ascendant social class, the bourgeoisie, composed of wealthy business owners, highly-placed civil servants, and financiers, emerged as the dominant group in French society. Together with allies amongst the petite bourgeoisie, which included members of the professions, artisans, and tradesmen living in cities and towns, and the urban masses, known as the "Sans-Culottes" because of their plain clothing, they created a secular republic committed to science, reason, and universal rights. The French Revolution transformed French and European society, but led to periods of "terror," reaction, and dictatorship under Napoleon. During the period known as the "Reign of Terror," the Committee of Public Safety wiped out people perceived to be enemies of the Revolution, including many former Revolutionary leaders, in an effort to protect France from foreign invaders committed to restoring the monarchy. The Committee of Public Safety increasingly lost favor and in the month of Thermidor (July–August), 1794, upper class counter-revolutionary forces gained power. Later, in a military coup, Napoleon seized power and the French Revolution, launched in the name of expanded rights, ended as a dictatorship led by a new monarch. Napoleon continued and expanded on some of the reforms introduced by the revolution, particularly in the areas of science and law. His invasion and conquest of much of continental Europe also generated new nationalist movements. Since that time, historians have debated whether all revolutions are destined to follow the same pattern as the French Revolution.

1. Was France under the Old Regime ripe for revolution?
   a. *Identify/define*: First, Second, and Third Estates, tithe, taille, gabelle, Old Regime, peasantry, aristocracy, clergy, established church.
   b. *Describe/analyze*: political, economic, and social conditions in France under the Old Regime.
   c. *Explain/analyze*: powers and privileges of First and Second estates.
   d. *Discuss*: Was the Old Regime ripe for revolution?
2. Did the writers of the Enlightenment prepare people's minds for revolution?
   a. *Identify/define*: Natural law, natural rights, checks and balances, separation of powers, Social Contract, "philosophes," civil liberties, laissez-faire, tyranny, Enlightenment, Age of Reason, physiocrats.
   b. *Explain*: criticisms of the Old Regime made by the philosophers and writers of the Enlightenment, including Locke, Montesquieu, Rousseau, Voltaire, Adam Smith, Diderot, Thomas Jefferson.

    c. *Explain/analyze*: views of the Enlightenment held by philosophers and writers of the era.

    d. *Assess*: Did the writers of the Enlightenment prepare people's minds for revolution?

3. Should the French have been satisfied with the changes enacted by the National Assembly after the fall of the Bastille?

    a. *Identify/define*: feudalism, assignats, abolition, emigres, limited monarchy, legislative assembly.

    b. *Explain*: how reforms enacted by the National Assembly changed the conditions existing under the Old Regime: (1) abolition of feudalism and special privileges; (2) Declaration of the Rights of Man; (3) seizure of Church lands; (4) Civil Constitution of the Clergy; (5) reform of local government; (6) Constitution of 1791.

    c. *Evaluate*: Should the French have been satisfied with the changes enacted by the National Assembly after the fall of the Bastille?

4. Did the Reign of Terror go too far to preserve the French Revolution?

    a. *Identify/define*: Danton, Marat, Robespierre, Committee of Public Safety, Jacobins, Girondists, Liberty, Equality, Fraternity, National Convention, Directory.

    b. *Explain*: how different groups responded to the Revolution of 1791: (a) émigrés; (b) churchmen; (c) radicals; (d) monarchs of Europe; (e) peasants; (f) bourgeoisie.

    c. *Explain*: how the National Convention protected and promoted the French Revolution.

    d. *Describe*: causes and results of the Reign of Terror in France.

    e. *Assess*: Did the French Revolution significantly improve the lives of the French people and change French government for the better?

5. Was Napoleon the right man to rule France?

    a. *Identify/define*: Directory, coup d'etat, plebiscite, the Consulate, sister republics.

    b. *Describe*: conditions in France that helped make Napoleon's coup d'etat possible.

    c. *Describe/analyze*: traits of character and personal achievements that helped Napoleon rise to power in France.

    d. *Evaluate*: advantages and disadvantages of one-man rule.

6. Did Napoleonic rule preserve or destroy the gains made by the French Revolution?

    a. *Identify/define*: Confederation of the Rhine, Grand Duchy of Warsaw, universal manhood suffrage, concordat, Code Napoleon, Continental System, exile, the Consulate, Legion of Honor, Bank of France.

    b. *Locate*: areas conquered and/or controlled by Napoleonic France.

    c. *List, describe, and analyze*: Napoleon's reforms in each area: law, education, taxation, money and banking, relations with the Catholic Church.

    d. *Explain and analyze*: Napoleonic measures that turned France into a dictatorship.

    e. *Explain*: Reason's for Napoleon's downfall.

    f. *Evaluate*: Did Napoleonic rule preserve or destroy the gains made by the French Revolution?

7. Was the Metternich system effective in stopping the spread of European nationalism?

    a. *Identify/define*: conservative, reactionary, liberalism, balance of power, legitimacy, compensation, Concert of Europe, Congress of Vienna, Holy Alliance, Quadruple Alliance, nationalism.

    b. *Explain*: how territorial changes made at the Congress of Vienna violated the principle of nationalism.

    c. *List and explain*: methods used by Metternich and his allies to suppress nationalist and democratic ideas: (1) military power; (2) alliances; (3) censorship and spies.

8. Did the French Revolution have global impact?

    a. *Describe*: the spread of nationalism to other nations and parts of the world: (1) Revolutions of 1820–1821 in Italy and Spain; (2) Latin American Revolutions from 1810 to 1832; (3) Greek Revolution from 1821 to 1829; (4) Revolutions of 1830–1832 in France, Belgium, Italy, and Poland; (5) Revolutions of 1848 in France, the Austrian Empire, Italy, and Germany.

    b. *Evaluate*: impact of the French Revolution on other revolutionary movements.

    c. *Evaluate*: Metternich's statement, "When France sneezes, all Europe catches cold." Discuss this statement in the light of events from 1830 to 1848.

Teaching Activity: Design a Content-based Unit

Try it yourself:
Using a high school social studies textbook and a collection of primary source documents, design a content-based unit plan (containing between 8 and 10 lessons) for a specific historical era or on a specific topic. Start with a brief essay explaining what is important to know and why.

Add your voice to the discussion:
How do you view the content-based approach to social studies unit planning? Why?

HOW IS A DOCUMENT-BASED THEMATIC UNIT ORGANIZED?

This social studies unit about the African-American civil rights movement in the United States after World War II is based on an inquiry approach to social studies curricula. It is organized so that students use historical documents to answer questions about the period and theme. Documents can be pictures, cartoons, songs, newspaper articles, quotes, artifacts, charts, or graphs (i.e., any materials that an historian might find useful).

While content information remains important in this unit, it is not the central element in planning or student learning. The educational principle underlying this type of unit is that, as students examine the documents, they become historians who understand broader concepts, draw connections between events, and formulate explanations (hypotheses). Academic and social skills and social studies content are learned while students examine documents and answer questions. A document-based unit allows a teacher to focus class time on questioning and guiding students, rather than on presenting information. Written homework assignments and textbook readings, along with class discussions, are used to provide narrative continuity.

This approach requires considerable historical knowledge on the part of teachers. You must have familiarity with the standard historical narrative, a sense of what is important to know about the topic, and familiarity with primary source documents from the period.

Initially, document-based units require more research and preparation time for teachers than the traditional content-based chronological unit. However, as a document file grows over time, it becomes easier to construct units and individual lessons. Some publishers provide document packages geared to their texts, either in the form of a collection of handouts or as a document book. I recommend the two-volume *The American Spirit,* 11th edition (Kennedy and Bailey 2006), which is published by Houghton Mifflin as a companion volume for its advanced placement text, *The American Pageant: A History of the Republic,* 12th edition (Kennedy et al. 2001). As a teacher, I adapted many of these documents for use in regular classes. The sourcebook that accompanies the middle school series, *A History of Us* (Oxford University Press, 1999), can also be used with high school classes. Howard Zinn and Anthony Arnove have developed a document book, *Voices of a People's History of the United States* (Seven Stories Press, 2004), that includes less traditional sources, such as statements by George Jackson, Chief Joseph, Nicola Sacco, Bartolomeo Vanzetti, Bruce Springsteen, Mark Twain, and Malcolm X. It is intended as a companion text for Zinn's pioneering book, *A People's History of the United States, 1492–Present* (HarperCollins 2003).

New York City publishes an excellent collection of edited and adapted multicultural documents designed for 7th- and 8th-grade classes. They can also be adapted for high school. Well-designed commercial document packages are available from *Jackdaws* (at: www.jackdaw.com, accessed April 23, 2007). The federal National Archives and Records Administration (available at: http://www.archives.gov/publications/teaching-aids.html#teach, accessed April 23, 2007) publishes *Teaching with Documents,* an excellent four-volume collection of primary source material. Document resources available on the Internet are discussed in Chapter 12.

Steps in Planning a Document-based Thematic Unit

Start by researching the main themes and issues related to the topic. Make a list or write a brief narrative explaining what is important to know and why.

Frame an historical question about the topic. Answering the question helps you to decide what to include in the unit.

Break the broad historical unit question into smaller pieces, statements, topics, or questions that need to be explored so the class can start to answer the broader question.

Assemble a list of available historical resources (primary source documents, secondary source interpretations, and audio- and videotapes) that allow students to discuss the smaller pieces, statements, topics, or questions.

Divide the questions, historical resources, social studies concepts, and research, communication, and social skills needed to utilize resources and answer questions into segments for organization into individual lessons. Because they are being used to answer specific questions, the documents may or may not be used chronologically.

Make decisions about the amount of time available for the unit and about the number of topics, documents, questions, etc., that can be included. These decisions need to be reconsidered continuously while the unit is taught. Depending on student involvement in class discussion, questions, and insights into historical issues, some of the documents may never be used.

Edit documents to an appropriate length for use in class. Adapted them if necessary. Individual lessons that use different formats and different types of sources are developed.

Unit Topic
The Post-World War II African-American Struggle for Civil Rights and Equality in the United States

The sample unit that follows provides more document choices than can possibly be integrated into the lessons. A teacher can decide that one document best illustrates a historical point and introduce only that document in class. Another option is to edit a series of documents so that each is a single paragraph long. Sometimes student teams work with different documents and bring insights based on their research into full class discussions.

Unit Question
Could the "promise" of the Declaration of Independence ("We hold these truths to be self-evident, that all men are created equal") be achieved in the post-World War II United States?

What is important to know about the Civil Rights Movement and why?

With the Compromise of 1877, the post-Civil War Reconstruction of the United States was suspended. The federal government ended the military occupation of the South and protection for the citizenship rights of African-Americans. The large majority of ex-slaves remained in the South as a largely agrarian work force economically dependent on former slaveholders who remained in control of the land and resumed control over local governments. During the next two decades, Southern states formalized the "Jim Crow" system of racial segregation in public and private facilities and denied African-Americans the right to vote. The legality of this system was confirmed by the United States Supreme Court in the 1896 Plessy v. Ferguson decision that "separate" was "equal." It was also given support by President Woodrow Wilson's endorsement of racial segregation in the nation's capital.

African-Americans challenged segregation in the courts, initially without much success, through organizations such as the National Association for the Advancement of Colored People (NAACP). Increasingly, African-Americans fled the Jim Crow South and resettled in Northern and Western cities, although they continued to face job and housing discrimination. During the 1920s, there was a cultural flowering known as the Harlem Renaissance. The Great Depression, however, adversely affected social mobility. One area where African-Americans made some progress was as members of the organized labor movement.

World War II placed new manpower demands on the nation. African-American activists pressured the federal government to enlist African-Americans as workers in the defense industries and in the military, although the armed forces remained racially segregated until 1948. An important symbolic change following the war was the desegregation of Major League baseball in 1947. However, of greater social import was continuing racial segregation in federal programs, especially those targeting veterans, and in newly expanding suburban communities.

At the end of the war, African-Americans and white allies launched major campaigns to mobilize people in a struggle to end racial segregation and secure full citizenship rights for all Americans. The campaigns were aided by pressure on the United States, as the leading western power during the Cold War, to live up to its democratic promises, and by the attention television news coverage was able to focus on Southern brutality and racism.

Ultimately two strategies bore fruit. The intensive 20-year legal campaign to overturn segregation by Thurgood Marshall and the National Association for the Advancement of Colored People (NAACP) led to the 1954 Supreme Court decision in Brown v. the Topeka, Kansas Board of Education that "in the field of public education, the doctrine of 'separate but equal' has no place. Separate educational facilities are inherently unequal." While opponents resisted implementation of the decree, the decision placed the federal government on the side of desegregation. During the next decade, court decisions, Presidential actions, and new federal laws gradually broke the legal system supporting Jim Crow.

The second strategy, mass organization and non-violent civil disobedience in defiance of segregation, led to one of the most dynamic social movements in the history of the United States. It drew on organizational networks and organizing experience in church and labor groups, and produced influential national organizations such as the Southern Christian Leadership Conference, the Congress of Racial Equality, and the Student Non-Violent Coordinating Committee. While a number of people played important leadership roles, including Rosa Parks, E. D. Nixon, Medgar Evers, Hosea Williams, John Lewis, Wyatt Walker, Ralph Abernathy, Fannie Lou Hamer, A. Philip Randolph, and Bayard Rustin, the movement was most closely identified with Martin Luther King, Jr., whose words and actions stirred the nation's consciousness. Some of its most dramatic organizing efforts were the Montgomery, Alabama Bus Boycott, the campaign to desegregate public facilities in Birmingham, Alabama, the 1963 March on Washington, and efforts to march from Selma, Alabama to Montgomery, which led to passage of the 1965 Voting Rights Act.

The Civil Rights coalition, which never succeeded in transforming racial consciousness in the United States, imploded after the passage of the 1965 Voting Rights Act. Most of its White supporters believed its goal, the end of legal segregation in the United States, had been achieved. Meanwhile, many urban Black communities, frustrated by ghettoization, deteriorating housing, high levels of unemployment, and the failure of the Great Migration North to rid people of the burden of racism, exploded into violent protest. New groups, ideologies, and leaders came into prominence, including Malcolm X, the Nation of Islam, and the Black Panther Party. The break up of the Civil Rights coalition was instrumental in the political shift in the late 1960s that propelled large numbers of Southern and suburban White voters into the Republican Party and brought conservative, often racist, forces into power in the United States.

The United States changed enormously as a result of the Civil Rights movement. In 1960, less than 20 percent of eligible Black voters were registered to vote in Virginia, Alabama, South Carolina and Mississippi. In 1964, less than 1 percent of African-American children in Arkansas, Alabama, Louisiana, Georgia, South Carolina, North Carolina and Mississippi attended interracial schools. Equality before the law created new opportunities and African-Americans responded by becoming important cultural, political and economic leaders. They are a visible presence in virtually every area of American society. The struggle for civil rights for African-Americans reinvigorated and redefined democracy in this country. It helped to extend rights to women, ethnic and racial minorities and to gays and lesbians.

Yet, despite significant gains, serious problems persist in the United States. School segregation intensified during the 1990s. The life expectancy of African-American men at the start of the twenty-first century was approximately seven years less than the life expectancy for White men; 24 percent of the Black population of the United States lived in poverty compared to 10 percent of the White population; and the average income for Black families was $18,000 per year less than the income for the average White family. A study by the Justice Policy Institute found that there are more African-American men in jail or prison than in college. One in every three Black American men faces the possibility of imprisonment during his lifetime (Singer 2004: 2).

The Civil Rights movement illustrates a number of major themes in the history of the United States. They include:

- The power of the idea, imbedded in the Declaration of Independence, that all people are equal and entitled to basic legal and human rights
- Racism has been a powerful force throughout United States history
- People acting collectively can pressure political leaders to adopt progressive policies and successfully struggle to improve their lives and the lives of others
- People of goodwill will join struggles to support the rights of others
- Citizens can change powerful institutions such as the government, churches, unions, and educational systems
- Organizations that involve large numbers of people in long term struggle, not just prominent individuals, are crucial to the success of social movements. The Civil Rights movement did not happen just because Rosa Parks sat down and Martin Luther King stood up
- Media, and technology in general, by informing the public and expanding democratic interaction, can support social change
- Principled national leaders, such as Supreme Court Justice Earl Warren, and Presidents Dwight Eisenhower and Lyndon Johnson, can have lasting impact on society if they are prepared to take political risks
- Social movements are fragile coalitions representing conflicting interests and may lose steam or become divided
- Change is neither linear nor gradual. After centuries of enslavement and racial segregation, the United States changed in a relatively short period of time
- Change, once it starts, can go off in new and unanticipated directions. The struggle for African-American rights contributed to the struggle for rights for women, immigrants, gays and lesbians, and the anti-war movement
- The United States remains an unequal society, in part because of its failure to resolve many of its internal inconsistencies during the Civil Rights movement

- The official story is not necessarily the true story. Martin Luther King, Jr. and Malcolm X, who are honored today, were vilified by the press and investigated by the government during their lifetimes.

Historical resources available for this unit include:

Video Documents:
- *Eyes on the Prize*, parts 1 and 2 (Prize 1/ Prize 2).
- Martin Luther King, *From Montgomery to Memphis* (King).

Internet sites (accessed April 27, 2007):
- African-American Odyssey: The Civil Rights Era, http://memory.loc.gov/ammem/ aaohtml/exhibit/aopart9.html
- Civil Rights Movement Veterans, http:// www.crmvet.org
- We Shall Overcome: Historic Places of the Civil Rights Movement, http://www.cr.nps .gov/nr/travel/civilrights
- USA History; Civil Rights Movement, http: //www.spartacus.schoolnet.co.uk/ USAcivilrights.htm
- Voices of the Civil Rights Movement, http:// www.voicesofcivilrights.org
- Timeline: Civil Rights Era, http://www. pbs.org/wnet/aaworld/timeline/civil_01.html
- Civil Rights Icons, http://video.google.com/ videoplay?docid=-3029468302589487153
- The King Center, http://www.thekingcenter .org
- The Civil Rights Coalition for the 21st Century, http://www.civilrights.org

Documents and collections:
Bracey, John H. Jr., Meier, August and Rudwick, Eliot. 1970. *Black Nationalism in America.* Indianapolis, IN: Bobbs-Merrill (Nationalism).

Carawan, Guy and Carawan, Candie, eds. 1990. *Sing for Freedom, The Story of the Civil Rights Movement through its Songs.* Bethlehem, PA: Sing Out (Songs).

Feder, Bernard. 1967. *Viewpoints: USA.* Woodstock, GA: American Book Company (Viewpoints).

Katz, William L. 1995. *Eyewitness: A Living Documentary of the African-American Contribution to American History.*

Englewood, NJ: Jerome Ozer Publishers (Eyewitness).

Kennedy, D. and Bailey, T. 2006. *The American Spirit: United States History As Seen By Contemporaries, volume II.* 11th ed. Boston, MA: Houghton Mifflin (Spirit).

Malcolm X and Haley, Alex. 1992. *The Autobiography of Malcolm X*, Westminster, MD: Ballantine.

New York City, Grade 8. 1995. *United States & New York State History* (NYC).

Washington, James, ed. 1991. *A Last Testament of Hope, The Essential Writings and Speeches of Martin Luther King, Jr.* San Francisco, CA: Harper.

Williams, Juan. 1988. *Eyes on the Prize, America's Civil Rights Years, 1954–1965.* New York: Penguin (Prize).

HISTORICAL QUESTIONS AND DOCUMENTS

1. What was life like for African-Americans at the end of World War II?

Documents

- Fourteenth Amendment to the Constitution of the United States (Viewpoints, 331).
- The Majority Opinion from *Plessy* v. *Ferguson* (1896) (Viewpoints, 332).
- Justice Harlan dissent from *Plessy* v. *Ferguson* (1896) (Viewpoints, 332–333).
- Gunnar Myrdal, *An American Dilemma* (New York: Harper; 1944), 1009–1021 (Viewpoints, 350–351).
- Carl Rowan, *South of Freedom* (1952) (NYC, 64).
- Kenneth Clark, The Doll Test (Prize, 23).
- Anne Moody writes about the Emmett Till murder in *Coming of Age in Mississippi* (Prize, 56).

Video

- Emmitt Till (Prize 1).

2. How did African-Americans respond to these conditions?

Documents

- Philip Randolph, testimony on desegregating the armed forces, Congressional Record, 80th Congress, 2nd session, part IV, 4313–4317 (Eyewitness, 471–472).
- The Highlander Folk School (Prize, 64–65).
- Jo Ann Robinson, Organizing before the Boycott (Prize, 70–71).
- The Story of the Montgomery Bus Boycott, http://www.montgomeryboycott.com/frontpage.htm (accessed April 27, 2007).

Video

- Montgomery bus boycott (King).

3. What were the responses of Southern whites and state and local governments?

Documents

- One Hundred Southern Congressmen Dissent, *Congressional Record*, 84, Cong. 2 session, 4515–4516, March 12, 1956 (Spirit, 847–848).
- Governor Faubus defies Desegregation, 1957 (Viewpoints, 335).
- Karr Shannon. 1958, *Arkansas Democrat*, March 10, (Spirit, 851–852).
- James Jackson Kilpatrick. The Southern Case for School Segregation (Prize, 28–30).
- A Dixie White's View (Prize, 54–55).
- *The Klan-Ledger*, Special Neshoba County Fair Edition, 1964 (Eyewitness, 501–502).
- White Backlash in Mississippi, *Memphis Press-Scimitar*, September 12, 1966, 1, 3 (Eyewitness, 532).

Video

- Governor Wallace blocks the door at the University of Mississippi (Prize).

4. How did the federal government respond to the Civil Rights movement?

Documents

- The Majority opinion from *Brown* v. *Board of Education of Topeka* (1954) (Kennedy, 846–847).
- President Eisenhower responds to southern defiance at Little Rock, Arkansas (1957) (Kennedy, 848–849).
- Elizabeth Eckford. First hand account of Little Rock school desegregation effort. From Daisy Bates, *The Long Shadow of Little Rock*. New York: David McKay, 1962, 73–76 (Eyewitness, 492–494).

- The Civil Rights Act of 1957 (Viewpoints, 336).
- President Kennedy Calls for Equal Rights, June 1963 (Eyewitness, 499–501).

Video
- Black students enter Little Rock High School (Prize 1).

5 & 6. What were the ideas and strategies of the Civil Rights movement?
Documents
- Guy and Candie Carawan, *Sing for Freedom, The story of the Rights movement through its songs,* Sing Out, Bethlehem, PA, 1990 (Songs).
- Sit-Downs: An Interview with Diane Nash (Prize, 130–131).
- Freedom Riders: James Peck, *Freedom Ride*. New York: Grove Press, 1962, 98–99 (Eyewitness, 495–496).
- *Desegregating Universities*: James Meredith, "I'll Know Victory or Defeat," *The Saturday Evening Post,* November 10, 1962, 17 (Eyewitness, 497).
- Birmingham, Alabama: Mary Hamilton, "Freedom Now," *Pacifica Radio* (Eyewitness, 498).
- *Mississippi Summer*: Excerpts from Dave Dennis' Eulogy for James Chaney (Prize, 239–240).
- *Voting Rights*: Fannie Lou Hamer, Hearing before a select Panel on Mississippi and Civil Rights at the National Theater. Washington, DC. Monday, June 8, 1964. *Congressional Record*, Cong. June 16, 1964 (Eyewitness, 503–504).
- Fannie Lou Hamer. *To Praise Our Bridges* (Prize, 245–247).
- *Selma, Alabama*: Sheyann Webb and Rachel West Nelson, *Selma, Lord, Selma*, Tuscaloosa, AL: University of Alabama Press, 1980.

Video
- Freedom Rides (Prize 1); Birmingham, 1963 (King); Selma, Alabama (Prize 2).

7. What was Martin Luther King, Jr.'s vision for US society?
Documents
- King, Martin Luther, Jr. 1987. *Stride Towards Freedom*. New York: Harpercollins, 212–217.
- King, Martin Luther, Jr. 1964. *Why We Can't Wait*. New York: Signet, 74–100.
- King, Coretta. 1992. *The Words of Martin Luther King*. New York: Newmarket Press.
- Washington, James, ed. 1991. *A Last Testament of Hope: The Essential Writings and Speeches of Martin Luther King Jr.* San Francisco, CA: Harper, 7–8, 50, 447, 647. Specifically, excerpts from: A Letter from Birmingham Jail (1963); March on Washington (1963); Nobel Prize Address (1964).

Video
- Birmingham, 1963 (King); Washington, 1963 (King); Norway, 1964 (King).

8. Did the Civil Rights movement significantly change the laws of the US?
Documents
- Lyndon Johnson, speech, March 15, 1965 (Kennedy, 868–874).
- Civil Rights Act of 1964
- Voting Rights Act of 1965

9. Why did African-American communities explode?
Documents
- Bayard Rustin. 1966. "The Watts Manifesto and the McCone Report." *Commentary,* March (Viewpoints, 341).
- Langston Hughes. 1964. "Harlem III," *New York Post*, July 23, 29 (Eyewitness, 535–536).
- Ernie Chambers. 1967. Official Transcript of Proceedings before the National Advisory Commission on Civil Disorders, Washington, DC, September 21, 1533–1596 (Eyewitness, 538–541).
- Eliot Asinof. 1968. "Dick Gregory is Not So Funny Now," *The New York Magazine*, March 17, 38–42 (NYC, 76).
- Excerpts from the Report of the National Advisory Commission on Civil Disorders. 1968. Washington, DC: US Government Printing Office. http://historymatters.gmu.edu/d/6545, accessed April 27, 2007.

Video
- Riots (Prize 2).

10. Why did a new generation of African-American activists challenge the ideas and strategies of the Civil Rights movement?

Documents
- Stokely Carmichael. 1966. "Black Power," Notes and Comments. SNCC (Nationalism, 470–476).
- Alvin Poussaint. 1967. "A Negro Psychiatrist Explains the Negro Psyche." *The New York Times Magazine*, August 20, 53 (Eyewitness, 533–534).
- Stokley Carmichael and Charles Hamilton. 1967. *Black Power*. New York: Random House, 44–49 (Eyewitness, 537–538).
- The Black Panther Party Program. 1968. *The Black Panther*, March 16, 4 (Nationalism, 531–534).

Video
- Black Panthers (Prize 2).

11. Who was Malcolm X and what did he teach?

Documents
- Malcolm X and Alex Haley. 1992. *The Autobiography of Malcolm X*. Westminster, MD: Ballantine, 35–36, 108–110, 149–152, 197, 315, 375–376.
- "Minister Malcolm X Enunciates the Muslim Program." 1960. *Muhammed Speaks*, September, 2, 20–22 (Nationalism, 413–420).
- Malcolm X press conference, March 12, 1964 (Eyewitness, 536).
- Malcolm X, "An Address to Mississippi Youth," December 31, 1964. George Breitman, ed., *Malcolm X Speaks*. New York: Pathfinder Press, 1965.

Video
- Malcolm X (Prize 2).

12. Did the Civil Rights movement succeed?

Documents
- Bayard Rustin. 1965. "From Protest to Politics," *Commentary,* February 25–26 (Viewpoints, 342–343).
- *The New York Times* Editorial, October 2, 1966, IV, I (Viewpoints, 341–342).
- *Life Magazine,* December 24, 1965, 106–120 (Viewpoints, 343).
- Kenneth Clark, in Peter Kihss, "Clark Scores 'Separation' at Antioch," *The New York Times,* May 23, 1969 (Eyewitness, 544–545).
- Eldridge Cleaver. 1967. *Soul on Ice*. New York: McGraw-Hill, 123–125 (Eyewitness, 545–546).

13. Why does racial discrimination continue to be an issue in the United States?

Documents
- Robert Coles. 1966. "The White Northerner: Pride and Prejudice," *Atlantic Monthly*, June 1966, 53–57 (Kennedy, 996–1000).
- Black Enterprise Champions Affirmative Action, August 1978, 7 (Kennedy, 991–992).
- George Will. 1978. "Reverse Discrimination," *Newsweek,* July 10, 84 (Kennedy, 993–996).

Teaching Activity: Design a Theme-based Unit

Try it yourself:
Using a high school social studies textbook and a collection of primary source documents, design a theme-based unit plan (containing between 8 and 12 lessons) for a specific historical era or on a specific topic.

Add your voice to the discussion:
How do you view this approach to social studies unit planning? Why?

Classroom Activity: Post-World War II African-American Experience

Examine Tables 7.1–7.6, and Figure 7.2, which illustrate different aspects of the African-American experience in the post-World War II United States. One of the side benefits of document-based lessons is that the same documents appear again on student assessments. I often provide students with a chart and have them "translate" it into a graph, or provide a graph that they must "translate" into a chart. Most of this data is from United States Census and Bureau of Labor Statistics reports. For more information, see Loury, G. 2002. *The anatomy of racial inequality*. Cambridge, MA: Harvard University Press.

Try it yourself:
Using the graph provided for Figure 7.2 as a model, select one of the other charts and create a graph.

It's your classroom:
Using the questions provided for Table 7.1 as a model, what questions would you ask students to guide their analysis of the information in the other tables?

Table 7.1 School segregation and voting rights in the US South (%)

State	African-American children in interracial schools, 1964	Eligible African-Americans registered to vote, 1960	Eligible African-Americans registered to vote, 1964
West Virginia	58.2	NA	NA
Delaware	56.5	NA	NA
Kentucky	54.4	NA	NA
Missouri	42.0	NA	NA
Oklahoma	28.0	NA	NA
Texas	5.5	32	46
Tennessee	2.7	59	64
Virginia	1.6	19	25
Florida	1.5	26	45
Arkansas	Less than 1	30	41
Alabama	Less than 1	14	19
Louisiana	Less than 1	22	31
Georgia	Less than 1	22	36
South Carolina	Less than 1	11	30
North Carolina	Less than 1	25	42
Mississippi	None	4	6

1. What percentage of African-American children attended interracial schools in Missouri?
2. What percentage of African-American children attended interracial schools in Florida?
3. In which of these states did the smallest percentage of African-American children attend interracial schools?
4. What percentage of eligible African-Americans were registered to vote in Texas in 1960?
5. Which of these states had the largest percentage of eligible African-Americans registered to vote in 1964?
6. Which state or states had the greatest percentage increase from 1960 to 1964?
7. What conclusions do you draw from this chart?

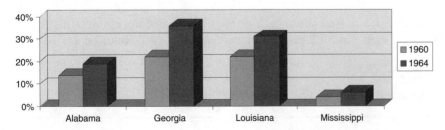

Figure 7.2 Eligible African-Americans registered to vote, 1960 and 1964.

Table 7.2 Standard of living by race, 1950–1970

Category	Year	All People	Whites	African-Americans
Unemployment (%)	1950	5.3	4.9	9.0
	1960	5.5	4.9	10.2
	1970	4.9	4.5	8.2
Median income (US$)	1950	3,319	3,334	1,369
	1960	5,620	5,835	3,233
	1970	9,867	10,236	6,516
Life expectancy (years)	1950		69	61
	1960		71	64
	1970		72	64

Table 7.3 Education of head of household of African-American families in poverty (%)

Education level	1978	1987
At least one years of college	12.6	11.2
High school graduate	18.7	27.8
High school dropout	34.2	39.4

Table 7.4 Income distribution by race, 2005 (%)

Income	White families	African-American Families
Over $75,000	27.9	15.1
$50–74,999	18.9	15.1
$35–50,000	14.9	15.1
$25–35,000	11.4	12.6
$15–25,000	12.0	16.1
Under $15,000	12.8	26.0
Median Income (US$)	48,554	30,858

Table 7.5 African-American males, incarcerated or in college, 1980 and 2000

Status	1980	2000	Percentage increase
Incarcerated	143,000	791,600	450
College	463,000	603,032	30

Source: Butterfield, F. 2020. "Study Finds Big Increase in Black Men as Inmates Since 1980," *The New York Times*, August 28, A14.

Table 7.6 Racial profiling, January 1, 2006 through September 30, 2007

Category	White	Black
Population of New York City (million people)	3.6	2.2
Police stops for searches	94,530	453,042
Police stops for searches that did not result in an arrest or summons	83,452	402,943
Police stops as percent of population	2.6% of Whites	21.1% of Blacks
Percent of police stops that led to arrest or summons	12%	11%

Source: Dunn, C., Lieberman, D. and Pressman, A. 2007. "Profiling by the numbers," *The New York Times*, November 18, CY11.

Teaching Activity: Design a Theme-based Unit

Try it yourself:
Using a high school social studies textbook and a collection of primary source documents, design a theme-based unit plain (containing between 8 and 12 lessons) for a specific historical era or on a specific topic.

Add your voice to the discussion:
How do you view this approach to social studies unit planning? Why?

WHAT IS A COMPARATIVE THEMATIC UNIT?

In the chronological global history curriculum, teachers tend to focus on different groups, nations, or regions during each historical epoch. A problem with this approach is that it can give students the impression that all peoples and nations were undergoing similar experiences at the same time.

In an area studies curriculum, students briefly and separately examine the histories, geography, and cultures of each region (e.g., Latin America and the Caribbean, sub-Saharan Africa, North Africa and the Middle East, South-east Asia, China, Japan, and the Indian sub-continent). A problem with this approach is that students do not learn to draw connections between events taking place in different parts of the world.

A comparative/thematic unit is one way to address the limitations in both of these approaches. It makes it possible for students to examine the similarities and differences in the ways that peoples, nations, and civilizations interact and confront historical forces. For example, a class can examine the problems related to industrialization and modernization, as well as solutions developed by people in different places during different historical periods. Another possibility is to study nationalist movements in various countries as people respond to colonialism and imperialism. A comparative/thematic approach can be used throughout the entire curriculum or as a way to organize occasional integrative units.

Comparative/Thematic Unit Outline

Nationalism vs. Imperialism = revolution
The goal of this unit is to examine similarities and differences in post-World War I revolutionary movements and to discover why some

movements are successful while others are defeated or deflected and lose track of their ideals.

The nineteenth-century industrial revolution in Europe gave European countries a tremendous economic and military advantage over other regions of the world. At the same time, it plunged them into intense competition for resources and markets. The result was capitalist consolidation over economic and political power in Europe and imperialist expansion around the world. Competition between the nations of Europe for dominance also led to two worldwide conflagrations, World War I (1914–1919) and World War II (1939–1945). These massive military undertakings put enormous strain on the European empires and created the potential for revolutionary uprisings against both capitalism and foreign domination. At the end of World War II, the United States supplanted Europe as the major expansionist military and economic force and brought it into sharp conflict with revolutionary movements around the world.

The Russian Empire was both a colonizer in central Asia and a victim of German and British imperial ambitions. The devastating impact of World War I led first to the collapse of the Czarist monarchy and then to a reform government. The revolution brought to power a small vanguard party committed to communist ideals, including internationalism and worker control over the government. However, the need to consolidate authority against hostile internal and external enemies led to increasingly autocratic practices and the creation of an authoritarian and bureaucratic state. The Russian Revolution became a model for, and supporter of, revolutions around the world for the next half century. The emergence of Russia, now known as the Soviet Union, as a world power following World War II led to its domination over much of eastern and central

Europe. In the late 1980s and early 1990s, a new wave of pro-democracy revolutionary movements challenged Soviet authority and overthrew Soviet power at home and abroad.

Ireland, the world's "oldest" colony, was under English control from the twelfth century until the end of World War I. Periodic insurrections, either with popular support or led by small vanguard parties, were readily defeated. Irish nationalists took advantage of British involvement in World War I to launch an "Easter Uprising" in 1916. It drew little support and was quickly put down. However, British authorities made a major miscalculation. The execution of rebels as traitors caused massive public outrage. At the end of the war, Irish soldiers who had served in the British army during World War I became the backbone of a new republican army and independence was secured in 1923.

The British consolidated power in India during the first half of the nineteenth century where they pioneered divide and conquer tactics and the use of "puppet" local authorities to govern. The economy of India was made completely subservient to the economic needs of the conquering power. After World War I, a broad coalition of Indian nationalists led by Gandhi and the Nehru family launched a non-violent campaign of civil disobedience to defy British authority. Military action by the British only bolstered the resistance and, weakened by World War II, the British withdraw. As independence approached, national unity quickly broke down and violence led to the relocation of millions of people and the partition of the Indian sub-continent into separate Hindu and Islamic states.

While European imperialist forces never directly governed China, Europeans did succeed in creating extra-territorial "spheres of influence" and were able to force the Chinese imperial state to accept their economic, political, and military dictates. The collapse of the empire on the eve of World War I brought a divided nationalist party (the Kuomintang) to power. Civil War was avoided until the late 1920s, when an alliance of non-democratic feudal warlords, the military, and pro-capitalist forces attacked and defeated more radical political parties and workers groups. The opposition retreated to the interior of the country under the leadership of Mao Zse-tung and the Chinese Communist Party. There they built model socialist communities and a new

army. When China was invaded by Japan prior to the Second World, the communists, rather than the Kuomintang dominated government, led the resistance. After the defeat of Japan, the communists, with broad popular support, seized power. Over the next three decades, they tried various strategies to build socialism in an economically backward and vastly overpopulated society. While their measures generally failed, the Communist Party was able to maintain control by generating new social movements in support of its ideals and through a restrictive authoritarian government. In the last two decades, China has remained undemocratic, but has increasingly transformed itself, creating its own version of a controlled capitalist economy.

After World War II, Great Britain, France, and the other European powers were no longer able to maintain control over their empires in Africa. Kenya and Algeria were colonies with relatively large populations of European settlers who controlled the land and resources and hoped to retain power, either through annexation (Algeria) or some type of "commonwealth' status (Kenya). In both countries, indigenous populations launched violent and ultimately successful revolutions that were dismissed by their European masters as terrorist and uncivilized. In both cases, the imperialist forces used repressive terrorist tactics against civilians and combatants in an effort to maintain control. In resource rich Nigeria and the Congo, independence brought civil war between ethnic groups that had been manipulated against each other by imperialist forces during the colonial period. These wars, which have cycled for decades, have been fed by continuing European economic interference.

The Vietnamese revolution, although led by nominal communists, was one of the most successful mobilizations of nationalism against foreign intrusion. Vietnamese nationalists opposed the French after World War I, fought against the Japanese during World War II, and defeated French efforts to reassert colonial control after the war. When the United States replaced the French and established a puppet government in the south, the Vietnamese fought a war of attrition until the US finally withdrew. The years of resistance came with a terrible price tag. The country was devastated, and although independent, never recovered economically.

Cuban revolutionaries had been stifled for the first half of the twentieth century and then were suddenly successful in a bloodless coup when a pro-US dictatorship under Batista lost all popular support and collapsed in 1959. Because of the new government's efforts to socialize the economy, which included the nationalization of US-owned properties, the United States placed Cuba under an international economic embargo that has left the country virtually bankrupt. Despite this the government, while non-democratic, was able to maintain popular support because of campaigns to create mass literacy, end poverty, and provide high levels of health care. Cuba supported other revolutionary movements around the world, and because of the hostility of the United States, developed close ties with the Soviet Union.

After World War II, Iran's elected government was overthrown by the United States and Great Britain, who feared that the country would nationalize foreign-owned oil assets. They installed an authoritarian monarchy and helped silence all secular opposition groups. The dictatorship was finally overthrown by a revolutionary movement in 1979 that established a new government under the direction of Islamic religious leaders. This government has supported other conservative religious groups in the Middle East in opposition to the United States and its allies.

Major themes examined in this comparative/thematic unit include:

- Foreign imperialist powers and domestic dictators rarely give up their power without costly and destructive revolutions and wars.
- It is generally a serious mistake to underestimate the ability and popular appeal of revolutionary leaders.
- The idea of revolution can be romantic, exhilarating, or frightening depending on your social position.
- Revolutionary wars have their own historical logic. Many revolutions began with public support and liberationist goals and then deteriorated into dictatorship and human rights abuses. Since the French Revolution of the late eighteenth century, the return of repressive government following a revolution is termed the Thermidorian Reaction.
- The direction of history can suddenly change. Major powers have hidden weak-

nesses. Apparently supine movements can suddenly win adherents and seize power.
- Revolutionary wars, whether against foreign occupiers or local oppressors, tend to be violent affairs that employ intimidation and attacks on civilians. Generally, all sides employ terror tactics. This raises the question of whether, or when, ends justify means.
- Revolutionary wars, fought to liberate the economic potential of societies, have often left them impoverished and unable to improve conditions for their citizens.
- Success in battle does not equate with success in building a just and democratic society. Often revolutions begin when wars are over.
- Non-violent social movements have succeeded in toppling oppressive forces (e.g., India, South Africa, and Eastern Europe), but have still been subject to turmoil and violence after achieving power.

Topic Calendar (Lessons can take more than one period)

1. Unit introduction
   - *Focus*: Underlying and immediate causes of World War I and the grievances of colonized peoples.
   - *Question*: How did imperialism and war lead to waves of revolution?
2. Communist Revolution in Russia
   - *Focus*: Conditions that led to the overthrow of Czarist rule and the coming to power of the communists.
   - *Question*: Why were communist revolutionaries able to seize power in a politically and economically backward society?
3. Nationalist Revolution in Ireland
   - *Focus*: Opposition to forced cultural and political assimilation.
   - *Question*: Why did a movement that was marginalized and repeatedly defeated suddenly succeed?
4. India challenges the British Empire
   - *Focus*: Gandhi and the idea and practice of nonviolent civil disobedience.
   - *Question*: Is it possible to build a unified nation in an ethnically, religiously, and linguistically diverse society?
5. Communist Revolution in China
   - *Focus*: Mao Zedong and violent revolution as a vehicle to gain power and change society.

- *Question*: Is Communism a viable alternative for oppressed people?
6. Anti-colonialism in Kenya and Algeria
   - *Focus*: Independence struggles in settler colonies (colonies where large numbers of people from the imperialist power have established permanent homes).
   - *Question*: Are attacks on civilian supporters of colonial regimes justified?
7. Nigeria and the Congo after Independence
   - *Focus*: Creating one nation out of different peoples.
   - *Question*: Do nations have the right to suppress internal nationalist movements?
8. Vietnam: winning but losing
   - *Focus*: Cultural and historical roots of resistance.
   - *Question*: How did a small traditional nation resist world superpowers?
9. Seizing power and building socialism in Cuba.
   - *Focus*: Building socialist institutions after the achievement of political power.

- *Question*: Can communism meet the economic, political, and social needs of people?
10. Islamic Revolution in Iran
    - *Focus*: Right-wing religious opposition as a revolutionary force.
    - *Question*: Are revolutions progressive by nature?
11. Anti-Communist Revolutions in Eastern Europe
    - *Focus*: Non-violent overthrow of Soviet-backed dictators and the collapse of the Soviet Union.
    - *Question*: Does capitalism bring democracy?
12. Unit conclusions
    - *Focus*: Compare nationalist revolutions in different countries.
    - *Questions*: How do we decide whether revolutionary movements are justified? How do we decide when revolutionary movements are successful?

Teaching Activity: Design a Comparative Unit

Try it yourself:
Using a high school social studies textbook and a collection of primary source documents, design a comparative unit plan (containing between 8 and 10 lessons) for a specific historical era or on a specific topic.

Add your voice to the discussion:
How do you view this approach to social studies unit planning? Why?

It's your classroom:
Which approach to unit planning do you prefer? Why?

Learning Activity: Drawing Connections between Events

Frequently students learn historical events in isolation from each other or from only one perspective. The following questions are intended to encourage people to draw connections between peoples and events.

1. The Jewish holiday of Hanukah is the celebration of ancient Hebrew resistance to conquest and assimilation between 100 and 200BC. Who were they battling against?
2. In 732AD, the victory of an army headed by Charles Martel at the Battle of Tours prevented the integration of medieval European societies into a vibrant international civilization that already extended from the Pyrenees to China. Which army was defeated in this battle?
3. In 1325, a voyager from the Mediterranean region began his travels across the Eastern Hemisphere, probably reaching India in 1333 and China in 1345. Later, he visited western Africa. As a result of his journals, dictated upon his return home, the known world became much more integrated. Who was this voyager?

4. Study of the "Age of Exploration" usually starts around 1450, with Portuguese voyages along the west coast of Africa. However, a half century earlier, this empire sponsored a series of major voyages to expand trade and find a water route connecting the east and west. One trip involved over 300 ships and nearly 28,000 people. The voyages stopped in 1433, when the empire decided it had little to learn about or acquire from the rest of the world. Which empire sponsored these voyages?

5. What is the oldest permanently established community in what is now the continental United States?

6. In 1608 a separatist group of Calvinists left England to stay with co-religionists in the Netherlands. Unhappy over the assimilation of their children into Dutch society, the "Pilgrims" returned to England a year later. In 1620, they left England again, this time to settle in the new world. Later in the seventeenth century, some of their former Dutch hosts followed their example and went into exile in the wilderness to establish a religious community. Who were they and where did they go?

7. The American colonies and the United States were involved in the French and Indian War from 1754–1763 and the War of 1812 from 1812 to 1815. Both wars were actually the North American fronts of broader European conflicts. Which wars were they? Who were the primary European combatants?

8. In 1831, he led a slave rebellion that shook the entire slave system and directly led to emancipation in a number of new world territories. Who was he and where was the rebellion?

9. Where did Mohandas Gandhi begin his involvement in opposition to British colonialism?

10. In the early twentieth century, this future world leader sought a position in the French bureaucracy so that he could help the French develop his homeland. He was refused. In 1919, he tried to represent his homeland at the peace conference at Versailles, but he was denied admission. As a revolutionary leader, he later helped his people defeat the Japanese, the French, and the United States. Who was he and what was his homeland?

Try it yourself:
How did you do on these questions? Answers are on the last page of this chapter.

Essay 1: Original Intent and the United States Constitution

An earlier version of this essay appeared in A. Singer (2006). Used with permission.

I want to start with an admission. Although Article 3, Section 1 of the United States Constitution lists no qualifications for judges other than "good behavior" while in office, I do not believe I am qualified to be a Justice of the United States Supreme Court. It is not because I am trained as a teacher and an historian instead of as a lawyer. It is primarily because I am an activist with a political commitment to my fundamental beliefs and not to the basic integrity of the legal system. One of my heroes is William Lloyd Garrison, who publicly burned a copy of the Constitution at an anti-slavery rally in Framingham, Massachusetts on July 4, 1854. Garrison (1845) believed the Constitution, because it permitted slavery, was a "covenant with death," an "agreement with Hell," and a "refuge of lies."

I see the courts and laws, including the US Constitution, as mechanisms for achieving broader social goals. However, Supreme Court Justices must defend the principles of the Constitution even when they run counter to their own views. It is because Justices swear an oath to defend the United States Constitution as the first law of the land, and for the other reasons that I disqualify myself, that I also describe Chief Justice John Roberts and Associate Justices Samuel Alito, Antonin Scalia, and Clarence Thomas as "Original Incompetents" who should never have been appointed to the Supreme Court. If Alito, Roberts, Scalia, and Thomas had any integrity, they would resign. Of course, if they had integrity, they never would have been nominated for the court by President Reagan, the first President Bush, and the most recent President Bush.

Discussion of the meaning of the Constitution, how it should be interpreted by judges, and the qualities the President of the United States and the Senate (who respectively nominate and approve candidates) should look for in potential appointees to the highest court, took on immediacy with the retirement of Associate Justice Sandra Day O'Connor and the death of Chief Justice William Rehnquist. Vacancies on the court give President George W. Bush an opportunity to reshape Constitutional jurisprudence and the future of the country. During the 2004 Presidential election campaign, he promised conservative audiences, who share his limited world view, religious beliefs, and [mis]conceptions of the United States Constitution, to appoint judges in what he called the Scalia-Thomas "mold" (Toner 2005: 1).

Recent Senate Hearings

Unfortunately, the Senate hearings preceding the appointment of John Roberts as Chief Justice (replacing Rehnquist) and Samuel Alito as Associate Justice (replacing O'Connor) shed little light on constitutional issues. Both nominees were lauded for their intellect and "judicial temperament," while they refused to answer questions about their philosophies. At a time when President Bush and his supporters were trying to move the court significantly to the right, the public was being told that ideas did not matter.

The debate over the meaning of the United States Constitution and how to uncover it is not new. In the early twentieth century, Finley Peter Dunne (Levy 1988: ix), speaking through his fictional character Mr. Dooley, a philosophical Irish bartender, wrote "Tis funny about th' constitution. It reads plain, but no wan can undherstant it without an interpreter." Part of the problem is that there is no official guidebook to the Constitution. The Constitution was written in secrecy and James Madison, Secretary of the Constitutional Convention and the 4th President of the United States (who certainly should know), warned that "As a guide in expanding and applying the provisions of the Constitution, the debates and incidental decisions of the Convention have no authoritative character" (Levy 1988: 1).

In his concurring opinion in *Graves* v. *New York*, 306 US466 (1939), United States Supreme Court Associate Justice Felix Frankfurter wrote, "[T]he ultimate touchstone of constitutionality is the Constitution itself and not what we [the Justices] have said about it." Yet despite this philosophical position on interpreting the Constitution, a cautious conservative judge like Frankfurter was able to support the unanimous 1954 *Brown* v. *Topeka, Kansas Board of Education* decision that drew on modern sociological evidence to demonstrate the impact of racial segregation on African-Americans. Evidently Frankfurter understood that textual analysis alone was insufficient for deciding issues that had not been clearly addressed in a document written 167 years before the case was decided.

The idea that the Constitution should be understood as a "living" document subject to continual reinterpretation was clearly endorsed by Thomas Jefferson, the third President of the United States and one of the primary authors of the Bill of Rights. In a letter written in 1810 that is quoted on the walls of the Jefferson Memorial in Washington DC, Jefferson explained, "I am not an advocate for frequent changes in laws and Constitutions, but laws must and institutions must go hand in hand with the progress of the human mind. As that becomes more developed, more enlightened, as new discoveries are made, new truths discovered and manners and opinions change, with the change of circumstances, institutions must advance also to keep pace with the times. We might as well require a man to wear still the coat which fitted him when a boy as civilized society to remain ever under the regimen of their barbarous ancestors" (Jefferson 1810). Clinton Rossiter, a relatively conservative political scientist writing in the 1960s, supported Jefferson's view. According to Rossiter, "The one clear intent of the Framers was that each generation of Americans should pursue its destiny as a community of free men" (Levy 1988: xiv).

Learning Activity: Historian Howard Zinn Discusses the Constitution

Source: "It's Not up to the Court," *Progressive*, November, 2005

According to historian Howard Zinn, "There is enormous hypocrisy surrounding the pious veneration of the Constitution and 'the rule of law.' The Constitution, like the Bible, is infinitely flexible and is used to serve the political needs of the moment. When the country was in economic crisis and turmoil in the Thirties and capitalism needed to be saved from the anger of the poor and hungry and unemployed, the Supreme Court was willing to stretch to infinity the constitutional right of Congress to regulate interstate commerce. It decided that the national government, desperate to regulate farm production, could tell a family farmer what to grow on his tiny piece of land. When the Constitution gets in the way of a war, it is ignored. When the Supreme Court was faced, during Vietnam, with a suit by soldiers refusing to go, claiming that there had been no declaration of war by

Congress, as the Constitution required, the soldiers could not get four Supreme Court justices to agree to even hear the case. When, during World War I, Congress ignored the First Amendment's right to free speech by passing legislation to prohibit criticism of the war, the imprisonment of dissenters under this law was upheld unanimously by the Supreme Court . . . It would be naive to depend on the Supreme Court to defend the rights of poor people, women, people of color, dissenters of all kinds. Those rights only come alive when citizens organize, protest, demonstrate, strike, boycott, rebel, and violate the law in order to uphold justice."

In this statement, Zinn makes a number of controversial claims. He accuses many who interpret the Constitution of hypocrisy. He argues that the courts have been inconsistent in applying the Constitution to different issues. He charges that the Supreme Court does not defend the rights of poor people, minorities, and political dissenters.

Add your voice to the discussion:
Write a brief reply to Howard Zinn expressing your views on his statement.

It's your classroom:
Develop a unit rationale summarizing main ideas about the Constitution you would use as the basis for a unit plan on the Constitution for an American history or government class.

Justice Taney and Dred Scott

While few of its proponents want to be identified with him, one of the principle nineteenth-century proponents of "original intent" was Supreme Court Chief Justice Roger Taney, author of the Dred Scott (1857) decision. In his decision calling for the re-enslavement of Dred Scott and the unlimited extension of slavery into the territories, Taney wrote, "No one . . . supposes that any change in public opinion or feeling, in relation to this unfortunate race . . . should induce the Court to give to the words of the Constitution a more liberal construction in their favor than they were intended to bear when the instrument was framed and adopted. Such an argument would be altogether inadmissible in any tribunal called on to interpret it . . . Any other rule of construction would abrogate the judicial character of this court, and make it the mere reflex of the popular opinion or passion of the day. This court was not created by the Constitution for such purposes" (Levy 1988: 325). No wonder William Lloyd Garrison wanted the Constitution burned!

According to historian Leonard Levy (1988 xii), the modern debate over interpreting the Constitution started in the 1980s when President Ronald Reagan, Attorney General Edward Meese and Supreme Court nominee Robert Bork started to promote the idea of "original intent." Up until that point, advocates of "original intent" had had no specific political ideology. However, as Reagan and Meese made clear (and as Bork, Scalia and Thomas have continually tried to obfuscate), their goal was not a more accurate interpretation of the Constitution, but finding judges who would ratify a right wing political agenda.

On July 9, 1985, at a meeting of the American Bar Association in Washington, DC, Meese argued that "The intended role of the judiciary generally and the Supreme Court in particular was to serve as the 'bulwarks of a limited constitution' . . . As the 'faithful guardians of the Constitution,' the judges were expected to resist any political effort to depart from the literal provisions of the Constitution. The text of the document and the original intention of those who framed it would be the judicial standard in giving effect to the Constitution . . . What, then, should a constitutional jurisprudence actually be? It should be a Jurisprudence of Original Intention . . . Those who framed the Constitution chose their words carefully; they debated at great length the most minute points. The language they chose meant something. It is incumbent upon the Court to determine what that meaning was."

Ronald Reagan and "Original Intent"

President Reagan gave his personal stamp to the idea of "original intent" in a February 11, 1988 speech to a Conservative Political Action Conference dinner. President Reagan claimed that his goal was respect for the original intent of the authors of the Constitution. "For two decades we've been talking about getting justices on the Supreme Court who cared less about criminals and more about the victims of crime, justices who knew that the words 'original intent' referred to something more than New Year's resolutions and fad diets . . . The great legal debates of the past two decades over criminal justice have, at their root, been debates over a strict versus expansive construction of the Constitution."

However, President Reagan's actual agenda had little to do with Constitutional principles. He argued in the same speech, without references or evidence, that "The Constitution, as originally intended by the framers, is itself tough on crime, and protective of the victims of crime" and he blamed liberalism for permissiveness in the national culture. The President wanted strict constructionists on the Supreme Court who would endorse conservative efforts to have the nation say "'no' to drugs, and 'yes' to family, and 'absolutely' to schools that teach basic skills, basic values, and basic discipline." If President Reagan had bothered to read the Constitution or the "Notes of Debates in the Federal Convention of 1787 Reported by James Madison" (Koch 1985), he would have discovered that none of the issues he listed were included in the document or discussed by the framers.

Presidents Reagan and both Bushes denounced "activist," supposedly liberal, judges who they believed were reinterpreting the Constitution to suit their personal agendas. However, between 1994 and 2004, it was the rightwing of the court, Justices Thomas (65 percent), Kennedy (64 percent), Scalia (56 percent) and Rehnquist (46 percent), who voted most consistently to declare newly enacted federal legislation unconstitutional (Gerwirtz and Golder 2005: A19).

Learning Activity: Interpreting the Law, or Writing It

During the 1960s, conservative critics accused Supreme Court Chief Justice Earl Warren and his allies on the court of writing the law instead of interpreting it. They were especially troubled by a series of cases that extended the rights of people accused of crimes.

Case. *Mapp* v. *Ohio*, 1961
- Issue. Can illegally seized evidence be used in a trial?
- Decision. No. This violates the rights of the accused.

Case. *Gideon* v. *Wainright*, 1963
- Issue. Do accused have the right to a lawyer?
- Decision. Yes, in felony cases, even if they cannot pay themselves.

Case. *Escobedo* v. *Illinois*, 1964
- Issue. Does the accused have a right to an attorney while being questioned by the police?
- Decision. Yes.

Case. *Miranda* v. *Arizona*, 1966
- Issue. Must accused be told their rights?
- Decision. Yes, especially that they have a right to remain silent and the right to a lawyer.

Case. *Berger* v. *New York*, 1967
- Issue. Can police tap phone conversations?
- Decision. Only when they have a legal and specific warrant.

Case. In re Gault, 1967
- Issue. Are juvenile accused entitled to the same legal protection as adults?
- Decision. Courts must respect legal rights of juveniles.

Add your voice to the discussion
1. In your opinion, did the Warren Court of the 1950s and 1960s go too far in protecting the accused from police authority? Explain.
2. In your opinion, was the Warren Court interpreting or writing the law? Explain.

Try it yourself:
Design a lesson for teaching about the Warren Court and the rights of the accused.

Robert Bork and "Original Intent" Theory

The philosophical champion of "original intent" was federal judge Robert Bork, whom President Reagan nominated for the Supreme Court in 1987. At his nomination hearings, Judge Bork argued, "when a judge goes beyond [his proper function] and reads entirely new values into the Constitution, values the framers and ratifiers did not put there, he deprives the people of their liberty." Bork, who was rejected by the Senate, later wrote that Justices must be guided by "the meaning understood at the time of the law's enactment . . . all that counts is how the words used in the Constitution would have been understood at the time . . . The interpretation of the Constitution according to the original understanding, then, is the only method that can preserve the Constitution, the separation of powers, and the liberties of the people" (Bork 1990: 144–147, 159).

The most articulate opponent of a doctrine of "original intent" was William Brennan, an actual conservative who was appointed to the Supreme Court by President Dwight Eisenhower in 1956. Brennan rejected the idea that it was possible to know "the intent of the Framers" and argued that "We current Justices read the Constitution in the only way that we can: as Twentieth-Century Americans." He accepted the responsibility to "look to the history of the time of framing and to the intervening history of interpretation," but felt "the ultimate question must be, what do the words of the text mean in our time?"

"The genius of the Constitution," according to Justice Brennan, "rests not in any static meaning it might have had in a world that is dead and gone, but in the adaptability of its great principles to cope with current problems and current needs. What the constitutional fundamentals meant to the wisdom of other times cannot be their measure to the vision of our time." He felt that Supreme Court Justices had no choice but to "adapt our institutions to the ever-changing conditions of national and international life."

Justices Scalia and Thomas

Justices Antonin Scalia and Clarence Thomas have attempted to skirt Brennan's criticism of "original intent" by defining their position as a combination of what they call "textualist" and "originalist"; however, the difference, as far as I can see, is largely semantic. In a speech at the Catholic University of America in 1996, Scalia argued that "If you are a textualist, you don't care about the intent, and I don't care if the framers of the Constitution had some secret meaning in mind when they adopted its words. I take the words as they were promulgated to the people of the United States, and what is the fairly understood meaning of those words . . . The words are the law." Scalia rejects the idea of an "evolving" Constitution that recognizes "all sorts of rights that clearly did not exist at the time." Justice Scalia conceded that "Originalism has a lot of problems . . . Sometimes it's awful hard to tell what the original meaning was . . . But the real problem is not whether it's the best thing in the world, but whether there's anything better."

Scalia may not like it, but the only way a judge can ascertain the original meaning of what are frequently vague phrases, is to examine the intentions of the authors. This problem arose very early in the national government in the case of *Chisholm* v. *Georgia* (1793) when neither the federal courts nor the legislative and executive branches could agree on the meaning of the Constitutional promise of state sovereignty because they could not agree on the implications of the word "sovereignty" as used in the text (Levy 1988: 56).

Justice Thomas echoes Scalia's position in a 2001 lecture at the American Enterprise Institute for Public Policy Research in Washington, DC. He conceded that "reasonable minds" might differ on the exact meaning of the Constitution, "but that does not mean that there is no correct answer, that there are no clear, eternal principles recognized and put into motion by our founding documents . . . The Constitution means what the delegates of the Philadelphia Convention and of the state ratifying conventions understood it to mean; not what we judges think it should mean."

Associate Justice Stephen Breyer has been sharply critical of justices who espouse "textualist" or "originalist" doctrines. In a series of lectures delivered at New York University in 2001, Breyer argued that Supreme Court Justices needed to focus on the consequences of laws and their decisions, and not just text. He felt that judges need to take "greater account of the Constitution's democratic nature when they interpret constitutional and statutory texts . . . [I]ncreased emphasis upon that objective by judges when they interpret legal text will yield better law—law that helps a community of individuals democratically find practical solutions to important contemporary problems" (Breyer 2005: 5–6). He warned, "Literalism has a tendency to undermine the Constitution's efforts to create a framework for democratic government" and is "inconsistent with the most fundamental original intention of the Framers themselves" (Breyer 2005: 131–132).

I know that this will come as somewhat of a surprise at this point in the essay, but I think Justice

Brennan is wrong when he says that we cannot know the original intent of the framers of the Constitution. I believe, and will attempt to demonstrate, that we can. For me, the real problem is that Reagan, Meese, Bork, Rehnquist, Scalia and Thomas are so blinded by rightwing ideology that they cannot see what the "original intent" or the meaning of the "text" is.

A clue to the "original intent" of the framers actually appears in Brennan's 1985 speech. According to Brennan, "The Constitution on its face is . . . a blueprint for government. And when the text is not prescribing the form of government it is limiting the powers of that government. The original document, before addition of any of the amendments, does not speak primarily of the rights of man, but of the abilities and disabilities of government." The "original intent" of the framers of the Constitution was not the institutionalization of a particular legal principle or a specific law, nor was it the resolution of the fundamental conflicts dividing the new country. It was the creation of a "blueprint for government" based on a complex system of checks, balances, and compromises that would allow the new country to resolve issues as they arose in the future. On every major substantive conflict, the framers took a pass, and opted for a mechanism rather than a solution.

This interpretation is consistent with what James Madison understood to be the purpose of the Constitution. One of the earliest debates in the first Congress was on a bill to establish the Department of Foreign Affairs. When Madison spoke to the issue, he explained "The decision that is at this time made will become the permanent exposition of the Constitution and on a permanent exposition of the Constitution will depend the genius and character of the whole government." Therefore, Madison stressed, the decision must "retain that *equilibrium* [italics added] which the Constitution intended" (Levy 1988: 6). This explanation of the "original intent" of the framers is also supported by Madison's arguments in favor of the ratification of th[e] tion in the Federalist papers.

Madison Explains "Original Intent"
In Federalist 10 (originally published in *The New York Packet*, November 23, 1787), Madison (Rossiter 1961) argued that the government created by the Constitution was specifically designed to "break and control the violence of faction" by making it difficult for majorities to change the way the national government operated. The framers were responding to worries that the existing state and national "governments are too unstable, that the public good is disregarded in the conflicts of rival parties, and that measures are too often decided, not according to the rules of justice and the rights of the minor party, but by the superior force of an interested and overbearing majority." According to Madison, "To secure the public good and private rights [minority rights, especially the property rights of the wealthy] against the danger of such a faction, and at the same time to preserve the spirit and the form of popular government, is then the great object to which our inquiries are directed." It is the "original intent" of the framers. They would do this by avoiding "pure democracy," which he considered turbulent and contentious. Instead the framers were proposing a republic with "the delegation of the government . . . to a small number of citizens elected by the rest" of the citizens [white, male, Protestant, property owners, including those who owned other human beings].

The great compromises at the Constitutional Convention and in the initial years of government were all designed to maintain national unity and government stability by promoting equilibrium through balance and compromise, by postponing potentially divisive decisions, and hindering movements for social reform movements or Constitutional change. This system largely worked until the 1850s, when increasingly intense sectional conflict over slavery finally plunged the nation into Civil War.

Classroom Activity: Can Judges or Teachers be Neutral?

During questions directed by Supreme Court Justices to opposing attorneys in the Morse v. Frederick case (2007), a majority of the Roberts Court seemed willing to limit student First and Fourth Amendment rights. One of the lawyers defending the decision by a local school district to suspend a student for behavior it considered unacceptable was Kenneth Starr, former Solicitor General of the United States during the administration of the first President Bush. *The New York Times* commented that Mr Starr's biggest ally on the court was the man who once worked as his deputy in the solicitor general's office, Chief Justice John G. Roberts Jr. The chief justice intervened frequently making clear his view that "schools need not tolerate student expression that undermines what they define as their educational mission" Greenhouse 2007: A16).

At one point during the question, Chief Justice Roberts asked, "Where does that notion that our schools have to be content neutral [come from]? I thought we wanted our schools to teach something, including something besides just basic elements, including character formation and not to use drugs."

Add your voice to the discussion:
Should Supreme Court Justices, schools, and teachers strive for neutrality? Is it even possible? Explain.

The Great Compromises

The great compromises included federalism, the division of governmental responsibility between state and national governments; built-in checks and balances that limited the power of each of the three independent branches of the national government; a bi-cameral legislature where one house had representation based on population and the other house had equal representation for each state no matter its size; the 3/5th Compromise which was intended to balance the voting strength of northern and southern states; the Bill of Rights, which protects the rights of individuals from state power; the amendment process, which protected the property rights of the wealthy, including slaveholders, by making it extremely difficult to modify the Constitution; and, the Missouri Compromise of 1820, which formalized a decision made in 1796 to balance the number of northern and southern states and ensure equal representation in the Senate.

The "original intent" of the framers had nothing to do with promoting family values and religious beliefs or a women's ability to secure an abortion. It had nothing to do with examining the minds of the authors of the Constitution to uncover their deepest biases and moral indiscretions. It had nothing to do with searching the text for the real eighteenth-century meaning of the words. Justice Brennan was right, even when he was wrong. The "original intent" of the framers was to create a government that would support our ability to read the Constitution in the only way that we can: as twenty-first-century Americans. "The ultimate question must be," as Brennan argued so eloquently, "what do the words of the text mean in our time?"

A rigid commitment to discovering ultimate meaning through a slavish examination of original "text" can be seen in a number of intellectual traditions, including Roman Catholic rationalism as developed by Thomas Aquinas, dogmatic Marxists in the Stalinist era, fundamentalists within all the major religions, and even academic Shakespearean scholars. Each of these traditions believes ultimate truth is imbedded in its document and can only be discovered through careful textural analysis. Because they believe their truths are universal, they act as if they were divinely inspired rather than the work of human beings, and they ignore as meaningless the historical contexts of the documents. Textualists may make good academics, but they make lousy judges. Warning against this type of dogmatism, Federal Judge Learned Hand (1944: 190–191) argued that "The spirit of liberty is the spirit which is not too sure that it is right; the spirit of liberty is the spirit which seeks to understand the minds of other men and women; the spirit of liberty is the spirit which weighs their interests alongside its own without bias."

In a 2002 speech at the Georgetown University Law Center, Senator Edward M. Kennedy suggested standards for judicial appointees that make a lot more sense. They include "A commitment to the core constitutional values embedded in the fabric of our democracy—freedom of speech and religion; the right to privacy; and equal protection and due process under the law . . . A dedication to equality for all Americans, especially those who have been denied their full measure of freedom, such as women and minorities. A respect for justice for all whose rights are too readily abused by powerful institutions, whether by the power of government itself or by giant concentrations of power in the private sector. Respect for the Supreme Court itself, for our constitutional system of government, and for the history and heritage by which that system has evolved, including the relationship between the federal government and the states, and between Congress and the President. And, finally, possession of the special qualities that enable judges to meet their own important responsibilities—qualities often described as fairness, impartiality, open-mindedness, and judicial temperament."

Whatever you may think of Senator Kennedy, it is an interesting set of criteria, especially the ideas of "respect for the Supreme Court itself, for our constitutional system of government, and for the history and heritage by which that system has evolved" and "fairness, impartiality, open-mindedness, and judicial temperament." Personally, I can live with Supreme

Court Justices who have different views than mine, true conservatives appointed by Republican Presidents such as Earl Warren and William Brennan (Eisenhower), Harry Blackmum (Nixon), Sandra Day O'Connor and Anthony Kennedy (Reagan) and David Souter (Bush I), if they remember Judge Hand's comments on the "spirit of liberty" and possess these qualities.

Classroom Activity: Debating Original Intent and the Meaning of the United States Constitution

Instructions

Working in your teams, examine each quotation and complete Table 7.7 below. The quotations are arranged chronologically. Working individually, use the information from your chart to write a 500-word essay explaining your views on the debate over original intent and the meaning of the Constitution. In your essay, refer to specific quotes and authors that agree or disagree with your point of view.

A. "I am not an advocate for frequent changes in laws and Constitutions, but laws must and institutions must go hand in hand with the progress of the human mind. As that becomes more developed, more enlightened, as new discoveries are made, new truths discovered and manners and opinions change, with the change of circumstances, institutions must advance also to keep pace with the times. We might as well require a man to wear still the coat which fitted him when a boy as civilized society to remain ever under the regimen of their barbarous ancestors."—Letter from former President Thomas Jefferson (1810)

B. "[T]he ultimate touchstone of constitutionality is the Constitution itself and not what we have said about it."—Associate Supreme Court Justice Felix Frankfurter (1939)

C. "The intended role of the judiciary generally and the Supreme Court in particular was to serve as the "bulwarks of a limited constitution." The judges, the Founders believed, would not fail to regard the Constitution as "fundamental law" and would "regulate their decisions" by it. As the "faithful guardians of the Constitution," the judges were expected to resist any political effort to depart from the literal provisions of the Constitution. The text of the document and the original intention of those who framed it would be the judicial standard in giving effect to the Constitution."—United States Attorney General Edwin Meese (1985).

D. "To remain faithful to the content of the Constitution . . . an approach to interpreting the text must account for the existence of these substantive value choices, and must accept the ambiguity inherent in the effort to apply them to modern circumstances . . . But our acceptance of the fundamental principles has not and should not bind us to those precise, at times anachronistic, contours . . . We current Justices read the Constitution in the only way that we can: as Twentieth-Century Americans. We look to the history of the time of framing and to the intervening history of interpretation. But the ultimate question must be, what do the words of the text mean in our time. For the genius of the Constitution rests not in any static meaning it might have had in a world that is dead and gone, but in the adaptability of its great principles to cope with current problems and current needs. What the constitutional fundamentals meant to the wisdom of other times cannot be their measure to the vision of our time. Similarly, what those fundamentals mean for us, our descendants will learn, cannot be the measure to the vision of their time?"—Associate Supreme Court Justice William J. Brennan, Jr. (1985)

E. "The judge's authority derives entirely from the fact that he is applying the law and not his personal values. That is why the American public accepts the decisions of its courts, accepts even decisions that nullify the laws a majority of the electorate or their representatives voted for . . . [W]hen a judge . . . reads entirely new values into the Constitution, values the framers and ratifiers did not put there, he deprives the people of their liberty.—Robert Bork, defeated nominee to become an Associate Justice of the Supreme Court (1987)

F. "The great legal debates of the past two decades over criminal justice have, at their root, been debates over a strict versus expansive construction of the Constitution. The Constitution, as originally intended by the framers, is itself tough on crime, and protective of the victims of crime."—President Ronald Reagan (1988)

G. "I belong to a school, a small but hardy school, called "textualists" or "originalists" . . . The theory of originalism treats a constitution like a statute, and gives it the meaning that its words were understood to bear at the time they were promulgated [written] . . . If you are a textualist, you don't care about the intent, and I don't care if the framers of the Constitution had some secret meaning in mind when they adopted its words. I take the words as they were promulgated to the people of the United States, and what is the fairly understood meaning of those words . . . The words are the law. I think that's what is meant by a government of laws, not of men. We are bound not by the intent of our legislators, but by the laws which they enacted, which are set forth in words."—Associate Supreme Court Justice Antonin Scalia (1996)

H. "When interpreting the Constitution and statutes, judges should seek the original understanding of the provision's text, if the meaning of that text is not readily apparent . . . [S]trict interpretation must never surrender to the understandably attractive impulse towards creative but unwarranted alterations of first principles."—Associate Supreme Court Justice Clarence Thomas (2001)

I. "Literalism has a tendency to undermine the Constitution's efforts to create a framework for democratic government, . . . it is inconsistent with the most fundamental original intentions of the Framers themselves."—Associate Supreme Court Justice Stephen Breyer (2004)

J. "In reviewing the record of a judicial nominee, I believe that the most appropriate standards include the following: A commitment to the core constitutional values embedded in the fabric of our democracy—freedom of speech and religion; the right to privacy; and equal protection and due process under the law. These are the cherished rights that we must preserve for generations to come . . . A dedication to equality for all Americans, especially those who have been denied their full measure of freedom, such as women and minorities. A respect for justice for all whose rights are too readily abused by powerful institutions, whether by the power of government itself or by giant concentrations of power in the private sector. Respect for the Supreme Court itself, for our constitutional system of government, and for the history and heritage by which that system has evolved, including the relationship between the federal government and the states, and between Congress and the President. And, finally, possession of the special qualities that enable judges to meet their own important responsibilities—qualities often described as fairness, impartiality, open-mindedness, and judicial temperament."—United States Senator Edward Kennedy (2002)

Table 7.7 Interpreting the Constitution.

Author	Year	Position	Views on interpreting the Constitution
A			
B			
C			
D			
E			
F			
G			
H			
I			
J			

Essay 2: Teaching About Work and Workers

An earlier version of this essay appeared in A. Singer (2004). Used with permission.

In economics classes, and in US history classes, examining industrial expansion after the Civil War, I usually begin lessons about the labor movement by asking students if their parents are members of labor unions and if they know the reasons for labor unions. Over the years, fewer and fewer students have raised their hands. When students do, the most common answer about the purpose of labor unions is that they provide dental insurance.

When I student-taught in 1971, a little more than a quarter of non-agricultural workers in the United States were labor union members, down from a peak of 36% in the mid-1950s. In 2007, the number of workers belonging to labor unions was only 12.5%. The change in union membership is actually even greater than indicated by this steep decline. Between the early 1950s and the late 1980s, union membership in the construction industry declined from 84 to 22 percent, in manufacturing from 42 to 25 percent, and in transportation from 80 to 37 percent. In 2007, only 7.8 percent of the workforce in private sector industries was unionized, compared with roughly 40 percent of public employees (see http://www.bls.gov/news.release/union2.nr0.htm, accessed September 25, 2007).

The weakening of the American organized labor movement since the 1960s has corresponded with three major historical shifts. Globalization has driven more and more industrial jobs overseas. Computerization, prefabrication, and other technological advances have transformed the way we work, ending the need for highly skilled workers in some of the industries where organized labor was traditionally the strongest. With the decline in labor movement membership there has been a parallel weakening of the Democratic Party and a near disappearance of an organized "left" and what have been described as "socialist" ideas in the United States.

Looking at labor unions today, it is hard to imagine the dynamic role they played in United States history, as a force for expanding democracy, limiting the power of big business, improving conditions for immigrants and in cities, pressuring local, state, and the national governments to provide social services, and as a progressive voice for social change. Despite their declining influence and importance, they were a vital force in the history of the United States, and as the expression of organized working people, they have the potential to take a leading role again in the future. Historically, social movements ebb and flow along with the material conditions of people's lives. Another Great Depression on the magnitude of the 1930s, or even a prolonged economic downturn, could lead to a revitalization of organized labor as a major force in the defense of worker rights and a decent standard of living.

Because so many people were members of unions, and because they operated on local as well as national levels, studying the labor movement introduces the role played by ordinary people as historical actors and allows teachers to use to examples from all over the country and a variety of racial and ethnic groups. In the second half of the nineteenth century, celebrated in song by both Black and White workers, was a fictional African-American "steel-driving man" named John Henry. In the midst of Jim Crow, dockworkers in New Orleans and coal miners in the Southern Appalachian Mountains organized labor unions that defied racial segregation. In 1919 alone, in response to World War I wage freezes, there were nationwide strikes by coal miners, steel workers, and railroad employees and a general strike by workers in Seattle. In New York City, 20,000 dockworkers, 50,000 garment workers, 40,000 cigarmakers, and 15,000 streetcar employees went on strike in the month of March. In Boston, municipal police went on strike (Asinof 1990: 132–141, 165).

AIM: HOW DO UNIONS HELP WORKERS DEFEND THEIR RIGHTS?

Instructions

Read the introduction and the lyrics to the songs and write the answers to the questions in your notebook.

Introduction

During the winter of 1936–1937, automobile workers in Flint, Michigan went on strike against General Motors. They faced a particularly difficult situation. It was the middle of the Great Depression, so jobs were scarce. The company refused to negotiate with the union. Picketing was illegal in Michigan. General Motors planned to move crucial machinery to another site so it could continue production. The workers finally decided on a novel strategy, the Sit-Down strike. For 44 days they occupied the Fisher Body plant and refused to leave until General Motors agreed to negotiate a contact recognizing the right of workers to join a labor union of their own choosing. To keep up their spirits during the strike, the autoworkers and the Women's Emergency Brigade that provided support, created union songs by adding new lyrics to popular tunes. *The Fisher Strike* was sung to the tune of the popular southern ballad called *The Martins and the McCoys* (Kraus 1947: 104–105). Another popular song among strikers during the 1930s was simply called *Sit-Down*.

The Fisher Strike

Gather round me and I'll tell you all a story,
Of the Fisher Body Factory Number One.
When the dies they started moving,
The Union Men they had a meeting,
To decide right then and there what must be done.

These 4000 Union Boys,
Oh, they sure made lots of noise,
They decide then and there to shut down tight,
In the office they got snooty,
So we started picket duty,
Now the Fisher Body Shop is on a strike.

Now this strike it started one bright Wednesday evening,
When they loaded up a boxcar full of dies.
When the union boys they stopped them,
And the Railroad Workers backed them,
The officials in the office were surprised.

Now they really started out to strike in earnest,
They took possession of the gates and buildings too.
They placed a guard in either clock house,
Just to keep the non-union men out,
And they took the keys and locked the gates up too.

Now you may think that this union strike is ended,
And they'll all go back to work just as before,
But the day shift men are "cuties",
They relieve the night shift duties,
And we carry on this strike just as before.

Sit-Down

When they tie the can to a union man, Sit down! Sit down!
When they give him the sack, they'll take him back, Sit down! Sit down!
When the speed-up comes, just twiddle your thumbs, Sit down! Sit down!
When the boss won't talk, don't take a walk, Sit down! Sit down!
When they smile and say, no raise in pay, Sit down! Sit down!
When you want the boss to come across, Sit down! Sit down!

Questions:

•According to these songs, how were the workers able to win their strike?
•How do these songs view the relationship between workers and employers?
•In your opinion, why were songs used in campaigns to organize labor unions?
•Labor unions might have been necessary for working people in the 1930s, when these songs were written. Do you think they are still necessary today? Why?

Teaching Activity: Analyzing a Song

It's your classroom:

What questions would you ask students about this topic or about these songs?

Try it yourself:

Design a lesson that uses the words to a song to provide students with information about a topic and helps generate discussion.

As part of a Teaching American History Grant in the summer of 2002, I helped develop material for teaching about the labor movement and the impact of industrial change on American society and the American people that centered on New York City. Modern industry, and with it, a modern working class, was created by the Industrial Revolution at the beginning of the nineteenth century. From 1788 to 1850, New York City witnessed the emergence of a working class, more quickly and with greater force than anywhere else in the United States (Wilentz 1984). At mid-century, New York City was the most productive manufacturing center in the country (Jackson 1995).

At the start of the industrial era, no one quite knew what was happening to the city, the nation, and the world. In one of his most famous poems, "I Hear America Singing," Walt Whitman, the poet laureate of the nineteenth-century United States and of New York City, rejoiced in both the growth of industry and the role of workers. He described the "singing" of mechanics, carpenters, shoemakers, and working girls. For Whitman, workers were the backbone of industrial change; they created the music and songs of industrial life. But while many people celebrated Whitman's poetry, not everyone shared his views about working people and the dignity of labor. During the Civil War, from 1861 through 1865, there were more than 90 major strikes in New York City demanding higher wages as a protection against wartime inflation. Then in 1872, 100,000 workers in the New York City building trades held a successful three-month strike to win an eight-hour workday.

What did it mean to be a worker in New York City during the early industrial era? In the 1840s and 1850s, Five Points in Manhattan, an overpopulated, swampy, and disease-ridden slum near what is now Chinatown, was the home to many recent immigrants and New York City's less skilled work force. Because of low wages and high unemployment, more than one-fourth of Five Point families were forced to take in boarders in order to make ends meet. In the poorest sections, on Baxter and Mulberry Streets, most apartment dwellers lived with boarders, who made up about fifteen percent of the total population of Five Points.

Although most of the boarders lived in private dwellings, there were also commercial boardinghouses. Often these were the worst places to live. The seediest, and cheapest, were located in cellars. A *New York Tribune* report in 1850 found that in the Sixth Ward, which included Five Points, there were 285 basement apartments with 1,156 occupants. They lived "without air, without light" in apartments "filled with damp vapor from the mildewed walls, and with vermin in ration to the dirtiness of the inhabitants." The residents of these cellar apartments were easily identified by their "whitened and cadaverous countenance" and "the odor of the person . . . ; a musty smell, which . . . pervades every article of dress, . . . as well as the hair and skin" (Anbinder 2001: 77–78).

Sadly, 40 years later, conditions in these communities had not improved significantly. Jacob Riis described tenement life in *How the Other Half Lives*, written in 1890. "The sinks are in the hallway, that all the tenants may have access—and all to be poisoned alike by their summer stenches . . . listen! That hack cough, that tiny, helpless wail—what do they mean? The child is dying with measles. With half a chance it might have lived; but it had none. Come over here. Step carefully over this baby—it is a baby, in spite of its rags and dirt . . . That baby's parents live in the rear tenement here. A hundred thousand people lived in rear tenements in New York last year" (Anbinder 2001: 43–44).

Living conditions in the working-class communities of New York City were made even worse, if that is possible, by the practice of homework in the garment industry. According to a memoir by one immigrant tailor, "we worked piece-work with our wives, and very often our children . . . We worked at home in our rooms. We had to buy fuel to heat the irons for pressing, and light in winter." A letter to the *New York Tribune* in 1850 described most of the tailors as "half-paid" and "half-starved." The local tailors finally organized a union in 1850 and called a city-wide general strike in July to win a higher wage rate (Anbinder 2001: 117–118).

Workers in other industries also suffered from horrendous working situations and tried to organize unions in order to win higher wages and better conditions. Americans have long been awed by the majesty of the Brooklyn Bridge, but few think about the human cost of its construction. There were between twenty and thirty deaths of workers, including that of John A. Roebling, who designed the bridge and led the initial construction team. In May 1871, laborers laying the foundation for a man-made island that would support the New York tower of the Brooklyn Bridge found blood spurting from their noses and mouths and began to experience terrible cramps. As they sank the shaft deeper, men began to die (Burrows and Wallace 1999: 936–937). Desperate, on May 8, 1871, the caisson men struck for a pay increase to three dollars for a four-hour shift. The bridge company agreed to $2.75, which the men turned down. The strike collapsed when the company threatened to fire all strikers.

Strikes, even when successful, usually only brought short-term relief, lasting until the next economic downturn. Irish sewer diggers struck in 1874, but were replaced by newly arrived Italian immigrants (Anbinder 2001: 377). During the Depression of 1877, a wage reduction led to strikes on train lines across the country. New York City workers scheduled a meeting for July 25 to vote on joining the strike. In preparation, the National Guard was called out, garrisons placed at rail depots, its Central Park headquarters surrounded by howitzers, and a US Navy warship dispatched to New York harbor. The 20,000 workers who attended a mass meeting at Tompkins Square Park in the East Village were attacked by charging, club-wielding policemen.

Nevertheless, workers continued to organize. There was a major freight handlers strike on the docks in 1882 (Anbinder 2001: 378). A series of short strikes in the 1880s led to the unionization of the New York-area streetcar companies. However, the union was later defeated in a bitter strike in Brooklyn during the winter of 1895, when police, armed company guards, and National Guard troops open fired on transit workers (Freeman 1989: 16).

In August 1883, a US Senate committee investigating the relations between labor and capital came to New York City. One of the workers they interviewed was a machinist named John Morrison. He was asked about "the prospect for a man now working in one of these machine shops, a man who is temperate and economical, to become a boss or a manufacturer of machinery." According to Morrison, "there is no chance. They have lost all desire to become bosses now. The trade has become demoralized. First they earn so small wages; and next, it takes so much capital to become a boss now that they cannot think of it, because it takes all they can earn to live ... I understand that at the present day you could not start in the machinist's business to compete successfully with any of these large firms with a capital of less than $20,000 or $30,000" (Litwack 1962: 11–15).

In this demoralized world, the labor movement offered working people their major hope. During this period, New York City was at the center of two new large labor organizations, the American Federation of Labor (AFL) and the Knights of Labor. Samuel Gompers, who was one of the founders of the AFL, was born in London in 1850, to Dutch-Jewish parents who brought him to New York City in 1863. He worked in his teens and early twenties making cigars in an East side tenement apartment with his father. Gompers, who attended free lectures and classes at Cooper Union in Greenwich Village,

became a socialist and an activist in the Cigarmakers Union. Following the failure of a Cigarmakers strike in 1877, he developed a philosophy of labor organization which came to be known as "pure and simple unionism." He helped make the Cigarmakers union more businesslike by charging high dues that would be used to create a strike fund and provide workers with sick benefits (Burrows and Wallace 1999: 1089–1090).

This same period saw the development of a New York City branch of the Knights of Labor. A January, 1882 rally at Cooper Union led to the formation of a citywide trades assembly and the creation of a Central Labor Union of New York, Brooklyn and Jersey City. It also led to the first "Labor Day" parade on September 5, 1882. Wearing the regalia of work and carrying banners, 20,000 marchers assembled near City Hall and moved up Broadway to Union Square. By 1884, the Knights had 36 affiliated unions in New York City and by 1886, over 200 organizations representing approximately 50,000 workers. While the AFL concentrated on organizing skilled workers to negotiate higher wages and better working conditions with their employers, the Knights welcomed skilled and unskilled labor and launched a political campaign for an eight-hour day and an end to child labor (Burrows and Wallace 1999: 1091–1092).

On May 1, 1886, the American labor movement launched a nationwide offensive. This series of strikes has long been identified with the "Haymarket Riot" on May 3 in Chicago, where a bomb was thrown as local police attacked a demonstration. Eight policemen died as a result of the bomb and when officers fired into the crowd. In New York City, 45,000 workers walked off their jobs in coordinated strikes. They included streetcar conductors, cigarmakers, building trades workers, and machinists. Employers tried to use the courts to quash the strikes. Leaders of the Musicians' Union were convicted of "conspiracy" for promoting a boycott of a non-union beer hall and the brand of beer it sold, and were sentenced to up to four years in Sing-Sing prison (Burrows and Wallace 1999: 1098).

In response, workers organized a United Labor Party which nominated Henry George for mayor of New York City. Business interests nominated Teddy Roosevelt as the Republican candidate, hoping he could stop the workers revolt. The Tammany Hall Democratic machine and the Roman Catholic Church backed a wealthy businessman, Abram Hewitt, in an effort to stop the labor movement. Hewitt eventually won with 90,552, to 68,110 for George and 60,435 for Roosevelt. Soon after the election, as a result of strains caused by an economic depression, the national response to the Chicago Haymarket Riot, and the anti-labor and anti-socialist stand of the Roman Catholic Church, the New York City labor coalition broke up. The national Knights of Labor also failed to survive.

Two of New York City's early labor organizing drives especially lend themselves to classroom exploration, one, because it was conducted by junior high school age and younger boys, and the other, because it is associated with the Triangle Shirtwaist factory fire, a transcendent event in the history of both the New York City and the American labor movements.

The New York City "Newsies" strike against the World and Journal newspapers was portrayed in a Disney movie (Newsies 1992) and by some of the contemporary newspapers as cute, with boys speaking in heavily accented, almost pidgin-English. However, in actuality, the strike was a serious struggle for social justice. According to the *New York Daily Tribune*, on July 20, 1899, "About 300 news-boys decided not to sell '*The Evening World*' and '*The Evening Journal*,' and went on strike . . . against an increase in the price of the papers from 50 cents a hundred copies to 70 cents." Jack Sullivan, leader of

the Arbitration Committee told the Tribune, "They tink we're cravens . . . but we'll show 'em dat we aint. De time is overripe fer action. De cops won't have not time fer us . . . Well, den, de strike is ordered. Der must be no half measures, my men. If you sees any one sellin' de 'Woild' or 'Joinal,' swat 'em . . tear 'em up, trow 'em in de river any ole ting."

The next day *The Tribune* reported on a strike meeting addressed by Grand Master Workman "Kid" Blink, alias "Mug Magee." He told the group, "Fr'en's, Brudders and Feller Citerzens: We is united in a patriotic cause. The time has cum when we mus' eder make a stan' or be downtridden by the decypils of acrice and greed'ness. Dey wants it all, and when we cums to 'em dey sez we must take the papes at der own price or leave 'em. Dis ain't no time to temporize. Is ye all still wid us in de cause?"

Unfortunately for the boys, the police were called in to break their strike. On July 24, 1899, *The Tribune* reported that "[f]our newsboys were arraigned before Magistrate Mott in the Centre Street police court yesterday morning, charged by Detective Allen and Policemen Distler and Snydecker, of the Oak Street station, with parading without the proper license."

Classroom Activity; "Newsies" Strike against the *World and Journal* (1899)

The Newsies strike lasted from July 18, 1899 through August 2, 1899. During their short strike, the "Newsies" demonstrated that workers, even children, could fight for rights against powerful employers and be successful.

Possible classroom projects include:
- Locate newspaper article on-line and create a "current events" portfolio.
- Design posters and flyers for a "pro-Newsies" demonstration.
- Write "letters" to the editors of the *World and Journal* expressing support for the "Newsies."
- Write a script and act out a play about the "Newsies."

It's your classroom:
Historically, the "Newsies" are not that important. Would you invest precious classroom time studying about them? Explain.

The second organizing drive, the 1909 walkout of 20,000 shirtwaistmakers in the New York City garment industry, was more successful, but also more problematic and much more tragic. The rally that led to this strike was described by the *New York Call*, a socialist newspaper, in an article on November 23, 1909. Clara Lemlich, who had been badly beaten by hired company thugs during an earlier strike, interrupted the speakers and demanded the right to address the audience. "Cries came from all parts of the hall, 'Get up on the platform!' Willing hands lifted the frail little girl with flashing black eyes to the

stage, and she said simply: 'I have listened to all the speakers. I would not have further patience for talk, as I am one of those who feels and suffers from the things pictured. I move that we go on a general strike!' As the tremulous voice of the girl died away, the audience rose en masse and cheered her to the echo. A grim sea of faces, with high purpose and resolve, they shouted and cheered the declaration of war for living conditions hoarsely."

According to historian Philip Foner (1980: 231), after Lemlich spoke, the chairman of the meeting called for a vote and three thousand voices shouted unanimous approval. He then demanded of the crowd, "Will you take the old Hebrew oath?" At that point, "three thousand right arms shot up, and three thousand voices repeated the Yiddish words: "If I turn traitor to the cause I now pledge, may this hand wither from the arm I now raise."

I called this union organizing drive both problematic and tragic. It was problematic because of the labor movement's, especially the AFL's, poor record on the organization of African-American workers. Because of anti-Black discrimination by the garment workers union, the employers' association was successful in recruiting Black strikebreakers, who with police protection were able to cross the picket lines (Foner 1980: 233). *The New York Age*, an African-American newspaper, ran an editorial where it charged that "Trade Unionism is hostile to the colored race and that the Negro will continue to be the pivot upon which future strikes will turn so long as labor will ignore his right to work and thwart his ambition to advance in the mechanical world" (Aptheker 1968: 844). Editors refused to condemn strikebreaking since Black workers had "no assurance that the union would in the future admit without discrimination colored girls to membership." The garment workers union, in a letter published by W.E.B. DuBois in *The Horizon*, defended its actions and claimed that "in both Philadelphia and New York, some of the most devoted members of the Ladies Waist Makers Union are colored girls" and that to promote participation by Black workers, strike meetings were being held at the "Fleet Street Methodist Memorial Church (colored) in Brooklyn and St. Marks Methodist Church in Manhattan."

Unfortunately, as with most things in life, there are no simple, happy endings. Employers continued to resist the union, and conditions in the shops remained horrible until the tragedy of the Triangle Shirtwaist Fire. The deaths of 146 young immigrant Jewish and Italian girls in this conflagration finally swung public sentiment to support of the union.

Rose Schneiderman (1911), an ILGWU organizer, gave a memorial speech at a mass funeral for these girls. It is one of the best statements I know defending the right of workers to form unions and the necessity for social struggle and collective action.

"This is not the first time girls have been burned alive in the city. Every week I must learn of the untimely death of one of my sister workers. Every year thousands of us are maimed. The life of men and women is so cheap and property is so sacred. There are so many of us for one job it matters little if 146 of us are burned to death.

We have tried you citizens; we are trying you now, and you have a couple of dollars for the sorrowing mothers, brothers and sisters by way of a charity gift. But every time the workers come out in the only way they know to protest against conditions which are unbearable the strong hand of the law is allowed to press down heavily upon us.

Public officials have only words of warning to us—warning that we must be intensely peaceable, and they have the workhouse just back of all their warnings. The strong hand of the law beats us back, when we rise, into the conditions that make life unbearable.

I can't talk fellowship to you who are gathered here. Too much blood has been spilled. I know from my experience it is up to the working people to save themselves. The only way they can save themselves is by a strong working-class movement."

Classroom Activity: "Eyewitness at the Triangle" (*Milwaukee Journal*, March 27, 1911)

William G. Shepherd, a United Press reporter, was present at the scene of the Triangle Shirtwaist Company fire that killed 146 young immigrant Jewish and Italian working girls.

"I was walking through Washington Square when a puff of smoke issuing from the factory building caught my eye. I reached the building before the alarm was turned in. I saw every feature of the tragedy visible from outside the building. I learned a new sound—a more horrible sound than description can picture. It was the thud of a speeding, living body on a stone sidewalk.

Thud—dead, thud—dead, thud—dead, thud—dead. Sixty-two thud—deads. I call them that, because the sound and the thought of death came to me each time, at the same instant. There was plenty of chance to watch them as they came down. The height was eighty feet.

The first ten thud—deads shocked me. I looked up—saw that there were scores of girls at the windows. The flames from the floor below were beating in their faces. Somehow I knew that they, too, must come down, and something within me—something that I didn't know was there—steeled me.

I even watched one girl falling. Waving her arms, trying to keep her body upright until the very instant she struck the sidewalk, she was trying to balance herself. Then came the thud—then a silent, unmoving pile of clothing and twisted, broken limbs.

As I reached the scene of the fire, a cloud of smoke hung over the building . . . I looked up to the seventh floor. There was a living picture in each window—four screaming heads of girls waving their arms.

"Call the firemen," they screamed—scores of them. "Get a ladder," cried others. They were all as alive and whole and sound as were we who stood on the sidewalk. I couldn't help thinking of that. We cried to them not to jump. We heard the siren of a fire engine in the distance. The other sirens sounded from several directions.

"Here they come," we yelled. "Don't jump; stay there."

One girl climbed onto the window sash. Those behind her tried to hold her back. Then she dropped into space. I didn't notice whether those above watched her drop because I had turned away. Then came that first thud. I looked up, another girl was climbing onto the window sill; others were crowding behind her. She dropped. I watched her fall, and again the dreadful sound."

Questions
1. What caught the attention of the author of this newspaper article?
2. Why were the firefighters unable to help the girls caught in the fire?
3. Why did the young man help the girls jump to their deaths?
4. How do you think the people of New York City and the nation responded to this story? Why?

Essay 3: Using Student Dialogues to Teach Social Studies and Promote Democracy

In the sample 11th-grade United States curriculum calendar presented in Chapter 6, I listed, but did not explain, lessons using "student dialogues" to introduce and review units. Suggested questions for examination by classes were "Should the United States have dropped the atomic bomb on Japan?" and "Did the Civil Rights movement succeed?"

The idea of using structured student dialogues to teach social studies content, concepts and skills, and as a vehicle for building classroom community and promoting democracy, has been pioneered by Michael Pezone of the New Teachers Network. Michael's work with recent immigrants and mainstreamed special education students in a middle school and hard-to-reach minority youth in a troubled high school has been described in *Social Education* (Pezone and Singer 1997), the *American Educational Research Journal* (Singer and Pezone 2001), a book on citizenship education (Miller and Singleton 1997), and the *New York State Great Irish Famine Curriculum Guide* (Pezone and Palacio 2001). It has been adopted and adapted by other members of the network, including Jennifer Quinn, Rachel Thompson, Stephanie Hunte, and Lauren Rosenberg, who have made student dialogues an important part of their own teaching.

In his social studies classes, Michael Pezone employs many of the practices advocated by progressive and transformative educators (Apple and Beane 1995; Banks 1991; Bigelow 1988; 1990). He believes that the success of the dialogues and the experience in democracy both depend on the gradual development of caring, cooperative communities over the course of a year (Noddings 1992; Kohn 1986). To encourage these communities, he works with students to create an atmosphere where they feel free to expose their ideas, feelings, and academic proficiencies in public without risking embarrassment or attack and being pressed into silence. He stresses with students that the dialogues are not debates; that as students learn about a topic the entire class "wins or loses" together.

The student dialogues are highly structured. Michael believes that structure maximizes student freedom by ensuring that all students have an opportunity to participate. It also helps to ensure that classes carefully examine statements, attitudes, and practices that may reflect biases and demean community members.

Michael uses dialogues to conclude units; however, preparation for the dialogues takes place all the time. At the start of the semester, he and his students decide on the procedures for conducting dialogues so that everyone in class participates, and on criteria for evaluating team and individual performance. Usually students want the criteria to include an evaluation of how well the team works together; the degree to which substantive questions are addressed; the use of supporting evidence; the response to statements made by the other team; whether ideas are presented effectively; and whether individual students demonstrate effort and growth. These criteria are codified in a scoring rubric that is reexamined before each dialogue and changed when necessary. Students also help to define the question being discussed. After the dialogue, students work in small groups to evaluate the overall dialogue, the performance by their team, and their individual participation.

During a unit, the class identifies a broad social studies issue that they want to research and examine in greater depth. For example, after studying the recent histories of India and China, they discussed whether violent revolution or non-violent resistance is the most effective path to change. On other occasions, they have discussed if the achievements of the ancient world justified the exploitation of people and whether the United States and Europe should intervene in the internal affairs of other countries because of the way that women are treated in some cultures.

The goal of a dialogue is to examine all aspects of an issue, not to score points at the expense of someone else. Teams are subdivided into cooperative learning groups that collect and organize information supporting different views. The teams also assign members to be opening, rebuttal, and concluding speakers. During dialogues, teams "huddle-up" to share their ideas and reactions to what is being presented by the other side. After dialogues, students discuss what they learned from members of the other team and evaluate the performance of the entire class.

An important part of the dialogue process is the involvement of students in assessing what they have learned. In Michael's classes, students help develop the parameters for class projects and decide the criteria for assessing their performance in these activities. The benefit of this involvement for students includes a deeper understanding of historical and social science research methods; insight into the design and implementation of projects; a greater stake in the satisfactory completion of assignments; and a sense of empowerment because assessment decisions are based on rules that the classroom community has helped to shape.

Michael uses individual and group conferences to learn what students think about the dialogues and

their impact on student thinking about democratic process and values. Students generally feel that the dialogues give them a personal stake in what happens in class and they feel responsible for supporting their teams. Students who customarily are silent in class because of fear of being ridiculed or because they are not easily understood by the other students, become involved in speaking out. For many students, it is a rare opportunity to engage in both decision-making and open public discussion "in front of other people."

From the dialogues, students start to learn that democratic society involves a combination of individual rights and initiatives with social responsibility, collective decision-making, and shared community goals. They discover that democracy frequently entails tension between the will of the majority and the rights of minorities and that it cannot be taken for granted. It involves taking risks and is something that a community must continually work to maintain and expand. Another benefit of the dialogue process is that it affords students the opportunity to actively generate knowledge without relying on teacher-centered instructional methods.

Michael finds that the year long process of defining, conducting, and evaluating dialogues involves students in constant reflection on social studies concepts, class goals, student interaction, and the importance of community. It makes possible individual academic and social growth, encourages students to view ideas critically and events from multiple perspectives, and supports the formation of a cooperative learning environment. He believes that when students are able to analyze educational issues, and create classroom policy, they gain a personal stake in classroom activities and a deeper understanding of democracy.

Students in Michael's ninth grade law elective and Jennifer Quinns's 12th grade participation in government classes participated in dialogues while helping to field-test a document packet that is part of the New York State Great Irish Famine curriculum. They researched and examined the question, was British policy in Ireland during the Great Irish Famine an example of genocide?

On Day 1, students read and discussed the definition of genocide by the United Nations that includes a number of different kinds of actions but requires proof of intent, and documents describing events that could be considered examples of genocide. The documents included the 1935 Nuremburg Racial Laws in Nazi Germany, an historian's account of Turkey's attack on Armenians during the era of World War I, an enslaved African's description of the middle passage, a newspaper photograph of an open burial site in Rwanda from 1994, a chart showing the decimation of native American population centers following the arrival of Europeans, and descriptions by contemporaries of famine-era Ireland. Students used the UN definition of genocide to evaluate the events described in the other documents. At the end of the first class period, students decided whether they wanted to be on the team that presented evidence that British policy was an example of genocide or on the opposing team.

On Days 2 and 3, student teams were sub-divided into work groups that examined a series of primary source documents from the Great Irish Famine curriculum and prepared opening and closing state-ments. These included newspaper articles, editorials and political cartoons, government documents, speeches, and charts showing evictions, emigration, food availability and population decline.

On Day 4, students held their dialogues. After opening round statements, teams caucused to prepare rebuttals. Following rebuttals, teams updated concluding statements. After the concluding state-ments, the classes discussed what students learned from the dialogue and each other.

On the final day of the project, individual students used the documents and what they learned from the dialogue to write a document-based essay.

Teaching Activity: Rules for Student Dialogues in Ms. Rosenberg's Class

Choosing Teams:
Students will select teams based on their opinions. Ms. Rosenberg may reassign some students so the teams are equally balanced.

Issues for the Dialogues:
- United States History: Should the United States be the police force for the world?
- Global History: Do revolutions improve people's lives?

Preparation for the Dialogues:
Student teams will be divided into study groups of three or four students. Each study group will research a topic. Using the research, individual students will prepare regents style essays supporting their position. Study group members will edit each other's essays before the dialogue.

Procedures for the Dialogue:
There will be four rounds during the dialogue. Before round one, teams will meet together and plan their presentation. Students from each team will take turns speaking. In Round 1, five students from each team will introduce the team's views. After Round 1, teams will "huddle up" to think about what the other team said. In Round 2, students will take turns responding to the ideas of the other team. Teams will huddle up again after Round 2 to plan how to conclude the dialogue. In Round 3, three students will summarize the main ideas of their team. After Round 3, teams will meet again to evaluate what students have learned. In Round 4, students will discuss what they learned from the other team.

During the Dialogue:
- Students should respect each other
- Students should not attack or interrupt each other
- One person speaks at a time. Everyone must participate
- After your turn to speak, take notes and share them with your team-mates
- The discussion should be as free and open as possible
- Students should speak loudly and clearly
- Team members should take turns. Don't speak too long
- Team-mates must make sure that everyone speaks
- Some people who are comfortable speaking to the whole class should wait until the end.

Things to Remember:
- People must listen to each other
- People must give reasons for their opinion
- People must present facts
- People have to believe what they are speaking

- People need to talk about the things that other people say
- Express your ideas clearly
- Learn and understand the ideas of other people
- Share opinions
- Discussion is more important than winning. There are no right answers.

Add your voice to the discussion:
1. How do you evaluate student dialogues as an approach to teaching social studies?
2. Would you consider using them in your classroom? Explain.

It's your classroom:
1. Michael Pezone spends time every year having students in each class reinvent the dialogue process. Lauren Rosenberg prefers to provide students with guidelines for the dialogues. Which approach to you prefer? Why?
2. Dialogues in Jennifer Quinn's classes tend to be less structured than they are in Michael's classes. Would you prefer a tighter or looser structure? Explain.

Try it yourself:
1. Assemble a set of documents (between five and ten) that can be used as the basis for a student dialogue.
2. What question would you have students discuss?

Topics for Democratic Dialogues
These topics offer students a spectrum of opinions to consider, research, and support. It is important for students to understand that there are more than just two sides in a political debate and that even allies have disagreements. An excerpt from a newspaper article introduces both topics. After reading and discussing the excerpt, students select the "position" that comes closest to their own.

A. Immigration Reform: Should the "golden door" be closed?

STATEMENT
"Comprehensive or Incomprehensible?" (Thompson, *National Review*, 2007)

"Most Americans know that we have an illegal immigration problem in this country, with perhaps as many as 20 million people residing here unlawfully. And I think most Americans have a pretty good idea about how to at least start solving the problem—secure our nation's borders ... We should scrap this "comprehensive" immigration bill and the whole debate until the government can show the American people that we have secured the borders—or at least made great headway. That would give proponents of the bill a chance to explain why putting illegals in a more favorable position than those who play by the rules is not really amnesty."

POSITIONS
1. We need to be honest. The United States is at least partly responsible for economic and political conditions in other countries. Undocumented immigrants should receive amnesty and be put on the path to citizenship. We should welcome immigrants seeking a better life. They have the same aspirations as earlier people who came to this country and will add to the richness our lives.
2. We need to be compassionate. The United States should recognize its special place in the world. We cannot accept everyone, but we should accept more and find a way to help undocumented people who are already here.
3. We need to compromise. People who are here should stay, but new undocumented aliens should be kept out.
4. We need to be realistic. Businesses need low-wage workers. This country needs a guest worker program, but it must be carefully regulated and it should not be a path to permanent residency or citizenship. Illegal aliens should be kept out.
5. We need to be vigilant. The United States must protect its borders and its citizens. Illegal aliens break the law. They should be expelled.

B. Third World: Who is responsible for the problems?

STATEMENT
"Report on Child Deaths Finds Some Hope in Poorest Nations" (Dugger, *New York Times*, 2007: 6)

"The rate at which young children perish has worsened most disastrously over the past 15 years in Iraq, hard hit by both sanctions and war, and in Botswana, Zimbabwe and Swaziland, devastated by AIDS, according to a report released yesterday by Save the Children. But researchers also found against-the-odds progress in

214

some of the world's poorest nations. Bangladesh has profoundly improved the chances that a child would survive by promoting family planning, a strategy that has enabled women to have fewer children, space births and strengthen their own health and that of their babies. Nepal, despite a decade-long Maoist insurgency, has halved the death rate of children under age 5. It has enlisted the help of 50,000 mothers, most of them illiterate, who have squeezed vitamin A drops into the mouths of every child, hauled laggards in for vaccinations and even diagnosed pneumonia and dispensed medicines to combat it. And Malawi, with an extreme shortage of doctors and nurses, has made surprising gains by taking simple steps that require no professional skills, for example distributing nets that protect children from malarial mosquitoes."

POSITIONS

1. The past is past. Giving aid to the Third World today is like pouring water down the drain. Only the people who live there can solve their problems.
2. Of course economically developed nations share responsibility for conditions in the Third World and must offer aid, but little will change until local people get their acts together.
3. The situation is very complex and I am not sure where I stand.
4. I am not excusing local corruption and brutality, but much of it is a result of outside involvement. Outside forces have to help clean up the mess.
5. Most problems in the Third World today are the direct result of continuing exploitation by outside forces. Little will improve until this ends.

References and Recommendations for Further Reading

Anbinder, T. 2001. *Five points*. New York: Free Press.

Apple, M. and Beane, J. 1995. *Democratic schools*. Alexandria, VA: ASCD.

Aptheker, H., ed. 1968. *A documentary history of the Negro people in the United States, II*. New York: Citadel.

Asinof, E. 1990. *America's loss of innocence*. New York: Donald Fine.

Banks, J. 1991. "A curriculum for empowerment, action and change," in C. Sleeter, ed. *Empowerment through multicultural education*. Albany, NY: SUNY Press, pp. 125–41.

Bigelow, W. 1988. "Critical pedagogy at Jefferson High School," *Equity and Choice* 4(2).

Bigelow, W. 1990. Inside the classroom: Social vision and critical pedagogy. *Teachers College Record*, 91(3).

Bork, R. 1987. "The Bork hearings; Bork statement: 'Philosophy of role of judge,'" *The New York Times*, September 16. http://query.nytimes.com/gst/fullpage.html?res=9B0DE7D81E31F935A2575AC0A961948260, accessed March 10, 2008.

Bork, R. 1990. "The tempting of America: The political seduction of the law," New York: The Free Press. Cited in J. Rader. 1998. Judicial interpretation: An introduction. *OAH Magazine of History*, 13(1). http://www.oah.org/pubs/magazine/judicial/rader.html, accessed July 1, 2005.

Brennan, W. 1985. Excerpts of Brennan's Speech on the Constitution. *The New York Times*, October 13, 36.

Breyer, S. 2004. *Tanner Lecture on Human Values at Harvard University*. http://www.law.harvard.edu/news/2005/01/20_breyer.php, accessed April 10, 2008.

Breyer, S. 2005. *Active liberty*. New York: Alfred Knopf.

Burrows, E. and Wallace, M. 1999. *Gotham: A history of New York City to 1898*. New York: Oxford University Press.

Dugger, C. 2007. "Report on Child Deaths Finds Some Hope in Poorest Nations," *New York Times*, May 8.

Foner, P. 1980. *The AFL in the Progressive era*. New York: International Publishers.

Frankfurter, F. 1939. *Graves* v. *New York, 306 US 466*. http://www.policyofliberty.net/quotes4.php, accessed July 1, 2005.

Freeman, J. 1989. *In transit*. New York: Oxford University Press.

Garrison, W. 1845. "The American union," *The Liberator*, January 10. http://teachingamericanhistory.org/library/index.asp?document=572, accessed July 1, 2005.

Gerwirtz, P. and Golder, C. 2005. "So who are the activists?," *The New York Times*, July 6.

Greenhouse, L. 2007. "Court hears whether a drug statement is protected free speech for students," *The New York Times*, March 20.

Greaves, R., Cannistratato, P. Zaller, R. and Murphy R. 1990. *Civilizations of the world: The human adventure*. New York: Harper & Row.

Hand, L. 1944. *The spirit of liberty*. http://www.commonlaw.com/Hand.html, accessed July 1, 2005.

Herszenhorn, D. 2005. "Teachers protest the methods of a regional superintendent," *The New York Times*, February 4.

Jackson, K., ed. 1995. *The encyclopedia of New York City*. New Haven, CT: Yale University Press.

Jefferson, T. 1810. *Quotations on the Jefferson memorial*. http://www.monticello.org/reports/quotes/memorial.html, accessed July 1, 2005.

Kennedy, D. and Bailey, T. 2006. *The American spirit: United States History as seen by contemporaries, volume II*. 11th ed. Boston, MA: Houghton Mifflin.

Kennedy, D., Cohen, L. and Bailey, T. 2001. *The American pageant: A history of the republic*. 12th ed. Boston, MA: Houghton Mifflin.

Kennedy, E. 2002. "Judiciary and Its impact on the rights of Americans," September. *Address at Georgetown*

University Law School. http://www.acslaw.org/views/September25EMK.htm, accessed July 1, 2005.

Koch, A. 1985. *Notes of debates in the Federal Convention of 1787 reported by James Madison.* Athens, OH: Ohio University Press.

Kohn, A. 1986. *No contest: The case against competition.* Boston: Houghton Mifflin.

Kraus, H. 1947. *The many and the few.* Los Angles, CA: The Plantin Press.

Levy, L. 1988. *Original intent and the framers' constitution.* New York: Macmillan.

Litwack, L., ed. 1962. *The American labor movement.* Englewood Clifts, NJ: Prentice-Hall.

Meese, E. 1985. "The great debate," *Address at American Bar Association,* July 25. http://www.fed-soc.org/resources/id.49/default.asp, accessed April 29, 2007.

Meyers, M., Cawleti, J. and Kern A., eds. 1967. *Sources of the American republic,* vol. I. Glenview, IL: Scott, Foresman.

Miller, B. and Singleton, L. 1997. *Preparing citizens, linking authentic assessment and instruction in civic/law-related education.* Boulder, CO: Social Science Education Consortium.

National Archives and Records Administration. 1989. *Teaching with documents,* vol. 1.

National Archives and Records Administration. 1998. *Teaching with documents,* vol. 2.

National Council for the Social Studies Task Force on Social Studies in the Middle School. 1991. "Social studies in the middle school," *Social Education* 55(5): 287–93.

Noddings, N. 1992. *The challenge to care in schools.* New York: Teachers College Press.

Oxford University Press. 1999. *A history of us, sourcebook and index, documents that shaped the American nation, Book 11.* New York: Oxford University Press.

Pezone, M. and Singer, A. 1997. "Empowering immigrant students through democratic Dialogues," *Social Education* 61(2): 75–9.

Pezone, M. and Palacio J. 2001. "Democratic dialogues about genocide," in M. Murphy and A. Singer, eds.

New York State Great Irish Famine Curriculum Guide, Albany, NY: State Education Department, pp. 430–40.

Reagan, R. 1988 "On the frontier of freedom," *Address at Conservative Political Action Conference,* February 11. http://www.historicaldocuments.com/RonaldReaganFrontierofFreedom.htm, accessed April 29, 2007.

Rossiter, C., ed. 1961. *The Federalist papers.* New York: New American Library.

Scalia, A. 1996. "A theory of constitution interpretation," *Address at Catholic University of America,* October 18. http://www.courttv.com/archive/legaldocs/rights/scalia.html, accessed July 1, 2005.

Schneiderman, R. 1911. "Lament for lost lives," The Survey, in Stein, L. 1962. *The triangle fire.* New York: Carroll & Graf, 144–5.

Shanker, A. 1985. *The making of a profession.* Washington, DC: American Federation of Teachers.

Singer, A. and Pezone, M. 2001. High school democratic dialogues: A response to Annette Hemmings. *American Educational Research Journal* 38(3): 535–9.

Singer, A. 2004. "Working people and organized labor in New York City in the era of industrialization, 1820–1920," *Social Science Docket* 4(1): 8–11.

Singer, A. 2006. "Original in[compe]tents: Rightwing ideologues and the Supreme Court," *Social Science Docket* 6(2): 2–9.

Thomas, C. 2001. "Be not afraid," *Francis Boyer lecture to the American Enterprise Institute,* February 13. http://www.freerepublic.com/forum/a3a8af14018e8.htm, accessed July 1, 2005.

Thompson, F. 2007. "Comprehensive or Incomprehensible?," *National Review Online,* May 18. http://article.nationalreview.com/?q=YjEzYTc5YjA2ZGNiZjlmZDJkMTllYmE4MjE3ZmY1OTY=, accessed September 16, 2007.

Toner, R. 2005. "After a brief shock, advocates quickly mobilize," *The New York Times,* July 2.

Wilentz, S. 1984. *Chants democratic.* NY: Oxford University Press.

Zinn, H. and Arnove, A. 2004. *Voices of a people's history of the United States.* New York: Seven Stories Press.

Answers to Drawing Connections Between Events

1. Between 334BC and 326BC, the armies of Alexander the Great conquered Asia Minor and the lands between Egypt and India. The Hellenistic Age that followed was a period of cultural, social, and commercial integration in the Mediterranean world. The rebellion between 166BC and 164BC was in opposition to Greek administration and culture and its local Jewish supporters.

2. Charles Martel (Charles the Hammer) defeated an Islamic army and halted the advance of Islamic culture and religion into Western Europe.

3. During his lifetime, Abu Abdallah Ibn Battuta of Tunisia traveled widely, serving as an emissary for a number of Islamic rulers. In 1356, the ruler of Morocco had a young scholar record Ibn Battuta's experiences and observations about the Islamic world. After completing the book, Abu Abdallah Ibn Battuta became a judge in a small Moroccan town. As far as we know, he never traveled again.

4. In 1405, the Ming rulers of China sent Zheng He on the first of seven expeditions to India, Arabia, and the east coast of Africa.
5. The Hopi village of Orabi in Arizona.
6. The Dutch establish a colony at the Cape of Good Hope in southern Africa in 1652. The Boers or Afrikaners soon declare Africans the descendants of the biblical "Ham," justifying their enslavement and *apartheid*.
7. Both wars centered on Anglo-French competition for empire and efforts to build alliances. The French and Indian War was part of the Seven Year War in Europe. The War of 1812 was a battlefront in the Napoleonic Wars.
8. Sam Sharpe, a literate slave preacher, led an eight-day rebellion that spread across the entire island of Jamaica. He was captured and hanged; however, his rebellion led to the abolition of slavery in the British Empire.
9. Mohandas Gandhi was a founding member of the African National Congress in South Africa in 1912.
10. Nguyen That Thanh of Vietnam, who was later known as Ho Chi Minh.

8. How Do You Plan a Social Studies Lesson?

Overview

- Explore issues related to lesson planning
- Present a rationale for formal lesson plans
- Discuss activity-based lessons
- Examine sample document-based activity sheets
- Illustrate lesson plan alternatives
- Alleviate lesson plan anxiety
- Develop strategies for promoting student literacy

Key Concepts

Planning, Structure, Flexibility, Choice, Literacy

Questions

- Why Have Written Lesson Plans?
- What Does it Mean to Plan a Lesson?
- Why are there Disputes over Lesson Planning?
- What do Students Understand from a Lesson?
- How do Lesson Plans Reflect Ideas about Learning?
- What do Beginning Teachers Worry about?
- What Should Beginning Teachers Consider When Planning Lessons?
- What are the Ingredients of an Activity-Based Lesson Planned?
- How is an Activity-Based Lesson Organized?
- How is a Developmental Lesson Organized?
- What Does an "Outcomes-Based" Lesson Plan Look Like?
- Does the "Workshop Model" Make Sense in Secondary Schools?
- How do you Translate your Plan into Practice?

Essays

1. Using "Text" and "Context" to Promote Student Literacies
2. Teaching About Presidential Elections
3. What are the Lessons of 9/11?

WHY HAVE WRITTEN LESSON PLANS?

Attitudes about formal lesson plans vary widely among social studies teachers, as do ideas about what needs to be included. In some school districts, lesson planning is treated as if it were a teacher's primary professional responsibility. Frequently, districts or departments insist that teachers use a standard lesson plan format and supervisors regularly examine teacher plan books to monitor the general quality of lessons. Supervisors also check whether curriculum goals are being met, ensure that departmental lesson calendars are being respected, and, some teachers suspect, guard against innovation and the introduction of controversial ideas into classroom discussions. Rationales for this approach to lesson planning include the ideas that quality lessons flow from quality lesson plans, that standardized lesson plan formats promote high-level and uniform instruction, and that the regular review of lesson plans is a way to ensure teacher accountability.

Many veteran classroom teachers are very critical of formal lesson planning. They argue that formal planning, especially standardized lesson plan formats, stifle creativity, create rigid teacher-centered classrooms, contribute to an authoritarian atmosphere in schools, deny students a say in their own learning, and undermine any notion that teachers are professional educators capable of deciding what should take place in their classrooms. This group of educators claims that elaborate lesson plans only represent teacher intentions. They insist that the only way supervisors can authentically evaluate how well teachers are teaching is by visiting classrooms where they can observe how their students are learning.

I tend to agree with most of the critics of formal lesson plans, but I draw a different conclusion from their criticisms. I am a strong advocate of lesson planning. I think the problems they identify are more related to the kind of lessons they plan, and the ways that plans are used, than to the idea of planning itself. For me, planning is an essential part of what it means to be a professional educator and an historian/social scientist. Proficiency in lesson planning is a key to effective social studies teaching. It is what makes possible student and teacher creativity, flexible and interesting lessons, and the creation of student-centered, democratic classrooms.

WHAT DOES IT MEAN TO PLAN A LESSON?

Lesson planning should not be a technical task that requires social studies teachers to fill in slots on a prepared form. It involves much more than planning the sequence, content, and activities a teacher will include in a specific lesson. Lesson planning is part of the process of making pedagogical, intellectual, and ideological choices. It is where teachers get to think about and figure out historical and social science ideas. It is where we start making choices about what is important to know, how we want to explain it, and how we can make it possible for our students to figure it out also. The most useful book on lesson planning that I am familiar with, a book that stresses the relationship between planning and goals,

is *Understanding by Design* (Wiggins and McTighe 2005).

Alan's Ten Reasons for Lesson Planning
1. Lesson planning is the process of figuring out the intermediate steps necessary to achieve long-term goals. It is like putting together an intellectual puzzle.
2. Lesson planning includes researching different historical, economic, anthropological, sociological, political, and geographical ideas and information.
3. Lesson planning means integrating knowledge about historical epochs and social science fields, and deciding what are the major ideas that students need to consider during a lesson.
4. Lesson planning involves breaking complex ideas down into manageable and understandable pieces.
5. Lesson planning involves translating abstract historical and social science concepts into concrete examples that teenagers can critically examine, struggle to understand, decide to accept or reject, and use to reshape their own conceptions of the world.
6. Lesson planning means figuring out the activity, document, or question that promotes a student to say "I got it!"
7. Lesson planning means making decisions about the most effective ways to organize classrooms and learning activities so students become involved as historians, social scientists, and citizens.
8. Lesson planning means finding, rewriting, or even creating, appropriate text so that students in your class can read material with understanding.
9. Lesson planning means establishing a context for lessons and thinking of creative ways to motivate students to explore topics that might not initially attract their interest and thinking of questions that help them draw connections between ideas and events.
10. In inclusive classes, lesson planning means developing multiple strategies for presenting material so that all students learn to standards.

Teaching Activity: Outlining a Lesson

Try it yourself:
1. Select a social studies topic you would like to teach and formulate a question about the topic.
2. Divide a page into two columns. In the first column, list the important ideas and information a student would need to answer the question.
3. In the second column, list ways that the information could be made available to students.

WHY ARE THERE DISPUTES OVER LESSON PLANNING?

Lesson plans outline what students will actually be taught and how they will learn it. As a result, they are hotly contested terrain in many educational battles. Take, for example, the disputes over multiculturalism in social studies and the value of the transmission model of teaching (e.g., lectures).

As multiculturalism has become more acceptable, new topics have been included in social studies curricula. There appears to be a consensus that Native Americans, African-Americans, women, working people, and immigrants should be included in the history of the United States, and that American students need to be familiar with the histories and cultures of other peoples. A typical high school social studies curriculum might expect students to compare and contrast the experiences of different groups, explain the values and cultures of different societies, and state opinions that are supported by evidence on the contributions of different civilizations or on the causes of events during different historical periods.

But what exactly will students be comparing, contrasting, explaining, and supporting with evidence? This is the area where guidelines become murky and arguments increase in volume. There is no general agreement on a wide range of issues. Examples include the following:

- The similarities and differences in the problems confronting Eastern and Southern European immigrants to the United States at the end of the nineteenth and beginning of the twentieth centuries, the situation faced by African-Americans during the Great Migration north, and the problems faced by immigrants to the United States or Western European countries today.
- The impact of different civilizations on world development (e.g., the contributions of West Africa to ancient Egyptian and Greek civilizations; the contributions of Native Americans to the United States).
- The relationships between different events (e.g., European imperialism and World War I, the nuclear attack on Hiroshima and conflict between the United States and Soviet Union).
- What constitutes sufficient evidence to support a controversial position (e.g., claims that communists infiltrated the US government during the 1930s and 1940s, that the FBI and the CIA tried to discredit black leaders during the 1960s, or that American soldiers were being held prisoner in Vietnam long after hostilities ended).

Teachers are continually required to make choices about what to teach about controversial topics as we create unit and lesson plans. For example, teachers must decide whether to include Malcolm X in lessons on the Civil Rights movement. If they decide to include him, what position should teachers take on his role? Was he a positive or negative force, an important advocate for his people, or a dangerous racist? If teachers want to leave it up to students to define Malcolm X's role, which contemporary and secondary sources do they bring into class for students to examine? The importance and difficulty of these decisions underscore the importance of lesson planning. It is one of the reasons that I list the sources I plan to use and the main ideas about a subject that inform my thinking and shape the direction of my teaching when I plan lessons and units.

Historian Sean Wilentz of Princeton University and the National Council for History Education has defined another major war as "content" vs. "process." In a widely distributed essay, Wilentz (1997: 4.15) divided the educational universe into two oppositional forces, "history-minded reformers" who are advocates of "more demanding history standards," and supporters of social studies who harbor "a fundamental disregard for history" characterized by a "one-dimensional" approach to the past, and an unwillingness to make serious demands on students or teachers. Wilentz declared that "the past is not a 'process'," and that social studies topics should not be selected based on their current "relevance to our own world."

But many historians, myself included (Singer 1997), disagree with Wilentz's conception of history and the role of the historian. For us, the practice of history involves a dialogue between past and present, and the process of understanding the past cannot be totally separated from the events themselves. E. H. Carr (1961: 32–35), for example, argued that historians are engaged in a "continuous process of molding facts to interpretation and of interpretation to the facts . . . The historian without facts is rootless and futile; the facts without their historian are dead and meaningless." This process of rethinking the past based on contemporary concerns and understandings is fundamental to the work of the historian and should play a central role in social studies education.

Part of my problem with Wilentz and his supporters is their disregard for the validity of knowledge generated by other academic disciplines, especially by educational researchers and secondary school classroom teachers. They advocate an approach to the study and teaching of history based on their experience with graduate seminars at Princeton, Columbia, and UCLA. But these may not be the best strategies for engaging teenagers in Appalachia, South Central Los Angeles, rural Nebraska, or suburban Chicago, who often believe that what happened before they were born is irrelevant to their lives.

Secondary school social studies teachers, as opposed to university professors, must create a context that convinces students of the relevance of studying the past, introduces them to the "process" of historical and social change, encourages them to think critically about both assumptions and received "facts," and create classroom environments and projects that bring the past alive. While university professors assume student interest, knowledge, and academic skill, secondary school social studies teachers must have both educational and content goals, the ability to assess where students in their classes are starting from, and teaching

strategies that make it possible for students to move from one place to another.

WHAT DO STUDENTS UNDERSTAND FROM A LESSON?

I frequently wonder what students actually understand about what I present in class. The problem is not simply inattention. Students create meaning by relating what they are studying with prior experience and understanding. Who they are often determines what they think and how they feel about the importance of what they are learning.

Students generally see everything before their birth as ancient history, and events from when they were young as a long time ago. I lived through the Vietnam War and it is part of my lived experience, but World War II was my father's war and, for me, it was always part of the historical past.

In 2007, I taught lessons to two groups of high students in the same school about "lessons of 9/11." It was located in a suburb of New York City and local residents had died in the attack on the World Trade Center. Eleventh graders who participated had been 11 years old in 2001. They discussed the events five years earlier as part of their lived experience. I also met with ninth grade students who were nine years old in 2001. These students discussed 9/11 as an academic topic, as a part of history with a lot less personal relevance to their lives.

Twice, I conducted relatively systematic research projects to explore deeper student understanding, rather than just testing for content and conceptual knowledge. A study of the gender stereotyping by high school students in United States history classes not only found differences in attitude between male and female students, but also identified a clustering phenomena within each group. Students from similar socioeconomic and cultural backgrounds had surprisingly similar responses to what they had learned during a unit on woman's rights, responses that were significantly different from students who were members of other groups (Singer 1995). Another study explored student attitudes about what is important to know about slavery. Teachers from the New Teacher Network and I had students in half a dozen racially segregated schools complete questionnaires about slavery in the United States that quizzed them on their content knowledge and asked them to list and explain the things they thought were important to know. We found that content knowledge was consistent across schools and demographic groups, but that ideas about what was important to know differed widely. For example, white students from predominately white schools emphasized that slavery was a thing of the past and felt it was time for the nation to move past recriminations. African-American students from predominately black schools were convinced that the nation still grapples with the impact of slavery on people and society and had to finally come to terms with this heritage.

Teachers assume that because something is meaningful to us, it will be meaningful to our students. It is a serious mistake. We cannot count on student's coming equipped with a meaningful context that will make it possible for them to see the importance or relevance of a topic. The context must be provided by the lesson, and even then, different students will see the same material in different ways. Just because you taught something does not mean students understood the main points you were trying to present, even if they were paying attention.

Learning Activity: Taking a Stand On Some Hot Issues

Think it over:
- In the late nineteenth and early twentieth centuries, US industry was expanding. Today the country is de-industrializing. What is the significance of this change for immigrants?
- In 1903, W. E. B. DuBois wrote that the major problem facing the United States in the twentieth century was the "color line." In your opinion, how has race affected the opportunities available to different groups in the United States at the start of the twenty-first century?

Add your voice to the discussion:
Where do you stand in the "content" vs. "process" debate? Explain.

It's your classroom:
The Smithsonian Museum's initial plan for an exhibit commemorating the 50th anniversary of the end of World War II became the subject of major political debate because it included questions about the decision to drop atomic bombs on Japanese cities. Would you involve students in your high school class in critically examining this decision? Why or why not? If you would, how would you do it?

Learning Activity: Quotes from Malcolm X

Think it over:
Source: Wood, J., ed. 1992. *Malcolm X. In Our Own Image*. New York: St. Martin's Press.
- "You don't stick a knife in a man's back nine inches and then pull it out six inches and say you're making progress" (p. 48).
- "No matter how much respect, no matter how much recognition, Whites show towards me, as far as I'm concerned, as long as it is not shown to every one of our people in this country, it doesn't exist for me" (p. 48).
- "One of the first things I think young people, especially nowadays, should learn is how to see for yourself and listen for yourself and think for yourself" (p. 59).
- "There's new thinking coming in. There's new strategy coming in. It'll be Molotov cocktails this month, hand grenades next month, and something else next month. It'll be ballots, or it'll be bullets. It'll be liberty, or it will be death" (p. 11).
- "There can be no Black-White unity until there is first some Black unity. There can be no worker's solidarity until there is first some racial solidarity. We cannot think of uniting with others, until after we have first united among ourselves" (p. 73).
- "By any means necessary" (p. 60).

Add your voice to the discussion:
Some of Malcolm X's ideas are considered very controversial. What do you think? Why?

HOW DO LESSON PLANS REFLECT IDEAS ABOUT LEARNING?

Lesson plans are also plans for how we will teach about a subject. Often students in my social studies methods classes write in their sample lesson plans that they will lecture about a topic. I always scribble in the margin of their plans, "Just because you say it, does that mean they learn it?" A report on what high school students think about during class supports my concern (Clinchy 1995). It found that, "in a typical history class where the teacher was lecturing about Genghis Khan's invasion of China and conquest of Beijing in 1215, only two out of 27 students were thinking about China." But that does not mean these two students were thinking about the lesson either. One of the students reported that, during the lecture, he "was remembering the meal he had when he last ate out with his family at a Chinese restaurant." The other student reported that he "was wondering why Chinese men wore their hair in a ponytail." This study certainly raises questions about the efficacy of lecturing.

Sometimes students in my social studies methods class write in their lesson plans that their secondary school students will "discuss" an issue. But making it possible for students to have a discussion takes a lot of planning. Over the years, I have had many "failed" discussions in my high school social studies classes. Sometimes no one had anything to say about what I thought would be a hot topic. Sometimes students had a lot to say, but took the discussion in a direction I was unprepared for or had not even considered. I always ask prospective teachers who plan to "discuss" an issue: "How will the discussion be organized?" "How do students know about the subject that they are supposed to discuss?"

The best ways to actively involve students in learning social studies, avoid lecturing, and have discussions where students know things that they can share and evaluate together, are activity-based lessons that are part of long-term projects. On a day-to-day basis, activity-based lessons are the key to successful social studies teaching and student learning. Every lesson is organized around things that students are reading, examining, analyzing, thinking, talking, and writing about a famous speech, a part of an essay, a newspaper article, an artifact, a song, a poem, a chart or graph, a picture, a political cartoon, or a hands-on activity. Every student has the ability to contribute to the lesson because they all have the material being studied in front of them.

Teaching Activity: What Did the Teacher Say?

Try it yourself:
Observe a secondary school social studies classroom where a teacher is lecturing. After the class is over, ask individual students what they remember about the lesson and what they were thinking about while the teacher spoke.

Teaching Activity: Promoting Student Discussion

It's your classroom:
Consider a topic you think middle school students would find interesting to discuss. What would you do to prepare students for this discussion? What would you do to promote student participation during the discussion? How would you bring discussion to a close?

WHAT DO BEGINNING TEACHERS WORRY ABOUT?

Students preparing to become teachers, and beginning teachers, always worry about lesson planning. I think their general sense of dread masks some particular issues that need to be examined.

Beginning teachers worry about "deadly silence": what will happen in the classroom if they have nothing to say and nothing for the students to do. I think every teacher remembers having nightmares about lessons petering out after ten minutes and being forced to ad lib through the rest of a terrifying period. Sometimes in your nightmares you are performing before an audience of sharks or wolves, trying to distract them with a song and dance routine, and hoping they will not move in for the kill.

Another worry that new teachers have is that their students will unmask them as frauds. Here you are, a social studies teacher who is supposed to have encyclopedic knowledge of everything; only you know how little you really know. Prospective teachers wonder if they are allowed to say, "That's a good question. I don't know the answer, but let's see if we can do some research and discuss it in another lesson."

Perhaps a beginning teacher's major in college was post-Renaissance European intellectual history, and now they find themselves teaching about the development of Southeast Asian cultures, the relationship between employment and inflation rates, or contemporary American social movements. To cover for their insecurity, beginning teachers often want foolproof lesson plans that anticipate every possible student question and include every conceivable fact about the topic. Sometimes they produce plans that are so long and unwieldy that they have limited usefulness.

Because many new teachers are also beginning the first job in their career, they almost always live in fear of supervisor expectations. Will department chairs demand complex detailed lesson blueprints that allow no deviation? Will they be judged inadequate as teachers and human beings because of lesson plan design lapses? How should they handle important but unanticipated student questions that "threaten" to give a lesson a different slant, especially when a supervisor is in the room? Another one of my recurring nightmares was that I arrived at school, began my first class, and simultaneously discovered that I left my plan book at home and that my supervisor was paying an unannounced visit to my class.

Even when classroom observations go well and students seem to respond to a lesson, beginning teachers may fear that their ideas about history and social studies, and about teaching methods, will be challenged by supervisors, administrators, or parents who disagree with "the latest styles" coming out of college classrooms. There is often a sense among new teachers that they are always "walking on eggshells." During my first year of high school teaching, my department chair wanted to know how I justified asking my students if they thought "imperialist goals" might have influenced US decisions during World War I. I knew my historical sources and the debate on this period, but I was still shaken. Finally, I managed to stammer, "It was just an opinion question." Since that time, I have learned that I need to carefully document my views, especially if they are out of the ordinary.

Classroom Activity: Was There an Economic Motive behind US Entry into World War I?

A. Secretary of State William J. Bryan (1914):
"It is inconsistent with the spirit of neutrality for a neutral nation to make loans to belligerent nations, for money is the worst of all contrabands . . . The government withdraws the protection of citizenship from those who do enlist under other flags—why should it give protection to money when it enters foreign military service?"

B. Secretary of State William J. Bryan (1915):
"It is not sufficient to say that according to international law, American citizens have a right to go anywhere . . . If the authorities of a city are justified in warning people off the streets of the city in which they reside, surely a nation is justified in warning its citizens off the water highways which belong to no nation alone."

C. Table 8.1 US Trade with Belligerents, 1914–1916 (in millions of dollars):

Nation	1914	1915	1916	Percentage of change
Great Britain	594	912	1,527.00	+257
France	160	369	629.00	+393
Italy	74	185	269.00	+364
Germany	345	29	0.29	–1,150

Source: Adapted from Bailey, T. and Kennedy, D. 1983. *The American Pageant*. 7th ed. Lexington, MA: D.C. Heath, p. 653.

Try it yourself:

What conclusion do you draw from these documents?

It's your classroom:

What questions would you ask to help students better understand this material?

WHAT SHOULD BEGINNING TEACHERS CONSIDER WHEN PLANNING LESSONS?

To allay some of these fears, and to prepare students to become effective social studies teachers, we spend a lot of time in our methods class experimenting with lesson ideas and plans. These are some general ideas I think you should consider in social studies lessons.

Alan's 14 Suggestions to Help Lesson Planning

1. *Lesson plans are necessary tools for teaching.* They are not works of art. They will never be perfect.
2. *Lesson plan formats are suggestions based on other people's experiences.* They are not etched in stone. What works for one person may not work for someone else. There are a number of different ways to plan effective lessons.
3. *Successful teachers, even the most experienced, always plan.* Some very good veteran teachers argue that they do not need *written* plans anymore because everything is in their heads. It may be possible for them to teach this way, and it may be possible for you in the distant future, but it has never worked for me. I find social studies too complex a discipline, and the effort to involve students in a lesson too demanding, for me to just rely on my memory during a lesson.
4. *Lesson plans are experiments.* Sometimes they get the expected results and sometimes they do not. Every teacher has

lessons that did not work the way they wanted. I try to include three or four possible activities in each lesson. If something does not seem to be working, I go on to the next activity.
5. *It is better to overplan than underplan.* An important part of teaching is making choices. You can always leave something out or decide to use it another day or in another way. As I became a more experienced teacher, I overplanned on purpose.
6. *Lesson plans should change.* If something does not work in one class, you can do it differently the next period, the next day, or the next year. At the end of a class or the day, I jot down comments on my lesson plans for future reference: what worked, what did not, and what to add, drop, or change.
7. *Many goals require more than one period to achieve.* Just because time can be subdivided into discrete packets does not mean that human beings think in 40-minute blocks or that every (or any) idea can be grasped in one class period.
8. *A structured plan makes it possible to be flexible in class.* You can choose from different built-in lesson alternatives based on student involvement in the lesson. Maybe you cannot change a horse in "midstream," but you can change a lesson.
9. *Lesson plans must be adjusted to meet particular circumstances, and they need to be different for different students.* A lesson

225

that makes sense for a class of 15 may not work with a class of 34. A lesson planned for a class that meets in the morning probably has to be modified for a class that tears into the room at 14:30. Lessons planned for heterogeneous classes will differ from lessons planned for homogenous classes. Lessons must be planned with students in mind.

10. *Lessons planned for middle school students differ from lessons planned for high school classrooms.* Usually middle school teachers have fewer time constraints. This makes it possible for students to approach an idea from different directions and learn about it in different ways.

11. *Sample lessons may look great on paper, but teachers need to adapt them to their classes and their own personalities.*

12. *The things a teacher includes in a lesson plan change as a teacher becomes more experienced.* Beginning teachers, knowing they will be nervous, should list possible questions in advance. Preparation makes it easier to think on your feet. Later on,

I found that I did not need to think up as many questions in advance because I was able to develop questions during the course of a lesson based on student questions and comments.

13. *Whatever your individual preferences are for a lesson plan format, when you first start out, you will likely have to use the format recommended by your district or department.* Beginning teachers are generally monitored closely until they establish a reputation for competence. But I think you will discover that, whatever format you are asked to use, you will be able to adapt it to what you believe should be included in a lesson plan.

14. *Personal computers were probably invented with social studies teachers in mind.* I design lessons, modify them as worksheets, rearrange them into homework assignments, and recycle homework and classroom questions when I make up tests. The next time I teach the subject, I start with a lesson plan database that I can easily reorganize.

Teaching Activity: What Would You Include in a Lesson Plan?

Think it over:
List the things you think you would want to include in a lesson plan. Why would you include these things? After you finish, compare your list with "Ingredients for an Activity-based Social Studies Lesson" that follows.

WHAT ARE THE INGREDIENTS OF AN ACTIVITY-BASED LESSON PLAN?

One of my students compared a lesson plan to a recipe. She said that when she first started cooking, she needed to follow all of the steps carefully. Later, as she became more experienced, she felt more comfortable varying

the ingredients and experimenting with her own ideas.

Following are the ingredients of an activity-based social studies lesson. Experiment with the ingredients you find useful in a lesson plan. Sometimes my lessons include some of these ingredients, sometimes they include others, and on a rare occasion they include all of them.

INGREDIENTS OF AN ACTIVITY-BASED LESSON

Unit:
Locates the lesson in the overall conceptual sequence.

Aim:
A question that a particular lesson is designed to answer or a statement or phrase introducing the topic of a lesson. Usually it is written on the board at the start of the lesson. Sometimes it is elicited from students during the early stages of a lesson.

Goals/objectives:

The skills, concepts, and content that students will learn about during the lesson. Can also include social/behavioral/classroom community goals. Goals are broad and achieved during a long period of time. Objectives are specific short-term goals that are achievable during a particular lesson.

Main ideas/understandings:

The underlying or most important ideas about a topic that inform a teacher's understanding and influence the way lessons and units are organized—the ideas that teachers want students to consider. Can be formulated as statements or as broad questions that become the basis for ongoing discussion.

Materials:

The maps, documents, records, and equipment needed by teachers and students during the lesson to create the learning activities.

Activities/lesson development:

The substance of the lesson. Explains how students will learn the goals and objectives. Includes discussions, document analysis, mapping, cartooning, singing, performing drama, researching, cooperative learning, teacher presentations, and so on.

Do now activity:

An introductory activity that immediately involves students as they enter the room.

Motivation(al) activity:

A question, statement, or activity that establishes a learning context and captures student interest in the topic that will be examined. Motivations connect the subject of the lesson to things that students are thinking about or are interested in.

Questions:

Prepared questions that attempt to anticipate classroom dialogue; designed to aid examination of materials, generate class discussions, and promote deeper probing. Medial summary questions make it possible for the class to integrate ideas at the end of an activity.

Transitions:

Key questions that make it possible for students to draw connections between the information, concepts, or understandings developed during a particular activity with other parts of the lesson and to a broader conceptual understanding.

Summary:

A concluding question or group of questions that make it possible for the class to integrate or utilize the learning from this lesson and prior lessons.

Application:

Extra optional questions or activities planned for this lesson that draw on and broaden what students are learning in the unit. These can be used to review prior lessons or as transitions to future lessons.

Homework assignment:

A reading, writing, research, or thinking assignment that students complete after the lesson. It can be a review of the lesson, an introduction to a future lesson, background material that enriches student understanding, an exercise that improves student skills, or part of a long-term project.

Teaching Activity: Outlining an Activity-based Lesson

Try it yourself:

Select a social studies topic you would like to teach. Outline a lesson using the categories for an activity-based lesson plan.

HOW IS AN ACTIVITY-BASED LESSON ORGANIZED?

There are probably as many different lesson plan formats as there are teachers. This section compares four different types of lesson plan formats and discusses how to use them in class. I learned the developmental lesson plan approach as a college undergraduate, and I thought it was an accurate description of the lessons I remembered from middle school and high school. It assumes that students did the homework the night before and come into class prepared to learn.

I should have realized from my own experience as a high school student that my friends and I usually were not prepared. Instead, we developed strategies to fake it or to get by. We would answer an easy question at the start of the lesson and then disappear into the woodwork. We would spend a lot of time in the bathroom, or we would try to throw the teacher off track by asking awkward, sweeping, or tangential questions (e.g., Is it true that Thomas Jefferson and George Washington had children with women who were their slaves? Is the Declaration of Independence the most important document in world history? Could the colonies still have gained independence if George Washington had been captured at the start of the war?). Usually, questions like these would launch a teacher into a lecture and we would be left alone.

Whatever I forgot about being a middle or high school student while I was sitting in my college methods classes, I quickly remembered when I started trying to teach 6th and 7th graders at Macombs Junior High School in the Bronx. Learning along with my students, I struggled to come up with a lesson plan design that made sense to me. It was an act of survival. After a number of years (and many headaches), I gradually developed an activity-based lesson plan that is based on six principles.

Alan's Six Principles for Planning Activity-based Lessons

1. Students are not inherently interested in social studies just because the clock says it is time for my class. It is my job to interest and motivate them. I must create a learning context for every lesson.
2. A lesson needs a clear structure. If students cannot figure out what I want them to do, they cannot do it.
3. Related to this, every lesson must have a beginning and an end, even if we will be discussing the same topic the next day.
4. Everyone can participate and learn if I organize a lesson around materials that I bring to class. If students do the homework in advance, their experience will be enriched. But even if they did not do the homework, they will be able to use the materials to participate in classroom activities and discussions.
5. Students have a range of reading facility, so that a lesson that involves everyone must include material written on different levels.
6. Broadly defined lesson goals and objectives give a class more freedom to explore ideas during a lesson than does a list of specific lesson outcomes.

Teaching Activity: Principles for Planning

Add your voice to the discussion:
Which of these principles do you agree with? Which would you change? What would you add?
Explain the reasons for your choices.

Over the years, I have had to use required lesson plan formats in different schools. But I always adapted the required format to what I knew was necessary for a successful lesson for my students. I generally start each lesson with an **Aim Question** and **Homework Assignment** written on the board and a brief **Do Now Activity**. I think about social studies a lot, I like it, and it is important to me. But I know my students have many other things on their minds. If nothing else, they have six or seven other subjects. The likelihood is that they have not thought about our last lesson since they left the room. Copying the **Aim Question** and **Homework Assignment** and starting the **Do Now** settles them, reminds them why we are here, and reintroduces the particular topic. When they are all ready, I start with a **Motivation**—an activity based on student interests and questions, but related to the issues we will be exploring. The rest of the lesson is organized around a series of related **Activities**, beginning with an examination of the **Do Now**. Some activities are done by individual students or groups and some are designed for a full class. Every **Activity** provides students with a document, idea, or exercise that they can examine and discuss. I try to end lessons with a **Summary Question** or activity, but the reality is that it is not easy to summarize each lesson in a neat little package. Often the **Summary Question** is the **Aim Question** that started the lesson. Sometimes a class will examine the same **Materials** and **Main Ideas** for a number of days. However, I try to have each lesson stand on its own.

I also try to build flexibility into my lessons. The same points can be made in different ways.

If something does not capture the interest of my students, if they are unable to understand a passage or get the point from the materials that I provide them with, I try using something else. I plan lessons in 10-minute increments, with extra activities available "just in case."

If something goes really well, I may decide to stay with it. If my students have good ideas, we explore them. If an activity bombs, we move on.

Teachers must constantly make choices while they teach. In New York City, many high school students take the subway to school and there are always "transportation delays" in the morning. Sometimes, during the first period, I begin in the middle, using an activity, document, or passage that is less crucial for understanding the main ideas of the lesson. I wait until all the students are present and physically and mentally ready before I begin the **Motivation** and key activities.

Teaching Activity: A Motivation is Not a Hook

Some teachers argue you should begin a lesson with an attention grabber or "hook" that catches student attention. The motivation, as I am describing it, is not a "hook." An attention grabber may or may not be related to the main ideas of a lesson. A motivation is always directly connected to what you will be teaching. For example, I use a balance scale as a motivation in a lesson on checks and balances in the Constitution, a giant elastic band to start a lesson on stretching the powers of Congress, and a giant puzzle to illustrate judicial review. In each case the motivation provides students with a visual metaphor for understanding the concept we will be examining.

Sometimes the motivation is simply listening to a song or speech from the historical era or looking at a cartoon or photograph that captures a piece of the story. Other times I draw connections between their lives and experiences and choices that confronted people in the past. I began a lesson on why the Puritans lost political control and moral influence in colonial New England by asking why their parents seemed to get stricter with them as they became teenagers. Inevitably they argue that rigidity and dogmatism are marks of declining authority and this leads into a discussion of the Puritans.

Add your voice to the discussion:
- Do you think motivations should be necessary parts of lessons? Explain.
- Should motivations be directly connected to the substance of the lesson? Explain.

Try it yourself:
Suggest a possible motivation for lessons on each of these topics from United States history.
- Underlying causes of the American Revolution (1763–1783)
- Westward and Manifest Destiny (1820–1880)
- Impact of Industrial Change on farmers (1860–1900)
- Life in Urbanizing America (1890–1920)
- Immigration restriction (1921–1924)
- Scopes "Monkey" Trial (1925)
- Election of Franklin D. Roosevelt (1932)
- Japanese Internment (1942–1945)
- African-American Protests during the Civil Rights Movement (1955–1965).

During the last period of the day, it usually takes students a little longer to settle down. I take more time with the **Do Now** and review it immediately. Students are already excited, although not about social studies, so I may use the lesson motivation at the end of the period as an application. At the end of the day, a class may be a little bumptious (maybe there will be a full moon that night, or they served a particularly bad lunch and everyone is starving), so a teacher can decide to have students work as individuals rather than in groups. In all cases, teachers have to be prepared to make decisions about how to use their plans when it becomes time to actually teach.

In the lessons that follow, I try to give some sense of the differences between a middle and high school lesson. In the middle school, a teacher usually has fewer time restraints, the ability to personalize discussions, and more freedom to utilize long-term projects and themes. In high school, the curriculum tends to be tighter, and more time is spent searching for evidence that supports historical conclusions. Materials aimed at middle school social studies classes tend to be modified from the original, using simpler vocabulary and shorter, edited passages. But these differences are not absolutes, and teachers have to make judgments about which materials to use and how much

time to spend on a topic, based on their own classes. I include side comments to try to give some sense of how a lesson actually goes. I have also included more questions than I would actually write in a lesson plan.

There is one last problem. Preservice teachers frequently ask, "Where do you start when constructing a lesson?" This is a more complicated question than it seems because I do not start planning each lesson the same way. First, I try to conceptualize what the entire unit or theme will look like. Then I look at the number of days I have available, as well as the topics, major ideas, documents, and skills activities I want to include in this unit. At this point, I block out individual lessons. Some of the lessons are built around answering an historical question (**Aim Question**). Sometimes I start with a skill activity, like map reading, or a particularly juicy primary source document for students to interpret. Many times I start with main ideas and I try to find ways to make them accessible to my students. To further complicate matters, some lessons are designed to take more than one day. Students act out an historical play on Day 1, analyze it in groups or as a full class on Day 2, and write about its implications on Day 3. I guess the answer is, I start constructing a lesson at the beginning.

MIDDLE SCHOOL ACTIVITY-BASED LESSON ON THE DECLARATION OF INDEPENDENCE

Unit:
Middle school (7th grade)—Revolutionary America

Aim:
Why did colonial Americans write a Declaration of Independence? [I try to keep aim questions simple.]

Goals/objectives:
[These include social and academic skills as well as conceptual goals.]

1. Read a primary source document with understanding
2. Write explanations that demonstrate their understanding
3. Work in teams
4. Recognize an analogy
5. Understand reasons for writing the Declaration of Independence
6. Examine the meaning of concepts of change, freedom, equality, responsibility, revolution, human rights, and government.

Main ideas/understandings:
[These are from the main ideas/understandings for the entire unit. They will be developed and reinforced in other lessons as well.]

1. People and societies are constantly *changing*. These changes affect their relationships with other people and societies.
2. As people's lives *change*, they may demand greater *freedom* and want to take on new responsibilities.
3. The authors of the Declaration of Independence felt a need to explain their *revolution*. They did not believe that *revolutions are always justified*.
4. The meaning of concepts like *equality*, *change* over time.
5. The authors of the Declaration of Independence believed that *human rights* come from "the Creator," not from *government*.
6. Human rights include the idea that "all men are created equal."
7. The purpose of *government* is to protect *human rights*.
8. When *governments* do not protect *human rights*, people have the right to *change* them.

Materials:
Activity Worksheet: The Declaration of Independence—In Your Own Words

Do now:
Read Passage 1 on your worksheet, The Declaration of Independence—In Your Own Words. Answer Questions 1–3 in your notebook. [Sometimes I have a class work in their notebooks and sometimes directly on the worksheets. The only rule is to give clear directions.]

Motivation:
Compare being a teenager in the United States today with the situation facing the maturing British colonies in the Americas after the French and Indian War. [Have students discuss the problems they are experiencing in their families now that they are in 7th grade and ready to become teenagers. Why are tensions between them and their parents escalating? How do they see the next few years? How have older sisters and brothers handled these problems? What will eventually happen between them and their families? Why do many families with teenagers seem to have similar conflicts?]

Activities/questions/transitions:
- [Transition] If you were going to write a letter of complaint to your parents about the problems in your relationship with them, what are some of the things you would include in your letter? Why? [List ideas on the board.]
- How would you organize the letter? (a) An introduction including main ideas. (b) A list of complaints or grievances. (c) A statement explaining your views about what would make things fairer. [Encourage multiple answers to questions and cross conversation.]
- [Transition] Let us say a number of years went by and the tension between you and your parents became so great that you felt you had to move out of their house. If you wrote them a letter at that point, what could you title it? Why? Do you think it is fair to compare the problems of teenagers in families today with the problems faced by the American colonies with Great Britain over 200 years ago? Why?
- [Transition] Have a student read the passage (from the do now assignment) aloud. According to this passage, why did colonial Americans write the Declaration of Independence?
- [Transition] The Declaration of Independence was written over 200 years ago. Many of its passages are hard to understand. Student teams will read the rest of the passages from the Declaration of Independence. In your notebooks, rewrite passages in language that is easier to understand today, but still includes the main idea of the passage. [Depending on time, each team can complete either the entire sheet or only one passage. While students are working, the teacher can circulate around the room, helping students or checking homework assignments.]
- The second passage is one of the most often quoted statements in the United States. Have a student read the passage aloud. Have a student explain how they rewrote the passage and why they wrote it this way. Why do you think this quote is so famous? What does this quote tell us about the reasons that Americans wrote the Declaration of Independence? [Other passages will be reviewed at the start of the next lesson.]

Summary:

Based on our discussion today, why did colonial Americans decide to write a Declaration of Independence?

Application:

[These questions will be major parts of future lessons.] Do you agree with the reasons for independence explained in these two passages? What else do you think the Declaration of Independence needs to include? Do you think the statement that "all men are created equal" meant the same thing in 1776 as it does today? Why?

Homework assignment:

Re-read pages _____ in your textbook. Using your textbook and based on our discussions in class, make a list of grievances (complaints) the colonies might have had against Great Britain. Explain why the colonists were upset by each of these actions by Great Britain. [The next night's homework will have students rewrite their translations of the Declaration of Independence based on class discussion.]

ACTIVITY WORKSHEET: THE DECLARATION OF INDEPENDENCE— IN YOUR OWN WORDS

Do now:

Read Passage 1 and answer Questions 1, 2, and 3 in your notebook.

"When in the course of human events, it becomes necessary for one people to dissolve the political bands which have connected them with another, and to assume, among the powers of the earth, the separate and equal station to which the laws of nature and of nature's God entitle them, a decent respect to the opinion of mankind requires that they should declare the causes which impel them to separation."

Questions:

1. What does "in the course of human events" mean?
2. What do the Americans want to do?
3. Why did Americans write the Declaration of Independence?

Activity:

In Your Own Words

1. "We hold these truths to be self-evident:—That all men are created equal; that they are endowed by their Creator with certain unalienable rights; that among these are life, liberty, and the pursuit of happiness."
2. "That, to secure these rights, governments are instituted among men, deriving their just powers from the consent of the governed."
3. "That, whenever any form of government becomes destructive of these ends, it is the right of the people to alter or to abolish it, and to institute new government, laying its foundation on such principles, and organizing its powers in such form, as to them shall seem most likely to effect their safety and happiness."
4. "Prudence, indeed, will dictate that governments long established should not be changed for light and transient causes, and, accordingly, all experience hath shown that mankind are more disposed to suffer, while evils are sufferable, than to right themselves by abolishing the forms to which they are accustomed."
5. "But when a long train of abuses and usurpation's . . . evinces a design to reduce them under absolute despotism, it is their right, it is their duty, to throw off such government, and to provide new guards for their future security."

Teaching Activity: Evaluating an Activity-based Middle School Lesson Plan

Think it over:
What do you see as the strengths and weaknesses of this lesson plan? Why?

It's your classroom:
1. How would you change this lesson plan? Why?
2. Rewrite the lesson so you feel comfortable with it.

HIGH SCHOOL ACTIVITY-BASED LESSON ON THE DECLARATION OF INDEPENDENCE

Unit:
High school (11th grade)—Revolutionary America

Aim:
What is the promise of the Declaration of Independence? [I try to keep aim questions simple.]

Goals/objectives:
[These include social and academic skills as well as conceptual goals]
- Read a primary source document with understanding
- Recognize the continuing importance of ideas and documents
- Place the Declaration of Independence within philosophical and political contexts
- Recognize connections between ideas in different historical eras
- Draw conclusions based on historical decisions and evidence
- Understand the benefits and problems of compromise and consensus
- Examine the meaning of concepts of change, human rights, government, revolution, equality, law, injustice, compromise, and consensus.

Main ideas/understandings:
[These are from the main ideas/understandings for the entire unit. They will be developed and reinforced in other lessons as well.]
1. The ideas about *human rights* and *government* expressed in the Declaration of Independence have roots in the scientific rationalism of seventeenth- and eighteenth-century European Enlightenment philosophy
2. The ideas about *human rights* and *government* expressed in the Declaration of Independence continue to have meaning in the contemporary United States. These ideas can be considered the promise of America
3. The meaning of concepts like *equality* change over time
4. The authors of the Declaration of Independence believed that *human rights* come from "the Creator," not from a monarch or *government*
5. Human rights include the idea that "all men are created equal"
6. The purpose of *government* is to protect *human rights*
7. When *governments* do not protect *human rights*, people have the right to *change* them
8. The authors of the Declaration of Independence believed that *laws* of nature and society determined whether a *revolution* was legitimate. They wanted to ensure that there were limits on the right to *revolution*
9. Enslavement, class hierarchy, and what we would consider social *injustice* were accepted in the communities where the authors of the Declaration of Independence lived
10. The Declaration of Independence is intentionally vague about the level of public support needed to justify a *revolution*. Partly, it was an attempt to convince the colonists of the legitimacy of independence

11. The general nature of the philosophical statements about *human rights* and *government* represented an effort at *compromise* and *consensus* by people who disagreed about many specific points, especially the continuing existence of slavery.

Materials:
Audio or Video recording of Dr Martin Luther King, Jr.'s "I Have A Dream" speech at the August 1963 Civil Rights march on Washington, DC and appropriate equipment.

Do now:
Read Passage 1 on your worksheet, Excerpts from the Declaration of Independence. According to this passage, why do the American colonies claim the right to "dissolve the political bands which have connected them with" Great Britain? [Sometimes I have students work in their notebooks and sometimes directly on the worksheets. The only rule is to give clear directions.]

Motivation:
Play excerpt from Dr Martin Luther King, Jr.'s "I Have A Dream" speech, where King quotes from the Declaration of Independence. Identify the source of the speech. (In your opinion) why is Martin Luther King, Jr. quoting from the Declaration of Independence in a speech at a rally in Washington, DC, over 187 years after it was written? Suffragists also quoted from the Declaration of Independence during their struggle to win women's right to vote. Why has the Declaration of Independence been quoted in this way throughout US history? Why is the Declaration often called "the promise of America?" [Ask a number of students. Encourage cross conversation.]

Activities/questions/transitions:
- [Transition] On July 2, 1776, the second Continental Congress approved a resolution by Richard Henry Lee of Virginia to declare colonial independence from Great Britain. The Congress decided to wait two days, until Thomas Jefferson and the committee could write a formal declaration, before making its decision official. Why do you think they made this decision to wait?
- [Transition] Have a student read the passage (from the do now assignment) aloud. Does this passage give a clue to why they felt a formal Declaration of Independence was necessary? What is the clue? What do you think is the reason? [Ask other students if they agree or disagree, and why.]
- [Transition] Following the introduction, the Declaration of Independence contains the statement of principles quoted by Martin Luther King, Jr. What does this passage mean? [Encourage multiple answers to questions and cross conversation.] We studied the ideas of European Enlightenment thinkers like Newton, Locke, Montesquieu, and Rousseau. Where do you think Jefferson got these ideas? Why? Why do you think they decided to include this statement of principle in the Declaration of Independence? What do you think they meant by the statement that these were unalienable rights granted by their "Creator?" Do you think the statement that "All men are created equal" meant the same thing then as it does to us today? Why?
- [Transition] Let's read through the third passage from the Declaration together. What is the main issue they are discussing in this passage? According to this passage, what is the source of government power? Why do you think they are concerned with the source of government power? According to this passage, when do people have the right to overthrow a government? Is this right limited or unlimited? How is it limited? What would you expect them to discuss in the next part of the Declaration of Independence? Why?
- [Transition] The third passage states that "it is the right of the people to alter or abolish it," meaning the government. Which people are they talking about? Does it require an election, a simple majority vote, a two-thirds vote, or a unanimous vote? In your opinion, why didn't the authors of the Declaration of Independence make this clear? What does this suggest about the reason for delaying a formal decree on independence until the Declaration was ready?

Summary:
Based on our examination of these passages and our discussion of American history, why do you think the members of the second Continental Congress decided to have Thomas Jefferson write the Declaration of Independence? Why has this document come to represent the "promise of American society?"

Application:

If you had the ability to rewrite these passages from the Declaration of Independence, would you change them? How? Why?

Homework assignment:

Read pages ___—___ [discussing the Declaration of Independence] and answer the following questions:

1. How is the Declaration of Independence organized?
2. Which section of the Declaration of Independence do you consider most important for people at that time? Why?
3. Which section of the Declaration of Independence do you consider most important for people today? Why?
4. Write a paragraph supporting your opinion on this question: Should people who signed a document stating that "all men are created equal," while owning slaves or profiting from the slave trade, be treated as national heroes or criticized as hypocrites?

ACTIVITY WORKSHEET/EXCERPTS FROM THE DECLARATION OF INDEPENDENCE

Do now:

Read Passage 1 on your worksheet, Excerpts from the Declaration of Independence. According to this passage, why do the American colonies claim the right to "dissolve the political bands which have connected them with" Great Britain?

1. "When in the course of human events, it becomes necessary for one people to dissolve the political bands which have connected them with another, and to assume, among the powers of the earth, the separate and equal station to which the laws of nature and of nature's God entitle them, a decent respect to the opinion of mankind requires that they should declare the causes which impel them to separation."
2. "We hold these truths to be self-evident:—That all men are created equal; that they are endowed by their Creator with certain unalienable rights; that among these are life, liberty and the pursuit of happiness."
3. "That, to secure these rights, governments are instituted among men, deriving their just powers from the consent of the governed; that, whenever any form of government becomes destructive of these ends, it is the right of the people to alter or to abolish it, and to institute new government, laying its foundation on such principles, and organizing its powers in such form, as to them shall seem most likely to effect their safety and happiness. Prudence, indeed, will dictate that governments long established should not be changed for light and transient causes, and, accordingly, all experience hath shown that mankind are more disposed to suffer, while evils are sufferable, than to right themselves by abolishing the forms to which they are accustomed. But when a long train of abuses and usurpations, pursuing invariably the same object, evinces a design to reduce them under absolute despotism, it is their right, it is their duty, to throw off such government, and to provide new guards for their future security."

Teaching Activity: Evaluating a High School Activity-based Lesson Plan

Think it over:

What do you see as the strengths and weaknesses of this lesson plan? Why?

It's your classroom:

1. How would you change this lesson plan? Why?
2. Rewrite the lesson so you feel comfortable with it.

HOW IS A DEVELOPMENTAL LESSON ORGANIZED?

The developmental lesson (Dobkin et al. 1985) is designed to teach about a major concept, event, or relationship, and it is tailored to one lesson period. A lesson has an *aim*, either in the form of a question or a statement that defines the topic for the day. Sometimes a social studies teacher will open the lesson with the aim already written on the board, and sometimes the aim question or statement will be elicited from students during a motivation. By the end of the lesson, students in the class should be able to answer the aim question or, if it is a statement, a question based on it. This developmental lesson includes performance objectives—specific short-term goals that are achieved during the lesson. Ideally, a lesson plan that contains performance objectives should also include some way of assessing whether students achieved these objectives.

The developmental lesson begins with a *Motivation* that introduces the topic or poses the problem that the class will examine during the period. The *Development* outlines the steps that the class follows as students master the content, skills, and concepts that allow them to answer the aim question. The class ends with a *Summary* question, which is frequently a restatement of the aim question. If there is enough time at the end of a developmental lesson, a teacher can introduce an *Application* that has the class apply the material learned during the lesson in a different context or to another topic. The application can also be a homework assignment that prepares the class for the next lesson.

Developmental lesson plans rely on student desire to perform well in class. Homework assignments introduce students to material prior to a lesson. Teachers craft questions that are designed to elicit the factual content from students, provide the answer to the aim question, and move the class from one point to the next in the lesson.

This sample lesson plan includes prepared questions and board notes. During the lesson, board notes can be modified based on student responses to questions. The lesson is tied together at the end with a broad conceptual summary question that a number of students are involved in answering. Teachers who use this method try for maximum student involvement in answering questions and discussions. The assumption is that students who do not actively participate learn the material by listening to the teacher and other students, from the notes, and from the homework assignments.

HIGH SCHOOL DEVELOPMENTAL LESSON WITH PERFORMANCE OBJECTIVE

Aim:

Does the Declaration of Independence justify revolution?

Performance objectives:
- Students will be able to define the basic rights described in the Declaration of Independence.
- Students will be able to list three colonial complaints against British rule.
- Students will be able to explain when the authors of the Declaration of Independence believe a revolution is justified.

Preparation:

Homework: Prior to this lesson, students read the Declaration of Independence for homework and answer the following questions:

1. The Declaration of Independence is organized into three sections: A Brief Introduction, a Statement of Principles, and a List of Complaints. What is the reason for each of these sections?
2. The Declaration includes a series of complaints against Great Britain. Which complaints do you consider the most serious? Why?
3. According to the Declaration of Independence, what rights do all people have?

Class work:

In the previous lesson, students learned about the basic rights described in the Declaration of Independence.

Motivation:

Throughout history, governments have been threatened by violent revolutions. Many revolutionaries today argue that the United States Declaration of Independence supports their right to overthrow existing governments. How would you respond to this claim? Why?

Development:

Questions
- Why was the Declaration of Independence written?
- What does most of the Declaration consist of? Why?

Notes I. Purpose of the Declaration
- Declare independence from Great Britain
- List basic human rights
- Establish a theory of government
- Justify the American Revolution.

Medial summary
- In your opinion, which is the most important purpose of the Declaration of Independence?

Questions
- What are unalienable rights?
- What does the Declaration of Independence mean when it says that men are all created equal?
- According to the Declaration of Independence, why do governments exist?

Notes II. Theory of government
- People have rights that governments cannot take away
- The power of governments comes from the people of the country
- The purpose of government is to protect the rights of the people
- US government is based on the idea that all men are created equal.

Medial summary
- Why would the American colonists want these ideas included in a new government?

Questions
- According to the Declaration of Independence, when would I be justified in leading a revolution against our government?
- What, if any, limits are there on my right to rebel?
- In your opinion, which rights are so important that violation of these rights by government would justify rebellion?

Notes III. The Right to Rebel
- When a government does not respect people's rights, citizens have a right to rebel against the government.
- People should only rebel against a government when:
- It has a long history of abusing their rights.
- It is a dictatorship.
- Other methods of changing the government have failed.

Medial summary
- Why did the authors of the Declaration of Independence believe that the colonies had the right to rebel against Great Britain?

Final lesson summary questions:

According to the Declaration of Independence, when are revolutions justified? Why? When are revolutions not justified? Why? Does the Declaration of Independence justify revolution against our government today?

Application:

In your opinion, does the Declaration of Independence continue to have relevance today?

Teaching Activity: Evaluating a Developmental Lesson

Think it over:
What do you see as the strengths and weaknesses of this lesson plan? Why?

It's your classroom:
1. How would you change this lesson plan? Why?
2. Rewrite the lesson so you feel comfortable with it.

While many veteran teachers that I respect swear by this lesson plan format, I have a number of disagreements with them. First, it is based on a teacher-centered transmission model of teaching and lends itself to content-driven curricula and student acquisition of discrete packets of factual information that can easily be measured (performance objectives). As an historian, I think this approach presents an oversimplified linear conception of historical development, and it masks important historical debates. There is also an underlying assumption that individuals will master complex ideas and relationships during 40-minute learning bytes while sitting in classrooms of over 30 people.

This format encourages choreographed lessons that limit the ability of teachers to adjust to student insights, questions, and contributions. A discussion of student views could take up more than one lesson. Insight becomes an interference with the progression of the lesson, rather than a goal. Eventually students get the message to keep quiet or give the answer that the teacher wants.

This format assumes academic interest and motivation on the part of students. The answers to the questions that direct the lesson are based on prior student knowledge. Usually teachers rely on students having done the homework the night before, having understood it, and being able to remember and explain it. I have observed many classrooms where teachers using this model end up talking to a small group of students sitting in the front of the room while everyone else is "lost in space."

Teaching Activity: Once You Were a Student in This Class

Think it over:
- When you were a high school student, were you aware of structure in the way teachers planned social studies lessons?
- During your secondary school student career, you probably participated in many lessons organized according to the developmental lesson format. Based on your experiences as a student, how do you evaluate this kind of lesson and the criticisms raised here? Why?

WHAT DOES AN "OUTCOMES-BASED" LESSON PLAN LOOK LIKE?

The federal "No Child Left Behind" Act and intensified standardized testing have contributed to a push for more "outcomes-based" instruction. One of the more widely used instruction models is a seven-step lesson design that is part of the "Madeline Hunter Teacher Effectiveness Training Program" (Hunter 1982; Wolfe 1987: 70–71). This design, which is intended to be applicable in all subject areas, tries to systematize lesson planning. In theory, it makes it easier for teachers to have clear learning objectives that students can master by the end of the instructional period.

Critics of the Hunter approach (Berg and Clough 1990/1991), myself included, are unhappy with its claim to be useful in all subject areas and adaptable for all types of lessons. They find it inflexible and fear it will stifle teacher and student creativity. Because of its emphasis on measurable results, it tends to be even more heavily scripted than traditional developmental lessons, and it relies on extrinsic motivations and rewards (grades, praise, and special favors). Many of the categories that I find most useful in lesson planning are missing in the Hunter model. Hunter and her supporters defend the model, claiming that, although it "is deceptively simple in conceptualization," it is "incredibly complex in application."

I also find that evaluating teachers and lessons based on whether students master specific measurable learning objectives by the end of a given time period ensures lessons that focus on teaching facts and low-level skills, rather than encouraging students to think about ideas and concepts and express opinions. When my students plan sample lessons, I forbid them to use the Hunter designation SWBAT (students will be able to). Maybe I am just a poor teacher, but I cannot predict with the type of accuracy or regularity claimed by advocates for this format what other human beings will be able to do after a brief intervention into their lives on my part.

ELEMENTS OF AN OUTCOMES-BASED "HUNTER" LESSON

Each section of the lesson plan may include questions that the teacher uses to measure student understanding up until that point.

Anticipatory set: A brief opening activity or statement that focuses students' attention on what they will be learning.

Objectives: A detailed list of what students will know or be able to do at the end of the instruction period. It includes information that a teacher provides to students about what they will be able to do at the end of the lesson and how the lesson is relevant to their learning.

Instructional input: Information that a teacher provides to students so they can perform a skill or complete a process. Questions that a teacher asks to ensure that students understand procedures.

Modeling the information: The teacher leads the class in an activity so students understand what they are supposed to do.

Checking for understanding: Teachers ask questions and examine student work to ensure that students possess the essential information and skills necessary to achieve the instructional objective.

Guided practice: Teachers assist students as they work on assignments to ensure that student efforts are accurate and successful.

Independent practice: Students have mastered the basic skills and understandings needed to complete activities without direct teacher intervention. This is the final measure of whether lesson objectives have been achieved.

Middle School Lesson on the Declaration of Independence Using an Outcome-based Model

Anticipatory set
Let's review yesterday's discussion of the human rights promised in the Declaration of Independence. Can anyone explain those rights to us? [If necessary, a teacher can ask students to reread the passage they examined the day before or to consult their notes or homework.]

Objectives
- Students will be able to explain the meaning of a passage from the Declaration of Independence in their own words.
- Students will be able to define the terms *citizen* and *government*.
- Students will be able to explain the relationship between government and citizens defined in the Declaration of Independence.
- Students will state three contemporary examples of the relationship between government and citizens in the United States.
- Students will be able to explain what the authors of the Declaration thought people should do when governments do not respect the rights of citizens.
- Students will be able to define the terms *limits* and *revolution*.
- Students will be able to write a letter that expresses their opinions on this concept from the Declaration of Independence.
- Students will be able to use evidence to support their opinions.

Main ideas/understandings
Today we will be working independently and in groups, examining the part of the Declaration of Independence that describes how governments must protect the rights of citizens. By the end of the lesson, each of you will be able to explain what the authors of the Declaration

thought people should do when governments do not respect these rights. Before we begin, I want to review some ideas from previous lessons and from your homework. [Encourage maximum class participation in discussion.]

- Can someone explain what a citizen is? According to the Declaration of Independence, what rights do citizens have?
- Does anyone think they can tell us what a government is and what it does?
- In the United States today, what responsibilities do citizens have to the government? What responsibilities does government have to citizens?

Instructional input
Each student will read the passage from the Declaration of Independence, rewrite it in their own words, and then answer the questions at the end of the worksheet. When everyone in your group is finished, group members should compare answers and see where they agree or disagree. Group members should try to resolve their differences. Does anyone have any questions?

Modeling the information
Before you begin to read on your own, let us go over the first passage together. The first passage says, "That, to secure these rights, governments are instituted among men, deriving their just powers from the consent of the governed." Can someone put this passage into their own words for us? [Encourage maximum class participation.]

Checking for understanding
While students work on their own, the teacher circulates around the room, asking questions

and ensuring that students understand the assignment.

Guided practice
The teacher helps individual students understand the reading passage and think about the questions. Students check their work with the other members of their group. The entire class discusses what the authors of the Declaration thought people should do when governments do not respect their rights. [Encourage maximum class participation in discussion.]

- Does the Declaration of Independence place limits on the power of government? What are these limits? Do you agree with them? Why?
- Does the Declaration of Independence place limits on the rights of citizens? What are these limits? Do you agree with them? Why?
- What do we call a decision by people to overthrow a government? Does the Declaration of Independence support all revolutions? Why?

Independent practice
To demonstrate your understanding of this part of the Declaration of Independence, each student will write a letter to Thomas Jefferson, explaining whether you agree with his ideas about what people should do when governments do not respect their rights. In your letter, be sure to explain the reasons for your opinion. Give at least three reasons to support your opinions.

Homework
Complete your letters to Thomas Jefferson. Continue collecting current events newspaper articles on revolutions in other parts of the world.

ACTIVITY WORKSHEET/DECLARATION OF INDEPENDENCE— CITIZENS AND GOVERNMENTS

1. "That, to secure these rights, governments are instituted among men, deriving their just powers from the consent of the governed; . . ."

_____

_____

_____

2. " . . . that, whenever any form of government becomes destructive of these ends, it is the right of the people to alter or to abolish it, . . ."

_____

_____

_____

3. "... and to institute new government, laying its foundation on such principles, and organizing its powers in such form, as to them shall seem most likely to effect their safety and happiness."

_____

_____

_____

4. "Prudence, indeed, will dictate that governments long established should not be changed for light and transient causes, ..."

_____

_____

_____

5. "... and, accordingly, all experience hath shown that mankind are more disposed to suffer, while evils are sufferable, than to right themselves by abolishing the forms to which they are accustomed."

_____

_____

_____

6. "But when a long train of abuses and usurpations, pursuing invariably the same object, evinces a design to reduce them under absolute despotism, it is their right, it is their duty, to throw off such government, and to provide new guards for their future security."

_____

_____

_____

Questions:
1. Does the Declaration of Independence place limits on the power of government? What are these limits? Do you agree with them? Why?

_____

_____

2. Does the Declaration of Independence place limits on the rights of citizens? What are these limits? Do you agree with them? Why?

_____

_____

3. What do we call a decision by people to overthrow a government? Does the Declaration of Independence always support this decision? Why?

_____

_____

_____

Teaching Activity: Evaluating an Outcomes-based Lesson

Think it over:
What do you see as the strengths and weaknesses of this lesson plan? Why?

It's your classroom:
1. How would you change this lesson plan? Why?
2. Rewrite the lesson so you feel comfortable with it.

DOES THE "WORKSHOP MODEL" MAKE SENSE IN SECONDARY SCHOOLS?

What has come to be known as the "Workshop Model" for teaching (see http://www.tqnyc.org/NYC052376/main_new.html, accessed May 14, 2007) was originally developed as a way to promote literacy in young children. In this approach, teachers model activities for the class and confer with and assess individual students while they work cooperatively in groups and individually to master specific skills. Its leading proponent is Lucy Calkins (2003), a Professor of Education at Teachers College—Columbia University. Strengths of the model as deployed in secondary schools are that it moves the teacher away from the front of the room, minimizes direct instruction, promotes student cooperation, and requires that students analyze documents. Proponents claim that in addition to improving student skills, it successfully promotes high order thinking.

Every "Workshop Model" lesson uses the same procedure. It starts with a five-to-ten minute Mini-Lesson with the teacher leading the class through a discussion of the topic for the day. Next, the teacher models the day's task for students for approximately five minutes, showing them how to analyze a quote, map, chart, graph, or cartoon. After Teacher Modeling, students, either individually or in groups, complete similar tasks for 20–25 minutes during Work Time. While they are doing this, teachers circulate around the room conferring with and assisting students and assessing their performances. Lessons end with a 5–10 minute Closing where teachers ask questions to further assess student mastery of ideas and skills.

Many secondary school teachers that I work with who have been forced by district administrators to use this model have been very critical of it. The biggest complaints are that lessons are too tightly scripted and cannot fit into the standard secondary school time allocated for a class period. I have used the "Workshop Model" in demonstration lessons in both middle schools and high schools. While I agree it can be too rigidly applied and difficult for students to do meaningful work in short, timed, blocks, I found it compatible with the activity-based approach that I prefer. My biggest problem with the "Workshop Model" is the same as my complaint about "outcomes-based" instruction using the Hunter model. Whatever proponents claim, I find they leave too little time for questioning, discussing, and thinking about the main issues that need to be addressed in secondary school social studies classrooms.

HOW DO YOU TRANSLATE YOUR PLAN INTO PRACTICE?

I want to emphasize that lesson plans are working documents, not works of art. Once they get the hang of planning, all teachers that I know modify lesson plan formats to fit their style of teaching. Different people include different things. Student teachers from the Hofstra program have found this simplified lesson plan designed for activity-based lessons to be especially helpful.

UNIT: _____

LESSON: _____

1. What are the main ideas (maximum of 3) students need to know about this topic?

   a. _____

   b. _____

   c. _____

2. What materials (e.g., ACTIVITY SHEET, MAP, SONG) will I present?

   _____

3. What (AIM) question will I ask the class to answer?

   _____

4. What activity, if any, will I use to settle students and establish a context (DO NOW)?

   _____
   _____
   _____

5. How will I open the lesson (MOTIVATION) and capture student interest?
_____
_____

6. What activities will I use to help students discover what they need to learn?
_____
_____
_____
_____
_____

7. How will we summarize and assess student learning (KEY QUESTIONS)?
_____
_____

8. Homework.
_____
_____

9. What topics come next?
Tomorrow: _____
Day After Tomorrow: _____

Essay 1: Using "Text" and "Context" to Promote Student Literacies

Many veteran social studies teachers, especially in the high schools, insist that their job is to teach content material to students who already possess the required academic skills. However, no matter what social studies content you are teaching, your students likely also need to learn how to learn, to find and evaluate information available in different formats, think systematically, support arguments with evidence, present ideas clearly, and to evaluate their own work and the work of others so they can participate in conversations within the subject discipline. Whatever your position is on this issue, social studies teachers are increasingly being required to be full partners in promoting student literacy in its multiple forms: critical literacy, which involves thinking, understanding and acting on the world and technical literacy, which include finding, processing and using information from different media and fields of study.

Maureen Murphy and I (MacCurtain et al. 2001) conducted a multi-year project developing interdisciplinary activities, lessons, and units for teaching about the Great Irish Famine in grades 4–12. Our initial plan was to prepare separate high school

(9–12) and upper elementary/middle-level (4–8) packages. High school material would be minimally *edited*, while the middle-level package would include documents that were *adapted* for classroom use.

Through field-testing the lessons in classrooms, participating in and observing of group work, and following up discussions with students, we discovered that our distinction between the two levels did not take into account the full range of student academic performance. Many high school students were more comfortable with the *adapted* documents, while some middle-level students were capable of reading with understanding the minimally *edited* text. In addition, in both middle and high school classes, some students with a record of poor academic performance could not read either set of material. Teachers working with these students recommended that documents be completely *rewritten*. As a result of their input, the final curriculum guide offers teachers the option of using differentiated edited, adapted, and rewritten text with major language revisions, either with an entire class on any grade level or with selected students.

Teaching Activity: Irish Immigrants in New Orleans, Louisiana

Source: Powers, T. 1836. *Impressions of America during the years 1833, 1834, and 1835.* (Binder and Reimers 1988)

Edited version:
One of the greatest works now in progress here is the canal planned to connect Lac Pontchartrain with the city of New Orleans. I only wish that the wise men at home who coolly charge the present condition of Ireland upon the inherent laziness of her population, could be transported to this spot. Here they subsist on the coarsest fare; excluded from all the advantages of civilization; often at the mercy of a hard contractor, who wrings his profits from their blood; and all this for a pittance that merely enables them to exist, with little power to save, or a hope beyond the continuance of the like exertion.

Adapted text:
One of the greatest works now in progress here is a canal. I only wish that the men in England who blame the condition of Ireland on the laziness of her people could be brought to New Orleans. Here the Irish survive on poor food and are at the mercy of hard employers who profit from their blood; and all this for a low wage that only allows them to exist, with little power to save or hope.

Rewritten text with major language revisions:
A great canal is being built in Louisiana. I wish people in England who think the Irish are lazy could see how hard they are working here. Irish immigrants in New Orleans are treated badly by their employers. Their wages are low. Their food is poor quality. They have little hope.

Add your voice to the discussion:
How would you respond to the charge that teachers "water down" the curriculum and lower standards when they modify text? Explain.

While field-testing the curriculum, we also learned that the way material was presented to students was fundamental for capturing their interest and promoting learning. When teachers engaged students in activities, used references that had meaning to a particular group of students, reviewed vocabulary and provided a context for language, provided readings that were accessible, and encouraged freewheeling discussions, every group of students responded enthusiastically to the curriculum. Inner-city and suburban students, immigrants and native-born, and students from different ethnic backgrounds were all fascinated by events prior to, during, and after the Great Irish Famine.

Some of our most successful lessons about the Irish were taught in low-performing inner-city middle schools, with students who were largely African-American, Caribbean and Latino/a. The keys to these lessons were our ability to create a context for literacy and learning, as well as to provide students with appropriate text. Students sang traditional songs like "Paddy on the Railway" and "No Irish Need Apply," examined political cartoons and newspaper illustrations downloaded from the Internet, and compared the experience of the Irish with their own experiences with discrimination and inequality. In a few classes, volunteers transformed the songs into contemporary "raps."

During opening discussions, a number of students testified about their personal experiences as immigrants or discussed problems faced by their families and relatives when they arrived from other countries. In concluding discussions, students drew connections between the treatment of immigrants in the past and present as they tried to understand the Irish experience. Our experience in these classes was consistent with Maxine Greene's (1995) idea that learning is a search for "situated understanding" that places ideas and events in their social, historical, and cultural contexts.

Teachers who field-tested the curriculum modified lessons to make them more appropriate for their classes and used different teaching strategies successfully. Adeola Tella and Nichole Williams both worked with students who had academic difficulties. They each spent a significant amount of class time having students read, sing, discuss, and rewrite the traditional Irish songs. Lynda Costello-Herrara (NTN) and Rachel Thompson (NTN) focus on team projects in their classes. Their students participated in creating exhibits for a "museum" about the Great Irish Famine.

Cheryl Smith, a cooperating teacher in the Hofstra program, worked primarily with inclusion classes and emphasized differentiated group-based instruction (Tomlinson 1999). Cheryl prefers mixed-level student teams and assigned edited, adapted, or rewritten versions of documents to individual students in each group based on their reading performance. When possible, each team member examined a different aspect of the topic by using a different source. In one lesson, each team member studied conditions faced by Irish immigrants in a different North American location: New Orleans, New York, New Brunswick, Canada, and Philadelphia. Students who examined New Orleans read *edited* text. Students who studied about New York and New Brunswick, Canada read *adapted* text. Students assigned Philadelphia read *rewritten* material.

Cheryl's approach makes it possible for every student to understand the material they are working with and requires that they each provide information for their group's final report to the class. Smith is a strong proponent of teacher-prepared organizers that help student teams arrange information and necessitate contributions from every team member. The organizer for this assignment required the team to report evidence of anti-Irish stereotypes, violence against immigrants, unsafe working and living conditions, and positive experiences in each locality.

I sometimes compare learning to read with weight lifting. If your goal is to bench press 200 pounds, you start with a lower weight and build up your skill and muscles over time. If you were given a bar with 200 pounds on the first day and told to lift, you would probably just give up. Using differentiated texts offers social studies teachers a strategy to maintain student interest while helping them gradually develop literacy skills and reach higher academic standards.

Learning Activity: Text and Context

1. Sample Lesson Organizer: Ms. Smith's Team Reports on Irish Immigration

Evidence of . . .	New Orleans	New York	Philadelphia	Canada
Anti-Irish stereotypes				
Violence against the Irish				
Unsafe working conditions				
Poor living conditions				
Fair treatment of Irish immigrants				
Success by Irish immigrants				

Add your voice to the discussion:
1. In your view, will the use of differentiated text and lesson organizers facilitate inclusive instruction?
2. The song "Paddy Works on the Railway" contains a nonsense phrase, "Filly-me-oori-oori-ay," that is repeated over and over again. Many students with weaker reading skills were stymied when they tried to decipher it and gave up reading the song. When we explained that it was a nonsense phrase before asking students to read the song, we eliminated the problem.

Think it over:
1. Can you remember a situation as a student when you were stymied trying to do an assignment? What kind of help would have made it possible for you to be successful?
2. In your opinion, are teachers lowering standards when they provide this kind of help? Explain.
3. In a number of classes, students compared their own experiences as members of immigrant families with what they learned about the Irish. Many students argued that immigrants in the United States are subject to discrimination today. Some spoke about personal experiences being harassed by police or storeowners.

It's your classroom:
Would you have permitted or even have encouraged these discussions in an effort to create "context"? Explain.

Essay 2: Teaching About Presidential Elections

An earlier version of this essay appeared in Singer (2008). Used with permission.

In January 2007, a year before the primary season would begin, a year and a half before the national conventions, and almost two years before the general election, Senator Hillary Clinton of New York declared her candidacy for the Democratic Party's presidential nomination. As the first woman, and first former "First Lady," to have a serious chance of winning the nomination of a major political party and election, she was an immediate front-runner.

Senator Clinton started her presidential election bid so early because the field was already crowded with candidates. Delay would make it difficult for her to line up campaign contributions, endorsements, advisors, and campaign workers for an election campaign estimated to cost as much as 500-million dollars. In the United States in the twenty-first century, only the rich, or those supported by the rich, can afford to run for elective office.

The presidential election cycle provides teachers across the country with a highly motivating subject that focuses national media and student attention on social studies and historical topics. Teachers generally use student interest in presidential elections to examine the idea of multiple perspectives on major issues and the importance of research, analysis, and dialogue about current events and candidates. Some have their classes study obscure or confusing topics such as the Electoral College system or actively promote citizenship through voter registration drives.

While all of these focal points can have educational value, I think in the end they sell students short. Too often, students get an MTV-lite version of news coverage. Quick blips. Unsupported opinions. Lots of music. Little actual analysis of issues, voting patterns, or the role of media and money in campaigns takes place in the classroom. Candidates are viewed as celebrities and mock elections become popularity contests. Minor candidates and third party campaigns are almost always ignored. Not many students change their minds or deviate very far from the attitudes of their parents and peers.

Few teachers use the election campaigns to seriously explore with their students what is taking place in American society, and I suspect those who do continually worry that they will be accused of partisanship or even unpatriotic behavior. Teachers, like the presidential candidates, end up being pushed to the middle where they act as if uncritical acceptance of compromise represents the best ideas our society has to offer. I fear that by focusing on the superficial, teachers contribute to the attitude that politics is entertainment and help place democracy in the United States at risk.

There is much that is serious about the presidency, presidential elections, and the national political climate, much that social studies teachers should think about themselves, and much that they can incorporate into the curriculum. These include both historical and contemporary issues and some very difficult questions.

Historical Issues

1. Can a system designed for a small, lightly populated, primarily agrarian country with semi-autonomous states effectively govern a centralized, modern, military and economic superpower? Does the expanding power of the modern presidency threaten historical checks and balances between the different branches of government, checks and balances that have provided core protection for the rights of Americans?

2. Why were so many nineteenth-century presidents irrelevant, incompetent, or simply forgettable? Try this simple test. Name the presidents between Andrew Jackson (number 7) and Abraham Lincoln (number 16) and those between Lincoln and Theodore Roosevelt (number 26)? Why are they so unmemorable? The first era was one of sharp sectional division. The leading statesmen were in the Senate where crucial governmental decisions were made. Webster, Clay, and Calhoun tended to obstruct each other's national ambitions. Presidents were compromise selections with few negatives rather than strong positives. As a candidate, Abraham Lincoln fits this profile. During the second era, capitalist industrial expansion reshaped the nation and the most memorable national figures are businessmen like Rockefeller, Carnegie, Vanderbilt, and Morgan. During the "Gilded Age," presidents and the presidency hardly rated as important.

3. Should presidential indiscretions and disabilities be exposed to public view? Thomas Jefferson and Grover Cleveland fathered illegitimate children, Ulysses Grant and Warren Harding were probably alcoholics, and John F. Kennedy and Bill Clinton were compulsive philanderers. Franklin D. Roosevelt ran for reelection while terminally ill

and it is suspected that Ronald Reagan was already exhibiting signs of dementia when he was reelected. Do inquiring minds have the right to know?

4. Do we remember presidents for the wrong reasons? Andrew Jackson promoted democracy for White people at the expense of Blacks and Native Americans. Woodrow Wilson is credited with winning a war that his Secretary of State argued the United States did not have to enter. Harry Truman is remembered for tough decisions. But were his decisions to authorize the nuclear attacks on Japan, start the Cold War, and attack domestic opponents as communists justified? Should our goal be to promote patriotism or analyze history?

5. Is Lord Acton's statement that "power corrupts, absolute power corrupts absolutely" an apt description of the twentieth-century American presidency? The economy and the American people suffered because Herbert Hoover and Jimmy Carter were narrowly focused technocrats unable, or unwilling, to adjust to changing economic circumstances. Lyndon Johnson was brought down by his blind commitment to defeat "communists" in Vietnam in much the same way that the Bush presidency has been seriously weakened by its unyielding campaign against supposed "terrorists" in Iraq and Afghanistan. Richard Nixon was forced to resign when he placed himself and the presidency above the law, and Bill Clinton faced removal from office for flouting moral codes and lying about it under oath.

Contemporary Issues

1. Is the presidential election system broken? Has the selection of a president become like *American Idol* or *Survivor*? Does the primary system as it is currently constituted produce the "best" candidates? Is the "best" candidate necessarily the best president?

2. Are we electing skilled and thoughtful leaders or the best-financed celebrity package? Ronald Reagan was an actor who looked presidential, but was he? Democrats Jimmy Carter, Bill Dukakis, Bill Clinton, Al Gore, and John Kerry campaigned as experienced managers and problem solvers. But can every problem be addressed by managerial fine-tuning?

3. Who does a president actually represent? It costs $500 million to mount a campaign. Does the president speak for the people as a whole, those who voted for the candidate, party loyalists, or his or her wealthy campaign contributors?

4. Is the Imperial Presidency, what conservative theorists call the "unitary executive," a threat to constitutional checks and balances that are at the core of the American political system? Can the nation afford to rest all power to wage war in the hands of a single individual? Should one person's religious views be able to prevent scientific research or limit access to birth control and sex education? Is the election of a "dictator" for a limited term of office the best way to preserve liberty and promote freedom?

5. How much ability to shape the national agenda does a president actually have? Are they agents of history or prisoners of powerful interest groups?

6. Are American voters, especially White male voters, trapped by their racial and ethnic bigotry? Does this leave a significant block of voters easily exploited by demagogues? Since the Civil Rights movement of the 1950s and 1960s granted greater equality to African-Americans, White male voters have increasingly voted as a block for Republican and conservative candidates.

7. Why do people with little chance of winning run for president? It seems as if every politician thinks they are three elections away from the presidency (win a local and then a statewide election and you are ready to rumble). Does the system promote reason and experience or put a premium on arrogance and a gambling mentality? Does it encourage nasty attacks in an effort to bring down campaign leaders and to cut off other potential rivals? Is the system bringing out the best of the American people, or the worst?

8. Why do some presidential elections mark major shifts in the national balance of power while others represent modest corrections brought about by reactions to excessive practices? The elections of 1828 (Andrew Jackson), 1860 (Abraham Lincoln), 1932 (Franklin Roosevelt), and 1968 (Richard Nixon) brought new coalitions to power along with new presidents. However, the elections of 1840 (Harrison), 1884 (Cleveland), 1912 (Wilson), 1952 (Eisenhower) and 1976 (Carter) did not reverse national political trends.

This last question is particularly important for the organization of a social studies-based United States history curriculum. Elections that signaled major shifts in political alignment also marked significant changes in economic and political relations within the country. Jackson's election was the result of both a broad extension of the franchise to less affluent White male farmers and urban residents and of the expansion of the country westward. Lincoln was elected when the Democratic Party divided along regional lines over the future of slavery. The ascendancy of the new Republican Party also was a response to an expanding role for the federal government in an industrializing nation. When the Republican Party failed to respond to economic crisis during the Great Depression, the Democrats, behind a New Deal philosophy championing activist government, were swept into power. This shift was made possible by a new national demographic as Eastern and Southern European immigrants and their children were increasingly eligible to vote and by the emergence of a powerful organized labor movement as a political force. Increasing conservative and Republican Party dominance in local and national politics since 1968 has paralleled the decline in labor union membership and influence as a global economy has shifted skilled industrial jobs overseas. Between 1983 and 2006, union membership declined from 20 percent of the workforce to 12 percent, undermining the Democratic Party's voter base and its financial backing. While political controversy during this recent period has often been attributed to cultural differences and questions of values, it has certainly been intensified by economic competition between different racial and ethnic blocks and between men and women as working people have been affected by economic change.

As teachers, there are many standard and effective classroom practices we can use to take advantage of student interest generated by presidential elections. Have students study national maps and chart poll numbers and election results. Organize a class blog. Design campaign posters, slogans, and songs. Collect current events articles, write position papers, interview local candidates and the representatives of national candidates.

But students also need to dig deeper, to question national assumptions, and their own beliefs, about the nature of the electoral system and the qualities of the candidates.

Essay 3: What are the Lessons of 9/11?

An earlier version of this essay appeared in Singer (2007). Used with permission.

In a series of speeches leading up to the 5th anniversary of 9/11/2001, President George W. Bush told audiences "I approach tomorrow with a heavy heart." He vowed, "I'm never going to forget the lessons of that day." In a televised address, President Bush declared, "on 9/11, our nation saw the face of evil" and that "the lessons of that day are clear." I am not so sure.

What exactly are the lessons of 9/11 and how should teachers help their students understand them? I have spoken and written about the events of 9/11 and the United States response previously, but I have done so cautiously, perhaps too cautiously. My concern was that a grieving nation needed time to heal before it could hear sharply dissenting voices. But politicians from both the Republican and Democratic parties continue to play on fear to manipulate the American people. As a result, the healing process has been stymied and the body politic is seriously infected.

I believe that as teachers and educated citizens in a democratic society, we have an obligation to critically examine President Bush's claims about the lessons of 9/11 and to engage our colleagues and students in broad, difficult, and potentially controversial discussions. Anything less is an abdication of our professional responsibility. There is no safety in playing it safe.

Our task is made harder, as Frank Rich points out in a recent book, by media that report official distortions and outright lies as reasonable parts of "balanced" coverage. It is made harder by former government officials such as Colin Powell, who refuse to publicly challenge failed policies, and politically ambitious opposition leaders such as Hillary Clinton, who criticize without posing alternatives. It has been made harder, in the words of Morris Berman, author of *Dark Ages America*, as "9/11 has entered our national mythology as a day in which the United States, a decent and well-meaning nation, was attacked by crazed fanatics hell-bent on destroying its way of life." And it is made harder by the self-censorship of teachers who are afraid of parental and administrative retribution if they express their views as part of an open classroom dialogue with their students.

Rarely do I quote former President Ronald Reagan favorably. But on June 8, 1982, he told the British House of Commons "If history teaches anything, it teaches self-delusion in the face of unpleasant facts is folly." Silent complicity with the Bush Administration's "self-delusion" is folly. It places our students, families and country, and perhaps even the world, in jeopardy. We need to ask some very difficult questions of our leaders and to demand answers that are supported by evidence and reason.

Based on my reading of President Bush's speech, he claims there are seven lessons to be learned from 9/11 (the full text is available on-line at: http://www.whitehouse.gov, accessed May 14, 2007).

1. The "nineteen men" who attacked the United States did so with "a barbarity unequaled" in the history of this country and "made war upon the entire free world." Their actions have forced the United States and its allies to take "the offensive in a war unlike any we have fought before."

Nineteen men attacked the World Trade Center and the Pentagon, and hijacked flight 93, which crashed in Pennsylvania. These 19 men killed about 3,000 people, caused billions of dollars in damage and terrified a nation. They terrified my family. But it was the work of 19 men, all of whom are dead. Declaring this as an act of unequaled "barbarity," a "war upon the entire free world," and an "offensive in a war unlike any we have fought before" blows it out of all proportion and is being used to justify unconscionable responses.

Do the events of 9/11 compare with the European holocaust and the extermination of six million Jews, the nuclear destruction of Hiroshima and Nagasaki, slavery and the trans-Atlantic slave trade, nineteenth-century genocidal policies against native Americans, or even Klan terrorism against African-Americans?

Do the events of 9/11 justify the destruction of Afghanistan and Iraq, and United States support for the Israeli bombardment of Lebanon, actions in the "war on terror" that have slaughtered tens of thousands of innocent civilians and created chaotic conditions that are breeding grounds for new recruits?

One of the supposed "lessons" of 9/11 is that the "nineteen men" attacked "civilian targets" without any regard for human lives. First, that is the nature of modern war. Civilians were not evacuated before the United States bombed Dresden, Tokyo, Hanoi, or Baghdad. In these cases the death of civilians was dismissed as "collateral damage," unfortunate but necessary for victory. Second, Americans need to recognize that these were not random targets. The Pentagon is the hub of American global military might. The Trade Center was the symbol of American economic domination of the world. Civilians died in these attacks, but again, that is the nature of modern war.

2. The enemy "is a global network of extremists who are driven by a perverted vision of Islam." They are "evil and kill without mercy—but not without purpose." They embrace "a totalitarian ideology that hates freedom, rejects tolerance, and despises all dissent." The battle against them is "the decisive ideological struggle of the twenty-first century, and the calling of our generation."

With this statement President Bush places the "nineteen men" within a larger "evil" conspiracy—Al Qaeda—that is led by the arch-villain Osama bin Laden. It is a conspiracy that embraces a totalitarian ideology, a "perverted vision of Islam," that allows them to "kill without mercy."

I do not, under any circumstances, defend bin Laden, Al Qaeda, or any religious fanatics who make war on non-believers—and that includes George W. Bush. But the question that plagues me, and should plague everyone, is why did bin Laden switch sides and go from being a CIA operative in the US war against the Soviet Union to an avowed enemy of the United States?

The key is the first Gulf War. As a religious Muslim, bin Laden cannot accept that United States troops occupy bases in Saudi Arabia. In fact, they still do 15 years later. This is a violation of basic Islamic beliefs that is tolerated by a dictatorial monarchy dependent on the United States military to remain in power. Bin Laden did not declare war on civilization. He declared war on the nation whose troops occupy the Islamic homeland.

According to a Rand Institute publication, "(t)he Islamic world feels itself under siege from the West in numerous vital political, military, cultural, social, and economic realms. This feeling of siege has several sources: the perception of victimization and Western onslaught based on historical and psychological grounds . . . ; 'objective' internal pressures generated by the process of modernization and related social and economic tensions . . . ; and conscious, direct pressure from the West in the policy arena" (Fuller and Lesser 1995: 81). Instead of President Bush dismissing opponents as "evil," the American people would be better served if the United States addressed some of these issues.

A foreign policy based on distortion places this country and the world in grave danger. During the Israeli bombardment of Lebanon in the summer of 2006, Americans were told that this was another front in the "war on terror" and that Israel was targeting Hezbollah, a radical organization that was occupying and victimizing Lebanon. To the surprise of everyone who listened to these propaganda assessments, Hezbollah turned out to have strong support among the Lebanese people. In September 2006, over 100,000 protestors attended a mass rally in Beirut in support of the group. Many had walked for days because the Israeli bombardment virtually destroyed the nation's transportation infrastructure.

3. It is a ruthless enemy, which if it had "weapons of mass destruction," would not hesitate to use them against us. Because of this, the United States cannot "distinguish between the terrorists and those who harbor or support them."

So far in world history, the United States remains the only country to use weapons of mass destruction and it continues to export dangerous weapon's technology to favored allies, including the unstable military dictatorship that rules Pakistan and possesses nuclear weapons. In fiscal year 2005–2006, in the midst of the so-called "war on terror," foreign sales by US arms makers doubled. Contracts were signed for a total of $21 billion in weapons, including a $5 billion order made by Pakistan for sophisticated F-16 jets. India and Indonesia, which were once barred from purchasing US weapons, were allowed to place large orders.

Meanwhile, President Bush has continually articulated a doctrine of pre-emptive attack that has no precedent in United States history. Essentially, any country that could potentially become a threat in the future is subject to attack now. It is a doctrine that places the entire world at risk, threatens global chaos, and establishes an impossible standard for deciding which nations harbor terrorists and are therefore justifiable targets. In the 1960s, the United States harbored paramilitary units that tried to assassinate Premier Fidel Castro of Cuba. In the 1980s, it supported death squads operating in Nicaragua and El Salvador and it armed Saddam Hussein in his war against Iran. It has imprisoned and tortured prisoners from the Iraqi war in violation of the Geneva Convention. During the recent Israeli bombardment of civilian targets in Lebanon, the United States supplied the Israeli air force with missiles in the middle of the war while the rest of the world was pushing for a cease-fire.

Do these policies make the US a terrorist state subject to regime change? Is it any wonder that the Bush administration has blocked an international effort to establish a world tribunal to investigate war crimes?

4. "America must confront threats before they reach our shores, whether those threats come from terrorist networks or terrorist states." This is the justification for the United States attack on Iraq, a nation that had nothing to do with the events of 9/11. According to President Bush, "the world is safer because Saddam Hussein is no longer in power."

However, it is not true that "the world is safer because Saddam Hussein is no longer in power." According to a classified assessment issued by American intelligence agencies and reported in *The New York Times* on September 24, 2006, the overthrow of Saddam Hussein and the occupation of Iraq has "helped spawn a new generation of Islamic radicalism." It has led to civil war in Iraq, destabilized the entire Middle East, and increased the overall threat of terrorist activities. The report, which is the most authoritative document that United States intelligence agencies prepared on the topic, and which was approved by the Director of National Intelligence, asserts that rather than retreating in the face of US military power, Islamic radicalism has "metastasized and spread across the globe."

The invasion of Iraq and the ensuing occupation has also led to the isolation of the United States from most of its former allies, the use of the American army as a police force, a role for which it is ill-prepared, and the dangerous over-stretching of American military power. The war in Iraq has been a recruiting magnet for groups opposed to the US role in the world and has demonstrated that a relatively small insurrectionary force can subvert a US military occupation for years. No matter what President Bush might say or believe, an occupying army is rarely, if ever, treated as a liberation force, and generally promotes coalitions among disparate and previously warring factions.

Part of the problem is that the Bush Administration has ignored standard military procedure because of its ideological blinders. In 1995, the US Army War College published a Rand Corporation study on "Force Requirements in Stability Operations" (Krugman 2006: A19). The study projected the size of an occupying army necessary to defeat insurgent forces in a country such as Iraq. Based on British experiences in Northern Ireland and Malaya, the authors estimated that the United States would need 20 troops per 1,000 inhabitants or, in the case of Iraq, 500,000 soldiers, three times the number of troops assigned to the operation.

Perhaps even more dangerous than the actual invasion is the idea that, for the United States, the ends justify the means. Since the end is protection of our own "shores" from attack, any overseas military action is acceptable. This is dangerous for two reasons. It demonstrates to the rest of the world that the United States, rather than standing for principle, is an imperial power intent on protecting its own interests without regard to the consequences. It excuses the inexcusable, the violation of human rights around the world, because it might, in the end, protect the United States. It also establishes that any other country that feels threatened has the same right to invade another country. This was the same justification used by Nazi Germany during World War II.

5. The "war on terrorism" is a war without gray areas and a war without a foreseeable end. Any hesitation or internal disagreement emboldens the terrorists and fuels their "extremist movement." President Bush believes that "We are now in the early hours of this struggle between tyranny and freedom" and he "committed America's influence in the world to advancing freedom and democracy as the great alternatives to repression and radicalism."

President Bush believes that it is possible to export freedom and democracy to other countries based on very weak historical arguments. His major evidence is Japan, which was a one-party state for years following World War II, and Korea and Taiwan, which may be democracies now, but were military dictatorships for decades. Bush's position even ignores the history of the United States, which was a slave-holding nation for "four score and seven years" until it was torn apart by a violent civil war.

President Bush prides himself on his conservative credentials and commitment to national security. During the 2006 campaign for control over the House of Representatives and the Senate, Bush and fellow Republicans argued that the Democrats would be ineffective in defending the nation from terrorist attack because they lacked the Republican Party's will to act and the commitment to America's democratic values.

However, in an unprecedented action by United States military newspapers, an editorial in the *Military Times* (as well as editorials in newspapers representing the different branches of the armed services), charged that the nation's leaders, President Bush, Vice President Cheney, and Defense Secretary Rumsfeld, were keeping the "truth about the Iraq war" from the American people. They joined top-level active duty military personnel in expressing misgivings about the war and called for the resignation of Secretary Rumsfeld, who "has lost credibility with the uniformed leadership, with the troops, with Congress and with the public at large" (*Army Times* 2006). Their actions played a major role in Rumsfeld's removal from office.

There are serious reasons to question what President Bush actually means by both conservatism and American values. The international "Coalition

of the Willing," assembled to fight the war in Iraq, includes some of the world's most corrupt and dictatorial regimes. Among the important US partners in the "war on terrorism" are Pakistan and Kazakhstan, placed by highly regarded Transparency International at the bottom of the barrel for honesty and good government. Access to American weapons has secured the support of Tajikistan, Serbia, Armenia, and Azerbaijan. The Saudi monarchy, one of the world's most anti-democratic regimes, was allowed to purchase $5.8 billion in weapons from US companies in 2005–2006, including a $3 billion order for Black Hawk helicopters. Black Hawks are also being sold to such "bastions" of democracy as Bahrain, Jordan, and the United Arab Emirates.

Fritz Stern, a prominent historian who specializes in the study of the Nazi rise to power, argued that in the wake of 9/11, the Bush Administration had broken with the nation's long-standing foreign and domestic policies. He charged that its actions demonstrated chaotic recklessness and subverted Constitutional principles. Rather than leadership committed to traditional conservative ideals, it was a government dominated by radical right-wingers.

6. "This struggle has been called a clash of civilizations. In truth, it is a struggle for civilization ... Winning this war will require the determined efforts of a unified country, and we must put aside our differences and work together to meet the test that history has given us."

The message here is that dissent is unpatriotic. Many critics of administration policies are concerned that the President is promoting an either/or mentality—you either support his policies without question or you are aiding a subtle and shifting enemy engaged in a war without end on the United States. If this view is accepted, domestic dissidents, like myself, become dangerous enemy agents and are subject to the suspension of constitutionally protected civil rights. There are precedents for this in Presidential decrees issued during the American Civil War and World War II.

7. God, "a loving God who made us to be free," is on the side of the United States and the West in this war.

This is simply pandering to a religious audience. Osama bin Laden in his speeches makes the same unverifiable claim as George Bush—God is on his side. This claim has been repeatedly made by combatants throughout recorded history to justify bloodthirsty slaughter. I am an atheist, so I am skeptical about any assertion of divine support.

Nevertheless, I am convinced that God, if there is a God, would not take side in wars.

There are people who would dismiss my opinions as either the arguments of a disaffected Democrat or a radical. I do not consider myself a Democrat and have had a series of public confrontations with Senator Charles Schumer, chairman of the Democratic Senatorial Campaign Committee. On the other hand, I do consider myself a radical, albeit one who is committed to reasoned discourse and taking positions based on evidence. The United States needs a real and open discussion about the lessons of 9/11 and a number of non-radicals have endorsed positions similar to mine. The most prominent is probably former US Marine Corps General Tony Zanni, who commanded US forces in Iraq. In *The Battle for Peace* (written with Tony Klotz, Macmillan 2006), Zanni argues that the attack against the United States on 9/11/01 was a logical outcome of the collapse of the Soviet Union, the end of the Cold War, and the emergence of a "uni-power" global system. This uni-power system replaced "manageable, super-power imposed stability . . . and nothing took its place. We expected a new world order of peace and prosperity to bless the Earth. We could not have been more wrong" (pp. 44–46). Instead of combating vast ideological conspiracies in a supposed war between civilizations, Zanni argues that the United States should pursue reasonable, narrow, military objectives, including reestablishing the local balance of power in international hot spots.

A major critic of the Bush foreign policy who has not received much mainstream attention is Chalmers Johnson, an expert on US-Japanese relations and author of *Blowback: The Costs and Consequences of American Empire* (2001) and *Sorrows of Empire: Militarism, Secrecy, and the End of the Republic* (2004a). His main theses are that many of the attacks by "terrorist" groups are a direct response to previous United States actions and that the situation has gotten worse since President Bush declared war on terrorism. According to Johnson, "between 1993 and 2001, including 9/11, al Qaeda managed to carry out five major bombings internationally. In the three years since 9/11, down to and including the attacks in Riyadh, the suicide bombings in Istanbul, the bombings of the commuter railroads in Madrid, they have carried out well over 20." Johnson believes that there is "something absurd and inherently false about one country trying to impose its system of government or its economic institutions on another. Such an enterprise amounts to a dictionary definition of imperialism." One result of American policy is that "the entire Islamic world are now passive supporters of al Qaeda" (Johnson 2004b).

Other "non-radical" commentators have been similarly critical of the Bush Administration response to 9/11. William J. Dobson, in an essay in *Foreign Policy* (2006), described September 11, 2001 as "the day nothing much changed."

In an op-ed piece in *The New York Times*, Joseph J. Ellis (2007: 17), a professor of history at Mount Holyoke College and the author of *His Excellency: George Washington*, raised two questions about the attacks on 9/11 in an attempt to evaluate the historical significance they have achieved. Where does Sept. 11 rank in the grand sweep of American history as a threat to national security? What does history tell us about our earlier responses to traumatic events? Ellis concludes that 9/11 does not make the top tier of the list of events which posed a serious challenge to the survival of the American republic and that in retrospect, none of the domestic responses to perceived national security threats in the past looks justifiable. "Every history textbook I know describes them as lamentable, excessive, even embarrassing."

A major thrust in social studies education is the evaluation, by students, of primary source documents in order to piece together an historical narrative, analyze claims about events, and formulate informed judgments about the past. These same approaches must be applied to understanding the present. And just as effective social studies teachers engage in discussion with students about the implications of Washington's Farewell Address, Monroe's Doctrine, Roosevelt's Corollary, the post-World War II Truman Plan, and Reagan's Evil Empire speech during the Cold War, we must participate in the discussion and evaluation of the Bush Doctrine and his administration's "War on Terror."

Dissent from government positions, even popular positions, has played an important role in American history. As a United States citizen I am proud to stand with Abraham Lincoln, who in 1847 risked his political career by defying a President who misled the American people in order to launch an imperialist venture against a neighboring country. I stand with Congressional Representative Jeannette Rankin and Secretary of State William Jennings Bryan who resisted pressure to support World War I and US involvement in a "commercial war." I stand with Senator Wayne Morse who denounced the Gulf of Tonkin Resolution and warned "that within the next century, future generations will look with dismay and great disappointment upon a Congress which is now about to make such a historic mistake." I stand with Congressional Representative Barbara Lee, who cast the only dissenting vote on September 14, 2001. Lee begged her colleagues not to rush to judgment, arguing, "Far too many innocent people have already died. Our country is in mourning. If we rush to launch a counter-attack, we run too great a risk that women, children, and other non-combatants will be caught in the crossfire. Nor can we let our justified anger over these outrageous acts by vicious murderers inflame prejudice against all Arab Americans, Muslims, Southeast Asians, or any other people because of their race, religion, or ethnicity."

We are fast entering the 2008 Presidential campaign. I believe the United States government, candidates for public office, and the American people must concern themselves with a global economic system that has produced gross international inequalities. It is a system, maintained by United States military power that permits one nation, with a mere 5 percent of the world's people, to consume 35 percent of its resources. It is the same system that consigns millions of people to the refugee camps, battered cities and desiccated villages and fields of the Middle East, and produces waves of young people with little hope of advancement and very little to lose.

As a historian, teacher, and citizen, I am not neutral on pressing political issues. I believe in teaching for democracy, social justice, and a world where people can live in peace. This requires teaching students to critically examine claims made by public officials as well as views espoused by their teachers. I welcome all of you, no matter what your views are, to join me in discussion. If the demand that students learn to think for themselves somehow constitutes an imposition on them, I plead guilty.

References and Recommendations for Further Reading

Army Times. 2006. Editorial. November 6. "Time for Rumsfeld to go," *Army Times.* http://www.truthout.org/cgi-bin/artman/exec/view.cgi/66/23614, accessed December 29, 2007.

Berg, C. and Clough, M. 1990/1991. Hunter lesson design: The wrong one for science teaching, *Educational Leadership,* 48(4): 73–8.

Binder, F. and Reimers, D. 1988. *The way we lived, essays and documents in American social history,* vol. I. Lexington, MA: D. C. Heath.

Calkins, L. and Colleagues from the Teachers College Reading and Writing Project. 2003. *Units of study for primary writing: A yearlong curriculum (grades K-2).* Portsmouth, NH: Firsthand.

Carr, E. H. 1961. *What is history?* New York: Vintage.

Clinchy, B. 1995. "Goals 2000: The student as object," *Phi Delta Kappan,* 76(5): 383–4, 389–92.

Dobkin, W., Fischer, J., Ludwig, B. and Koblinger, R. 1985. *A handbook for the teaching of social studies.* Boston, MA: Allyn & Bacon.

Dobson, W. 2006. "The day nothing much changed," *Foreign Policy* 156: 22–5.

Ellis, J. 2007. "Finding a place for 9/11 in American history," *The New York Times,* January 28.

Fuller, G. and Lesser, I. 1995. *A sense of siege: The geopolitics of Islam and the west.* Boulder, CO: Westview Press.

Greene, M. 1995. *Releasing the imagination, essays on education, the arts, and social change.* San Francisco: Jossey-Bass.

Hunter, M. 1982. *Mastery teaching.* El Segundo, CA: TIP Publications.

Johnson, C. 2001. *Blowback: The costs and consequences of American empire.* New York: Owl Books.

Johnson, C. 2004a. *Sorrows of empire: Militarism, secrecy, and the end of the republic.* New York: Metropolitan Books.

Johnson, C. 2004b. "Evolving empire: Chalmers Johnson on Bush's major troop realignment," *Democracy Now!* http://www.democracynow.org/article.pl?sid=04/08/17/1354236, accessed May 14, 2007.

Krugman, P. 2006. "The arithmetic of failure," *The New York Times,* October 27.

MacCurtain, M., Murphy, M. Singer, A., et al. 2001. "Text and context: Field-testing the NYS Great Irish Famine curriculum," *Theory and Research in Social Education* 29(2): 238–60.

Singer, A. 1995. "Challenging gender bias through a transformative high School social studies curriculum," *Theory and research in social education* 33(3): 234–59.

Singer, A. 1997. "Forum on teaching: Divisions real and imagined," *OAH Newsletter* 25(3): 3.

Singer, A. 2007. "What are the lessons of 9/11?," *Social Science Docket,* 7(2): 4–8.

Singer, A. 2008. "Making sense of presidential elections," *Social Science Docket* 8(1): 4–6.

Tomlinson, C. 1999. *The differentiated classroom.* Alexandria, VA: ASCD.

Wiggins, G. and McTighe, D. 2005. *Understanding by design.* 2nd ed. Alexandria, VA: ASCD.

Wilentz, S. 1997. "The past is not process," *The New York Times,* April 20, 4.15.

Wolfe, P. 1987. "What the "Seven-Step Lesson Plan" isn't," *Educational Leadership* 44(5): 70–1.

Zanni, T. and T. Klotz. 2006. *The battle for peace.* New York: Macmillan.

9. What Are the Building Blocks of an Activity-based Lesson?

Overview

- Explore an activity-based approach to lesson planning
- Examine parts of an activity-based lesson
- Design document activity sheets
- Compare different questioning strategies
- Develop classroom strategies for involving all students

Key Concepts

Activity, Document, Document-based Instruction, Motivation, Transition, Questioning, Applications, Lesson Organizers, Cooperative Learning

Questions

- How can Lessons Actively Involve Students in Learning?
- What is Document-based Instruction?
- How do Teachers Organize a Social Studies Activity?
- How do Teachers Open an Activity-Based Lesson?
- Are there Perfect Questions?
- How can Teachers Reinforce Student Understanding?
- Are Activities always Appropriate?

Essays

1. Which Document Do You Choose?
2. Cooperative Learning in Social Studies Classrooms
3. Founders Discuss the Reasons for a New Constitution

HOW CAN LESSONS ACTIVELY INVOLVE STUDENTS IN LEARNING?

People in our society adopt a wide range of styles in the ways that they dress, work, and live their lives. Their styles suit their personalities, talents, preferences, and experiences. Teachers are no different. Some prefer and consider themselves more effective using one style or method of teaching, some prefer others, and some experiment with different approaches. Early in my teaching career, my lessons tended to be teacher-centered largely because I was unsure of myself and afraid of what would happen if students experienced freedom in the classroom. Whether I was struggling with students to get them to complete a particular assignment or was entertaining them in an attempt to draw them into lessons, I tried to hold the classroom reins tightly in my hands. It was not until I became more confident of my own knowledge of social studies and in my ability as a teacher that I was comfortable organizing a classroom where students actively participated as historians and social scientists, and were allowed to make choices about what and how they would learn.

Although I am an advocate of student-centered, activity-based, lessons, I do not believe there is only one way to teach a social studies lesson, or that it is desirable to always teach the same way. A strength of the activity-based approach is that the types of activities are very different. They include analyzing primary source documents, discussions, graphing and mapping, singing and dancing, dramatics, or creating cartoons, posters, and poems. What the activities have in common is that they all involve students in learning by doing. Variety in instructional methods helps keep students interested, and flexibility in lesson design allows teachers to take into account the dynamic of a particular class.

Classroom Activity: Dancing Social Studies

As part of global history, I involve students in learning international folk dances. Although I know the steps, I am not much of a dancer or dance teacher. The activity has been most successful when we jigsaw. I teach the dances to a small group of volunteers (between 3 to 5 students) during free periods, and then they teach the dances to the rest of the class. I have a small repertoire of dances from different cultures and time periods that I use to teach different social studies concepts. While dancing, the class discusses the dances, their similarities and differences, and the roles that dance and the arts play in different cultures.

1. *Pata Pata* is a dance from South Africa that was part of the anti-apartheid movement. It blends traditional African dance steps with contemporary music. It is an example of art as a form of social protest.
2. *Tanko Bushi* is a nineteenth-century Japanese pantomime dance with precise stylized movements. In this dance, the dancers reenact the work of pre-industrial women coal miners.
3. *Alunelul* is a Romanian harvest celebration dance. It is a vigorous dance with a lot of stomping because the dancers are symbolically breaking open the shells of hazelnuts. Young men and women dance in separate lines demonstrating their physical fitness in an effort to attract prospective mates.
4. *Tininkling* is a dance from the Philippines where dancers step between sticks and act out efforts to capture a bird. It is an example of the blended Asian and European culture of the archipelago.
5. *Mayeem* is an Israeli dance that originated on collective farms called *kibbutzim* and represents a hopeful call for rain. It is an example of efforts to create new cultural symbols after Israel became an independent nation in the 1940s.
6. *Misilou* is a Macedonian and Greek dance that celebrates resistance against oppressors. The legend behind the dance is that in ancient times Macedonian women danced to their deaths over a cliff rather than surrender to conquerors. During the 1940s, the dance symbolized Greek resistance to Nazi forces that occupied their country.

Instructions for Alunelul, Mayeem, and Misilou are available at: http://www.recfd.com/folknote.htm. Instructions for Tininkling and Pata Pata are available at: http://www.edb.utexas.edu/coe/depts/kin/Faculty/slacks/crpac/folkdances/. Instructions for Tanko Bushi are available at: http://www.daytonfolkdance.com/mvfd/instructions/tankobushi.html (These sites were last accessed November 5, 2007).

It's your classroom:
How could you use dance or other art forms to teach social studies concepts about culture?

Add your voice to the discussion:
Is it worth the investment of time to involve secondary school students in this kind of activity in social studies classes? Why?

Acknowledging that competent teachers can have different teaching styles does not mean that all teaching is equally effective for every grade level and for achieving every classroom goal. Advocates of direct instruction (e.g., lecturing, "chalk and talk"—the teacher says something and then writes it on the board) claim that students in their classrooms learn because the classrooms are well structured and students remain focused. Students are told what they need to know, drilled to impress it on their memories, required to copy from the board, tested, and either punished or rewarded based on their scores.

I am suspicious about what students actually learn in this kind of classroom. If John Dewey is correct, and experience is the most significant teacher, then, whatever the content presented in these classes, the primary lessons students learn are related to values and behavior. Students learn to be passive, to submit to authority without questioning, to blend in, to remain silent and hidden, to memorize enough data so they can pass a test, to avoid the consequences of a poor grade, and that people should compete rather than work together. They learn that some people's ideas are not valued and that, although teachers have the right to choose a teaching style that suits them, there is no room for individual difference in student learning styles.

Direct instruction classrooms run counter to the kind of classrooms and effective teaching described by people like Dewey, Paulo Freire, Maxine Greene, and James Banks. I think this is the case in any secondary school subject, but especially for social studies, where our expressed goals include developing active citizens and critical thinkers prepared to offer leadership in a democratic society.

Sometimes preservice teachers ask, "Is it ever okay to lecture?" They are talking about lessons dominated by extended presentations of information or long, detailed answers to student questions. For middle school social studies classes, my answer is always "no." When teachers do this, they only lose the students.

In high school, I think that this kind of "teacher talk" should be avoided. At best, it is a last resort, when a teacher is unable to find a way to involve students in examining materials and questions. I do not mean that a teacher is not allowed to express any ideas or answer a question. Rather, I am suggesting that, instead of launching into long extemporaneous monologues, we need to find materials that make it possible for students to participate in our lessons.

Formal lectures—the kind we associate with college classes, where a teacher thinks out loud about an idea while students are jotting down their reactions and questions—can be consistent with an activity-based approach. High school students need to be able to gather, organize, and evaluate information that is presented in a number of forms. When a teacher has a clear skills goal for students, an engaging manner, an interesting topic, and uses the technique judiciously, formal lecturing can be an effective approach.

Michael Pezone (NTN) and I organized a series of short lectures of about 20 minutes each for students in his inner-city high school who wanted to experience a college-style classroom. Prior to the lectures, students were given a list of the main themes that were going to be introduced and spent a class period examining the primary source documents that would be referred to in the presentation. During the lecture they took notes and then they met in small groups to discuss their understanding of the material and their questions. This was followed by a full class discussion. For homework, they were assigned a 500-word, two-page essay answering a question posed during the lecture. These essays were presented in class and discussed the next day.

This chapter focuses on the building blocks of activity-based lessons—lessons that involve students as historians and social scientists who learn social studies content and skills as they examine documents and are engaged in activities. It looks at ideas and strategies for stimulating students' interest, expanding their ability to understand the world, encouraging them to think and ask questions, and making it possible for them to draw connections between different disciplines, the past and present, and the academic world and their own experiences. This chapter also includes strategies for dealing with heterogeneous ability groups.

WHAT IS DOCUMENT-BASED INSTRUCTION?

The most common activity in a social studies classroom is probably document analysis. Recently there has been a big push in a number of states for document-based assessment (see Chapter 10), but I prefer to talk about document-based instruction. Document-based instruction gives students the opportunity to act as historians and social scientists and draw their own conclusions. It also helps enhance analytic and literacy skills. Many textbook companies and social studies organizations now publish original, edited, and modified versions of primary source material organized on ready-to-use activity sheets. Some of this material can be downloaded directly from the Internet (see Chapter 13).

I define the term "document" very broadly to include both written sources and non-written artifacts, pictures, and photographs that can be used to understand or tell a story. In the Pacific Northwest, pre-literate societies created totem poles whose symbols described the history of their tribes and clans. In the American Southwest, the Navaho people use sand paintings to explain their religious beliefs. In medieval Europe, stained glass windows performed a similar function. The totem poles, sand paintings, and stained glass are all "documents" that students can "read" to learn about these people.

Ideally our goal as social studies teachers is to prepare students to "read" historical documents in their original or unedited form. But this is a goal, and students need to develop their skills working with material that takes into account their level of interest and performance. I would also like students to be able to pick up a document and analyze it on their own, but until they develop this ability, I provide questions that guide them and help them discover key information and patterns.

Teaching Activity: Reading a Photograph

Try it yourself:
This photograph (Figure 9.1) is from a 1999 trip to the Irish countryside. Read the photograph. Describe what you see. What story does it tell about life in rural Ireland today?

Figure 9.1 Irish countryside (1999).

It's your classroom:
What questions could you ask students about the photograph?

Teaching Activity: Constructing a Document-based Activity Sheet

1. Define a broad question that the lesson examines. The documents provided in the lesson should make it possible for students to answer the question.
2. Select a photograph, graph, political cartoon, chart, song or quote, or a series or mixture of photographs, graphs, political cartoons, charts, songs and quotes appropriate to the reading and interest level of your students. Analysis of the documents should make it possible for students to draw broader conclusions about a person, event or era.

3. Provide students with directions so they know what you want them to do.
4. Provide either three or four guiding questions to assist in analysis of the document. One or two questions should be on the content of the document (WHAT, WHERE, WHO, DESCRIBE or IDENTIFY). This directs student attention to key information. These are followed by a conclusion (WHY or HOW) and an opinion question. The conclusion question asks students to draw a connection (Why is something happening?) between different information provided in the document or between information in the document and what they already know about the person, events, or era. The opinion question asks students to evaluate the importance of what they have learned for understanding the broader historical context.

Grade/subject:
High School-level United States History

Aim question:
What was the impact of the Transportation Revolution on the new nation?

Directions:
Work in pairs. Examine the chart (Table 9.1) and answer questions 1–4.

Table 9.1 Impact of the Erie Canal on central New York cities, population and (national rank), 1810–1840

City	1810	1820	1830	1840
Albany	10,762 (10)	12,630 (11)	24, 209 (9)	33,721 (9)
Buffalo	—	—	8,668 (28)	18,213 (22)
Rochester	—	—	9,207 (25)	20,191 (19)
Troy	—	5,264 (35)	11,556 (19)	19,334 (21)
Syracuse	—	—	—	—
Utica	—	—	8,323 (29)	12,782 (29)

Source: Campbell Gibson. 1998. *Population of the 100 largest cities and other urban places in the United States: 1790 to 1990.* Washington, DC: US Bureau of the Census.

Questions
1. What is the population of Buffalo in 1830?
2. What is the national ranking of Rochester in 1840?
3. How did the Erie Canal affect this region of New York State?
4. In your opinion, what other changes would you expect to find in this part of the country? Why?

HOW DO TEACHERS ORGANIZE SOCIAL STUDIES ACTIVITIES?

ACTIVITIES

The ways that students will learn the goals and objectives of a lesson. Activities include document analysis, mapping, cartooning, singing, writing, reading, dramatic presentations, research, and creating projects. Instructional methods include class discussion, group work, cooperative learning, teacher and student presentations/demonstrations, and coaching work teams.

This is the part of planning I like the most—finding the quote, picture, chart, or cartoon that opens everything up for the students. It can also be frustrating when you cannot find what you want, or when none of the students understand or are interested in your "perfect" illustration. To protect myself from ill-founded assumptions about what will work in class, I usually plan three or four activities for a 40-minute period. If all goes well, the class may only look at one or two of them. But just in case, I always have other materials and activities available.

For example, analyzing the song *Talking Union* (Seeger and Reiser 1986) is a way to promote class discussion of why workers organized unions in the past and the role of unions in today's US economy. The song gives students some information about why workers organize labor unions. In the discussion, students can supplement this with information they learned from other readings, charts and graphs, current events articles, or discussions with union members or employers. When using a song in class, I usually give students a copy of the lyrics to read and also play it for them (a selection from the song is available at: http://www.last.fm/music/Pete+Seeger/_/ Talking+Union, accessed November 5, 2007). When I really feel adventurous, I try to get them to sing along.

The questions at the end of the song help focus student attention on the subject of the lesson, and gives them a chance to think about their own ideas before full class discussion begins. The questions can be on the song sheet or the board, or the teacher can just read them aloud. Students can work on answering them individually, in pairs, or in groups. If combined with current events headlines or articles about recent labor union–employer conflicts, and assuming that students get involved in discussion, this activity will span an entire class period.

AIM: SHOULD WORKERS JOIN UNIONS?

Instructions

Read the lyrics to the song *Talking Union* and write the answers to the questions in your notebook.

According to Pete Seeger, this song almost wrote itself while he and the other songwriters were helping to organize labor unions for the Congress of Industrial Organizations in 1941. The song has eight stanzas. Parts of four are included here.

TALKING UNION by Lee Hays, Millard Lampell, and Pete Seeger, Copyright © 1947 by Stormking Music, Inc. All rights reserved. Used with permission.

1. If you want higher wages,
   Let me tell you what to do:
   You got to talk to the workers
   In the shop with you;
   You got to build you a union,
   Got to make it strong,
   But if you all stick together,
   Now, 'twont be long.
   You get shorter hours,
   Better working conditions.
   Vacations with pay,
   Take the kids to the seashore.

2. It ain't quite this simple,
   So I better explain
   Just why you got to ride
   On the union train;
   'Cause if you wait for the boss
   To raise your pay,
   We'll all be waiting
   Till Judgment Day;
   We'll all be buried –
   Gone to Heaven –
   Saint Peter'll be
   The straw boss then, folks.

3. Now, you know you're underpaid,
   But the boss says you ain't;
   He speeds up the work
   Till you're about to faint.
   You may be down and out,
   But you ain't beaten,
   You can pass out a leaflet
   And call a meetin' –
   Talk it over –
   Speak your mind –
   Decide to do something
   About it.

4. Suppose they're working you so hard
   It's just outrageous,
   And they're paying you all
   Starvation wages:
   You go to the boss,
   And the boss would yell,
   "Before I raise your pay
   I'd see you all in hell."
   Well, he's puffing a big cigar
   And feeling mighty slick,
   He thinks he's got your
   Union licked.

Questions

1. According to this song, what are three benefits of belonging to a labor union?
2. How does this song view the relationship between employers and employees?
3. In your opinion, why were songs used in campaigns to organize labor unions?
4. Labor unions might have been necessary for working people in 1941, when this song was written. Do you think they are still necessary today? Why?

Teaching Activity: Analyzing a Song

It's your classroom:
What questions would you ask students about this topic or about this song?

Try it yourself:
Design a lesson that uses the words to a song to provide students with information about a topic and helps generate discussion.

HOW DO TEACHERS OPEN AN ACTIVITY-BASED LESSON?

Much of the time, the hardest part of a lesson is getting started. You planned a brilliant lesson. You thought about it for days, and gathered engaging and appropriate learning materials. But your students have not thought about social studies since they left your classroom the last time, or if you are lucky, since they did their homework. They have been too busy with the important things in their lives—friends, family, food, jobs, sports, music, and movies. In addition, they are squirming in their seats because it is hot or cold in the room; half asleep because its eight in the morning or falling asleep because it's two in the afternoon; starving because they have not had lunch yet, or all charged up because of the fight in the hall, the basketball game in gym, or the fire drill. Their last class was boring. Hormones are kicking in. Four students walk in late without a pass. Maybe your students are just a rambunctious group. In any event, it is not a perfect setting for social studies. Clearly a lesson needs some kind of activity designed to get the class started.

Do now activity:
A brief introductory activity that immediately involves students as they enter the room.

Motivation(al) activity:
A question, statement, or activity that captures student interest in the topic to be examined. Motivations connect the subject of the lesson to things that students are thinking about or that interest them.

Transitions:
Key questions that make it possible for students to draw connections between the information, concepts, or understandings developed during a particular activity with other parts of the lesson, and to broader conceptual understanding.

Step 1
A **Do Now** is a quick way to establish that class has begun, to introduce a topic to students, or to remind them of what they are going to be studying. The do now activity does not have to be a big deal. Have a regular spot on the board where students can find the do now assignment as they enter the room. Students can copy some notes or a definition; think about answers to a question, read a quote from the board or a passage from a handout, and answer a couple of questions.

While they are working—individually, in pairs, or in small groups—you have the chance to move among them as a calming presence. You can chat with individual students, give instructions to the class or to groups, check homework, collect excuses, and get feedback from students on what they do and do not understand about the topic or their assignments. I usually carry a memo pad as I travel around the room so I can jot down student responses to the do now assignment. This helps me draw students into the discussion as the lesson progresses.

SAMPLE DO NOW ACTIVITIES

Subject: US History
- Lesson topic: World War II Home Front
- Objective: Examine efforts to mobilize the public to support the war effort
- Do Now: Examine the poster (Figure 9.2) "The World Has Ears" and use it to answer questions 1–3.

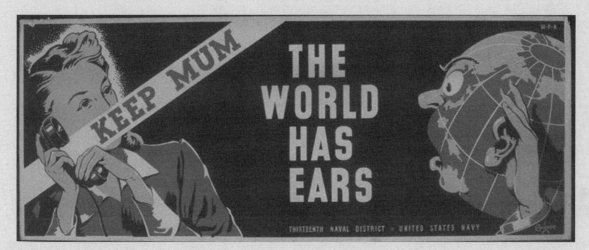

Figure 9.2 World War II poster.
Source: Library of Congress Prints and Photographs Division. Reproduction Number: LC-USZC2–5554.

Questions
1. What is happening in the poster?
2. When do you think the poster was made?
3. In your opinion, what was the purpose of the poster?

Subject: Economics
- Lesson topic: The changing nature of the US economy
- Objective: To show the relative importance of the agricultural, manufacturing, and service components of the economy.
- Do Now: Use the information from the chart to complete 1–3.

Questions
Construct a line graph comparing income in the three sub-categories.

Describe the trend for each sub-category.

What conclusion can you draw about changes in the United States economy during this period?

Table 9.2 National income by industry, 1930–1970 (US$ billions)

Year	Total income	Agriculture, forestry, fishing	Manufacturing	Services
1930	75.4	6.4	18.3	8.4
1940	81.1	6.1	22.5	8.0
1950	241.1	17.6	76.2	21.8
1960	414.5	16.9	125.8	44.5
1970	800.5	25.6	217.5	102.9

Source: US Department of Commerce. 1975. *Historical Statistics of the United States. Vol. 1.* Washington DC: Government Printing Office.

Subject: Government
- Lesson topic: Federal responsibility for health programs
- Objective: To examine the debate over the responsibility of the federal government to provide health programs for the poor, aged, and uninsured.
- Do Now: Examine these headlines from *The New York Times* from September 22–24, 1995.

"House G.O.P. Plan Doubles Premiums of Medicare Users," September 22, 1995

"Democrats Say Republicans Are Pushing Medicare Plan Too Fast," September 22, 1995

"Gingrich Threatens US Default If Clinton Won't Bend on Budget," September 22, 1995

"Republican Blitz Shakes Congress / Democrats Aghast as Pillars of US Health Care Crack," 9 September 23, 1995

"Redesign of 2 Vast Systems Advances," September 23, 1995

"Medicare Prognosis for New York Is Grim / Cuts to Teaching Hospitals in G.O.P. Plan Could Mean Less Care," September 23, 1995

"State Lawmakers Prepare to Wield Vast New Powers / Republicans Plan to Transfer Authority Over Welfare and Safety to Legislatures," September 24, 1995

Based on the information in these headlines:
1. What issue(s) are being debated in the federal government?
2. What positions are being taken in this debate?

Subject: Sociology
- Lesson topic: Comparing class and caste
- Objective: To examine different systems of social stratification.
- Do Now: Copy vocabulary words

Questions
1. *Stratification.* The formal or informal division of society into groups that receive different levels of power, prestige, and economic rewards.
2. *Class.* A social group whose members have similar occupations or income levels. Status is not hereditary. People can change their class position.
3. *Caste.* A social group whose members are born into the group. People cannot change their caste status. Caste status is passed to descendants.

Subject: Global History
- Lesson topic: Golden Age for India.
- Objective: To examine the factors leading up to the creation of a powerful civilization during the early history of India.
- Do Now: Copy the chronology of events.

Table 9.3 Golden Age for India

Year(s) BC	Events
500	Persia controls the Indus Valley and the Punjab.
400	Kingdom of Magadha rules plain of the Ganges and northern India.
323	Alexander and the Greek army defeat Persian and Indian forces.
300	Under Maurya, Magadhan Empire expands north and west.
261–232	Asoka rules Mauryan Empire. Era of growth, stability, and peace.

Teaching Activity: Using Activities in a Lesson

It's your classroom:
How could you use these activities as parts of lessons?

Step 2
Once students are settled and the subject of the lesson is established, you need to establish a context for what students will be learning, grab their attention and hold onto it. A motivation can flow from the do now activity, or the do now can be set aside for later discussion. The key to motivation is capturing the imagination of stu-

dents by creating a metaphoric image or analogy that connects who and where they are with the topic under discussion. The motivation does not have to be directly related to the main idea of the lesson, but it is more effective if it is. The motivation should also provide a transition from the activity to the social studies concepts that are going to be explored during the lesson.

SAMPLE MOTIVATIONAL ACTIVITIES

Opening a Lesson with a Demonstration:
US History: Understanding the Constitution

Checks and balances. A balance scale and loose change (or blocks, rocks, etc.) are on a desk in front of the room. Students take turns using the change to balance the scale. If we have enough scales, students can work in groups. Why is it hard to balance the scales? Why is it hard to keep things in balance? Why would the authors of the US Constitution want to make certain that the powers of the different branches of the government were balanced?

Unconstitutional. In *Marbury* v. *Madison* (1803), the US Supreme Court concluded that, in the Judiciary Act of 1789, Congress had violated the guidelines established by the US Constitution. Therefore, the law was null and void. I hang a piece of oak tag on the front board with a strangely shaped piece cut out. The oak tag is labeled, CONSTITUTION. While the class reviews the process of how a law is made, I cut a series of shapes out of cardboard to represent laws. At the last step, we hold the cardboard pieces up to the cut-out in our oak tag Constitution. What happens to the "laws" that do not fit? What happens to the laws that do?

Stretching the Constitution. Article 1, Section 8, Part 18, the Elastic Clause, empowers Congress "to make all laws which shall be necessary and proper for carrying into execution the foregoing powers and all other powers vested by this Constitution in the government of the United States, or in any department or office thereof." The extent that these powers can legitimately be stretched has been debated for 200 years. While students discuss the meaning of the clause, I have two students pull on a large piece of elastic. Beware when they pull too far; the elastic snaps back.

Opening a Lesson with Questions and a Discussion:
Global History: Impact of Technology on History
- Think of a small thing or event that has had a major impact on world history.
- What thing or event did you choose? Why did you choose it?
- How do you think changes in technology have influenced world history?

Government: The Changing Powers of the Presidency
- In your opinion, what are the major problems facing the United States today?
- Would you support expanding the power of the president of the United States if you believed it was the only way to solve the problems of the country? Why?
- Would you allow the president to become a dictator? Why?

US History: The Importance of National Symbols to the New Nation
- What are some important symbols to different groups of teenagers today?
- Why do think teenagers from different communities and groups have their own symbols?
- Why are symbols important to teenagers?
- What are the symbols of the United States? Why are symbols important?
- Why do you think symbols were important to the creation of a new nation?

Opening a Lesson with a Dramatic Guest:
Most of this material is available on the internet. In the press conference, the teacher acts out a speech by an historical figure. The students listen to the speech and make up questions they would ask if it

were a press conference. Some interesting speeches include President William McKinley's explanation of how he decided that the United States should annex the Philippines (1898), Senator Margaret Chase Smith's statement against the excesses of McCarthyism (1950), Richard Nixon's resignation as President (1974), or President Ronald Reagan's State of the Union Address, where he explained his "Second American Revolution" (1985). In addition, many recent public figures can "visit" your classroom on videotape. Students can design questions to ask Martin Luther King, Jr., John F. Kennedy, or Malcolm X.

Sometimes I wrap a toga (sheet) around my clothes and pretend I am Socrates. I illustrate the Socratic method by asking students to define an inanimate object (What is a chair?) and then a concept (What does good mean?).

Student volunteers can do a dramatic reading of a brief statement. Examples include the conclusion of Patrick Henry's 1775 "Give me liberty or give me death" speech, Anne Hutchinson's 1637 statement to the Massachusetts General Court, William Lloyd Garrison's 1831 editorial in *The Liberator*, where he warned his opponents that he will not be silenced on the issue of slavery, Susan B. Anthony's statement to the 1860 National Women's Rights Convention on the "one-sided" nature of marriage, excerpts from Frederick Douglass' 1883 speech at the National Convention of Colored Men, where he demanded that the nation abide by the promises of the Constitution, or Bartolomeo Vanzetti's statement to the court during his politically charged trial for murder during the 1920s.

Teaching Activity: Motivational Activities

It's your classroom:
- What other demonstrations can you think of to illustrate constitutional principles?
- How would you use them?
- How would you connect the interests of teenagers to the subject of the lesson?
- What historical guests would you invite to your class? Why?
- Which of these motivational activities would you use in middle school? Which would you use in high school?

Step 3

The next step is to move the class from the do now or motivational activity to the content, concepts, and skills of the lesson. There needs to be some sort of transition—a question by the teacher that connects the introduction with the lesson, a question by a student, or even a "Eureka" statement, where students explain what they discovered about the topic. Three samples follow that illustrate the progression from do now to motivation to transition.

MOTIVATIONS WITH TRANSITIONS

US History
- **Aim:** Why did the British colonists demand independence?
- **Do now:** Examine the map of Boston Harbor in 1775 (Figure 9.3).
  1. Locate Breed's Hill, Bunker Hill, Colonial forces, roads, and British troops and ships.
  2. On what type of land formation are Bunker and Breed's Hills located?
  3. If you wanted to capture the colonial forces, how would you attack? Why?
  4. According to the map, how did the British launch their attack?

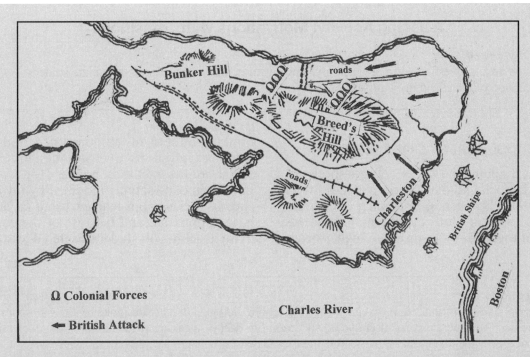

Figure 9.3 Boston Harbor. Key: Ω, Colonial forces; A, British ships; ⋯, Roads; ⇐, British attack route.

- **Motivation:** Review the "do now" assignment (for more information on the Battle of Bunker Hill, see http://www.masshist.org/bh/, accessed July 13, 2007). Why do highly regarded sports team lose to inferior opponents? What makes it possible for an underdog to win these games? (Overconfidence) You've examined the map of Boston Harbor. Why do you think the British launched a frontal assault instead of cutting off the colonists at the neck of the peninsula?
- **Transition:** What would be the impact of the British defeat in this battle? Why?

Economics
- **Aim:** How did industrialization change the world?
- **Do Now:** Make a list of what you consider to be the ten greatest inventions in human history.
- **Motivation:** Hold up a small can and rattle it. In this can is what I consider the greatest invention of the nineteenth century. Can anyone guess what it is? Open the can. In the can are ten bolts. A washer and a nut are on each bolt. Pass the bolt-washer-nut assemblage to ten students and have the students take them apart. Pass the bolts, washers, and nuts around the classroom until they are all mixed up. Now have each person with a bolt collect a washer and a nut and reassemble. Do they fit together? How can they if we mixed them up? What invention have we illustrated? Why is this an important invention?
- **Transition:** In your opinion, what makes an invention "great?"

Economics
This lesson was developed with Brendalon Staton (NTN).

- **Aim:** What is money?
- **Do now:** Answer Questions 1 and 2:
  1. How much money do you spend in an average week?
  2. What are your major purchases?
- **Motivation:** Offer inflated prices to purchase a student's backpack. When a student agrees to sell, pull out a wad of enlarged photocopies of $20 bills (the teacher's picture can replace Andrew Jackson). When students ask what they are, tell them "big bills."
- **Transition:** When the student denies that it is real money, ask the class to define real money.

Teaching Activity: Motivations with Transitions

Try it yourself:
Design an aim question, a do now activity, a motivation, and a transition to stimulate student discussion of apartheid in South Africa.

ARE THERE PERFECT QUESTIONS?

My ideas about the kinds of questions to include in social studies lesson plans draw on traditional approaches, including Benjamin Bloom's system for classifying questions based on their ability to promote higher order thinking by students (Bloom 1985), and on the emphasis given to question design in most social studies methods books. However, they have been considerably modified by my experience as a classroom teacher using an activity-based approach, and because of the emphasis in my teaching on student-centered lessons.

Questions:
Prepare questions that attempt to anticipate classroom dialogue, that are designed to aid examination of materials, generate class discussions, and promote deeper thinking. Medial summary questions make it possible for the class to integrate ideas at the end of an activity.

Summary:
A concluding question or questions that make it possible for the class to integrate or utilize the learning from this and prior lessons.

In my college teacher education program and during my early years as a teacher, the emphasis in lesson planning was on designing predetermined "perfect questions" that would stimulate student interest, invoke higher order thinking, and, in theory, unleash sustained student discussions. After ten years of teaching high school social studies, I finally asked my first "perfect question" at the end of a unit on the emergence of the United States as a world power between 1870 and 1920. I asked the class: "Do you think the United States acted as an imperialist power during World War I?" In previous lessons, students had examined a package of quotes, cartoons, maps, and charts that included excerpts from essays by historians Arthur Link, Harry E. Barnes, and William Appleman Williams, and statements by Secretaries of State William Jennings Bryan and Robert Lansing, Senators La Follette and Norris, and by President Woodrow Wilson. Based on this document package, students could effectively support a number of different positions. There was no single right answer.

I still remember that a student started the discussion by citing William Jennings Bryan to support the idea that US actions were imperial-ist. His comments unleashed a period-long argument among the students as they sorted through the documents to find references needed to make their points. My role for the rest of the period was trying to get them to listen to each other and occasionally asking questions like, "Why do you believe that?" "How do you respond to what so-and-so said?" "What evidence do you have to support your position?"

I had been asking the question, "Do you think the United States acted as an imperialist power during World War I?" for years without getting this kind of response. It was not the question that made the discussion possible. Rather, it was made possible by all of the work done by students during the unit, and their sense of a classroom community where they could express their opinions without fear of being dismissed. My job during this discussion was to listen to students, hear what they had to say, and encourage them to think their ideas through more completely. If I had asked any of my other prepared questions, I am convinced that I would have stifled their discussion.

A Handbook for the Teaching of Social

Studies (Dobkin et al. 1985: 37–65), published by the Association of Teachers of Social Studies (ATSS), recommends that teachers plan lessons around carefully crafted pivotal questions that focus on higher order thinking skills. The chapter on "The Art of Questioning" stresses that "the nature of the questions asked by the teacher" and "the sequence in which they are asked" (p. 37) are keys to successful social studies teaching. Predetermined questions play such a crucial role in this version of lesson plan design that the book offers nine rules for designing questions, seven rules for wording them effectively, 14 common pitfalls to avoid when asking questions, and directions on how to react to student responses. In addition, new teachers are provided with 159 sample pivotal questions from different social studies disciplines that they can incorporate in their lesson plans or use as models.

This approach to lesson planning is frequently coupled with Benjamin Bloom's hierarchical question classification system (Manson and Clegg 1970). Bloom classifies questions based on whether they encourage critical thinking by students. The lowest level of questions asks students to recall information, whereas the highest level requires them to exercise judgment. Bloom's system is useful because it emphasizes that students should be learning to use information to formulate and support their ideas.

Benjamin Bloom's classification system organizes questions into six categories based on the "level of thought" required from students. They are ranked here from lower-level to higher-level thinking. I have to confess that I am not clear how *application* differs significantly from *synthesis* or why *evaluation* ranks higher than *analysis*. Consider the following categories:

Table 9.4 Benjamin Bloom's classification system

Category	Definition	Example
Knowledge	Students are asked to recall or describe information that they have been provided in an assignment or by the teacher.	According to the document, what was the author's first job?
Comprehension	Students are asked to interpret or explain information.	Explain why the author decided to return to school.
Application	Students use information to explain other related events, solve a problem, or speculate about broader causes or issues.	What other reasons would a person have to give up a job and return to school?
Analysis	Students use information to draw conclusions.	Which of the author's statements are facts and which ones are opinions?
Synthesis	Students use information to arrive at a new understanding.	What would you do if you were faced with a similar situation?
Evaluation	Students use information and established criteria to make a judgment or support an opinion.	Which experience was most significant in shaping the author's ideas?

Teaching Activity: Designing Questions for a Lesson on the Scopes Trial

Examine the edited transcript of William Jennings Bryan's testimony at the 1925 Scopes ("Monkey") trial in Dayton, Tennessee (from *The New York Times*, July 21, 1925). John Scopes was a high school biology teacher who was put on trial for violating a Tennessee law that prohibited teaching about evolution. The trial, including this dialogue between Bryan and defense attorney Clarence Darrow, was immortalized in the play, *Inherit the Wind*. Bryan, a member of the prosecution, was called to the stand by the defense as an expert witness on the Old and New Testaments. This document is useful in an elective course studying law, a government class examining religious freedom, or a high school US history class.

Excerpts from the Transcript of the Scopes Trial:
Darrow: You have given considerable study to the Bible, haven't you Mr. Bryan?
Bryan: Yes, sir. I have tried to.

Darrow: Well, we all know you have; we are not going to dispute that at all. But you have written and published articles almost weekly, and sometimes have made interpretations of various things?

Bryan: I would not say interpretations, Mr. Darrow, but comments on the lessons . . .

Darrow: Do you claim that everything in the Bible should be literally interpreted?

Bryan: I believe everything in the Bible should be accepted as it is given there; some of the Bible is given illustratively. For instance: "Ye are the salt of the earth." I would not insist that man is actually salt, or that he had the flesh of salt . . .

Darrow: The Bible says Joshua commanded the sun to stand still for the purpose of lengthening the day, doesn't it, and you believe it?

Bryan: I do.

Darrow: Do you believe at that time that the entire sun went around the earth?

Bryan: No, I believe that the earth goes around the sun.

Darrow: Do you believe that the men who wrote it thought that the day could be lengthened or that the sun could be stopped?

Bryan: . . . I think they wrote the fact without expressing their own thoughts.

Darrow: Have you an opinion as to whether whoever wrote the book, . . . thought the sun went around the earth or not?

Bryan: I believe that he was inspired . . . I believe that the Bible is inspired, and an inspired author, whether one who wrote as he was directed to write, understood the things he was writing about, I don't know.

Darrow: Whoever inspired it, do you think whoever inspired it believed that the sun went around the earth?

Bryan: I believe it was inspired by the Almighty, and he may have used language that could be understood at the time . . . (to the court) His purpose is to cast ridicule on everybody who believes in the Bible, and I am perfectly willing that the world shall know that these gentlemen have no other purpose than ridiculing every person who believes in the Bible.

Darrow: We have the purpose of preventing bigots and ignoramuses from controlling the education of the United States, and you know it, and that is all.

Bryan: I am glad to bring out that statement . . . I want to defend the Word of God against the greatest atheist or agnostic in the United States. I want the papers to show that I am not afraid to get on the stand in front of him and let him know that agnosticism is trying to force agnosticism on our colleges and on our schools, and the people of Tennessee will not permit it to be done . . .

Darrow: I object to your statement. I am examining you on your fool ideas no intelligent Christian on earth believes.

Learning Activity: Evolution, Creation, and Religion

Think it over:

Religious issues can be very controversial in the classroom. How would you prepare students for this lesson?

Add your voice to the discussion:

In your opinion, does the debate over evolution and creationism belong in the social studies classroom? Why?

Try it yourself:

Design a question for each of the categories in Bloom's taxonomy for use in a lesson based on excerpts from the transcript of the Scopes ("Monkey") trial.

Although I support encouraging students to think critically, as well as carefully planned lessons, a fixation on question design can be counterproductive. Predetermined questions are intended to elicit preconceived responses that are directed back to the teacher, not to the class. Answers that deviate the least from teacher expectations are judged to be the best. Lessons tend to be teacher-centered and scripted, with little space for students to think. Although the ATSS handbook recommends "an effective teacher should not insist upon a particular phraseology or pattern of thinking unless accuracy or precision of thought is involved," it warns that "regardless of interest or absolute value, digressions are ill-advised" (pp. 122–124). I also think that Bloom's system, because it encourages teachers to think of certain types of questions as inherently more worthwhile, lends itself to rigid application.

An anecdote told to me by a high school student illustrates the problem with this approach. The student's biology teacher asked the class the difference between studying science and history—a higher order question that requires comparison and synthesis. The student raised his hand and responded, "I don't think there is that much of a difference." Before he could elaborate or explain, the teacher shouted out: "Wrong!" Then the teacher called on the next volunteer.

Clearly, predetermined questions are useful for teachers. They help us think about main ideas and goals, and to plan logical lessons. They are good to have written down in reserve just in case we get stuck during a lesson. They are especially useful for directing students as they analyze a document. But once the information is on the table, once discussion has begun, predetermined questions can become a hindrance to examination and discussion in a student-centered classroom. If we want to promote higher order thinking, teachers need to worry less about designing and asking perfect questions, and more about listening to and responding to the ideas of our students.

While I do not believe there are perfect questions, there are pretty good ones. A retired English teacher, who works with the New Teachers Network, spoke with a group of social studies teachers about using poetry in their classrooms. He raised with us that when teachers ask students the "meaning" of a poem, they are usually met with silence because students are afraid they will not have the "right" answer. However, when teachers ask, "What does this poem mean to you?" it becomes an opinion question and students are more willing to discuss what they think. The same holds true for document analysis. It is much easier for students to respond when teachers ask, "What does the opening passage of the Declaration of Independence mean to you?" than when they demand the "correct" historical analysis.

Teaching Activity: Designing Questions for a Primary Source Document

Students might read excerpts from the United Nation's Universal Declaration of Human Rights (United Nations General Assembly, 1953) while studying US or global history, or the US government.

"Whereas recognition of the inherent dignity and of the equal and inalienable rights of all members of the human family is the foundation of freedom, justice and peace in the world,

Whereas disregard and contempt for human rights have resulted in barbarous acts which have outraged the conscience of mankind, and the advent of a world in which human beings shall enjoy freedom of speech and belief and freedom from fear and want has been proclaimed as the highest aspiration of the common people,

Whereas it is essential, if man is not to be compelled to have recourse, as a last resort, to rebellion against tyranny and oppression, that human rights should be protected by the rule of law, whereas it is essential to promote the development of friendly relations between nations, whereas the peoples of the United Nations have in the Charter reaffirmed their faith in fundamental human rights, in the dignity and worth of the human person and in the equal rights of men and women and have determined to promote social progress and better standards of life in larger freedom, . . .

> Now, therefore, The General Assembly, Proclaims this Universal Declaration of Human Rights as a common standard of achievement for all peoples and all nations . . ."

Try it yourself:

1. What AIM question would you use for a lesson on the Universal Declaration of Human Rights?
2. Which sections of the preamble to the Declaration of Human Rights would you have students read in class? Why?
3. Design different types of questions (content, comparison, opinion, and analysis) to help students understand the meaning of the document, its historical context, and its implications for today's world.
4. Would you have students write the answers to these questions as a classroom activity or homework assignment, or would you ask the questions during class discussion? On what basis would you make your decision?
5. What SUMMARY question would you use for a lesson on the Universal Declaration of Human Rights?

HOW CAN TEACHERS REINFORCE STUDENT UNDERSTANDING?

Applications:

Extra questions or activities that draw on, broaden, or review what students learned in a lesson or unit. They can be part of a lesson, a follow-up homework assignment, or a new lesson. They can be used to review prior lessons, as transitions to future lessons, or to bring units to a close and prepare students for exams. At the end of a class period, many teachers have students write a summary of what they learned during the lesson in their social studies journal.

Applications allow teachers to assess student learning. They are also a way for a class to review for a test. Written applications can be completed in class as part of a lesson, during a separate period, or as a homework assignment. A simple application is to have students keep a social studies learning log. After each lesson, they informally write down their thoughts about what they learned. Applications can also be more complicated, like the cooperative learning team dramatic activity included later in this chapter.

Sample Lesson Organizers

Jeannette Balantic, Laura Pearson, and Rozella Kirchgaessner (NTN) provide their classes with structured lesson organizers to guide discussions and writing. They find that the organizers provide students with clear directions and visual representations that are particularly useful in classes where students have a wide range of writing skills. Organizers can be visual aids, like diagrams, charts, and idea webs that allow students to see the relationships among people, places, ideas, and events, or a list of questions that help direct their writing.

Jeannette, Laura, Rozella, and I share a commitment to designing thought-provoking lessons that involve all students in our classes. Organizers are one of the tools that makes this possible. Jeannette's sample organizers are used to review broad content areas in global history classes. Students use the first organizer to write speeches supporting their candidate for "Best Leader in Indian History." After the speeches are presented in class, students use the second organizer to evaluate the candidates before they cast their ballots.

ORGANIZER 1: ELECTION FOR BEST LEADER IN INDIAN HISTORY

Candidates:

Asoka of Maurya, Akbar of Mughal, Chandragupta of Gupta, Jawaharlal Nehru, Indira Gandhi

Directions:

You have been hired as speechwriters for one of the candidates for "Best Leader in Indian History." You must write a speech for your candidate so he or she can persuade the people of India to support his or her candidacy. Use the following organizer to help you write the speech.

My name is:

_____

I was the leader of India during:

_____

I should be elected "Best Leader in Indian History" because (give at least three reasons)

_____
_____
_____

My opponents will criticize me because:

_____
_____
_____ , but my accomplishments outweigh my setbacks.

There are good reasons not to elect my opponents.

_____ should not be elected because (give at least three reasons):

_____
_____
_____

ORGANIZER 2: EVALUATING THE CANDIDATES FOR BEST LEADER IN INDIAN HISTORY

Leader/Empire	*Positive achievements*	*Negative actions*
Asoka of the Maurya Empire		
Akbar of the Mughal Empire		
Chandragupta of the Gupta Empire		
Jawaharlal Nehru of modern India		
Indira Gandhi of modern India		

Cast your ballot wisely. Which candidate do you support for Best Leader in Indian history? Why?

_____
_____
_____

Laura uses formal organizers to help middle school students, working individually, to evaluate supplemental primary source documents at the end of a lesson. As an application, Rozella has her law elective classes write in their social studies logs at some point during nearly every lesson. She always provides students with prepared questions, which helps connect their experiences and understandings with the main ideas of the lesson.

ORGANIZER 3: DOCUMENT REPORT

Document Title:
_____

Who is speaking/writing/illustrating? _____

What is the date (make an educated guess if necessary)? _____

What is the *explicit* meaning of this document (what is in the lines)?
_____
_____

Does the document have a hidden or implicit meaning ("between the lines")?
_____
_____

Is this document a primary or secondary source? _____

In your opinion, is this a reliable source? Explain.
_____
_____

ORGANIZER 4: MAKING DIFFICULT DECISIONS

Please answer these questions in your social studies log:

1. Have you ever had to make a difficult decision about who should get something? Explain.
2. When your friends are planning an activity, how does the group decide what to do?
3. If you had free tickets to a special event, but were not able to attend, how would you decide to whom to give them?
4. If you had enough rare medicine for two people, but six people were sick, how would you decide who would receive it?
5. What factors would you consider when making a difficult decision?
6. How would you weigh a person's need, ability, and past history when making decisions about the distribution of scarce resources?

Teaching Activity: Constructing Lesson Organizers

Try it yourself:

Select a primary source document or a newspaper article. Design a series of questions, a chart, or a graphic organizer that will guide students as they read and analyze the material.

ARE ACTIVITIES ALWAYS APPROPRIATE?

While I am a strong advocate of an activity-based approach to teaching social studies, this chapter is not intended as a blanket endorsement of all classroom "activities." I have my own pet peeves. I do not like classroom "games" and competitions and I am leery about the use of role-play.

Before the start of student teaching, I warn student teachers that I do not, under any circumstances, want to see them playing "Jeopardy" or "Bingo" with classes during an observation lesson. If a cooperating teaching insists that they conduct a specific lesson this way on a day I am scheduled to visit, they should reschedule the observation.

"Jeopardy" and "Bingo" may be more fun than a regular review lesson, but they are essentially just forms of rote recall. They have nothing to do with establishing an historical setting or illustrating why something is important to know. In addition, they teach students that the acquisition of knowledge is a competitive rather than a cooperative venture. They may build team spirit, but it is at the expense of classroom community. Students are active, but these are not social studies learning activities.

I am also cautious about using role-play to "get inside the head" of an historical character, explain ideologies, or reenact historical events. During role-play complex events and ideas are vastly oversimplified and students believe they have experienced things they actually have not. Based on a role-play, do students really understand what people experienced in concentration camps, on the Trail of Tears, or during the Middle Passage? Meryl Landau (NTN), who is a very imaginative young teacher, created a webquest that required students to write diaries about their "experience" on the Underground Railroad. The problem was that it was illegal for enslaved Africans to learn to read or write so they were overwhelmingly illiterate. The project ended up teaching students the wrong lesson. Meryl later modified the assignment so that after arriving in the north the newly free men and women told their stories to abolitionists who wrote them down.

Role-play can also teach students the wrong lessons. One of the best-known role-plays is the Blue Eyes/Brown Eyes Exercise pioneered by Jane Elliot (available at: http://janeelliott.com/videos.htm, accessed November 5, 2007) as a way to address racial discrimination in American society following the assassination of Martin Luther King. Elliot originally conducted the project with third-graders in the racially homogenous farming community of Riceville, Iowa during the late 1960s. I saw a video of the exercise conducted with adults. In the video, a facilitator alternated between discriminating against people with brown eyes and people with blue eyes. In a closing session, participants explained how they felt when their group was considered inferior and how new empathy with others would help them combat racial prejudice. While the exercise focused on personal biases and the arbitrariness of stereotypes, it did not explore systemic racism in American society and the ways some groups benefit from it. I was left skeptical about the depth of the personal testimonies and the long-term impact of the transformations.

I actually witnessed a facilitator leading a Blue Eyes/Brown Eyes exercise during a staff development workshop for public school teachers and I was a bit outraged. It was in New York City and there was nobody in the group with blue eyes. There are also almost no blue-eyed children in a school system where ninety percent of the students are African-American, Hispanic, or Asian. Someone in the workshop suggested, and the suggestion was seriously considered, that participants could be divided into Blue Eyed/Brown Eyed teams based on their skin color. The suggestion was finally rejected when I argued that this would more likely reinforce existing racial and ethnic tensions than alleviate them.

Effective role-plays can have a tendency to get out of control, especially if they stimulate the intense feelings the simulated situations are supposed to create. In an ABC After School Special (*The Wave* 1984) supposedly based on a true story, a high school history teacher who is teaching about Nazi Germany divides his class into hierarchical social groups and forces them to wear colored armbands designating their status in society. Groups are required to follow different sets of rules and have different privileges while they are in school. Eventually fights break out, there are threats of broader violence, and the teacher explains that many students are endorsing the same set of ideological beliefs advocated by Adolf Hitler (see http://www.thewave.tk/, accessed November 5, 2007).

While the development and final resolution of this role-play is too pat (after all it is a made-for-television movie), I was involved in a similar educational disaster as a teacher. In a summer youth program during the 1980s, we involved middle school age students in the campaign to end apartheid in South Africa. To give them a sense of what apartheid meant, we had an apartheid day at our residential camp. After breakfast the entire camp discussed the purpose of the program and then children were divided into castes. During the day, camp resources, including space in the cafeteria, would be allocated unequally with higher caste individuals receiving the best benefits. We had to cancel the program before lunch as fights repeatedly broke out between participants when higher caste individuals bossed around members of groups that were being discriminated against. When we evaluated the program, we realized that the children were too upset by their treatment by people they thought of as friends to draw any meaningful connections with apartheid in South Africa.

All this having been said, carefully constructed role-plays can be meaningful for students if teachers have clear and limited goals. Suzann Schmanski (NTN) and her colleague Jeff Krautheimer have developed an effective role-play to help their middle school students understand McCarthyism and the Red Scare. They open the class by saying that honesty and integrity are an essential part of their school's philosophy and something the teachers take very seriously. Teachers and administrators discovered that several students were cheating on tests and homework assignments. The principal requested that all teachers generate lists of students who they believe are part of this cheating ring. Students whose names are on these lists will be questioned by the principal and assistant principals. Students who do not cooperate with the investigation will be removed from the honor role, kicked out of honor society, and will not be permitted to take honors classes in high school. In addition, their grade averages will be adjusted down. Students who cooperate and reveal the names of other cheaters will receive significantly lesser punishments. After the charges are made and procedures are explained, students are asked how they feel about the accusations and whether they will cooperate. After some discussion, the teacher explains that this investigation is not really happening in their school, but that something similar happened in the United States during McCarthyism and the Red Scare, and that people named the "names" of others, including their friends, in order to avoid persecution.

Essay 1: Which Document Do You Choose?

Critics accuse the Fox Television News of tailoring news reports to support the political positions of its management. They claim it gives prominent airtime to charges made against individuals or groups the network does not like, and either ignores or buries responses. In the lead up to the United States invasion of Iraq in 2003, the network continually reported on supposed connections between the government of Iraq and Al-Qaeda, the organization that attacked the World Trade Center in 2001, and the presence of weapons of mass destruction in Iraq. While both claims were later proved to be false, one-third of Fox's viewers believed they were true (see http://www.worldpublicopinion.org/pipa/articles/international_security_bt/102.php?nid=&id=&pnt=102&lb=brusc). Because of Fox's reputation, during the early days of the 2008 Presidential campaign, the anti-war group MoveOn.org called for a boycott of Fox and some Democratic candidates refused to participate in debates organized by the network (see http://www.cnn.com/2007/POLITICS/03/10/debate.canceled/index.html). Fox generally defended its decisions as legitimate journalistic choices tempered by the demands of its audience.

Social studies teachers have a problem similar to the television networks. While document-based instruction gives social studies students the opportunity to act as historians and social scientists, to draw their own conclusions, and to enhance analytic and literacy skills, there are drawbacks. Depending on the primary source document, or even the way it is edited, students can learn very different versions of history. As you can see from these selections, document-based instruction requires that teachers have a broad and deep understanding of events.

The New York Times article below about the Pennsylvania coal miners seems like a good illustration of anti-war and anti-draft sentiments among both Copperheads and immigrants in the North during the Civil War, and raises questions about the need to punish violence and prevent treason. But the article only tells a small part of the story. Based on War Department correspondence in the National Archives, it seems that the military draft was being used by coal mine owners allied with local Republican Party officials to break strikes by impoverished miners who were seeking higher wages.

According to a report from General Rausch, the arrival of troops returned the mines to operation, and the operators proposed to "discharge the bad characters" if they were assured of government support. The military eventually arrested about 70 miners, but found little to prove disloyalty or resistance to conscription. Charges against most of the accused were dropped. Yet despite the lack of evidence, a military tribunal convicted 13 defendants, who spent the remainder of the war in a prison camp. This part of the story did not appear in *The New York Times* until December 2002 in an article discussing military tribunals proposed by President George W. Bush (Bulik 2001).

Learning Activity: Which Document do you Choose?

It's your classroom:

1. Do you have questions about the news article and headlines? What are they? Why?
2. In your opinion, are the accompanying questions effective for guiding students through the passage? Explain.
3. Would you use the activity sheets in your high school class in a lesson on the "home front" during the Civil War? Explain?

The New York Times, Saturday, November 7, 1863:
The Pennsylvania Coal Mines/An Irish, Welsh And German Row At Mauch Chunk
The Fruits of Copperhead Teachings
The Buckshots and the Molly McGuires On The Rampage/Four Men Killed

> "Last night Mr. C. K. Smith, coal operator at Yorktown, Carbon County, was murdered in a most brutal manner in his house, in the presence of his family, by a gang of Irish outlaws, known as "Buckshots." Mr. Smith was a loyal and highly respected gentleman, and was suspected of giving certain information to the Deputy Provost-Marshal, by which the latter, with the military under Capt. Yates, was enabled to arrest the drafted men.
>
> No Union man's life is safe in. . . . Beaver Meadows and other mines of the middle coal fields. Seven or eight murders were committed there within the last few weeks. . . .
>
> Last August, a peaceable law abiding citizen, residing in Beaver Meadows, was made the object of an attack from a riotous crowd of Irishmen, who, under the names of *buckshots* and *Molly McGuires*, have disciplined themselves into an organization. . . .
>
> The success of this insolent violation of law and order inaugurated the reign of terror which has settled down on the district. Mob orators from Mauch Chunk have told these deluded miners that 'they must not submit to the Lincoln tyranny, . . . that they must stand in the door and resist every officer connected with the draft who comes near them . . .'
>
> The draft enrollment has been made from the books of the mine owners. No man alive dare serve the notice. . . . These men have openly boasted that 'no draft dare ever be made amongst them, . . . that they would murder any soldier or body of soldiers that came near them.'"

Questions:

1. What is going on in the United States at the time of these events?
2. According to this news article, what is going on in the coal towns of Pennsylvania?
3. According to the news article, who is responsible for these actions?
4. In your opinion, should the people involved in these actions be punished? Why? How?

Sometimes it is helpful to provide students with multiple documents presenting different perspectives on a subject so they can see how difficult it is to establish historical truth. In January 1895, five thousand workers employed on Brooklyn, New York trolleys went on strike. Their employers recruited "scab" labor, and seven thousand state troopers and National Guard troops were sent to Brooklyn by the state governor to protect private property and break the strike. When workers responded by attacking trolleys and strikebreakers and fighting against soldiers, the strike became the focus of both the local and national press. The coverage of the strike and sympathy towards the workers varied widely from publication to publication.

On January 21, 1895, the *Brooklyn Eagle* published a statement released by strikers explaining their position (*Social Science Docket* 2004: 26). "The employees of the Brooklyn trolley lines were driven from their posts by soulless corporations, because they were human beings and unable to work another year under the terrible strain put upon them by being compelled to run trolley cars through crowded streets at a high rate of speed for 14 hours as a day's work . . . We offered to continue our contracts with our masters for another year at the same wages if we were guaranteed against more than ten hours' work. The companies refused."

However, an editorial in *The Brooklyn Eagle* on the same day placed full blame for the strike on workers and declared, "A great advance has been made when the president of a large corporation asserts that the corporation has some rights which it can insist upon. It has been common for the unions to do the insisting and they have acted as if business enterprises were undertaken solely for their benefit."

On February 2, 1895, *Harper's Weekly* declared its opposition to the strike. According to *Harper's Weekly*, "Whether or not the wages paid by the Brooklyn street-car lines were inadequate, and whether or not their regulations were oppressive to the men, cannot be decided by rumor, by the resolutions of striking unions, nor by any evidence now before the public. These are proper questions for the State Labor Commissioners."

An article in the Chicago, Illinois *Times* was much more sympathetic to the strikers and critical of management. It argued that "The fundamental trouble is not in the strike itself . . . The fault lies in the fact that a community through its corporate authorities has given away rights of the public . . . in order that greedy, merciless corporations, . . . shall increase the profits."

Students can also benefit from looking at multiple sources when they examine contemporary news stories. On February 5, 2003, United States Secretary of State Colin Powell presented the US case against Iraq to the United Nations Security Council (see http://www.cnn.com/2003/US/02/05/sprj.irq.powell.transcript/). In his argument for war, Powell claimed that US intelligence proved that Saddam Hussein had weapons of mass destruction including mobile bio-weapons labs mounted on trucks. A *New York Times* editorial (A38) credited Powell with presenting "the most powerful case to date that Saddam Hussein stands in defiance of security council resolutions and has no intention of revealing or surrendering whatever unconventional weapons he may have." The editorial praised President Bush's "wise concern for international opinion."

The day after the speech, *The Guardian*, a British newspaper ran the headline "Powell Raises the Banner for War but the World Remains Divided."

According to the article, "the presentation appeared to do little to heal the deep rifts in the UN security council. America and Britain claimed the evidence proved Iraq was in 'material breach' of its UN obligations, justifying 'serious consequences'. France and Russia said that the evidence only strengthened the case for further inspections. Iraq rejected the presentation as a fraud" (see http://www.guardian.co.uk/Iraq/Story/0,,889828,00.html). On May 8, 2003, *Le Monde*, a French newspaper reported: "Almost a month after the fall of Baghdad, none of the weapons the US government accused Saddam Hussein of possessing have been found . . . In mid-January, a senior State Department official nevertheless stated that, as soon as they had control of the country, US forces would be able to establish the veracity of these accusations. 'Do you know where to find these weapons?' one journalist asked. The reply was categorical: 'Yes, absolutely'" (http://www.worldpress.org/Mideast/1140.cfm). All of Powell's assertions at the United Nations about weapons of mass destruction in Iraq have now been proven to be untrue.

Important goals in document-based instruction are teaching students to construct a story from component pieces, having them base opinions on evidence, helping them understand why people often have multiple perspectives on an issue, and encouraging them to seek out more information when possible. I say this cautiously, but I think these are more important goals than for them to get the facts "just right." To "force" students to think and to promote debate in class, I try, as often as possible, to find sources that disagree about events.

For the lesson that follows, students are introduced to the documents and to our task as historians by a "do now" activity. They read the statement by John Hains and answer questions that focus attention on key points in his testimony. As a motivation, they discuss their own experiences with the police, the problem of historical objectivity, and the need to weigh evidence carefully. We may also discuss the responsibility of a jury at a trial. After reviewing the Hains testimony as a full class, students work in teams to complete the rest of the activity. At the end of the period, teams report back to class on their investigations and conclusions.

Teaching Activity: Did New York City police Participate in anti-Black Riots in 1900?

Do Now
Read the statement by John Hains and answer the following questions:

1. What happened to John Hains on the evening of August 15, 1900?
2. According to his account, how was Mr Hains treated by the police?
3. In your opinion, why would Mr Hains swear to his testimony before a "Notary Public"?

John Hains, being duly sworn, desposes and says: I reside at No. 341 West 36th Street. I am a laborer, and am at present employed as a longshoreman at Pier 16, North River. On the evening of August 15, 1900, I went to bed as usual at 9:30 o'clock. About two o'clock in the morning I was awakened by somebody beating me on the back with a club. When I awoke, I found six policemen in the room; they had broken in the door. They asked me for the revolver with which they said I had been shooting out of the window. I told them I did not have a revolver. One of the officers said that he had seen me shoot out of the window. Three officers then began to club me, while the other three were searching the house . . . They dragged me out of the house, and proceeded to take me to the station house. I was only in my undershirt, being asleep at the time they broke into the house, and begged them to allow me to put on my trousers and my shoes. They only sneered at this, and one of the officers said, "You'll be d–d lucky if you get there alive." Here another of the officers pulled out a revolver and said, "Let's shoot the d–d nigger," to which a third officer replied, "We can take the black son of a b– to the station house as he is." When I got to the station house, I was bleeding from my head and other parts of my body, as a result of these clubbings. Sworn before me this 28th day of August, 1900. GEORGE HAMMOND JR., Notary Public.

Team Activity: Acting as Historians:
1. Summarize the events described in the newspaper articles below.
2. Do you believe New York City participated in anti-Black riots in 1900
3. What evidence supports your position?
4. Why do you reject alternative explanations?
5. What other evidence would you want to examine to better understand what took place?

A. *The New York Times*, "Race Riot On West Side," August 16, 1900
For four hours last night Eighth Avenue, from Thirtieth to Forty-second Street, was a scene of the wildest disorder that this city has witnessed in years. The hard feeling between the white people and the Negroes in that district, which has been smoldering for many years and which received fresh fuel by the death of Policeman Thorpe, who was shot last Sunday by a Negro, burst forth last night into a race riot which was not subdued until the reserve force of four police precincts, numbering in all over 100 men, headed by Chief Devery himself, were called to the scene and succeeded in clearing the streets by a liberal use of their night sticks.

B. *The New York Times*, "Police In Control In Riotous District," August 17, 1900
The race trouble which was first encountered by the New York police force Wednesday night is now practically at an end. The burial of Policeman Thorpe and the arrest of the Negro Harris, who, it is alleged, killed him, both had much to do with quieting the feeling in the neighborhood of Ninth Avenue and Thirty-seventh Street, where the rioting started . . . That policemen were not too active in stopping the attacks on the Negroes, and even went so far as to use their clubs on colored men who had been arrested, was fully developed at the West Thirty-seventh Street Station yesterday. The policemen, according to their own statements, are feeling vindictive against the colored people generally.

C. *New York Times Editorial*, "A Disgrace To The Police," August 17, 1900
The record of the police in the riotous attacks on the Negroes in their quarter on Wednesday night may briefly be summed up. They stood idly by for the most part while the Negroes were being beaten except when they joined savagely in the sport, until the rioting threatened to extend dangerously; then they gradually dispersed the crowds, arresting almost no whites and many

blacks, most of the latter being clubbed most unmercifully. This record is fully established by the testimony of many eye-witnesses, and there is nothing in the official reports so far published to contradict it.

D. *The New York Times*, "Negro Aliens Complain," August 18, 1900
Dr. M. S. N. Pierre of 318 West Forty-first Street, a Negro from British Guiana, and 200 of his fellow-British subjects have prepared a petition to Percy Sanderson, British Consul, asking him to take the necessary steps for their protection. The petition alleges that the signers were brutally attacked by the mob in the recent riots, and that the police, instead of giving them protection, actually urged and incited the mob to greater fury.

E. *The New York Times*, "Race Riot Investigation," September 20, 1900
The investigation conducted by President York of the Police Board into the charges of brutality made against the police during the late race riots on the west side was continued yesterday afternoon in the courtroom at Police Headquarters . . . President York said: "I am going to examine these witnesses, and don't care whose cases they insure."

F. *The New York Times*, "Police Are Exonerated," December 9, 1900
Bernard J. York, President of the Board of Police Commissioners, who conducted the investigation made by the Police Board into the charges made against policemen in connection with the Negro troubles on the west side last August, made public yesterday a report on his investigation. The report fails to fix the blame for the clubbings on any policeman. It goes into details in several cases, and states in substance that the police did no more than their duty during the days of the race riots.

Piecing together the historical narrative from documents that provide only part of a puzzle or support a variety of interpretations about events central to what historians do. Whatever the difficulties, document-based instruction and assessment should be at the core of the social studies curriculum. This document-based essay is based on a lesson developed by the American Social History Project (ASHP) and available on its website at http://ashp.cuny.edu/video/s-act1.html (accessed October 20, 2007). It can be supplemented by a video documentary, *Savage Acts: Wars, Fairs and Empire*, available from ASHP. I learned about this lesson and the website from an article written by John DeRose (2007), a teacher at Whitefish Bay High School in Wisconsin, for *Rethinking Schools*. He used their lesson, a series of primary source documents, and the book *History Lessons: How Textbooks from Around the World Portray U.S. History* (Lindaman and Ward 2004), to help his students evaluate coverage of what was happening in the Philippines in their regular textbook, McDougal Littell's *The Americans: Reconstruction to the 21st Century* (Danzer et al. 2002). A question that his students debated was whether it should be remembered as the "Philippine-American War" or the "War of Philippine Independence"? Each of the documents has been edited (Singer 2008).

Classroom Activity: Annexation of the Philippines

Aim question
Was the Annexation of the Philippines by the United States an act of Imperialism?

Historical Background
In 1899, the United States was sharply divided over whether to add the Philippines to an expanding overseas American empire. In the 1900 presidential campaign, William Jennings Bryan, the Democratic Party made anti-imperialism a central issue of his campaign. President William McKinley, a Republican who was running for reelection on a record that included the acquisition of new colonies in the Caribbean and the Pacific, won the election by a large margin of popular and electoral votes. Walter LaFeber (1998), a prominent historian, argues that McKinley's reelection shows that the American public had reached a fundamental consensus in favor of American expansionism abroad.

Task
Examine the maps and ten primary source documents from the debate over American annexation of the Philippines and answer the questions that follow each document. As a summary activity, write a newspaper editorial expressing your views on whether or not the United States should annex the Philippines. In the editorial, be sure to refer to the maps and at least five of the documents.

Political Map of East Asia
http://www.lib.utexas.edu/maps/middle_east_and_asia/east_asia_pol_95.jpg, accessed October 22, 2007.

Physical map of the Philippines
http://www.lib.utexas.edu/maps/middle_east_and_asia/philippines_rel93.jpg, accessed October 22, 2007.

Questions
1. Why were the Philippines an attractive base of military and economic operations for the United States?
2. How did geography make the Philippines difficult to pacify and control?

A. British Newspaper Views Annexation
[The United States government] should break an injudicious pledge to Congress [rather] than allow Cuba and the Philippines to be independent or to return to the cruel Spanish dominion. Since it is equally inadmissible to grant independence or to transfer the Philippines to any other power, it is best that the United States should assume the heavy responsibility involved, which will serve to bring out the best qualities of the American Nation. *Source*: *London Spectator*, July 29, 1898 (reprinted in *The New York Times*, July 30, 1898).

Questions
1. What did President McKinley pledge to Congress when the country went to war with Spain?
2. Why does the *Spectator* believe the US should break this pledge?

B. Permanent Dependencies—*New York Times Editorial*
If the Democratic leaders will take a firm position against making our new possessions a part of the territory of the United States they will have the support of a very great majority of the people of the country. We do not want the Filipinos as citizens of the United States. We have a very firm belief that if we ever try to make citizens of their people we shall raise up for ourselves untold trouble and embarrassment. *Source*: *The New York Times*, December 21, 1898.

Questions
1. What did *The New York Times* want the Democratic Party to do?
2. Why did the *Times* make this recommendation?

C. President William McKinley (Republican)
When I next realized that the Philippines had dropped into our laps I confess I did not know what to do with them. And one night late it came to me this way. 1) That we could not give them back to Spain—that would be cowardly and dishonorable; 2) that we could not turn them over to France and Germany—our commercial rivals in the Orient—that would be bad business and discreditable; 3) that we not leave them to themselves—they are unfit for self-government—and they would soon have anarchy and misrule over there worse than Spain's wars; and 4) that there was nothing left for us to do but to take them all, and to educate the Filipinos, and uplift and civilize and Christianize them, and by God's grace do the very best we could by them, as our fellow-men for whom Christ also died. *Source*: *The Christian Advocate*, January 22, 1903.

Questions
1. What did President McKinley decide to do?
2. Why did he believe this was necessary?

D. William Jennings Bryan, Democratic presidential candidate in 1896 and 1900
Imperialism is the policy of an empire. A republic cannot be an empire, for a republic rests upon the theory that the government derive their powers from the consent of the government and colonialism

279

violates this theory. We do not want the Filipinos for citizens. They cannot, without danger to us, share in the government of our nation and moreover, we cannot afford to add another race question to the race questions which we already have. Neither can we hold the Filipinos as subjects even if we could benefit them by so doing. Our experiment in colonialism has been unfortunate. Instead of profit, it has brought loss. Instead of strength, it has brought weakness. Instead of glory, it has brought humiliation. *Source*: *Speeches of William Jennings Bryan.*

Questions

1. Why did Bryan reject imperialism?
2. What does he believe will be the outcome of the conquest of the Philippines?

E. Senator Alfred Beveridge (Republican-Indiana)

We will not renounce our part in the mission of our race, trustee of God, of the civilization of the world. They [the Filipinos] are a barbarous race, modified by three centuries of contact with a decadent race [the Spanish]. It is barely possible that 1,000 men in all the archipelago are capable of self-government in the Anglo-Saxon sense. The Declaration [of Independence] applies only to people capable of self-government. How dare any man prostitute this expression of the very elect of self-government peoples to a race of Malay children of barbarism, schooled in Spanish methods and ideas? *Source*: *Congressional Record* 1900.

Questions

1. What was Senator Beveridge's position on the annexation of the Philippines?
2. Why did he believe the US Declaration of Independence did not apply?

F. Samuel Gompers (President of the American Federation of Labor)

If the Philippines are annexed what is to prevent the Chinese, the Negritos [an ethnic minority group native to the Philippines] and the Malays coming to our country? Can we hope to close the floodgates of immigration from the hordes of Chinese and the semi-savage races coming from what will then be part of our own country? If we are to retain the principles of law enunciated from the foundation of our Government, no legislation of such a character can be expected. If we attempt to force upon the natives of the Philippines our rule, and compel them to conform to our more or less rigid mold of government, how many lives shall we take? Of course, they will seem cheap, because they are poor laborers. They will be members of the majority in the Philippines, but they will be ruled and killed at the convenience of the very small minority there, backed up by our armed land and sea forces. *Source*: *Imperialism—Its Dangers and Wrongs* 1898.

Questions

1. Why did Gompers oppose Philippine migration to the United States?
2. According to Gompers, which group from the Philippines would support annexation?

G. Petition from the "Colored Citizens of Boston"

The colored people of Boston in meeting assembled desire to enter their solemn protest against the present unjustified invasion by American soldiers in the Philippines Islands. While the rights of colored citizens in the South, sacredly guaranteed them by the amendment of the Constitution, are shamefully disregarded; and, while frequent lynchings of Negroes who are denied a civilized trial are a reproach to Republican government, the duty of the President and country is to reform these crying domestic wrongs and not attempt the civilization of alien peoples by powder and shot. *Source*: *The Boston Post*, July 18, 1899.

Questions

1. What position on the Philippines was taken by the "Colored Citizens of Boston"?
2. Why did the people who signed the petition take this position?

H. Emilio Aguinaldo, President of the Independent Philippine Republic

The constant outrages and taunts, which have caused misery of the people of Manila, and, finally, the useless conferences and the contempt shown the Philippine government prove the premeditated transgression of justice and liberty. I have tried to avoid, as far as it has been possible for me to do so, armed conflict, in my endeavors to assure our independence by pacific means and to avoid more costly sacrifices. But all my efforts have been useless against the measureless pride of the American government. *Source: Report of Military Operations and Civil Affairs in the Philippine Islands* 1899

Questions

1. Why is Aguinaldo upset with the United States?
2. What is the implied threat in this statement?

I. Clemencia Lopez, Activist in the Philippine Struggle for Independence

In the name of the Philippine women, I pray the Massachusetts Woman Suffrage Association do what it can to remedy all this misery and misfortune in my unhappy country. You can do much to bring about the cessation of these horrors and cruelties which are today taking place in the Philippines, and to insist upon a more human course. You ought to understand that we are only contending for the liberty of our country, just as you once fought for the same liberty for yours. *Source: The Woman's Journal*, June 7, 1902.

Questions

1. Where was Lopez speaking?
2. Why did she expect a positive response from this group?

J. Philippine Newspaper Editorial

It seems that the magnanimous spirit which in the American Congress cried out so indignantly against the proceedings in Cuba is unconcerned about conditions in the Philippines. We say frankly and with deep sorrow that this measure which causes so much suffering is not justified by the good at which it claims to aim. There are created by it feelings of animosity and rancor that will not be forgotten for many years,—perhaps never. Does America desire to establish herself in the hearts of the Filipinos? Does she not at least desire to refrain from creating resentment in their minds? Then let her rectify these deeds! "Whoever sows hatred will reap wrath and hatred twofold." We are not ignorant of the object of this rigorous campaign to suppress the outlaws, but the people, especially the lower classes, do not reason, they can only feel, and what affects them are ruin, hunger and nakedness. We can only trust that the authority put into the hands of the governor-general may lie dormant. *Source: El Renacimiento.* June 30, 1905

Questions

1. Why does the newspaper editorial compare Cuba and the Philippines?
2. What did the newspaper fear would be the outcome of the campaign against the "outlaws"?

Essay 2: Cooperative Learning in Social Studies Classrooms

Based on Alan Singer, "A Teacher's Guide to Cooperative Learning in Middle School Social Studies Classrooms," *In Transition, Journal of the New York State Middle School Association*, 10(2), Winter 1993: 16–21.

Social studies classes have heavy responsibilities. Students must learn content and concepts while mastering the skills needed for analytical thinking and information processing. In addition, they are expected to become members of learning communities, where they develop the ability to work with people from diverse backgrounds and explore the values they need to be productive citizens in a multicultural, democratic society. Making the situation for teachers even more complicated, in many districts there is pressure to de-track schools so that students are no longer grouped into classes based on past academic performance. Often this change includes the mainstreaming of students who had previously been assigned to special education classes because of difficulties learning in traditional settings.

There is no magic wand that will transform students into avid social studies fanatics and change them from passive recipients of "knowledge" to active participants in learning. However, teachers have discovered strategies that can increase student involvement and interest in learning social studies, and enhance the social skills they need to work together. One of the most effective strategies is "cooperative learning."

Cooperative learning is not new. Students taught and learned from each other in colonial and frontier America; fans of author Laura Ingalls Wilder know that cooperative learning was used in her one- room prairie schoolhouse. As a result of the ideas of educators like John Dewey and Francis Parker, cooperative learning was popular in the late nineteenth and early twentieth centuries, and many social studies teachers continue to use elements of cooperative learning in group work, projects, and reports. Frank Maniscalco, a science teacher who is a member of the New Teachers Network, argues that cooperative learning teams are at the core of any successful science laboratory program. He was actually surprised to learn that this "lab" approach is also used in social studies and recommends cross-discipline cooperation by teachers so they can learn from each other.

As with any other educational "innovation," advocates of cooperative learning frequently disagree with each other about the best approaches and the most important goals. However, some common points do emerge in the educational literature and in teacher discussions:

- Cooperative learning enhances student interest in social studies and other subjects because it gives them a greater stake in what is happening in their class and in their education. In large classes, it provides students with more "individual attention" because they are involved in helping each other. Students at all academic levels, including students who need remediation and students who are academically advanced, seem to learn more, and to learn more effectively, in cooperative learning teams.
- Cooperative learning is an especially effective way to teach inclusive classes. While students work together and help each other, content and support

teachers (also known as regular and special education teachers) are free to circulate around the room and provide assistance where it is needed.

- Cooperative learning enhances the social skills and values that are so important for future academic and economic success, and that are essential for participation in a multicultural, democratic society.
- Teachers must be able to define their own classroom goals and to experiment with the approach or approaches that successfully involve their students in learning.

I used cooperative learning teams in large high school classes with over thirty students, and I consistently found three major benefits. First, there is significant improvement in the willingness of students to write and in the quality of their writing. Working in cooperative learning teams, students are able to stimulate and support each other and to edit each other's work. Second, participation in discussions in cooperative learning teams gave students an opportunity to test their ideas before presenting them to the full class and in front of me. It enabled students who generally did not participate in class discussions to participate more freely, either presenting their own ideas or representing their teams. As a result, class discussions were enriched by the addition of diverse viewpoints. Third, class attendance and punctuality in handing in assignments improved because students were able to make demands on their team members and follow up on each other. People having difficulty were less likely to get lost in the shuffle.

Before you experiment with cooperative learning in your classroom, I recommend reading additional resource material, participating in workshops sponsored by school districts, union-sponsored teacher centers, or local colleges. You should also talk with your colleagues. Someone may already be using cooperative learning in your school. Someone might want to start with you. It is easier to experiment with something new when you have a support group.

Teaching Activity: Goals and Objectives for Cooperative Learning

In classrooms using cooperative learning teams, students will learn to:

1. Work cooperatively in small groups.
2. Work cooperatively with students from other racial, ethnic, and religious backgrounds, and across differences created by gender, class, interest, and academic achievement level.
3. Give leadership to and accept leadership from others.
4. Respect the abilities and contributions of others.
5. Understand the roles of cooperation, compromise, and consensus in democratic decision- making.

6. Participate in group and class activities with greater confidence in their individual abilities.
7. Explain their ideas orally and in writing more effectively.
8. Score higher on class and standardized tests.

Think it over:
Based on your experience as a student and your knowledge about the way that you and other people learn, how do you evaluate cooperative learning as a teaching strategy for social studies?

It's your classroom:
Many claims are made about the importance of cooperative learning. Which of these objectives would you consider most important in your classrooms? Why?

How Do You Begin?

Once you are committed to using cooperative learning in your classroom, the first step is defining your goals. What do you want to achieve? Do you want to focus on content or skills learning? Do you want to concentrate on group process and the development of democratic values? Do you want to address inter-group tensions in your class?

I advise beginning teachers to set achievable goals and integrate cooperative learning into their regular classroom approach. It also makes sense to involve students from the start in discussions about the goals and processes involved in cooperative learning. Listening to their ideas can be helpful, and it gives them a sense of ownership and responsibility from the beginning.

How Do You Organize Cooperative Learning Teams?

How you organize teams depends on your goals. In general, a teacher has to make two basic decisions: Will students be permitted to choose their groups or will they be assigned to groups? Will groups be homogenous (students are more alike) or heterogeneous (students are more different)? If students choose their own cooperative learning groups, the groups will most likely be based on friendships or shared interests.

Advantages of student choice are: (a) group members will more likely have prior experience working together; (b) group members will share more interests in common; (c) there may be fewer intra-group conflicts for the teacher, the group, and the class to deal with; and (d) students may have a greater sense of identification with the process if they feel that they selected their own groups.

Disadvantages of student choice are: (a) groups will more likely be segregated by race, ethnicity, gender, class, or academic achievement levels; (b) friendship bonds can be socially constraining as students try to learn and experiment; (c) some students will feel left out because they do not have a group of friends in the class; (d) teams based on friendship groups may tend to compete with each other in destructive ways; and (e) students will not have the opportunity to work with a new and diverse team of people where they all start out on an equal footing.

Sometimes teachers prefer to assign students to academically homogenous cooperative learning teams. Usually this happens when a class has a wide range of achievement or reading levels. Homogenous groupings allow cooperative learning teams to focus on particular skills. They allow teachers to help some students with remediation while others are allowed to accelerate.

The disadvantage of homogenous grouping is that it imitates academic and social tracking. Students are separated out and can be stigmatized. Frequently students feel trapped in "lower level achievement" groups and so are unwilling to invest in learning. Meanwhile, other students, working in accelerated groups, can become arrogant about their placement and contemptuous of their classmates. Instead of teaching students how to live and work with people who are different from them, homogenous groupings can reinforce the divisions that already exist in our society. Heterogeneous cooperative learning teams require more work from teachers. Student differences can contribute to group conflict, so teams will need active teacher involvement. Despite this, I recommend heterogeneous cooperative learning teams because they can provide students with a unique learning experience that helps teachers achieve key social goals.

Heterogeneous teams: (a) provide settings where people from different racial, ethnic, class, gender, and achievement groupings learn to work together in a structured, supportive, and mutually respectful environment; (b) allow students to learn from each other's strengths; (c) allow students to share across their differences, thereby enriching everyone's experience; (d) allow students to learn about shared interests, concerns, and humanity; (e) help teachers create miniature multicultural democratic communities that prepare students for active citizenship roles; and (f) stimulate all team members as students grapple with new ideas, concepts, and skills, and try to explain them to each other.

Students should discuss the advantages and disadvantages of choosing their own cooperative learning teams, and of heterogeneous versus homogenous groupings. After discussion, a teacher has the option to allow the class to make a decision or to make the decision for the class. Often, after a discussion of the goals of cooperative learning, a class will reach consensus that it wants teams to be heterogeneous, and that the fairest way is for the teacher to set them up.

Some parents and educators have questioned whether heterogeneous cooperative learning teams penalize "high-achieving" students. Studies conducted by cooperative learning specialists from the University of Minnesota show that "high achievers" working in heterogeneous cooperative learning teams do at least as well on standardized academic tests as high achievers who work in competitive individualized settings. "Low-level achievers" and "middle-level achievers" who are involved in heterogeneous cooperative learning teams almost always do better on these types of tests. Meanwhile, all groups of students benefit from the important social skills they develop by working in cooperative learning teams.

Teaching Activity: Organizing Cooperative Learning Teams

It's your classroom:
Considering the different goals in social studies classrooms, how would you organize cooperative learning teams? Why?

How Do I Insure That All Students on a Team Are Involved in the Team's Activities?
Cooperative learning teams are not just a group of students who are given an assignment and left alone to complete it. In our society, young people, as well as adults, need to learn how to work cooperatively. For cooperative learning teams to work successfully, teachers and students must have clear group process goals. There must be a clear structure for democratic group decision-making, and there must be a sense of shared group responsibility for the team. In *Circles of Learning* (Johnson et al. 1984), David Johnson, Roger Johnson, Edythe Johnson Holubec, and Patricia Roy suggested that the following should be built into the cooperative learning process:

- Teams need to depend on all of their team members to achieve the team's goals; students have to work together.
- Team members must be held collectively and individually accountable for learning by group members; everyone is responsible for the group.
- Responsibilities are divided up so that all team members have the opportunity to play both leadership and supporting roles.
- Teams are concerned with learning, and with maintaining cooperative group relations.
- Team members need to learn how to run meetings, make decisions, organize projects, divide responsibilities, and evaluate progress. Teachers cannot assume that students already have social and organizational group work skills.
- Teams must evaluate themselves, and be evaluated by teachers as teams, on both group process and the completed team product.

How Are Team Responsibilities Divided up Among Students?
Responsibilities can be divided up among students and then rotated on a regular schedule or when a team finishes a project. Team members will need to learn how to perform all of these important assignments. Sometimes a student will assume more than one responsibility. When team responsibilities are divided up, possible tasks include:

- Chairperson/Facilitator: The person responsible for leading team meetings.
- Recorder: The person who keeps a record of what is said at meetings and of team decisions.
- Reflector: A person assigned to listen carefully

during discussions so they can summarize key points at the end of meetings.

- Reporter: A person who reports on team problems and progress when the class meets as a whole.
- Liaison: A person who meets with representatives of other teams to share ideas.
- Organizer: A person who makes sure that work is completed on schedule and is ready to be presented or submitted.
- Mediator: A person who attempts to resolve internal conflicts between team members

Kristin Joseph, a middle school teacher who is part of the New Teacher Network, has cooperative learning teams in her social studies classes do a number of art-related projects. Among the jobs she assigns is a "Supplies Manager." She also finds it useful to designate someone to be the "Reader," the person whose reads project instructions aloud to the team before they begin.

How Big Should the Cooperative Learning Teams Be?

There must be at least two students, but more than six is probably unmanageable. Every group does not have to be the same size. Generally, I recommend groups of four. That way, if one person in a group is absent, there are still three people in class who can work together. But it makes sense to experiment. See what works.

How Long Should Groups Be Together?

If they are going to learn to work together, groups have to have some permanence. They should at least have an opportunity to finish a major project and a chance to evaluate what they have learned. However, some cooperative learning teams may never work well together. The class may need a new mix. It may make sense to reorganize teams every marking period or every semester. Why not see what your students think?

How Frequently Should Teams Meet?

It is impossible to answer in advance. You have to evaluate what makes sense in terms of the projects that the students are involved in, how well cooperative learning seems to be going in your classroom, and the other demands that you want to make on them.

Teaching Activity: Setting up a Classroom

The way you set up a social studies classroom depends on what makes sense to you and your class, what you are doing on any particular day, and what you have available. Do you have moveable desks, tables, and chairs? Is the room crowded, or is there space to breathe?

If I have a choice, I prefer moveable chairs with fixed arms. Even when I use cooperative learning with a class, I usually start every lesson with the room organized into rows. It makes it easier for me to perform clerical tasks (e.g., take attendance, check homework) and to get students started with the lesson. From there, we switch the room around depending on what we are going to do that day. Students can work individually, with a partner in the next row, or four chairs can be made into a pinwheel so that student cooperative learning teams can work together. If there is a student or teacher presentation, if we are watching a video, or if something needs to be copied off the board, we can keep the desks in rows. For a full- class discussion, we can "circle up."

Think it over:
When you were in middle school and high school, how did you like the room set up? Why?

What Does the Teacher Do While Students Are in Their Cooperative Learning Teams?

The teacher is busy, very busy, being an ex officio member of each cooperative learning team: You may (a) stick your head in a team meeting, listen for a while, say and do nothing, and then move on to another team; (b) ask a team a question or give it direction, helping a team solve an especially difficult academic problem; or (c) ask questions about how a team is working together. Perhaps some people are being left out or are disruptive. You may decide to ask team members to stop what they are doing and examine how they are working together. They may need you to mediate. They may need the entire class to get involved in their problem. They may only need to reflect on what they are doing in order to figure it out by themselves.

Further Reading on Cooperative Learning

"Cooperative Learning," *Educational Leadership* 47(4) (December 1989/January 1990). [This is a theme issue focusing on cooperative learning. Articles present research on the effectiveness of cooperative learning, different cooperative learning approaches, and selected resources for using cooperative learning.]

Johnson, D., Johnson, R. T., Holubec, E. J. and Roy, P. 1984. *Circles of learning: Cooperation in the Classroom*. Alexandria, VA: ASCD. [This book is a brief presentation of how to use cooperative learning in a classroom. It explains the goals, procedures, and problems in a cooperative learning program.]

Kohn, A. 1986. *No Contest: The Case Against Competition*. Boston, MA: Houghton Mifflin. [This book presents the case for cooperation in the classroom as part of a shift toward a more democratic, productive, and cooperative society.]

Essay 3: Sample Cooperative Learning Activity: Founders Discuss the Reasons for a New Constitution

In middle school social studies classes, fewer topics are examined than in high school, and they are covered in less detail. As a result, more time can be set aside for cooperative learning projects, individual and group research, book reviews, and student presentations. I would explain the project to the class before we began studying the US Constitution. Student cooperative learning teams could work on researching and writing parts for presentation as a culminating unit activity.

Introduction

The authors of the US Constitution were mostly wealthy and conservative. They were lawyers, merchants, investors, bankers, landlords, and plantation and slave owners. The original government under the Articles of Confederation owed money to 40 of these men. Not one of the 55 delegates who met in Philadelphia during the summer of 1787 was a woman, an African-American, a slave, an indentured servant, an urban craftsman, a Native American, or a poor white farmer.

Our final project goal is to produce a "television roundtable discussion," where we will try to answer this question: Could these men write a constitution and create a new government that would be fair to all Americans?

This package contains primary source documents from the time of the writing of the US Constitution. These documents discuss the rights of people and the job of government. Some of the people who speak here favor the US Constitution, some of them oppose it, and some of them are not sure whether it is a good idea.

For this project, each student team will be assigned one of the speakers:

- Find out as much as you can about your person and prepare a one-page biography of his or her life.

- Work together to translate the speaker's statement into more modern English.

- Use the biography and the translation to prepare a statement your person might make about whether the new US Constitution is a good idea.

- Select a team representative to portray your historical figure during the "television roundtable discussion." Team representatives will explain their historical figure's ideas about the US Constitution and join in a panel discussion discussing its merits and problems.

- After all of the roundtable participants speak, the studio audience asks them questions and joins in the discussion.

Roundtable Participants

Abigail Adams, Correspondent, wife of John Adams

John Adams, 1st vice-president, 2nd president of the United States

Benjamin Banneker, a free African-American who lived in Maryland, a scientist and architect

Benjamin Franklin, member of the Continental Congress and the Constitutional Convention

Alexander Hamilton, 1st secretary of the treasury, an author of the Federalist Papers, member of the Constitutional Convention

Patrick Henry, governor of Virginia

Thomas Jefferson, principal author of the Declaration of Independence, 3rd president of the United States

James Madison, secretary of the Constitutional Convention, an author of the Federalist Papers, 4th president of the United States

George Mason, Virginia delegate to the Constitutional Convention

Amos Singletary, delegate to the Massachusetts Convention to Ratify the Constitution

George Washington, president of the Constitutional Convention, 1st president of the United States

Robert Yates and James Lansing, New York State delegates to the Constitutional Convention

Other participants can be a small farmer from New York, a skilled worker from New England, an indentured servant from Virginia, an enslaved African from South Carolina, and people living on the Appalachian frontier.

SOURCES FOR QUOTES

Aptheker, H., ed. 1951. *A Documentary History of the Negro People in the United States*, vol. 1. Secaucus, NJ: Citadel.

Bailey, T. and Kennedy, D., eds. 1984. *The American Spirit*, vol. 1, 5th ed. Lexington, MA: D. C. Heath.

Farrand, M. 1911. *Records of the Federal Convention*, vol. 1. New Haven, CT: Yale University.

Feder, B. 1967. *Viewpoints: USA*. New York: American Book Company.

Fitzpatrick, J., ed. 1939. *The Writings of George Washington*, vol. 28. Washington, DC: Government Printing Office.

Madison, J. 1966. *Notes of Debates in the Federal Convention of 1787*. Athens, OH: Ohio University.

Rossiter, C., ed. 1961. *The Federalist Papers*. New York: New American Library.

Primary Source Statements

Thomas Jefferson wrote in the Declaration of Independence:

> 1776 – "We hold these truths to be self-evident; that all men are created equal; that they are endowed with certain unalienable rights; that among these are life, liberty and the pursuit of happiness. That to secure these rights, governments are instituted among men, deriving their just powers from the consent of the governed."

Thomas Jefferson discussed Shays' Rebellion:

> 1787 – "I hold it that a little rebellion now and then is a good thing, and as necessary in the political world as storms in the physical . . . It is a medicine necessary for the sound health of government."

> 1787 – "What country can preserve its liberties, if their rulers are not warned from time to time that this people preserve the spirit of resistance? Let them take arms! . . . What signify a few lives lost in a century or two? The tree of liberty must be refreshed from time to time with the blood of patriots and tyrants."

Thomas Jefferson commented on the new Constitution:

> 1787 – "I will now add what I do not like. First the omission of a bill of rights providing clearly . . . for freedom of religion, freedom of the press, protection against standing armies, restriction against monopolies . . . and trials by jury in all matters . . . Let me add that a bill of rights is what the people are entitled to against every form of government on earth."

Alexander Hamilton explained why the country needs a new US Constitution:

> 1787 – "We may . . . be said to have reached the last stage of national humiliation. There is scarcely anything that can wound the pride or degrade the character of an independent nation which we do not experience . . . Do we owe debts to foreigners and to our own citizens . . .? These remain without any proper or satisfactory provision for their discharge. Have we valuable territories and important posts in the possession of a foreign power which, by express stipulations, ought long since to have been surrendered? These are still retained . . . Are we in a condition to . . . repel the aggression? We have neither troops, nor treasury, nor government . . . Are we entitled by nature and compact to a free participation in the navigation of the Mississippi? Spain excludes us from it . . . Is commerce of importance to national wealth? Ours is at the lowest point . . ."

Alexander Hamilton defended the new US Constitution:

> 1787 – "Inequality would exist as long as liberty existed . . ., it would unavoidably result from that very liberty itself . . . Inequality of property constituted the great and fundamental distinction in Society."

> 1787 – "All communities divide themselves into the few and the many. The first are the rich and the well-born, the other the mass of the people . . . The people are turbulent and changing; they seldom judge or determine right."

Amos Singletary feared what would happen if the US Constitution were approved by the states:

> 1788 – "These lawyers, and men of learning, and moneyed men, that talk so finely and gloss over matters so smoothly, to make us poor illiterate people swallow down the pill, except to get into Congress themselves. They expect to be the managers of this Constitution, and get all the power and all the money into their own hands. And then they will swallow up all us little folks . . . This is what I am afraid of."

George Washington was critical of the Articles of Confederation:

1785 – "The confederation appears to me to be little more than a shadow without the substance . . . Indeed, it is one of the most extraordinary things . . . that we should confederate as a nation, and yet be afraid to give the rulers of that nation . . . sufficient powers to order and direct the affairs of the same . . . From the high ground on which we stood, we are descending into the vale of confusion and darkness."

1786 – "The better kind of people, being disgusted with these circumstances, will have their minds prepared for any revolution whatever. We are apt to run from one extreme to another . . . Would to God that wise measures may be taken in time to avert the consequences we have but too much reason to apprehend."

1786 – "We have probably had too good an opinion of human nature in forming our Confederation. Experience has taught us that men will not adopt, and carry into execution, measures the best calculated for their own good, without the intervention of coercive power . . ."

George Washington discussed Shays' Rebellion:

1786 – "Mankind, when left to themselves, are unfit for their own government. I am mortified beyond expression when I view the clouds that have spread over the brightest morn that ever dawned upon any Country."

1786 – "Without an alteration in our political creed . . . we are fast verging to anarchy and confusion . . . What stronger evidence can be given of the want of energy in our government, than these disorders? . . . Thirteen sovereignties pulling against each other, and all tugging at the federal head, will soon bring ruin on the whole . . ."

George Washington defended the new US Constitution:

1787 – "The legality of this Constitution I do not mean to discuss, . . . that which takes the shortest course to obtain them, will, in my opinion, under the present circumstances, be found best. Otherwise, like a house on fire, whilst the most regular mode of extinguishing it is contended for, the building is reduced to ashes."

Benjamin Banneker wanted to extend rights to enslaved Africans:

1791 – "I freely and cheerfully acknowledge, that I am of the African race, and in that color which is natural to them of the deepest dye . . . Suffer me to recall to your mind that time, in which the arms and tyranny of the British crown were exerted, with every powerful effort, in order to reduce you to a state of servitude . . . This, Sir, was a time when you clearly saw into the injustice of a state of slavery . . . But, Sir, how pitiable is it to reflect, that although you were so fully convinced of the benevolence of the Father of Mankind, . . . that you should at the same time counteract his mercies, in detaining by fraud and violence so numerous a part of my brethren."

Abigail Adams discussed Shays' Rebellion:

1787 – "With regard to the tumults in my native state which you inquire about, I wish I could say that the report had exaggerated them. It is too true Sir, that they have been carried to so alarming a height as to stop the courts of justice in several counties. Ignorant, restless desperadoes, without conscience or principles, have led a deluded multitude to follow their standard, under pretense of grievances which have no existence but in their imaginations. Some of them were crying out for a paper currency, some for an equal distribution of property. Some were for annihilating all debts, others complaining that the Senate was a useless branch of government, that the court of common pleas was unnecessary, and that the sitting of the General Court in Boston was a grievance. By this list you will see the materials which compose this rebellion, and the necessity there is of the wisest and most vigorous measures to quell and suppress it. Instead of that laudable spirit which you approve, which makes people watchful over their liberties and alert in the defense of them, these mobbish insurgents are for sapping the foundation, and destroying the whole fabric at once."

John Adams wanted a strong national government:

1787 – "Property is surely a right of mankind as really as liberty. Perhaps, at first, prejudice, habit, shame or fear, principle or religion, would restrain the poor from attacking the rich, and the idle from usurping on the industrious; but the time would not be long before courage and enterprise would come, and pretexts be invented by degrees to countenance the majority into dividing all the property among them . . . The moment the idea is admitted into society, that property is not as sacred as the laws of God . . . anarchy and tyranny commence . . ."

Patrick Henry feared the new US Constitution would create a new king:

1788 – "This constitution is said to have beautiful features; but when I come to examine these features, sir, they appear to me horribly frightful: among other deformities, it has an awful squinting; it squints toward monarchy."

1788 – "Our rights and privileges are endangered . . . The rights of conscience, trial by jury, liberty of the press, all our immunities and franchises, all pretensions to human rights and privileges are rendered insecure, if not lost, by this change."

James Madison believed the US Constitution solved many problems:

1787 – "The diversity in the faculties of men from which the rights of property originate is . . . an . . . obstacle to a uniformity of interests. The protection of these faculties is the first object of government . . . The possession of different degrees and kinds of property immediately results, and . . . ensues a division of society into different interests and parties."

1787 – "The most common and durable source of factions has been the various and unequal distribution of property. Those who hold and those who are without property have ever formed distinct interests in society."

1787 – "A pure democracy can admit no cure for the mischief of factions. A republic promises the cure for which we are seeking."

Robert Yates and John Lansing refused to sign the new US Constitution:

1788 – "A general government, however guarded by declarations of rights, ... must unavoidably, in a short time, be productive of the destruction of the civil liberty of such citizens who could be effectively coerced by it."

George Mason condemned the new Constitution:

1787 – "This government will set out a moderate aristocracy: it is at present impossible to foresee whether it will, ... produce a monarchy or a corrupt, tyrannical aristocracy. It will most probably vibrate some years between the two, and then terminate in the one or the other."

Benjamin Franklin was not completely sure:

1787 – "I confess that there are several parts of this constitution which I do not at present approve . . . I agree to this Constitution with all its faults, . . . because I think a general Government necessary for us."

1787 – "Few men in public affairs act from a mere view of the good of their country, whatever they may pretend; and though their activity may bring real good to their country, they do not act from a spirit of benevolence."

Teaching Activity: Dramatic Presentation of Constitutional Controversies

The historical background for this activity comes from Charles Beard (1913), *An Economic Interpretation of the Constitution of the United States* (New York: Macmillan) and Howard Zinn (1995), *A People's History of the United States* (New York: HarperCollins).

Add your voice to the discussion:
This activity is based on a particular interpretation of the Constitutional Convention. In your opinion, is it legitimate to introduce it into a middle school classroom? Why or why not?

It's your classroom:
As a middle school teacher, would you be willing to invest the time necessary for this type of project? Why or why not?

Teaching Activities: Sample Social Studies Cooperative Learning Activities

Project Teams:
Cooperative learning teams can be organized to conceptualize, research, outline, write, and present group reports. Cooperative learning team projects can include craft activities like Navaho sand paintings, dramatic presentations, preparing international foods, teaching the class folk songs, spirituals, or presenting a traditional folk dance. These kinds of activities allow students with skills that are not usually drawn upon in social studies classes to play important leadership roles. A cooperative learning team project can involve producing a current events newspaper, a dramatic presentation in class, or radio/television news broadcast. Cooperative learning teams can design questionnaires and conduct interviews.

Class Work Teams:
Instead of students working individually on class assignments, teams can work together and help each other with problem-solving activities, reading comprehension questions, map assignments, or worksheets.

Study Groups:
Students can meet regularly in cooperative learning study teams to prepare for tests and quizzes.

Writing Pairs:
Students can be paired off within their cooperative learning teams to read each other's written work, respond to each other's ideas, edit, and suggest alternatives.

Add your voice to the conversation:
1. As a secondary school student, how did you respond to cooperative learning activities and projects?
2. How would you use your own experiences to better organize cooperative learning?

References and Recommendations for Further Reading

Beard, C. 1913. *An Economic Interpretation of the Constitution of the United States*. New York: Macmillan.

Bloom, B., ed. 1985. *Taxonomy of educational objectives, handbook 1: Cognitive domain*. New York: Longman.

Bulik, M. 2001. "American Gothic: Terrorists' and tribunals in the Civil War era," *The New York Times*, December 30.

Danzer, G., Kor De Alava, J., Kreiger, L., et al. 2002. *The Americans: reconstruction to the 21st century*. Boston, MA: Houghton Mifflin.

DeRose, J. 2007. "History textbooks 'theirs' and 'ours'," *Rethinking Schools* 22(1): Fall.

Dobkin, W., Fischer, J. Ludwig B. and Koblinger R., eds. 1985. *A handbook for the teaching of social studies*. New York: The Association of Teachers of Social Studies.

LaFeber, W. 1998. *The new empire: An interpretation of American expansion, 1860–1898*. Ithaca, NY: Cornell University Press.

Lindaman, D. and Ward, K. 2004. *History lessons: How textbooks from around the world portray U.S. history*. New York: New Press.

Manson, G. and Clegg, A. 1970. "Classroom questions: Keys to children's thinking," *Peabody Journal of Education* 47(5): 302–7.

Seeger P. and Reiser, B. 1986. *Carry it on!* New York: Simon and Schuster.

Singer, A. 2008. "DBQ: Annexation of the Philippines," *Social Science Docket*, 8(2): 4–7.

Social Science Docket. 2004. "Documenting New York state labor history," *Social Science Docket*, 4(1): Winter-Spring.

United Nations General Assembly. 1953. *The universal declaration of human rights: A guide for teachers*. Paris: UNESCO.

Zinn, H. 1995. *A People's History of the United States*. New York: HarperCollins.

III. Implementing Your Ideas

10. How Can Social Studies Teachers Plan Controversy-Centered, Thematic, and Interdisciplinary Units?

Overview

- Refine educational goals
- Discuss the role of controversial issues
- Explore thematic and interdisciplinary alternatives for unit planning
- Find ways to connect educational goals with unit planning

Key Concepts

Themes, Controversy, Complexity, Academic Freedom, Interdisciplinary Teaching, Connections, Inclusion

Questions

- How Should Controversial Issues Be Addressed in Social Studies Curricula?
- Why Teach Thematic Units?
- How Do You Organize a Controversy-Centered, Thematic Curriculum?
- How Should We Deal With Sensitive Topics?
- Should Thematic Units Focus on Particular Social Groups?
- How Can Different Subjects Be Connected in the Social Studies Classroom?

Essays

1. Expanding Our Concept of Inclusion
2. Women's History Month Curriculum
3. Responding to Crisis: What Can Social Studies Teachers Do?

HOW SHOULD CONTROVERSIAL ISSUES BE ADDRESSED IN SOCIAL STUDIES CURRICULA?

In the spring of 1989, while my 11th-grade US history classes were examining the US Supreme Court's 1973 *Roe* v. *Wade* decision, five young women approached me after class and asked if I would take them to Washington, DC, to participate in a "pro-choice" demonstration. I told them that I would be glad to accompany them if it were organized as an official school trip. I recommended that they speak with the school's student political action club (I was the faculty advisor) about sponsoring them. The students agreed; the club and the school's administration gave approval; the trip was arranged; and we went to Washington with a contingent from a local public college.

Because reproductive rights, abortion, and anything else that relates to teenage sexuality are controversial subjects in nearly every American community, most teachers avoid them like the plague. I could have sidestepped the issue entirely ("I'm sorry but I'm not able to go") or simply referred the young women to the local college group. However, I made a decision that supporting these young women's interest in active political involvement created a potential "learning moment" for them and other students in our school. The next fall, these young activists spurred the political action club to organize a school-wide dialogue on the reproductive rights of teenage women, and to send an entire bus-load of students to participate in another pro-choice rally in the nation's capital.

The excitement generated by these young women, and amplified by the political action club, spilled over into my social studies classrooms. Because of their uncertainties about, and encounters with, human sexuality, the controversy over reproductive rights was already on the minds of many students and emerged as a major theme in my "Participation in Government" classes. That semester, students considered moral, philosophical, and political attitudes about reproductive decisions. They became avid readers of the newspaper and engaged in meaningful writing activities that helped them achieve higher literacy standards. They wrote and circulated petitions supporting their individual positions and attended public meetings. They designed posters and flyers; wrote speeches and letters; and examined the division among national, state, and local authority under the federal system, the balance of power within the federal government, how a bill becomes a law, the constitutional amendment process, Judicial Review, and the local social service budget. Students also debated the roles of citizens and government in a democratic society, the relationship between church and state in the United States, and their ideas about other First Amendment principles. If I had avoided this controversial issue out of concern with becoming embroiled in community battles over abortion and teenage sexuality, none of this would have been achieved.

The official position of the National Council for the Social Studies (NCSS) is that social studies teachers should "face up to controversy and ... assume the special responsibility to teach students how to think." In the forward to its 45th Annual Yearbook, which focused on teaching controversial issues, Council President Jean Tilford wrote (Muessig 1975): "With the Watergate debacle etched on every mind, with disputes over school textbooks providing many pages of copy for newspapers, and with nations continuing to tear at each other's boundaries, teachers of social studies have been living closely with controversy." She concluded that the secondary school social studies curriculum was the best place to prepare young people to become active citizens armed with the critical thinking and problem-solving skills needed to form opinions and address these controversies. However, Tilford also noted that, "[I]n spite of the dissent of the 1960s, Vietnam, and proliferating energy crises, some social studies classrooms have ignored all aspects of controversy. Perhaps in fear, or because of feelings of inadequacy about coping with volatile issues, they have ignored the critical examination of contemporary events. As one observer of the current social studies scene commented, 'Better the artifacts than the actualities of the present'" (p. viii).

These ideas were reaffirmed most recently in 2007 in an NCSS position statement on academic freedom that called for the study of controversial issues "in a spirit of critical inquiry" that exposes "students to a variety of ideas, even if they are different from their own" (NCSS 2007: 282).

Although I agree with the NCSS concern with educating a probing, critical citizenry, I believe that this requires social studies teachers to emphasize, not just introduce, controversial, contemporary, and historical issues in the curriculum. Recognizing and discussing controversies offers students a much more accurate picture of human societies and history. It also legitimizes student's perceptions of the existence of class, ethnic, racial, gender, ideological, and generational conflicts. It makes students uncomfortable with pat answers and their own preconceptions, and it stimulates them to delve for deeper meaning, to reconsider their own ideas, and to buttress their conclusions with supporting evidence. Last, but not least, a thematic focus on a controversial issue makes social studies learning a lot more exciting.

Teaching Activity: Is History Too Straight?

Among the "blanks" in history is recognition of achievements by gay men and lesbians. For example, evidence suggests that prominent historical figures, including Hadrian, Leonardo da Vinci, Michelangelo, Walt Whitman, and Eleanor Roosevelt were homosexuals. Many gay and lesbian activists argue that ignoring their sexual identity contributes to the sense that homosexuals are somehow dangerous aliens, who should be kept separate and denied rights by the rest of society.

Think it over:
In your opinion, should teachers identify the sexual preference of prominent historical figures where strong evidence exists that they were gay or lesbian? Why or why not?

It's your classroom:
During discussion in class, a student refers to a historical figure, someone in the news, or another student as a "faggot." What do you do? Why?

WHY TEACH THEMATIC UNITS?

Important and/or controversial social studies issues cannot be addressed effectively in a single class period. Issues are too complicated and lessons will be messy. When a class is excited by a topic, everyone wants to speak. Students often go off on extended tangents. When disagreements are real, rather than fabricated, people can be short-tempered and dismissive of each other. Outspoken, forceful students who present controversial views may upset classmates. Many days are needed to clarify issues, gather supporting evidence for positions, develop and give a fair hearing to alternative voices, examine criteria for evaluating positions, and reach either consensus or respectful disagreement.

A controversy-centered approach to social studies requires long-term careful planning, and it is best addressed in thematic units or with long-term themes that are woven throughout the curriculum. Possible social studies topics that allow students to explore multiple points of view on controversial issues through a series of lessons include the following:

1. Struggles for women's rights in the United States or around the world
2. Racial and ethnic similarities and differences, and their cultural or biological roots
3. The role of religion in history, in our society, and in world events
4. The impact of scientific thinking on societies, including the debate over evolution and creationism
5. The existence and origin of universal human rights
6. The possibility of social justice in the United States or other countries
7. Whether racism, imperialism, and exploitation are peripheral or fundamental elements of civilizations
8. The possibility of a more equal distribution of economic resources in society without jeopardizing either its ability to satisfy human needs and wants or individual freedom.

With broad themes that extend an entire year, students can: (a) compare the promise vs. the reality of US society throughout its history; (b) explore the thesis that democracy is a unique product of Western history with roots in the ancient Hellenistic world; or (c) examine theories about human nature while attempting to understand the institution of slavery or periodic genocides. As students study history, they can also become involved in exploring and critiquing historical explanations. Does history record gradual and inevitable human progress? Is multiculturalism an effort to combat forced assimilation, or a divisive ideology that threatens the survival of the United States as a nation?

Thematic teaching does not necessarily have to focus on controversial issues. Long-term themes that explore relationships between geography and history, the causes of historical events, the impact of technological development on societies, or the importance of cultural diffusion and exchange do not necessarily involve classroom controversy. But isn't social studies more exciting for both students and teachers when we examine whether environmental disasters are caused by acts of nature or people, whether individuals or groups can change the course of history, who benefits from technology and who suffers, and the impact of cultural, economic, and political imperialism on conquered peoples?

Classroom Activity: Behind the Headlines

At the start of the term or a unit, student teams examine recent newspapers to identify broad social, economic, and political issues and raise their own questions about current events. Lists of issues and questions are compared, consolidated, and developed into underlying themes for repeated exploration during the semester.

Try it yourself:
Using a recent edition of the newspaper, make a list of broad issues behind the headlines and questions about these issues.

Add your voice to the discussion:
In your opinion, can students identify useful themes for long-term study? Why or why not?

It's your classroom:
Would you use the same theme or themes for an entire unit, a semester, or a year? Why or why not?

HOW DO YOU ORGANIZE A CONTROVERSY-CENTERED, THEMATIC CURRICULUM?

Conflicting ideas about the nature of human rights makes an exploration of human rights issues an excellent thematic focus for a high school social studies curriculum. It can be adapted for use in classes studying the history and government of the United States, the origins and development of Western civilization, or the history and cultures of the non-Western world. During the course of a semester or a year, students can examine the origin of ideas about human rights and human nature, different notions about what constitutes a human right, and the impact of ideas about human rights on different societies and social groups (Banks and Gregory, 1996: 4–5; Singer, 1996: 16–23).

A thematic focus on human rights issues provides a lens for examining social conflicts, as well as social and individual choices. It involves students in understanding the complexity of ideas and issues, how the same events can be viewed from multiple perspectives, and the importance of making informed judgments based on evidence, thoughtful consideration of individual and social values, and respect for difference.

I have used songs and children's literature to open up class discussions on struggles for human rights. *Die Gedanken Sind Frei* ("Ideas Are Free," available at: http://www.diegedankensindfrei.com/, accessed November 5, 2007) and *Die Moorsoldaten* ("Peat Bog Soldiers," available at: http://flag.blackened.net/revolt/hist_texts/songs_moorsoldaten.html, accessed November 5, 2007) are songs of the Germany anti-Nazi resistance. I also use more recent popular songs, especially *Rebel Music* by Bob Marley and the Wailers (available at: http://web.bobmarley.com, accessed November 5, 2007) and the work of Public Enemy (available at: htttp://publicenemy.com, accessed November 5, 2007), and Pink Floyd (available at: http://www.allfloyd.com/lyrics/Lyrics.html, accessed November 5, 2007).

My wife and colleague, Judith Singer (2001: 61–62), was a day-care director and is now an elementary school social studies educator. She "turned me on" to using children's literature, especially the work of Eve Bunting, to introduce human rights issues in the classroom. Bunting has written extensively on the right of children to be protected from "terrible things." Judi recommends reading Bunting's books with preschoolers and their parents and with "children" of all ages.

Exploring questions (e.g., Are there such a things as inalienable human rights? Where do human rights come from? How are human rights defined and by whom? Do human rights include the right or obligation to resist injustice?) involves students in broad discussions of philosophy, religion, anthropology, political science, and history, and an examination of a number of controversial issues. For example, students can examine whether the idea of inalienable human rights is a uniquely Western invention, or also has roots and relevance in other cultures.

Classroom Activity: United Nations Charter

"[T]he peoples of the United Nations have in the Charter reaffirmed their faith in fundamental human rights, in the dignity and worth of the human person and in the equal rights of men and women and have determined to promote social progress and better standards of life in larger freedom" (Universal Declaration of Human Rights, United Nations General Assembly, December 10, 1948).

Think it over:

In your opinion, what are the origins of "fundamental human rights?" Why do you believe these are the origins?

Try it yourself:

Suppose you were on the United Nations committee drafting the "Universal Declaration of Human Rights." Make a list of the specific rights you would want to include in this document. Write a brief explanation of why you would include each of these rights.

A human rights theme lends itself to the kind of animated classroom dialogue that engages secondary school students. Students can discuss whether belief in the idea of higher laws and human rights requires belief in a supreme being, or whether these ideas can be based on human consensus and shared social values. A related question, premised on belief in divine law is this: Who interprets God's will? In the United States in the first half of the nineteenth century, both pro-slavery and abolitionist groups argued that the Christian Bible justified their position. More recently, feminists, including practicing Christians, have argued that the right to control one's body and freedom of reproductive choice are fundamental human rights. They are challenged by the Roman Catholic Church hierarchy, for example, which continues to declare abortion a violation of God's commandments and of an inalienable human right to life.

Examining the question "Do human rights include the right or obligation to resist injustice?" involves students in the issue of whether it is ever right to break a civil law in the name of fundamental human rights. Most students would argue that complicity with the Nazi regime in Germany was immoral, and that violating Nazi laws through armed resistance or efforts to help people targeted for extermination were morally justified. But choices are generally not so easy. For example, does a nation committed to a belief in human rights have an obligation to intervene in contemporary genocidal conflicts in the Balkans or Africa? Or, should citizens refuse to pay taxes that are used to build nuclear weapons or that support dictatorial regimes?

Because of its tolerance of slavery, William Lloyd Garrison denounced the US Constitution as a "covenant with death" and an "agreement with hell" (Feder 1967: 127). Henry David Thoreau declared that he could not "recognize that political organization as my government which is the slave's government also" (Feder 1967: 127). He insisted that "if the law is of such a nature that it requires you to be an agent of injustice to another," people should "break the law." Was the United States guilty of massive human rights violations? Do descendants of enslaved Africans or Native Americans have a right to reparations? In US history classes, students can discuss these questions and whether efforts to help enslaved people escape from bondage, including armed resistance to slavery, were justified as a defense of human rights.

Thomas Jefferson, who owned enslaved Africans, is perhaps the best-known US advocate of unalienable human rights, including the idea that resistance to oppression is a fundamental human right. In the Declaration of Independence, Jefferson asserted, "whenever any Form of Government becomes destructive of these ends (achieving inalienable rights), it is the Right of the People to alter or to abolish it ..." (Bailey and Kennedy 1984: 101).

During the debate over the ratification of the US Constitution, Jefferson expanded on his position regarding the legitimacy of resistance to oppression. In a letter to James Madison, he declared, "I hold that a little rebellion now and then is a good thing ... It is a medicine necessary for the sound health of government." In a letter to William S. Smith, he argued, "What country can preserve its liberties, if their rulers are not warned from time to time that this people preserve the spirit of resistance? ... The tree of liberty must be refreshed from time to time with the blood of patriots and tyrants. It is its natural manure" (Feder 1967: 45).

In the United States in the twentieth century, the idea of resistance to oppression as a funda-mental human right is central to the type of nonviolent civil disobedience championed by Martin Luther King, Jr. In King's Easter 1963 letter to the clergy of Birmingham, Alabama, he referred both to traditional Christian beliefs and to the ideas of the founders of the United States in order to defend direct action and resistance to oppression as crucial components of human rights. In other statements, King even suggested that the right to resist oppression might be the only human right that cannot be taken away.

Classroom Activity: Declaration of Independence

"We hold these truths to be self-evident, that all men are created equal, that they are endowed by their Creator with certain unalienable Rights, that among these are Life, Liberty and the pursuit of happiness" (United States, Declaration of Independence, July 4, 1776).

Think it over:
- In your opinion, did the United States inherit a commitment to human rights from the European Enlightenment? Explain.
- Does this statement represent a sufficient commitment to human rights for today's world? Why?

Try it yourself:
If you could rewrite this statement, how would you change it?

Classroom Activity: Ideas of Martin Luther King, Jr.

"We have not made a single gain in civil rights without determined legal and non-violent pressure. Lamentably, it is an historical fact that privileged groups seldom give up their privileges voluntarily. . . . We know through painful experience that freedom is never voluntarily given by the oppressor; it must be demanded by the oppressed."—Martin Luther King, Jr., Letter from Birmingham Jail, April 16, 1963 (King 1963).

Think it over:
What forms of resistance by oppressed people do you believe are justified when oppressors do not respect human rights? Why do you support these methods? Why do you reject other methods?

Try it yourself:
King argued that "freedom is never voluntarily given by the oppressor; it must be demanded by the oppressed." Can you cite some historical examples that support this position? Can you cite some historical examples that contradict this position?

It's your classroom:
How would you help your students consider the morality of violence?

Groups and individuals representing more conservative and traditional ideas have also advanced the notion of resistance to oppression as a basic human right. For example, in March 1995, in an encyclical condemning abortion and euthanasia, Pope John Paul II (1995: 133–136) called on Roman Catholics and other people of good will, "under grave obligation of conscience not to cooperate formally in practices which, even if permitted by civil legislation, are contrary to God's law." He declared that resisting an injustice is "not only a moral duty—it is also a basic human right."

A thematic focus on resistance to oppression makes possible a comparative study of resistance movements in different societies around the world. Students can discuss similarities and differences in the philosophies and strategies of the Mau Mau rebellion against the British in Kenya, the African National Congress campaign against apartheid in South Africa, Gandhi and the Indian independence movement, Irish struggles against the British for home rule, and various anti-Nazi resistance movements in Europe during World War II. Frequently students will discover that people with whom they sympathize engage in activities that violate other human rights that they value.

Clearly, a human rights theme has the potential to introduce many complex issues into a social studies curriculum. One of its most important contributions is this: It encourages students to discuss individual responsibility, how they would respond to human rights claims and violations of civil law by people with whom they agree, and by people who hold ideas and embrace causes that they find unacceptable or even disturbing. It also helps them understand that explaining and justifying an event or social movement are not the same things.

Learning Activity: Anti-Slavery Resistance

Adapted from A. Singer (1996) with the permission of *Social Science Record.*

In 1850, the US Congress passed a Fugitive Slave law as part of the Compromise of 1850. Under the new law, anyone who helped enslaved Africans escape to freedom was subject to heavy fines and jail sentences. This law incited northern opposition to slavery. Especially hated was a clause requiring white northerners to join the slave-catching posses. Ralph Waldo Emerson, an abolitionist, declared, "The act of Congress . . . is a law which every one of you will break on the earliest occasion—a law which no man can obey . . . without loss of self-respect . . ." (Singer 1996).

William Parker was the head of a local African-American self-defense organization in Christiana, Pennsylvania. In September 1951, he received word that slavecatchers were in the area. Parker, two other African-American men, and two African-American women, decided to protect local escapees. A battle ensued, and one of the slavecatchers was killed. Following the skirmish, 36 local African-Americans and five local whites, most of whom were bystanders during the battle, were charged with treason against the United States for resisting a US Marshall, with violating the Fugitive Slave law, and with rebellion against the government. Their trial, which drew national attention, involved the largest group ever charged with treason at one time in US history. Among the defense lawyers was prominent abolitionist and Congressman, Thaddeus Stevens.

Eventually, the people brought to trial were found "not guilty" of treason, and other charges were dropped. The trial helped convince southerners that their "property rights" would never be respected by a northern-dominated federal government. It left northerners increasingly angered by what they perceived as southern attempts to force them to participate in maintaining and defending slavery. As a result of the anti-slavery resistance at Christiana, the country moved another step closer to civil war and the abolition of slavery.

For high school students, the story of the Christiana anti-slavery resistance and the trial provides the opportunity to examine the meaning of human rights, especially the right to resist oppression. William Parker and his supporters clearly broke the law, and in the process of breaking the law, a member of the US Marshall's posse was killed. Students can discuss the following questions:

1. Did a higher law give William Parker and the other Christiana defenders the right to break civil laws and resist returning the escapees to slavery?
2. Did free African-Americans and formerly enslaved Africans have an obligation to obey the laws of the United States, or did they have the human right to resist the injustice of enslavement, even if it meant killing a slave owner?
3. What happens when rights are in conflict (e.g., the right to own property and the right to personal freedom)?
4. What happens to a country if resistance to its laws is recognized as a human right?

5. Was resistance to slavery in the name of human rights a cause of the Civil War?
6. Could slavery have ended without civil war if the people who wanted to abolish slavery had been willing to compromise, instead of insisting on the human rights of enslaved Africans?
7. What would you have done if you were William Parker? Why?
8. What would you have done if you were a local white person ordered by a marshal to join a slave-catching posse? Why?

Teaching Activity: Resistance at Christiana, PA

As follow-up activities, teachers can try some of these ideas.

- Students can stage a trial of William Parker and the Christiana defenders for treason and/or murder, using primary source documents as evidence.
- Students can write editorials for an 1851 newspaper about the anti-slavery resistance and the trial for treason. They can either express their own views or the views held by different groups in the United States at the time.
- Students can create a portfolio of current events articles about contemporary resistance movements that resort to violence in the name of "higher laws" or human rights. They can compare their reactions to these movements with the resistance at Christiana.
- As a final project for a thematic curriculum based on an exploration of human rights issues, a class or school can sponsor a convention where students discuss historical and contemporary issues relating to human rights, and draft their own statement on human rights. At the convention, students can represent themselves or different nations and historical groups.

It's your classroom:
1. Would you use activities like these in your classroom? Why or why not?
2. Would the race or ethnicity of your students influence your approach to these questions and activities? Why or why not?

HOW SHOULD WE DEAL WITH SENSITIVE TOPICS?

Earlier in this chapter, I wrote that because some issues are emotionally charged, sensitivity is required whenever teachers express their views. I have had to deal with this repeatedly when doing lessons on the impact of the events of September 11, 2001. I have been a strong opponent of the United States invasions of both Afghanistan and Iraq. I believe the wars were unjustified and made a difficult situation worse, rather than better.

In the New York metropolitan area where I teach, views on the invasions are tempered by people's personal experiences and feelings about the attack on the World Trade Center. I have spoken with high school and college classes where students and teachers had family members, friends, and neighbors who died in the attack or the rescue effort. In these lessons, I generally open with a question on the board, "What are the lessons of 9/11?" and a handout for students to read with a brief excerpt from a newspaper article about September 11th itself or about the debate leading up to the attacks on Afghanistan and Iraq. This establishes for students what we will be discussing in the class. Then, before I say anything else, I ask if anyone has a comment or a question they would like to make to the group. If people are quiet, I prod them a little by saying that I am sure people have talked about it before. I even ask if someone is willing to share personal experience from that day.

When students speak, and they eventually do, I ask then to explain a little more and jot down notes on the board based on what they say. Students talk about their fears and anger. They also express misconceptions and factual errors that we can later examine. This part of the activity can take half of my allotted time, but I do it because students must know they are respected before they can hear me.

Once others have finished speaking, I start. Often I put on a T-shirt I made that accused

George Bush of war crimes and demanded his impeachment. This always gets students to ask questions and provokes great discussions. Sometimes the discussions are so good and students are so knowledgeable that I say little else. Usually, however, students want me to explain my views, and are interested in what I have to say because I already demonstrated that I was interested in what they had to say.

SHOULD THEMATIC UNITS FOCUS ON PARTICULAR SOCIAL GROUPS?

Throughout human history, including most of US history, women have been, at best, second-class citizens. Their continuing second-class status is reflected in many social studies classrooms, where the roles played by women in society and their achievements in the past and present continue to remain virtually invisible. Although the names and faces of women now appear more frequently in social studies textbooks, their inclusion is generally an addition to an already existing curriculum. Female heroes are discovered and fit into previous topics and categories. There is little exploration of the role of women in earlier societies—the ways they lived, the accommodations they were forced to make to patriarchal and oppressive social mores, the familial and community networks and institutions they built, or the struggles women engaged in to achieve legal, political, and economic rights. Nel Noddings (1992: 230–241) argues that a completely reconceptualized social studies curriculum should focus on women's culture, the realm of the home and family, the idea of women's work, and the role of women as community and international peacemakers.

Over the years, Andrea Libresco became so frustrated with the gaps in textbooks that she encouraged her students to place post-it notes in their social studies books adding new information about women and other groups. Each new "generation" of students learns from the previous generations and provides insights of its own.

In the first edition of *Social Studies for Secondary Schools* (1997), I examined how major middle school, high school, and advanced placement United States history textbooks reported on Woman's Suffrage. In the second edition, I decided to see how some of the publishers had changed their coverage. One of the first things I noticed was that publishers had expanded the membership of the teams that write and edit textbooks and have included more women. Whether this is the reason for the change or not, coverage of the struggles of women in the United States for full citizenship rights seems to have improved.

Women's History—A Middle School Textbook (1984)

Ernest R. May, in *A Proud Nation* (1984), mentioned campaigns for woman's suffrage six times. An insert containing the Constitution, the Amendments, and comments informed students that "the right to vote was finally extended to women in 1920" (p. 266). The unit on "An Era of Improvement" discussed movements for reform, including the women's rights movement. It included a photograph of Susan B. Anthony and a caption that recounts her arrest and conviction for voting in the 1872 Presidential election (pp. 370–371). This unit also included a full-page focus on "Lucy Stone's Solitary Battle" for women's rights (p. 374). Campaigns for women's rights were reintroduced in the section on post-Civil War corruption and reform. This section contained a map showing when women gained the right to vote in different states, two pictures representing the suffragist campaign of the World War I era (pp. 525–529), and a full-page focus on Abigail Scott Duniway's leadership in the battle for woman's suffrage in Oregon (p. 536). The right of women to vote also received brief mention in the section on reforms during Woodrow Wilson's administration, but the book failed to mention that Wilson opposed woman's suffrage and only agreed to it as an emergency wartime measure (p. 553).

Women's History—A Middle School Textbook (2002)

In 2002, McDougal, Littell replaced *A Proud Nation* as a middle school textbook with Jesus Garcia et al., *Creating America, A History of the United States* (2002). This book had expanded coverage on the struggle for the right of women to vote. The 19th amendment was discussed in the section on the Constitution (p. 273), which included a photograph of women marching with the banner "I Wish Ma Could Vote" and a photograph of members of the Congressional caucus for Women's Issues. A unit on "A New Spirit of Change, 1820–1860" included a chapter on "Abolition and

Women's Rights." It included three pages (pp. 443–445) on women reformers, photographs of Lucretia Mott, Susan B. Anthony and Elizabeth Cady Stanton with extended captions quotes from the Seneca Falls Manifesto and Sojourner Truth, and a political cartoon on family "discord" resulting from the women's rights campaign. Women were discussed again in a chapter on westward expansion, which described the battle by the Wyoming territory legislature to ensure that woman could vote (p. 569). In Unit 7, "Modern America Emerges," the battle for suffrage took center stage. A march by suffragists in Washington, D.C. in 1914 and a quote from Susan B. Anthony opened the unit. The third section of Chapter 22, "Women Win New Rights," discussed women in the Progressive Movement and had two pages on the successful campaign for suffrage (pp. 652–653). This included a map showing when women gained the right to vote in different states. The material on Abigail Scott Duniway's leadership in the battle for woman's suffrage in Oregon was dropped. The impact of suffrage on the ability of women to run for office was discussed in the section of the 1920s (p. 714). The book still failed to mention that President Wilson opposed woman's suffrage and only agreed to it as an emergency wartime measure (p. 653).

Women's History—A High School Textbook (1985)

Winthrop D. Jordan, Miriam Greenblatt, and John S. Bowes, in *The Americans, The History of a People and a Nation* (1985), mentioned campaigns for woman's suffrage in three places. The section on amendments to the Constitution included a drawing of women attempting to vote for Susan B. Anthony for president of the United States. The caption read: "Forty years after the first introduction of a bill in Congress, women secured voting rights. Susan B. Anthony was arrested for voting in 1872" (p. 191). The chapter, "Populism, 1876–1910," contained a two and a half-page sub-chapter, "Women Continue Their Struggle for Suffrage." It included a picture of Susan B. Anthony and Elizabeth Cady Stanton, and a discussion of feminist objections when the 15th Amendment failed to make provisions for women. It also mentioned the formation of the National American Woman Suffrage Associ-

ation in 1890, local initiatives and legal efforts to secure the right to vote, attempts to pass a constitutional amendment, and anti-suffrage opposition (p. 478–480). The final discussion of woman's suffrage occurred in three paragraphs on social change in the 1920s. They mentioned suffragist protests in front of the White House during World War I, Woodrow Wilson's decision to support voting rights for women, and a quote by Carrie Chapman Catt describing the long campaign by women to secure the right to vote. This section included a picture of women picketing the White House. The caption read: "The 1920s saw many changes, and one of the first and most important was the 19th Amendment" (p. 566).

Women's History—A High School Textbook (2005)

The 2005 edition of *The Americans* (2005) was edited by a team including Gerald Danzer, J. Jorge Klor de Alva, Larry Kreiger, Louis Wilson and Nancy Woloch. The major shift in this edition is the way in which women are integrated into the regular flow of the text and in images without specifically designated sections on women. A photomontage on the title page directs readers to coverage of George Washington, Abraham Lincoln, Dwight Eisenhower, and Martin Luther King, Jr., but also to sections on Abigail Adams, Dorthea Lange, Harriet Tubman, and Eleanor Roosevelt. An illustrated chapter index includes images of Molly Pitcher, two enslaved African woman, a Sioux man and woman, Zora Neale Hurston, a female Holocaust survivor, and a female participant in the Montgomery bus boycott. These illustrations set the tone for a textbook where women seem to appear at least as regular, if not full, participants in every era of history.

One of the reasons women are more prominent is because of an expanded focus on social history. There are sections on life in Native American (pp. 8–13), West African (pp. 14–19), and European (pp. 20–25) societies prior to the Columbian exchange, Colonial Courtship patterns (pp. 90–91), young people in the early republic (pp. 188–189), work and working conditions in the nineteenth century (pp. 266–267), the impact of the Great Depression on families (pp. 680–683), and suburban life in post-World War II America (pp. 840–857). Early in the text (pp. 124–125), a two-page

"Tracing Themes" section discussed the struggle by women for a political role in the United States from early protests against British authority through battles for the vote, equal rights, and political representation. Women's rights and roles are still treated separately in discussions of their struggles to achieve equality in American society, but in these cases it is appropriate. Generally, however, prominent women are just included in the text. Mercy Otis Warren is featured in a section on colonial patriots without designating her as a woman (p. 107), as is Dorthea Dix in a section on Jacksonian reformers (p. 244).

Women's History—An Advanced Placement Textbook (1983)

Thomas A. Bailey and David M. Kennedy, in *The American Pageant, A History of the Republic*, 7th edition (Bailey and Kennedy 1983) briefly mentioned woman's suffrage in four places. The chapter, "The Ferment of Reform and Culture, 1790–1860," contained a two-page subsection, "Women in Revolt." It included a picture of Susan B. Anthony and a caption that identified her as "a foremost fighter in the women's rights movement, as well as in that for temperance and abolition." The caption mentioned her arrest in 1872 for voting. The section concluded, "The crusade for woman's rights was eclipsed by that against slavery in the decade before the Civil War . . . Yet women were being gradually admitted to colleges, and some states . . . were even permitting wives to own property after marriage" (pp. 317–318). Two hundred pages later, four paragraphs discussed "Women's Rights and Wrongs." This section emphasized gains made by women after the Civil War, including securing the right to vote in some local elections and in western territories. It concluded that, "American females had long enjoyed a degree of freedom unknown in Europe," and that their "gradual emancipation" brought problems—an increasing divorce rate—as well as benefits (pp. 515–516). In the section on the Progressive movement, Bailey and Kennedy mentioned the revival of woman's suffrage, and included an extended quote from a statement by President Theodore Roosevelt. Roosevelt offered lukewarm support for women's right to vote. He wrote, "Personally I believed in woman's suffrage, but I am not an enthusiastic advocate of it, because I do not regard it as a very important matter" (p. 603). In the chapter, "The War to End War, 1917–1918," a paragraph (accompanied by a picture of women picketing the White House) announced the passage of the 19th Amendment, crediting Woodrow Wilson's decision that woman's suffrage was "a vitally necessary war measure" (p. 685).

Women's History—An Advanced Placement Textbook (2002)

The 12th edition of *The American Pageant, A History of the Republic* (2002), edited by David M. Kennedy, Lizabeth Cohen and Thomas A. Bailey, has undergone significant revision. The disenfranchisement of women is mentioned in an early section on the Massachusetts Bay colony (p. 47) and the rights, and lack of rights, of women in colonial society America receives extended coverage (pp. 73–83) in a chapter on "American Life in the Seventeenth Century, 1607–1692." The temporary New Jersey experiment with woman's suffrage is also mentioned (pp. 167–168) in a section that discusses the incomplete pursuit of equality in the new nation. The chapter, "The Ferment of Reform and Culture, 1790–1860," still contains a subsection, "Women in Revolt," that is largely unchanged, however the picture of Susan B. Anthony has been replaced by a picture of Anthony with Elizabeth Cady Stanton. The caption now discusses their commitment to suffrage, but not Anthony's arrest (pp. 330–332). The new text contains a section on the outrage of Anthony and Stanton when the 14th amendment and 15th amendments granted African-American males the vote, but not women (pp. 490–491). Sections on the urbanization of the United States, immigration, the labor movement, and the Progressive era now highlight the role of women with new pictures and text. The voting breakthroughs in the west (p. 601) and the revitalization of the suffrage movement in the Progressive era (pp. 668–669) are included; the quote by Theodore Roosevelt has been dropped. The chapter, "The War to End War, 1917–1918," now contains a two-page section with pictures, "Suffering Until Suffrage" (pp. 711–713), that documents the final successful campaign for the vote. Woodrow Wilson's decision to support woman's suffrage as "a vitally necessary war measure" (p. 712) is mentioned, but he no longer receives credit for passage of the amendment. *The American Pageant* (p. 755) also describes how in the 1920s, the Supreme Court used the Nineteenth Amendment as a justification for removing minimum wage and workplace rules that had protected women workers.

Learning Activity: Evaluating Textbooks

Add your voice to the discussion:
1. What do you think of this textbook coverage? Is it sufficient? Is it good? Why?
2. Would textbook coverage be more effective if the sections on women were consolidated into one overall unit? Why or why not?

Try it yourself:
1. Become a textbook detective. Compare the way that different US history textbooks discuss the struggle for Woman's Suffrage or another issue related to women in US history. Do you feel coverage is adequate? Why or why not?
2. Language influences the way we think about others and ourselves. Examine a social studies textbook for possible sexist language. How would you address this use of language in your class?

It's your classroom:
1. Would you involve middle school (or high school) students as textbook detectives? Why or why not?
2. What would you do if classroom discussion showed that reactions to the textbook coverage differed between male and female students? Why?

In his book, *The Disuniting of America, Reflections on a Multicultural Society* (1991), Arthur Schlesinger, Jr. argued that the attention given to difference by multiculturalists and ethnocentrists threatened to reinforce "the fragmentation, resegregation, and tribalization of American life" (pp. 73–99). He was particularly concerned that school curricula that focus on specific ethnic or aggrieved social groups are celebratory, rather than academic and critical. For most of my secondary school teaching career, I resisted efforts to have separate units on African-Americans, immigrants, or women because I wanted their histories integrated into more comprehensive social studies curricula. However, what I have been forced to accept, and what Schlesinger evidently refused to consider, is that in most secondary school social studies curricula the experiences of racial and ethnic minorities and the roles and contributions of women in our society are rarely considered unless separate units or classes are organized.

A "Women's History Month" unit can be included in social studies curricula on every grade level and in every subject area. In middle and high school US history classes, a unit can focus on the participation of women in the development of the country. It can include the struggles waged to change the condition of, attitudes toward, and opportunities for women in the past and present. In a global history class, units can focus on women in a particular country, region, or century, and examine findings from the United Nations Beijing Conference on the Status of Women (see http://www.un.org/Conferences/Women/Pub Info/Status/Home.htm, accessed November 5, 2007). An economics unit could examine the changing role of women in the economy as producers and consumers. Units in American government could focus on the struggle for women's rights, ideas about gender equity, and a comparison of the voting patterns of men and women. Contemporary issues of particular importance in an American government curriculum include an Equal Rights Amendment, equal pay for equal work, reproductive freedom, women in government, and women in the military.

Teaching Activity: Women's History Month

Add your voice to the discussion:
Would you prefer a separate Women's History Month unit in the US history curriculum, an independent Women's History elective, or the integration of lessons about women into the regular curriculum? Why?

HOW CAN DIFFERENT SUBJECTS BE CONNECTED IN THE SOCIAL STUDIES CLASSROOM?

In the movie version of the *Wizard of Oz*, the Cowardly Lion sings, "If I Were King of the Forest." In the song, the lion explains what he would do if he were in charge of everything. If I were in charge of secondary education, students would define the questions they want to explore, all learning would be integrated, and social studies themes and projects would be at the center of our inquiry-based curriculum. But although I am not in charge, social studies can still be the focal point for interdisciplinary learning in our classrooms.

An interdisciplinary approach to teaching has a number of advantages. Subject classes explore similar ideas and reinforce similar academic and intellectual skills. Metaphors from one subject help students create meaning in other areas. Because knowledge is connected instead of atomized in unrelated pieces, it is easier for students to understand and remember information. Many middle schools now have a team approach that requires all subject area teachers to meet regularly and encourages integrated instruction.

In Chapter 2, I called social studies teachers the intellectual imperialists of secondary education. Because all knowledge is part of human experience, and the creative arts and literature are central to human culture—social studies, especially when taught thematically—is interdisciplinary by its very nature. One reason for stressing the same social studies concepts over the course of years is that social studies understanding requires a tremendous breadth of knowledge and experience, and familiarity with a number of different academic disciplines.

In high schools that use block programming, thematic houses, or teaching teams, social studies is generally paired with language arts. For a number of years while I was teaching US history at Franklin K. Lane High School, I shared students with an English teacher.

Working together informally, we drew up a list of historical novels for students to read during summer vacation, coordinated written assignments so that our classes emphasized similar skills, consulted on individual student performance, introduced common historical and literary references in our classes, and scheduled units so that the English teacher could cover novels, stories, and poetry from the time periods students were studying in history class.

Social studies is easily integrated with other subjects as well. In my high school US history classes, I used the 1925 *Tennessee* v. *John Scopes* "Monkey" trial to explore scientific concepts like fact and theory, and to examine how scientists test their understanding of our world. In both US history and global studies, the study of slavery and race prejudice provide opportunities to examine genetics, human origins, and human similarities and differences. Topics like the development of river valley civilizations highlight the impact of the environment on human history. The Bronze Age, repeated agricultural revolutions, the era of industrialization in Europe, the study of modern wars, and the Space Age all illustrate the impact of technology on society. Students can study how technological development, especially during the US Civil War, led to the defeat of native peoples living on the Great Plains, and the transformation of the plains from semiarid pastureland to the "breadbasket" of the United States.

A number of teachers with whom I have worked have been very successful at interdisciplinary teaching. Henry Dircks (NTN) uses geography to integrate biology, physics, chemistry, earth science, and mathematics into the global history curriculum. He works with teams of students to create demonstrations illustrating scientific principles behind seasonal monsoons in southern Asia, global warming, the depletion of the ozone layer, and the Pacific basin volcanic ring of fire. Daniel Bachman (NTN) organized a small band and chorus in his social studies classes so students could use music to study US history. Sheila Hanley taught a 10th-grade Western Civilization course using works of art to illustrate changes in European society. Many teachers use poetry and popular songs to examine the ideas of an historical period.

Interdisciplinary Ideas for Social Studies Classrooms

Science and Social Studies

Henry Dircks uses this activity in his global studies class to illustrate the impact of air currents and energy transformation on climate.

1. Place a large map of India on the floor. Cover the map with a sheet of oak tag. Blow up four balloons, tie ten-inch long strings to each balloon, and place the balloons roughly where the Bay of Bengal and the Arabian Sea are located. Tape the ends of the strings to the floor.
2. Have students quickly lift the oak tag. This represents the upward movement of heated summer air rising over the northern mountains. As the hot air rises, clouds (balloons) are drawn off the water onto the land. The monsoons arrive in India.

Poetry and Social Studies

The poetry of Walt Whitman, especially poems like *O Captain! My Captain!*, *I Hear America Singing*, and *Thou Mother With Thy Equal Brood*, provides vivid images of the United States in the era before and after the Civil War. In *Thou Mother With Thy Equal Brood*, Whitman ascribes a special mission to the United States as a ship of democracy that carries the past and future of the entire world. The Harlem Renaissance poets, especially Claude McKay and Langston Hughes, are primary source commentators on conditions facing African-Americans in the interwar years. I have had students read Hughes' work and write their own "I, Too Sing America" poems. Many poems, including many by Whitman, McKay, and Hughes, are available on the internet at: http://www.poets.org/poems (accessed November 5, 2007).

Students can compare Robert Frost's poem prepared for the 1960 Kennedy inauguration with the poem by Maya Angelou delivered at the 1992 Clinton inauguration. They both define what it means to be an American, but they do it very differently. These poems are available on the internet at: http://www.lib.virginia.edu/exhibits/frost/english/images/dedicat1.jpg and http://eserver.org/poetry/angelou.html (accessed October 10, 2007).

In *Tae A Moose* [To a Mouse] the eighteenth-century Scottish poet, Robert Burns (see http://www.electricscotland.com/burns/mouse.html, accessed October 10, 2007) explains that, despite human pretensions, human life and aspirations are just as fragile as the hopes of a humble field mouse. After reading this poem, students can discuss the role of individual action and will in shaping historical events and the contingent nature of history.

William Butler Yeats' poem, *The Second Coming* (1922) is an important historical document describing conditions in Europe and a sense of impending doom at the end of World War I (see http://www.online-literature.com/yeats/780/, accessed October 10, 2007).

Literature and Social Studies

Chinua Achebe. *Things Fall Apart*. Garden City, NY: Doubleday, 1994. Jeannette Balantic has students in her global history classes read *Things Fall Apart* while they study nineteenth-century European imperialism in Africa. In this novel, Achebe examines the culture of the Ibo people of Nigeria as they struggle to preserve their way of life in the face of European intrusion into their world. As students read the novel, Jeannette provides them with "organizers" that point them toward specific events and issues, help them gather information, and encourage them to think and draw conclusions about the experience of the Ibo people. For example, one organizer has students compile a list of "Aspects of Traditional Ibo Life" on the left-hand side of the page and "The Impact of Europeans" on these traditions on the right-hand side. They are asked to specifically consider family life, religious beliefs and rituals, village customs, community values, diet, government, and the division of labor. Another "organizer" has students draw a picture of the Ibo village of Umuofia as it is portrayed in the story.

Margaret Goff Clark's *Freedom Crossing* (New York: Scholastic, 1991) is the story of a young white girl named Laura who returns to her family's farm in western New York State after living with an aunt and uncle in Virginia. She discovers that her brother and a childhood friend are now conductors on the underground railroad and that the farm is a station on the route to Canada. She must decide whether she is willing to violate fugitive slave laws and help a 12-year-old boy named Martin Paige escape to freedom. Rachel Thompson of the NTN strongly recommends this book.

Music and Social Studies
The song *Paddy on the Railway* dates back to the 1840s. In the first edition of this book, I identified it as the story of Irish immigrants to the United States during the potato famine in Ireland. I was wrong. Paddy leaves Ireland in 1842 and the potato blight does not begin until 1845. Large scale Irish emigration to the United States, industrial England, and Australia actually started in the 1820s. Although their labor was crucial for the construction of the canals and railroads that bound the American north and west, they were generally not welcomed in this country. Lyrics are available on the internet at: http://ingeb .org/songs/oineight.html (accessed August 10, 2007).

Asikatali was sung by members of the African National Congress on picket lines as they protested against apartheid in South Africa. It is based on a traditional Zulu folk song. A recorded version is on the internet at: http://www.rednoteschoir.org.uk/Asikatali%20 (range).mp3 (accessed October 10, 2007). The lyrics and music to *Asikatali* and many other folk songs are available in the book *Rise Up Singing*, edited by Peter Blood and Annie Patterson (Bethlehem, PA: Sing Out Publications, 2004).

Art and Social Studies—Comparing Madonnas
In Christian European societies, the Madonna (the mother of Jesus) and her baby have been continuous subjects of paintings since the European Middle Ages. A classroom can be set up as an art gallery and students can view pictures from different periods and countries. The portraits give insight into the way that people viewed both religion and the natural world. For example, in early paintings, the baby Jesus is drawn as a little man. Over the centuries, he is gradually transformed into an infant. Thousands of samples of the "Madonna and Child" can be downloaded from the internet. You can also do special sub-searches using the name of a painter. I usually include modern portrayals of the Madonna by Chagall, Picasso, a controversial one by Chris Ofili that uses elephant

dung as one of its elements, and a photograph of the pop singer Madonna with one of her children.

Math and Social Studies
Usually math and social studies cross paths when students need to read maps to calculate size and distance, or to gather and use information from charts and graphs. The following activities use geometry to answer puzzling social studies questions. Sharon Whitton at Hofstra helped me design these examples.

1. How did people in the ancient Mediterranean world know the size of the earth? If we know the length of a section on the circumference of a circle (arc) and the angle created by lines drawn from either end of the arc to the center of the circle, we can calculate the size of the entire circle. In the third century BC, Eratosthenes, a Greek mathematician living in Egypt, used geometry to calculate the circumference of the earth.

 At Syene, a city on the Nile River (now known as Aswan), the sun was directly overhead at noon on the day of the summer solstice (the first day of summer). The sun's reflection could be seen at the bottom of a deep well, while a vertical pole cast no shadow. However, at noon on the same day in Alexandra, about 500 miles north, the sun cast a shadow. Eratosthenes used a vertical pole and its shadow to create a right triangle, and then measured the other angles. He then used a geometric principle (alternate interior angles created by a line crossing two parallel lines are equal) to figure out the angle created by imaginary lines drawn from Alexandra and Syene to the center of the earth (Figure 10.1). This angle represented approximately 1/50 of a circle (7°12). So when Eratosthenes multiplied the distance from Alexandra to Syene by 50, he got the approximate circumference of the earth.

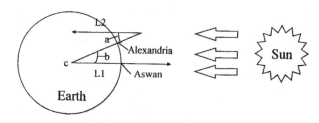

Figure 10.1 Calculating the circumference of the earth.

2. Did the Mayans learn how to build pyramids from Africans? Some Afrocentric scholars have argued that pyramids built by the Mayan people on the Yucatan Peninsula (in current day Mexico) are evidence that African (or Egyptian) civilization spread to the Americas before the European arrival. Geometry suggests another explanation for the architectural similarities. Triangles are the most stable geometric shapes, and pyramids are the most stable large-scale structures. Attempts to build large temples and funeral monuments would lead both civilizations to these structures independently. Students can demonstrate the use of the triangle in construction with the following activity: Student teams are given glue, masking tape, scissors, and an equal number of plastic straws. The goal is to build the largest stable structure using these materials. One team is required to build its structure using triangles as the basic building unit. The other teams can try anything but triangles.

Essay 1: Expanding Our Concept of Inclusion

The 1974 federal "Individuals with Disabilities Education Act" requires that all children with disabilities receive a "free, appropriate education" that meets their individual needs. The act also requires that support services be provided in the "least restrictive environment" so that special-education students are not unnecessarily segregated from the general school population. Unless the severity of a disability prevents it, children with disabilities should be educated in inclusive classrooms along with other children (*Michigan in Brief:* 2002–03).

In many of the school districts I visit, inclusion remains largely a euphemism on the secondary-level. In these districts, only the exceptional special-needs student ever ends up placed in advanced academic classes or even has much academic interaction with the general student population. Classes designated as inclusive are usually tracked to include special-needs students and mainstream students who need remediation. Often these mainstream students have histories of disruptive behavior. In some schools, the separation between inclusion and regular academic classes has been used to maintain racial segregation. Clearly, this is not how the system is supposed to work.

For the last few years, I have floated a proposal for de-tracking secondary schools that would provide for genuine inclusion. So far there have been no takers. Hopefully some of you will find it an interesting idea and can advocate for it in your schools.

In 14 years as a public school teacher I taught social studies on virtually every academic level including advanced placement and self-contained special education classes for emotionally and conceptually challenged students. At Franklin K. Lane High School, what we called the advanced placement class was largely made up of students with ordinary academic skills who were willing to work hard and do more. Most would not have been eligible for advanced classes at other schools. Students in regular classes at Edward R. Murrow High School, where I taught for one year, had scores on standardized exams at least as high as the advanced students did at Lane. The important thing is that the Lane students performed at a higher level than they would have in regular classes at the school because they responded to the challenge.

The issue is how can teachers and schools balance conflicting goals. We want to maximize the integration of special-needs students with the general student population, challenge students to perform at higher academic levels, and at the same time, to realistically appraise student performance so we can design appropriate lessons and activities.

My solution is to have social studies recitation sessions and learning laboratories. This idea is standard practice in science classes and has proved successful in second language instruction.

A triad of social studies teachers would have parallel programs. Three days a week, students would be organized heterogeneously for recitation sections and divided among the teachers. While the teachers in the triad would plan together, during these recitation sessions they would teach pretty much the way they normally do. Push-in inclusion teachers would be available in the classrooms to help special-needs students on recitation days.

Twice a week, students and teachers would meet in separate social studies learning laboratories organized to provide instruction on advanced, regular, and "extra-help" levels. One of the differences between the laboratories would be the academic difficulty of primary source material. Learning laboratories could also do different kinds of writing activities and research projects. Inclusion teachers and one of the subject specialists would work with the "extra-help" lab guaranteeing smaller class size so individual academic needs could be addressed. Ideally there would be some fluidity between the groupings so that students who felt they could do more advanced work would be able to shift to another laboratory.

Essay 2: Women's History Month Curriculum

This thematic middle school unit on the history of women in the United States is based on the work of Jeannette Balantic and Andrea Libresco, and was part of their celebration of the 75th Anniversary of the 19th Amendment to the Constitution. They received support from a National Endowment for the Humanities teacher–scholar fellowship. At the time they did this work, they were both high school teachers. Jeannette is now a district curriculum coordinator and Andrea, who has completed her doctorate, is a teacher educator.

Jeannette and Andrea believe that their ideas on women's history can be taught as a unit in a US history class or as a US women's history elective, but they prefer to integrate individual lessons throughout the regular social studies curriculum. This middle school level "Women's History Month" unit focuses on social history and includes nineteen lessons (presented chronologically). The lessons mix attention to the achievements of individual women with an examination of women collectively. They include full-class, group, and individual activities.

As an initial activity, students list either five or ten women they believe made major contributions to the history of the United States (no entertainers please). After completing their individual lists, students meet in small groups to consolidate lists and discuss evidence supporting their choices. After group ideas are written on the board, the class discusses criteria for deciding which individuals made major contributions to US history. After establishing criteria, the class evaluates the initial list of famous women, and discusses whether women and men are equally important in US history.

Many teachers have started to question whether a special focus on women's history, such as this one is still needed now that textbooks and curricula have been rewritten to make them more inclusive. Margaret Smith Crocco, a social studies educator at Teachers College-Columbia University has a very interesting answer for them. Crocco believes that while the names of prominent individuals have been added, the issues that confronted women in the past and continue to confront them in much of the world today—inequality, discrimination, abuse, and lack of healthcare, birth control, and access to education—continue to be largely ignored in the curriculum. She is calling for a much broader reorganization of what we teach (Crocco 2006: 171–193).

1. Are women and men equally important in US history?

Students discuss the significance of Women's History Month and establish criteria for evaluating the contributions of both men and women in US history. Activities from this lesson can also be used as part of a final assessment of student learning at the end of the unit.

2. What roles did women play among Native American peoples?

This lesson helps students understand that women have had different roles and rights in different societies. Students read short passages about and discuss the position of women in different Native American societies.

3. What was life like for women in colonial America?

This lesson helps students imagine life on a colonial farm before the development of electricity and modern appliances. Students read and discuss excerpts from diaries of women from this era. It can include a visit to an historical restoration site, and involve students in a discussion of the ways that life differed from today. Students can also recreate colonial or early American crafts.

4. How did women view the War for Independence and the founding of a new government?

Some activities are considered valuable contributions to society when performed by men, but are often minimized when performed by women. For example, Alexander Hamilton was an important advisor to George Washington during the Revolutionary War and the early years of the new government. Is his contribution to the revolutionary cause significantly different from that of Abigail Adams, whose correspondence with Thomas Jefferson and John Adams kept them aware of events affecting the nation and its people and advised them on the need for new laws and the Constitution? Students read and discuss excerpts from letters from Abigail Adams to John Adams and Thomas Jefferson.

5. What role did women play in the industrialization of the United States?

Because of traditional limits on the roles of women and legal restrictions on their property rights, women in the United States during the first half of the nineteenth century had little opportunity to acquire an education, enter a profession, or start a business. However, when workers were needed for the new factory system, New England farmwomen became the primary source of labor. Student teams examine different primary source documents and report their findings about conditions for women in early mill towns and factories. An excellent supplemental source is the young adult novel *Lyddie* by Katherine Paterson (New York: Puffin, 2005).

6. What role did women play in westward expansion?

A number of women documented the western expansion by the United States in their diaries and letters. Prudence Higuera, the daughter of a Spanish rancher, wrote about her impressions of the early US settlers in California. Louise Clappe described the California gold rush in letters to her sister. A diary by Lydia Milner Waters reported on her family's experiences as they crossed the Great Plains and Rocky Mountains in 1855. Students can read and discuss excerpts from these sources. The "Little House on the Prairie" series by Laura Ingalls Wilder gives students insight into life on the frontier as the United States moved westward. Middle school students will also enjoy *My Antonia* by Willa Cather (Boston, MA: Houghton Mifflin, 1918), a novel about the settlement of the prairie states during the 1870s.

7. Why did women rewrite the Declaration of Independence?

At the 1848 Women's Rights Convention at Seneca Falls, New York, Elizabeth Cady Stanton presented a "Declaration of Sentiments" that paraphrased the Declaration of Independence and declared "all men and women are created equal." Students analyze the Declaration of Sentiments and compare it to the Declaration of Independence. The class discusses which grievances were most serious and whether the grievances outlined at Seneca Falls have been redressed in the United States in the last century and a half. As follow-up assignments, students compose a new Declaration of Sentiments that represents the views of other groups in American society in either the past or present (e.g., students, Native Americans, immigrants, or gay men and lesbians).

8. How did women help end slavery in the United States?

Women authors played a major role in the struggle to end slavery in the United States. Poetry and novels were used to express the hardship of slavery, protest against injustice, and celebrate resistance. Students read and discuss excerpts from the work of Harriet Beecher Stowe, Phillis Wheatly, and Ellen Watkins Harper. Students write poems expressing their views on slavery.

9. How did women help save the union during the Civil War?

Military action in the Persian Gulf in 1991 was the first time that large numbers of American women served as military personnel in a combat zone. But it was not the first time that American women went to war. Thousands of women served as nurses in World War II, Korea, and Vietnam. In other wars, including the US Civil War, women secretly disguised themselves as men in order to fight for their country and their families. Students read and discuss accounts of women who served in the Union Army during the US Civil War (1861–1865). These accounts become the starting point to discuss whether women should participate in combat in the US armed forces today.

10. How were women stereotyped in nineteenth-century society?

During the nineteenth century, middle-class women were taught to see themselves as fragile and ineffective. Despite these stereotypes, housekeeping and "women's work" changed as increasing numbers of people moved from farms to cities. Changes also reflected the growing number of educated women. Students examine nineteenth-century advice columns and children's books for examples of stereotypes about girls and women and compare them with attitudes today. The class compares life in contemporary families with nineteenth-century families. Students write to advice columns as nineteenth-century women. They exchange letters and answer each other's questions.

11. Why did women emerge as leaders of reform campaigns?

During the nineteenth and early twentieth centuries, women were at the forefront of many American reform movements. Women reform leaders included women's rights advocates Sojourner Truth, Lucy Stone, and Lucretia Mott; labor organizers Mary Harris "Mother" Jones and Elizabeth Gurley Flynn; populist orator Mary Lease; anti-lynching campaigner Ida B. Wells-Barnett; muckraking journalist Ida M. Tarbell; temperance leaders Frances E. Willard and Carrie Nation; Jane Addams, a founder of the settlement house movement; Clara Barton, who established the American Red Cross; Charlotte Perkins Gilman, a radical feminist; Florence Kelley, an advocate of protective wage and labor laws for women and an end to child labor; and Emma Goldman, an anarchist. Student teams research female reform leaders. They present three- to five-minute persuasive speeches that explain a reform leader's view of American society, the changes she advocated, and the tactics she used to achieve her goals. The class discusses issues that students are willing to support and how they would do it.

12. What did women experience as immigrants and workers?

From the 1880s to the 1920s, millions of women immigrated to the United States, where they became workers, wives, mothers, and, eventually, citizens. These women and their families frequently suffered great hardships as they struggled to preserve families and build communities in a new country. Many women went to work in factories, especially in the garment industries, and became active labor union organizers. Students read stories about women immigrants and workers, and write "diaries" describing their lives.

13. Why did working women demand "bread and roses"?

In 1912, 20,000 workers walked out of the mills in Lawrence, Massachusetts, in a spontaneous protest against a cut in their weekly pay. During one of the many parades conducted by strikers, young girls carried a banner with the slogan: "We want bread and roses too." Students read and discuss the song "Bread and Roses" by James Oppenheim (available at: http://www.fortunecity.com/tinpan/parton/2/breadrose.html , accessed January 7, 2008), and

design and paint a wall mural depicting the struggle of women during the Lawrence strike.

14. How did women win the right to vote?

It took 133 years of struggle from the Constitutional Convention of 1787 until the ratification of the 19th Amendment to the US Constitution for American women to secure the right to vote. The campaign for woman's suffrage produced outstanding women leaders, including Elizabeth Cady Stanton and Lucretia Mott, who organized the first women's rights convention in the United States at Seneca Falls, NY; Susan B. Anthony, a founding member of the National Woman Suffrage Association in 1869; and Carrie Chapman Catt and Alice Paul, who led ultimately successful campaigns for the right to vote during World War I. Students create half-hour news broadcasts of different historical topics, including the campaign for woman's suffrage. Student teams research an event; write a script that includes props, scenery, and costumes; and prepare a full-length video or act out a live broadcast in class. Every production includes an anchorperson, news reporters, and historical actors with different views of the event.

15. How did women reformers shape the twentieth century?

During the twentieth century, suffragists and feminists were frequently involved in other reform issues. Student teams research the lives of twentieth-century women reformers, including Ella Baker, Myra Bradwell, Rachel Carson, Marian Wright Edelman, Fannie Lou Hamer, Frances Perkins, Jeannette Rankin, Eleanor Roosevelt, Margaret Sanger, Mary Church Terrell, and Lillian Wald. After their research is completed, students organize their information into bio-poems.

Bio-poem Format
First name of person: _____
  Title or role: _____
Descriptive words: _____
  Lover of . . . _____
Who believed . . . _____
Who wanted . . . _____
  Who used . . . _____
  Who gave . . . _____
  Who said . . . _____
Last name of person: _____

16. Why did African-American women sing the blues?

Between 1900–1945, African-American women experienced and described the "Great Migration" north, World War I, the "Roaring 20s," the Great Depression, and World War II. This interdisciplinary lesson draws heavily on art, music, and literature. Students examine and discuss work by women writers Zora Neale Hurston, Jesse Redmond Fauset, Nella Larsen, Anne Spencer, Georgia Douglas Johnson, Gwendolyn Brooks, and Margaret Walker; Laura Wheeler Waring, a painter and illustrator; Meta Warrick Fuller, a sculptor; and musical performers Marian Anderson, Ann Brown, Sippie Wallace, Camilla Williams, Gertrude "Ma" Rainey, and Bessie Smith. They also examine work by men who described conditions faced by women, including poetry by Langston Hughes ("Mother to Son") and Fenton Johnson ("The Scarlet Woman" and "The Lonely Mother"), and the mural art about the "Great Migration" by Jacob Lawrence.

17. Why did women lead opposition to war?

Throughout US history, women have played leading roles in antiwar movements, even when this meant they risked being labeled as *traitors*. Examples include Jane Addams, president of the Women's Peace Party, Emily Greene Bach, 1946 Nobel Peace Prize winner, Congresswoman Jeannette Rankin, Coretta Scott King, a Civil Rights and anti-Vietnam War activist, and Dr Helen Caldicott, a leader in the campaign to eliminate nuclear weapons. Students research the life of a woman in US history who was an activist for peace. Students design a "quilt square" that presents the ideas, struggles, and achievements of the woman they researched. When all of the pieces are completed, squares are assembled into a giant "peace quilt."

MATERIALS NEEDED FOR A PEACE QUILT

- Felt or paper (a large piece or pieces for the background; the number of square feet equals the number of students in the class)
- 12 × 12″ pieces of felt or construction paper for the individual quilt pieces
- Assorted colors of felt or construction paper
- Markers
- Glue sticks and glue guns
- Scissors
- Curtain rod for hanging

---

18. What role did US women play in World War II?

Women's adaptation to the new roles created during World War II produced mixed feelings for women, men, and society in general, and forced many people to reevaluate their perceptions of a woman's capabilities. Women proved they could build planes, tanks, and ships. Although thankful for the end of the war, many women were reluctant to give up their new jobs. Students examine articles in local newspapers about women during World War II.

19. How have women's lives changed since World War II?

Students interview their mothers, grandmothers, and other female relatives about changing attitudes toward women and new opportunities for women during their lifetimes. Topics include work, education, family roles, women's health issues, and access to political power. Women can be invited to come to class and discuss their experiences.

Recommended Sources on United States Women's History

American Social History Project. 1989. *Who built America?* New York: Pantheon.

Eisler, B., ed. 1977. *The Lowell Offering: Writings by New England mill women (1840–1845)*. Philadelphia, PA: Lippincott.

Millstein, B. and Bodin, J. 1977. *We, The American Women: A Documentary History.* Chicago: Science Research Associates.

National Council for the Social Studies. 1994. "Homefront to Homelines," *Social Education*. Washington, DC: NCSS.

National Council for the Social Studies. 1995. "75th

Anniversary of Woman's Suffrage," *Social Education*. Washington, DC: NCSS.

Schissel, L. 1992. *Women's diaries of the Westward Journey*. New York: Schocken.

Schneiderman, R. and Goldthwaite, L. 1967. *All for One*. New York: Paul S. Eriksson.

Seller, M., ed. 1981. *Immigrant women*. Philadelphia, PA: Temple University Press.

Tanner, L. 1970. *Voices from Women's Liberation*. New York: New American Library.

Wenner, H. and Freilicher, E. 1987. *Here's to the women*. New York: The Feminist Press at CUNY.

Wertheimer, B. 1977. *We were there: the story of working women in America*. New York: Pantheon.

Essay 3: Responding to Crisis: What Can Social Studies Teachers Do?

Maureen Murphy, S. Maxwell Hines, and Sandra Stacki, faculty advisors to the Hofstra New Teachers Network, helped with this essay. Other versions have appeared in Singer, et al., *Teaching to Learn/Learning to Teach* (Mahwah, NJ: Lawrence Erlbaum and Associates, 2003) and the newsletter of the New York State Council for the Social Studies.

This essay is about my experience on the morning of September 11, 2001, and subsequent efforts to provide support for students and teachers related to the Hofstra University program and in the New York metropolitan area in general. Crises can be localized or national and international in scope. Young people experience tremendous stress and are often the hardest hit victims. Psychological injuries can have both short-term and long-term consequences. We have seen this during and after violent attacks at schools in Columbine and Virginia Tech and in the aftermath of Hurricane Katrina in New Orleans. Teachers become, in effect, "first-line" responders.

On September 11, I was visiting a student teacher and two members of the New Teachers Network at a junior high school in Queens, New York. We first learned of events at the World Trade Center when one of the teachers received a cell phone call from his sister. She was sobbing because her husband worked on a top floor in one of the towers and she feared he was dead.

Within minutes, school administrative personnel circulated around the building briefing teachers and telling us the school was in "lock down"—no one was permitted to enter or leave. Administrators and teachers were calm and professional, but clearly there was no broader plan to address what was happening and how to respond to students who suspected something was going on, heard rumors about catastrophe and war, or simply wanted to know why they could not leave. Within an hour, a crowd of concerned parents were outside the building and visible from classroom windows. Many were crying.

That afternoon, teachers in the New Teachers Network began to exchange e-mail messages. They described their experiences and fears with each other

in an effort to come to terms with what had happened and to figure out how to help their students understand events. Mentors teachers from a number of schools in the area and teachers educators also met with over 30 new teachers for three hours on Saturday morning, September 15.

What emerged from our conversations was a picture of what had taken place in the area's secondary schools on the day of the attack and the days that followed. In a number of schools in the city and the suburbs, students and teachers, alerted by cell phone calls or late arrivals to school, witnessed the second plane crash and the collapse of both towers from school windows. In some of these schools, teachers and students discussed what they saw and turned on news broadcasts to try to learn what was happening. But in others, teachers were ordered to remain silent and carry on with business as usual in their classes.

Each school and district seemed to go in a different direction. On the following days, some school districts tried to return to normalcy and pretended that nothing had happened, while others provided counseling for upset students, but little else. A number of schools held memorial assemblies and then told students and teachers to get back to work. Some schools designated specific subject classes where events would be discussed, while other schools left it up to the discretion of individual teachers. Many New York City districts provided teachers with lesson plans. Some of these encouraged teachers to involve students in open discussion and to challenge ethnic stereotyping. However, other plans limited teachers to responding to student questions with scripted answers.

Not one teacher in our network reported that districts involved them either in discussion of the events or asked how they thought they should respond to students. All they received were directives.

In a time of national and local crisis, when they were in the best position to help adolescents make meaning of events, the professionals most directly connected with young people were disempowered by our school systems. A number of teachers involved in the network reported to the group that as adults who know and are trusted by their students, they felt they had to act. They decided to "shut their doors," ignore the directives and proceed on their own, whatever the later administrative consequences. Many stressed that their decisions helped to establish their classrooms as communities where students were able to speak out, could depend on each other, and felt safe.

Maureen Murphy, the English educator working with the New Teachers Network, put together a package of poetry to help students understand their feelings, and suggested writing exercises that would allow them to express their thoughts and emotions. Many classes wrote letters of condolence to victims of the attack. Michael Pezone's social studies classes published an entire magazine of student essays, drawings, and poems.

As the social studies educator working with the network, I distributed a simple lesson that a number of the teachers used in their classes. We divided the front board into four columns. What We Know. What We Need To Know. How We Feel About What Happened. What We Think Should Happen Next. Working individually, in groups, or as a full class, students filled in the columns and then discussed what they had written. Our goals were to help students distinguish between fact and opinion, substantiated information and rumor, and emotion and reason. We challenged stereotypes and stressed the difference between Islam, a religion of over a billion believers, many of whom live in the United States, and the actions of one organized group or a few individuals. We also wanted to lay the basis for a long-term investigation of why the attack took place so students could analyze underlying and immediate causes, understand why many people in other countries believe they have been injured by the United States and its allies, and participate in debate over United States policy decisions.

Many of the teachers followed up by having students use the internet to collect newspaper articles from around the world on the attack and the United States response. Comparing reports helped students see multiple perspectives that were overlooked in the local media.

At the Saturday network meeting following the attacks, a biology teacher asked how she could be involved since events did not easily fit into her subject area. The group recommended that every teacher press schools and districts as part of professional development to involve teachers in discussion of these events and in designing a response strategy that included lessons for different subjects. The teachers also felt that whatever their individual areas of expertise, they needed to be there for their students as emotional supports and as role models to promote tolerance and to champion reason at a time when all of us might get swept up in a wave of irrationality.

Teaching Activity: Is it Acceptable to Question Government Policies in a Time of National Emergency?

It can be very difficult and politically risky to challenge government policies during a time of national emergency. The following elected representatives spoke out against war at different times in United States history. Examine each statement carefully and use your textbook or other sources to learn more about the situation the United States was facing at the time.

1. What is the main point raised by the speaker?
2. In your opinion, were they wrong to dissent in this way? Explain.
3. If you were a constituent, would you have voted for them for reelection? Explain.

Resolution introduced by congressman Abraham Lincoln (1847)
"Whereas the President of the United States has declared that 'the Mexican Government . . . has at last invaded our territory and shed the blood of our fellow-citizens on our own soil.' And whereas, This House is desirous to obtain a full knowledge of all the facts which go to establish whether the particular spot on which the blood of our citizens was so shed was or was not at that time our own soil; there, Resolved by the House of Representatives, that the President of the United States, be respectfully requested to inform the House . . . (w)hether the people of that settlement, or a majority of them, or any of them, has ever, previous to the bloodshed mentioned in his message, submitted

themselves to the government or laws of Texas, or of the United States, by consent, or by compulsion, either by accepting office, or voting at elections, or paying taxes, or serving on juries, or having process served upon them, or in any way."

Representative Jeannette Rankin Opposes US Entry into World War I (1917)

"I knew that we were asked to vote for a commercial war, that one of the idealistic hopes would be carried out, and I was aware of the falseness of much of the propaganda. It was easy to stand against the pressure of the militarists, but very difficult to go against the friends and dear ones who felt that I was making a needless sacrifice by voting against the war, since my vote would not be a decisive one . . . I said I would listen to those who wanted war and would not vote until the last opportunity and if I could see any reason for going to war I would change it."

Senator Wayne Morse votes "NO!" on the Gulf of Tonkin Resolution (1965)

"I believe that history will record that we have made a grave mistake in subverting and circumventing the Constitution of the United States . . . I believe that within the next century, future generations will look with dismay and great disappointment upon a Congress which is now about to make such a historic mistake."

Statement by Representative Barbara Lee (September 14, 2001)

"I rise today with a heavy heart, one that is filled with sorrow for the families and loved ones who were killed and injured in New York, Virginia, and Pennsylvania. Only the most foolish or the most callous would not understand the grief that has gripped the American people and millions across the world. This unspeakable attack on the United States has forced me to rely on my moral compass, my conscience, and my God for direction . . . There must be some of us who say, let's step back for a moment and think through the implications of our actions today—let us more fully understand its consequences . . . .We must not rush to judgment. Far too many innocent people have already died. Our country is in mourning. If we rush to launch a counter-attack, we run too great a risk that women, children, and other non-combatants will be caught in the crossfire. Nor can we let our justified anger over these outrageous acts by vicious murderers inflame prejudice against all Arab Americans, Muslims, Southeast Asians, or any other people because of their race, religion, or ethnicity."

Senator Robert Byrd Questions War with Iraq (February 12, 2003)

"This nation is about to embark upon the first test of a revolutionary doctrine applied in an extraordinary way at an unfortunate time. The doctrine of preemption—the idea that the United States or any other nation can legitimately attack a nation that is not imminently threatening but may be threatening in the future—is a radical new twist on the traditional idea of self-defense. It appears to be in contravention of international law and the UN Charter. And it is being tested at a time of world-wide terrorism, making many countries around the globe wonder if they will soon be on our— or some other nation's—hit list . . . We may have massive military might, but we cannot fight a global war on terrorism alone . . . In my heart of hearts I pray that this great nation and its good and trusting citizens are not in for a rudest of awakenings. To engage in war is always to pick a wild card. And war must always be a last resort, not a first choice. I truly must question the judgment of any President who can say that a massive unprovoked military attack on a nation which is over 50% children is "in the highest moral traditions of our country.""

It's your classroom:

Would you discuss these issues in class with students during a time of national emergency? Explain.

References and Recommendations for Further Reading

American Textbook Council. 1994. *History textbooks, a standard and guide: 1994–95 ed.* New York: Center for Education Studies/American Textbook Council.

Bailey, T. and Kennedy, D. 1983. *The American pageant, A history of the republic.* 7th ed. Lexington, MA: D. C. Heath.

Bailey, T. and Kennedy, D. 1984. *The American spirit,* Vol. 1, 5th ed. Lexington, MA: D. C. Heath.

Banks, D. and Gregory, G. 1996. Introduction to the special issue on human rights. *Social Science Record,* 33:(1).

Crocco, M. 2006. Gender and social education, what's the problem?, in E. W. Ross, ed. *The social studies curriculum.* New York: SUNY Press.

Danzer, G., Klor de Alva, J., Krieger, L. *et al.* 2005. *The Americans.* Evanston, IL: McDougal Littell.

Feder, B., ed. 1967. *Viewpoints: USA.* New York: American Book Company.

Garcia, J., Ogle, D., Risinger, C. et al. 2002. *Creating America, a history of the United States.* Evanston, IL: McDougal, Littell & Company.

Jordan, W., Greenblatt, M. and Bowes, J. 1985. *The Americans, the history of a people and a nation.* Evanston, IL: McDougal, Littell & Company.

Kennedy, D., Cohen, L. and Bailey, T. 2002. *The American Pageant, A History of the Republic,* 12th ed. Boston, MA: Houghton-Mifflin.

King, M. Jr. 1963. *Why we can't wait.* New York: Harper & Row.

May, E. 1984. *A proud nation.* Evanston, IL: McDougal, Littell & Company.

Michigan in Brief: 2002–03. 2003. Lansing, MI: Public Sector Consultants. http://www.michiganinbrief.org/edition07/Chapter5/SpecialEd.htm accessed July 16, 2007.

Muessig, R., ed. 1975. *Controversial issues in the social studies: A contemporary perspective.* Washington, DC: National Council for the Social Studies.

NCSS National Council for the Social Studies. 2007. Academic freedom and the social studies teacher. *Social Education* 71(5).

Noddings, N. 1992. Social studies and feminism. *Theory and Research in Social Education* 20(3): 230–41.

Paterson, K. 2005. *Lyddie* New York: Puffin, 2005.

Pope John Paul II. 1995. *The gospel of life.* New York: Times Books.

Schlesinger, A. Jr. 1991. *The disuniting of America.* New York: Norton.

Singer, A. 1996. Exploring human rights in a thematic social studies curriculum: With lesson ideas on the Christiana, Pennsylvania, anti-slavery resistance of 1851. *Social Science Record* 33(1).

Singer, J. 2001. Teaching children about human rights using the work of Eve Bunting. *Social Science Docket* 1(1).

11. What Is a Project Approach to Social Studies?

Overview

- Introduce a project approach to social studies
- Examine current and past ideas for implementing a project approach
- Experiment with different project ideas

Key Concepts

Project approach, Interdisciplinary learning, Integrated curriculum

Questions

- How do you Include Projects in Social Studies Curricula?
- What are the Advantages of a Project Approach to Social Studies?

Essays

1. Oral Histories: A Project Approach to Social Studies
2. Technology-based Project Ideas
3. Middle School Immigration Museum

I think he made history in his own little way. I enjoyed this report because I got to know someone very special to me. Now I understand him better and I love him more. This report taught me that history can be made in many different special ways.—An 11th-grade high school student comments on her oral history of the life of a Haitian immigrant to the United States.

My grandfather passed away on his 74th birthday, April 7, 1989. This was only two days after our second interview for this report. I am grateful that I had to do this oral report. It gave me precious time to spend with my grandfather. It let me see a side of him not too many people knew. He told me many stories. My favorite ones were of his childhood. He was a good man who I loved and will miss.—A note attached to an oral history report submitted by a high school junior.

HOW DO YOU INCLUDE PROJECTS IN SOCIAL STUDIES CURRICULA?

Over the years, many of my students have concluded oral history projects with personal statements about how important the class project was to them and their family. I believe that the most successful social studies projects achieve their goals because the projects connect the subject matter of the class with the lives of students. These projects engage students as historians or social scientists, and stimulate them to want to know more about the events and people they investigate. They also encourage students to read and write, playing an important role in the development of student literacy.

During the last decade, a project approach to social studies education came under sharp attack from advocates of content-based instruction, stricter standards, and a greater concentration on assessment. Critics like E. D. Hirsch (2000) charged that projects waste valuable instructional time that would be better spent in teacher-directed lessons where students learn concrete information. Gilbert Sewall (2000: 42–43) of the American Textbook Council suggested that "time-consuming, trivializing activities" were "displacing the cultivation of active minds."

Hirsch and Sewell are correct that in-class projects will take time away from direct instruction and test preparation. What I hope to show in this chapter is that a project approach is actually a more effective way to achieve higher social studies academic standards. I strongly

317

recommend it as an organizing principle for middle school curricula (grades 6 through 8) and as an essential part of the high school curriculum.

Project approaches to social studies can be used in secondary school classrooms in different ways, depending on the particular subject or grade level and on a teacher's or school's curriculum goals. Students can work as individuals or in learning teams. Projects can originate from student discussions or teachers can present previously developed ideas to their classes. The focus of a particular social studies project can be on skill development, the research and development process, the product created by individuals or groups, or on student presentations in class. It can also be a combination of all of these. Projects can be at the center of the curriculum or they can be used to supplement what students are learning.

Long-term projects are especially valuable because they help provide continuity from lesson to lesson. In a government class, an entire curriculum might be organized around citizenship participation projects. An oral history project can be integrated into a history curriculum so that the biographies researched and written by students become the primary sources that are used to introduce topics and events.

Project-based learning has its origins in the work of John Dewey (1938/1972), William Heard Kilpatrick (1934), and the movement for progressive education in the early decades of the twentieth century. Progressive educators argued for project-based learning as a way to promote democratic citizenship. Their projects encouraged critical thinking and allowed students to construct their own knowledge about the world around them. In addition, student decision-making during the projects, and the group nature of the activities, provided students with democratic experiences.

Charles Howlett (1999) a former cooperating teacher in the Hofstra program, is an avid defender of the project approach. He had students in his United States history classes research and write about the local history of their town and they have published a local history journal. As part of the project, students conducted interviews with long time town residents and examined diaries, autobiographies, letters, census data, official community documents, and local newspapers. Chuck found that this project not only helped students understand the story of their town and its place in regional and United States history, but also gave them an irreplaceable experience as practicing historians. I strongly agree with him. A project approach to teaching social studies supports calls for developing curriculum and activities that involve students in the work of historians and social scientists. These activities include developing hypotheses, organizing and conducting research, gathering data, answering questions, discovering trends, drawing conclusions, preparing and making presentations of findings, and conducting discussions with colleagues (teachers and fellow students).

A project approach to learning is a major component of the educational practice proposed by the Coalition of Essential Schools (CES); it is implemented at the Central Park East Secondary School (Meier 1995; Meier and Schwarz 1995) and in Foxfire programs. According to Ted Sizer (1984), the director of CES, student learning is best promoted through a program emphasizing that "less is more." The in-depth exploration that is part of a long-term project makes possible greater personalization of learning, more active involvement by students in shaping their education, and more authentic assessment of what students have actually mastered.

Foxfire programs (available at: http://www.foxfire.org/, accessed November 5, 2007), which began with efforts to motivate students and preserve southern Appalachian culture through the creation of a series of student-written publications, have formalized project-centered learning during the last three decades. In the Foxfire approach, students choose and design their projects, and they are involved in monitoring their own learning. The process tries to ensure that a project belongs to the students from start to finish.

In classrooms using the Foxfire approach, teachers act as mentors, not classroom bosses. Mistakes are expected and considered part of the learning process. Because reflection is crucial to learning, time is structured into the day so that students can think about and discuss their projects. Because learning is a social activity, projects are presented in the class, school, and broader community.

In 2007, I saw an example of this approach put into action in the small rural Anderson Valley school district in northern California. Boonville was a community in transition as the grown children of older, long-established European American families moved away and were replaced in the schools by a new, largely Hispanic, immigrant population. To build multigenerational bridges between the old and new residents, in 1997 a group of teachers began the "Voices of the Valley Documentary Project" (see http://www.calhum.org/programs/story_ voices.htm, accessed October 10, 2007). As part of the project, middle and high school students tape, transcribe, and publish the life stories of elderly valley residents. The interviews were also broadcast on a local public radio station.

In another approach, Dean Bacigalupo (NTN) provided his middle school students with a "project menu" at the start of the year. Each project is assigned a different point value based on complexity and the amount of work involved. Students select both the type of individual and group projects they want to complete and the topics they wish to explore so that the total point value of all their projects is equal to 100 points. Sample projects include maintaining a current events packet, oral histories, "spontaneous" poems, keeping a diary/journal/memoirs, illustrating a thematic children's alphabet book, developing a Power-Point presentation, research papers, political cartoons, and original works of art. Topics include immigration, imperialism, World War II/Holocaust, Civil Rights, the Cold War, and globalization.

A problem that I always had while students were working on in-class individual and group projects was staying out of their way so I would not stifle their creativity. The project approach requires a lot of pre-class preparation on the part of teachers and a different way of looking at class time. Eventually I realized that project time could also be an opportunity for me to work with individual students who were having difficulty in their academic work and needed additional assistance.

Teaching Activity: The Foxfire Approach—Perspectives and Core Practices

Source: http://www.foxfire.org/teachi.html, accessed November 5, 2007

1. The work teachers and learners do together is infused from the beginning with learner choice, design, and revision.
2. The academic integrity of the work teachers and learners do together is clear.
3. The role of the teacher is that of facilitator and collaborator.
4. The work is characterized by active learning.
5. Peer teaching, small group work, and teamwork are all consistent features of classroom activities.
6. There is an audience beyond the teacher for learner work.
7. New activities spiral gracefully out of the old, incorporating lessons learned from past experiences, building on skills and understandings that can now be amplified.
8. Reflection is an essential activity that takes place at key points throughout the work.
9. Connections between the classroom work, the surrounding communities, and the world beyond the community are clear.
10. Imagination and creativity are encouraged in the completion of learning activities.
11. The work teachers and learners do together includes rigorous, ongoing assessment and evaluation.

It's your classroom:
The basic tenet of the Foxfire approach is that the interests and actions of students are central to a project and to learning. The teacher is seen as a facilitator and collaborator. Do you think this is a feasible way to organize a social studies curriculum? Explain your reasons.

WHAT ARE THE ADVANTAGES OF A PROJECT APPROACH TO SOCIAL STUDIES?

In discussions of student portfolios and the authentic assessment of student learning, many teachers offer formal and informal methods for evaluating the learning that goes on during student projects. George Wood (1991) of the Institute for Democracy and Education recommends that teachers take several points into consideration when they evaluate student projects. First, the criteria for evaluation should be clear, public, reflect student-generated goals, and include student ideas on what is important and well done. Wood believes that an evaluation should include discussion of how students have worked together as researchers, as well as an examination of the final results of the project. He encourages the use of multiple evaluation points so that evaluations become part of reflection and learning.

Other useful organizing principles for a project approach to social studies include the following:

- Learning should be challenging as well as fun. Keep the projects interesting.
- Students need to take responsibility for their learning. Do not be afraid to ease up on the controls. Student work will not be as polished without constant teacher involvement, but the projects will be theirs.
- Invest time in student projects. Cover content by having students do things. Projects by their nature are hands-on.
- Encourage students to become historians and social scientists. What questions would they like to think about and answer? Have students consider hypotheses, design research, collect data, and discuss explanations.
- The best projects tend to be interdisciplinary. Human understanding is not compartmentalized. Encourage students to use their talents from other areas. Include art, literature, music, and drama in social studies projects and presentations. Let students build on concepts they learn in science or math.
- Projects should involve students in intellectual interaction with their colleagues. Learning is social. Knowledge spreads through exchange. Classrooms may get a little noisy.
- Let students become teachers and present their findings to each other in classroom conferences and student publications. Let them use their imaginations to figure out creative ways to present their work to the class.
- Projects should be long-term learning activities. This makes continuity possible in learning. Students think about what they are studying in between classes, and look forward to coming to school the next day.
- Group projects provide students with experiences in democratic living and group decision-making.

A. Interdisciplinary Middle School Project Ideas

1. Historical restoration site guidebook and document-based questions

Laura Pearson (NTN) takes her 7th grade class to a local historical restoration site. Students prepare for the trip by reading about life in colonial America and the new nation. They travel around the site in teams and must answer questions about homes and buildings, food and farming, occupations and trades, education, clothing, recreation and religion in the village. Teams take photographs that document their discoveries and prepare a guidebook based on their visit. As a concluding activity, students examine each others' photographs and must refer to them as "documents" in a document-based essay where they describe life in the United States in the pre-Civil War era. If you are located too far from an historical restoration site, students can do virtual tours on-line to historic sites, such as Mesa Verde (http://www.nps.gov/archive/meve/home.htm); Jamestown (http://www.virtualjamestown.org/); Colonial Williamsburg (http://www.history.org/); Plymouth Plantation (http://www.plimoth.org/); Mount Vernon (http://www.mountvernon.org/virtual/index.cfm/ss/29/); New Orleans (http://www.oakalleyplantation.com/); and South Carolina plantations (http://www.nps.gov/chpi/); or the Gettysburg Battlefield (http://www.virtualgettysburg.com) (all sites accessed October 10, 2007).

2. Dioramas and museum displays

The New Teachers Network sponsors an annual "middle school museum" on a different social studies theme at the Hofstra University School of Education and Allied Human Services Building. Students from different schools prepare dioramas, posters, "artifacts,"

PowerPoint presentations, and plays to present to each other. Recent themes have included Slavery in the Americas, the Great Irish Famine, African-American History, and Immigration to the United States (see Essay 1 at the end of this chapter).

At the museum, exhibits are displayed on tables or hung up, along with a card that explains what is being depicted. After every one has a chance to browse, each student or student team presents their exhibit to the entire group. At the end, students discuss with the whole group what they learned from participation.

Teachers approach preparation for the "museum" differently. Some have students work outside of class, independently or in small groups, to create a series of 3-dimensional displays. Others have students work both individually and as a full class to create their exhibit. Teachers have organized an entire unit on the theme of the museum with learning packages for student teams and the final team projects were used to assess student learning.

In preparation for creating their class museums, students can visit major museums on-line. Among my personal favorites are: the American Museum of Natural History (http://www.amnh.org/); Ellis Island (http://www.ellisisland.org); the Lower East Side Tenement Museum (http://www.tenement.org/); the Metropolitan Museum of Art (http://www.metmuseum. org/); the Smithsonian (http://www.si.edu/museums/); the United States Holocaust Memorial Museum (http://www.ushmm.org/); the Louvre (http://www.louvre.fr/llv/commun/home.jsp?bmLocale=en); and the British Museum (http://www.britishmuseum.org/). When there was concern during the United States invasion of Iraq that looters would steal prized Mesopotamian artifacts from Iraqi museums, I joked that scholars did not have to worry because the British Museum in London, the Louvre in Paris, and the Metropolitan Museum in New York had stolen the best ones a long time ago.

Amanda Ahern, April Francis, Richard Tauber, and Kiesha Wilburn of the New Teachers Network have developed a number of museum projects with their students at their middle school in Uniondale, New York. For a Museum of the Iroquois, Amanda and April helped students put together stations with traditional foods, artifacts borrowed from a local museum, pictures, readings, a video (available on-line from Discovery Education, at: http://streaming.discoveryeducation.com), and an on-line guide to Iroquois languages (see http://www.iroquois.net/).

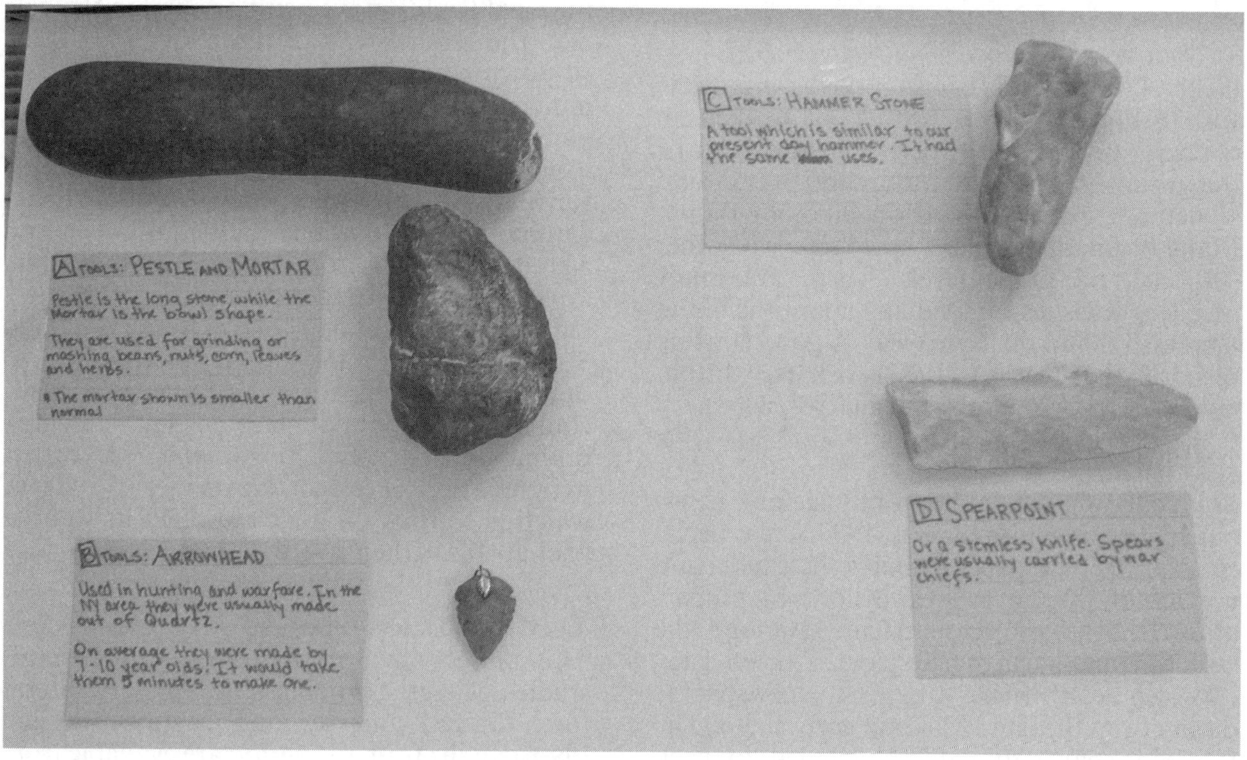

Figure 11.1 Artifacts.

Figure 11.2 Amanda Ahern and students work with stone tools.

3. The Great Depression and the New Deal

Henry Dircks (NTN) developed these projects with 8th-grade classes. Students worked in cooperative learning teams. Sometimes all of the groups in a class did the same project and sometimes teams worked on different things. Many of the projects can be adapted for other subjects and grade levels. There are many excellent websites for studying about the Great Depression and the New Deal. A good starting place is the New Deal Network (see http://newdeal.feri.org, accessed January 7, 2008).

FRONT-PAGE NEWS

Student teams create the front page of a newspaper. The date is January 1, 1930. This special issue of the newspaper explains the causes and impact of the Great Depression. In preparation for the project, students examine the structure and parts of newspaper articles. They can also read articles from local newspapers dating from the late 1920s and early 1930s. The following parts should be included in each story:

- A headline that discusses a specific cause of the Great Depression
- An introductory paragraph that explains this cause and its role in creating the depression
- The source on which the article is based: quote(s) from one or more imaginary or real local people that discuss the impact of the depression on your community
- An explanation of the impact of this cause of the Great Depression on the entire country.

All of the stories should be typed and laid out as the front page of the local newspaper, either through "cut-and-paste" or using a desktop publishing program. The page should include a masthead and appropriate pictures and editorial cartoons. Students in a team can work on individual articles independently or as a group. The team is evaluated on the quality of its overall product.

Other front-page topics from US history can include responses to the Declaration of Independence; reports on the completion of the Erie Canal or Transcontinental Railroad; coverage of Yorktown, Gettysburg, Pearl Harbor, Normandy, or Hiroshima; a Native-American perspective on the arrival of Columbus or the Trail of Tears; Woman's Suffrage or the Civil Rights movement; or a union struggle like the Homestead Strike, the 1937 GM sit-down strike, or Mother Jones and the coal miners' union. This project can also be used in global studies classes. They can focus on broad topics like the French, Russian, or Chinese Revolutions; people such as Winston Churchill, Mahatma Gandhi, Nelson Mandela, or Corazon Aquino; or individual events such as Cinco de Mayo in Mexico, battles like Dunkirk, Dien Bien Phu and Stalingrad, the Warsaw Ghetto and Soweto uprisings, and historic elections or peace conferences. A good place to start research on-line is *The New York Times* (see http://nytimes.com, accessed November 5, 2007), which has articles available though its website back to 1851 when it started publication.

GREAT DEPRESSION DRAMAS

This project involves English, art and social studies classes. Students study history, literature, drama, and set and costume design. Photographs from the period are available from the Library of Congress American Memory website (http://memory.loc.gov/ammem/index. html, accessed January 7, 2008). Teams should be organized at the start of the unit and work on their production while the class is studying the time period. The goal for students is to demonstrate their understanding of the impact of the Great Depression on the American people. Sample dramatic settings can include these:

1. Members of a family and their lives in a "Hooverville"
2. A public meeting where local government officials and citizens discuss New Deal relief proposals
3. Workers organizing a union or farmers responding to evictions
4. Life on the road or in a Civilian Conservation Corps camp

Questions for dramatizing a historical event:

- In what setting will your play take place?
- What events will provide the drama for your production?
- Who are the people in your production?
- What ideas from class and your research will you include in the play?
- How have events and social position affected the people in your play?
- How will your dialogue show the feelings of participants in your play?
- What message do you want viewers to learn from your play?
- What props and costumes will you need?
- What will be the background for your stage?
- How long will the play last?

FIRESIDE CHATS

Franklin D. Roosevelt (FDR) became President of the United States during a time of bank failures, high unemployment, and suffering by many people. At his inauguration, he promised a "New Deal" for Americans. In order to secure public confidence in the economy, FDR promoted recovery, relief, and reform. Periodically, FDR addressed the nation by radio to discuss his proposals. These talks are known as "fireside chats." They explained new legislation or programs, calmed public fears, and enlisted political support.

In this project, students write, perform, and audiotape a "fireside chat" designed to explain and sell a New Deal reform proposal to the American public. Students submit both a transcript and the audiotape for evaluation. Topics include the Emergency Banking Relief Act, the Federal Deposit Insurance Corporation, the National Recovery Administration, the Wagner Act, Social Security, the Security and Exchange Commission, Home Relief proposals, public housing projects, the Works Progress Administration, the Civilian Conservation Corps, or proposed Supreme Court reform. Each "fireside chat" should include the following:

- Explain the purpose of the proposed reform. Tell how the proposal will benefit individual Americans and the nation as a whole.
- Ask for the American people's support to make the new proposal work.

ALPHABET AGENCY POSTERS

The New Deal introduced the idea that active government was the solution to the problems created by the Great Depression. A number of government agencies were created to address these problems. Many of the agencies were best known to the public by their initials: the TVA, NRA, CCC, AAA, and WPA. For this project, students investigate the purpose of an agency, and design and create a poster or mural that explains its role to the American people. This project works best when done in conjunction with an art teacher. As students design their posters, they should consider the following:

1. Does the poster show the work being done by the agency?
2. How is the work being portrayed?
3. Does it illustrate the way the agency benefits the public?
4. Will this poster win public support for the program?
5. How does this poster present the New Deal's broader idea of active government as a solution to the problems created by the Great Depression?

THE WPA GUIDE TO YOUR COMMUNITY

In the 1930s, the Works Progress Administration (WPA) sponsored Federal Writers' Project Guides to communities all over the United States. In addition, the Farm Security Administration funded professional photographers to document life in the United States. In this full-class project, students can examine sample guides and photos and use them as a model to create a WPA-style guide to their own community. Student teams can subdivide the project. Teams can investigate and write about the community's geography, history, architecture, local businesses, community resources, and important individuals.

4. Bridges and the city

Judith Singer and I (Singer et al 1999/2000) developed this middle level US History project as part of a summer school program. Part of its strength is that it is an interdisciplinary project that combines history, science, math, art, literature and writing. As the final activity of the summer, students created a Museum of the City of New York that focused on the bridges that help unify its five boroughs and three major islands.

At the center of the museum was an 8-foot long, 7-foot tall, replica of the Brooklyn Bridge that students could walk across. The actual bridge, completed in 1883, is a suspension bridge that spans the East River separating Manhattan Island and Long Island in New York harbor. Since the original New York City was located on Manhattan Island and Brooklyn is located on Long Island, the bridge played a major role in creating one city out of two.

Building the replica of the Brooklyn Bridge was a multi-step process. Students began by reading *The Brooklyn Bridge* by Elizabeth Mann (1996) and preparing short reports about the history of the city and its bridges. The "Brooklyn and Manhattan Bridge," as the Brooklyn Bridge was originally known, was opened on May 24, 1883 (McCullough 1972). At the time, the span between its towers was the longest in the world and the bridge dwarfed surrounding structures. It was the inspiration of an engineer named John Roebling, the inventor of a process for manufacturing wire cable, who first proposed building the bridge in 1867.

The project continued with a trip to the promenade overlooking New York harbor and a walk across the Brooklyn Bridge. On the promenade, students saw and discussed the bridge, the Statue of Liberty, Ellis Island, and the Manhattan skyline. They also sketched the bridge and read the poem, *The New Colossus*, by Emma Lazarus. In the poem, written in 1883, Lazarus describes how the Statue of Liberty commanded the harbor shared by the twin cities of New York and Brooklyn.

As they walked across the bridge, students and teachers discussed what made it a suspension bridge. They examined the set of four woven steel cables that drape across the giant granite towers that stand near the opposing shores and the network of wires hanging from the cables that hold up the roadway. They could also see the Williamsburg Bridge (opened in 1903) and the Manhattan Bridge (opened in 1905) slightly upriver. These bridges were built decades after the Brooklyn Bridge when steel production had expanded and new technology was available. They have steel towers and can carry greater weight. As a result, subway lines connecting Brooklyn and Manhattan still run across these bridges.

When they returned to school, students discussed what they had learned and mapped out the activities for the next few days. They touched up and painted their sketches, wrote stories and poems about the history of New York City, and worked in teams to design and build model suspension bridges. The sketches, paintings and models were all exhibited at the end-of-summer museum. When their models were complete, ten students met with a community volunteer who is an amateur carpenter. He helped them design a wood-and-polyethylene rope suspension bridge that they could walk across. Students helped calculate the quantity of material that was needed to build the suspension bridge, measured and helped cut the wood, and assembled and painted it.

Even if they do not have the Brooklyn Bridge in their neighborhood, teachers can use interdisciplinary projects to help students discover the relationship between technology, history, and geography. Since ancient times, bridges have been constructed using different designs because of the variety of geographical conditions and the availability of technology and materials. There are bridges made of rope, wood, rock, bricks, and concrete and steel. Modern suspension bridges like the Verrazzano-Narrows in New York harbor and Golden Gate in San Francisco Bay span large open spaces. Arch bridges generally span shorter distances. Often an arch bridge consists of a series of connected arches that stand on a row of natural or human made islands. Very long bridges like the Chesapeake Bay Bridge in Maryland are actually a series of different types of bridges attached to each other. Students can study ancient Roman arches and learn how this technological discovery made possible the construction of aqueducts, buildings, and bridges. They can search for examples in their communities and build miniature keystone arches. Excellent websites about bridges (accessed October 10, 2007) with plenty of pictures include *howstuffworks* (http://science.howstuffworks.com/bridge.htm) and *About Bridges* (http://www.nireland.com/bridgeman/index.htm).

Just as bridges allow roads to cross over rivers, canals make it possible for rivers to cross dry land. The construction of canals in the nineteenth century created a vast transportation network across the eastern United States. The remnants of famous canal systems have been turned into parks in New York, New Jersey, Pennsylvania, and along the Potomac River in Washington, DC and Maryland. Classes can visit the canals, study how they transformed society, and construct models of locks used to raise and lower boats along the canals. Similar interdisciplinary units can focus on the idea of crossroads or the way towns grew up along railroad lines. Websites for studying about canals include: *The Erie Canal* (http://www.eriecanal.org/); the *Panama Canal Authority* (http://www.pancanal.com/eng/); and a teacher-created website on the Suez Canal (http://www.mrdowling.com/607-suez.html). Websites for studying about railroads include: the Smithsonian (http://memory.loc.gov/ammem/gmdhtml/rrhtml/rrintro.html); and the Central Pacific Railroad Photographic History Museum (http://cprr.org/Museum/Exhibits.html). (These sites were accessed October 10, 2007.)

5. Coming-of-age ceremony mask project
Many cultures have coming-of-age ceremonies that celebrate a young man or a young woman's entry into adulthood and the assumption of expanded responsibility within the community. Frequently they include special gifts from family and community elders that acknowledge puberty and the possibility of reproduction. Gifts can also be related to the acquisition of knowledge and expertise. Sometimes a coming-of-age ceremony includes taking a new name that symbolizes changed social status and spiritual transformation. In the contemporary United States, birthday parties and school commencements mark transformations in the lives of young people. Other coming-of-age ceremonies are religious in nature. They include the Roman Catholic confirmation, adult (or teenage) baptism among certain Protestant church groups, and the Jewish bar or bat mitzvah.

Mask making can also have religious or spiritual significance. In West African cultures, wood carvers envision the spirit hidden within a piece of wood and hand-carve a mask that liberates it. They do not start with an image and then construct it out of plaster, plastic, or papier mâché. In many traditional cultures, creating and wearing masks are part of the way people tell stories and pass along knowledge of tribal customs. Masks can represent spirits that protect or threaten a tribe and they are often integral to dances and dramatic performances. The Barong dance on the island of Bali in Indonesia and similar dances in India and Sri Lanka use masks to tell the story of the struggle between good and evil. In an example of cultural diffusion, mask dances became an integral part of Buddhist religious ceremonies and spread with Buddhism into Myanmar (Burma), Cambodia, Thailand, and Tibet. In Tibetan Buddhism, masks are used in sacred mystery plays aimed at exorcizing malignant demons, and the masks are believed to possess the qualities of the characters they depict. These masks are generally made of papier mâché and brightly painted.

In China and Japan, mask dances celebrate national history, while in Korea they tend to have a more local focus. Over 100 different masks were used in traditional Japanese No dramas to represent Gods, demons, animals, and human beings. In Korea, mask dances have political overtones. In the past, dancers used masks to hide their identities as they ridiculed the local elite. In Africa, masks often honor ancestors and are used in ceremonies that evoke their support for difficult personal or community decisions. Among the Ibo and Yoruba people of contemporary Nigeria and the Bambara of Mali, masks play an important role in initiation ceremonies for adolescents. In an example of parallel cultural development, they play a similar role in initiation rites among the people of Papua New Guinea in Oceania. In the ancient Mediterranean world, Egyptian, Greek, and Roman civilizations all had mask making traditions. Until a thirteenth-century papal order forbidding the practice, Roman Catholic clergy in Europe wore masks during some ceremonies and while dramatizing Bible stories. The earliest known Japanese masks are made of clay and shell and are over 2,000 years old.

Today, mask making remains important throughout Africa, among Native American people, and in the Pacific Rim areas of Asia. Masks are also part of carnival celebrations in many European, Latin, and Caribbean societies.

This interdisciplinary activity developed with Stephanie Hunte (Singer et al. 1998) combines a coming-of-age ceremony with mask making. Instead of creating inauthentic versions of traditional masks, students create their own spirit masks using modern materials. The masks represent their hopes for their teenage years and adulthood.

MATERIALS

Clean plastic gallon jugs, any color (milk, water, paint, cooking oil, laundry soap, etc); hammer, nails, and small wood block; retractable knife; latex acrylic paint (black, brown, white, blue, red, yellow, and green); brushes; markers; glue; scissors; construction paper; stapler; wool; straw; feathers; corn husks; needle and thread; buttons, cloth strips, index cards (*Note: Tempera paint cracks and peels off plastic jugs*).

PROCEDURE

1. Close your eyes. Imagine a face that represents your inner spirit as it is transformed at a crucial point in your life. Is the spirit angry or happy, supportive or threatening? Are you an adolescent preparing for religious commitment or entering a new school or new grade, a teenager entering adulthood, an adult entering a new career, a person preparing for marriage or parenthood? Think of symbols and colors that describe the image in your mind.

2. Open your eyes. Draw a sketch of the face from your inner vision. Why do you make the choices that you make? Explain them to your neighbor.

3. Think of ways to transform your drawing into a three-dimensional mask.

    a. Select a plastic jug. Holding it so the handle faces you (it will become part of the mask face), cut up from the mouth of the jug until it is divided in half (discard the back piece).

    b. Use markers to sketch the face on the jug. Use the retractable knife to cut out the eyes and mouth (*With younger students, teachers should do this part or else the eyes and mouth can be painted on later*). Use the hammer, nails, and wood block to punch small holes for attaching wool hair, feathers, or buttons.

    c. Paint the entire mask with a base coat of paint and allow it to dry over night.

    d. Paint on the mask face and symbols. Again, allow it to dry over night.

    e. Add wool, straw, cloth strips, buttons, cornhusks, feathers, and paper designs. With thinner plastic water or milk jugs, it is easy to staple or sew on items. If the plastic is too thick, use paste.

4. On the index card, describe the transformation in life depicted by the spirit in the mask. Describe the spirit and the role it plays in your life. Describe the special symbols used in your mask.

RESOURCES ON MASK-MAKING

Print (Reference books and pictures):

Brooklyn Museum of Art. 1998. *Ancestors and Art, African Gallery Guides.* Brooklyn, NY: Brooklyn Museum of Art.

Lechuga, R. and Sayer, C. 1994. *Mask Arts of Mexico.* San Francisco: Chronicle Books.

Mack, J., ed. 1994. *Masks and the Art of Expression.* New York: Harry N. Abrams.

Segy, L. 1976. *Masks of Black Africa.* New York: Dover Publications.

Singer, A., Gurton, L., Horowitz, A., et al. 1998. "Coming of age ceremonies: a mask project," *Social Education Middle Level Learning* 3: M14–M16.

Print (for students):

"Masks," *Faces* 3(2); 1987.

Price, C. 1978. *The mystery of masks.* New York: Charles Scribner's Sons.

Hunt, K. and Carlson, B. 1961. *Masks and mask makers.* New York: Abingdon Press.

Teaching Activity: Respecting Cultural Integrity

Some educators (Bigelow et al. 1992) are concerned that social studies art and craft projects, by removing traditional activities out of their cultural and technological contexts, trivialize religious rituals and mislead students about the high level of skill these crafts require. For example:

- West African wood carvers envision the spirit hidden within a piece of wood and hand carve a mask that liberates it; they do not start with an image and then construct it out of papier maché.
- Navaho religious leaders scatter sand paintings in the wind at the end of communal healing ceremonies to show reverence to the spirit world and to protect the secrets of their people from outsiders. Traditional sand paintings, which portray Navaho religious beliefs, are never made permanent, displayed, or sold.
- Critics of these types of projects argue that few teachers would consider involving students in reenacting Judeo-Christian rituals or making models of our religious symbols.

Add your voice to the discussion:
In your opinion, should students engage in art and craft projects that are modified versions of traditional crafts or religious activities? Why or why not?

Think it over:
How would you address this issue in your class?

Try it yourself:
Create an art or craft project to use in a global studies class. Teach the students in your class how to do them. How would you use the project to teach social studies concepts?

It's your classroom:
What do you do if you do not have artistic ability?

B. Global History Projects for 9th and 10th-grade Classes

1. Cultural festivals
A number of network members have experimented with international festivals and culture days as part of the global studies curriculum. In some communities, they find parents or community residents who will come to school and share foods, clothes, stories, music, and family treasures. Stavros Kilimitzoglou (NTN), who lived in Greece for many years, uses a jigsaw approach to teach Greek culture to his class. Student volunteers learn Greek dances, perform them in class, and teach the dances to the other students. Lois Ayre (NTN) and her students organize classroom stations where students can sample ethnic foods, listen to music, and examine cultural artifacts. Christina Agosti-Dircks (NTN), who has taught both regular and special education social studies classes, takes students on trips to visit international restaurants. After sampling a national cuisine, they buy ingredients and prepare international foods as part of her global studies class.

2. Craft ideas for global history classes
For the Great Irish Famine curriculum, Maureen Murphy and I included a series of traditional craft projects. We involved students in wool dyeing, Crios (belt) weaving, making a

traditional Irish drum called the Bodhrán, dip candlemaking, and weaving children's toys and religious emblems out of straw. The New York State Great Irish Famine curriculum is available on-line at: http://www.emsc.nysed.gov/nysssa/gif/index.html (accessed January 7, 2008).

The following project is recommended by Christina Agosti-Dircks (NTN). Among the Jalisco and Nayarit people of Mexico, "Ojo de Dios" (God's Eye) is a sacred decoration that promises good luck, prosperity, health, and a long life. A father presents one to an infant at birth and on each birthday until the child is five years old.

MATERIALS
2-foot long pieces of yarn (multiple colors), 2 ice cream sticks per student

INSTRUCTIONS
1. Cross pairs of sticks. Staple or tie them together with yarn. Tie a piece of yarn to the center.
2. Weave the yarn around a stick and then around the next stick, circling the cross. When a piece of yarn is almost finished, tie on a different colored piece of yarn and continue to weave.
3. When the eye is complete, put a knot at the end so it does not unravel.

3. Cultural museum exhibits

Classes or student teams collect or re-create the material culture of a society or group of people. Artifacts and cultures are described on museum cards and displayed for the entire school. Students can give tours of the exhibit at scheduled times. One year I had a group of students who were born in Russia in my class. It was the first time that many of them had been instructed in English and they were almost all reticent about participating in class discussions. During one marking period, I assigned them to be a project team and worked with them to create a museum display focusing on their Russian heritage. They brought in family artifacts and Russian products available at stores in their community that they presented to the other students in our class.

4. Hallway maps for the social studies corridor

Cover an entire wall with sections of white paper. Use an overhead projector and a transparency to project a map on the wall. Trace the map on the paper. Add political subdivisions, geographic features, or pictures illustrating local cultures or attractions. Paint and display. Students in the class, or in the entire school, can mark their family's point of origin on a world map.

5. Puppet folk theater and plays

Middle and high school students can take traditional, historical, or contemporary social studies stories written for elementary school age students and rewrite them as plays or puppet shows. They can create puppets and scenery and then present the shows in local elementary school classrooms. With this project, students in remedial classes can work with social studies ideas and materials, improve their reading and writing skills, and become positive role models for younger students.

Stories and books that can be dramatized include *Terrible Things* by Eve Bunting (Philadelphia, PA: Jewish Publication Society, 1989), an allegory of the European Holocaust; *Hiroshima No Pika* by Toshi Maruki (New York: Lothrop, Lee & Shepard, 1990), a book about the effects of the dropping of the atomic bomb on Hiroshima; *The People Could Fly* by Virginia Hamilton (New York: Alfred A. Knopf, 1985), a collection of African-American folk tales; *The Banza*, a Haitian story by Diane Wolkstein (New York: Dial Books); and traditional European and US folk tales.

Linda Shank, who I met at a Teaching American History program in Sonoma, California, has developed a very systematic approach to student-created skits. She recommends keeping them short (4–6 minutes), limiting the number of scenes and characters, and having lots of movement. Actors should do something rather than just speak. To make it easier for the audience to follow, narrators introduce characters that wear simple, but distinctive, costumes or carry identifying props. Her skits focus on a conflict to create dramatic tension.

I developed this "play" with Jen Debler (NTN) and her student teacher, Kara McEneneany, for a 7th grade class. It can be presented as either a pantomime or a puppet show. It is based on a story from *In The Beginning* by Virginia Hamilton (New York: Harcourt Children's Books, 1988).

Classroom Activity: The Iroquois Story of Creation

Characters—Narrators, Sky Chief, Sky Woman, Fire Dragon, Birds, Great Turtle, Daughter, Twins

Narrator 1: Long before there were human beings, there were Sky People. They lived in their own Sky World. In those days there was no sun. All light came from the large white blossoms on the tree that stood in front of the Lodge of the Sky Chief. Sky Chief married Sky Woman. In time, Sky Woman began to show signs that she would bear a child. (Sky Chief and Sky Woman walk hand-in-hand through Sky World. They are smiling).

Narrator 2: In Sky World there was a troublesome being known as Fire Dragon. Fire Dragon was always spreading rumors. He whispered to Sky Chief that the child would not be his. In a fit of anger and jealousy, Sky Chief uprooted the great tree in front of his lodge. He pushed his wife through the hole where the tree had stood. (Fire Dragon swoops in and flies around. He makes loud and scary noises. He whispers in the ear of Sky Chief. An outraged Sky Chief screams and uproots the tree. He pushes Sky Woman through the hole.)

Narrator 3: Sky Woman fell rapidly down toward the vast dark waters below. The birds, feeling sorry for her, flew underneath and gently supported her, breaking her fall and carrying her slowly downward. At the same time, the water animals hurried to make a place for her. Great Turtle said that he would support a world on his back. The sea animals plunged down into the water looking for some earth. Muskrat succeeded and came up with a large mouthful of earth, which he placed on Great Turtle's back. The light from the blossoms of the fallen celestial tree shone through the hole where it had stood and became the sun. When Sky woman landed, everything was in readiness for her, with grass and trees beginning to grow. (Sky Woman is falling but is saved by the birds. Great Turtle swims through the dark waters. He rises to the surface. A globe is on his back.)

Narrator 4: Sky Woman gave birth to a daughter. When this daughter grew to womanhood, she began to be with child. No one knows whether her husband was Great Turtle or the West Wind, but she gave birth to two remarkable twin boys—one good and one evil. The Good Twin was born in the usual way. But the Evil Twin was in a hurry and pushed thought his mother's side to be born. In doing so, he killed his mother. (Daughter is heavy with child. She pulls one doll from her side. She is in great pain and falls to the ground and is dead.)

Narrator 5: Sky Woman buried her daughter and plants miraculously began to grow from various parts of the daughter's body. This is the origin of the tobacco plant, cornstalks, bean bushes, and squash vines. These plants will become important to the human beings. (Sky Woman stands over her dead daughter and cries. She spreads magic seeds in the air and plants grow.)

Narrator 6: The Good Twin and the Evil Twin quickly grew to manhood. The Good Twin creates all plants, animals, medicinal herbs, rivers, and streams. The Good Twin creates people to live in this new world. The Evil Twin tries to spoil his brother's work. He puts rapids and boulders in the rivers. He creates poisonous plants, thorns, and briars. He spreads disease and releases monsters. The Good and Evil Twins fight but neither is able to win, so good and evil both survive. This is how our world began. (The Good Twin and Evil twin have their backs to each other and make their creations. They turn and fight but neither wins.)

It's your classroom:

1. Would you use plays, pantomimes, and puppet shows to illustrate history and social studies? Explain.
2. How would you help students identify key social studies themes in this play?

---

6. Archeological grab bag

The premise of this project is that you learn to be a social scientist by being a social scientist. Brendalon Staton (NTN) begins the project by giving each student team a mystery bag containing artifacts from a "lost society." Bags can contain dried bones and seeds, shaped rocks, plant fibers, plastic and metal items, coins, children's toys, cans, written items, and so on. Teams examine the artifacts, reconstruct the society, and report to the class about their findings. During the reports, fellow archeologists ask questions about interpretations and possible inconsistencies. Erin Hayden (NTN) has the artifacts buried in a sandbox and students have to carefully grid the archeological site. William McDonaugh (NTN) likes to begin by modeling the activity. The entire class gathers around him as he sits at a table in the center of the room and tries to reconstruct an animal from pieces of bone. As he works, he explains to students what he is doing and carefully writes down a description of each bone or fragment. In another variation, one team analyzes a website with artifacts from an ancient society. For example, the Heraklion Archaeological Museum in Crete has a website with artifacts from the ancient Minoan world at: http://www.scholarsresource.com/browse/museum/119 (Accessed July 16, 2007).

Depending on the amount of time you want to invest in the project, student teams can assemble their own artifacts and construct new societies. When they present these societies in class, they include the "history" of their society, a description of how people have adapted to their environment, and an anthropological discussion of its beliefs and values. Reports can include "maps" and dioramas. Once again, fellow archeologists ask questions about interpretations and possible inconsistencies.

Some museums and universities make available collections of artifacts for classroom use. The Anthropological Studies Center at Sonoma State University in Sonoma, California (http://sonoma.edu/asc, accessed November 5, 2007) has traveling boxes with artifacts from local Native American cultures. The Crow Canyon Archaeological Center (http://www.crowcanyon.org, accessed November 5, 2007), based in the four corners region near the borders of Colorado, Utah, Arizona, and New Mexico, runs both on-site and on-line educational programs. On-line programs include a virtual tour of Castle Rock Pueblo that allows students to "visit" three different time periods (1200s, 1800s, and 1900s) and "Archaeologists On-line," where students can e-mail questions about archaeology, archaeologists, and Pueblo Indian history (see arch_online@crowcanyon.org, accessed November 5, 2007).

Because of growing concern with global warming, there has been much speculation about the impact of climate change on traditional societies. *Collapse* (2005) by Jared Diamond and *The Winds of Change* by Eugene Linden (2006) look at the breakdown of civilizations in the Yucatan, the US Southwest, on Easter Island, and in Mesopotamia as populations outstripped resources. The Archeological Grab Bag project is an excellent way to introduce students to this vital topic.

7. Ancient world alphabet book

Tammy Manor (NTN) has students create an illustrated alphabet book (with topics ranging from A to Z) using history and myth from the ancient world. Students can focus on one society or include material from many groups. Each letter introduces a topic, person, or event and contains a written description and an illustration (Xerxes of Persia invades Greece in 480BC). Some of the illustrations are their own. Others are downloaded from the internet or scanned from magazines and tourist fliers.

C. High School US History Projects

1. Music videos

Folk music from the nineteenth and the first half of the twentieth centuries was rooted in the culture of ordinary people. We can study lyrics to learn about popular social, religious, and political concerns. If this music were written today, it would be very different. Vocabulary would change, and it would reflect different musical genres. An exciting project is to have students take the ideas expressed in a traditional song and present them in a contemporary musical context. An ambitious team could perform their work in class or produce a music video. The following example, based on the song "Union Maid," was written and produced as a video by students in one of my high school classes. The original version of "Union Maid" is available on the internet at: www.geocities.com/Nashville/3448/unionm.html (accessed October 10, 2007).

UNION MAID RE-MIX
A long time ago, way back in the dayz
There once was a group called the union maids
A bunch of brave souls who were never afraid
Of goons and ginks and company finks
or deputy sheriffs who made a raid!
As often as possible meetings were called
At a place by the name of the union hall.

But the meetings weren't always so pleasant
and kind
The cops would come around next to no time
And try to chase everyone outta town
But the union maids would stand their
ground and say. . .
We're sticking to the union (3×)
(you can't scare us) till the day we die.
These union maids were very wise
Wise to the tricks of the company spies
They'd never be fooled by the company
stools
And made sure they'd always organize the
guys
And always, always got their way
And made sure they struck for higher pay
They'd show their cards to the company
guards
And this is what they'd say.
We're sticking to the union (3×)
(you can't scare us) till the day we die.
When the union boys had finally seen
the mad pretty, pretty, pretty union queens
They stood up and sang in the deputies' faces
They laughed and yelled in all of the places
And don't you know what the deputies done?
When they heard this song, they tucked their
tails and began to run.
We're sticking to the union (3×)
(you can't scare us) till the day we die.
All you women that wanna be free
I got a little to you from me
When all of the workers come and unite

We'll be able to fight every fight
And instead of many we'll all be one—
sticking to the union!
We're sticking to the union (3×)
(you can't scare us) till the day we die.

2. Political cartoon history of the United States
One year I found myself challenging my classes at the end of each period to design political cartoons illustrating an idea from the lesson. Students would shout out their ideas and I would sketch them on the board. I shared the room with another teacher who liked the idea and started doing it also. Soon classes were competing with each other to come up with the best cartoons, and students with artistic ability replaced the teachers at the blackboard.

An interesting long-term project is to have student teams create a "Political Cartoon History of the United States." This is a good way of recognizing and encouraging students with artistic talents who might otherwise be lost in social studies classrooms. These cartoons are recreations of cartoons by students in an 11th grade class when we studied Industrialization and the Progressive Era. The one on the left is about the battle between farmers and railroads in the west. The one on the right shows bloated monopolies supported by workers. The Library of Congress (see http://memory.loc.gov/learn/features/political_cartoon/resources.html, accessed November 5, 2007) has a special site for examining political cartoons from the past.

Figure 11.3 Populist cartoon.

Figure 11.4 Monopoly cartoon.

D. Economics, Government, and Citizenship Projects

1. Investigative reporters
Students research local and state consumer laws, and visit supermarkets and restaurants to find out if they are in compliance. Stores that violate consumer laws can be reported to appropriate authorities. Students can create commendations and award them to stores that are in compliance. The results from student investigations can also be sent to local newspapers and radio stations and posted on the internet.

2. Product tests
Students decide on product standards, evaluate products, examine advertising, interview consumers, and compare prices. One test that students have particularly enjoyed is measuring vertical and horizontal jumps wearing different brands of sneakers. They can compare their results with studies by *Consumer Reports* (see http://www.consumerreports.org/, accessed November 5, 2007) or other consumer advocacy groups and publish their own newsletter.

3. Public advocates
Students analyze local budgets, zoning codes, and laws, and make presentations at public meetings. They can take stands on controversial issues such as the way their school and community responds to undocumented immigrants.

4. News reports
Television news broadcasts aim for short sound bytes and older audiences. Students videotape and edit broadcasts into more in-depth thematic presentations. They can include their own research presented by student broadcasters and interviews with students, staff, and community residents.

E. Psychology and Sociology Projects

1. What is normal human behavior?
Answering the question "What is normal human behavior?" provides an overall theme for a high school psychology course developed by Jeannette Balantic (NTN). This activity is designed to help students understand that *normal human behavior* is defined differently in different cultures, and that the definition of *normal* can be very broad. Students can work individually or in groups. As they read about actual individuals, they discuss and answer these questions:

- What types of behavior are considered normal behavior in this society?
- How does this individual behave?
- Is this behavior within the culturally defined boundaries of normal? Why or why not?

2. Who stops at stop signs?
This project, designed by Andrea Libresco (NTN), gives students experience using a structured scientific method. Working individually or in groups, students develop hypotheses about the types of people who stop at or drive through traffic stop signs. Variables can include: vehicle type, location, characteristics of the driver (age, gender, race), and number and types of passengers in the vehicles. Stopping categories can include: full stop, rolling stop, and no stop. After completing observations and sharing information with classmates, students write reports describing their results and conclusions. Reports include the following elements:

- Identification of hypotheses being tested
- Identification of variables
- Discussion of how observations were conducted
- Description of results
- Analysis of results
- Discussion of problems with the experiment (e.g., impact of stereotypes on hypotheses and assignment of categories)
- Conclusion: assessing the validity of the initial hypotheses and suggestions for further experiments.

F. Writing Projects

1. Global pen pals

Over the years, I have made contacts with schools in other countries through UNICEF, UNESCO, and government missions in the United States. However, the vagaries of international mail always made a global pen pal project difficult. The internet offers an entirely new set of possibilities for global pen pals. Responses to e-mail are virtually instantaneous. Students get answers to their questions while they are still interested in them. However, teachers and parents need to be careful before approving partners. While the United Nations does not administer a pen pal program, its website refers visitors to: http://www.worldpeace.org/peacepals.html. Internet sites that help arrange for pen pals include *ePals*, which advertises as the leading provider of school-safe collaborative learning products for K-12 across 200 countries and territories (http://www.epals.com/). *ePals* and other sites reviewed and recommended by Yahoo! are listed at: http://dir.yahoo.com/Social_Science/Communications/Writing/Correspondence/Pen_Pals/Children/. (These sites were accessed October 10, 2007.)

2. Messages to world leaders

In the spring of 1995, the United Nations invited youth worldwide to use the internet to send statements on international development, poverty, unemployment, and social conflict to world leaders attending the World Summit for Social Development in Copenhagen, Denmark. Lynda Costello-Herrara (NTN) had her 9th-grade global studies students send in their ideas (see http://www.youthlink.org/, accessed October 20, 2007).

3. Zen Buddhist Haiku

Michael Pezone (NTN) (Singer and Pezone 1996) and his 9th-grade students study traditional Japanese culture with a focus on Zen Buddhism. The Zen spirit of humor and irreverence particularly intrigues students. They are fascinated as well by the Zen emphasis on "immediate," as opposed to conceptual, knowledge. This emphasis is clearly evident in the Zen tradition of haiku writing. Haiku are short, three-line poems that employ "imagistic snapshots" to evoke profound perceptions. Students are encouraged to depart from a rigid syllable rule. After all, the duration or spoken tempo of Japanese is much more rapid than that of English. Students thoroughly enjoy writing haiku and reading each other's creations. Frequently their works focus on unexpected comparisons and metaphors.

4. Poems about life in the United States

Students can write poetry that shows their understanding of social movements or major historical developments in US history. In the poem that follows, an 11th-grade student discusses the impact of mechanization on working people and their families (Singer 1994).

NEWSPAPER MEN
by Nicole Paciello

The busy hustle of the city streets,
The noise, the excitement, keys to the big city.
The trains make my insides rattle—
People run to catch it,
Or stop at the stand for the morning paper.
So easy in their strides, people hardly notice
Newspapers are dwindling in number.
Newspaper men on the sidelines,
Machines have their jobs now.
They watch the game,
Waiting to be called in,
They sit in their cardboard shelters
Watching the world run by.
The noise, the excitement,
The strange faces hurrying by are noticed easily—
Your eyes fix on their attaché cases, their hard-hats,
And the morning paper under their arms.
The others are overlooked,
Others who don't read the morning paper,
They wear it.

I never noticed these people before,
When they were out in the cold clutching
their cardboard homes,
Or inside their concrete houses, yet still cold.
One day, I stop and take a long hard look
As I hear the train above me.
The train drowns out all else
As I pass by the newsstand and head home.
My father's waiting for me,
Way before the 5:15 train.
There's a carpet mark behind the corner,
Where his attaché used to be.
I ask him what he's done today.
He looks at me,
With his glassy eyes,
And his five o'clock shadow.
He tells the youngest of his three daughters,
"I pressed the clothes in the dryer."
I reassure him—again,
A machine can do many jobs,
But it can't replace him as my father.
Newspapers are dwindling in number.
Newspaper men on the sidelines,
Machines have their jobs now.
They watch the game,
Waiting to be called in,
They sit in their cardboard shelters
Watching the world run by.

5. Editorials and speeches

The Forum Club was an extracurricular political action student group organized by students in "Participation in Government" classes as part of a student civics program (Singer 2003: 22). Club activities included encouraging people to complete census surveys, voter registration, lobbying for a health clinic for their school, sponsoring a school forum and debate on abortion rights, and testifying on a condom availability proposal. Students in the club worked together in groups to help each other write political advocacy speeches and editorials. The following are excerpted from a speech presented by a member of the Forum Club at a public hearing organized by the New York Pro-Choice Coalition and from an essay printed in *New York Newsday* on January 14, 1990.

POLITICAL ADVOCACY SPEECH

I think it is a good idea to talk to your parents about a pregnancy and an abortion. But I also understand that you may not be able to do this. Some teenagers are afraid to tell their parents. Some teenagers have good reasons why they cannot tell them . . . A law cannot take a distant relationship and make it a close one. That's why there are hotlines to call and all sorts of counselors, so that a pregnant teenager does not end up boxed into a corner unable to get out . . . My mom has said to me, "If you make mistakes in your life, you are the one who has to live with them. But always remember that I am here for you." I think all teenagers should be able to talk with their parents. I wish all parents were like my mom, but I know that it's not that way. That's why I am fighting against parental consent and parental notification laws.

STUDENT OP-ED PIECE

The members of the Forum Club strongly disagree with the behavior of some of the pro-choice demonstrators at Saint Patrick's Cathedral. We believe that it was uncalled for and inexcusable to disrupt the mass and interfere with communion. We believe that the demonstrators who entered the church were wrong and hurt the ability of the pro-choice movement to win people over to our ideas on human freedom and the rights of Americans.

However, we also believe that the newspaper coverage of events on that day misrepresented the pro-choice movement. Out of 5,000 people who demonstrated at Saint Patrick's Cathedral on that day, only 43 were arrested inside the church. Furthermore, only one person disrupted Holy Communion.

Meanwhile, the media buried reports about another demonstration that took place on the same day. In New Jersey, 125 members of Operation Rescue, an anti-abortion group, were arrested at a health clinic. They had blocked the entrance to the clinic to prevent women from choosing to have safe and legal abortions. Six of these demonstrators had chained themselves together.

We believe that on this Sunday, both the pro-choice and anti-abortion groups did things that violated the rights of other Americans. What we don't understand is why the pro-choice group was singled out for the harsher criticism.

Teaching Activity: Evaluating Interdisciplinary Project Ideas

Think it over:

1. How could you modify these projects to make them appropriate for students on different grade levels and in different subject areas?
2. How would you ensure that the projects include social studies content and concepts?
3. How would you incorporate the projects into your overall curriculum?
4. How would you assess student learning?
5. How much voice and choice would you allow students in defining the projects, especially when they touch on controversial issues?
6. How would you respond to critics who charge that the students are not really learning social studies?

Try it yourself:

Select and complete three of the projects described in this section.

Essay 1: Oral Histories: A Project Approach to Social Studies

Based on A. Singer and B. Brody. 1990. On Teaching—Franklin K. Lane High School oral history project and history magazine. *OAH Magazine of History* 4(4); and A. Singer. 1994. Oral history and active learning. *Social Science Record* 31(2). Used with permission.

Oral history is a way to actively involve students in thinking about and understanding history and the contemporary world. It allows teachers to bring the cultural and historical experiences of students and their families directly into the classroom and the learning process. In many schools, it creates possibilities to enhance the multicultural nature of social studies curricula. An oral history class project has the potential to become the centerpiece of class discussions on recent US and global history.

There are different methods to introduce students to oral history projects, depending on the interest and academic level of the class. Students can bring in and discuss family heirlooms that allow the class to examine cultural similarities and differences. Classes can complete family histories that help students pinpoint where their family's story has intersected with broader historical events. Classes can also read oral histories to figure out what questions the interviewer asked the subject, and to allow students to think of questions they would like to ask.

Students can participate in oral history projects as individuals or in cooperative learning teams. However, a heterogeneous cooperative learning format is strongly recommended. It helps students learn how to work supportively in groups, and it allows them to learn more about their teammates' families and cultures. Cooperative learning teams of three or four students can create their own interview

questionnaires, or use questions prepared by the class or the teacher.

Interview subjects can be neighbors, family friends, members of senior citizens centers, participants in church or veterans' programs, and the school's older staff members. An entire cooperative learning team can interview one person, the team can interview a member of each student's family, or students can interview their family members by themselves and then meet to write their reports together.

Open-ended interviews using prepared questions as starting points encourage people to tell stories about their past. Sometimes during an interview, students ask all of their prepared questions, sometimes only part of their questions, and sometimes they think of new follow-up questions in the middle of the interview.

Before teams do their interviews, it is useful to conduct a practice interview in class. One of the student teams can interview a staff member, a family member, or a community resident. The practice interview teaches students how to conduct open-ended interviews that stimulate interview subjects into telling their stories.

Students can take notes during an interview, or audio- or videotape them. When the interviews are completed, cooperative-learning teams can work together to write up their findings as biographical sketches or in a question–answer form. Team members compose, write, and edit the reports together. Sometimes interviews are conducted in languages other than English, and students need to work together to translate what they have learned.

Interview subjects should be asked for permission to include their stories in student magazines. Magazines can be used as student-created texts to teach about the Great Depression, World War II, the Civil Rights movement, the problems of workers in modern America, and the hopes and problems confronting immigrants and ethnic minorities.

As they conduct interviews and edit oral histories, students are confronted with what it means to be an historian. A person's memories are their memories, but they may not be historically accurate. To establish their validity, a historian must seek out corroborating evidence. One student interviewed a grandmother who claimed that during World War I the federal government gave public assistance to Jews in her community, but not to her family because they were Ukrainian Catholics. As a result of additional research, she learned that there was neither a national or local welfare system in place during World War I and that religious groups provided most charity to members of their churches. Because her grandmother was a non-Jew living in a largely Jewish community, she experienced this system of aid distribution as a form of official discrimination.

Follow-up activities can include trips to local museums like the Ellis Island Immigration Museum in New York City or the creation of a school exhibit using family photographs and artifacts. Students can also become involved in checking personal testimonies against primary sources and history books. They can discuss the subjectivity of our knowledge of the past and the importance of examining multiple sources before arriving at conclusions. The oral histories that follow were included in an article published by the New York State Council for the Social Studies.

Excerpts from Oral Histories Written by High School Students

Life in Sicily
I was born on December 17, 1913 in agricultural Sicily. My birth took place in my great grandfather's house, a house which had been handed down from generation to generation. It was always inherited by the eldest son in the family. My family was one of the more fortunate families in our village. We were a small family in comparison to the enormous families with an average of ten children per household. That number decreased with time; for it was almost inevitable. Disease and sickness struck most families from all walks of life. I frequently heard neighbors gossiping late at night discussing deaths. "Poverino era piccolo, simpatico." Poor child, so young, so beautiful . . .

Though poverty seemed to be in every direction your eyes led you, people still found it in their hearts to share what little they possessed with the more needy. Frequently neighbors would gather collections of blankets, bread, cheese, whatever they could afford to give. The package was then placed on the doorsteps of a family that was having a hard time. The person offering one month never knew if she would be receiving the following month.

A Black family comes North
When he was almost ten years old, Marcus and his brother and sister got word that they'd soon be moving to the North. His father had gotten a job in Chicago, Illinois. In October of 1924, Evelyn and Cyril and their children headed for the train station. When he and his family boarded the train, the children were all surprised to see how many other men and families were making the same move. The ride was the most memorable moment of Marcus' young life. The trip meant a complete and total change from the way things were and had always been, to something very foreign and far off. Once Marcus and his family left the train and he could see the new place, he grabbed his younger sister and held her by the back of her collar. He never took his eyes off of the signs in the station. He was amazed that any place could be so big and afraid that it would swallow him whole. In Chicago, they were driven to a large brick monstrous building that gobbled up entire families of people. There was an empty room in the beast's belly where Marcus and his family settled. The tiny rooms stacked on top of one another and squished together side by side were different from the homes Marcus had known. Many things in the North took a lot of adjusting to.

Holocaust survivor
My grandpa is a Holocaust survivor. When he was younger he lived in a small town called Cozova in Poland. There were five children in his family—Seymore, Carl, Yossel, Aliva, and his sister Hencha. It all started in the summer of 1941. The Jews of his town knew that when the Jewish policeman threw up his nightstick it was a warning to hide because the Germans were coming. When Carl's family saw the Jewish police, they jumped into a small covered ditch by their horse stables. When the Germans found them they yelled at them to get out or they would shoot. They grabbed Carl's three brothers, Aliva,

Yossel, and Seymore and dragged them off. His mother, sister and Carl were shoved into a truck and were rushed to a train station a few miles away. They were being taken away to concentration camps. There were many people on the train with him—so many that you couldn't even sit. The trains the people were packed in were mainly used to transport the cows. They still had the odor. The Germans didn't give them any food or water; not even a pail to urinate in. Everybody on the train was screaming and crying because they knew where they were headed. A man in the car with my grandfather had a razor. My grandpa started to cut away at the door by the latch. He finally cut a hole big enough for his fingers to fit through to lift the latch. He shoved the door open and jumped out of a speeding train. The last memory of the train was that his mother was very sick.

Life in Puerto Rico and New York

My grandfather was born on December 6, 1930, on the southeastern part of a beautiful island called Puerto Rico. He lived in a small town called Patillas with his native Puerto Rican parents and two brothers and a sister. My grandfather's reasons for coming to the United States were simple. First, he wanted to see a new country. Second, he wanted to look for new origins. He was hearing all the talk about how wonderful the US was, so he decided to find out by himself. He secretly went and sold a cow they had by the name of Manuela, and with the money bought a plane ticket to New York.

Discrimination was something he remembers too well. When looking for jobs or apartments, he tells how there were signs put up saying, "NO SPANISH PEOPLE WANTED," or "NO P.R.'S WANTED!" I found it amazing when he told me how he had to sign the name Mike Maccio in order to get a lease on an apartment. He had to try to pass as an Italian. Using his real last name, Rodriguez, wouldn't have helped the situation. Because of his looks, he got away with acting as an Italian.

A Greek war hero

Vangeli was born in 1921. In 1938, he was drafted into the Greek military. While he was in the military, World War II broke out and Vangeli was sent to the Albanian side of Greece. He fought many great battles and received the rank of sergeant. In 1945, World War II ended. Vangeli led his soldiers back home, but to his amazement, the war was not over. A civil war had started in Greece. Vangeli was very tired of fighting and did not want to see any more bloodshed. But he had no choice in the matter. Vangeli's father, Georgo, was killed by a Communist party member. Vangeli then sent his younger brother Fotis to America with an old friend to look after him until he was finished fighting the civil war. Vangeli was in a town called Nea Smirna. He was stationed there for seven months. During that time he and his soldiers captured many Communist followers and killed them. Vangeli often killed them himself, letting some of his anger out for his father's death ... He was slightly going mad and insane from all of the bloodshed and killing he had seen his whole life ... Vangeli wrote to his wife about his feelings. Vangeli wanted to move to America with Maritsa and live with his brother Fotis ... That night as Vangeli was fast asleep there was a Communist attack on the town. Vangeli ordered his men to open fire on anyone not wearing their uniform. Vangeli's men were outnumbered seven to one. There was no hope for victory. The next morning Vangeli was shot by a firing squad just like his father had been. Vangeli lived his whole life fighting wars. He died at the age of twenty-eight. The war ended in 1949, just two months after his death.

Life in Haiti and the United States

Antoine was born in Haiti on March 20, 1930. On January 2, 1950, at the age of 20 years old, Antoine was arrested for speaking out against the government. The President of Haiti was Francois Duvalier. Nobody had the right to speak out against him. Antoine had spoken against the President for ordering the killing of peasants in Port-au-Prince, the capital of Haiti. He refused to let them hurt innocent people who did not do anything wrong. The police officers arrested Antoine and put him in a jail for three months before he could go before a jury. The jury was appointed by Duvalier. When Antoine finally went to court, he was convicted before he even had a trial. The jury didn't even bother to listen to his reasons for going against the President's wishes. They sentenced him to a lifetime of imprisonment.

After five years of hell, little food and beatings by the officers at the jail, his mother found a way for him to escape to freedom in America. He had to use a fake passport and a fake name but he made it through the American immigration.

Life in China

I was born in 1907 in a big city in the south of China whose name is Guangzhou. My family was not very rich, but it couldn't be considered a poor family. My father was a professor in a university. We lived in a big mansion even though we didn't have much money. I had five brothers and sisters and I am the second daughter. My father died suddenly when I was only nine years old and we were forced to leave the mansion because we didn't have the money to pay for the rent. My mother brought her six children to live in a 10-meter-square room. Seven people lived in a small place without a bathroom. When we had to go, we went to the public bathroom.

My mother was working 18 hours per day. My sisters and brother felt hungry every single day, especially my brother. He got sick all the time. Unfortunately, we really didn't have money to send him to see a doctor. After thinking of it for several nights, my mother decided to sell my brother! She told us that instead of the whole family dying together, we should sell our brother to a wealthy family and let him have a good life. We could get the money to live on also. After she sold our brother, she cried all day. Instead of letting her son die of starvation, she wanted him to be alive even though she couldn't see him any more.

Learning Activity: Writing Oral Histories

Try it yourself:
Design a questionnaire and interview a senior citizen about life in the United States or in another part of the world. Using your notes and tapes, write a first- or third-person account of the person's life.

It's your classroom:
How would you help students verify information they learned during their interviews?

FOR FURTHER READING ON ORAL HISTORY

Brecher, J. 1988. *History from Below*. New Haven: Advocate Press.
Brody, B. and Singer, A. 1990. "Franklin K. Lane High School oral history project and history magazine," *Organization of American Historians Magazine of History* 4(4): 7–9.
Hickey, M. G. 1991. "And then what happened, Grandpa?," *Social Education* 55(4): 216.
Singer, A. 1994. "Oral history and active learning," *Social Science Record* 31(2): 14–20.
Terkel, S. 1970. *Hard times*. New York: Pantheon.

Essay 2: Technology-based Project Ideas

Warning: I know this is not what the band "Rage Against the Machine" was referring to, but I am notorious among tech support personnel on my college campus for screaming over the phone every time something goes wrong with my computer. I am not cursing at them, but at the machine on my desk, which I am convinced plots against me and freezes just to drive me crazy. Given these "credentials," you need to take whatever I have to say about technology in the classroom with a grain of salt. (All sites mentioned in this essay were last accessed October 10, 2007.)

As the mobster played by Robert Di Nero in the movie *Analyze This* (1999) tells his therapist who he is preparing to murder, "I'm conflicted." I am not ashamed to say that I consider myself a Luddite, a spiritual descendant of early nineteenth-century English hand-loom weavers who smashed mechanized looms that were driving down wages and destroying their way of life. I may not like computers—after all they are machines not living things—but I use them a lot and I have for a long time. Since the early 1980s, I have written and rewritten lessons, activity sheets, and tests on desktop computers at home and at work. I am in near constant contact with friends, family, colleagues, students, and alumni via email. This edition of *Social Studies for Secondary Schools* was written on a PowerMac and a MacBook. I use the internet for research and occasionally illustrate presentations with PowerPoint. But I am still not sure what the hullabaloo over technology in the social studies classroom is all about. It seems to me that most of the better social studies activities and projects that involve computers could be, and in the past were, done without them.

The National Council for the Social Studies has vigorously promoted the use of technology through ongoing features in all of its publications, a special NCSS bulletin on social studies in the digital age (Bennett and Berson 2007), and themes issues of *Social Education* (April 2007) and *Theory and Research in Social Education* (2007). Michael Berson, a major proponent for enhancing social studies instruction through the use of technology has been involved in many of these projects.

But I also have allies. In 2000, Neil Postman wrote an essay for a special edition of *Theory and Research in Social Education* where he argued, "the new technologies both in and out of the classroom are a distraction and an irrelevance" (p. 580). Bill Tally of the Center for Children and Technology, who is a supporter of the use of technology in social studies classrooms, reminds enthusiasts that educators need to be concerned with the undermining of print literacy and the inability of technology so far to substantively transform education (2007: 305). Tally argues that contrary to what its advocates generally anticipate, new technologies will be most useful when they "slow down learning," rather than accelerating it. Potentially, this will allow students and teachers to focus on thinking and the evaluation of more complex materials and problems. He concedes that unfortunately, when new technologies have been used in social studies classrooms, they have been used to promote routine rather than creativity. Students use the internet to find predigested information, word processors to write formulistic reports, and PowerPoint to present glossy but unsubstantive findings. According to Tally, even the webquests he has observed, which are supposed to represent the best integration of social studies pedagogy with the new technologies, largely promote ritualized process over critical understanding. Despite these reservations, Tally remains a hopeful proponent of the use of new technologies in the social studies classroom. I am not sure why, but he just does.

Because of my continuing resistance to technological innovation, this essay is basically a compilation of technology-based project ideas for the social studies classroom developed by members of the New Teachers Network. I think these projects are very good ones. I am just not sure how much the computers add to the projects.

Recommendations from Middle School Teachers

Jennifer Debler (2002) is a middle school social studies teacher who has grappled with a series of problems that emerge when students surf the web doing research. Many waste a lot of time, others get distracted, and some end up discovering and using questionable information. To alleviate these problems, she created her own website. Jennifer previews websites that she plans to have students visit and links them to her site. This allows students to go directly to her homepage when they are working on an assignment. Increasingly, school districts are providing teachers with dedicated webspace. A number of companies also offer teachers free webspace. These include: http://www.cyberbee.com/freeweb.html; http://www.education-world.com; and http://www.schoolnotes.com/. Others, including http://teacherweb.com, provide inexpensive webspace along with other useful services. (All sites in this section were last accessed December 6, 2007.)

On her site, Jennifer includes homework assignments, project directions, class guidelines, her e-mail address so students and parents can contact her, and links to the school and district webpages. Research connections are organized by units and projects. She also has "just for fun" links to interesting social studies related sites that are not necessarily tied into what students are studying in class. She finds that her students like to visit these sites, so she continually updates them, which encourages students to visit her webpage on a regular basis.

Jennifer advises that before teachers begin computer projects, there are some things they need to consider. Teachers must be familiar with their school or district's internet policies. Many require that students have written parental consent before they use the internet. Some computer labs have filters that block certain websites. Often these blocks appear to be irrational. When choosing sites for a project, check to make sure they are not blocked by the school's filter.

Jennifer recommends the program *Inspiration* (see http://www.inspiration.com) for creating graphic organizers. Teachers and students can use the organizers for planning, organizing, outlining, webbing, and concept mapping. She recommends *PowerPoint Palooza* (see http://www.pptpalooza.net/) for sample PowerPoints and PowerPoint formats useful for both teachers and students. Social Studies teachers can use PowerPoint to create and present slide shows, overhead transparencies, instructions for lessons and projects, maps and charts, class notes, and quiz or test reviews. Students can use PowerPoint to create presentations on topics that they research. Using slide shows to support oral presentations helps even the most nervous student learn to speak more easily in the classroom.

Some districts have video conferencing technology available for classroom use. Video conferencing allows students to take field trips and "visit" remote locations using video, computer, and communications technology. Students can conference with other classrooms or visit real life locations such as the American Museum of Natural History, the Museum of Modern Art, the National Science Center, the Baseball Hall of Fame, and NASA.

African colonial experience project

For this project, students utilize Microsoft Word and the internet to create class "books" about the experiences of Africans during the colonial period. Working in pairs, students select and research specific topics and create a page for our class book.

Students learn about and write pages on African kingdoms, trade within Africa, and the Atlantic slave trade, the Middle Passage, the evolution of African-American culture and customs, and individuals like Phillis Wheatley, Benjamin Banneker, Prince Whipple, and Olaudah Equiano. Students use the internet for their research. All sites are categorized and book marked in advance. Students write their own text but can include images pasted from the internet. Each group presents its page to the full class. At the end of the project, every student receives a printed copy of the entire project.

RECOMMENDED WEBSITES:

Africans in America (http://www.pbs.org/wgbh/aia/home.html)
HarpWeek: Towards Racial Equality (http://blackhistory.harpweek.com/)

George Washington art project

This assignment was designed as an enrichment activity for grade 7 "modified" classes. Students evaluated works of art featuring George Washington. Each student chose three paintings or works of art and created a PowerPoint presentation to share with other students. Students cut and pasted the artwork from a website and then formatted the work into their presentation. They had to use the art to

explain the historical period of Washington's life (Pre-Revolution, Revolution, Presidency, Final Days), provide information about the artist and the time when the work was created, and evaluate how the painting portrayed Washington. A painting such as "Washington Crossing the Delaware" by Emanuel Leutze gave students the opportunity to learn about historical accuracy, themes, and artist perspective.

RECOMMENDED WEBSITES:

George Washington Picture Gallery (http://www.historyplace.com/unitedstates/revolution/wash-pix/
    gallery.htm)
The Life of George Washington (http://earlyamerica.com/lives/gwlife/index.html)

Federal agencies

This project is another enrichment activity for a grade 7 "modified" classes. Students compile a class book explaining various federal agencies. Many

government agencies offer student pages explaining their function. Students used Microsoft Word to format their information.

RECOMMENDED WEBSITES:

Central Intelligence Agency (https://www.cia.gov/kids-page/index.html)
Department of justice (http://www.usdoj.gov/usao/eousa/kidspage/)
Federal Bureau of Investigation Kid's page (http://www.fbi.gov/fbikids.htm)
Social Security Administration (http://www.ssa.gov/kids/kids.htm)

Supreme Court cases

This project requires student teams to research Supreme Court cases involving the Bill of Rights

and present individual cases to the class using PowerPoint. The Oyez Project at the Northwestern University website provides students with both case abstracts and actual Supreme Court decisions. The abstracts provide information appropriate for the middle-level students.

PowerPoint presentations explain the issues in the case, the constitutional amendment under examination, and the decision made by the court. Students are required to integrate two quotations from the court decision into their reports.

For this project, students utilized government websites to copy and paste photos and graphics into their presentation. They also practiced using

PowerPoint features such as animation and layouts. Presentations were made in the school library on a large screen television that was connected to the computer lab.

Cases included *N.J.* v. *TLO*; *Gideon* v. *Wainwright*; *US* v. *Eichman*; *Abington Township* v. *Schempp*; *Lee* v. *Weisman*; *Miranda* v. *Arizona*; *Hazelwood, S.D.* v. *Kuhlmeier*; *Tinker* v. *Des Moines*; *BOE* v. *Pico*; *Texas* v. *Johnson*; *Bethel S.D.* v. *Frasier*; *Schenk* v. *US*; *Goss* v. *Lopez*; and *Engel* v. *Vitale*.

RECOMMENDED WEBSITE:

Supreme Court Database (http://www.oyez.org/)

Letter to Congress
In conjunction with English classes, students write business letters to their United States Congressional Representative regarding their views on a bill she or he has sponsored. One year, students researched the National Language Act, HR 280, a bill to declare English the official language of the US Government. As part of this project, students learned how a bill was drafted and identified where HR 280 was in the law-making process. They discovered when it was introduced, its sponsors and committee assignments, interpreted its meaning, and debated its implications. Students found the text of the bill through a local Congressional Representative's webpage at the Congressional Website (http://www.house.gov/king)

and THOMAS, a legislative information site of the Library of Congress (http://thomas.loc.gov/).

The Transportation Revolution
For this project, students examine the movement of people and goods, human-environment interaction, technology, and interdependence during the nineteenth-century transportation revolution. Using internet sites, students created brochures publicizing different types of transportation innovations including roads, steamboats, canals, and railroads. Students used Print Shop Deluxe or Microsoft Publisher to format their brochures. Again, students copied and pasted photos and graphics from the internet to use in their projects.

RECOMMENDED WEBSITES:

Erie Canal (http://www.history.rochester.edu/canal/)
History of the National Road (http://www.nationalroad.org/html/history.html)
National Railroad Museum (http://www.nationalrrmuseum.org)

Rachel Thompson is the middle school technology specialist in her school district and a major proponent of both a project approach to teaching social studies and the integration of technology into the middle school social studies classroom.

Industrialization project
Students examine the period of industrialization in the United States, roughly 1870–1915, and prepare a HyperStudio or PowerPoint slide show with a series of 13 slides. Presentations must address major historical questions, including "Did industrialization improve conditions for all or lead to social

inequality?" "Did changing technology make life in the United States better or worse?".

Travel brochure
Students use the internet to create a tri-fold brochure that describes one of the American states. The goal is to encourage tourism to the state. Each brochure must include:

- Front cover: Name of the state, a picture or graphic, and an advertising slogan.
- Inside folds: Introduce the state including a bit about its history, interesting or unusual facts

about the state, pictures, things to do and places to visit.
- Back cover: Include a map of the state and traveling instructions.

Recommendations from High School Teachers

Ken Dwyer is a high school social studies teacher who is a strong advocate of examining essential questions in Global History (see Chapter 3). This projects uses technology to engage students as historians to answer essential questions. As students review ancient civilizations they focus on three questions: "Is geography destiny?" "To what degree does religion provide order in society?" "To what degree does government provide order in society?" Their assignment is to use the internet to find at least five documents (quotes, artifacts, maps, artwork, etc.) from or about societies they are studying that address one of the essential questions. When students locate the documents, they are imported into a word processing file. When students are satisfied with their selections, they develop a "scaffolding question" for each document that can be answered using information provided by the document.

Activity Sheet—Creating a Global History DBQ

These essential questions guide our study of ancient civilizations and early empires:
- Is geography destiny?
- To what degree does religion provide order in society?
- To what degree does government provide order in society?

Task:
Using the internet, research information about the civilizations we have studied. Evaluate the information and select sources that provide evidence to support your views. Assemble a set of documents that provide evidence for one of the essential questions. Each student must assemble a minimum of five documents. The documents should be imported into a word processing file and a scaffolding question must be written for each document.

Types of Documents:
Each packet of documents must include at least three different types of sources. Possible sources include the following: Charts, graphs, illustrations, maps, pictures, written primary sources (at least one is required), and written secondary sources.

Civilizations Studied:
Each set of documents must include sources from at least three of these civilizations: Egypt, Mesopotamia, Indus River Valley, Chinese River Valleys, early empires of India, early empires of China.

Format:
Topic: _____
Essential question: _____

Document 1.
Type of document: _____
Civilization represented: _____
Is the document the appropriate length? _____
Is the document understandable? _____
Does the document provide evidence for the essential question? _____
Can the scaffolding question be answered from the document? _____
Suggestions for improvement. _____

Kenneth W. Leman (2002) uses a package of websites and a set of questions to help high school economics students participate in the debate over globalization. While many of these sites require a high level of academic skill to understand, Ken encourages students to use as many of them as possible. Students can use multiple sites to write extended research reports or be responsible for reporting to class on a specific site.

Essential questions on globalization

- What is a global economic system? How do international capital systems work?
- How does globalization affect local, national, regional, and international economies?
- How does globalization affect wages and prices?
- Does globalization promote the removal of production and jobs from developed to underdeveloped countries? What are the social costs to both groups?
- Why has globalization promoted child labor, environmental degradation, and poor health in many underdeveloped countries?
- How have the power of multinational corporations and trade agreements affected the balances of national, international, and regional power around the world?
- What will be the impact of globalization on movements for democracy and human rights?
- Why should citizens and consumers care about globalization?
- Can globalization occur without disrupting traditional cultures, religions, and economies?
- Can the current global system more uniformly benefit all people?
- What can businesses, organized labor, governments, and citizens do to make globalization more just?
- If globalization cannot be made fairer, can and should the world undo or modify the current global business systems? Can the clock be turned back?

Sites for research on globalization

1. **Center for Economic Policy and Research** (http://www.cepr.net/). This private think-tank site offers a balanced and critical view of economic globalization, discussing many of the relative advantages and disadvantages to countries around the world. *Globalization: A Primer* is an excellent overview of the interrelated factors affecting the world economy. Vocabulary may challenge students with lower reading abilities.
2. **International Monetary Fund** (http://www.imf.org/). Posted by one of the two supranational organizations that controls international capital, this site offers its own primer on economic globalization. It makes good use of graphs and requires prior understanding of key economic terms. The bias of this site is clearly in favor of globalization as an evolving process of expanding the market economy to all countries. While it freely acknowledges bad consequences of globalization, it takes the approach that such

consequences are the by-product of change rather than systemic inequality.
3. **The World Bank Group** (http://www.worldbank.org/). An excellent site for the better reader. It contains a wealth of information on World Bank policies and practices and explains how money moves around the world and why.
4. **Clearing House Interbank Payments System** (http://www.chips.org) and **Asian Development Bank** (http://www.adb.org/). The CHIPS site explains international monetary exchange. The ADB site shows how the ADB provides funding for local economic and infrastructure development in Asia. These two are very accessible for students of all reading abilities.
5. **JusticeNet** (http://www.justicenet.org/). This site provides articles and links to sites that take a more critical view of globalization. Articles discuss the social and economic disruption that IMF and World Bank practices cause. It includes links to sites that expressly address issues related to children.
6. **Youth for International Socialism** (http://www.newyouth.com/). This is a key site in the anti-globalization movement. It offers a fairly balanced but critical view of global inequalities and explanations of protests at WTO, G-8, and IMF meetings.
7. **Worldwatch Institute** (http://www.worldwatch.org/). This site provides a wide variety of alternative analyses of globalization's downside. Its focus is on environmental degradation.
8. **Global Challenge Initiative** (http://www.challengeglobalization.org/). This organization's sole purpose is challenging the current global system. The site offers access to a wealth of information, training programs, and advocacy support to oppose the status quo and a collection of political cartoons.
9. **Mother Jones** (http://www.motherjones.com/) and **AFL-CIO** (http://www.aflcio.org/). Mother Jones contains easy to read reports on globalization's ill effects. The AFL-CIO site provides organized labor's view of issues.
10. **The Fair Trade Federation** (http://www.fairtradefederation.org/). This site focuses on the FTF's activities to promote fair wages for overseas workers engaged in global production. The FTF's eight Practices and Principles challenge students to think about fair wages and employment practices whether these can be promoted within the global economy.
11. **Human Rights for Workers** (http://www.senser.com/). This site addresses globalization and human rights issues such as child labor.

12. **United Nations University** (http://www.unu.edu/). This site focuses on UN activities. Material on Africa and the global economy compares current African problems with Asia's earlier experience, and suggests possible local, national and international initiatives.

Essay 3: Middle School Immigration Museum

The Hofstra New Teachers Network is nominally made up of recent graduates of the Hofstra University teacher education program, however some of our "new teachers" have been active for over fifteen years and all local teachers are welcome to participate. NTN sponsors two annual conferences, distributes regular e-mail "updates" that allows teachers to discuss classroom, curriculum, and contemporary issues, and develops curriculum projects.

Middle school social studies teachers from the Hofstra University New Teachers Network organize an annual theme-based "Middle School Museum of History" with a weeklong display of student-made exhibits in the Hofstra University School of Education building. The themes for the museum are selected from the New York State human rights curriculum. Recent themes have been the Great Irish Famine and the right to food, Slavery in the United States and the right to freedom, and African-American History and the struggle for Civil Rights. A committee of teachers meets and decides on the museum's theme during the summer and creates lesson materials. They involve their students in planning and creating exhibits as soon as the new school year begins. The displays are assembled at the Hofstra School of Education and students present their work to each other on the Friday before Thanksgiving.

For Fall 2007, the theme was Immigration to the United States: Past and Present. One of the reasons teachers selected immigration as a theme was because the United States, New York State, and Long Island where they teach, are sharply divided over recent immigration reform proposals. In conjunction with the museum, teachers developed a series of lessons and projects exploring the history of immigration to the United States and contemporary controversies. A goal of the museum program was bringing together in an academic setting, students from different school districts, many of which are racially and ethnically segregated. Students who participated in the program were from very diverse backgrounds. A significant number were either immigrants or the children of immigrants and some of them were from families that are undocumented.

Exhibits at the Museum of Immigration included a chronological (paper) tapestry illustrating the entire history of immigration to the United States; 5-foot by 3-foot "images of immigration" painted on foam board and suspended from the atrium ceiling; tri-board posters and dioramas presenting the experiences of different immigrant groups; readings of oral histories based on interviews with recent immigrants; student made plays presenting the immigrant experience from earlier historical epochs; family artifact displays presenting immigrant cultures; poetry readings and "raps" about immigrant life; PowerPoint presentations; and a debate on the future of immigration to the United States. Kimberly Cahill (Brooklyn) developed a virtual museum project for use by all of the participating schools.

Dawn Sumner (Hempstead) had her class research, write, and film a documentary on recent immigrants designed to dispel stereotypes. As they studied the history of nineteenth-century immigration to the United States, Bill Hendrick (Queens) and Cherisse Irons (Westbury) had students become immigrants and write journals about their experiences, hopes, and apprehensions. They later compared what they had written with stories told by immigrants who were members of their families or who lived in their community. Richard Tauber and Kiesha Wilburn (Uniondale) had students write poems about the experience of immigrants. Kristin Joseph (Bellmore-Merrick), Birthe Seferian (East Williston) and Lauren Borruso (Farmingdale) had students create dioramas illustrating immigrant life.

Jennifer Debler (Baldwin) prepared a project sheet to introduce the museum to 7th grade students. Her students worked individually. Adeola Tella (Uniondale) developed ideas for eighth-grade students and an evaluation rubric. Her students were assigned to work in teams. Kristin Joseph (Bellmore-Merrick) prepared an organizer for students to complete as they visited museum exhibits.

Over 300 middle school students from nine schools visited the museum. Twenty of Eric Sorenson's high school (Comsewogue) students who were studying about immigration to the United States attended and acted as docents helping teach the middle school students about conditions portrayed in the displays. Exhibits were arranged chronologically so visitors passed through six historical eras: The First Americans (Pre-Columbian Native Americans); Colonial American and the New Nation (1500–1820); New Groups Begin to Arrive (1820–1880); Industrialization and Immigration Transform the Country (1880–1924); Closed Doors and Internal Migration (1920–1965); Doors Are Re-Opened (1965 to the Present).

I opened the activities in my *Reeces Pieces* persona by performing an "immigration rap," where I described my family's arrival in the United States at the beginning of the twentieth century. According to coverage in a local newspaper (Winslow 2007), "Singer's enthusiastic, though rather wooden delivery, elicited raucous laughter from the more than 300 students, but it nevertheless laid out the themes the students had delved into themselves for the museum."

One exhibit that drew particular attention at the museum was a carpenter's box with an old-fashioned wooden plane that was brought to the United States from Clifden, Ireland, by the great-great-great-grandfather of one of the middle school students.

Bill Hendrick, whose school sent 90 students to the museum, described it as "very successful in displaying and encouraging diversity in America. This was a day for children to come together and exchange thoughts, display knowledge, highlight hard work, and learn about different cultures from each other."

A. 7th grade Immigration Museum Social Studies Project

Create a museum exhibit about the early American or modern day immigrant experience. Since grade 7 social studies focuses on America's beginning until the Civil War time period, please pick a topic that occurred before 1865 or a current events topic. Exhibits can be posters, but "artifacts" and three-dimensional items like dioramas are preferred. All exhibits should include typed "museum cards" explaining the exhibit. Computer slides. Videos and live presentations (plays) are also welcomed. These will be presented in class and at the Hofstra Immigration Museum. This event will be held on Friday, November 16 in Hagedorn Hall at Hofstra University. You may choose from among the suggested topics or one of your own (with approval).

Topic ideas (pre-1865)

- Jamestown, Virginia: America's first successful English settlement was founded in 1607

- Pilgrims and Puritans: The first English settlers in Massachusetts
- Africans in British America: The first enslaved Africans were brought to Virginia in 1619
- Trans-Atlantic Slave Trade
- First US Census (1790): Half of the population of the original 13 states was of English ancestry. One-fifth of the population was enslaved Africans. The rest were Scots/Irish, German, Dutch, French, Swedish, Welsh, or Finnish
- Early Settlers to New France, New Spain, or New Netherlands
- Quakers of Pennsylvania
- Early European Settlers of New York, especially Long Island
- Naturalization Act of 1795: Restricted citizenship to "free white persons" who resided in the United States a minimum of 14 years
- Alien and Sedition Acts. Gave the President the authority to deport any foreigner thought to be dangerous
- Immigrant Workers on the Erie Canal. Many of the workers on the canal were part of the first wave of Irish immigrants to the United States
- New Immigrants: Famine and war at home and hope for a new life spur new immigrants from Ireland, Germany, and Scandinavia
- Treaty of Guadalupe Hidalgo (1848). Ended the Mexican-American War and extended citizenship to approximately 80,000 Mexican residents of the Southwest who lived in areas acquired by the United States
- Chinese Migrants: Most come as temporary workers. They help build the towns, railroads, and mines in the west.

Topic ideas (Current Events)

- Family Artifacts: Present real or "created" artifacts representing your family's culture and tell the story behind the artifact
- Immigration Trunk: Create a trunk or suitcase of items brought to the United States by recent immigrants
- Newest Immigrants: Write a report and create a display about a recent immigrant group
- An Immigrants Story: Interview someone you know about his or her first hand experience as an immigrant. Include pictures with your report
- Local Immigration Issues: Use newspaper articles to prepare a report on how immigrants live and work on Long Island
- Preserving their Culture: Report on how immigrants try to preserve their culture once they have arrived in the United States.

B. 8th grade Immigration Museum Social Studies Group Projects

Each cooperative learning team will select and complete one of these projects:

Restricting immigrants

Research immigration laws from the late 1800s, the 1920s, and the 1960s and proposed changes in the law being discussed today. Create a PowerPoint presentation where you compare and contrast immigration laws in these time periods. Be sure to include excerpt from immigration laws, charts and graphs that explain what was happening at the time, and photographs and political cartoons that illustrate conditions faced by immigrants and the debate over changes in immigration laws.

Musical diary

Assemble a collection of song lyrics that document the experience of immigrants before they leave their countries of origin and in the United States.

Create a "musical diary" using PowerPoint that includes the songs and photographs or drawings that illustrate the things described in the songs. Songs that you can start with include *Paddy on the Railway* about Irish immigrant and *When I First Came to This Land*, and *Deportee* by Woody Guthrie about undocumented Mexican immigrant workers (see http://alri.org/ltc/immigration/Songs/Songs_about_Immigrants.html, accessed October 16, 2007).

Diorama

Create a three-dimensional depiction of the immigrant experience. Possibilities include arrival at Ellis Island, ethnic neighborhoods, the Statue of Liberty, images of the American Dream, working conditions, and life in tenements. Every diorama must include a museum card. A museum card is a brief report describing the scene in the diorama and explaining its historical importance.

C. Immigration Project and Virtual Museum

Task

You are an investigative reporter writing about contemporary immigration to the United States. As historical background for a series, your newspaper editor wants you to include an article comparing about two very different immigrant experiences from the early twentieth century (1900–1920)—one of a person who entered the United States through Ellis Island in New York City and the other of a person who entered through Angel Island in San Francisco. This assignment requires that you to look at immigrants from all parts of the world, not just Europe. To prepare for writing the story you should gather the following items for both entry ports (Ellis Island and Angel Island): Photographs illustrating the immigrant experience (at least five for each); statistical information; at least one personal document for each (birth certificate, passport, personal diary, immigration form); at least one other primary source document for each; and at least one image of a physical artifact representing each immigrant experience.

Presentation format

Your newspaper article must be at least 1,000 words and typed. In addition, your information will be presented in a PowerPoint that will become part of the newspaper's on-line virtual "museum."

RECOMMENDED INTERNET RESOURCES

http://www.pier21.ca/ (Canadian Immigration)
http://www.cobhheritage.com/index2.html (Exodus from Ireland)
http://www.danishmuseum.org/Welcome.html (Immigration from Denmark)
http://www.angelisland.org/historic2.htm (Angel Island)
http://www.libertystatepark.com/immigran.htm (Liberty State Park)
http://www.ellisisland.org/genealogy/ellis_island.asp (Ellis Island)
http://www.nps.gov/archive/stli/serv02.htm#Ellis (Ellis Island)
http://teacher.scholastic.com/activities/immigration/seymour/index.htm (Immigration Story)
In addition, these sites will give you some ideas and materials for your PowerPoint.
http://museumvictoria.com.au/ (Australian Immigration)
http://www.history.sa.gov.au/migration/about.htm (Australian Immigration)

D. Peopling of America, Background Information

Table 11.1 Types of immigrants.

Type	Group	Experience
Indigenous	Native peoples	In Latin America they are the workforce, but in the US they are either invisible or considered an obstruction to be removed. Seen as incapable of assimilation
Settlers	English, original Dutch, French, Spanish	Come for different reasons, economic, political, adventure, looting, "City on the Hill." Establish early institutions
Captives	African	Denied rights and humanity; debt peonage and non-citizenship after emancipation
Exiles	Irish, Cuban, Vietnamese, some of the early German	Mixed migration, often includes skilled, strong ethnic identity and institutions, unclear about future status
Immigrants	Later Irish immigrants, Jews, Slavs, most Germans, Scandinavians, Greeks, Armenians, Italians (after initial communities were established)	Emphasis on assimilation, language acquisition and education—Americanization
Migrant labor	Mexican, Chinese, Japanese, Southern Italian (initially)	Seen as temporary, work as need for labor expands, return home as need for labor contracts, retention of home language and culture

Table 11.2 Waves of migration.

Wave	Years	Groups
I	50,000–20,000BC	Migratory peoples from Asia become indigenous Native Americans
II	1500–1820	Great Britain (English, Scots/Irish), Africa, Netherlands, Spain, France, British West Indies.
III	1820–1880	Ireland, Germany, Scandinavia, China
IV	1880–1924	Russia (including Jews and Slavs), Austro-Hungarian Empire (including Jews, Slavs, Bohemians, Magyrs), Italy and Sicily, Balkins/Asian Minor (including Greeks, Turks, Armenians and Arabs)
V	1917–1965	Internal Migration: South Blacks and Whites, Puerto Ricans
VI	1965 to present	Latinos (Mexico, Dominican Republic, Central America, Andes), West Indies (Jamaica, Trinidad, Grenada, Guyana, Haiti), Asians (China, Korea, Vietnam and the Philippines), Eastern Europe and Middle East

E. Immigration Museum Activity Sheet

Directions

There are several time periods for US immigration history that you can learn more about by exploring the museum. Your task is to record at least three facts for each category. Write down the source of your information (such as the student name from the exhibit, their school, the presenter you spoke with, etc). If you cannot locate the information from the exhibit, ask someone. Meet some new historians today!

First Americans (before Columbus):
1.
2.
3.

Colonial American and the New Nation (1500–1820):
1.
2.
3.

New Groups Begin to Arrive (1820–1880):
1.
2.
3.

Industrialization and Immigration Transform the Country (1880–1924):
1.
2.
3.

Closed Doors and Internal Migration (1920–1965):
1.
2.
3.

Doors Are Re-opened (1965 to the Present):
1.
2.
3.

Homework:

- What were the most interesting things you saw and learned about at the Hofstra Immigration Museum? Explain.
- If you could do your exhibit over again, what would you change? Why?

F. "Immigration Rap" by Reeces Pieces (also known as Dr. Alan Singer)

My grandfather's name was Solomon Singer
He fled Eastern Europe for a better life
The work was hard and they were unwanted
But they let him in and he brought his wife.

He was a presser in the garment district.
His job was to iron rich people's clothes.
Sweatshop wages and sweaty conditions
How hard they worked, nobody knows.

He was a religious man who prayed to his
  God
He carried the torah and supported the shul
But he also worshiped the ILGWU
A better life was tied to the union rule.

Katie and Abbie, Manny and Bernie.
Four children born on the Lower East Side

No work for years during Great Depression
With little to eat, they almost died.

But he knew as a Jew it was better here.
Only death for the people who stayed behind.
The Nazis wiped out his entire village
So he worked when he could to ease his mind.

Where would I be if he stayed in Europe?
Where would I be if they'd locked the door?
It was hard enough when they were legal
Where would I be if they'd said no more?

They were Jews, Italians, Irish, and Poles.
Russians, Slavs, Armenians, and Greeks.
They spoke no English, never went to school,
They wanted only what everyone seeks.

How different were they from Manuel and
  Rosalita?
Do we shut the door because they're not White?
How different were they from Mohammed and
  Maria?
Shutting the door on them just is not right.

My grandfather's name was Solomon Singer.
He left Eastern Europe with only a dream.
We cannot say no to the newest arrivals
If our grandfathers knew they would start to
  scream.

Teaching Activity: Creating a History Museum

Add your voice to the discussion:
1. What are the strengths and possible weaknesses of a project such as the immigration museum?
2. Bill Hendrick (NTN) felt that the immigration museum project successfully displayed the diversity of the United States and "was a day for children to come together and exchange thoughts, display knowledge, highlight hard work, and learn about different cultures from each other." Do you agree with his assessment? Explain.

Classroom Activity: Rapping History

Students take a current issue or a newspaper article and explain the issue or article as a rap, poem, or song.

It's your classroom:
1. Would you have students perform their ideas in your classroom?
2. Would you share your rap, poem, or song with your class? Explain

References and Recommendations for Further Reading

Bigelow, W., Miner, B. and Peterson, R., eds. 1992. *Rethinking Columbus.* Milwaukee, WI: Rethinking School.

Bennett, L. and Berson, M. eds. 2007. *Digital age, technology-based k-12 lesson plans for social studies, NCSS bulletin 105.* Silver Spring, MD: National Council for the Social Studies.

Berson, M. and Bolick, C. eds. 2007. "Technology and the social studies," *Theory and Research in Social Education* 35(2).

Debler, J. 2002. "Ideas for using computers in your seventh grade social studies class," *Social Science Docket,* 2(2).

Dewey, J. 1938/1972. *Experience and education.* New York: Macmillan,

Diamond, J. 2005. *Collapse: How societies choose to fail or succeed.* New York: Viking.

Doane, C. 1993. "Global issues in 6th grade? Yes!" *Educational Leadership* 50(7): 19–21.

Hirsch, E. 2000. "'You Can Always Look It Up' . . . Or Can You?" *American Educator* 24(2): 4–9.

Howlett, C. 1999. "Teach history students can touch," *Newsday,* October 4.

Hunte, S., Thompson, R. and Kurtz, R. 2002. "Middle school museum of slavery project," *Social Science Docket* 2(2).

Kilpatrick, W. 1934. "The essentials of the activity movement," *Progressive Education* XI(October): 346–59.

Leman, K. 2002. "Website directory on economic globalization," *Social Science Docket* 2(1): 40–2.

Linden, E. 2006. *The winds of change.* New York: Simon and Shuster.

Mann, E. 1996. *The Brooklyn Bridge.* New York: Mikaya Press.

McCullough, D. 1972. *The great bridge.* New York: Simon and Schuster.

Meier, D. 1995. *The power of their ideas: Lessons for America from a small school in Harlem.* Boston, MA: Beacon.

Meier, D. and Schwarz, P. 1995. "Central Park East Secondary School: The hard part is making it happen," in M. Apple and J. Beane, eds. *Democratic schools.* Alexandria, VA: ASCD, pp. 26–40.

Mossman, L. 1940. *The activity concept.* New York: Macmillan.

Postman, N. 2000. "Will our children only inherit the wind?" *Theory and Research in Social Education* 28(4): 580–6.

Sewall, G. 2000. "Lost in action," *American Educator* 24(2): 4–9, 42–3.

Singer, A. 1994. "The impact of industrialization on American society: Alternative assessments," *Social Education* 58(3): 171–2.

Singer, A. 2003. Student clubs: A model for political organizing. *Rethinking Schools* 17(4).

Singer, A., Dircks, H. and Turner, V. 1996. "Exploring the Great Depression and the New Deal: An interdisciplinary project approach for middle school students," *Social Education* 60(5).

Singer, A. and Pezone, M. 1996. "Interdisciplinary projects that explore traditional Japanese culture," *In*

Transition, Journal of the New York State Middle School Association Spring: 28–9.

Singer, A., Gurton, L., Horowitz, A, et al. 1998. "Coming of age ceremonies: A mask project," *Middle Level Learning, Supplement to Social Education* 62(5): M14–M16.

Singer, J., Goodman, C., Ridley, T. and Singer, A. 1999/2000. "Bridges and the city: An interdisciplinary project," *Childhood Education* 76(2): 100–3.

Sizer, T. 1984. *Horace's compromise*. Boston, MA: Houghton Mifflin.

Tally, B. 2007. "Digital technology and the end of social studies education," *Theory and Research in Social Education* 35(2): 305–21.

Wiggins, G. 1993. "Assessment to improve performance, not just monitor it: Assessment reform in the social sciences," *Social Science Record* 30(2): 5.

Winslow, O. 2007. "Hofstra shows immigration through students' eyes," *Newsday On-Line*. http://www.newsday.com/news/local/ny-liimmi1117, 0,3527256. story, accessed November 16, 2007.

Wood, G. 1991. "Project-centered teaching: A tool for the democratic classroom," *Democracy & Education*, 6(1): 3–6.

12. How Should Teachers Assess Student Learning and Our Own Practice?

Overview

- Examine reasons for assessing student learning
- Discuss ways of integrating assessment with learning
- Develop sample test strategies
- Explore alternative assessment strategies

Key Concepts

Assessment, Performance Assessment, Authentic Assessment, Portfolio Assessment

Questions

- Does Assessment Equal Testing?
- What do the Tests Actually Measure?
- Why Should Educators Assess Student Learning?
- How can Testing Become Part of Learning?
- What do Teachers Want to Measure?
- What does a Social Studies Portfolio Look Like?
- How can Teachers Integrate Instruction and Assessment?
- How do Teachers Design Fair Exams?
- How can Teachers Grade Fairly?
- Should Students be Involved in Assessing Their Own Learning?

Essays

1. How Do We Move from Instruction to Assessment?
2. What Does a Research Paper Look Like?
3. Assessing Our Teaching Practice

Attitudes toward assessment reflect the way teachers think about their goals, their students, and teaching social studies. This chapter includes discussion and examples of both traditional and alternative methods of assessing student learning. I hope it provides teachers and pre-service teachers with an opportunity to assess their own thinking about the ideas and issues raised in this book.

ASSESSMENT:

The ways students demonstrate understanding of concepts, mastery of skills, and knowledge of and ability to utilize information. Assessment devices include, but are not limited to, teacher-designed and standardized tests. Assessments are used to evaluate student performance, teacher effectiveness, and the success of social studies curricula and programs.

DOES ASSESSMENT EQUAL TESTING?

On November 2, 1995, newspaper headlines across the country announced that American students "Don't Know Much About History." The press was not promoting Sam Cooke's classic rock and roll ballad, "(What A) Wonderful World" (see http://artists.letssingit. com/sam-cooke-wonderful-world-don-t-know-much-wzxlmlw, accessed October 10, 2007); it was reporting the latest "failure" of the American education system. Fifty-seven percent of the country's high school seniors had been unable to achieve "basic competency" on a US history examination administered by the National Assessment of Education Progress (NAEP), an independent agency that conducts tests for the US government. According to William T. Randall, who was the Education Commissioner of Colorado and chair of the citizens' board that oversees the NAEP, "The strikingly poor performance . . . indicates a major problem in how history is taught and learned—or not learned—in American schools." Randall concluded that, unless students master this information, "our system of democratic self-government, which depends on knowledgeable citizens, will be weakened" (*The New York Times*, 1995: A22).

Two days after this report was released, the education commissioner of the state of New York announced his plan to raise the state's educational standards by instituting a policy of more rigorous testing. Most high school students in New York State were already taking standardized Regents examinations in global studies at the end of 10th grade and in US history after 11th grade. Students who failed these exams were denied high school diplomas unless they could pass alternative statewide subject area competency exams. The State Commissioner wanted to discontinue the competency exams and require students to pass more difficult versions of the Regents to graduate (Dao 1995: 1).

Emphasis on expanding student social studies content knowledge is often coupled with the demand for more rigorous testing. For people who support this view of social studies education, testing serves multiple functions. Tests direct classroom curricula, and measure student knowledge, the competence of teachers, and the performance of schools and districts. In addition, fact-based multiple-choice exams are considered cost-efficient objective measures of performance.

In 2002, as he prepared the nation for a war against Iraq, President George W. Bush called for improving the teaching of history and civics in United States schools. He argued, "To properly understand and love our country, we must know our country's history" and understand that, "America is a force for good in the world, bringing hope and freedom to other people." However, according to President Bush, "ignorance of American history and civics weakens our sense of citizenship" and the ability of Americans to understand the critical issues confronting the United States in a dangerous world. He was concerned because standardized test results showed "nearly one in five high school seniors think that Germany was an ally of the United States in World War II. Twenty-eight percent of 8th graders do not know the reason why the Civil War was fought. One-third of 4th graders do not know what it means to 'pledge allegiance to the flag'" (information available at: http://www.whitehouse.gov/news/releases/2002/09/20020917-1.html, accessed November 6, 2007).

Most of you have some familiarity with the "No Child Left Behind" Act of 2001 (NCLB). Proponents of this law, which was the centerpiece of President Bush's education initiatives, claimed that it would promote standards-driven and outcomes-based education nationally. NCLB did not define national achievement standards—it left this to individual states—but it did lead to a wave of high stakes testing. As the law came up for renewal in 2007, it met with stiff resistance from critics who charged that test prep was replacing education and that subjects that were not being tested were squeezed out of the curriculum (Menken 2006). Rethinking Schools branded NCLB a "hoax" and a "test and punish" law, rather than a school improvement plan (see http://www.rethinkingschools.org/special_reports/bushplan/index.shtml, accessed October 10, 2007). Even supporters of the bill wanted to give states greater flexibility in implementation.

The National Education Association (NEA, http://www.nea.org), a professional organization and advocacy group for teachers that also represents many as a labor union, played a leading role in efforts to revise the No Child Left Behind Act (National Education Association 2007a). It supported the Coalition of Essential Schools' (CES, http://www.

essentialschools.org, accessed October 10, 2007) declaration of the month of May as National Exhibition Month, a time when teachers and schools could demonstrate that exhibitions are a "better and more comprehensive way than standardized tests to measure student performance."

In its Congressional lobbying efforts, the NEA stressed that professional accountability "should be based upon multiple measures of student learning and school success." It demanded that states be granted the "flexibility to design systems that produce results, including deciding in which grades to administer annual statewide tests" and to "utilize growth models and other measure of progress that assess student achievement over time" (National Education Association 2007b).

WHAT DO THE TESTS ACTUALLY MEASURE?

What do national or state standardized tests actually tell us about student understanding in social studies? Is there any correlation between more rigorous testing of content knowledge and the expansion of either critical understanding or a commitment to active citizenship?

Walter Parker (1989), who remains a leader in defining citizenship education for the National Council for the Social Studies (NCSS), argues, "Knowledge of government and history is necessary to but not sufficient for cultivating civic virtue." He stresses that "more so than knowledge, civic virtue is a disposition to think and act on behalf of the public good," and that social studies classrooms should be organized "to encourage that disposition rather than discourage it." For Parker (1989: 353–354), "open, free, authentic talk is the coin of participatory citizenship."

Focusing on content and testing does not promote this kind of "free, authentic talk"; it encourages teachers to prep students for tests. Social studies teachers drill students in basic skills and present them with long lists of facts to memorize. At best, this approach reduces the time available for the kind of education the Colorado State Education Commissioner cited above claimed to value. At worst, it destroys any hope that students will enjoy or value learning about social studies.

An examination of one of the questions on the 1995 NAEP test illustrates some of the problems with this kind of test, and with social studies assessment in general. Some 72 percent of the 12th graders who took the NAEP test got the answer to this question wrong:

President Carter played a major role in negotiating the Camp David Accords, which promoted peace between . . .

A. The Soviet Union and China
B. The Palestinians and the Jordanians
C. Egypt and Israel
D. North Korea and the United States

Personally, I wish more US high school seniors knew about the peace conference between Egyptian President Anwar al-Sadat and Israeli Prime Minister Menachem Begin, but I am not shocked that such a large percentage got the answer wrong. I do not think many veteran social studies teachers were surprised either. The Camp David Accords were in 1979. In curricula that are littered with thousands of years of detail, how many US or World history classes actually get to 1979? Think back for a minute; when you were a high school student, how close did your class get to recent decades?

In addition, between 1979 and 1995, other events in world affairs, especially in South-west Asia and North Africa (the Middle East), grabbed the historical and media spotlight away from the Israeli–Egyptian settlement. These events included the hostage situation and the Islamic Revolution in Iran, the death of 260 US marines in Lebanon, the *Intifada*, the assassinations of both Sadat and Yitzhak Rabin, the Persian Gulf War, and the continuing negotiations between the Palestine Liberation Organization (PLO) and the nation of Israel. The Camp David Accords, which held out so much initial promise, did not succeed in bringing lasting peace to the Middle East. Since then, they have been overshadowed by the emergence of Hamas as a new force in the Palestinian movement, the war between Islamic fundamentalist groups and the West, and the US occupations of Iraq and Afghanistan. At 30 years after the event, it is not a major focus in most social studies classrooms.

A third problem with this question is that it is poorly designed. The number of correct answers would have been substantially higher if the question provided a historical or geographical context. For example, the question could have been reworded to read:

"President Carter played a major role in negotiating the Camp David Accords, which promoted peace *in the Middle East* between . . ." or,

"President Carter played a major role in negotiating the Camp David Accords, which promoted peace between *Arabs and Jews* in . . .".

A fourth problem raises an even more significant issue for assessment in the social studies. A factual recall question requires no broad understanding of world events. Even when students get the answer right, we learn nothing about their understanding of social studies or their ability to be knowledgeable, thinking citizens. Will the ability to recall some detail about the Camp David Accords help students formulate informed opinions about current US policy in the Middle East and its financial, political, and military support for an Israeli government that as of 2007 continued to occupy Palestinian territory seized in a 1967 war?

A 2003 study by Jonathan Rees (2003) is even more critical of the NAEP history test than I am. According to Rees, "test designers, in their effort to design questions that are as relevant as possible, approximate an unattainable consensus by creating questions that legitimate established social, political and economic authorities. These questions tend to stress the importance of institutions over individuals, conservative actors over reformers and agreement over dissent. In other words, they tend to reflect conservative political values." He charges, "Conservative politicians and educational reformers exploit standardized test scores to promote the idea that a crisis exists in history and civics education."

Although the NAEP test tells very little about what students actually know and understand, it does suggest a lot about the failure of testing and test-driven curricula to stimulate students to think about history and the social sciences. It also raises many questions about the significance and purpose of assessment in social studies classrooms.

WHY SHOULD EDUCATORS ASSESS STUDENT LEARNING?

According to the NCSS (1991), "the overriding purpose of testing in social studies classrooms is to improve learning." Unfortunately, that is not always the case.

As an education student in college, I was taught techniques to design "fair" tests with "good" questions. At the end of the marking period, we were supposed to average up test scores; add or subtract a few points based on factors like class participation, attendance, and handing in assignments punctually; and then assign a scientifically precise numerical grade that summarized a student's performance in class. In theory, teachers did not evaluate students; our job was to calculate and record the grade they had earned.

We were also advised to do the following:

1. Encourage competition between students for higher grades. This would ensure that they studied
2. Make all of the choices on multiple-choice tests the same length. Unequal length would tip off students to the right answer
3. Avoid making "B" the right answer too often. It is the most popular "wild guess" answer
4. Be careful not to make "All of the Above" a choice only when the answer we want is "All of the Above"
5. Use different types of questions (e.g., fill-ins, matching, multiple choice, short description, and longer essays) so students cannot anticipate the kinds of questions you will ask. If they do, they will not study as hard

6. Throw in a few questions about really obscure points. This rewards students who do all of the homework, encourages the others to work harder, and gives you a spread of grades (One of my high school teachers once gave us a fill-in question: Who invented barbed wire?).

Although some of this advice is useful, something is seriously wrong with this approach to assessment. Testing and grading are only indirectly related to instruction and the assessment of learning. Additionally, the assumption here is that education is a series of contests between students and between students and teachers.

In these methods classes, we never discussed why we test in social studies, the relationship between assessment and learning, or even why we test like this. The principles of testing and grading and the forms of tests were presented as eternal truths. Teachers gave tests. Students took tests. Parents and supervisors expected tests and test scores. The school system judged and sorted students based on test results.

The purpose of testing was to assign grades. Tests and grades were weapons to control classes and make students do the work through extrinsic rewards and punishments. Students who tried, but did not do very well, were offered extra help, but ultimately put in "slower" classes where they could "experience success." Those who failed the tests because they did not seem to care were cajoled with threats, calls or letters home, low grades, or failure for the course. Students who did well on tests were rewarded with high grades, certificates, and recommendations for better high schools and colleges. In theory, better test scores eventually meant admission to more prestigious colleges and ultimately to more successful careers and greater financial rewards.

As a beginning teacher, I used tests pretty much the same way they had been used in my classes when I was a student (although, of course, I considered myself fairer than the teachers who had tormented me). Sometimes I gave short weekly tests. At the end of units, I gave more comprehensive full-period tests. I worked with colleagues to design standard departmental midterms and finals. My students were supposed to know the information that had been presented in class, especially what I wrote on the board, and what they had been assigned for homework in the textbook. Like most of my colleagues, I fell into the pattern of tailoring lessons to prepare students for these tests.

Over the years, my relationships with students and my commitment to finding ways to motivate them to want to learn history and social studies, forced me to think about my goals in assessing student learning. One incident from early in my career still stands out. A middle school student who loved social studies, was a leader in class discussions, and always made interesting points, refused to do any of the homework assignments, and failed each test miserably. I gave him chance after chance, but I could not get him to do the work. Finally, I pleaded with him to go home and study and retake the same test the next day. He was a remarkably tolerant and patient kid. He complied with my requests, took the test, and failed again. In desperation, I decided to try an experiment. During lunch I read him the multiple-choice questions and choices, and he checked off his selections. This time he scored in the high 80s. He understood what we were studying in class, but he did not know how to read well enough to do the homework assignments or distinguish between the choices on the multiple-choice tests.

Unfortunately, in teaching, as in life, there are few fairy tale endings. At the time, I had no idea what to do, and there was no one in the school who was able to help us. The student passed my class, but very few others. Because he was already overage for middle school, he was passed on to high school the next year. Although this example is an extreme case, it is not unusual to have students who work very hard and are excited by social studies topics, but still get a lot of questions wrong on tests because of inadequate literacy skills. One strategy I tried was to make tests easier, but then the more literate students got high grades without doing any work at all. To paraphrase the King of Siam from the Broadway musical *The King and I*, "Testing policy is a paradox."

HOW CAN TESTING BECOME PART OF LEARNING?

It seems to me that the only way out of this testing paradox is to make assessment part of learning, and to use a variety of assessment tools to discover what individual students understand. There are good reasons for testing and evaluating students. Students have a right to know how they are doing compared with other people doing similar work. This makes it possible for them to assess their activities, make decisions about their priorities, and evaluate their goals. In addition, as teachers, there are things we need to know so we can do our jobs effectively. Assessing student learning helps us evaluate our teaching. Assessment helps us think about some important questions including these:

1. Does the curriculum make sense to the students? Does it connect with who they are? Does it take into account their level of academic and social studies skills, and help to improve them?
2. Am I teaching effectively? Is the class as a whole learning? Are the books and materials appropriate? What do I need to change?
3. Do individual students understand what they are studying?
4. How can I respond to their specific needs and motivate them to try again or try harder? How do I help students assess their own learning so they can use this knowledge as a way to expand their understanding? What will make it possible for every individual to succeed in class?
5. Are students doing the classroom and homework assignments? Are the assignments reasonable and interesting? Which assignments should be kept? Which ones should be modified? Which ones should be dropped?
6. Are my assessment tools accurate measures of what I am trying to assess? Am I testing recall, the ability of students to read and write, or their understanding and ability to use ideas?

7. Can I assign students composite grades at the end of marking periods and semesters that have meaning to them and will encourage them, rather than just reward or punish them?

Assessment is not an easy task. It is the area of my teaching practice where I am frequently the least comfortable with my decisions and judgments. I find I am always sweating over grades and offering students other opportunities to demonstrate what they have learned and what I have taught.

As a high school teacher, I was regularly called down to an assistant principal's office to explain why I had so many missing grades on my roster sheets. In the "old days," I passed it off as a clerical error. Later, I blamed those "damned computers." I did not know how to explain that I could not figure out a grade because people are too complicated and learning is always incomplete. Something I try to remind myself as well as my students is that grades do not measure your qualities as a human being. At best, they tell teachers and students how someone performed on a task at a particular moment in time, under a particular set of circumstances, compared to other people whose life conditions and opportunities may have been very different.

By the way, historians usually credit Joseph F. Glidden, who was issued a patent in 1874, with the invention of barbed wire. I looked up the answer after I found out about the question during lunch from a student who took the test in the morning. As lifetime residents of urban communities, neither she nor I understood the importance of barbed wire in US history. In our neighborhoods, it was used to keep kids off the roofs of buildings or out of vacant lots. But with her help, I got the answer right on the test.

Learning Activity: How Did Technology Transform the Great Plains?

A major theme in social studies is the impact of technology on history. While a graduate student in history, I read *The Great Plains* by Prescott and finally understood the importance of barbed wire as part of the technological changes that supported US expansion west and made possible agricultural development on the Great Plains. Years later, to help my urban students understand both the broader theme of the impact of technology on history and a world that was distant from them in time, space, and culture, I designed a learning activity that I have since augmented with Internet research assignments. I introduce the lessons by passing around samples of different types of barbed wire that I found at a gift shop at the Denver, Colorado Airport. Students discuss why an innovation as simple as barbed wire can have a major impact on history. I think this learning activity, if used as an assessment of student learning rather than as part of a lesson, models authentic assessment of conceptual understanding as opposed to simple factual recall. Most of the initial questions require students to locate information. The key question is the last one, which requires that students formulate an opinion and support it with evidence.

Aim: How did new technology transform the Great Plains?

In the 1820s, a government-sponsored expedition explored and mapped the Great Plains. A map produced by the expedition labeled the center of the North American continent "the Great American Desert." Its report described the Great Plains as "almost wholly unfit for cultivation, and of course, uninhabitable by a people depending upon agriculture for their subsistence. Although tracts of fertile land considerably extensive are occasionally to be met with, yet the scarcity of wood and water, almost uniformly prevalent, will prove an insuperable obstacle in the way of settling the country" (Meinig 1993: 76).

Nineteenth-Century Technological Innovations that made Possible Settlement of the Great Plains

- Railroad—transport of goods and people
- Barbed wire—fencing
- Steel-typed plough—breaking the sod (hard-packed dirt)
- Repeating rifle—defeating native people
- Steel windmill—pumping subsurface water for agriculture
- Telegraph—communication

Questions

1. Locate the Great Plains on a map of the United States. What current states are located in whole or part on the Great Plains?
2. According to this quote and other sources, how did Americans initially view the Great Plains?
3. What problems faced Americans who wanted to settle on the Great Plains?
4. How did each of these technological innovations impact on American settlement of the Great Plains? Write one paragraph describing each technology, its uses, and its impact on the settlement of the Great Plains.
5. In your opinion, which three of these technological changes had the greatest impact on the development of the Great Plains? Why?

It's your classroom:

Would you use assessments like this one in your classroom? Explain.

Teaching Activity: Why Test?

The following points were raised in discussions about testing and grading by graduate and undergraduate students in social studies methods classes at Hofstra University:

- "I don't like tests. They push for regurgitation of information. Teachers use them to sort people out and define them."
- "Tests help me discipline myself. They force me to think and get my ideas together. They help me bring something together, to finish it."
- "I like tests because I like to compete."
- "If we lower standards, kids are just pushed ahead without learning anything."
- "I'd try to see if students understand the main points and follow the directions."
- "It's hard for me to mark papers. It feels very uncomfortable being judged or judging."
- "I try to give my students tests that require them to organize information."
- "Why are we having a final exam in this class? Tests are oppressive."

Add your voice to the discussion:

1. With which statement(s) do you agree? Why?
2. How would you respond to the people with whom you disagree?
3. What points would you add to this discussion?

WHAT DO TEACHERS WANT TO MEASURE?

What do teachers measure when they give their classes a surprise quiz?

1. Student short-term memory
2. Student resistance to what is taking place in class
3. Whether the morning class told the afternoon class about the quiz
4. How intimidated students are
5. If students copied the answers to the homework questions from the book
6. What students understand about social studies and history
7. All of the above choices, except 6.

In the last few years, increasing numbers of teachers and politicians have argued for more accurate and authentic assessment of student learning. In October 2007, when I ran a Google search on *social studies assessment*, there were almost 55-million hits. However, there is little general agreement about what constitutes more accurate assessment. Proposals for the social studies include intensive testing of student skills and content knowledge, broader testing to include student performance as historians and social scientists as they evaluate primary source documents, and de-emphasis of testing and evaluation of students based on work assembled over the course of a year or a span of a number of years (portfolio assessment). An issue always raised in discussions of authentic assessment is the reliability and validity of standardized multiple-choice tests. There is disagreement whether they discriminate against particular groups or measure what they claim to measure. The problem of subjectivity is even more pronounced when it comes to designing and evaluating essay questions and student projects. In general, people who argue for authentic assessment do not repudiate the idea of assessing students to see what they learned during a semester or year, but they do want fairer evaluations (Wolf et al. 1992; Meyer 1992).

> *Standardized Assessment:*
> Standardized assessment devices, especially multiple-choice tests, measure narrow areas of competence. Advocates for this type of assessment argue that results on these tests accurately and objectively measure a student's general level of achievement.
>
> *Performance Assessment:*
> This is direct evaluation of student competence in a number of different areas using a variety of assessment devices, including standardized tests. Performance assessment attempts to directly measure a student's ability to think critically, write clearly, express ideas orally, and work cooperatively.
>
> *Authentic Assessment:*
> This is a form of performance assessment that minimizes the use of tests and encourages the direct assessment of student performance during learning activities and through the evaluation of student work.

A different approach to assessing student learning is closely related to what John Dewey called developing "habits of mind." In Dewey's view, assessing (comparing, analyzing, sorting, organizing, exploring, experimenting) is how human beings learn. What teachers need to assess is not the information that students know, but how effectively students are assessing and integrating the information into their worldview. The Coalition for Essential Schools has tried to incorporate this view of assessment into programs at its affiliated schools. In these schools, teachers and students both learn and assess learning by trying to answer five basic questions:

1. How do you know what you know? (Evidence)
2. From what viewpoint is this being presented? (Perspective)
3. How is this event or work connected to others? (Connections)
4. What if things were different? (Suppositions)
5. Why is this important? (Relevance)

A significant question is whether teachers can effectively measure Deweyan "habits of mind" by using standard social studies assessment devices: short answer tests, essays, written reports, and classroom presentations.

Teaching Activity: How Do We Know What We Know?

For centuries, philosophers have been puzzled over this question: How do we know what we know? Plato's "Euthyphro" (Tredennick 1980) is the story of a young man who charges his father with manslaughter because he caused the death of a servant. In the dialogue, Socrates questions Euthyphro about the certainty of his knowledge of right and wrong:

Socrates: "Do you really believe that you understand the ruling of the divine law, . . . so accurately that in the circumstances that you describe you have no misgivings? Aren't you afraid that . . . you may turn out to be committing an act of impiety yourself?"
Euthyphro: "No Socrates; I shouldn't be worth much, . . . if I didn't have accurate knowledge about all that sort of thing."

Socrates continues the dialogue with a series of questions that press Euthyphro to clearly define *piety*. Euthyphro tries to distinguish between pious and impious actions, but each definition he offers proves to be unsatisfactory because it includes categories of behavior or ways of knowing which Euthyphro cannot accept as pious. Eventually, Euthyphro tells Socrates that he has another engagement, but promises to continue the discussion the next time they meet.

I am not sure I would have done much better than Euthyphro if Socrates questioned me about a social studies concept like justice, democracy, or human rights. How much would anyone's knowledge stand up to grilling by Socrates?

Uncertainty, however, is not necessarily bad. Twentieth-century French philosopher John-Paul Sartre's existentialist philosophy suggests that people can never be absolutely certain of anything. Human beings have to make the best choices that they can, based on limited knowledge. Contemporary postmodernist thinkers go one step further than Sartre to argue that there is no such thing as absolute knowledge or certainty because all knowledge is shaped by the experiences and understanding of the knower. Perhaps what Socrates, Sartre, and the postmodernists are all suggesting is that the key to understanding is not what we know, but how we know: the Deweyian "habits of mind" that we use to understand our world.

Think it over:
Is Euthyphro's problem his lack of knowledge about the meaning of piety, the unfair nature of Socrates' questions (the assessment device), or some other factor(s)? Explain the reasons for your answer.

Add your voice to the discussion:
Should social studies teachers focus assessment on content knowledge, skills competence, student ability to understand and use concepts, or "habits of mind"? Explain the reasons for your answer.

It's your classroom:
If Euthyphro were a student in your class, how would you assess his "habits of mind"? Explain the reasons for your assessment.

Grant Wiggins, a major advocate of performance assessment, is critical of most social studies testing for measuring the least complex levels of human thought (Nickell 1992; Wiggins and McTighe 2005). Wiggins challenges social studies educators to assess student performance on the higher order thinking skills identified in Bloom's taxonomy. For example, a student's ability to synthesize information and create new understanding requires creativity and judgment. This kind of thinking stimulates diverse and unexpected responses that are not easily measured on a multiple-choice exam.

Wiggins (1992; 1993; Wiggins and McTighe 2005) argues that the key to employing Deweyan ideas about learning in social studies assessment is to view assessment as an ongoing part of a learning process, where people repeatedly test their knowledge and their skills, and adjust what they do and how they do it based on what they discover. This is very different from creating tests that measure a limited form of knowledge at a particular point in time. Wiggins suggests that teachers think of their students as workers (historians and social scientists) who are continually enhancing their skills as they create increasingly more complex products. The difficult task for teachers is establishing criteria for evaluating these products during the process of creation and after they are completed.

I believe that certain principles can guide social studies teachers as we work to discover more authentic ways of assessing student understanding. These principles include:

1. We should assess student performance based on the full range of what is being taught in class. That includes content knowledge and academic skills. It also includes the acquisition of social skills; an understanding of historical and social science concepts; the ability to gather, organize, present, integrate, and utilize information; and the ability to explore values and ideas, and use new understandings to reconsider the ways people think and live.

2. Assessment should be part of the learning process. It should be continuous so that students have feedback on how they are doing. We should use tests to discover what students know, not what they do not know. A reasonable assumption is that when students are excited about what they are learning and do well on tests, they will want to learn more.

3. If test scores are going to reflect what students are learning, they need to be designed for specific classes. Prepackaged and standardized tests are based on the assumption that the same things are happening in widely diverse settings.

4. Although the criteria for assessment should be clear to students, they should also be flexible. Assessment is relative, not absolute. It involves judgments about which people can legitimately disagree.

5. Assessment is most effective when it includes individual self-assessment.

6. Authentic assessment of student learning requires examining a number of types of activities at a series of points in the learning process, and using different criteria and assessment devices to evaluate student performance. We do not measure temperature with a speedometer. How can a matching quiz measure a student's understanding of democratic values?

7. The goal of assessment is to encourage and assist learning. Tests and projects should not be used to punish or sort students. Everyone who works hard and does well should be able to receive the highest evaluation.

8. If the ability to work hard in an organized and disciplined fashion is one of the things we want students to learn, then effort should count in an evaluation of students' work.

9. If we want students to learn how to work collectively, take responsibility for group activities, respect the value and contributions of other people, and play leadership roles, performance on group activities should be factored into an evaluation of a student's work.

10. Students with limited academic skills should be able to demonstrate their knowledge and understanding of a subject in ways that are appropriate to their skills. Imagine you are a chef being tested on your ability to cook a new dish, but the recipe is written in a language you cannot read. Would this be a fair assessment of your ability or knowledge?

11. We are assessing knowledge and understanding of a subject, and academic and social skills, not a student's qualities as a human being.

WHAT DOES A SOCIAL STUDIES PORTFOLIO LOOK LIKE?

Writing about assessment practices for the NCSS, Pat Nickell (1993) explains that, "If our intended outcome is to enable all students to become competent citizens, we must give less emphasis to mere recall and low-level comprehension of facts and concepts, and more emphasis to applying knowledge to tasks that require high-level cognition . . . 'Doing' social studies, like doing mathematics, science, or art is imperative . . ."

Organizing project-based social studies classrooms where the primary method for evaluating student understanding is an evaluation of the products of their activity and research introduces a new dimension into social studies assessment: the *portfolio*. One group of West Coast educators defined the portfolio as "a purposeful collection of student work that tells the story of the student's efforts, progress, or achievement in (a) given area(s). This collection must include student participation in selection of portfolio content; the guidelines for selection; the criteria for judging merit; and evidence of student self-reflection" (Arter and Spandel 1992: 36–44).

> **Portfolio Assessment:**
> Students' performance is evaluated based on a collection of their work assembled over an extended period of time. The portfolio demonstrates growth as well as final achievement.

A portfolio is not simply a collection of student work. For it to be a useful document that symbolizes a student's mastery of a subject area during a class or a whole course of study, it must be integrated into the instructional and assessment fabric of a school's social studies program. Effective portfolio programs need to provide students and teachers with specific guidelines for creating, assembling, and evaluating student work.

A multitude of questions have to be addressed when a teacher or school establishes a social studies portfolio program:

1. Who defines what goes into a portfolio: individual students and teachers, the social studies department, school or district administrators, or a state's regulatory body?
2. Can portfolios accurately measure the full range of skills, attitudes, content knowledge, and conceptual understanding developed during a social studies course or multiyear program?
3. Will students be involved in defining portfolio topics and projects, deciding on the products that will be evaluated, and the evaluation process itself?
4. Are portfolios comprehensive documents showing the full span of a student's work, or do they contain a selection of typical, or perhaps exemplary, efforts?
5. How much weight will be given to effort, the process of creation, and the final product in assessing student work?
6. Does individual growth count, or only a student's final achievement?
7. How will growth, the process of creation, and effort be measured?
8. Can portfolios include group as well as individual work? If they can, how will a student's participation in a group project be evaluated?
9. What standards should be used to evaluate the quality of work at different points in a student's secondary school career?
10. Can evaluation be objective or even systematic?
11. How do programs avoid the mechanical application of portfolio design and assessment?
12. Will schools and districts sacrifice student experimentation and creativity as they try to ensure that minimum guidelines are met?
13. Can portfolio assignments and even entire portfolios receive meaningful number or letter grades?

Grant Wiggins, formally affiliated with Center on Learning, Assessment, and School Structure, addresses some of these questions in proposals for integrating portfolio creation and assessment into regular social studies classrooms (Wiggins and McTighe 2005). Wiggins recommends involving students in clearly defined and guided multiple step projects that are evaluated at different points in the creative process. He also recommends detailed assessment rubrics that examine both content and presentation. The following sample scoring rubrics can be used to evaluate student oral presentations and written work. To learn more about Wiggin's approach to teaching and assessment, check out the *Relearning By Design* website at http://www.relearning.org (accessed October 12, 2007).

Table 12.1 Scoring rubric for oral presentations/demonstrations.

Content (55%): Poor 0–3 pts., Average 4–6 pts., Good 7–9 pts., Excellent 10–11 pts.	
Worthwhile and relevant information	( )
Information is sufficient	( )
Ideas clearly explained	( )
Ideas logically explained	( )
Effective organization	( )
Delivery (35%): Poor 0–1 pts., Average 2–3 pts., Good 4 pts., Excellent 5 pts.	
Contact with audience	( )
Effective use of notes	( )
Confidence	( )
Articulation	( )
Projection	( )
Enthusiasm	( )
Avoids distractions	( )
Overall (10%): Poor 0–4 pts., Average 5–6 pts., Good 7–8 pts., Excellent 9–10 pts.	
Coordination with group	( )
Comments:	
Grade (100%) ( )	

Table 12.2 Scoring rubric for written analysis or critique paper.

Weak (0–3) Satisfactory (4–7) Strong (8–10)

Clear, interesting, and informative introduction, summary, and conclusion	( )
Each paragraph has a main idea	( )
Identifies and explains social forces	( )
Explains different perspectives	( )
Author's views are clearly identified	( )
Appropriate information	( )
Effective use of details and examples	( )
Connections with current issues	( )
Satisfies writing requirements	( )
Satisfies project requirements	( )
Total Points/Assignment Grade ( )	( )

Jennifer Parente (NTN) is a middle school social studies teacher who has worked in urban and suburban communities and with diverse student populations. Projects and portfolio assessment have consistently been a major part of her approach to teaching. This is a sample guideline she gives to students and a portfolio check-off sheet students use to ensure that they have completed the entire assignment.

JENNIFER PARENTE'S 7TH-GRADE SOCIAL STUDIES PORTFOLIOS

You are to keep a portfolio detailing your progress and personal achievements in social studies every marking period. You are responsible for handing in your portfolio four (4) times this year. Every portfolio should be your own unique creation. Your portfolio will contain a minimum of 15 assignments each marking period.

Each marking period you **MUST** include:

1. Three Tests
2. Five Homework Assignments (you choose which ones)
3. Five Journal Entries (you choose which ones)
4. Two Required Assignments

In addition, you will also include special projects, essays, or reports that you did during the marking period.

REMEMBER: These are **not** additional assignments. Your portfolio contains work that you already completed during the marking period.

Portfolio Guidelines:

Each entry must be dated, and each area should be clearly defined (e.g., tests, homework, journal entries). You should use dividers to clearly mark the sections of your portfolio.

- Entries should be in chronological order (in order of their dates).
- All pages should be neatly arranged (no shredded paper) and written neatly in pen!
- Pages that are colorful and neat are more interesting and make a better impression on the reader.
- There should be a Title page with your name, school, grade and class, an introductory page, a Table of Contents and a "check-off" page.
- Some of you may wish to write a narrative introduction, indicating your progress, your personal learning style, and describing some of the talents you possess.
- Entries should focus attention on your progress in Social Studies during the marking period and year. Your portfolio should provide visible signs that show your growth and development.

Include the things that you are most proud of, even if they are not all "A" or "B" papers.

- Things you worked hard on and gained personal satisfaction from, regardless of the grade, should be included.
- At the bottom of each entry, you should write a brief paragraph explaining your reasons for including it. Ask yourself the following questions (include the answer to at least three of them for each entry):
    - Why did I select this item?
    - What makes this my best piece?
    - How does this work show what I learned?
    - If I could work on this assignment again, what would I do differently?
    - What do I think of the teacher's evaluation of my work?
    - What grade would I give this work? Why?
- You should spend a **minimum of one hour per week** preparing your portfolio. When there is no other homework assignment, your assignment is to work on your portfolio.
- There will be a "portfolio check" mid-way through the marking period so I can see if you are making good progress. The due date for your portfolio will be at the end of the marking period.
- You should come see me during "Extra Help" periods to ask questions and discuss your portfolio.
- Your portfolio is worth two (2) test grades.

PORTFOLIO CHECK-OFF SHEET

Name _____

_____ included a Title page?

_____ included a Table of Contents?

_____ included 3 Tests?

_____ included 5 Homework Assignments?

_____ included 5 Journal Entries?

_____ included Special Assignments?

_____ checked to make sure all entries are in pen?

_____ checked to see if entries are dated and in chronological order?

_____ wrote a personal statement about each piece?

_____ wrote an introduction to my portfolio?

Signature _____

Table 12.3 Portfolio rubric.

Quality	Possible score	Your score
Have you included 3 tests?	15	
Have you included 5 homework assignments?	25	
Have you included 5 journal entries?	25	
Have you included special assignments?	5	
Are papers in chronological order?	5	
Is there a written reflection for each piece?	20	
Have you included an Introduction?	5	
TOTAL	100	

The portfolio creation and assessment program at the Central Park East Secondary School (CPESS) in New York City, which is part of the *Coalition for Essential Schools*, is a more radical departure from traditional assessment. CPESS requires that seniors create and defend 14 portfolios to graduate. Each student selects seven major areas and seven minor areas for portfolio development. Four of the major areas are required of every student: "Science/ Technology," "Mathematics," "History and Social Studies," and "Literature." Social studies subjects that can be used as electives for either major or minor area portfolios include "Ethics and Social Issues" and "Geography" (Meier and Schwartz 1995).

Portfolios reflect cumulative knowledge and skills acquired by students while at CPESS. They demonstrate students' command of information about the subject, their ability to explain their own and other people's points of view, their ability to draw connections between different topics, their ability to think creatively about the subject, and their ability to explain the broader relevance of their work. Students work with staff advisors to prepare their final portfolios and present all 14 areas to a graduation committee for review and evaluation. The graduation committee members assess portfolios using an established scoring grid that weighs both the substance and style of the work. When portfolios need to be modified or expanded, students are given the opportunity to complete the necessary work and resubmit the portfolio for approval.

The majority of the material included by students in their portfolios is originally done as coursework. The inclusion of collaborative work is encouraged. Interdisciplinary projects can be submitted in more than one portfolio area. Because each student works at a different pace and in a different way, and because students bring a diversity of academic, social, and cultural experiences with them to their work, CPESS has no single prescribed formula for completing the portfolio assessment process. To learn more about *Coalition for Essential Schools*, check out their website at: http://www.essentialschools.org (accessed October 12, 2007).

Teaching Activity: What Are Student Exhibitions?

The Coalition for Essential Schools and the National Education Association launched a major campaign to promote student exhibitions as a form of assessment of learning during their campaign to reform the No Child Left Behind Act. This description of student exhibitions is taken from the NEA website (http://www.nea.org/esea/exhibitmonth07.html, accessed August 30, 2007).

- Exhibitions are an alternative way to assess student achievement.
- Exhibitions are presentations by students to teachers, parents, and other community members.
- Exhibitions offer a 360-degree view of a student's academic performance.
- Exhibitions demonstrate mastery of academic material, presentation skills, and critical thinking ability.
- Exhibitions are often held at the end of the school year—like final exams—to determine a student's ability to complete a course, move to the next grade, or to graduate.
- Exhibitions are also held throughout the school year to better understand a learner's strengths and needs, and to plan for future assistance.

- Exhibitions show students, teachers, parents, colleges, and employers how well students can do in real-world situations.
- Exhibitions can be aligned to meet and exceed State Learning Standards.

Add your voice to the discussion:
1. The NEA and CES argue that exhibitions allow students to demonstrate "mastery of academic material, presentation skills, and critical thinking ability." Do you agree or disagree? Why?
2. In your opinion, are exhibitions or standardized tests more effective measures of student learning? Explain.

It's your classroom:
1. Would you use student exhibitions as part of your assessment of student learning? Explain.
2. Would you involve parents and students on assessment teams? Explain.

Performance assessment, such as the evaluation of a portfolio is not as revolutionary as it sounds. Laboratory experiences and a practicum have long been part of assessment in the sciences and have been factored into student scores on standardized exams. The integration of portfolio assessment with more traditional unit and final examinations may be a key for maintaining both generalized curriculum goals and academic standards in diverse authentic assessment and portfolio assessment programs. Final student portfolios can contain a wide range of social studies projects, as well as their scores on different types of classroom and standardized tests.

The following are suggestions for activities to include in middle and high school social studies portfolios. Some of the activities can also be included as interdisciplinary items in portfolios for other subject areas. In their final portfolios, students should strive to show the increasing sophistication of their work over time.

EXAMPLE: PORTFOLIO ASSESSMENT

Sample Middle School Social Studies Portfolio (Grades 6, 7, 8):
- **Active reader/thinker.** Student develops a series of questions based on a primary source reading passage.
- **Outline of a textbook chapter.** Student demonstrates the ability to select and organize social studies information presented in a textbook.
- **Mapping, graphing, chart interpretation.** Student demonstrates the ability to interpret and create maps, graphs, and charts based on social studies and/or historical information.
- **Dramatic presentation.** Student participates in a dramatic presentation or role play that demonstrates an understanding of an historical era and the character and experiences of an historical figure. This is a group activity.
- **Narrative (expository) essay.** Student describes and explains an historical event.
- **Persuasive essay.** Student develops a position on an issue, supports the position with evidence, and tries to persuade the audience to accept this position.
- **Book report.** Student reads a work of historical fiction, summarizes the work, and analyzes it for historical accuracy.
- **Biography report.** Student reads the biography of an historical figure, summarizes the main events in the person's life, and explains the person's role in history.
- **Secondary source research report.** Student selects and researches a topic using multiple secondary sources. Report includes a bibliography. This can be an individual or group activity.
- **Interview.** Student develops a questionnaire and interviews a person or people about their involvement in local issues or major historical events. This can be an individual or group activity.
- **Social studies journal.** Student maintains a journal that includes comments on material studied in class and reports on progress on class projects.
- **Current events scrapbook.** Student collects current events newspaper and magazine articles and maintains a scrapbook and commentary on a specific subject.

- **Cultural art or craft project**. Student creates an art or craft project that represents the culture of a group studied in class. Student presents the project and background information in class. This can be an individual or group activity.
- **Class presentations**. Student presents different portfolio assignments to the class. This can be an individual or group activity.
- **Tests**. Traditional unit essay and short answer exams, quizzes, and standardized examinations.

Sample High School Social Studies Portfolio (Grades 9, 10, 11, 12):

- **Active reader/thinker.** Student develops a series of questions based on a primary source reading passage.
- **Outline of a textbook chapter**. Student demonstrates the ability to select and organize social studies information presented in a textbook.
- **Outline of a lecture**. Student demonstrates the ability to select and organize social studies information presented in a class lecture.
- **Mapping, graphing, chart interpretation**. Student demonstrates the ability to interpret and create maps, graphs, and charts based on social studies and/or historical information.
- **Dramatic presentation.** Student participates in a dramatic presentation or role play that demonstrates an understanding of an historical era and the character and experiences of an historical figure. This is a group activity.
- **Document summary**. Student demonstrates the ability to summarize the main points in a primary source historical document and explains the historical significance of the document.
- **Comparison essay**. Student demonstrates the ability to summarize and compare the main points in two or more primary source historical documents, or historical or social science monographs.
- **Analysis essay**. Student demonstrates the ability to summarize, compare, and analyze the main points in two or more primary source historical documents, or historical or social science monographs.
- **Opinion essay**. Student demonstrates the ability to summarize, compare, and analyze the main points in two or more primary source historical documents, or historical or social science monographs, and develops an interpretation based on these sources.
- **Book review**. Student reads a full-length historical or social science monograph, summarizes the work, and comments on the implications of the study.
- **Primary source research report**. Student selects and researches a topic using multiple primary sources. Report includes a bibliography and footnotes. This can be an individual or group activity.
- **Interviews**. Student develops a questionnaire and interviews people about their involvement in local issues or major historical events. Information from the interviews is verified and expanded using published sources. Materials are integrated into an essay or essays. This can be an individual or group activity.
- **Social studies journal**. Student maintains a journal that includes comments on material studied in class and reports on progress as historians and social science researchers during class projects.
- **Current events scrapbook.** Student collects current events newspaper and magazine articles and maintains a scrapbook and commentary on a specific subject. Student develops a position on the issue and writes a persuasive essay that supports the position with evidence, and tries to persuade the audience to accept this position.
- **Cultural art or craft project**. Student creates an art or craft project that represents the culture of a group studied in class. Student presents the project and background information in class. This can be an individual or group activity.
- **Cultural comparison project**. Student compares different aspects of cultures examined in the curriculum, including their own culture. Report can be written or oral. It should include examples of cultural similarities and differences. This can be an individual or group activity.
- **Creative display of social studies conceptual understanding**. Student creates one or more of the following: a book of the student's political cartoons and/or political poems; a poster display on an historical or contemporary topic; an audio- or videotape of social and political music and songs, including the student's own compositions; a photo essay on an historical or contemporary topic that includes the student's own work; a museum exhibit on an historical or contemporary topic. This can be an individual or group activity.

- **Oral presentations and comments**. Student participates in panel presentations to class, both as a presenter and a commentator. This is a group activity.
- **Journal of civic responsibility**. Student maintains a journal, where they comment on involvement and learning as a community volunteer or in political or social action campaigns.
- **Tests**. Traditional unit essay and short answer exams, quizzes, and standardized examinations.

Teaching Activity: Constructing Social Studies Portfolios

Add your voice to the discussion:

Do you think portfolios or examinations provide more accurate assessment of student learning? Why?

It's your classroom:

1. Select one of the social studies-related portfolio areas (history and social studies, geography, or ethics and social issues) from the CPESS, and develop guidelines for an acceptable (or an excellent) "major" portfolio.
2. What kind of reports and projects would you require?
3. Would you allow students to submit group work to fulfill part of their individual requirements? Why?
4. Would you include unit and standardized test results as part of a portfolio requirement?

HOW DO TEACHERS DESIGN FAIR EXAMS?

I used multiple forms of assessment in my high school social studies classes, including standard short answer and essay tests geared to the academic level of my students. Most students found my tests challenging, but not tricky. There is no simple rule for the frequency of tests, the number of questions on a test, the type of questions, the vocabulary level used in questions, the time allocated for a test, or the weight assigned to different kinds of questions. A lot of test design is based on a teacher's judgments about her or his class and the points and skills stressed in a particular unit. I tend to give short tests on a more frequent basis to classes where students have greater academic difficulty. I find that this gives more structure to their studying, and allows me to target specific academic skills. Otherwise, I give full-period exams at the end of a unit as part of the process of pulling together what we have been learning.

One rule I had is that everybody got to finish the test. If students needed more time, they could come back later in the day, during lunch or a free period. If necessary, a student could finish the test after school or the next day. I found that this takes some of the pressure off students who score poorly because they get anxious or because of academic difficulties.

Another rule was to test what I taught and what I considered important. There were no tricks or obscure references on my tests.

My tests usually included multiple-choice questions and a selection of essays. I generally only used matching questions when I want students to identify places on a map or the people who said or wrote particularly important quotations that we examined in class. As a policy, I did not use fill-in or true-false questions. I hated them as a student, and I am not convinced they tell teachers very much about what students know or understand.

I usually took the multiple-choice questions on an exam directly from the homework assignments and classwork activities. A typical homework assignment that could be adapted for a test would be: Read "Wars in China and Korea," pp. 697–700 in *The Americans* (Jordan et al. 1985), and answer the questions from your homework sheet. If there were 4 questions to an assignment, and 10 assignments to a unit, this gave me 40 questions from which to choose. Approximately 20 of them would be on the test. They would be supplemented by between 10 and 20 questions based on charts, graphs, quotes, or cartoons examined in class during the unit.

Homework Assignment:

A reading, writing, research, or thinking assignment that students complete after the lesson. It can be a review of the lesson, an introduction to a future lesson, background material that enriches student understanding, an exercise that improves student skills, or part of a long-term project.

The section "Wars in China and Korea" starts with a discussion of the impact of World War II on China, explores problems with the Nationalist government, and examines differences between the Communists and the Nationalists. It continues with a discussion of the post-World War II US role in Asia and in the conflict in China, and the US response to the fall of the Nationalist regime. Increasing US diplomatic and military involvement in Korea is explained as a response to Communist victory in China. The ability of the United States to enlist the United Nations in support of US policy is credited to a Soviet boycott of the Security Council.

In its suggested homework assignment, the text recommends two activities: "Developing Vocabulary" and "Mastering Facts." In "Developing Vocabulary," students are asked to explain the following terms: *mediate*, *Long March*, *limited war*, and *police action*. In "Mastering Facts," students are asked to answer four questions:

1. What were three reasons for the downfall of Chiang Kai-shek's Nationalist government?
2. How did the 38th parallel come to be the dividing line between North Korea and South Korea?
3. What was Truman's objective in Korea?
4. Why did the Soviet Union not veto the UN recommendation to send UN troops to Korea?

For an assignment like this one, most students skim the chapter to locate the vocabulary words and facts that answer the homework questions. Instead of using the questions provided in the book, I ask homework questions that require students to draw conclusions based on the information in the chapter. I also try to provide context clues in the questions that help students focus on the chapter's main ideas. Students know that these questions will appear on the unit test in multiple-choice form. If they read the chapter and do the written assignment conscientiously, they should do well on the tests.

Sample homework questions for this reading from *The Americans* follow:

1. What were the main reasons for the downfall of Chiang Kai-shek's Nationalist government? In your opinion, which reason was most significant?
2. US General Wedemeyer recommended that the United States send troops into China to support its Nationalist allies. President Truman was unwilling to commit US soldiers. Do you agree with General Wedemeyer or President Truman? Why?
3. The Truman administration was bitterly attacked by conservatives for "losing China to the Communists." Do you agree with the conservatives? Why?
4. North Korea considered its government the legitimate ruler of all of Korea, and considered the war in Korea a civil war. However, President Truman compared North Korean actions to those of "Hitler, and Mussolini, and the Japanese" during the 1930s. In your opinion, was the United States right to enter the Korean War? Why?

On the unit test, these homework questions become the following multiple-choice questions:

1. Why was Chiang Kai-shek's Nationalist government in China defeated by Communist forces?
   a. Many people considered the Nationalist government dictatorial and corrupt.
   b. Many Chinese peasants supported the communist program to redistribute land from the large landowners to the poor farmers.
   c. Nationalist leaders used poor military strategy. Troops remained isolated in cities while their supply lines were cut.
   d. Chiang Kai-shek was unwilling to change economic policies that favored the wealthy and his friends.
   e. All of these reasons.
2. Why was the Truman administration

bitterly attacked by conservatives for "losing China to the Communists?"

a. President Truman refused to send any financial support to US allies in China.
b. President Truman was unwilling to use US troops to support the Nationalist government.
c. President Truman sent thousands of US soldiers to China without adequate weapons.
d. President Truman gave the Communist forces financial help so they could win their war against the Nationalists.
e. All of these choices.

3. In his memoirs, President Truman compared North Korean actions to those of Hitler, Mussolini, and the Japanese during the 1930s. Why did Truman believe US troops had to be sent to Korea?

a. Truman thought North Korea would join with Germany and Japan to rebuild the World War II Axis alliance.
b. Truman believed that if communist aggression went unopposed in Korea, communism would keep expanding until there was a third world war.
c. Truman did not trust the UN or other countries to help defend freedom.
d. The North Korean army was the second most powerful army in the world, and only the United States could effectively oppose it.
e. All of these choices.

Teaching Activity: Designing Homework and Test Questions

Add your voice to the discussion:
What do you think about these kinds of homework and test questions? Why?

It's your classroom:
Select a three- to five-page reading assignment from a standard secondary school text. Design four homework questions based on the selection. Rewrite the homework questions as multiple-choice questions for a unit test. In the chapters on unit and lesson planning, we discussed the development of document-based lessons. Reusing the documents on a test helps determine whether all of the students understand the material presented during lessons.

EXAMPLE: ADAPTING CLASSWORK TO CREATE TEST QUESTIONS

Wealth in the US:
A sample document-based activity in an economics class might involve students in analyzing and discussing Figures 12.1a, 12.1b, and 12.1c on the growing disparity of wealth in the United States from 1973 through 1993. *Source: The New York Times Magazine,* November 19, 1995, 78–79.

1. Why is information in Figures 12.1a and 12.1b shown in "constant dollars?"
2. What was the median income for men working full time in 1973?
3. What happened to the median income for men working full time between 1973–1993?
4. Whose earnings are included in "median household income?"
5. What happened to the median household income from 1989 to 1993?
6. What happened to the share of the nation's total net worth held by the top one half of one percent (0.5%) of the population from 1983 to 1993?
7. Describe the trend (pattern of change) in each Figure.
8. What general conclusions can you draw based on these trends?
9. Based on your analysis of these Figures, what further information would you want to know about the US economy during this period?
10. In your opinion, what potential problems do these trends suggest for the United States?

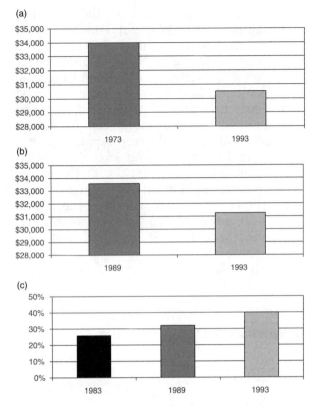

(a)

(b)

(c)

Figure 12.1 (a) Median wage for all men working full-time (shown in constant dollars). (b) Median household income (shown in constant dollars). (c) Share of the nation's total net worth held by the top 1/2 of 1 percent (0.5%) of the population.

On a short answer test, these questions could appear "as is" or reappear in the following form:

1. Why is information in Figures 12.1a and 12.1b shown in "constant dollars?"
   a. The value of money was constant from 1973 to 1993.
   b. The only people included are men who remained at the same jobs.
   c. Economists removed the impact of inflation on wages from the graph.
   d. All of these choices.
2. What was the median income for men working full-time in 1973?
   a. $34,048 b. $30,407 c. $33,585 d. $31,241
3. What happened to the median income for men working full time from 1973 to 1993?
   a. It rose by approximately 10 percent.
   b. It declined by a little less than 10 percent.
   c. It rose by over 25 percent.
   d. It declined by over 25 percent.
4. What earnings are included in "median household income?"

a. Only income earned by the head of the household.
   b. All income earned by people living in a household.
   c. Only the salaries of full-time wage earners living in a household.
   d. All income earned by the people or person who owns the house.
5. What happened to the median household income from 1989 to 1993?
   a. It rose by approximately 5 percent.
   b. It declined by over 5 percent.
   c. It rose by over 25 percent.
   d. It declined by over 25 percent.
6. What happened to the share of the nation's total net worth held by the top 1/2 of 1 percent (0.5 percent) of the population from 1983 to 1993?
   a. It rose by approximately 35 percent.
   b. It declined by over 35 percent.
   c. It rose by less than 10 percent.
   d. It declined by under 10 percent.
7. Notice the trend in Figure 12.1c. How does the share of the nation's total net worth held by the top 1/2 of 1 percent (0.5 percent) of the population change from 1983–1993?
   a. A slow but constant increase in the share of wealth held by the wealthiest people.
   b. A slow but constant decline in the share of wealth held by the wealthiest people.
   c. The share of wealth held by the wealthiest people is increasing at a faster rate.
   d. The share of wealth held by the wealthiest people is increasing, but the rate of increase is slowing down.

I would probably use the last three questions as the basis for the following essay.

Use the information provided by the graphs, discussions in class, and other relevant sources, to discuss the following:

- Trends in the US economy you can identify in these graphs.
- General conclusions you can draw based on these trends.
- A list of further information you want to know about the US economy during this period, and the reasons you want to know this information.
- Your opinions on potential problems these economic trends could pose for the United States.

Teaching Activity: Creating Short Answer Test Questions

Add your voice to the discussion:
What do you think about these questions? Why?

It's your classroom:
Select a document (quote, graph, chart, picture, or cartoon) you would use during a lesson in a middle or high school social studies class. Design at least four questions based on the document. Rewrite the questions as multiple-choice questions for a unit test.

I tried to design essay questions utilizing the same principles I employed in developing short answer tests. Generally, essay questions were rewritten versions of AIM or SUMMARY questions. For example, a unit in a US government class might explore the changing role of the Supreme Court through an examination of selected landmark court decisions and different theories for interpreting the Constitution. Sample lesson AIM questions during the unit could include the following:

1. How does the Constitution describe the Judicial Branch?
2. What was the origin of Judicial Review?
3. The Dred Scott Decision: How did the Supreme Court attempt to resolve the debate over slavery?
4. How did the Supreme Court redefine equal protection of the law in the *Brown* v. *the Topeka, Kansas Board of Education* decision?
5. Why did the Supreme Court support abortion rights?
6. Continuing the debate: Should Supreme Court Justices reinterpret the Constitution?

The three essay questions that follow are based on these AIM questions. The first question is a structured essay that tests whether students understand the main ideas examined during the unit and can recall and use specific information about cases discussed during the lessons. It also calls upon students to formulate their own views and support them with evidence.

The second essay question is more open-ended. Students are provided with a quote that has been discussed in class, and directions for answering the question.

The third essay question is completely open-ended, and is taken directly from an "AIM" question. Based on earlier work, students understand that an effective essay must present a clear point of view, provide supporting evidence, and address arguments made by people who hold alternative viewpoints.

Essay 1
The US Supreme Court has repeatedly reinterpreted the meaning of the Constitution during the last 200 years.

1. Explain the concept of Judicial Review. In your answer, discuss the origin of the idea of Judicial Review in the *Marbury* v. *Madison* decision.
2. Select three of the five cases listed next, and describe how the Supreme Court's decision in each case changed our understanding of the Constitution.
   - *Brown* v. *Topeka Kansas Board of Education* (1954)—School segregation.
   - *Engle* v. *Vitale* (1962)—School prayer.
   - *Miranda* v. *Arizona* (1966)—Rights of the accused.
   - *New York Times* v. *United States* (1971)—Freedom of the press.
   - *Roe* v. *Wade* (1973)—Abortion rights.
3. Select one of the cases and discuss the legal, social, or political issues involved in that case.
4. Conclude with a discussion of your views on the role of the Supreme Court in the US system of government. In your answer, provide specific examples to support your viewpoint.

Essay 2
Read the excerpt from a speech by former Supreme Court Justice William Brennan (*The New York Times*, October 13, 1985, p. 36), and then answer the question that follows it:

"We current Justices read the Constitution in the only way that we can: as twentieth-century Americans. We look to the history of the time of framing and to the intervening history of interpretation. But the ultimate question must be, what do the words of the text mean in our time? For the genius of the Constitution rests not in any static meaning it might have had in a world that is dead and gone, but in the adaptability of its great principles to cope with current problems and current needs."

Decisions by the US Supreme Court have been criticized by citizens, including Supreme Court Justices, who hold different views of the way that the Court should interpret the Constitution and decide particular cases. Explain and evaluate at least three different points of view of how the Supreme Court should interpret the Constitution. In your answer, discuss the ways that advocates of these views might (or did) view a particular issue.

Essay 3
Write an editorial expressing your views on the question: Should US Supreme Court Justices reinterpret the Constitution?

Teaching Activity: Designing Essay Questions

Think it over:
1. As a high school student, which essay would you have preferred to answer? Why?
2. As a teacher, which do you consider the most effective essay question? Why?

Try it yourself:
Write sample answers to the essay questions that you would consider appropriate for high school students.

It's your classroom:
Design a structured and a less structured essay question for a unit of your own design.

Generally, I use relatively structured homework and classwork assignments, like the samples included here, to direct students toward key information that they need to think about, analyze, and study. I also use these as the basis for test construction.

Assessment can also be based on more open-ended activities. Social studies teachers Bill Bigelow and Bob Peterson (1994) designed a project for grades 5–12 that they call "Students as Textbook Detectives." In this project, students research social studies topics and use their knowledge to examine classroom texts for biases, distortions, and omissions. Their goal is to make it possible for students to frame their own questions about the way knowledge received from textbooks shapes our understanding of the past and present.

I did a similar project in an advanced placement US history class using the text, *The American Pageant*, by Thomas A. Bailey and David M. Kennedy (1983). Bailey and Kennedy are "consensus historians"; their text focuses on broad areas of agreement and continuing growth and development in US history. Points of conflict and tension are minimized, and injustices are presented as unfortunate aberrations from the main democratic thrust of US history. Demands for radical change are dismissed as extremist, unnecessary, and disruptive. For example, in the chapter "The South and the Slave Controversy," Bailey and Kennedy argue that the US Civil War was avoidable if extremists on both sides, but especially among the northern abolitionists, had not undermined compromises and plunged the nation into catastrophic war.

Bailey and Kennedy believe that White southerners were "Slaves of the Slave System" who would have eventually accepted calls by "reasonable" abolitionists for the gradual elimination of slavery. Unfortunately for the United States, "Garrisonian Militants" shattered "the atmosphere of moderation" by provoking violence until "The South Lashes Back." Garrison is described as "the emotionally high-strung son of a drunken father." The historians conclude, "Abolitionist extremists no doubt hastened the freeing of the slave by a number of years. But emancipation came at the price of a civil conflict that tore apart the social and economic fabric of the South." In addition, as a result of the Civil War, "bewildered blacks were caught in the middle . . . Emotionalism on both sides thus slammed the door on any fair adjustment" (p. 344).

During this unit, students examined the underlying causes of the Civil War in class using primary source documents. Their homework assignment was to read and outline the main ideas of the chapter, and to compile a list of their questions and responses to the authors'

ideas. At the unit's conclusion, students drew on their notes from the text and classwork to examine the different interpretations of the causes of the Civil War. As part of this discussion, they explored the ideological biases of the textbook's authors and the way these shaped their interpretation of historical events.

On the unit test, students were asked to answer the following essay question:

Essay Question

According to the authors of *The American Pageant*, extremists, especially northern abolitionists, were the primary cause of the US Civil War. Explain why you agree or disagree with Bailey and Kennedy. Provide evidence from the text and from class document packets to support your position.

HOW CAN TEACHERS GRADE FAIRLY?

Even when tests are "fair" assessment devices, teachers have to decide how much to weigh different parts of a test and how to evaluate student answers on essay questions. Frequently, I assign a point value to questions after I see how students perform on a test. If many students do poorly on one part, I assume the problem was either in my teaching or with the test itself, and I count those questions for less. By being flexible, I get a more accurate measure of what students understand, I avoid demoralizing students with low test

scores, and I eliminate the practice of curving grades.

Evaluating essay answers requires a grading strategy. The three major approaches are "holistic" grading of entire essays, assigning a specific number of points for each section of an essay, or using an assessment rubric that gives students credit for including different types of evidence and arguments and for the effectiveness of their writing. I have used all three strategies, and I do not think there is one correct approach. However, whatever approach you take, a teacher needs to be as consistent as possible so students know what to expect when they write essays.

Table 12.4 Sample rubric for assessing an essay answer.

15 points total	Weak	Satisfactory	Strong
Introduction **3 points**	**0–1 pts**. Confused and incomplete	**2 pts**. A clear but brief statement	**3 pts**. A clear and well developed statement
Use of evidence to support argument **6 points**	**1–2 pts**. Insufficient or inaccurate evidence	**3–4 pts**. Sufficient evidence, but not well developed (or) well developed, but in need of additional evidence	**5–6 pts**. Sufficient information that strongly supports the position taken in the introductory statement
Conclusion **3 points**	**0–1 pts**. Insufficient; Unclear. Not based on the evidence	**2 pts**. Some problems with either the clarity or logic of the argument	**3 pts**. A clear concluding statement that follows from the introduction and the evidence
Quality of writing **3 points**	**0–1 pts**. Serious problems with clarity, spelling, grammar, and paragraph structure	**2 pts**. Some problems with clarity, spelling, grammar, and paragraph structure	**3 pts**. A well-written essay with minimal problems

---

Teaching Activity: Grading Essay Questions

It's your classroom:
1. Select one of the essay questions suggested in this chapter or a question of your own design. If you were grading an answer to this question "holistically," what would you look for in an essay? Why?

2. If you were assigning a set point value to each part of this question, how many points would each part be worth? Why?

3. If you were developing a grading rubric, how much value would you place on the quality of writing? Why?

SHOULD STUDENTS BE INVOLVED IN ASSESSING THEIR OWN LEARNING?

For many teachers, involving students in the assessment of their own learning is a touchy subject. They worry whether students are capable of objectivity in grading themselves or others, and about the dangers of surrendering some of the teacher's authority in the classroom. However, instead of seeing student involvement in assessment as a problem of fairness or a question of classroom management, we need to view it as a social studies teacher's commitment to developing critical thinkers and democratic citizens. Involving students in assessment can, but does not necessarily, mean they participate in deciding their own grades. It definitely means that students are involved in developing the parameters for class projects and deciding the criteria for assessing their performance in these activities. The benefits of this student involvement include: a deeper understanding of historical and social science research methods; insight into the design and implementation of projects; a greater stake in the satisfactory completion of assignments; and a sense of empowerment because assessment decisions are based on rules that the classroom community has helped to shape.

Michael Pezone (NTN) discusses assessment with students as part of discussions of social justice (Pezone and Singer 1997). Often he poses a problem for students to examine. For example, they own a plot of land that is covered by a forest, and they hire two workers to harvest the timber. Worker 1 is a large, strong, experienced lumberjack. While Worker 1 proceeds at a relaxed pace and takes extended breaks, this worker is able to cut down and trim 50 trees a day. Worker 2 is on the small side, and has never done this type of work before. Worker 2 gives a full effort from sun up to sun down, but is only able to harvest an average of 35 trees a day. The class is asked to discuss how much a fair employer should pay each of these workers. During the course of the discussion, the issue of fair payment is connected to the question of how to fairly assess student performance in class. Michael uses this story and student responses to involve the class in establishing grading procedures for tests, projects. and class participation.

Writing in *Educational Leadership*, Walter Parker (1995) recommends the development of performance criteria and scoring rubrics for assessing "civic discourse" in social studies classes. The evaluation of these discourses makes it possible for teachers to assess a student's ability to put "democratic principles into action." I think student involvement in defining civic discourse, in establishing procedures and criteria for assessment, and in evaluating performance, as they did in Michael Pezone's class, is a particularly useful way to encourage and evaluate democratic "habits of mind." It also provides a model that can be adapted by programs where students are expected to make presentations and assemble portfolios that demonstrate the depth and breadth of their work.

I am always willing to discuss grading criteria with students and to explain individual grades. If a student feels I have made a mistake in my evaluation, I will consider new evidence, but I try not to negotiate grades. Students must be helped to realize that grades are assessments of performance, not measures of their individual worth as human beings.

Teaching Activity: Should Students Assess Their Own Learning?

Add your voice to the discussion:
Do you believe that students should be involved in assessing their own learning? Why? How?

Essay 1: How Do We Move from Instruction to Assessment?

As I have argued repeatedly, authentic assessment means testing what we taught. This essay follows two sets of documents as they are transformed from activity sheet to unit examination. The first set, intended for high school, starts as part of a group project that can be organized in different ways depending on your students. There are five documents. An entire team can examine and report to the class on one of the documents, or each member of a team can examine a different document and help prepare a team report. The level of difficulty of the documents varies, so the package lends itself for use in heterogeneous classes. The documents from the first package (Murphy et al. 2001) reappear along with multiple-choice questions on the unit exam.

Sometimes at the end of a lesson I ask students, "What questions are answered by the information in these documents?" Their questions and the document package can appear on the unit exam as a document based essay.

The second set of documents is designed for use in middle school. In this case, the activity and the exam are both more "directive."

Document-based Assessment:

Students are asked to act as historians and social scientists as they examine and explain individual or sets of documents and artifacts. It is a form of performance assessment.

HIGH SCHOOL LEVEL ACTIVITY SHEET: NINETEENTH-CENTURY IRISH IMMIGRATION TO THE UNITED STATES

Instructions

Examine your assigned document. What does the document tell us about conditions faced by Irish immigrants to the United States in the nineteenth century?

A. Letter from Michael Hogan, Albany, NY, to Catherine Nolan, Pollerton, Co. Carlow:

I take this opportunity of writing those few lines to you hoping to find you and your family in good health as this leaves us all in good health at present. I thank God for his mercies to us all. I received a letter from Patrick Kelly on the 24th of December '51 which gave us all great pleasure to find that all friends were well. We were sorry to hear of my grandmother's death but yet thankful to God for taking her out of this wicked world.

I got a situation [job] on the 12th of February 1851 which I occupy up to this time. My wages is 6 dollars a week from the 1st of April until the 1st of January. The following three months I get 4 dollars per week. I board myself. My work is but 10 hours in the day. Dennys is working at boot and shoe making since we came here with the exception of four months which he worked in a foundry last summer. Patrick is idle at present but I expect to get him work in a few days. As the girls, Mary and Ann and Margaret are in good situations in the city, and Eleanor is learning the tailoress trade.

I would not encourage any person to come here that could live middling well at home as they might meet with many difficulties by coming here but any boy or girl that has to labor for their living, this is the country for them. Winter is a bad time for any person to come here as it is almost impossible to get anything to do and expensive to travel.

B. Traditional Song—Paddy Works on the Railway:

In eighteen hundred and forty four, I landed on America's shore, I landed on America's shore, to work upon the railway. Filly-me-oori-oori-ay (3×), to work upon the railway.

In eighteen hundred and forty five, I found myself more dead than alive, I found myself more dead than alive, from working on the railway. Filly-me-oori-oori-ay (3×), to work upon the railway.

In eighteen hundred and forty six, they pelted me with stones and sticks, and I was in one hell of a fix, from working on the railway. Filly-me-oori-oori-ay (3×), to work upon the railway.

It's "Pat, do this!" and "Pat, do that!", without a stocking or cravat (scarf), and nothing but an old straw hat, to work upon the railway. Filly-me-oori-oori-ay (3×), to work upon the railway.

C. A writer describes Irish Immigrants in New Orleans, 1833:

One of the greatest works now in progress here, is the canal planned to connect Lac Pontchartrain with the city of New Orleans. I only wish that the wise men at home who coolly charge the present condition of Ireland upon the inherent laziness of her population, could be transported to this spot. Here they subsist on the coarsest fare; excluded from all the advantages of civilization; often at the mercy of a hard contractor, who wrings his profits from their blood; and all this for a pittance that merely enables them to exist, with little power to save, or a hope beyond the continuance of the like exertion. The mortality amongst them is enormous. At present they are, where I have seen them working here, worse lodged than the cattle of the field; in fact, the only thought bestowed upon them appears to be, by what expedient the greatest quantity of labour may be extracted from them at the cheapest rate to the contractor. Slave labour cannot be substituted to any extent, being much too expensive; a good slave costs at this time two hundred pounds sterling, and to have a thousand such swept off a line of canal in one season, would call for prompt consideration.

D. Political Cartoon

Figure 12.2 Political cartoon.

Thomas Nast, "The Day We Celebrate: St. Patrick's Day, 1867," *Harper's Weekly*, April 6, 1867 (http://www.haverford.edu/engl/faculty/Sherman/Irish/19thc..htm, accessed November 6, 2007).

E. Immigration from Ireland to the United States, 1842–1854:

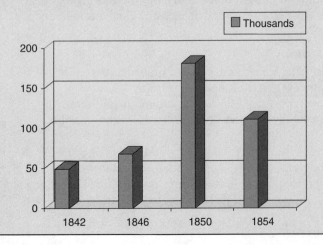

Figure 12.3 Immigration from Ireland to the United States, 1842–1854.

HIGH SCHOOL LEVEL UNIT TEST: NINETEENTH-CENTURY IMMIGRATION TO THE UNITED STATES

Instructions

Examine each document and answer the questions that follow it.

A. Letter from Michael Hogan, Albany, NY, to Catherine Nolan, Pollerton, Co. Carlow

I got a situation [job] on the 12th of February 1851 which I occupy up to this time. My wages is 6 dollars a week from the 1st of April until the 1st of January. The following three months I get 4 dollars per week. I board myself. My work is but 10 hours in the day. Dennys is working at boot and shoe making since we came here with the exception of four months which he worked in a foundry last summer. Patrick is idle at present but I expect to get him work in a few days. As the girls, Mary and Ann and Margaret are in good situations in the city, and Eleanor is learning the tailoress trade.

I would not encourage any person to come here that could live middling well at home as they might meet with many difficulties by coming here but any boy or girl that has to labor for their living, this is the country for them. Winter is a bad time for any person to come here as it is almost impossible to get anything to do and expensive to travel.

1. Where is Michael Hogan when he writes this letter?
   a. Pollerton, County, Ireland.
   b. A ship crossing the Atlantic on a voyage to America.
   c. New York State in the United States.
   d. Hofstra University, Hempstead, NY.
2. Why did Michael Hogan settle in this place?
   a. It is the place where he always dreamed of living.
   b. He was able to find a job here.
   c. Irish immigrants are required to live in this town.
   d. All of these choices.
3. What does Michael Hogan recommend to people in Ireland?
   a. He encourages everyone that he knows to move to the United States.
   b. He feels that people who are poor in Ireland will do better if they move here.
   c. He suggests that the Irish people would be better off if they remain in Ireland.
   d. He is sorry that he came to America and plans to return home as soon as possible.

B. Immigration from Ireland to the United States, 1842–1854

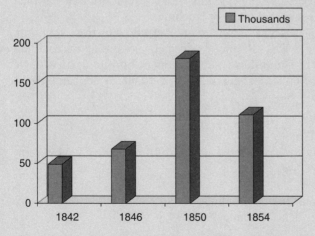

Figure 12.4 Immigration from Ireland to the United States, 1842–1854.

1. Approximately how many people migrated from Ireland to the US in 1842?
   a. 50,000
   b. 200,000
   c. 50,000,000
   d. 1 million
2. In which of these years did the most people migrate from Ireland to the United States?
   a. 1842
   b. 1846
   c. 1850
   d. 1854
3. What was the "PULL" that brought Irish immigrants to the United States?
   a. They liked the way they were treated by Americans and were immediately given citizenship rights.
   b. They were able to get high paying professional jobs and live in luxury in the finest homes.
   c. While jobs paid low wages and living conditions were harsh, the situation was better than in Ireland.
   d. All of these choices.

MIDDLE-LEVEL ACTIVITY SHEET—THE SOUTH AFTER RECONSTRUCTION

Introduction

Conditions were very difficult for African-Americans in the America South after the end of Reconstruction. The four documents that follow describe one of the most unjust periods in United States history. Examine each document carefully and answer the questions at the end of the document. Be prepared. They are very upsetting.

Document A. Mrs Ida Wells-Barnett Writes a Letter to President William McKinley, 1898:

Source: Aptheker, H. 1968. *A Documentary History of the Negro People in the United States*. New York: Citadel Press, p. 798.

"Mr. President, the colored citizens of this country . . . desire to respectfully urge that some action be taken by you as chief magistrate of this great nation . . . for the apprehension and punishment of the lynchers of Postmaster Baker, of Lake City, S.C. . . . (W)e most earnestly desire that national legislation be enacted for the suppression of the national crime of lynching.

For nearly twenty years lynching crimes . . . have been committed and permitted by this . . . nation. Nowhere in the civilized world save the United States of America do men, possessing all civil and political power, go out in bands of 50 and 5,000 to hunt down, shoot, hang or burn to death a single individual, unarmed and absolutely powerless. Statistics show that nearly 10,000 American citizens have been lynched in the past 20 years."

Questions

1. In what year was this letter written?
2. Ida Wells-Barnett wrote President Wilson about the "colored citizens of this country." What term would we use to describe this group of people today?
3. What problem did Ida Wells-Barnett describe?
4. How many times did this happen in the 20-year period she describes?
5. What does Ida Wells-Barnett demand of President McKinley?

Document B. Photograph of a Lynching (see opposite):

1. Describe what you see in this picture.
2. Why is this picture so frightening?

Figure 12.5 A lynching. Credit: Library of Congress, Manuscript Division, Frederick Douglass Papers.

Document C. How Many People Were Lynched in the South?

Table 12.5 How many people were lynched in the south?

Year	Total victims	Whites	Blacks	Percentage of victims who were Black
1882	113	64	49	43
1885	184	110	74	40
1890	96	11	85	88
1895	179	66	113	63
1900	115	9	106	92

Source: Adapted from Bailey, T. and Kennedy, D. 1983. *The American Pageant*. 7th ed. Lexington, MA: D.C. Heath, p. 447.

1. How many years are shown on this chart (Table 12.5)?
2. How many people were lynched in the South in 1882?
3. How many of these people were White? How many were Black?
4. How many people were lynched in the South in 1900?
5. How many of these people were White? How many were Black?
6. What has changed from 1882 to 1900?

Document D. Strange Fruit, a song sung by Billy Holiday in the 1930s:
Lyrics are available at: http://www.pbs.org/independentlens/strangefruit/film.html. A clip of Billie Holliday singing Strange Fruit is available at: http://www.youtube.com/watch?v=h4ZyuULy9zs (accessed October 12, 2007).

1. According to the lyrics to this there is blood on the leaves and blood at the root of the trees in the South. What is the "strange fruit" described in this song?
2. What images does the song use to create a picture in your mind?
3. Draw a picture or write your own poem, song, or rap about lynching in the South.

Middle-level Document-based Essay on Reconstruction:
A. Examine each of the documents in your package.
B. Make a list of three pieces of information you learn from each document.
C. Using this information, write a letter to your hometown newspaper describing what is happening in the South.
D. Conclude your letter with your ideas on what should be done.

Essay 2: What Does a Research Paper Look Like?

Jim Divers, Erika Lopes, Paul Jenssen, Samatha Siff, and Dominick Veneziano of the New Teachers Network contributed ideas for internet sites for this research project.

Many states have called on social studies departments to help promote student literacy in the content area. This has often meant increased attention in social studies classes to instruction in how to research, write, and edit reports, which was previously primarily the responsibility of Language Arts teachers. The website *Literacy Matters* links to a number of sites with social studies lesson ideas that promote reading and writing skills (see http://www.literacymatters.org/content/socialstudies.htm, accessed October 12, 2007).

A. 11th-grade Great Events in United States History Research Paper
You will be writing a research paper on a "Great Event" in the history of the United States between the years 1851 and 1991.

Possible topics
Other topics can be chosen but they require prior approval.

1. Christiana, Pennsylvania Rebellion Against Slavecatchers (1851)
2. New York City Draft Riots (1863)
3. Assassination of Abraham Lincoln (1865)
4. Brooklyn Bridge (1869–1883)
5. Haymarket Square Riot (1886)
6. Spanish-American War (1898)
7. Alice Paul and the Woman's Suffrage Movement (1914–1920)
8. Sinking of the Lusitania and the Push towards War (1915–1917)
9. Prohibition (1917–1933)
10. Red Scare and the Sacco and Vanzetti Trial (1919–1927)
11. Scopes "Monkey" Trial (1924)
12. Stock Market Collapse and the Start of the Great Depression (1929)
13. Hoover v. Roosevelt Presidential Campaign (1932)
14. New Deal's First 100 Days (1933)
15. Flint, Michigan Autoworkers Sit-down Strike (1937)
16. Japanese Internment (1942–1945)
17. Nuclear Attack on Hiroshima (1945)
18. Jackie Robinson and the Integration of Major League Baseball (1947)
19. McCarthyism (1950–1954)
20. *Brown* v. *Topeka, Kansas Board of Education* (1954)
21. Montgomery Bus Boycott (1955–1956)
22. Impact of Sputnik (1957)
23. Cuban Missile Crisis (1962)
24. Urban Riots (1965–1967)
25. Tet Offensive and the Vietnam War (1968)
26. New York City Teachers Strike (1968)
27. Moon Landing (1969)
28. Watergate and Nixon's Resignation (1972–1974)
29. End of the Cold War (1987–1991)
30. Desert Storm (1990–1991)

Resources
Our primary resource will be *The New York Times*, which started publication in September 1851. Free access to *The New York Times* historical archive is available through the school library webpage. You

should use a **minimum of ten articles** from *The New York Times*.

You should consult other websites linked to the school library webpage. You must keep a log of all web visits.

Your log and a copy of material from online encyclopedias and non-linked web sources must be submitted with your notes.

Secondary source books remain acceptable resources.

Submission schedule

1. The topic you selected with a one paragraph preliminary summary of events describing what you already know about what took place and its historical importance. Due _____.
2. Preliminary outline of your report in standard outline form. The outline requires that you narrow your topic based on your initial research. You should also try to change your "topic" into a question that your paper will attempt to answer. Due _____.
3. Research notes, weblog, and copies of material from online encyclopedias and non-linked web sources. Due _____.
4. First draft of your research paper. Due _____.
5. Final draft of your research paper. Due _____.

Final draft submission guidelines
Your final paper should be typed, double-spaced, ten-pages with one-inch margins, and printed using the Times New Roman 12 point font. It will be approximately 3,000 words long. You should have a cover page with the title of your paper, the question you are answering, your name, and optional illustrations. References should be listed on a separate page at the end of the paper using our standard format.

B. 8th-grade Local History Online Research Report
You will be writing a research report on the history of a local community. Your final paper should be typed, double-spaced, four-pages of text with one-inch margins, and printed using the Times New Roman 12 point font. It will be approximately 1,200 words long. Ideally it should include pictures and maps on separate pages. You should have a cover page with the title of your paper and your name. References including a list of all Internet sites visited should be listed on a separate page at the end of the paper using our standard format.

Most of your research will be conducted online using links to the school website. During your research you should consult the following sources:

1. These websites are data collections on local towns and are a good starting point for your research: http://city-data.com; http://www.epodunk.com; http://www.citytowninfo.com; http://www.hometownlocator.com; http://www.topix.net (accessed October 12, 2007)
2. Web resources available from the town, local public library, or historical society
3. Local newspaper reports on the history of the community
4. Census material that shows changes in local population between 1900 and 2000
5. Online state and local reports on the community and school district
6. Historical images and maps of the community (search Google Image and Google Earth)
7. Real Estate reports on the community
8. Websites of local elected officials.

Submission schedule

1. Outline of your report in standard outline form. Due _____.
2. Research notes. Due _____.
3. First draft of your research paper. Due _____.
4. Final draft of your research paper. Due _____.

Reminder: You can consult Wikipedia and other online encyclopedias, but they are not substitutes for visiting the other sites.

Essay 3: Assessing Our Teaching Practice

Overview:
- Discuss reflective practice and action research strategies
- Examine an action research project

Key Concepts:
Reflective Practice, Action Research

Questions:
- Why Should Teachers Assess Their Teaching Practice?
- How Does Action Research Improve Teaching Practice?
- Can Teachers Assess Changes in Student Values and Ideas?

Why Should Teachers Assess Their Teaching Practice?

One of the main reasons for social studies teachers to assess student learning is to understand our own performance. Examining student work makes it possible to evaluate the effectiveness of curricula and to decide whether individual lessons and activities connect to and scaffold on prior student understanding and experience. The assessment of students helps social studies teachers figure out how to better prepare, to more successfully present ideas in class, and to achieve goals. It makes possible what John Dewey and other educators have called *reflective practice*.

In *Reflective Practice in Social Studies* (Ross 1994), the NCSS examines a number of school programs where a systematic effort to promote reflective practice has both enhanced instruction and supported comradery among teachers. For example, teachers at the Mifflin International Middle School in Columbus, Ohio described how they "work hard to share their university level, inservice, and workshop learning with staff . . . They exchange resources and instructional ideas gained from these conferences during team meetings or special staff meetings . . . Continued reflection . . . is helping them creatively plan and implement" the school's program (p. 21).

Reflective Practice:

A process of professional self-examination where classroom teachers, working individually or with colleagues, review and reconsider educational goals, strategies, classroom decisions, curricula, and school organization.

Action Research:

Part of reflective practice; it entails testing assumptions about curricula, pedagogy, and student achievement, through the systematic organization, observation, and examination of what takes place in our own classrooms.

How Does Action Research Improve Teaching Practice?

John Dewey (1933) believed that human beings have "an innate disposition to draw inferences, an inherent desire to experiment and test. The mind . . . entertains suggestions, tests them by observation of objects and events, reaches conclusions, tries them in action, finds them confirmed or in need of correction or rejection" (p. 9). In my experience, what Dewey called an *innate disposition* can best be understood as *potential*. Human beings have the capacity to reevaluate, draw connections, and learn, but that does not mean we always engage in reflective practice. The value of including action research in our teaching is that it encourages us to more systematically evaluate our ideas about history and social studies and our teaching methods. Using action research in class, teacher/researchers can identify particular issues or questions, develop strategies for addressing them, and, through recurring cycles of teaching, observation, and reflection, test and revise our teaching strategies.

Myles Horton and Paulo Freire (1990) suggested an additional dimension for action research. He called on teacher/researchers to "Experiment with people, not on people . . . They're in on the experiment. They're in on the process" (p. 148). This is a valuable idea for a number of reasons. Involving students in action research projects adds to their sense of ownership over what goes on in social studies classes, and it helps teach them what it means to be an historian or social scientist. Additionally, when students are part of the research team, assessment of student learning becomes less a battle of wills and more a part of the learning process.

Can Teachers Assess Changes in Student Values and Ideas?

As a high school social studies teacher, I was particularly concerned whether students were using academic learning from class to reevaluate their values and ideas. I decided to develop an action research project involving students in determining whether the study of struggles for civil rights and gender equity influenced attitudes about gender differences and bias (Singer 1995). At the start of the semester, I explained the idea of action research and asked students to participate in an undefined experiment. If students agreed, I explained that they would be informed of the details of the experiment after activities were completed in class, so that their participation would not be influenced.

Learning Activity: Cartoon Dialogue

Try it yourself:

- Examine the cartoon panels in Figure 12.6. These female high school students are having a serious discussion.
- Write a dialogue for their discussion.
- Why did you decide to create this dialogue?

Figure 12.6 Gender cartoon.

The attitudes of young men toward young women, and of young women about themselves and toward each other, continually emerge in social studies classroom discussions and activities. As part of a unit on the changing role of women in the contemporary United States, I asked students to design "dialogues" between two female high school students who are having a serious discussion. Students could imagine any dialogue they chose, and had approximately ten minutes to complete blank dialogue boxes on a cartoon. They were also asked to explain why they created a particular dialogue.

Later in the unit, I explained that the cartoon dialogues provide us with raw data for an experiment measuring the impact of what we studied in class on student ideas and values. Cooperative learning teams examined the dialogues and sorted them by topic and according to student explanations for why they believed the young women were having a particular conversation. After general results were discussed in class, cooperative learning teams met to discuss (1) what students were trying to show in their dialogues, (2) why students chose particular topics, (3) why students felt that these female students were discussing these particular topics, and (4) whether gender stereotypes or biases influenced topic choices and dialogue content.

Generally, discussion in cooperative learning teams, and later in the class as a whole, was heated. Many students argued that some of the "cartoon dialogues," either by choice of subject or because of the content of the dialogue, expressed stereotypes about teenage women. Usually, however, students were divided over which dialogues and which explanations constitute gender bias.

Eventually, discussion of the "cartoon dialogues" extended into broader discussion of continuing gender bias in American society and modern American youth culture. In general, female students reacted most strongly to the impact of stereotyping. Male students, with a few exceptions, were less vocal than female students. What was striking in these discussions, however, was the absence of flippant and derogatory remarks about women, which male students often make in class.

It is difficult for teachers to get students to express their opinions on issues that are important to them, especially when the experience of so many young people is one of being vulnerable and silenced by both adults and peer groups. Even when students speak up in class, much of their effort is aimed at presenting the answers they believe teachers want to hear or that other students will accept. I believe that action research projects, like the one described here, provide students with opportunities to state and discuss what they are really thinking. Because of this, student choices on the "cartoon dialogues" and the discussions that followed helped me evaluate what was actually taking place in my classes.

From this action research project, I learned that I could not assume that students are making the intellectual connections I would like them to make. Academic knowledge by itself, even knowledge of social struggles against racial and gender prejudice, did not prompt students to reconsider their basic ideas and values. Knowledge remained compartmentalized until cooperative learning teams evaluated the student-created "cartoon dialogues" for potential gender bias. For me, the study suggests that if social studies teachers want students to make connections between school topics and life, we must find ways to make parallels clear, and help students make their understandings explicit.

References and Recommendations for Further Reading

Arter, J. and Spandel, V. 1992. "Using portfolios of student work in instruction and assessment," *Educational Measurement: Issues and Practice* 11(1): 36–44.

Bailey, T. and Kennedy, D. 1983. *The American pageant*, 7th ed. Lexington, MA: D. C. Heath.

Bigelow, B. and Peterson, B. 1994. "Students as textbook detectives," in *Rethinking our classrooms; Teaching for equity and justice.* Milwaukee, WI: Rethinking Schools, pp. 158–9.

Dao, J. 1995. "New York plans higher standards for high schools," *The New York Times,* November 4.

Dewey, J. 1933. *How we think: A restatement of the relation of reflective thinking to the educative process.* Boston, MA: Heath and Company.

Horton, M. and Freire, P. 1990. *We make the road by walking.* Philadelphia, PA: Temple University Press.

Jordan, W., Greenblatt, M. and Bowes, J. 1985. *The Americans, the history of a people and a nation.* Evanston, IL: McDougal Littell.

Meier, D. and Schwartz, P. 1995. "Central Park East Secondary School: The hard part is making it happen," in M. Apple and J. Beane, eds. *Democratic Schools,* Alexandria, VA: ASCD, pp. 31–2.

Meinig, D. 1993. *The shaping of America: A geographical perspective on 500 years of history, vol. 2: Continental America, 1800–1867.* New Haven: Yale University Press.

Menken, K. 2006. "Teaching to the test: How No Child Left Behind impacts language policy, curriculum, and instruction for English language learners," *Bilingual Research Journal* 30(2): 521–46.

Meyer, C. 1992. "What's the difference between authentic and performance assessment?" *Educational Leadership* 49(8): 39.

Murphy, M., Miletta, M. and Singer, A. eds. 2001. *New York State Great Irish Famine curriculum guide.* Albany, NY: State Department of Education.

National Council for the Social Studies. 1991. "Testing and evaluation of social studies students," *Social Education* 55(3).

National Education Association. 2007a. *Accountability: If not standardized tests, what?* http:/nea.org, accessed August 30, 2007.

National Education Association. 2007b. *ESEA: It's time for a change!* http:/nea.org, accessed August 30, 2007.

The New York Times. 1995. "Most 12th Graders Know Little History, Survey Says," *The New York Times,* November 2.

Nickell, P. 1992. "'Doing the stuff of social studies': A conversation with Grant Wiggins," *Social Education* 56(2): 91–4.

Nickell, P. 1993. *Alternative assessment: implications for social studies.* ERIC Document 360219.

Parker, W. 1989. "Participatory citizenship," *Social Education* 48(2): 353–4.

Parker, W. 1995. "Assessing civic discourse," *Educational Leadership* 54(8): 84–5.

Pezone, M. and Singer, A. 1997. "Empowering immigrant students through democratic dialogues," *Social Education* 61(2): 75–9.

Rees, J. 2003. "A crisis over consensus: Standardized testing in American history and student learning," *Radical Pedagogy* 5(2). http://radicalpedagogy.icaap.org/content/issue5_2/03_rees.html, accessed November 6, 2007.

Ross, E. W., ed. 1994. *Reflective practice in social studies, NCSS bulletin 88.* Washington, DC: National Council for the Social Studies.

Singer, A. 1995. "Challenging gender bias through a transformative high school social studies curriculum," *Theory and Research in Social Education* 23(3): 234–59.

Tredennick, H., trans. 1980. *The last days of Socrates.* New York: Penguin, p. 23.

Wiggins, G. 1992. "Creating tests worth taking," *Educational Leadership* 49(8): 26–32.

Wiggins, G. 1993. "Assessment to improve performance, not just monitor it: Assessment reform in social sciences," *Social Science Record* 30(2): 5–10.

Wiggins, G. and McTighe, J. 2005. *Understanding by design.* Alexandria, VA: ASCD.

Wolf, D., LeMahieu, P. and Eresh, J. 1992. "Good measure: Assessment as a tool for educational reform," *Educational Leadership* 49(8): 8–13.

13. What Resources Exist for Social Studies Classrooms and Teachers?

Overview

- Promote ongoing professional development
- Discuss the planning of trips
- Discuss technology in the classroom
- Examine issues related to copying materials for the classroom
- Locate sources for teaching materials, speakers, etc.

Key Concepts

Professional Development, Trips, Videos, Movies, Documentaries, Fair Use, Computers, internet, E-mail, Resources

Questions

- How can you Develop Your Skills as a Social Studies Teacher?
- How Useful are Computers in Social Studies Classrooms?
- How do You Plan Field Trips?
- Should I Show my Class a Movie?
- What can I Copy for my Class?
- Who Provides Resources for Social Studies Teachers?

All websites cited in this chapter were last accessed October 12, 2007.

HOW CAN YOU DEVELOP YOUR SKILLS AS A SOCIAL STUDIES TEACHER?

After ten years of high school teaching, I had enough of what was euphemistically called "staff development." Periodically, we would be required to sit in the library or auditorium, sometimes as a social studies department, and sometimes as a full faculty, where we were harangued about the latest fail-safe directive from the central administration or miracle solution to the problems of urban education being promulgated by edu-businesses, university consultants, or politicians. To maintain my sanity, I sat in the back of the room and tried to unobtrusively do paperwork. At one point, Barry Brody, my department chairperson at Franklin K. Lane High School, made a suggestion that ultimately changed my career path. I had been doing a number of interesting projects in my classes and he suggested that I could make presentations about them to the social studies department at staff development workshops. Because of my own dread about being lectured to, I made the workshops as interactive and hands-on as possible, and they were generally well received.

Barry also encouraged me to present the workshops at the local chapter of the National Council for the Social Studies (NCSS) and to write about them for social studies magazines. He later recommended me as a curriculum writer for a New York City effort to develop a package of lessons plans and activity sheets for teaching United States history with a multicultural focus in middle schools. These new activities not only got me out of attending the regular staff development meetings—I was given the rest of the time to prepare workshops—but they helped me organize my ideas about teaching social studies and history and reflect on my teaching practice in general. Whatever other people got out of the workshops, they became my own hands-on learning experience.

Staff and professional development remains a hit or miss proposition. To paraphrase a children's nursery rhyme, when they are good, they can be very, very, good, but when they are bad, they are horrid. If you have choices about what you can attend and where you can be involved, a good place to start is by joining your local, regional, or state chapter of the NCSS, which probably has an annual conference and offers other workshops during the year. NCSS local and national publications, which are distributed to members, also provide a range of useful classroom ideas. You can join the national organization and find out about affiliates at: http://socialstudies.org. At conferences, I look for workshops offered by classroom teachers and by authors whose ideas have interested me. I also try to present a workshop because I find it attracts teachers who have interests in common with mine. I avoid presentations by publishers representatives who are basically trying to sell their product, and avoid lectures unless there will be audience participation at some point. I suffer from poor impulse control and I have been known to interrupt speakers who make provocative points but have not left enough time for discussion.

In recent years, federal Teaching American History grants have funded high quality professional development collaborations between school districts and university, community, and museum partners. These usually involve presentations by historians, and interactive workshops lead by teacher educators. They sometimes provide help and funding for teachers developing their own curriculum projects and classroom support. Information on participating in an existing program or for applying for a grant for your school district is available at: http://www.ed.gov/programs/teachinghistory/.

Organizations that provide low cost, free, or even subsidized workshops and programs that focus on history include the Organization of American Historians (http://www.oah.org), the American Historical Association (http://www.historians.org), and the Gilder Lehrman Institute of American History (http://www.gilderlehrman.org). Regional branches of the Federal Reserve Bank (http://www.ny.frb.org) sponsor workshops for economics teachers. Information about the Fulbright Teacher and Administrator Exchange Program, which involves one-on-one exchanges of administrators and teachers from K-12 schools with more than thirty countries, is available at http://www.fulbrightexchanges.org/.

There are groups that offer workshops for social studies teachers that you need to be careful of because of their agendas. For example, the National Council for History Education (see http://www.nche.org), which runs an annual conference for teachers, is committed to replacing social studies in the secondary school curriculum with a more limited focus on history.

I find some groups are highly ideological and care more about indoctrination than education. For example, the Foundation for Teaching Economics (http://www.fte.org) requested that Hofstra University co-sponsor workshops for economics teachers, including one called "Is Capitalism Good for the Poor?" but refused to allow members of our staff or of the Hofstra New Teachers Network to participate as presenters. We declined their offer.

Independent travel can also be viewed as professional development and its costs are tax deductible if you document its classroom application. Over the years I have visited and prepared slide presentations (now Power-Points) on the Machu Picchu ruins in the Peruvian Andes, the palace of Versailles outside of Paris, Chichen Itzu and other Mayan pyramids, Cuba, ancient Roman and Greek sites, and Islamic Spain (Seville, Cordoba, and Grenada). I have also participated in two historical restoration projects that I highly recommend. La Sabranenque is a program in southern France for rebuilding castles and medieval towns using traditional materials and techniques (see http://www.sabranenque.com). The Crow Canyon Archaeological Center (see http://www.crowcanyon.org) operates an archeological dig and school exploring fourteenth-century Anasazi villages near Mesa Verde National Park in Colorado.

Figure 13.1 An Anasazi village at Mesa Verde National Park.

Teaching Activity: Read and Read Some More
(You Have 30 Years Until You Retire!)

During the last few years I have developed two interdisciplinary content-based courses for social studies teachers in response to requests from both pre-service and working teachers.

"Cultural Diversity and Global Perspectives" explores different ideas about cultural diversity, multiculturalism, and globalism through an examination of insights provided by different social studies disciplines and what I call "indigenous literature," literature that was written by people who are part of the cultural groups they are describing. The entire class reads *Cows, Pigs, Wars, and Witches* by Marvin Harris (New York: Random House, 1974) and *Guns, Germs, and Steel* by Jared Diamond (New York: Norton, 1997), and we discuss them during the first few sessions to evaluate our own ideas and establish shared reference points. During the concluding class meetings, students use the insights gained from these books and our discussions to report on a work of "indigenous literature" and their understandings about the culture of the group. The works of "indigenous literature" include the following:

Chinua Achebe (Nigeria). 1994. *Things Fall Apart*. New York: Anchor.
Monica Ali (Bangladesh). 2003. *Brick Lane*. New York: Simon & Schuster.
Julia Alvarez (Dominican Republic). 1995. *In the Time of the Butterflies*. New York: New American Library/Plume.
Andre Brink (South Africa). 2006. *A Dry White Season*. New York: HarperCollins.
Elisabeth Burgos-Debray (Guatemala). 1984. *I, Rigobertu Menchu*. New York: Verso.
Patrick Chamoiseau (Martinique). 1997. *School Days*. Lincoln, Nebraska: University of Nebraska Press.

Edwidge Danticat (Haiti). 1999. *The Farming of Bones.* New York: Penguin.
Khaled Hosseini (Afghanistan). 2005. *The Kite Runner.* New York: Riverhead Books.
Yu Hua (China). 2004. *Chronicle of a Blood Merchant.* New York: Anchor.
Duong Thu Huong (Vietnam). 2002. *Paradise of Blind.* New York: HarperCollins.
Witi Ihimaera (New Zealand). 2003. *The Whale Rider.* New York: Harcourt.
Bette Bao Lord (China). 1996. *The Middle Heart.* New York: Random House.
Frank McCourt (Ireland). 2000. *Angela's Ashes.* New York: Simon & Schuster.
Rohinton Mistry (India). 2002. *A Fine Balance.* New York: Knopf.
Boris Pasternak (Russia). 1997. *Dr. Zhivago.* New York: Pantheon.
V.S. Naipaul (British Colonialism). 1997. *A Bend in the River.* New York: Modern Library.
Orhan Pamuk (Turkey). 2005. *Snow.* New York: Vintage.
Arundhati Roy (India). 1998. *God of Small Things.* New York: HarperCollins.
Mongane Wally Serote (South Africa). 1981. *To Every Birth Its Blood.* New York: Raven Press.
Ngugi wa Thiong'o (Kenya). 1994. *Matigari.* Lawrenceville, NJ: Africa World Press.
Emile Zola (France). 1970. *Germinal.* New York: New American Library.

"Race, Ethnicity, and Class in United States: Past and Present" explores the political and economic ramifications of race, ethnic, and class identity and divisions on individuals, groups, and the overall society. In *One Drop of Blood: the American Misadventure of Race*, Scott L. Malcomson (New York: Farrar Straus Giroux, 2000) asks why a nation supposedly "dedicated to freedom and universal ideals produces, through its obsession with race, an unhappily divided people." This class examines the work of a number of social scientists, historians, and commentators in an effort to answer this question. Seminar participants bring their own experiences and a discussion of local conditions to the table in an effort to understand race, ethnic, and class relations in the United States in the past and present. The entire class reads Ronald Takaki, *A Different Mirror* (San Francisco, CA: Back Bay Books, 1994) and Studs Terkel, *Race: How Blacks and Whites Think and Feel About the American Obsession* (New York: The New Press, 2005). Individuals read and report to class on a number of different books from different disciplines. They include the following:

Science:
Stephen Gould. 1996. *The Mismeasure of Man.* New York: Norton.
Joseph Graves. 2001. *The Emperor's New Clothes.* New Brunswick, NJ: Rutgers University Press.

History:
Eric Foner. 2005. *Forever Free, The Story of Emancipation and Reconstruction.* New York: Knopf.
Nancy Foner. 2000. *From Ellis Island to JFK.* New Haven, CT: Yale University Press.
George Fredrickson. 2002. *Racism: A Short History.* Princeton, NJ: Princeton University Press.
Harvard Sitkoff. 1981. *The Struggle for Black Equality.* New York: Hill and Wang.
C. Vann Woodward. 2001. *The Strange Career of Jim Crow.* New York: Oxford University Press.

Personal Accounts:
Claude Brown. 1999. *Manchild in the Promised Land.* New York: Touchstone.
Alex Haley, ed. 1999. *The Autobiography of Malcolm X.* New York: Ballantine Books.
Kay Mills. 1994. *This Little Light of Mine, the life of Fannie Lou Hammer.* New York: New American Library/Plume.
Anne Moody. 1992. *Coming of Age in Mississippi.* New York: Random House.

Commentaries:
Martin Luther King, Jr. 1989. *Where Do We Go From Here?* Boston, MA: Beacon Press.
Cornell West. 2001. *Race Matters.* Boston, MA: Beacon Press.

Analysis:
Andrew Hacker. 2003. *Two Nations, Black and White, Separate, Hostile, Unequal.* New York: Simon & Schuster.
Ira Katznelson, I. 2005. *When Affirmative Action was White: An Untold History of Racial Inequality in Twentieth-Century America.* New York: Norton.
Glenn Loury. 2002. *The Anatomy of Racial Inequality.* Boston, MA: Harvard University Press.
Manning Marable. 2000. *How Capitalism Underdeveloped Black America.* London: Pluto Press.

The New York Times. 2005. *Class Matters.* New York: Times Books.

Stephen Steinberg. 2001. *The Ethnic Myth: Race, Ethnicity, and Class in America.* Boston, MA: Beacon Press.

William J. Wilson. 1987. *The Truly Disadvantaged.* Chicago, IL: University of Chicago Press.

Literature:

Zora Neale Hurston. 2000. *Their Eyes Where Watching God.* New York: HarperCollins.

Toni Morrison. 1998. *Beloved.* New York: Columbia University Press.

Walter Mosley. 1998. *Always Outnumbered, Always Outgunned.* New York: Norton.

Alice Walker. 2003. *The Color Purple.* New York: Harcourt.

Richard Wright. 1998. *Native Son.* New York: HarperCollins.

Add your voice to the discussion:

1. Do you think reading works of fiction is useful for social studies teachers? Explain.
2. What works of fiction would you recommend to other teachers? Why?
3. What history and social science books would you recommend to other teachers? Why?

HOW USEFUL ARE COMPUTERS IN SOCIAL STUDIES CLASSROOMS?

In the early 1990s, when I began working on the first edition of *Social Studies for Secondary Schools*, I turned to James Screven, Daniel Bachman, and Darren Luskoff of the New Teachers Network to help me with this section. As social studies teachers, they were technology pioneers and I really had not had much experience using computers in the classroom, for research, designing lessons, or desktop publishing.

During the last 15 years everything has changed. There was no internet to speak of when I started and e-mail was clumsy to use. Few people reading the third edition of this book are computer novices and in all probability much of what is discussed here will soon be outdated. This section is only intended as a starting point. I strongly recommend keeping up with new developments in technology for the social studies through membership in organizations like the National Council for the Social Studies (see http://www.socialstudies. org), which includes a subscription to its magazine, *Social Education.* In 2007, *Social Education* (71(3)) published a theme issue on "Going Digital in the Social Studies" and the NCSS distributed a special bulletin, *Digital Age, Technology-Based K-12 Lesson Plans for Social Studies* (Bennett and Berson 2007). Look for more updates from them in the near future.

Computers are useful in the social studies classroom, but teachers need to be cautious. *Jibjab* has some very funny and pointed videos, including one, Big Box Mart (http://www. jibjab.com/originals/big_box_mart) that is highly critical of Wal-Mart. However, a lot of material on the site is inappropriate for classroom use. *YouTube* has Universal Newsreels that were originally prepared to show to movie audiences. They offer historical footage and give insight into popular culture from other time periods. However, many *YouTube* videos have been altered and give students a distorted view of the past.

1. Information Processing

Word processing, database, desktop publishing, and spreadsheet programs are used for recording and organizing information, and for writing, editing, and printing reports. Using a word processing program, student researchers can record data in prepared organizers and write reports using a set format. They can also import scanned pictures and images (maps, cartoons, photographs, etc.) downloaded from the web. With a database program, students can compile a list of current events topics from the newspaper, enter a synopsis of each article, and make information accessible through keyword searches. Desktop publishing programs facilitate the production of student magazines. Popular desktop publisher programs include QuarkXPress, Adobe InDesign, Scribus, Microsoft Publisher, and Apple Pages.

2. Discovery/Reference

Students find information and sources for information. Discovery programs are designed to engage student interest in subjects that are often taught through rote memorization. There are numerous comprehensive multimedia resources available online including Encarta (http://encarta.msn.com), the CIA-sponsored World Factbook (http://www. odci.gov/cia/publications/factbook) and the Information Please Almanac (http://www. infoplease.com). One of my favorites is Sparta-cus Educational (http:// www.spartacus. schoolnet.co.uk) that is produced for British schools. There has been major controversy about student use of Wikipedia, both because there are questions about its reliability and because students download reports and hand them in as their own work (What a surprise!). Teachers need to stress that a visit to "Wiki" should be the beginning of student research, rather than the end (Cohen 2007). Historical documents and government-sponsored research reports are frequently available at museum or government web sites (e.g., Library of Congress). Using the internet, a student can locate, transfer, and work with the latest decision by the US Supreme Court or a recent Presidential speech. A number of news services are also available on the internet, including: *NewsLink* (http://www.newslink.org), with links to newspapers all over the United States and the world, the *British Broadcasting Company* (http://www.bbcnc.org.uk), and *The New York Times* (http://www.nytimes. com). Road maps and travel guides are available at a number of websites. They include Mapquest (http://www.mapquest.com) and Yahoo Maps (http://maps.yahoo.com/).

3. Communication/Participation

Using the internet, e-mail, chat rooms, and the web, students can discuss and share ideas and information as part of a worldwide intellectual community. A simple web design program allows a class to create its own web site to disseminate information. Students can petition the president using either an e-mail address or the White House website (President@white-house.gov or http://www.whitehouse.gov). Access to the internet requires a modem, a phone or cable line, and a connection through a public (e.g., university) or commercial service provider. Some commercial providers offer forums designed to facilitate conversations between people who share common interests. There are also many special interest groups, or ListServs, that will interest teachers. They focus on specific areas in history and the social sciences, and on teaching at different levels.

H-serv lists are described at (http://h-net.org/lists/).

4. Cooperation

The ability to merge files, transport disks, and send information electronically to different sites increases the possibility of students working together. A student can take a portable memory device home, pop it into a computer, and work on a project begun by someone else in school or everyone in the group can access information through e-mail or at a website.

5. Webquests and Simulations

Commercial simulation programs, such as Sim City and Sim Isle (http://simcity.htmlplanet. com) require students to balance human needs with ecological concerns. *Chronic Logic* offers a highly recommended simulation game, Pontifex, (http://www.chroniclogic.com), where students design and test bridges. San Diego State University (http://webquest.org/search/index.php) supports a webquest site with links to hundreds of social studies related problem-solving adventures for middle school and high school students. It also provides a program, *QuestGarden*, and space where teachers can design and store their own webquests. It charges a minimal registration fee for this service. Other sites where teachers and create and store webquests include *Filamentality* (http://www.kn.pacbell.com/wired/fil/) and *Teacher-Web* (http://teacherweb.com/TWQuest.htm). The Nebraska Schools Partnership for Middle School Students houses a number of useful teacher created webquests at its website (http://webquests.lps.org/).

6. Virtual Tours

Museums and historical restoration sites make it possible for students to "tour" their facilities online. Some of my favorites include the British Museum in London (http://www.thebritish museum.ac.uk/explore/introduction.aspx), the American Museum of Natural History in new York (http://www.amnh.org), the Metropolitan Museum of Art in New York City (http://www.metmuseum.org), the National Museum of American history in Washington, D.C. (http://americanhistory.si.edu/), the Louvre in Paris (http://www.louvre.fr/llv/commun/home. jsp?bmLocale=en), the United States Holocaust Memorial (http://www.ushmm.org), and

Colonial Williamsburg (http://www.history.org). Because of centuries of colonialism and imperialism, these museums have better artifacts from around the world than do the national museums of other countries.

7. Review/Practice

Individual students, working at their own pace, can review what they have learned and practice skills. Specific programs are designed to prepare students for standardized tests. Review programs also provide teachers with prepared testing materials that are geared to the level that students are expected to achieve.

8. Teacher and School Sites

Finding appropriate material on the internet is a problem. In September 2007, a search using the keyword social studies on Google (my preferred search engine) listed over 300-million websites compared to about 60,000 sites in 2002. New sites are constantly being developed and older ones are abandoned. Clearly there are too many places to just drop in and visit. Searches must be limited and directed. Many internet problems are avoided when teachers, social studies departments, or school create their own websites with links students can use as portals to the internet and guides for research.

9. Emerging Web-based Technologies

Two of my colleagues at Hofstra University, Roberto Joseph and Marlene Munn-Joseph (2008), are strong advocates of new web-based technologies that support the development of higher order thinking skills. *Blogs* allow a student to create an online portfolio where teachers and classmates can comment on their work. Social studies teachers can also create their own classroom blogs. For help getting started, they recommend Edublogs (http://edublogs.org/) and Wordpress (http://drrob.wordpress.com/). *Wikis* are websites that promote collaborative work. They allow students, without the use of special tools or skills, to write and edit online documents. For help using wikis and for instructional ideas, visit Peanut Butter Wiki (http://pbwiki.com), Education World (http://www.education-world.com/a_tech/sites/sites079.shtml), and Wiki in a K-12 Classroom (http://wik.ed.uiuc.edu/index.php/Wiki_in_a_K-12_classroom).

Another collaborative tool are *Social Bookmarking* sites that allow students to access each other's bookmarks over the internet. One of the most popular social bookmarking websites is 'Del.icio.us' (http://del.icio.us/). Using *RSS*, students can receive current events updates from a number of news sources. Popular RSS readers include Bloglines (http://www.bloglines.com) and Google Reader (http://reader.google.com). *YouTube* allows students to display their own educational videos.

10. New Problems

Students always seem to be at least one step ahead of teachers, and when it comes to the latest technology, the gap is probably wider. Downloading information and word processing have made copying reports easier. Some schools are investing in sophisticated search engines that help teachers uncover web-based plagiarism. Another solution, one that I prefer, is to have students hand in outlines, notes and rough drafts of their work so that the process is an important part of their learning. A teacher has the right to reject finished student work when they have not submitted the preliminary assignments.

As I wrote in the essay on technology-based projects, the use of computers in the social studies classroom is not a strong part of my approach to teaching and I remain skeptical about its widespread use. However, I do agree with my colleagues at Hofstra University, such as Blidi Stemn who is a math educator, that in a world where being comfortable using computers is a minimum requirement for a college education and middle-class employment, all students, but especially minority youth, must have considerable practice working with them. Blidi is concerned with what he calls the "digital divide," where students, especially students from poorer families and minority groups, who are least likely to have access to computers at home, attend schools with the worst computer facilities.

In 2007, Lauren Borruso (NTN), a second-year middle school social studies teacher from a middle-class suburban school district, was my teaching assistant in a class for pre-service teachers. I asked Lauren, who is generally a strong supporter of the use of technology in the classroom, about her experiences.

As a teacher, Lauren uses computers continuously for research, lesson design, and to prepare visual and audio classroom aids. These include photographs that provide students with "an idea of what the people we study look like" and allows them to "visualize different historic events and periods" and primary source document packages that she edits to make them appropriate for 7th and 8th graders. She frequently incorporates photographs into lessons using PowerPoint slides and will include video clips that allow students to hear speeches delivered in their original setting while they read them.

Lauren feels fortunate to work in a school with two online computers per classroom for the use of teachers and students. But she has had many problems using them effectively. Because of limited availability, she has been unable to figure out a way for students to use the internet in the classroom during class time. She can schedule classes in the library or computer lab but this must be done in advance and interferes with the kind of spontaneity you hope to generate during lessons. Her students have computers at home with high-speed internet access so she is able to give them research assignments for homework. This is vital because the school district deploys what she describes as an "extreme web filter" making it difficult to do research in the library or computer lab because many useful sites are blocked.

Working with Lauren Borruso and other members of the New Teachers Network, I have put together a series of internet sites that beginning teachers should find useful. They are organized into teaching sites for lesson planning and other support services, sites specific to teaching social studies, general reference sites such as online encyclopedias, content area sites useful for teachers and possibly students, and content area sites specifically intended for students, and current issues. Sites are listed alphabetically within each category.

Members of the New Teachers Network who recommended websites include: Lauren Borruso, Kimberly Cahill, Laura Carnevale, Tanya DiMambro, Kelly Dooley, Jaqueline Ford, Alison Kelly, Nazia Khan, Jessica Knobler, Meryl Landau, Patty Mangiocco, Heather Maselli, April McCarthy, Kara McEneney, Suzie Mellen, Michael Mullervy, Katharine Murawski, Billie Phillips, Scott Raulsome, Krystle Rogala, Ayesha Sheth, and Eric Sorenson.

Teaching sites

4teachers.org (http://www.4teachers.org). Helps teachers use technology in their classrooms. It includes support for creating rubrics, quizzes, and organizing heterogeneous classrooms.

Education World (http://www.education-world.com). This site provides help in lesson planning, suggestions for professional development, support for technological integration, and discussion of current school issues. It offers special lessons and resources on mandated topics such as Constitution Day and major themes such as teaching tolerance.

Evaluating Web Pages (http://www.ithaca.edu/library/training/think.html) or (http://www.lib.berkeley.edu/TeachingLib/Guides/internet/Evaluate.html). Teaches students how to evaluate websites according to a variety of criteria. The Ithaca College site is especially useful for teaching younger students.

Lesson Plans (http://www.lessonplanspage.com). This site provides a useful lesson plan template and hundreds of sample lesson plans on a wide variety of topics.

Prentice Hall (www.phschool.com). An assortment of material that supports Prentice Hall textbooks.

Research papers (owl.english.purdue.edu/owl/). A free online writing lab that offers tips on researching and writing papers.

School Notes (http://www.schoolnotes.com). A free site that allows teachers to create their own websites.

Social studies and history sites

ABC-CLIO (http://socialstudies.abc-clio.com). This site has valuable resources and lessons, but access is restricted.

Best of History Websites (http://www.besthistorysites.net). An award-winning portal that contains annotated links to over one thousand history web sites, lesson plans, teacher guides, history activities, games, and quizzes.

Daryl Cagle's Professional Cartoonists index (http://cagle.com). A treasury of contemporary political cartoons.

Edusolution.com (http://www.edusolution.com). A teacher created site with extensive links.

Free Federal Resources for Educational

Excellence (http://www.free.ed.gov). Lessons and documents.

History Channel (http://www.historychannel.com). Video Gallery, study guides, "This Day in History", timelines, etc.

History Matters (http://historymatters.gmu.edu). This site has all the material for teaching an Advanced Placement level US history class.

History Teacher (http://historyteacher.net). Curriculum, lessons, and documents, especially useful for advanced placement classes.

Hyperhistory Online (http://www.hyperhistory.com/online_n2/History_n2/a.html). Documents, maps, etc. organized chronologically and topically.

Mr. Dowling (http://mrdowling.com). Mike Dowling is a social studies teacher from Florida. This is probably the most extensive teacher created and maintained web site in the world.

National Archives (http://www.archives.gov). Documentary-based lessons in line with national history standards.

National Council for the Social Studies (www.socialstudies.org). The website of the national social studies organization.

New York Times (http://www.nytimes.com/learning/teachers/lessons/socialstudies.html). Includes historical and current items and ideas for teaching.

PBS Teachers (http://www.pbs.org/teachers/socialstudies/). Teaching ideas and materials geared to PBS broadcasts organized by grade and topic.

PBS Thirteen (http://thirteen.org/edonline/wideangle). Multimedia lessons for global history.

Social Studies Sources from the University of Indiana (http://education.indiana.edu/~socialst/). Extensive links.

Yale-New Have Teachers Institute (http://www.yale.edu/ynhti/curriculum/). Teaching ideas and materials crated out of a partnership between Yale University and the New Haven, Connecticut public school system.

Reference sites and online encyclopedias

Answers (http://www.answers.com). Allows students to search by asking a question.

Corbis (http://www.corbis.com). An extensive private photograph library that charge for reproduction rights.

Encarta Online (http://encarta.msn.com).

Encyclomedia (http://encyclomedia.com). A video encyclopedia.

Encyclopedia Britannica (http://www.britannica.com).

Idea Finder (http://www.ideafinder.com/history/). An online encyclopedia that focuses on inventions and inventors.

Library Thinkquest (http://library.thinkquest.org).

Spartacus (http://www.spartacus.schoolnet.co.uk). My personal favorite.

Wikipedia (htttp://wikipedia.org).

Worldbook Online (http://www.worldbookonline.com). Some materials require subscriptions.

Content sites primarily for teachers

Authentic History Center (http://www.authentichistory.com). Includes artifacts and sounds from American popular culture.

Court TV (http://www.courttv.com/trials/famous/). Transcripts from recent celebrity trials.

Ehistory (www.ehistory.osu.edu). An extensive collection of documents, maps and media resources hosted by the History Department at Ohio State University.

Environmental Protection Administration (http://www.epa.gov/highschool/). Environmental concerns.

Eyewitness to History (http://www.eyewitnesstohistory.com). First-hand accounts of historical events.

Gilder Lehrman Institute for American History (http://GilderLehrman.org) and (http://HistoryNow.org). Documents from United States with a special focus on slavery.

Harper Magazine (http://www.harpweek.com). Reprints of articles from the era of slavery. Civil war, and Reconstruction.

Internet Global History Sourcebook (http://www.fordham.edu/halsall/global/globalsbook.html). The internet's best English language source for primary source documents.

Landmark Supreme Court Cases (landmarkcases.org). Documents and lesson ideas with material at different reading levels.

Library of Congress, American Memory (http://memory.loc.gov/ammem/). Highlights documents from the Library of Congress collections including photographs.

New Deal Network (http://www.newdeal.feri.org). Links, lessons, and documents about the New Deal. Extensive photograph collection useful for teaching local history.

New York Times Historical (http://www.nytimes.com). Searchable database for articles since 1851. Uploading of articles requires a modest fee.

Protest Movements in US History (http://www3.niu.edu/~td0raf1/history498/index.htm). A thematic collection of primary source documents on protest movements maintained by a professor at Northern Illinois University.

TerraServer USA (http://www.terraserverusa.com). Maps and demographic and topographical information.

US Census Bureau (http://www.census.gov). Both recent and historical census data, especially useful for local studies.

US History (http://www.ushistory.org). Focus on the American Revolution. Created by Independence Hall in Philadelphia.

World Factbook (http://www.cia.gov/cia/publications/factbook/). Current information from the US Central Intelligence Agency organized by country.

World History (http://worldhistorymatters.org). World history sources and themes.

Student-friendly content sites

Bill of Rights Institute (http:// http://www.billofrightsinstitute.org/). Has materials for teachers, but is especially useful for student research.

Kidipede—History for Kids (http://historyforkids.org). Organized chronologically and by region.

History Learning (http://historylearningsite.co.uk). Excellent resource from Great Britain that is easily navigated by students.

History Place (http://www.historyplace.com). Timelines of American history.

National Geographic (http://nationalgeographic.com). Rich in visuals.

PBS Online (http://www.pbs.org/history/) and PBS Kids (http://pbskids.org).

United Nations (http://www.un.org/Pubs/CyberSchoolBus/). Helps students study about conditions for children around the world.

United States Congress (http://www.congressforkids.net). Learn about the United States government.

Current issues

Amnesty International (http://www.amnesty.org). An organization that works to protect human rights around the globe. Provides research material and promotes activism.

BBC (http://www.bbc.co.uk). News and commentary from the British Public Broadcast system.

CNN (http://www.cnn.com). Resources from the American cable news network.

Common Dreams (http://www.commondreams.org). An online magazine with news commentary from a progressive perspective.

Counterpunch (http://www.counterpunch.com/). An online magazine with news commentary from a progressive perspective.

Heritage Foundation (http://www.heritage.org/). News commentary from a conservative perspective.

Prevent Genocide International (http://www.preventgenocide.org). Provides research material and promotes activism.

Teachable Moment (http://www.teachablemoment.org). A project of the Morningside Center for Teaching Social Responsibility. A large selection of lesson plans and documents for teaching about current issues.

United Nations International Children's Emergency Fund (http://www.unicef.org). Provides research material and promotes activism.

Teaching Activity: Computers in the Social Studies Classroom

Add your voice to the discussion:

In your opinion, will computer resources revolutionize the study of history and the social sciences, or will they end up being a temporary fad that gradually fades into disuse? Explain the reasons for your answer.

Try it yourself:

Browse the Web. Locate and list social studies-related sites you think will interest social studies teachers and students.

Join the conversation:

Sign up for a social studies listserv.

HOW DO YOU PLAN FIELD TRIPS?

For me, field trips are more than an add-on. Field trips provide students with a hands-on environment that supports content and conceptual learning taking place in the classroom. They are crucial ways for students to "experience" the past.

The following suggestions by Christina Agosti-Dircks, Jeannette Balantic, Laura Pearson, and Henry Dircks of the New Teachers Network are based on their experiences organizing field trips for middle and high school social studies classes to museums, government offices, courts, historical restoration sites, public gardens, and cultural centers. Christina, Jeannette, Laura, and Henry advise that cooperative learning projects are an excellent way to follow up on what students learn during a trip. For example, student teams can edit a video or slide program, write a play, design their own museum exhibit, create a photograph display or Website, or re-create crafts or cultural activities.

- Field trips should be part of overall unit planning and relevant to the subject matter classes will be studying at the time of the trip.
- Discuss possible trips with students in advance so they can participate in making decisions and plans.
- Organize trips that are appropriate to the students' academic and maturity levels. Museums often have naked statues. Alert students in advance and allow any who may be uncomfortable to by-pass these exhibits.
- Contact sites in advance. Allow sufficient time for them to send curriculum or tour materials for pre-trip discussions.
- Ask about hours and prices, recommendations on chaperones, targeted grade level of exhibits, number of students they can accommodate, type of the exhibits (paintings, interactive, etc.), special exhibition dates, dining facilities, activities and tours, and available dates. If it is an overnight trip, ask about group accommodations and rates. Make tentative reservations.
- Receive permission from the school administration and department. Arrange for students to get parental permission to participate. Arrange transportation. For an overnight trip, arrange for accommodations.
- If possible, organize a pre-trip guided tour for teachers, chaperones, and student team leaders. Assess the appropriateness of the exhibits. Decide on a theme or focus, and prepare activities (worksheets, questions, or scavenger hunts) for the full-class visit.
- Prepare a preliminary instruction guide for students. Explain the purpose of the trip, transportation and entrance fees, the proposed trip schedule, meeting times and places, and materials they need to bring (bagged lunch, pen, notebook, cameras, etc.). Discuss appropriate behavior on the trip. Ask about parents who might be available to chaperone.
- Confirm all arrangements.
- Prepare lessons to discuss the subject of the trip prior to going and as a follow-up.
- Prepare a trip schedule that includes arrival and departure times, bathroom stops, meals, and a visit to the gift shop.
- On the day of the trip, review goals and assignments with students, and discuss appropriate behavior and procedures for the trip. Assign students to groups and chaperones. Remember to take head counts at the beginning of the trip and throughout the day.
- Try to enjoy the trip with your students.

SHOULD I SHOW MY CLASS A MOVIE?

Selecting a movie to show your class involves a number of considerations. For example, Michael Ferrarese (NTN) originally planned to show segments from the French documentary, *Night and Fog* (1955), to his global history classes as part of a lesson on personal responsibility and the European Holocaust. The narration of the film is in French and the screen is dark and unadorned. As a result, a number of students in his first class found it difficult to follow what was happening on screen. For his other classes, Michael decided to substitute a small segment from the Hollywood produced movie *Judgment at Nuremberg* (1961). In the scene he showed his classes, an actor, playing the prosecutor at the trial, provides an English narration of some of the same documentary footage. In addition, there are maps that show exactly where the concentration camps are located. Michael found that these lessons were much more successful.

Before you show a movie or part of a movie in class, a teacher needs to ask the following questions:

- Is the movie, or at least the section you want to show, historically accurate?
- Will students be able to understand it?
- Are its biases clear, or at least accessible for examination?
- Does it present important social studies concepts?
- How will you integrate the movie into class discussion?
- What questions will I ask?
- Is it entertaining enough to hold the attention of your students?
- How will they react to violence, racism, and human sexuality?
- How much time will it take to watch?
- How will students demonstrate what they learned from the movie?
- Given other options for instruction, is showing the movie educationally justified?

Even the most interesting documentaries and historical movies have problems that social studies teachers need to consider. Documentaries often have limited interest, whereas fictional accounts frequently sacrifice accuracy for dramatic considerations. Movies like *JFK* (directed by Oliver Stone 1991), *Mississippi Burning* (directed by Alan Parker 1988), and *Robin Hood: Prince of Thieves* (directed by Kevin Costner 1991) have been widely accused of distorting the past; even an otherwise excellent documentary, *The Liberators: Fighting on Two Fronts* (PBS 1992), was flawed by historical inaccuracies.

Even when accuracy is not an issue, there can be other problems. For example, story lines in a number of movies center on a mainstream character, rather than on a member of the culturally marginalized social group it is supposed to portray. *Dances with Wolves* (1990) tells the story of a Civil War veteran living among Native American people. *Glory* (1989) is the story of a White army officer who commands an African-American Civil War unit. In *Cry Freedom* (1987) and *Gandhi* (1982), the narrators are White newspaper reporters. In *Schindler's List* (1993), the central character is a Nazi industrialist. *Missing* (1982) is about an American searching for his son in Chile after the overthrow of the Allende government.

Movies can also offer a legitimate, but narrow, ideological perspective on historical figures or events. Examples include *Malcolm X* (directed by Spike Lee 1992); *Patton* (1970);

Nixon (directed by Oliver Stone 1995); *Exodus* (1960); and *Braveheart* (directed by Mel Gibson 1995). Sometimes even accurate portrayals contribute to faulty generalizations by students (e.g., based on a viewing of *Glory*, students have concluded that Union troops during the Civil War were overwhelmingly African-American.)

Many teachers (especially male teachers) like to show segments from war movies. In my experience, few are very good for classroom use and some popular movies are very bad. Many are celebrations of machismo or patriotism and glorify death and destruction. The portrayal of villainous "enemies" tends to be simplistic and their elimination by whatever means available is always justified. The movie *Black Hawk Down* (2001), which claims to be about American military intervention in post-Cold War Somalia, has other not so subtle messages. Elvis Mitchell, who reviewed the film for *The New York Times*, charged that it "converts the Somalis into a pack of snarling dark-skinned beasts—intended or not, it reeks of glumly staged racism" (Mitchell 2001). Brendan Sexton, an actor who appeared as a US soldier in the movie, later denounced it at an anti-war forum. According to Sexton, the Somalis were "portrayed as if they don't know what's going on, as if they're trying to kill the Americans because they—like all other "evildoers"—will do anything to bite the hand that feeds them . . . In fact, many were upset because the US military presence propped up people tied to the old, corrupt Barre regime." Unfortunately, students would never know about this aspect of the US role in Somalia by watching the movie (Sexton 2002).

Even when it is relatively accurate, a movie's point of view may be subtly biased. For example, a university-based historian, William Leuchtenburg (Carnes 1996), considered *All the President's Men* (1976) one of his favorite movies, and showed it in his classes on recent US history. After repeated viewings, he uncovered a subliminal message in the movie. Scenes from government offices were always poorly lighted, whereas scenes of the *Washington Post* office were well lit. Leuchtenburg believes that the lighting was designed to suggest that the Nixon White House was evil and that the *Washington Post* newsroom represented truth.

I usually select a short segment from a movie or documentary (5–15 minutes) that illustrates a particular point, and I use it instead of a document as the basis for class discussion. But as with a document, I give students specific questions to consider or write about. A typical assignment includes:

- Describe the events (characters, settings) in the movie.
- What point of view about the event is expressed in the movie?

- In your opinion, does this movie (documentary) provide an accurate portrayal of this period (topic)?

Cynthia Vitere, a high school social studies teacher, uses a set of general questions to help her students compare historical movies. She also has specific questions geared to each film. Below are questions for viewing the movie *Spartacus* (1960).

General Questions to Consider While Viewing Historical Movies:
- What are the historical themes that are developed by the film?
- Does the film's portrayal adhere to the historiography of the era?
- How does the filmmaker use light and color, or its absence, to enhance the story?
- How does the filmmaker use the camera to express action in a contemporary or historically appropriate manner?
- How is music used to enhance or detract from the narrative?
- Is the casting of actors appropriate: age, race, and ethnicity?
- Does the film develop the characters fully?
- Does the film rely on simple dichotomies, or does it express the full range of character and story development?
- What visual symbols and metaphors does the film utilize?
- How does the film reflect the culture, politics, and economics of the era it portrays?
- How does the film reflect the culture, politics, and economics of the era in which it was produced?

Questions to Consider While Viewing Spartacus:
- How does Spartacus depict the social distance between free and slave, rich and poor?
- What is the connection between love, friendship, and death in the gladiator school?
- What is the symbolic role that family and children play?
- How does the author's experience with anti-communism in the US emerge in the "I'm Spartacus" scene?
- Explain and describe the domestic world of slavery?
- What is the emotional and visual impact of the filming of major battle scenes?
- Discuss the moral predicament of the gladiator school: how do you kill someone for whom you have no animosity?

Adapted from C. Vitere. 2001. "Viewing history? Films and historical memory," *Social Science Docket* 1(2): Summer-Fall. Used with permission.

Alan's eclectic list of recommended documentaries and historical movies, with some ideas for classroom use, follows.

1. United States History

- *Roots* (1977) is the classic 12-hour made-for-television story of an African-American family based on a book by Alex Haley on his family's history. The early segments focus on life during slavery. I prefer to use sections from the movie, *Half Slave, Half Free* (1984 also distributed as *Solomon Northup's Odyssey*), which was directed by Gordon Parks and stars Avery Brooks as Solomon

Northup. It is based on Northup's autobiography, *Twelve Years a Slave* (Eakin and Logdon 1968), which was originally published in 1853. I show students the sections that illustrate the brutality of slavery, efforts by African-Americans to build community under adverse conditions, and the development of a blended African-American Christianity. This movie is especially useful because of its focus on slavery as a work system. For homework, I have students read and write about parallel sections in the book. There is also an audiocassette of the book narrated by Wendell Brooks that is available from the Social Studies School

Service. I found *Amistad* (1997) to be a very uneven movie; however the scenes depicting the middle passage are both incredibly powerful and accurate. *Beloved* (1998) is metaphysical, mystical, and difficult to follow.

- Two of the best-known movies about Native Americans are *Dances with Wolves* and *I Will Fight No More Forever* (1975). *Dances with Wolves* has excellent sections on life on the Great Plains. *I Will Fight No More Forever* is the story of Chief Joseph and the Nez Percé people. It raises important questions about the way the US government treated native peoples. *Little Big Man* (1970) has a powerful scene about Wounded Knee.

- *The Civil War* (1990), the award-winning PBS series directed by Ken Burns, is eleven hours long. To portray the horror and irrationality of the war, I prefer to use the opening scene from *Dances with Wolves* where the shots of the boots and the medical instruments are powerful and painful. The early scenes of the Clint Eastwood movie, *The Outlaw Josie Wales* (1976), present a southern view of the end of the war.

- Good movies about efforts to farm the Great Plains include *Sarah, Plain and Tall* (1990) and *O Pioneers* (1992). There are also episodes from the television series *Little House on the Prairie*. All three productions are based on books so that students can read along. *The Wizard of Oz* (1939) is based on a book by Frank Baum, which is an allegory about Populism (Littlefield 1964).

- PBS produced *A Walk Through the 20th Century with Bill Moyers*. Highlights of this nineteen part series include: the evolution of the automobile (*America on the Road*), social change in the 1960s (*Change, Change*), New Deal programs (*The Helping Hand*), labor struggles (*Out of the Depths*), and the cold war (*Post-War Hopes, Cold War Fears*).

- *The Inheritance* (1978) is a documentary about immigration (primarily Jewish and Italian) during the 1880–1920 period. Other movies about immigrants include *Hester Street* (1975), about Jewish immigrants in New York; the *Godfather* saga, particularly *The Godfather, Part 2* (1974); *Picture Bride* (1995), about Japanese immigrants to Hawaii; *The Joy Luck Club* (1993), about Chinese immigrants on the west coast; and *My Family* (1994), about a Mexican family in Los Angeles. Many excellent movies focus on problems faced by newer immigrants to the United States or by older Mexican American communities including *The Milagro Beanfield War* (1988), *Lone Star* (1996), and *Real Women Have Curves* (2002). While *The Gangs of New York* (2002) is a flawed movie with many historical inaccuracies, it has a useful scene showing Irish immigrants disembarking on the New York water front in the period just prior to the Civil War. *Titanic* (1997) is another movie with limited classroom use, but it has some good scenes depicting conditions in below deck steerage facilities for poor immigrants on trans-Atlantic voyages.

- *Bound for Glory* (1976) is the story of Woody Guthrie and life during the Great Depression. *The Cradle Will Rock* (1999) is about art, artists, left-wing politics, and the New Deal WPA program. My favorite movie about this period remains *The Grapes of Wrath* (1940).

- There are numerous documentaries on World War II. I usually show sections on Rosie the Riveter and the bombing of Hiroshima. I still use *The Liberators*, but discuss its inaccuracies with my classes. Among fictional works, *Come See the Paradise* (1990) focuses on the internment of Japanese Americans. *Tora! Tora! Tora!* (1970) and *Saving Private Ryan* (1998) have classic war scenes. Two recent movies directed by Clint Eastwood, *Flag of Our Fathers* (2006) and *Letters from Iwo Jima* (2006), are powerful depictions of the War in the Pacific as seem from both American and Japanese perspectives. *Fat Man and Little Boy* (1989) tells the story of the nuclear attacks on Hiroshima and Nagasaki.

- There are many excellent documentaries and movies on the Civil Rights movement. I always show sections from *King: Montgomery to Memphis* (1970): the Montgomery bus boycott, the use of dogs and fire hoses against demonstrators in Birmingham, and the 1963 March on Washington; *Eyes on the Prize* I (1986) and II (1990) has footage on the murder of Emmett Till, the desegregation of Little Rock High School, the voting rights march from Selma to Montgomery, Alabama, and Malcolm X. Movies include *The Great Debaters* (2007), which includes a powerful scene that depicts a lynching; *Separate But Equal* (1991), with a reenactment of Kenneth Clark's doll experiment;

To Kill a Mockingbird (1962); and *Nothing But a Man* (1964). The continuing impact of race in American society is explored in the Academy Award winning movie *Crash* (2004).

- Movies and documentaries make possible a thematic examination of the impact of the cold war and anti-communism on American culture in the 1950s and 1960s. The documentary *Nuclear Strategy for Beginners* (PBS Nova, 1983) explores the history of nuclear weapons and their role in the cold war. Many popular movies had underlying anti-communist themes, including: *The Invasion of the Body Snatchers* (1956), *The Village of the Damned* (1960), and *The Manchurian Candidate* (1962 and 2004). The more recent *Starship Troopers* (1997) is based on a 1950s anti-communist novel by Robert Heinlein. The mindless arachnids manipulated by a powerful leader represent the communist Chinese. In 1962, the US Defense Department produced a twenty-five minute propaganda film called *Red Nightmare*. Movies that challenge McCarthyism and blind anticommunism include *Fail Safe* (1964), *The Way We Were* (1973), *The Front* (1976), *Julia* (1977), *Guilty by Suspicion* (1991), and *Good Night, and Good Luck* (2005), which tells the story of Edward R. Murrow's opposition to censorship and blacklisting. *Thirteen Days* (2000) is about the Kennedy administration and the Cuban missile crisis. *Charlie Wilson's War* (2007) tells the story of an obscure congressman who organizes US support for Afghani rebels battling a Soviet-backed government.

- The 13-hour *Vietnam: A Television History* (1983) is another PBS production that has to be carefully edited to be useful. I usually show the opening sequence, which introduces a series of issues in the course of about twenty minutes. Depending on student questions, I show other segments. Movies include *Good Morning Vietnam* (1988), *Platoon* (1986), *Coming Home* (1978), *Apocalypse Now* (1979), *Born on the Fourth of July* (1989), *Casualties of War* (1989), and *Forrest Gump* (1994).

- Good movies that examine post-Cold War conflicts include *The Siege* (1998), which is about a terrorist attack on Brooklyn, New York. It raises questions about both American foreign policy and the fragility of civil rights in a time of war. *Syriana* (2005) looks at the actions of American secret agencies and *Jarhead* (2005) tells the story of the first Gulf War from the perspective of a soldier caught up in the battle.

- *The China Syndrome* (1979) and *Silkwood* (1983) are powerful movies about nuclear hazards. *Erin Brockovich* (2000), which starred Julia Roberts in an Academy Award winning role, is about legal efforts to award damages to people injured by toxic waste released into the environment by a large corporation. *Michael Clayton* (2007) is about lawyers defending and litigating against a powerful agrichemical company.

2. Economics

- US labor struggles are explored in a number of movies. My favorites include *Salt of the Earth* (1954), about New Mexican miners, *Norma Rae* (1979), about southern textile workers, and *Matewan* (1987), about West Virginia coal miners. Many recent movies about workers also focus on the experiences of recent, sometimes undocumented, immigrants. *Bread and Roses* (2001) recounts efforts to organize exploited Hispanic workers who clean offices at night in Los Angles.

- *Modern Times* (1936), starring Charlie Chaplin, is a classic about the assembly line. Business ethics are examined in *Wall Street* (1987) and *It's A Wonderful Life* (1946). The documentary *Hungry for Profit* (1985) questions whether problems in Third World countries are caused by underdevelopment or misdevelopment and exploitation by the industrialized world.

- Michael Moore has produced a series of movies examining economic inequality in the United States. *Roger and Me* (1989) examined the impact of the closing of a GM plant on Flint, Michigan. He continued his barbed assault on capitalist greed in *The Big One* (1998) and *Sicko* (2007). Moore's movies tend to focus a little too much on him, and communities and special interests he has reported on, especially people living in Flint, Michigan, often feel he exaggerates the situation to make his point. The movies certainly make for lively classroom discussions.

3. Political Science/Citizenship/Participation in Government

- *Amazing Grace and Chuck* (1987) is about middle school students who challenge the nuclear arms race. *Mr. Smith Goes to Washington* (1939) is about an ordinary citizen elected to Congress. *All the President's Men* (1976) is about Watergate and freedom of the press. *The Candidate* (1972) and *Bob Roberts* (1992) are about the shallowness of contemporary politics. Recent movies taking a critical look at political power and politics include *Wag the Dog* (1997), *Primary Colors* (1998), *Bulworth* (1998) and *The Contender* (2000). *V for Vendetta* (2005) takes place in England and challenges dictatorship in the tradition of *1984* (1984) and *Brave New World* (1980 and 1998). It offers a libertarian, almost an anarchist, perspective on social change.

- A number of movies examine the US legal system, including *The Verdict* (1982), which has excellent scenes of a courtroom cross examination, *Twelve Angry Men* (1957), which focuses on a jury, and *Inherit the Wind* (1960). The *Law and Order* television franchise in its different formats is an excellent vehicle for examining the legal process and issues. It is also probably the best television show for studying about police investigations.

- Movies that explore contemporary issues in interesting ways include *Dead Men Walking* (2005), which challenges the humanity of the death penalty, *John Q.* (2002) and *Sicko* (2007), which are about the inadequacies of the American health care industry, *Thank You for Smoking* (2005), which attacks the cigarette companies and advertising campaigns, *Bowling for Columbine* (2002), which looks at gun control, and *An Inconvenient Truth* (2006), an Academy Award documentary produced by former Vice-President Al Gore on the threat of global warming. Movies that look at potentially dark futures include *On the Beach* (1959), *Planet of the Apes* (1968), *The Children of Men* (2006), *The Day After Tomorrow* (2004), and *28 Days Later* (2002).

- Many movies include not-so-subtle stereotypes about women and their historical and cultural roles. An interesting class project can involve students in comparing the way women were presented in the movies in the 1950s and 1960s, with more recent movies like *Julia* (1977), *Norma Rae* (1979), *The Terminator* (I and II, 1984/1991), the *Alien(s)* series (1979, 1986, 1992 and 1997), *Thelma and Louise* (1991),

A League of Their Own (1992), and *Tank Girl* (1995).

4. Global History

- Australia, New Zealand, and Oceana: *Rabbit-Proof Fence* (2002) is about European efforts to forcibly assimilate Australian aborigines and tells the story of three young mixed race girls who escape from a boarding school and attempt to rejoin their extended matriarchal families. *Whale Rider* (2002) is about efforts to preserve Maori culture in New Zealand and asks: What does it mean to be part of a traditional cultural community in contemporary society?

- Latin America and the Caribbean: When I was 19 years old, I traveled in the Andes from Bogotá, Columbia to Lake Titicaca in Bolivia and spent a week on a barge in the Amazonas. I relived many of these scenes while watching Diarios de Motocicleta *(The Motorcycle Diaries*, 2004), a movie based on a journal kept by a youthful Ché Guevara while making a similar voyage of discovery. The opening scenes of *El Norte* (1984; Spanish with English subtitles) are about political and economic oppression in Guatemala. They effectively illustrate the world described by Rigoberta Menchú in her autobiography. Other movies about recent political conflict in Central America include *Hombres Armados, Men With Guns* (1997), *Romero* (1989), and *Under Fire* (1983). *The Emerald Forest* (1985) and *The Burning Season, The Chico Mendes Story* (1994) examine the impact of Amazonian development on native peoples and Brazilian rubber workers. *Missing* (1982) is about the overthrow of the Allende government in Chile; *The Official Story* (1986; Spanish with English subtitles) is about military dictatorship in Argentina; and *The Mission* (1986) is about Spanish settlement. *Sugar Cane Alley* (1984; French with English subtitles) examines life on a plantation in the French-speaking Caribbean. *Burn!* (1970) is about European colonialism in the Caribbean. *The Last Supper* (1976) is about slavery in eighteenth-century Cuba. *In the Time of the Butterflies* (2001) tells the story of four sisters known as Los Mariposas (the butterflies) who helped to topple the dictatorial Trujillo regime in the Dominican Republic. Brazil has a developing movie industry that has produced a number of excellent movies. *Kiss of the Spiderwoman* (1985) looks at the repression of the political opposition. *Central Station* (1998) explores the relationship between a retired teacher and an orphan. *City of God* (2002) is a painful examination of poverty and youth gangs in the notorious shantytown near Rio de Janeiro.

- Asia: *Gandhi* (1982) has many dramatic scenes about Indian life, the struggle for independence, and conflicts between Hindus and Muslims. Especially useful is the depiction of the Salt March. Scenes from *The Last Emperor* (1987) illustrate the opulence of the Forbidden City during the last Chinese dynasty, whereas scenes from *The Empire of the Sun* (1987) show the privileged European community and the extreme poverty of ordinary people living in Shanghai. *Little Buddha* (1994) offers both a look at life in the Himalayas and insights into Buddhist religious beliefs. *The Year of Living Dangerously* (1983) is about revolutionary uprisings in Indonesia. *Beyond Rangoon* (1995) and *Indochine* (1992) are about revolutionary times in South East Asia. *The Killing Fields* (1984) examines the Khmer Rouge in Cambodia. *Ran* (1985; Japanese with English subtitles) is about conflict in the royal family in fifteen-century Japan. *Shogun* (1980) is a made-for-television miniseries about European merchants in Japan. Interesting movies to recently come out of China include *Raise the Red Lantern* (1991), about an educated woman who becomes the fourth wife of a feudal nobleman in the 1920s, *The King of Masks* (1999), about an itinerant performer who adopts a homeless boy as an apprentice, only to discover that the boy is a girl, and *Not One Less* (1999), about education in rural China.
- Sub-Saharan Africa: *Cry the Beloved Country* (1951/1995), *Cry Freedom* (1987), *A World Apart* (1988), *A Dry White Season* (1989), *Sarafina!* (1992), and *In My Country* (2004) are about apartheid in South Africa. *A Dry White Season* includes scenes where the police attack student protesters in Soweto. *Sankofa* (1993) examines the Atlantic Slave Trade. A number of movies have focused on recent conflicts in Africa, which are often rooted in the European colonial past. *Lumumba* (2001) looks at the continuing impact of colonialism on the Congo.

Hotel Rwanda (2004) and *Sometimes in April* (2005) are both about the Rwandan genocide. *Blood Diamond* (2006) is about the impact of the illegal diamond trade on West African societies. *The Last King of Scotland* (2006), which stars Academy Award winner Forrest Whitiker as Idi Amin, is about his brutal reign in Uganda. *The Constant Gardener* (2006) looks at the exploitation of vulnerable African communities by European pharmaceutical companies.

- North Africa and the Middle East: *Hidalgo* (2004), about a trans-Arabia horse race, has beautiful scenes of the desert and offers a somewhat respectful look at people and customs. *Ararat* (2002) is confusing but does provide some background on the Armenian Genocide in Turkey during World War I. *The Battle of Algiers* (1966; French with English subtitles) is about the Algerian uprising against French colonialism. It raises the question, who are the terrorists? Terrorism is also addressed in the movie *Paradise Now* (2005), about two Palestinian young men plotting a suicide bomb attack in Tel Aviv. *Babel* (2006) is about the inability of people to connect with each other in a global age. It includes stark scenes of life in rural Morocco. Movies have explored the Israeli-Palestinian conflict from different perspectives. They include *Munich* (2005), about the Israeli retaliation for a Palestinian attack on Israeli athletes at the 1972 Olympics and the documentary *Blood and Tears* (2007).
- Ancient and pre-industrial Europe: *Spartacus* (1960) is about a slave rebellion during the Roman Republic and is much better than *Gladiator* (2000). *The Return of Martin Guerre* (1981; French with English subtitles) is about French peasant life during the Crusades. *Beckett* (1964) and *A Man for All Seasons* (1966) are about conflicts between church and king in England. *Amazing Grace* (2007) was produced in commemoration of the 200th anniversary of the abolition of the trans-Atlantic slave trade. It tells the story of English abolitionists at the turn of the nineteenth century.
- Modern Europe: Movies about the early industrial era include *David Copperfield* (with Daniel Radcliffe a/k/a Harry Potter, as the young David, 1999) and *Germinal* (1993; French with English subtitles), which examines the impact of industrialization on French coal miners. There are excellent

Resources for Social Studies Classrooms and Teachers

scenes of work, a strike, and women organizing against local merchants. *The Organizer* (1963; Italian with English subtitles) examines similar scenes of industrial unrest. *All Quiet on the Western Front* (1930 and 1979) portrays trench warfare during World War I. Similar scenes are depicted in *Legends of the Fall* (1994). *Paths of Glory* (1949) is about the way French troops are treated by their officers. In *Gallipoli* (1981), young Australians enlist in the British army to see the world and are used as cannon fodder on the Turkish Front. *Enemies at the Gate* (1991) is about the Battle of Stalingrad, perhaps the major turning point of World War II. *The Guns of Navarone* (1961), about the Greek resistance, remains my favorite movie about World War II. *Good-Bye Lenin* (2003) is a humorous look at the end of communism in Eastern Europe, while *Welcome to Farewell to Sarajevo* (1997) and *No Man's Land* (2001) looks at civil war in the Balkans after the collapse of Yugoslavia. *Strike* (2006) tells the story of Polish dockworkers and the Solidarity campaign that helped overthrow a pro-Soviet communist regime.

- The European Holocaust: *The Garden of the Finzi-Continis* (1971; Italian with English subtitles)*, The Diary of Anne Frank* (1959), *Judgment at Nuremburg* (1961; with scenes from the concentration camps), *Playing for Time* (1980), *Schindler's List* (1993), and *The Truce* (1996), examine Nazi efforts to exterminate European Jews. *Night and Fog* (1955; French with English subtitles) and *Weapons of the Spirit* (1990) are important documentaries. *Weapons of the Spirit* focuses on French Huguenots who help Jews

escape the Nazis. *Genghis Cohen* (1993) and *Life is Beautiful* (1998) are comedies about the Holocaust. They are excellent movies but not appropriate as an introduction to issues and events.

- Ireland: The history of Great Britain's first colony is an important topic to explore and deserves more attention than it generally receives. In Ireland, Great Britain experimented with divide-and-conquer, forced acculturation, and laissez-faire economic policies. Ireland is also important because, unlike in most of the colonized world, the exploited people are White Christian Europeans. Unfortunately, there are no movies I can recommend about the British conquest of Ireland or the Great Irish Famine. *The Wind that Shakes the Barley* (2006) and *Michael Collins* (1996) are about the post-World War I Irish independence movement and civil war. *In the Name of the Father* (1993), *The Crying Game* (1992), *Veronica Guerin* (2003), and *Bloody Sunday* (2002) explore different aspects of the ongoing conflict between Catholics and Protestants in Northern Ireland, which remains under British authority. A consistent theme in all of these movies is the difficulty in deciding the difference between a freedom fighter and a terrorist. *My Left Foot* (1989), *The Commitments* (1991), and *Angela's Ashes* (1999) portray working-class urban Irish life. *Waking Ned* (1998) is about contemporary life in a small Irish village. *The Magdalene Sisters* (2002) is a painful movie about young Irish women victimized by an oppressive Roman Catholic Church that wants to stamp out female sexuality.

Teaching Activity: Choosing Movies

Add your voice to the discussion:
What do you think about the historical value of using movies in class? Why?

Think it over:
How would you use movies or documentaries in your class? Why?

It's your classroom:
What movies would you remove from this list? What additional movies would you consider? Why?

WHAT CAN I COPY FOR MY CLASS?

According to US copyright laws (Demac, 1996), copyright holders have the exclusive right to authorize the reproduction, distribution, performance, and display of their work. However, there is a significant exception to this rule, the *fair use* doctrine. Teachers are permitted to make single copies for their own use of a chapter from a book, an article from a magazine or newspaper, a short story or short poem, a chart, graph, or cartoon. Court rulings against *Napster* appear to have extended these rules to use of material from the internet. Broadcasts can be recorded from television and radio for use in class, but copies are not supposed to be permanent. Guidelines on multiple photocopies for classroom use permit one copy per pupil of copyrighted material, as long as six criteria are satisfied:

1. Copies include the notice of copyright.
2. Copies must be brief. An entire article must be less than 2,500 words long, an excerpt must be less than 1,000 words. Sections from a poem must be under 250 words.
3. It should be a spontaneous decision that does not allow time to secure permission to reproduce from the copyright holder.
4. Copied material should be used for only one course. Only one complete piece or two excerpts can be by a particular author.
5. Students cannot be charged beyond the actual cost of the photocopying.
6. Material was not designed to be consumable (workbooks).

In addition, the following are considerations:

1. Teachers are permitted to make a single copy of a sound recording of copyrighted material purchased by the individual teacher or school.
2. Nonprofit institutions are permitted to make off-air video recordings of television programs at the request of a teacher and keep copies for a maximum of 45 days. Recordings can be used once during relevant teaching activities. They can be used again, when necessary, to reinforce student learning.
3. Software is considered leased, rather than purchased. It is illegal to make and distribute unauthorized copies of commercial software. One backup copy can legally be made.

4. Clear legal guidelines for the fair use of electronic information have not been established.

WHO PROVIDES RESOURCES FOR SOCIAL STUDIES TEACHERS?

Web searches are now the most effective way to locate classroom resources. Web addresses have been noted throughout this edition of *Social Studies for Secondary Schools* wherever possible. This list is sharply paired down from previous editions. It highlights a few organizations that merit special attention. Internet addresses were accessed October 2007.

American Association for State and Local History, 1717 Church Street, Nashville, TN 37203, http://www.aaslh.org. Works to preserve, interpret, and promote local history. Publishes *History News* and a monthly newsletter.

American Bar Association, 740 15th Street, NW, Washington, DC 20005–1019, http://www.abanet.org. National organization of lawyers. Sponsors a Youth Education for Citizenship program.

American Civil Liberties Union, 125 Broad Street, New York, NY 10004, http://www.aclu.org. Supports legal cases to protect and expand constitutional rights. Publishes pamphlets on legal issues.

American Federation of Labor/Congress of Industrial Organizations, 815 16th Street, NW, Washington, DC 20006, http://www.aflcio.org.

American Federation of Teachers, 555 New Jersey Avenue, NW, Washington, DC 20001, http://www.aft.org. One of two national teacher's unions. Its publication, *American Educator*, frequently discusses issues for social studies educators. Sponsors an Education for Democracy program.

American Historical Association, 400 A Street, SE, Washington, DC 20003, http://www.historians.org/. Primarily for university-based historians. Promotes history teaching in secondary schools. Publishes the *American Historical Review*, *Perspectives*, a newsletter, and a pamphlet series on historical ideas. Co-sponsor of the History Teaching Alliance and National History Day.

American Political Science Association, 1527 New Hampshire Avenue, NW, Washington, DC 20036, http://www.apsanet.org.

American Social History Project, Center for Media and Learning, The Graduate Center, CUNY, 365 Fifth Avenue, New York, NY 10016, http://www.ashp.cuny.edu. Produces teaching videos, texts, and curriculum guides that focus on social history.

American Sociological Association, 1307 New York Avenue, NW, Suite 700, Washington, DC 20005, http://www.asanet.org.

Anti-Defamation League, 823 United Nations Plaza, New York, NY 10017, http://www.adl.org. Combats hatred and bigotry in US society. Documents and publishes accounts of bias, promotes laws against hate crimes, and develops anti-bias programs.

Association for Supervision and Curriculum Development, 1703 North Beauregard Street, Alexandria, VA 22311, http://www.ascd.org. Publishes *Educational Leadership*. Thematic issues frequently discuss topics relevant to social studies.

Association of American Geographers, 1710 16th Street, NW, Washington, DC 20009, http://www.aag.org.

Center for Civic Education, 5146 Douglas Fir Road, Calabasas, CA 91302–1467, http://www.civiced.org. Creates resources and curricula for civics education. Publishes a newsletter, *Center Correspondent*; a curriculum guide, *CIVITAS: A Framework for Civic Education*; and middle school and high school editions of *We The People*.

Center for Research on Women, Wellesley Centers for Women, Wellesley College, Wellesley, MA 02481, http://www.wcwonline.org. Sponsors research, publications, and conferences on issues related to women and gender bias.

Children's Defense Fund, 25 E Street NW, Washington, DC 20001, http://www.childrensdefense.org. Advocacy organization that conducts and publishes research on poor and minority children.

Close Up Foundation, 44 Canal Center Plaza, Alexandria, VA 22314–1592, http://www.closeup.org. Non-partisan organization that promotes citizen involvement in government and student trips to Washington, DC.

Cobblestone Publishing, 30 Grove Street, Suite C, Peterborough, NH 03458–1454, http://www.cobblestonepub.com. Publishes thematic magazines for classroom use, Grades 4–9. Calliope (world history), Cobblestone (US history), and Faces (world cultures).

Common Cause, 1250 Connecticut Ave., NW #600, Washington, DC 20036, http://www.commoncause.org. Nonpartisan group that campaigns for responsive and responsible government. Publishes *Common Cause*.

Consumers Union of the United States, 101 Truman Avenue, Yonkers, NY 10703, http://www.consumersunion.org. Tests and reports on consumer products. Publishes *Consumer Reports* and *Consumer Reports for Kids*.

Educators for Social Responsibility, 23 Garden Street, Cambridge, MA 02138, http://www.esrnational.org. Promotes active citizenship and conflict-resolution programs. Offers a resource catalog and curriculum materials. Publishes *Forum* and *Making History*.

Facing History and Ourselves, 16 Hurd Road, Brookline, MA 02445, http://www.facing.org. Produces curriculum material that uses the Holocaust as a starting point for understanding conflict and moral choices in the past and present.

Greenpeace, 702 H Street NW, Washington, DC 20001, http://www.greenpeace.org. Campaigns against the dumping of toxic waste, in support of nuclear disarmament, and to protect the environment. Publishes *Greenpeace Magazine*.

Jackdaw Publications, P.O. Box 503, Amawalk, NY 10501, http://www.jackdaw.com. Thematic primary source document packages from both US and world history.

League of Women Voters, 1730 M Street, NW, Suite 1000, Washington, DC 20036, http://www.lwv.org. Non-partisan political group that supports voter registration and discussions of issues.

Morningside Center for Teaching Social Responsibility (formerly ESR Metro), 475 Riverside Drive, Room 554, New York, NY 10115, http://www.morningsidecenter.org. Pioneers curriculum material on conflict resolution in the classroom and on a global scale. Lesson materials are at: http://teachablemoment.org.

National Archives and Records Administration, Education Branch, 700 Pennsylvania Avenue, NW, Washington, DC 20408, http://www.nara.gov. Preserves and makes documents available to the public. Provides sample documents and lesson plans.

National Association for the Advancement of Colored People, 4805 Mt. Hope Drive, Baltimore, MD 21215, http://www.naacp.org. Organizes young people for social action. Publishes monthly magazine, *The Crisis*.

National Center for History in the Schools, Department of History, UCLA, 6339 Bunche Hall, 405 Hilgard Avenue, Los Angeles, CA 90095, http://www.sscnet.ucla.edu/nchs. UCLA/NEH program coordinates the National History Standards Project.

National Council for History Education, 26915 Westwood Road, Suite B-2, Westlake, OH 44145, 440/835–1776, http://www.nche.net/. Promotes the importance of history in schools and society. Publishes *Building a Curriculum: Guidelines for Teaching History in the Schools*, and a monthly newsletter, *History Matters*.

National Council for the Social Studies, 8555 Sixteenth Street, Suite 500, Silver Spring, MD 20910, http://www.socialstudies.org. National organization dedicated to the professional development of social studies educators. Annual conferences and publications are available to members. Annual membership dues include a subscription to the newsletter, *The Social Studies Professional*, and a choice between two magazines: *Social Education* and *Social Studies and the Young Learner*. Also publishes curriculum bulletins and a quarterly journal for university-based social studies educators, *Theory and Research in Social Education*. State and local chapter memberships support national efforts.

National History Day, 0119 Cecil Hall, University of Maryland, College Park, MD 20742, http://www.historynet.com/national historyday.

National Issues Forums, 100 Commons Road, Dayton, OH 45459, http://www.nifi.org. Sponsors public forums for adults and students. Publishes booklets presenting multiple views on controversial issues.

National Organization for Women, 1000 16th Street, NW, Suite 700, Washington, DC 20036, http://www.now.org. National organization that influences public issues of concern to women.

National Women's History Project, 3343 Industrial Drive, Suite 4, Santa Rosa, CA 95403, http://www.nwhp.org. Dedicated to including women in school curricula as equal participants in history.

Network of Educators on the Americas, PO Box 73038, Washington, DC 20056 http://www.teachingforchange.org. Works with schools to develop and promote teaching methods and resources for social and economic justice in the Americas. Publishes *Teaching for Change* and curriculum materials.

North American Congress on Latin America, 475 Riverside Drive, Suite 454, New York, NY 10115, http://www.nacla.org. Concerned with political and economic development in Latin America.

Northern Sun Merchandising, 2916 E. Lake Street, Minneapolis, MN 55406, http://www.northernsun.com. Catalog provides products for progressives, especially posters and shirts.

Organization of American Historians, 112 N. Bryan Street, Bloomington, IN 47408, http://www.oah.org. Organization of US historians and history educators. Publishes *Journal of American History*, *OAH Newsletter*, and *OAH Magazine of History*.

People for the American Way, 2000 M Street, NW, Suite 400, Washington, DC 20036, http://www.pfaw.com. Promotes voter education in secondary schools. Publishes newsletter, *First Voter*.

Phi Alpha Theta, National Headquarters, University of South Florida, SOC 107, 4202 East Fowler Avenue, Tampa, FL 33620, http://www.phialphatheta.org. National history honor society. Organizes conferences and publishes *The Historian* and a newsletter.

Political Economy Research Center, 502 S. 19th Avenue, Suite 211, Bozeman, MT 59718, http://www.perc.org. Publishes curriculum on environmental issues.

Rethinking Schools, 1001 East Keefe Avenue, Milwaukee, WI 53212, http://www.rethinkingschools.org. Dedicated to reforming elementary and secondary schools with an emphasis on progressive values. Publishes newsletter, *Rethinking Schools*, which frequently includes social studies teaching materials and curriculum ideas.

Southern Poverty Law Center, 400 Washington Avenue, Montgomery, AL 36104, http://www.splcenter.org. Monitors and mounts legal challenges to racism. Publishes *Teaching Tolerance*.

Teachers' Curriculum Institute, PO Box 1327, Rancho Cordova, CA 95741, http://www.teachtci.com. Develops middle and high school activity-based curriculum guides that emphasize engaging all learners in diverse classrooms. Produces *History Alive*.

Teaching for Change, PO Box 73038 Washington, DC 20056–3038, http://teachingforchange.org. Books, films, and posters from a "social justice" perspective.

United States Public Interest Research Group, 218 D Street, SE, Washington, DC 20003, http://www.uspirg.org. Lobbies for environmental and consumer protection. Publishes *Citizen Agenda*.

Veterans of Foreign Wars, 406 West 34th Street, Kansas City, MO 64111, http://www.vfw.org. Local chapters provide speakers for social studies classes.

Women's International League for Peace and Freedom, 1213 Race Street, Philadelphia, PA 19107, http://www.peacewomen.org. Works for social, political, economic, and psychological conditions necessary to ensure international peace and freedom.

References and Recommendations for Further Reading

Bennett, L. and Berson, M., eds, 2007. *Digital age, technology-based k-12 lesson plans for social studies, NCSS bulletin 105*. Silver Spring, MD: NCSS.

Braun, J. and Risinger, F. 1999. *Surfing social studies. National Council for the Social Studies Bulletin 96*. Washington, DC: NCSS.

Carnes, M. 1996. "Beyond words: Reviewing moving pictures," *Perspectives: American Historical Association Newsletter*, 34(5): 1.

Cohen, N. 2007. "A history department bans citing Wikipedia as a research source," *The New York Times*, February 21.

Demac, D. 1996. *Is any use fair in a digital world?* New York: Columbia University, The Freedom Media Studies Center.

Eakin, S. and Logdon, J., eds. 1968. *Twelve years a slave*. Baton Rouge, LA: Louisiana State University Press.

Joseph, R. and Munn-Joseph, M. 2008. "Overcoming the 'digital divide' in social studies," *Social Science Docket*, 8(2).

Littlefield, H. 1964. "The Wizard of Oz: Parable on Populism," *American Quarterly* 16(1): 47–58.

Mitchell E. 2001. Mission of mercy goes bad in Africa. *The New York Times*, December 28. http://movies.nytimes.com/movie/review?_r=1&res=9903E3D61031F93BA15751C1A9679C8B63&oref=slogin, accessed on September 14, 2007.

Sexton, B. 2002. "An actor speaks out—what's wrong with Black Hawk Down," *CounterPunch's Booktalk*, March 1. http://www.counterpunch.org, accessed on September 14, 2007.

Author Index

Achebe, Chinua 153
Acton, Lord 247
Adams, Abigail 286, 288, 309
Adams, Henry Brooks 44
Adams, John 286, 288, 309
Adler, M. 104, 151
Agosti-Dircks, Christina 124, 327, 328, 396
Aguinaldo, Emilio 280–1
Ahern, Amanda 321
Alcoff, L. 155
Ali, Tariq 33
Alito, Samuel 196, 197
al-Sadat, Anwar 353
Anbinder, T. 207–8
Angela, Aurora d' 47–8, 49
Angelou, Maya 306
Anthony, Susan B. 301, 302, 303, 311
Appiah, Kwame A. 160
Applebome, P. 114
Apple, Michael 138
Aristotle 53, 104, 107
Armstrong, Karen 162
Arnove, Anthony 183
Asimov, Isaac 41
Atwater, Lee 13–14
Ayre, Lois 327

Bachman, Daniel 305–6, 390
Bacigalupo, Dean 319
Bailey, T. 183, 303–4, 372–3
Baker, D. 70
Balantic, Jeannette 270, 306, 309, 332, 396
Balch, Emily Greene 142
Baldacci, John 113
Banerjee, N. 15
Banks, D. 296
Banks, James 119, 160
Banks, Russell 33
Banneker, Benjamin 286, 288
Barbaro, Michael 74–5
Barry, Kevin 158–9
Beagle, Peter S. 6
Beck, R. 162
Becker, Carl 3, 35
Begin, Menachem 353
Bell, Madison Smartt 33
Bell, N. 12
Berenson, R. 141
Berg, C. 238
Berk, L. 86
Berman, Morris 248

Bernal, Martin 54
Bernstein, J. 70
Berra, Lawrence "Yogi" 29–30, 45
Berson, Michael 339
Beveridge, Alfred 280
Bigelow, William 120–1, 372
bin Laden, Osama 27, 46, 249, 251
Bismarck, Otto 45
Blake, William 39–40
Bloom, Allan 82, 359
Bloom, Benjamin 266, 267, 268
Blum, J. 23
Boas, Franz 63, 64
Bonhoeffer, Dietrich 33
Bork, Robert 198, 200, 203
Borruso, Lauren 344, 392–3
Bowes, John S. 302
Brecht, Bertolt 35
Brennan, William 200, 201, 202, 203
Breyer, Stephen 200, 204
Brody, Barry 386
Brookhiser, Richard 127
Brown, H. Rap 17
Bryan, William Jennings 26–7, 224, 252, 267–8, 278, 279–80
Bunting, Eve 296, 328
Burke, Peter 52, 55
Burns, Robert 306
Burrows, E. 207, 208
Bush, George 13, 15, 17–18, 46, 83–4, 107, 108, 114–15, 196–7, 247, 248–52, 301, 352
Butler, Michael 149
Byrd, Robert 18, 315

Cahill, Kim 89–90
Calkins, Lucy 86, 242
Calvin, John 43
Carr, E. H. 25–6, 28, 29, 36–7, 41, 43, 221
Cartalucci, Jessica 122
Carter, Jimmy 247, 353–4
Carton, A. 86
Castro, Fidel 250
Cather, Willa 310
Chapman Catt, Carrie 311
Chavez, Hugo 45
Cheney, Dick 251
Cheney, Lynne 25, 141, 142
Christensen, Linda 120–1
Churchill, Winston 85
Clairmont, Robert 25
Clappe, Louise 310
Clark, George 28, 29

Author Index

Clark, Septima 86
Cleveland, Grover 246
Clinchy, B. 223
Clinton, Bill 108, 246, 247
Clinton, Hillary 115, 246, 248
Clough, M. 238
Code, L. 155
Cohen, Lizabeth 303–4
Cohen, Sarah 75–6
Cohn, Norman 163–4
Coleman, John 54–5
Collins, G. 127, 142
Columbus, Christopher 30, 121
Coolidge, Calvin 71
Cornbleth, Catherine 150
Costello-Herrara, Lynda 244, 333
Crocco, Margaret Smith 16, 142, 309
Croce, Benedetto 34
Crook, J. 124
Cross, Christopher T. 110

Dalberg, J. E. E. (Lord Acton) 28, 29
Danzer, G. 109, 278, 302–3
Darwin, Charles 43
Davis, J. 61
Davis, Mike 62
Debler, Jennifer 328, 339, 344
DeRose, John 278
de Tocqueville, Alexis 84
Dewey, John 8, 82, 88, 89–90, 112, 117–18, 137–8, 256, 282, 318, 358–9, 382
Diamond, Jared 33, 52, 61, 62, 165
Diderot, Denis 44
Dillon, S. 113–14
Dircks, Henry 305, 306, 322, 396
Disraeli, Benjamin 107
Dobb, Maurice 38
Dobkin, W. 236, 267
Dobson, William J. 252
Donnach, A. 114, 132
Douglas, Frederick 130–1
Doyle, Arthur Conan 37
Doyle, R. 113
DuBois, W. E. B. 64, 84, 210, 222
Duniway, Abigail Scott 301, 302
Dunne, Peter Finley 197
Dwyer, Kenneth 102, 122, 342

Edwards, John 115–16
Elliot, Jane 273
Ellis, Joseph J. 252
Emerson, Ralph Waldo 299
Engels, Frederick 45
Engvick, W. 25
Epstein, Rhoda L. 158
Equiano, Oloudah 154
Evans, R. 141

Ferrarese, Michael 396
Finley, M. I. 53
Finn, Chester E. Jr 25, 82, 113–14, 128
Finn, R. 113
Foner, Eric 33, 141
Foner, Philip 209
Ford, Henry 25
Francis, April 321

Frankfurter, Felix 197, 203
Franklin, Benjamin 128, 286, 289
Freeman, J. 208
Freire, Paulo 8, 12, 82, 86, 89, 103, 111, 117–18, 382
Freud, Sigmund 43
Frost, Robert 306
Fukuyama, Francis 43

Gage, Frances 14
Galileo Galilei 56
Gandini, L. 86
Gans, Herbert 68–9
Garcia, Jesus 301–2
Gardner, Howard 87
Garrison, William Lloyd 196, 297
Gaul, Gilbert M. 75–6
George, Henry 208
Giardina, Denise 33
Gilder, Richard 126–7, 142
Gillenwater, Vance 93
Giroux, Henry 8, 87
Giuliani, Rudolph 115
Glidden, Joseph F. 356
Gogg Clark, Margaret 306–7
Gompers, Samuel 208, 280
Goodman, Paul 171–2
Gould, Stephen Jay 25, 26–7, 29, 42
Grant, Ulysses 246
Gray, Yance T. 116
Greaves, R. 178
Greenberger, S. 148
Greenblatt, Miriam 302
Greene, Maxine 8, 82, 89, 118–19, 160, 244
Greenhouse, Steven 74–5
Gregory, G. 296
Gul, Hamid 27
Guthrie, Arlo 3
Guthrie, Woody 23–4

Hains, John 276, 277
Hamill, Jackie 122
Hamilton, Alexander 142, 174, 286, 287, 309
Hamilton, Virginia 328
Hand, Learned 202
Hanley, Sheila 306
Harding, Warren 246
Hardwick, M. 37
Harris, Marvin 64
Hartocollis, A. 25, 128
Hawke, S. 61
Hawking, S. 42
Hayden, Erin 330
Hegel, Georg W. F. 43
Heisenberg, Werner 41–2
Hellerman, L. 141
Hendrick, Bill 344, 345
Henry, Patrick 286, 288
Herbert, B. 14, 16
Herszenhorn, D. 173
Hertog, Roger 127
Hewitt, Abram 208
Higuera, Prudence 310
Hildebrand, J. 113
Hilton, R. 38
Hirsch, E. D. 82, 142, 317
Hobsbawm, Eric 33, 38–9, 45, 164

Hofstadter, Richard 26
Hogan, Michael 375, 377
Holson, L. 128
Holtzmann, L. 86
Hoover, Herbert 174, 247
Horton, Myles 86, 111, 119, 382
Howlett, Charles 318
Hughes, Langston 306
Hunter, Madeleine 238–9
Hunte, Stephanie 140, 326
Hussein, Saddam 250, 276
Hymowitz, Kay 127–8

Imus, Don 73
Irons, Cherisse 344

Jackson, Andrew 30, 34, 174, 247
Jackson, K. 141, 207
Jardine, Lisa 55
Jayamaha, Buddhika 116
Jefferson, Thomas 12, 60, 117, 129, 161, 174, 197, 203, 246, 286, 287, 297–8, 309
John Paul II, Pope 298–9
Johnson, Chalmers 252
Johnson, David 284
Johnson Holubec, Edythe 284
Johnson, Lyndon 247
Johnson, P. 55
Johnson, Roger 284
Jones, Thomas Jesse 60
Jordan, Winthrop D. 302
Joseph, Kristin 285, 344
Joseph, Roberto 392

Kafi, Patricia 65
Katznelson, Ira 33
Kennedy, D. 183
Kennedy, David M. 303–4, 372–3
Kennedy, Edward M. 202, 204
Kennedy, John F. 246
Kilimitzoglou, Stavros 327
Kilpatrick, William Heard 318
Kimball, Roger 127
King, Martin Luther Jr 117, 130–1, 185, 186, 188, 298
Kirchgaessner, Rozella 270–2
Klein, Laurence 16, 124, 180
Klor de Alva, J. Jorge 302–3
Kohl, Herbert 131
Kohn, Alfie 87
Kolko, Gabriel 42
Krautheimer, Jeff 274
Kreiger, Larry 302–3
Krugman, P. 107, 250

Ladson-Billings, Gloria 87
LaFeber, Walter 278
Landau, Meryl 273
Lansing, James 287, 289
La Place, Pierre-Simon 43
Leakey, Richard 162
Lee, Barbara 18, 252–3, 315
Lefkowitz, Mary 54
Lehrman, Lewis E. 126–7, 142
Leman, Kenneth W. 342
Lemisch, Jesse 142
Lemlich, Clara 12, 209

Leonardo da Vinci 56
Leuchtenburg, William 397
Levine, Molly Myerwitz 54
Levy, Leonard 198
Libresco, Andrea 30, 65, 301, 309, 332
Lincoln, Abraham 89, 117, 246, 252, 314–15
Linden, Eugene 62, 330
Litwack, L. 208
Lopez, Clemencia 281
Luskoff, Darren 124, 390

Mabrouk, Maram 40, 159
McCain, John 115
McCarthy, Joseph 110
McClintic, James 48
McCunn, Ruthann Lum 121
McDonaugh, William 330
McEneneany, Kara 328
Machiavelli, Niccolo 107
McIntosh, Peggy 87
McKay, Claude 306
McKenzie, R. 141
McKinley, William 278, 279
McNamara, John 180–1
McTighe, D. 219
McTighe, J. 56
Madison, James 197, 201, 286, 288–9
Malaguzzi, Loris 86
Malcolm X 185, 186, 189, 220, 222–3
Maniscalco, Frank 282
Mann, Horace 117
Manor, Tammy 330
Marable, Manning 69
Marshall, Thurgood 185
Maruki, Toshi 328
Marx, Karl 43, 44
Mason, George 286, 289
May, Ernest R. 301
Mead, Margaret 63, 64
Meese, Edward 198
Meese, Edwin 203
Meier, Deborah 90
Mejias, Monica 2
Mellen, Suzy 45
Merriam, John 60
Meyers, M. 178–9
Mill, J. S. 45
Mistry, Rohinton 153
Mitchel, John 103
Mitchell, Wesley 60
Montesquieu 43
Mora, Omar 116
Morgan, Dan 75–6
Morrison, John 208
Morse, Wayne 252, 315
Mott, Lucretia 311
Munn-Joseph, Marlene 392
Murdoch, Rupert 142
Murekatete, Jacqueline 4, 5
Murphy, Don 120
Murphy, Jeremy A. 116
Murphy, M. 103, 243, 314, 327–8, 375
Musa, Mansa 35, 110

Napoleon Bonaparte 109, 181, 182
Nasaw, David 142

Nash, G. 110, 141, 142
Newman, F. 86
Newton, Isaac 59
Nickell, Pat 360
Nieves, E. 13
Nixon, Richard 247
Noddings, Nel 87, 142, 301
Norton, Mary Beth 141

Obama, Barack 13, 15, 116
Oppenheim, James 311
Ortiz, Fernando 32
O'Shea, S. 56

Paciello, Nicole 333–4
Paige, Rod 24, 29
Paine, Thomas 68
Palmer, B. 40
Parente, Jennifer 362–3
Parker, Francis 282
Parker, Walter 353, 374
Parker, William 299, 300
Parrish, Lucian 48
Paterson, Katherine 310
Patterson, Orlando 53
Paul, Alice 311
Paz, Octavio 160
Pearson, Laura 270–2, 320, 396
Pericles 54
Peterson, Bob 372
Petraeus, General George 114, 115–16
Pezone, Michael 8, 67, 93, 105, 122–3, 181, 211–12, 256, 314, 333, 374
Pierre, M. S. N. 12, 278
Pogrebin, R. 127, 142
Porter, Eduardo 74
Postman, Neil 339
Powell, Colin 84, 248, 276
Powers, T. 11–12, 244

Quinn, Jennifer 212

Rabinowitz, Richard 142
Randall, William T. 352
Randolph, Arthur 28
Rankin, Jeannette 252, 315
Ravitch, Diane 14, 18, 25, 53, 82, 110, 127, 128, 141, 160
Reagan, Ronald 30, 174, 198–9, 200, 203, 247, 248
Rees, J. 24, 354
Reiber, R. 86
Reiser, B. 258–9
Rich, Frank 248
Riis, Jacob 207
Roberts, John 84, 196, 197, 201–2
Roberts, S. 17
Robeson, Paul 2
Robinson, Bobbie 69
Rochester, J. Martin 128
Roebling, John A. 207
Roebuck, Jeremy 116
Rogers, Guy 54
Roosevelt, Franklin D. 30, 174, 246, 323
Roosevelt, Theodore 208, 303
Ross, E. W. 382
Rossiter, Clinton 197
Rothschild, M. 111

Roy, Patricia 284
Rugg, Howard 90
Rumsfeld, Donald 251
Rush, Benjamin 60
Russell, Bertrand 41

Sacco, Nicola 47, 48, 49
Sanderson, Percy 12
Sandmeier, Edward 116
Sartre, John-Paul 359
Scalia, Antonin 196, 200–1, 204
Schlesinger, Arthur Jr 6–7, 44, 110, 111, 161, 304
Schmanski, Suzann 274
Schneiderman, Rose 210
Schumer, Charles 252
Schuster, K. 13
Scopes, John 267–8, 305
Screven, James 390
Seeger, P. 24, 258–9
Seferian, Birthe 344
Seldes, G. 25
Sen, Amartya 33
Serote, Mongane 153
Sewall, Gilbert 317
Shanker, Albert 110, 161, 171–2
Shank, Linda 328
Sheehan, Kevin 102
Shepherd, William G. 210–11
Shor, I. 117
Singer, Judith 296, 324
Singletary, Amos 286, 287
Sizer, Ted 90, 318
Sleeter, Christine 11, 12, 152, 161
Smith, Adam 71
Smith, C. 17, 178, 245
Smith, John 178–9
Smith, Wesley D. 116
Sobel, D. 56
Socrates 53
Sorenson, Eric 344–5
Spiegelman, A. 153
Stanton, Elizabeth Cady 311
Starr, Kenneth 201
Staton, Brendalon 329–30
Stearns, Bear 142
Stemn, Blidi 392
Stern, Fritz 251
Stevens, Adam 121–2
Sullivan, Jack 209
Sumner, Dawn 344

Takaki, Ronald 120
Tally, Bill 339
Tan, A. 153
Taney, Roger 198
Tauber, Richard 321, 344
Tella, Adeola 124, 244, 344
Thayer, Webster 48
Thernstrom, Abigal 53
Thiong'o, Ngugi wa 33
Thomas, Clarence 196, 200–1, 204
Thomas, J. 110
Thompson, B. 56
Thompson, E. 153
Thompson, Edward P. 39–40, 64
Thompson, Fred 116

Thompson, Rachel 16, 244, 307, 341
Thoreau, Henry David 297
Tierney, Patrick 64
Tilford, Jean 294
Torre, Joe 137
Truman, Harry 247
Truth, Sojourner 14
Turk, Pat 122

Uris, Leon 158

Vanzetti, Bartolomeo 47, 48, 49
Vitere, Cynthia 16, 398
Voltaire 44
Vosswinkel, Laura 122
Vygotsky, Lev 86

Walker, Alice 158
Wallace, M. 207, 208
Warren, Earl 84, 199
Washington, George 30, 174, 287, 288, 309, 340
Waters, Lydia Milner 310
Waugh, Dexter 150
Wells-Barnett, Ida 378
West, Cornel 69

Whitman, Walt 207, 306
Whitton, Sharon 307
Wiggins, G. 56, 103, 219, 359–60, 361
Wigginton, Eliot 88
Wilburn, Kiesha 321, 344
Wilder, Laura Ingalls 282, 310
Wilentz, S. 150, 207, 220–1
Williams, Nichole 244
Wilson, Louis 302–3
Wilson, Woodrow 184, 247, 301, 302, 303–4
Wolfer, Sondra 123
Wolkstein, Diane 328
Woloch, Nancy 302–3
Wood, George 320
Worley, James 171, 176
Wu, Joseph 151

Yates, Robert 287, 289
Yeats, William Butler 306
York, Bernard J. 278
Yoshizawa, Akira 151

Zanni, Tony 252
Zinn, Howard 86, 87, 120, 183, 197–8

Subject Index

abortion 133, 293–4, 297, 298–9
acculturation 32
action research 9, 382, 384
activism 12, 25, 114, 121, 122
   community 124
   metal detectors 123
   multiculturalism 160
   planning 293
   "Social Predators" 132–4
   women anti-war movements 312
activity-based lessons 223
   appropriateness 272–4
   building blocks 254–90
   opening 260–4
   plans 226–35, 242–3
   understanding reinforcement 270–2
activity sheets
   document-based 257–8
   immigration museum 347–8
   Irish immigration 375–6
   South after Reconstruction 378–80
activity worksheets
   Declaration of Independence 232, 235
   outcome-based model 240–1
Afghanistan 17, 18, 300
AFL-CIO 343
African National Congress 307
agriculture
   ancient world 62–3
   Ireland 61
aims
   developmental lessons 236
   lesson plans 226, 228, 229, 230, 233
Algeria, revolution 193, 195
alphabet book 330
Al Qaeda 249, 252, 274
American Association for State and Local History 404
American Bar Association 404
American Civil Liberties Union 116, 404
American Federation of Labor (AFL) 208, 210, 404
American Federation of Teachers (AFT) 116, 171, 404
American Historical Association (AHA) 24, 59, 60, 130, 387, 404
American Political Science Association 59, 404
American Social History Project (ASHP) 278, 405
American Sociological Association 59, 405
analysis, facts 37
Anglican Church, gay rights 13, 15
The Answers 25
anthropology 63–6
anticipatory set 239

Anti-Defamation League 116, 405
anti-Semitism 120, 157–8, 163–4
apartheid 133, 273–4
applications
   activity-based lessons 270
   developmental lessons 236
Arab-Israeli Conflict 40–1
archeological grab bag 329–30
art
   George Washington project 340
   interdisciplinary approach 307
artifacts 64, 330
Asian Development Bank 343
assessment
   portfolios 365–7
   self 374
   student learning 351–85
   teacher practice 351–85
assimilation 32
Association of American Geographers 405
Association for Supervision and Curriculum Development 405
Association of Teachers of Social Studies (ATSS) 267, 269

Ballad for Americans 2
banking method 82
beginning teachers, lesson planning 224–6
behavioral sciences 68–70
Bethel School District v. Fraser ruling 114
Bethlehem Steel 74
Bill of Rights 202
bio-poems 311
Blackboard Jungle 9
blogs 392
Blue Eyes/Brown Eyes Exercise 273
Bradley Foundation 127
brainstorming 10, 47, 175
bridges project 324–5
Brooklyn Bridge 207, 324
Brooklyn strike 275–6
Brown v. Topeka, Kansas Board of Education (1954) 185, 197
Burgess Shale 26

California 143
Camp David Accords 353–4
canals project 325
capitalism 38–9, 85
capitalist development 153–5
cartoons
   dialogues 383–4
   Irish immigration 376

Mr Block 72
  political 67, 331
case study approach 32
causality 61, 103
celestial mechanics 43
Center for Civic Education 108, 405
Center for Economic Policy and Research 343
Center for Research on Women 405
Certainly, Lord 158
Charting a Course 141–2
charts, unit plans 175, 177
Cherokee nation 13
child labor 71
Children's Defense Fund 405
China, nationalism 193, 194–5
Chisholm v. Georgia 200
chronological approach 143–52
chronological plans 180
citizenship 60–1, 133, 157, 353
  active 134
  movies 400–1
  projects 332
Civics and Citizenship Standards 133
Civics and Government Standards 92
Civil Rights Movement 79, 147, 148, 158, 184–91, 220
Civil War 145, 148, 207, 310, 372–3
classroom activities
  Annexation of the Philippines 278–81
  A Worker Reads History 35
  Behind the Headlines 296
  Can Judges or Teachers Be Neutral? 201–2
  Cartoon Metaphors 18–19
  Current Events and Talking Points 113
  Dancing Social Studies 255
  Debating Original Intent and the meaning of the US
      Constitution 203–4
  Declaration of Independence 298
  Eating Social Studies 156
  Economic Literacy 73, 74–6
  "Eyewitness at the Triangle" 210–11
  Family Artifacts 16
  History is Messy 30
  Ideas of Martin Luther King Jr 298
  Inventing the European Renaissance 55
  The Iroquois Story of Creation 329
  Mock Trial in a US Government Course 148–9
  My Life and History 4–5
  "Newsies" Strike Against the *World* and *Journal* 209
  Post-World War II African-American Experience 190–1
  Rapping History 349
  Steps to Revolution 42
  United Nations Charter 297
  Was There an Economic Motive Behind US Entry into
      World War I? 224–5
  When Does American History Begin? 99–101
  Who Am I? 9, 10, 11
Clearing House Interbank Payments System 343
climate change 330
Close Up Foundation 405
Coalition of Essential Schools 90, 141, 318, 352–3, 358, 364
Coalition of the Willing 251
coal miners, draft avoidance 274–5
Cobblestone Publishing 405
Cold War 147
collaboration, unit plans 175
coming-of-age ceremonies 325–7

Common Cause 405
communication, technology 391
Communism, China 193, 194–5
community 143
community political groups 134
comparative thematic units 192–6
conceptual approach 97
conflict resolution 125
Confucianism 163
Congo, civil war 193, 195
Constitution of the US 101, 140–1, 145, 196–204
  activity-based lessons 263–4, 286–90
  slavery 297
Consumers Union of the US 405
content-based approach 97, 141, 180–3
context 24
  literacy 243–5
  student-centered curriculum 180
controversy-centered units 293–316
cooperation, technology 391
cooperative learning 281–6
  cartoon dialogues 383–4
  field trips 396
  sample activities 286–90
copyright laws 404
craft ideas 327–8
creative maladjustment 131
critical literacy 243
critical thinking 267, 269
Cuba, revolution 194, 195
cultural diffusion 152
cultural diversity 179–80
cultural relativism 25, 64, 128
culture
  dance 255
  festivals 327
  integrity 327
  museum exhibits 328
curriculum
  calendar 143–8, 172, 194–5, 211
  planning 137–67
  student-centered 176, 180
Curriculum Standards for Social Studies 92–3

dance 255, 327
Darfur genocide 122
Dawes Rolls 13
decision-making, curriculum 139–40
Declaration of Independence 2–3, 117, 157, 184, 186, 236–7
  activity-based lessons 230–5
  activity worksheet 232
  human rights 297–8
  missing passage 157
  outcome-based model 239–41
  re-written by women 310
Declaration of Sentiments 310
democracy 31, 53
  Churchill 85
  Greece 54
  multiculturalism 157
  Portland 120–1
  social justice 117
  student dialogues 211–15
  teaching 89–90
  transformative education 124–5
democratic educators 8

demographics 61
Department of Education 108, 130, 141
determinism 43
developmental lessons
    organization 236–8
    plans 228
differentiated text 178, 245
dioramas 320–1, 346
direct instruction 255–6
discovery programs 390–1
discussion 223
Disney 128
documentaries 396–403
document-based instruction 256–8
document-based thematic unit 183–9
documents
    activity-based lesson 269
    choice 274–81
    Civil Rights Movement 186–9
    literacy 243
    multiple sources 275–6
    primary source 140, 178–9, 183, 269–70, 274
Do Now activities 227, 228–9, 230, 231, 232, 234, 235,
    260–2, 276
Dragnet School 34, 82, 128
drama 77–9
Dred Scott decision 198
drug laws 69

ecological disasters 62
economics 70–6, 174–5
    activity-based lessons 265
    Do Now activity 261
    movies 400
    projects 332
editorials 334
educational theory 88–9
    translation into practice 119–24
Educators for Social Responsibility 405
Egypt
    Greek influence 54–5
    nationalism 159
elections 246–8
electorate, race 16
empowerment 118–19, 132
environment, geography 61
equality, classroom examples 120–1
essays
    Are Activist Teachers "Social Predators"? 132–4
    Are We Teaching "Greek Myths" in the Global History
        Curriculum? 51–2
    Are We Teaching Religious Myth Instead of the History
        of Religion? 161–6
    Assessing Our Teaching Practice 381–4
    Cooperative Learning in Social Studies Classrooms
        281–6
    Expanding Our Concept of Inclusion 308–9
    How Can Teachers Promote the Economic and Civic
        Literacy of Students? 73
    How Can Teachers Use Drama to Promote Literacy
        While Teaching Social Studies Content and
        Concepts? 77–9
    How Do We Move from Instruction to Assessment?
        375–80
    Middle School Immigration Museum 344–9
    Multicultural Social Studies 152–61

Oral Histories: A Project Approach to Social Studies
    335–8
Original Intent and the US Constitution 196–204
Responding to Crisis: What Can Social Studies Teachers
    Do? 313–15
Sample Cooperative Learning Activity: Founders Discuss
    the Reasons for a New Constitution 286–90
Social Studies Under Attack 125–8
TAH Means "Traditional" American History 129–32
Teaching About Presidential Elections 246–8
Teaching About Work and Workers 204–11
Teaching Global History 149–52
Technology-based Project Ideas 338–44
tests 371–4
Using Student Dialogues to Teach Social Studies and
    Promote Democracy 211–15
Using "Text" and "Context" to Promote Student
    Literacies 243–5
What Are the Essential Questions? 102–5
What are the Lessons of 9/11? 248–53
What Does a Research Paper Look Like? 380–1
What Social Studies is all About 46–51
What We Should Teach 99–101
Which Document Do You Choose? 274–81
Why Multiculturalism Still Matters 11–19
Women's History Month Curriculum 309–13
Eurocentrism 54
euthanasia, religion 298–9
evaluation
    activity-based high school lesson plan 235
    activity-based middle school lesson plan 233
    developmental lessons 238
    Hunter model 239
    interdisciplinary projects 335
    outcomes-based lessons 241
    project approach 320
evolution 26–7, 29, 36, 43, 267–9
exams, fair 367–73
exhibitions 364–5
Expectations of Excellence 141

Facing History and Ourselves 405
facts 44
    analysis 37
    Fordham Foundation 128
    historians 36–7
    or thinking skills? 142–3
    vs theory 36
    what are? 34–5
"Fahrenheit 9/11" 128
Fair Trade Federation 343
Federal Reserve Bank 387
feminism 87
    see also women
    human rights 297
    positionality 155
    social studies curriculum 142
feudalism 38–9
field trips 396
Five Points families 207
flexibility
    lesson planning 225, 229
    unit plans 176
flip-flop planning 175
food 156
Fordham Foundation 127, 128

Forum Club 133–4, 334
Foundation for Teaching Economics 85, 387
Foxfire programs 318, 319
Fox Television 274
France, immigration 17
freedom 113–16, 294
free will 43
French Revolution 163, 181–2
Fugitive Slave law 299
Fulbright Teacher and Administrator Exchange Program
    387

games 272–3
gay rights 13, 15
gender 179–80
    see also women
    stereotypes 221
General Motors 205
genocide 212–13
geography 61–3
Georgia's Performance Standards 97
Gilder Lehrman Institute of American History 126–7,
    131–2, 142, 387
Global Challenge Initiative 343
global history 143, 149–52, 162–4
    curriculum 56, 84–5
    essential questions 102–3
    movies 401–3
    projects 327–30
    standards 162
    technology-based projects 342
global interdependence 61, 70–1
globalization 32
    technology-based projects 343–4
global warming 61–2
globes 62
goals 81–106
    see also objectives
    classroom practice 95–6
    cooperative learning 282–3
    curriculum 140
    historians 44–6
    lesson planning 225, 227, 230, 233
    state standards 96–9
    types 82
    unit plans 173
government 148–9
    movies 400–1
    projects 332
grading tests 373–4
Great Depression 119, 146, 184, 205, 208, 248, 322–4
Great Plains 356–7
Greece 51–5
Greenpeace 405
group membership 10
guided practice 239, 240
Gulf War 249

habits of mind 358
haiku 333
hallway maps 328
Harlem Resistance 184
Haymarket Riot 208, 209
heterogeneous groups 88, 178, 283–4
Hezbollah 249
hidden curriculum 138, 139–40

hidden government 67
high school
    activity-based lesson plan 233–5
    activity sheet 375–6
    cooperative learning 282
    developmental lessons 236–8
    history projects 330–1
    interdisciplinary approach 305
    Irish famine 243
    lectures 256
    lesson planning 226, 230
    technology-based projects 342–4
    unit plans 180–92
    unit test 377–8
    women's rights 302–3
The History Channel 127, 128, 142
Holocaust 157–8
homework 367–9, 372
    developmental lessons 236
    lesson plans 227, 228, 232, 235
    outcome-based model 240
homogeneous groups 88, 283–4
homophobia 53
homosexuality 13, 15, 53
hooks, lesson plans 229
human relations 152
Human Relations Day 122
human rights, controversy-centered units 296–300
Human Rights Campaign 116
Human Rights for Workers 343

immigration 47–51, 180
    Cartoon Metaphors 18–19
    France 17
    Irish 244, 245, 375–8
    laws 13, 15, 17
    learning activities 48
    middle school museum 344–9
    student dialogues 214
    women 311
imperialism, comparative thematic units 192–5
inclusion 152, 153
    expanding 308–9
    special education students 179
    unit planning 177–8
independent practice 239, 240
India 176
    Indian removal 30
    nationalism 193, 194
Individuals with Disabilities Education Act (1974) 308
industrialization 145–6, 153
    project 341
    women's role 310
Industrial Revolution 192, 207
inequality 16
    see also race; racism; women
    behavioral sciences 68–9
    racial 184–91
    social justice 117–18
information processing 390
infusion approach 152
inquiry-based learning 83
integrated curriculum 141
intelligence, multiple 87
interdisciplinary approach 305–6, 320–7
interdisciplinary units 293–316

interior monologue 121
International Monetary Fund 343
Internet 83
  canals project 325
  Civil Rights Movement 186
  computers in classrooms 390–5
  current issues sites 395
  history sites 393–4
  immigration museum 346
  mask making 327
  reference sites 394–5
  research papers 380–1
  resources location 404–7
  social studies sites 393–4
  student-friendly content sites 395
  teaching sites 393
  technology-based projects 338–4
  webquests 273, 391
interviews, oral history 335–8
investigative reporting 332, 346
Iran 194, 195, 250
Iraq 2, 17, 18, 84, 132, 134, 250–1, 276, 315
  classroom discussion 122
  Fox Television 274
  lesson aims 114–15
  sensitivity 300
  war discussion 113–16
Ireland
  famine 61, 103–4, 212, 213, 243–5, 327–8
  immigration 375–8
  independence 158–9
  nationalism 193, 194
Islam 35, 249
  fundamentalism 164
  rise 163
Israel 249–50

Jackdaw Publications 405
Jim Crow laws 184, 185, 205
JusticeNet 343

Kazakhstan 251
Kenya, revolution 193, 195
Knights of Labor 208, 209
Ku Klux Klan 110, 120

Labor Day 208
Lambda 116
leadership 125
League of Women Voters 405
learning activities
  Another Brick in the Wall 8
  Anti-Slavery Resistance 299–300
  Are these Quotations "Traditional" Enough? 130–1
  Athens during the Age of Pericles 52
  Attitudes Towards Immigrants 48
  Ballad for Americans 2
  Cartoon Dialogue 383–4
  Changing Complexion of the US 17
  Creative Imagination and Literature 119
  Decision-making in a Democratic Classroom 14–15
  Drawing Connections between Events 195–6, 216–17
  Evaluating Textbooks 304
  Evolution, Creation and Religion 269
  Historian Howard Zinn Discusses the Constitution 197–8
  Historical Knowledge of College Freshmen 125–6, 129

How Did Technology Transform the Great Plains? 356–7
  Impact of Capitalist Development 153–5
  Interpreting the Law, or Writing It 199
  The Intersection of Life and History 121
  Lens to the Past 11–12
  The Missing Passage 157
  The Nature of History 44
  Origami Paper Crane 152
  Political Protest 47–8
  Quotes from Malcolm X 222–3
  Reading History and the Social Sciences 33
  Songs of Resistance and Struggle 158–60
  Taking a Stand on Some Hot Issues 222
  Text and Context 245
  Understanding the Civil Rights Movement 79
  Which Document Do You Choose? 275
  Why Test? 357
  Writing Oral Histories 338
learning assessment 351–85
Lebanon 249, 250
lectures 82, 256
lessons
  aims, Should the US occupation of Iraq continue? 114–15
  design 173
  examples, The People Could Fly 95–6
  outlines 220
  planning 171–2, 176, 218–53
    perfect questions 266–7
    politics 172–3
  sample
    anthropology 63–6
    behavioral science 69
    economics 70–2
    geography 62–3
    political science 67–8
  sample organizers 270–2
listening to students 118
literacy 124
  context 243–5
  level disparity 178
  test problems 355
literature
  human rights issues 296
  interdisciplinary approach 306–7
local government, participation 124
Louisiana Purchase 109
Luddites 153–4

McCarthyism 274
Madeline Hunter Teacher Effectiveness Training Program
    238–9
Magdeburg 103
Magna Carta 178
The Making of a Profession 171
Manhattan Institute (MI) 127–8
maps 62
mask making 325–7
Massachusetts 98
maths, interdisciplinary approach 307–8
Mayan people 308
media, ownership 128
Michigan 97–8
middle school
  activity-based lessons 286–90
  activity sheet 378–80
  interdisciplinary approach 305

Irish famine 243
lectures 256
lesson planning 226, 230–2
outcome-based model 239–41
project menu 319
projects 320–7
technology-based projects 339–42
unit planning 176–7
women's rights 301–2
Missouri Compromise 202
moral judgments 45
moral relativism 156
Morningside Center for Teaching Social Responsibility 405
Morse v. Frederick 201–2
mortgage interest deductions 71–2
Mother Jones 343
motivation
activity-based lessons 260, 263–6, 276
developmental lessons 236, 237
lesson plans 227, 229, 231, 234
MoveOn.org 274
movies 396–403
multiculturalism 12–13, 15–18, 119, 143, 179–80, 304
see also race
essays 11–19, 152–61
lesson planning 220
September 11th 25
terrorism 128
multiple-choice questions 367–9
multiple perspectives 153
museums
displays 320–1, 328, 330
middle school immigration museum 344–9
music
see also songs
interdisciplinary approach 307
videos 330–1

National Archives and Records Administration 183, 405
National Assessment of Education Progress (NAEP) 352, 353–4
National Association for the Advancement of Colored People (NAACP) 184, 185, 405–6
National Center for History in the Schools 24, 108, 109, 110, 162, 406
National Council for Economic Education 108
National Council for Geographic Education 108
National Council of Geography Teachers 59
National Council for History Education (NCHE) 127, 141, 387, 406
National Council for History in the Schools 97
National Council for the Social Studies (NCSS) 1, 12, 24, 60–1, 92–3, 109, 131, 156, 386–7, 406
academic freedom 113
civic virtue 353
controversial issues 294
Hymowitz attack 127–8
integrated curriculum 141
reflective practice 382
Task Force report 176–7
technology 339, 390
thematic strands 91–2, 97, 141–2, 161–2, 174
National Education Association (NEA) 60, 116, 352–3, 364
National History Day 406
National History Standards 24, 92, 108–10, 141, 162, 180

national identity 44
nationalism
comparative thematic units 192–5
Egypt 159
National Issues Forums 141, 406
National Museum of Natural History 155
National Organization for Women 116, 133, 406
National Standards for Civics and Government 92
National Women's History Project 406
nation-state building 31
Native Americans 121
natural economic laws 71
Nazi regime 140, 157–8, 251, 297, 396
Network of Educators on the Americas 406
neutrality 119, 132, 201–2
New Deal 34, 174, 322–4
New Mexico 98–9
Newsies strike 209
newspaper article project 322
news reports 332
New Teachers Network 113, 124, 132, 211, 221–2, 313–14, 320–1, 390
New York Historical Society (NYHS) 131–2, 142
Nigeria, civil war 193, 195
No Child Left Behind (NCLB) 16, 73, 82, 238, 352
North American Congress on Latin America 406
Northern Sun Merchandising 406
note-taking 81–2
Now Foundation 128
Nuremberg Defense 30–1

objectives
see also goals
cooperative learning 282–3
developmental lessons 236
Hunter model 239
lesson plans 227
unit plans 173
Oceanside High School 102
opinions
teachers 111–12, 132–3
what to do if under attack 116
oral history 335–8
projects 317, 318
organization
activities 258–60
cooperative learning 283–4
developmental lessons 236–8
Organization of American Historians (OAH) 24, 110, 127, 387, 406
origami 151–2
original intent 198–204
originalists 200
outcomes-based lesson plans 238–41

Pakistan 250, 251
parallel cultural development 151, 152
parental bonding 69
peace quilt 312
pedagogical goals 87
pen pals 333
People for the American Way 406
Phi Alpha Theta 406
Philippines annexation 278–81
photographs 257
plagiarism 392

planning
    controversy-centered units 293–316
    curriculum 137–67
    interdisciplinary units 293–316
    lessons 176, 218–53
        perfect questions 266–7
        politics 172–3
        principles 228
    social studies unit 171–217
    thematic units 293–316
plays 328–9
Pledge of Allegiance 123
Plessy v. Ferguson (1896) 184
poetry
    bio-poems 311
    interdisciplinary approach 306
    projects 333–4
political action clubs 293–4
political advocacy speech 334
political donations 67–8
Political Economy Research Center 406
political science 66–8, 400–1
political teaching 107–36
portfolios 360–7
positionality 155
predestination 43
preservice teachers, lectures 256
primary source documents 140, 183, 274
        editing 178–9
        question design 269–70
pro-choice rallies 293–4, 334
product tests 332
project-based approach 141, 317–50
    portfolios 360
psychology 68–70, 332–3
public advocates 332
punctuated equilibrium 26
puppet folk theater 328

questions
    classification 266, 267, 269
    essential 102–5
        religion 165
        unit plans 173
    lesson plans 227, 228
    multiple-choice 367–9
    perfect? 266–70
    predetermined 269
    summary 227, 229, 232, 234, 236, 237

race 15–17, 95–6
    see also multiculturalism; slavery
    African colonial experience 340
    anti-black riots 277–8
    Civil Rights Movement 147
    cultural diversity 179–80
    Greek culture 54
    segregation 184–91
    teaching ideas 84
    union discrimination 210
racism 73
    apartheid 273–4
    behavioral sciences 68–9
    Blue Eyes/Brown Eyes Exercise 273
    Brooklyn 120
    Cherokees 13

drug laws 69
    lynching 378–80
    N-word 13–14
    post World War II 184–91
Rand Corporation 250
Rand Institute 249
reading
    learning 245
    level disparity 178
Red Scare 274
reflective practice 9, 82, 382
relevance 87
religion
    evolution 267–9
    history of 163–4
    human rights 297
    myths instead of history 161–6
    war justification 251–2
Renaissance 55–6
research papers 380–1
resistance 158–60
resources 386–407
responsibilities, cooperative learning 284–5
restoration sites 320
Rethinking Schools 116, 352, 406
revolution, comparative thematic units 192–5
Riceland Foods 76
role-play 272, 273, 274
Roman Catholic Church 55–6, 165–6, 297, 298–9
Russian Revolution 192–3, 194

Saudi Arabia 251
scaffolding 86
science, interdisciplinary approach 306
scientific method, history 41–2
Scopes Trial 267–8
scoring
    oral presentations/demonstrations 362
    written analysis 362
Seeds of Change exhibit 155
self-esteem 152
sensitivity 300–1
September 11th 17–18, 25, 113, 140, 221
    activism 134
    Fordham Foundation 128
    Hymowitz article 127–8
    lessons of 248–53
    Pledge of Allegiance 123
    responding to crisis 313–15
    sensitive topics 300–1
single group studies 152
situated understanding 118, 244
skills 92–5
    development 386–90
    or facts? 142–3
    unit plans 173
slavery
    addressing racism 120
    capitalist development 154
    classroom activity 30
    colonial New York 138–9
    curriculum calendar 145, 148
    Dred Scott decision 198
    Frederick Douglas 130
    Gilder Lehrman Institute 127
    Greece 54

perspective differences 153
religion 297
resistance 299–300
student understanding 221–2
TAHG 129–30
US Constitution 297
women's role 310
Smithsonian Institution 155, 156
social action projects 124
social bookmarking sites 392
social Darwinism 26–7
social justice 117–18, 122, 134
sociology 68–70
Do Now activity 261–3
projects 332–3
Socrates 359
songs 305, 379–80
African-American women 312
analyzing 206, 260
"Bread and Roses" 311
"Freedom is a Constant Struggle" 124
human rights issues 296
immigration museum 345, 346, 348
interdisciplinary approach 307
Irish immigration 375
projects 330–1
resistance and struggle 158–60
Talking Union 258–60
union 205–6
South Africa, apartheid 273–4
Southern Poverty Law Center 406
Spanish Inquisition 56
special education students 177–8, 179, 211
special-needs students 308–9
staff development 386–7
standardized exams 104
standards 96–9
Civics and Citizenship 133
Civics and Government 92
Georgia's Performance Standards 97
global history 162
national history 24, 92, 108–10, 141, 162, 180
Social Studies 92–3
starving time 178–9
stereotypes, women 310
student-centered curriculum 176, 180
student-centered education, activity-based lessons 254–90
student choice, cooperative learning 283
student dialogues, democracy 211–15
student horizons, expanding 121–2, 143
student rights 122–3
student voice 125
summary questions
developmental lessons 236, 237
lesson plans 227, 229, 232, 234
Supreme Court 340–1
surveys 69

taboos 64
Talking Union 258–60
Teachers' Curriculum Institute 406
teaching activities
Addressing Homosexuality in History 53
A Motivation is Not a Hook 229
Analyzing a Song 206, 260
Anthropology in the Curriculum 66

Breaking the Law 50
Can a Social Studies Curriculum be Non-political? 111
Choosing Movies 403
Computers in the Social Studies Classroom 395
Concepts, Understandings, and Controversies 92
Conspiracy, Conservative Campaign or Coincidence? 129
Constructing a Document-based Activity Sheet 257–8
Constructing Lesson Organizers 272
Constructing Social Studies Portfolios 367
Content, Concepts, or Skills? 95
Creating a History Museum 349
Creating Short Answer Test Questions 371
Dealing with Diversity 180
Defining a Freirean Curriculum 118
Defining History 28–9
Defining a Unit in US History and Economics 174–5
Design a Comparative Unit 195
Design a Content-based Unit 183
Designing Essay Questions 372
Designing Homework and Test Questions 369
Designing Questions for a Lesson on the Scopes Trial 267–8
Designing Questions for a Primary Source Document 269–70
Design a Theme-based Unit 189, 192
Did New York City Police Participate in Anti-Black Riots in 1900? 277–8
Does Social Justice Require Activism? 134
Dramatic Presentation of Constitutional Controversies 289
Economics in the Curriculum 73
Editing a Primary Source Document 178–9
Educational Theory 89
Evaluating an Activity-based Middle School Lesson Plan 233
Evaluating an Outcomes-based Lesson 241
Evaluating a Developmental Lesson 238
Evaluating a High School Activity-based Lesson Plan 235
Evaluating Interdisciplinary Project Ideas 335
Examining a Curriculum Calendar 148
Facts and Theories 36
Facts or Thinking Skills? 142–3
Foreign Criminals in New York 50–1
The Foxfire Approach- Perspectives and Core Practices 319
Geography in the Curriculum 63
Goals of Historians 46
Goals and Objectives for Cooperative Learning 282–3
Grading Essay Questions 373–4
Heterogeneous or Homogeneous Grouping? 88
History is a River 101
How Do We Know What We Know? 359
How Representative is a Primary Source Document? 140
Including Academic Skills in Social Studies Lessons 93–5
Including Goals and Understandings 96
Irish Immigrants in New Orleans, Louisiana 244
Is History Too Straight? 294–5
Is It Acceptable to Question Government Policies in a Time of National Emergency? 314–15
Join the Multicultural Debate 160–1
Models of Social Studies Learning 83
Motivational Activities 264
Motivations with Transitions 266
New Teacher's Debate "Point of View" 45
Once You Were a Student in This Class 238
Ordinary People 49

Organizing Cooperative Learning Teams 284
Outlining an Activity-based Lesson 227
Outlining a Lesson 220
Outlining Units on India and sub-Saharan Africa 176
Political Science in the Curriculum 68
The Politics of Lesson Planning 172–3
Principle for Planning 228
Problem Solving and Critical Judgment 90
Promoting Student Discussion 223
Reading a Photograph 257
Read and Read Some More 388–90
Resistance at Christiana, PA 300
Respecting Cultural Integrity 327
Rules for Student Dialogues in Ms Rosenberg's Class 213–14
Sample Social Studies Cooperative Learning Activities 289–90
Setting Up a Classroom 285
Sherlock Holmes 37
Should the Curriculum Depend on Your Students? 6–7
Should Students Assess Their Own Learning? 374–5
Should Teachers Express their Views? 112
Sociology and Psychology in the Curriculum 70
Student Discussions 50
Student Voice 49
Taking Risks 132
Teaching about the Arab-Israeli Conflict 40–1
The Tree of Liberty 101
Using Activities in a Lesson 262
What Are Student Exhibitions? 364–5
What Did the Teacher Say? 223
What did the US Purchase in 1803? 109
What Does It Mean To Be An Historian? 27–8
What Role Would You Play? 123
What was Life Like in Colonial New York city? 138–9
What Would You Include in a Lesson Plan? 226
Where Do You Stand? 86
Who Decides What Gets Taught? 108
Why Test? 357
Women's History Month 305
Teaching American History Grant (TAHG) program 1, 24, 82, 127, 129–32, 207, 387
teaching assistants, special education students 179
"Teaching the Culturally Different" 11
Teaching For Change 407
teaching ideas, How Important is Race in American Society? 84
Teaching Tolerance 116
technical literacy 243
technology
    see also Internet
    computers in classrooms 390–5
    Great Plains 356–7
technology-based projects 338–4
Tennessee v. John Scopes 305
terrorism 17–18
    see also September 11th
    multiculturalism 128
    war on terror 249–53
tests 353–60
    cf assessment 352–3
    grading 373–4
    standardized exams 104
    what do they measure 353–4
    Why Test? 357
textbooks, unit plans 173–4

textualists 200, 202
thematic strands 91–2, 97, 99, 141–2, 161–2, 174
thematic units
    comparative 192–6
    document-based 183–9
    planning 293–316
Third World, student dialogues 214–15
This Land Is Your Land 23–4
Tinker v. Des Moines ruling 114
tracked programs 177
traditional history curriculum 24, 31, 129–32
Trail of Tears 30
transculturation 32
transformative education 8, 90, 119–21, 124–34, 152
transitions
    activity-based lessons 260, 264–6
    lesson plans 227
transmission model 82–3, 90
Transparency International 251
transportation revolution 341
travel 387
travel brochure 341–2
Triangle Shirtwaist factory 210–11
truth 104

unemployment 70
unions 71, 116, 204–11
    decline 204–5
    Talking Union 258–60
uni-power system 252
United Nations 333
    Charter 297
    University 344
United States Public Interest Research Group 407
units
    controversy-centered 293–316
    interdisciplinary 293–316
    planning 171–217
    thematic 293–316

values 382–3
Veterans of Foreign Wars 407
videos
    conferencing 339–40
    documents 186
    music 330–1
Vietnam 147, 193, 195
virtual museum 346
virtual tours 320, 330, 391–2
1965 Voting Rights Act 185

Wal-Mart 74–5
weapons of mass destruction 250, 276
webquests 63, 273, 391
wikis 392
women
    see also feminism
    cartoon dialogues 383–4
    Greece 54
    History Month 305, 309–13
    subjugation 156–7
    suffrage 301–4, 311
    thematic units 301–5, 309–12
Women's International League for Peace and Freedom 407
working class 39
workshop model 172–3, 242

Works Progress Administration (WPA) 323–4
World Bank Group 343
World War I 104, 224–5, 315
World War II 146, 148, 157–8, 312
Worldwatch Institute 343
writing
  level disparity 178
  projects 333–4

Yoruba naming ceremony 63, 65–6
Youth for International Socialism
  343

Zen Buddhism 333
Zog Nit Keyn Mol 158